Professional XML Meta Data

Kal Ahmed

Danny Ayers

Mark Birbeck

Jay Cousins

David Dodds

Joshua Lubell

Miloslav Nic

Daniel Rivers-Moore

Andrew Watt

Robert Worden

Ann Wrightson

Wrox Press Ltd. ®

Professional XML Meta Data

Published by Wrox Press Ltd,
Arden House, 1102 Warwick Road, Acocks Green,
Birmingham, B27 6BH, UK
Printed in the United States
ISBN 1861004516

Trademark Acknowledgements

Wrox has endeavored to provide trademark information about all the companies and products mentioned in this book by the appropriate use of capitals. However, Wrox cannot guarantee the accuracy of this information.

Credits

Authors
Kal Ahmed
Danny Ayers
Mark Birbeck
Jay Cousins
David Dodds
Josh Lubell
Miloslav Nic
Daniel Rivers-Moore
Andrew Watt
Robert Worden
Ann Wrightson

Additional Material
Paul Spencer

Technical Architect
Dianne Parker

Technical Editors
Richard Deeson
Sarah Larder
Martin Lau
Simon Mackie
Nick Manning

Category Managers
Dave Galloway
Sonia Mullineux

Project Administrator
Beckie Stones

Author Agent
Marsha Collins

Proof Reader
Fiona Berryman

Technical Reviewers
Dave Beauchemin
Martin Beaulieu
Arnaud Blandin
Geert Bormans
Natalia Bortniker
Pierre-Antoine Champin
Robert Chang
Chris Crane
Paul Houle
Jim MacIntosh
Thomas B. Passin
Phil Powers-DeGeorge
J. Andrew Schafer
David Schultz
Ian Stokes-Rees
Andrew Watt
Ann Wrightson

Indexers
Martin Brooks
Andrew Criddle

Production Manager
Simon Hardware

Production Co-ordinator
Evelyn Tension

Diagrams
Paul Grove

Additional Layout
Paul Grove

Cover
Dawn Chellingworth

About the Authors

Kal Ahmed

Kal has worked with markup languages for more years than he cares to remember. He is a founder member of TopicMaps.Org and a contributor to the XTM 1.0 specification. Kal has worked for companies specialising in workflow systems, content management systems and topic map systems – mostly as a systems integrator and consultant. He is now working as an independent consultant and as lead developer of the Open Source topic map toolkit TM4J (http://www.techquila.com/tm4j.html).

I would like to thank and apologise in print to those members of my family that I haven't seen enough of (sorry, Mum). I would also like to thank the lovely people at Wrox and the thorough reviewers that helped knock my work into shape...and then make that shape readable (though I still take the blame for all mistakes!). Finally, and above all, I would like to thank my incredibly patient girlfriend Agata from the bottom of my heart.

Danny Ayers

Danny Ayers has a 20-year history of trying to make the best of inhuman operating systems, which in recent years have been less of an issue thanks to the Java language. Professionally he has been primarily involved with networking technologies, and as an independent information engineer he is currently working on tools that may help in the development of a semantic web. His other interests include music, woodcarving and travel. His personal web site may be found at http://www.isacat.net.

Thanks to my wife Caroline for being incredibly tolerant during my bad code days.

Mark Birbeck

Mark Birbeck is Technical Director of Parliamentary Communications Ltd. where he has been responsible for the design and build of their political portal, ePolitix.com. He is also managing director of XML consultancy x-port.net Ltd., responsible for the publishing system behind spiked-online.com. Although involved in XML for a number of years, his special interests lie in meta data, and in particular the use of RDF. He welcomes Wrox's initiative in trying to move these topics from out of the shadows and into the mainstream.

Mark would particularly like to thank his long-suffering partner Jan for putting up with the constant smell of midnight oil being burned. He offers the consolation that at least he is already up when their first child Louis is demanding attention during the small hours.

Jay Cousins

Jay Cousins is an Analyst/Consultant at RivCom, a consultancy specialising in helping businesses adopt XML technologies for the creation, management, and distribution of information. Jay works in information analysis and modeling, specializing in the development of NewsML and XML-based architectures.

Jay has an M.Sc. in Analysis, Design, and Management of Information Systems from the London School of Economics, and a BA in English with Comparative Literature from the University of East Anglia. He also studied at the Universität Salzburg, Austria under the ERASMUS exchange programme. Before joining RivCom, Jay worked as a Research Assistant at the LSE, and wrote and developed content for the Web and for PR. Private interests include art and literature.

David Dodds

David Dodds is based in Alameda California, and has worked with computers since 1968, when he wrote Continuous Systems Models at university. Later he developed a program to operate a multichannel analog speech synthesizer, which produced recognizable Coast Salish, an Indian language. He also wrote neural network simulations in 1972. After playing with programs to model human personality types and writing code to simulate a town council in a Von Forrester "Limits to Growth" type model, and teaching computing science at university for a while, he joined Nortel (Northern Telecom) where he wrote text understanding software, and expert systems in C and Prolog.

He has been working the last few years on the various emerging XML technologies, was on the W3C SVG workgroup to develop the specification for SVG 1.0; and on the early committee to develop XML Topic Map specification. David has published numerous papers in robotics and in fuzzy systems. He has a passion for "what is intelligence?" He works on systems of representation, designing UKL (Unified Knowledge Language), and pursues designs of systems of meta data and meta-programming representation.

Josh Lubell

Josh works at US National Institute of Standards and Technology (NIST) where he applies markup technology toward solving data exchange problems between manufacturing applications. He is a contributor to various standards efforts and speaks regularly at XML-related conferences. His pre-NIST experience includes artificial intelligence systems design and prototyping as well as software development for the building materials industry. He has an M.S. in Computer Science from the University of Maryland at College Park and a B.S. in Mathematics from Binghamton University. Josh lives in Maryland with his wife and sons, ages six and two.

Josh is thankful for NIST's support in writing the "Process Descriptions" chapter of "Professional XML Meta Data". He is also grateful for the helpful feedback and suggestions received both from NIST colleagues and from Wrox Press throughout the editorial process.

Miloslav Nic

Miloslav Nic started his career as an organic chemist (with a Masters degree from ICT Prague and a PhD from the University of London). After spending several years as a lecturer of organic chemistry in ICT Prague he came across XML (in 1999) and founded Zvon (http://www.zvon.org). It quite dramatically changed his life and some months later he became an employee of Idoox (http://www.idoox.com), a Web Services company.

Mila lives in Slany, a small town near Prague, with his wife and daughter Klarka. His favorite hobby is what he calls scientific decathlon and he is looking forward to the time when he is an impractical scientist again.

Daniel Rivers-Moore

Daniel Rivers-Moore is Director of New Technologies at RivCom, a UK-based consultancy specializing in helping companies and organizations adopt leading-edge technologies for information management and delivery. Daniel was actively involved from the outset in the development of XML and its related technologies. He has served as Joint Project Leader of the STEP/SGML Harmonization initiative for bringing together technical documents with engineering data, and is editor of NewsML, the XML-based standard for the management and delivery of multimedia news. A founder member of TopicMaps.org, Daniel served as chair of the subgroup that developed the XML Topic Maps Conceputual Model. Daniel is a member of the board of management of Knowledge on the Web (KnoW), a collaborative initiative aimed at furthering the development of the latest generation of Web technologies in the service of knowledge management and knowledge sharing. Daniel has a BA in Philosophy and Psychology from the University of Oxford. He spent the first 15 years of his adult life working in the field of voice and theatre before getting a "real job" in publishing in 1986.

Daniel is married and lives in Tetbury, a small market town in the Cotswold district of England.

Andrew Watt

Andrew Watt is an independent consultant who enjoys few things more than exploring the technologies others have yet to sample. Since he wrote his first programs in 6502 Assembler and BBC Basic in the mid 1980's he has sampled Pascal, Prolog, and C++, among others. More recently he has focused on the power of Web-relevant technologies including Lotus Domino, Java and HTML. His current interest is in the various applications of the Extensible Markup Meta Language, XMML, sometimes imprecisely and misleadingly called XML. The present glimpse he has of the future of SVG, XSL-FO, XSLT, CSS, XLink, XPointer, etc. when they actually work properly together is an exciting, if daunting, prospect. He has just begun to dabble with XQuery. Such serial dabbling, so he is told, is called "life-long learning".

In his spare time he sometimes ponders the impact of Web technologies on real people. What will be the impact of a Semantic Web? How will those other than the knowledge-privileged fare?

To the God of Heaven who gives human beings the capacity to see, think and feel. To my father who taught me much about life.

Robert Worden

Dr. Robert Worden is a consultant with Charteris plc in London. During the 70s he did research in high energy physics, writing Fortran programs to analyse bubble chamber data and test theories of high energy scattering. He then joined Logica and alternated between management and technical jobs for twenty years. He built a relational database management system which sold well before being wiped out by Oracle. He moved into AI and built expert systems for medical diagnosis; then for four years he managed Logica's advanced research centre at Cambridge (UK). Next he became a consultant specialising in project management and large-scale data architectures, continuing this role at Charteris. In his spare time, until recently, he published papers on cognitive science, writing papers about the hippocampus, primate social intelligence and child language learning. He has built working computer models of all these. Spare-time science stopped with the birth of Jonathan Worden two years ago.

Ann Wrightson

Ann has specialized in SGML & XML since 1985. She is well known in the XML field, presenting at conferences and participating actively in the continued development of international standards for XML/SGML-family technology. Following a varied and successful early career in electronic publishing, Ann spent ten years lecturing, researching, and consulting in an academic context, including, in 1998, developing the first UK postgraduate course in XML technology. More recently, she has been employed by a major UK publisher as an XML/SGML technical authority, and as a consultant by a leading-edge XML technology development company. Ann is also a founding board member of KnoW, a non-profit research and development organization bringing together industrial, commercial, governmental and academic partners for projects furthering the development of Web technologies.

Ann is married with three children. In her spare time plays in her local brass band, on bass trombone, alongside two of her kids.

Meta DataProfessionalXMLMeta DataProfessionalXMLMeta DataProfessional

Table of Contents

Table of Contents

Table of Contents

Table of Contents

Table of Contents

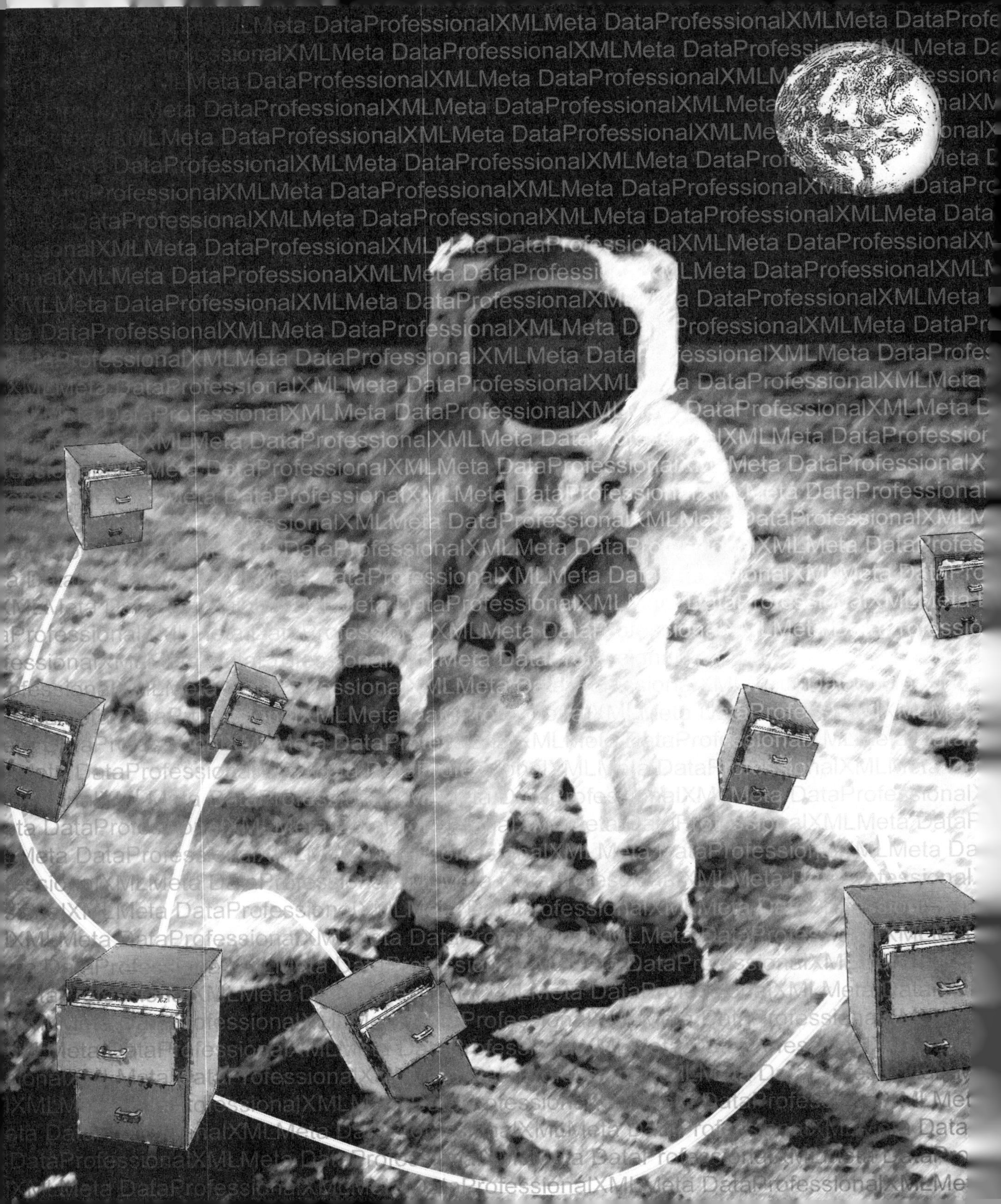

Introduction

In today's IT-dominated world we have an increasing amount of information available in electronic formats – not surprisingly, we need better ways of dealing with and managing the volume of data we store and exchange. In order to help us do this we can use **meta data**, which, put simply, is data about data.

XML is a very general file format that can be specialized for creating documents that look like "data" (structured formally, like a database table, tree and graph structures) and "text" (intermixed text and XML tags, such as XHTML.) A strength of XML is that it has some rather formalized ways of thinking about structure – with ideas such as well-formedness, validity, and schemas.

Since XML is both a *good* format and an *open* format (documented, tools for all kinds of platforms and languages, and human readable) it's naturally an ideal format for meta data – because often meta data is part of a scheme of sharing data between multiple sources.

In this book we'll cover a range of issues regarding, and implementations of, meta data; in particular those that use XML-based technologies as part of the solution. All of the initiatives covered aim to improve the way we build web/intranet applications that use meta data to:

- ❑ describe data

- ❑ describe "processes" used to process the data (such as executable programs which carry out business transactions)

- ❑ discover what information (content and knowledge) is held, including the vast amount of information "hidden" in legacy systems

- ❑ discover what processes are used to process the data

- ❑ retrieve selected information

- ❑ share the data/processes or description of the data/processes with others, such as in e-business scenarios

Such a vast topic area can be divided into three conceptual sections:

❑ **Describe** – build the data/process description. This involves creating order from the mass of information held by most organizations in electronic formats. Much of this information is not utilized to its full potential, often because people do not know (or forget) where this information lies, or how to access and use it, or because the media decays, or the file format changes, which often results in heavy duplication. Techniques include reading and writing DTDs and other schema languages; using RDF and its extensions; creating topic maps; linking resources with XML linking languages; and building XML representations of process descriptions.

❑ **Retrieve** – resource discovery/retrieval. This involves looking at how to make use of the data/process descriptions, to find out what information is held and to make retrieval of the data more straightforward. This includes the use of XML querying languages; using logical inferencing systems; creating database wrappers around traditional relational databases to help discover and access the information they contain; and using schemas for data discovery.

❑ **Communicate** – exchange/share information. There is an increasing trend in and between organizations to share data – from inter-department sales information to cross-company syndication of intellectual property. This will also be driven by the ability to be explicit about what information is available, in other words how to share the descriptions and retrieval tools with others. These techniques are what will enable us to take the enterprise meta data and inferencing systems we have built and use them to achieve something like a "Semantic Web" in our applications.

Most of the technologies covered in this book are at the very cutting edge of XML development, so understandably implementations are scarce. Where possible in this book we have demonstrated the techniques with working examples, and where implementations are not quite there yet we've provided enough detail to help you "get ahead of the field" in understanding how these technologies can help you in your business systems.

What's Covered in this Book

Chapter 1 – Why Meta Data? Why XML?

We will start with an introduction to what meta data actually is and why XML is an ideal format for representing it. This chapter describes a current project involving meta data to give a flavor of what is to come.

Chapter 2 – XML Schemas

In the broadest sense, schemas are design patterns or templates for XML structures and vocabularies. Within the XML technology family there are several ways in which XML document structures can be defined, for example Document Type Definitions (DTDs) – these are specifications for a single XML document type, which is a class of tree structures for a whole XML document.

The W3C XML Schema recommendation provides ways of describing the structures of parts of documents, including the detailed content of individual elements. Other schema notations have also been proposed, for example RELAX and TREX (now combined into RELAX NG), which have a more concise notation, more familiar to data designers with conventional computer science training. This chapter covers how to write and understand schemas, in this broad sense of the word, and also discusses the usefulness of schemas themselves as meta data describing the structures and content types to be found in XML documents.

Chapter 3 – XML Linking and Querying

This chapter covers basic concepts that are essential for understanding the following chapters on RDF and topic maps. The WWW has demonstrated convincingly the need for techniques to describe links between data, resources, and parts of resources (XML and non-XML). However, simple HTML links are very limited in their capabilities; this chapter introduces the extended linking supported by XLink, XPointer/XPath, and XInclude. These links are themselves useful as simple meta data, providing a basic mechanism for annotating and cross-referencing both HTML and XML resources. However, the full potential of linking requires additional concepts, which are found in later chapters of this book.

Querying of XML resources is still the subject of intense debate and controversy. The Document Object Model (DOM) provided a simple searchable structure for relatively small XML documents, and has been used effectively for many purposes. However, for effective querying of large amounts of XML there are two competing approaches. To simplify, one approach says that the structure of the XML document (or document set) itself should be queried; the other says that an XML document is not suited to querying, so queries should happen using meta data. As usual with such controversies, there is an element of truth in both approaches, and it is likely that different solutions will emerge in different application areas.

This chapter takes a look at the practical details of some currently available techniques; however, this is an area that can be expected to change fast over the next few years.

Chapter 4 – RDF Model and Syntax

Resource Definition Framework (RDF) is by now a stable and well-regarded meta data standard for use with XML. This chapter covers the basics of RDF, both as a syntax-independent model enabling automated processing of web resources, and as an XML syntax for encoding properties according to this model. Balancing theory and practice, examples are used to introduce the node-and-arc diagrams used by the RDF community, the grammar and parsing of the syntax, and the advantages that RDF gives you over just designing XML structures for your data.

Chapter 5 – RDF Schema

Having mastered the basics of RDF, this chapter brings in the additional modeling capabilities that make RDF a firm plank in the platform of protagonists of the "Semantic Web". Again using a mixture of theory and examples, you will learn about the key benefits gained from RDF when the concepts it models are also part of a consensus vocabulary in an industry or business domain, and how RDF Schema can model these concepts, using DAML+OIL, and define their relationships to your local system's data model.

Chapter 6 – Parsing RDF

This chapter takes a look at the practicalities of parsing RDF, since it is the foundation of any application that will use the RDF model and syntax for meta data. It then steps through the construction of an RDF framework and a modular, event-driven RDF parser application. Although you may not want to build your own parser, stepping through the process should enable you to understand how to integrate RDF parsers into your own applications.

Chapter 7 – Topic Maps and XTM

From the resource-based meta data of RDF, we now go to the current leader in subject-based meta data. Topic maps can organize any kind of resources, not just XML or HTML; they have been much hyped recently, and their generality and wide range of potential applications can make it difficult to see just where they fit into the overall picture. This chapter gives a thorough introduction to the core concepts of topic maps, and also explains the central problems they solve by means of a real example, the handling of news stories in press newsfeeds and newspaper editorial systems.

Chapter 8 – Meaning Definition Language

This chapter describes one way of using schema adjuncts to provide meta data for XML document structures. The rationale for Meaning Definition Language (MDL) is that the meta data provided by the schema alone is not generally sufficient to tell a receiving system how to process the XML. MDL provides additional information, such as associating system-specific information, or generic processing parameters, with schema-defined document structures.

Chapter 9 – Meta Data Architectures

Meta data is available in many different places, both within an organization and across the World Wide Web in general. This chapter discusses the approaches needed to locate and make use of meta data wherever it exists by introducing some of the architectures of meta data and the techniques for its implementation. It explore the different ways in which meta data manifests itself "in the wild", and then looks at ways in which each of these different manifestations may be required to be put to use, and what kinds of techniques can be used to turn "wild" meta data into productive, "domesticated" meta data.

Chapter 10 – Processing Techniques for Meta Data

This chapter provides a comprehensive survey of meta data from a practical applications perspective. Most of the book so far has looked at XML meta data from an XML standpoint; here is the other side, a chapter which brings to the table a wealth of experience with meta data and its processing in many different systems.

The chapter includes a look at the Meaning Definition Framework, and builds a simple web spider application.

It is one of the prevailing weaknesses of XML technology that when XML is applied to some area where other technologies have gone before, the lessons learned from the older technology are not always carried through, with predictable results – the same old mistakes happen round again. This chapter is your chance NOT to do that with meta data – don't miss it!

Chapter 11 – Further Topic Map and RDF Developments

One of the key problems in applying topic map technology to real problems is building the topic map; although some interesting ones have been built by hand, it is inevitable that the real payoffs will only come with large scale automated creation. Expanding on Chapter 7 (which briefly mentioned automatic means but mainly focused on manual creation of topic maps), this chapter will describe and demonstrate an example of the automatic construction of topic map from existing information resources.

The second future development we'll consider is the combination of RDF and topic map representations. This chapter contains discussion of how to mix TM and RDF representations, leveraging both. There are intensive efforts ongoing as we write between the RDF and topic maps communities to clarify and improve this relationship.

Chapter 12 – Exposing Relational Databases

Relational databases already hold a significant amount of data in most organizations. This chapter is a technical case study that describes ways of making the content of relational databases available to XML-technology-driven applications. This includes serving database content in XML, sending updates to the database in XML, extracting a database schema from a database using JDBC and recasting that information in RDF.

Chapter 13 – Data Validation and Mining with Schematron

This chapter is a short technical case study, taking advantage of the different virtues of XSLT, RDF, and XTM, to design an environment, and an application working in that environment, supporting data discovery and validation.

Chapter 14 – Process Descriptions

Process descriptions are a very important kind of meta data for both documents and applications, so it is no surprise that they too are emerging in XML. This chapter discusses business processes, and manufacturing engineering processes, together with their representations in XML. Representing and automating business and manufacturing processes in IT systems is a well developed field, with its own problems and accumulated wisdom; here again we have a good opportunity to avoid making some crass mistakes in XML, by learning from an experienced hand in this field.

Chapter 15 – Inferencing Systems

This chapter explains how some of the technologies which have survived the test of time (and real system requirements!) from the AI hype of the 1970s, can be used together with XML meta data to build systems using "knowledge technologies". The promise is great, but it needs strong discipline and consensus in use of meta data to really reap the benefits – "garbage in, garbage out" will be never so true as for meta data in the "Semantic Web".

Chapter 16 – Advanced Meta Data Use Cases

As stated before, XML meta data technologies are still at an early stage of development, but the future potential uses open up a realm of exciting possibilities. This chapter presents a couple of use cases for meta data applications in the future, using the W3C's Scalable Vector Graphics (SVG) language. The first use case is a discussion of self-describing (content aware) XML files, specifically a system that uses meta data embedded in an XML file to infer what the file describes. The second use case discusses the use of meta data to provide document integrity and data recovery.

Appendices

We've also included a glossary of the main terms in the book, and a compilation of some useful resources for further reading.

Who is this Book For?

This book is for developers who are already familiar with basic XML concepts and who:

- ❑ Need to understand the data that resides on a network, for example who need to catalog information for resource discovery.

- ❑ Need to provide some kind of navigation/linking/searching of the data or processes within their enterprise.

- ❑ Are looking for a better search engine technology, especially one which can do inferencing-based searches, thus finding information which is not explicit.

- ❑ Need to make that information available to others, either by providing a conventional user interface to do these things in a human-readable way (say, produce a report in HTML or PDF format, or do order tracking out of a relational database) or providing machine-readable, XML-format information, for people outside the "enterprise" to do automated things with (for example, object models serialized as XML).

- ❑ Need to incorporate data from external sources into their web pages, for example from weblogs, directories, search engines, etc.

- ❑ Are using XML in their applications – meta data applications range from simply writing schemas to automated resource discovery.

What You Need to Use this Book

For the book, you will need:

- ❑ Java SDK 1.3 for some of the chapters.
- ❑ Xalan 1.1.2 and Xerces.
- ❑ A simple text editor.
- ❑ A C++ compiler, such as Microsoft Visual C++ 6.0, for the RDF parser application.
- ❑ A database and JDBC driver for the exposing relational databases application.

Several other free tools are required; we'll tell you where to obtain these throughout the book.

Source Code

The complete source code from the book is available for download from the page for this book at: http://www.wrox.com.

Conventions

To help you get the most from the text and keep track of what's happening, we've used a number of conventions throughout the book.

For instance:

> **These boxes hold important, not-to-be forgotten information that is directly relevant to the surrounding text.**

The background style is used for asides to the current discussion.

As for styles in the text:

- ❑ When we introduce them, we **highlight** important words.
- ❑ We show keyboard strokes like this: *Ctrl-A*

- ❑ We show filenames and code within the text like so: `<topic id="conventions">`
- ❑ Text on user interfaces and URLs is shown like this: Menu

Example code is shown like so:

```
In our code examples, the code foreground style shows new, important,
    pertinent code...
While code background shows code that's less important in the present context,
    or code that has been seen before.
```

Customer Support

We want to know what you think about this book: what you liked, what you didn't like, and what you think we can do better next time. You can send your comments, either by returning the reply card in the back of the book, or by e-mail (to feedback@wrox.com). Please be sure to mention the book title in your message.

Errata

We've made every effort to make sure that there are no errors in the text or the code. However, to err is human and, as such, we recognize the need to keep you informed of any mistakes as they're spotted and corrected. Errata sheets are available for all of our books at http://www.wrox.com. If you find an error that hasn't already been reported, please let us know.

E-mail Support

If you wish to directly query a problem in the book with an expert who knows the book in detail, then e-mail support@wrox.com with the title of the book and the last four numbers of the ISBN in the subject field of the e-mail. A typical e-mail should include the following things:

- ❑ The **name**, **last four digits of the ISBN**, and **page number** of the problem in the Subject field.
- ❑ Your **name**, **contact info**, and the **problem** in the body of the message.

We *won't* send you junk mail. We need the details to save your time and ours. When you send an e-mail, it will go through the following chain of support:

- ❑ Customer Support – Your message is delivered to our customer support staff who are the first people to read it. They have files on the most frequently asked questions and will answer anything general immediately. They answer general questions about the book and the web site.

- ❑ Editorial – Deeper queries are forwarded to the technical editor responsible for that book. They have experience with the programming language or particular product and are able to answer detailed technical questions on the subject. Once an issue has been resolved, the editor can post the errata to the web site.

- ❑ The authors – Finally, in the unlikely event that the editor can't answer your problem, they will forward the request to the author. We try to protect our authors from any distractions from writing. However, we are quite happy to forward specific requests to them. All Wrox authors help with the support on their books. They'll mail the customer and the editor with their response, and again all readers should benefit.

P2P.WROX.COM

For author and peer support, join the XML mailing lists. Our unique system provides **programmer to programmer**™ **support** on mailing lists, forums, and newsgroups – all *in addition* to our one-to-one e-mail system. Be confident that your query is not just being examined by a support professional, but by the many Wrox authors and other industry experts present on our mailing lists. At p2p.wrox.com, you'll find a number of different lists aimed at XML programmers that will support you, not only while you read this book, but also as you develop your own applications.

Why this System Offers the Best Support

You can choose to join the mailing lists or you can receive them as a daily digest. If you don't have the time or facility to receive the mailing list, then you can search our online archives. Junk and spam mails are deleted, and your own e-mail address is protected by the unique Lyris system. Any queries about joining or leaving lists, or the lists in general, should be sent to listsupport@p2p.wrox.com.

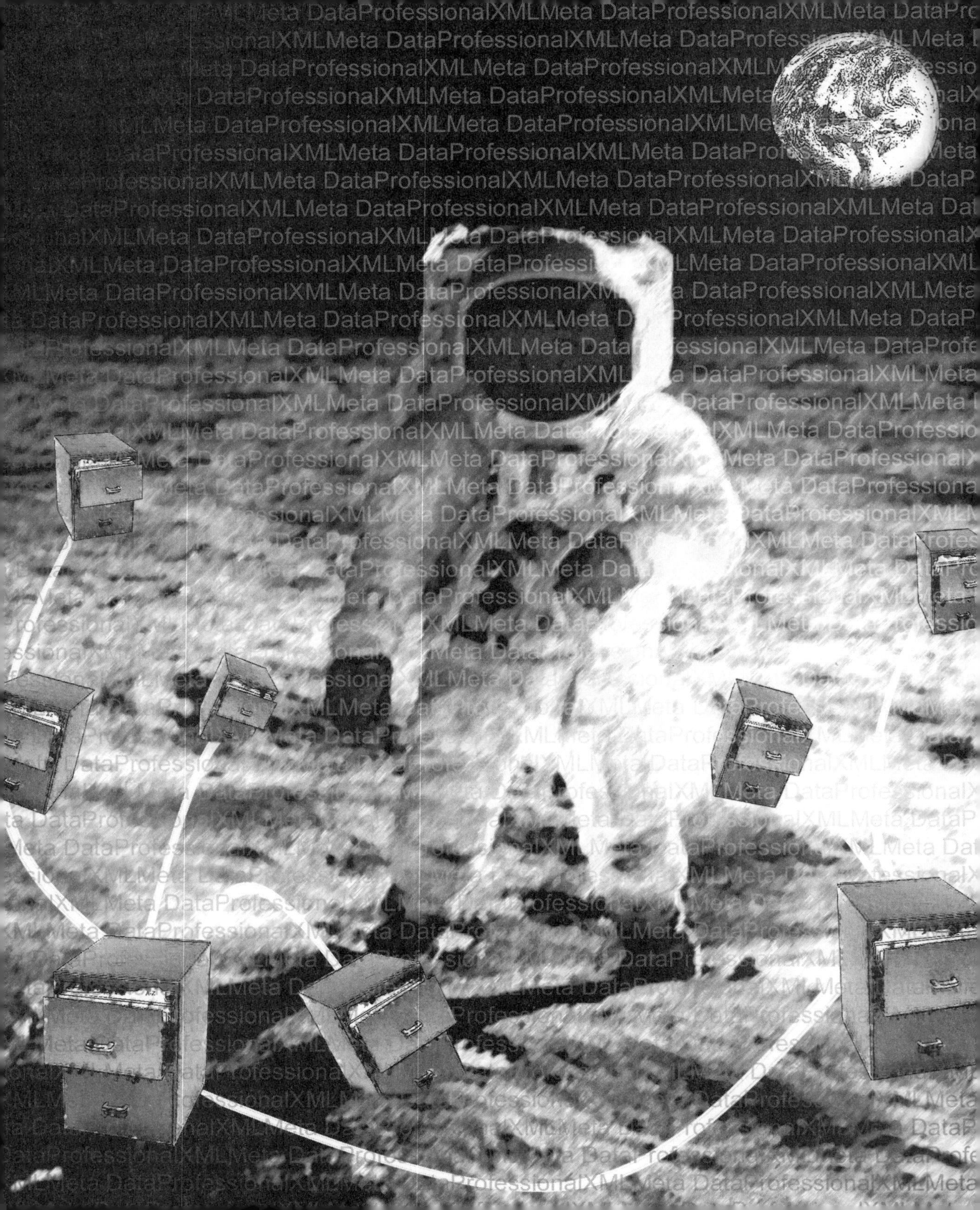
Meta DataProfessionalXML

1

Why Meta Data? Why XML?

Meta data is the essential "glue" which enables large collections of documents and data to function as organized libraries rather than disorganized junkyards. Nowadays, such collections are very rarely held on just one computer or even one network. Because of this, XML is an ideal medium for meta data because it can be understood by many different applications and systems.

However, that is only about 1 percent of the story. Meta data supports many functional requirements, such as electronic libraries, application integration, and web resource discovery – and is needed in many different system environments, such as local networks, large modular corporate intranets, and the WWW. So, as you might expect, there are about as many proposals for XML meta data technologies as there are combinations of requirements and environments. This book will help you make sense of this complex and rapidly evolving subject.

You may well be wondering why there are so many XML meta data solutions. This is partly because there are several possible technical approaches, all of which can work well; partly because different meta data content is required for different purposes; but mostly it is just because there are so many people and organizations working in parallel. Along with this go different motivating applications, and many competing dreams and visions – ultimate personal freedom, ultimate business success, ultimate targeted advertising, etc. In addition, there are numerous legacy technologies that have established techniques to offer (for example library cataloguing, software and hardware configuration management, distributed databases and data warehouses, networking protocols, business filing systems) – as well as people meeting these problems for the first time and inventing their own solutions.

To be fair, many, if not most, of the people and organizations involved *do* want to generate common, interoperating standards – but in the current state of development of the WWW and XML technology, this just means that there are many *groups* of people working on XML meta data technologies, rather than many individuals. The next twenty years or so may well lead to a gradual harmonization and "shake-out", but for now, a complex evolving pattern is what we've got. It is difficult to judge which technologies will emerge as clear leaders; I am sure that the technologies chosen for this book will not *all* be in use in five years time.

The unique strength of this book is that it combines in-depth introductions to a handful of the most prominent XML meta data technologies, with shorter overviews of some more specialized approaches (we can't cover them all – there are far too many!), together with mini-case studies to help you make sense of the whole picture. If this book helps you to choose appropriate technologies for your project's technical architecture, then we have succeeded.

The rest of this chapter contains an introduction to meta data and XML meta data technologies, followed by a detailed use case, which will hopefully help you understand some of the complex requirements which have driven the development of these technologies. Finally, there is a short discussion of the future of XML meta data technologies.

Meta Data and XML Meta Data Technologies

Our first question is, what exactly is **meta data**? A common short definition of meta data is that it is "data about data". In fact, meta data can be data about pretty much anything; what makes it meta data is its purpose and usage rather than its content or structure. Most often, meta data is designed to support people or programs in locating and retrieving information resources. A piece of data can be meta data to one application, and just data to another; meta data is also usually short and has a simple structure – and it's so familiar that you may not realize that you use meta data every day.

Think about using a collection of videotapes or CDs; if they were all just blank boxes, and you had to play each one to see what was recorded on it, then finding a particular film or track would be a long, tedious job. Add a label on each item giving a title, and picking out the right one immediately becomes very much easier. If the outer case of each one has a list of its contents, then finding the specific recording you are interested in should be straightforward. For a larger collection, you might add a searchable list or a subject index, together with a numbering system or shelf locations.

When you go beyond a few shelves of videos and CDs to a large library, or the World Wide Web, then the problem of finding exactly what you are looking for grows enormously – but the basic nature of the solution remains the same: make some simple, relevant, searchable information available, together with location information, and searching and retrieval becomes much easier. However, with this ease of location comes another problem: filtering and ranking results so that each user gets what they want – and not 10,000 other things they don't.

XML meta data technologies have been motivated by all levels of this problem – from adding simple labels to otherwise opaque data (such as weather station instrument readings), to providing for the WWW user the equivalent experience to walking round a well-organized IT or history section in a good conventional library.

Meta Data in XML

Meta data is an area where many different kinds of systems need to work together. For example, databases, AI-based search agents, even CAD systems, may use and hold meta data – and each of these technologies has its own characteristic approach and terminology.

The approach taken in this chapter is grounded in XML/SGML, as you might expect from a book entitled "Professional XML Meta Data", and is also inevitably influenced by the fact that the systems with meta data that I have worked with have been mostly concerned with technical publications, educational resources and course management, content management, and online information services. I also have some experience with application data integration using XML, and with inference-based systems. And of course this is why books such as this need a team of authors; you will meet a number of other perspectives later in this book.

*As we're looking at XML and meta data you might be thinking that the tags in XML documents could be considered to be meta data, but they are not included here – that deserves an explanation, so here it is. The tags embedded in an XML document do resemble meta data, for example if you look at the content alone, forgetting that it is an XML document, then you will see the XML tags as additional information providing structure and names for elements. However, an XML document is not just character data with embedded tags – it is a complete structure made up of elements with content, and character data with embedded tags is a common way of representing that structure. There is a different approach to representing XML document structure, called **standoff markup**, where the representation of the XML document structure is separated from the content, which is typically a pre-existing document such as an ancient Greek play. Standoff markup is meta data, but one of the many less-used techniques which have been left out of this book; embedded markup in data designed as XML is borderline, and for the purpose of this chapter, the wrong side of the border.*

> **From my perspective, the key characteristic of meta data is that, from the point of view of the application which is using it as meta data, it is ancillary information which is there for a specific purpose.**

XML meta data can take many different forms. It may be embedded in an XML document alongside the information it is about, or it may be held in a separate XML document. In the latter case it could identify what it is about by using, for example, a URI or an XPath expression. Perhaps the best way to understand this variety is by means of some examples of different kinds of meta data, along with their intended purposes:

❑ **Annotations**: These are side notes added to a document for a specific purpose; they will only be used by some readers, or by all readers but at different times and for different purposes. For example, comments added to a Microsoft Word document using the inbuilt "Comment" facility, or explanatory notes added to a literary text in XML, using XLink links to paragraphs held in a separate document.

Why are these meta data, rather than part of the content? This does depend on your point of view. For example, I am rewriting this paragraph during my first revision of this chapter, and the file I am modifying contains comments from reviewers and editors to me, and comments from me to them. From the perspective of the editing process, these can be seen as an integral part of the text; however, from your point of view as a reader, they are ancillary information belonging to the authoring process, and not part of the book as published. This kind of meta data is not the central concern of this book, so is not discussed further here. If you are interested in this aspect of meta data usage, a good starting point is the Text Encoding Initiative (TEI) home page (at http://www.tei-c.org/).

❑ **Cataloguing and identification**: This kind of meta data tends to associate specific properties and their values with whatever the meta data is about. For example, a library catalogue record for a printed book, giving its title, author, publisher, and date published. Another example is the identifying information held about me as a taxpayer, which enables me to conduct my tax affairs by post or electronic transaction rather than in person. In XML applications, this meta data is usually information about the properties of information resources, leading to the general name **resource based meta data** for this kind of meta data.

❑ **Subject indexes**: This refers to data which represents subjects and their interrelationships, and also usually designates specific information resources as belonging to these subjects. For example, a subject index to a library of books; an "index page" web page that gives collections of links to other documents, with the links organized using a list of subject areas. A closely related kind of meta data is the conventional back of book index; also the multiple hierarchical indexes found in technical manuals, where a part such as a valve in a pipe may be indexed by its place in a structure of sub-assemblies, and also by its role in some maintenance procedure. When it is implemented in XML, this kind of meta data can look very similar to resource based meta data, since the subjects can be modeled as properties of the information resources associated with them. However, it is useful to understand the difference between the underlying concepts, especially since that difference is a subtle but very important part of the difference in design intent and motivation between RDF and topic maps, two of the XML meta data standards discussed in depth in this book. **Subject based meta data** is a convenient general name for this kind of meta data.

❑ **Cross references**: Like annotations, these may not look like meta data from your point of view. However, cross references are an important kind of meta data for long-lived collections of documents, where documents are often cross referenced in ways not foreseen by their original authors. Cross references can have specific meanings, for example "see also" or "superseded by". In complex interdependent collections such as legal codes and cases, cross references grow into being **structural mappings**. Structural mappings are also found in engineering product data (historically in SGML, now often migrating to XML), where for example you can have a web interface for a field engineer making use of detailed interlinking between a maintenance manual for a complex piece of equipment; supplementary data from its design documentation; and a parts manual used for ordering spares.

I find that when I am learning about a new XML meta data technology, it is often very helpful to ask myself whether it is fundamentally resource based or subject based, or whether it provides a structural mapping. In practice, most technologies include aspects of both resource based and subject based meta data. This is partly because if you want to represent a subject inside a computer, you will probably end up doing so either by identifying the subject with an information resource such as a thesaurus entry, or by using a name for the subject as a value of a property. Also, if you have many resources with properties, you will want to control and structure which properties are used, and how they relate to each other, and the properties will take on a life of their own.

Examples of XML Meta Data Technology

This section contains short descriptions of just a few of the many XML meta data technologies. All of them are described in more detail later in this book; this section gives you a first glance at them, and hopefully also a feel for the range and diversity of XML meta data technologies available.

Schema Adjuncts

XML schemas describe elements within an XML document, in a way that allows the elements to be used anywhere in a well-formed XML document. (For further information see Chapter 2 of this book or *Professional XML 2nd edition*, ISBN 1-861005-05-9, and *Professional XML Schemas*, ISBN 1-861005-47-4, both from Wrox Press.) This notion of document structure and validity is a lot more adaptable, modular and reusable than DTDs. In particular, schema-defined structures from a number of different schemas can be combined and recombined for different purposes. So far so good – but apart from any human-readable information conveyed by tag names or schema namespace names, this does nothing to indicate why these syntactic structures are significant for any purpose. If you are just using XML schemas, the receiving system must still know exactly what to do with each schema-defined structure it receives – and this may mean a programming change for any modifications to the original designed XML structure.

Schema adjuncts are designed to overcome this problem by providing meta data for schema-validated XML documents. This is resource based meta data where the resources in question are the XML elements validated using the schema element type definitions. For example, you might have an XML application where the content of each element type is processed using a different set of parameters. The schema adjunct can either provide these parameters itself, or else provide a link (an XLink, URI, filename, or other identifier) to parameters held elsewhere. (There are some detailed examples of this in Chapter 8 when we look at Meaning Definition Language, MDL.)

Schema adjuncts have been hailed as providing semantics for schemas – this is a bit of an overstatement, but schema adjuncts can certainly help relate schema-driven XML data to other system resources within a distributed information processing system.

Schema adjuncts are not yet "mainstream", but the full realization of the potential of XML schemas does depend on systematic ways of associating processing with schema-validated elements. So, this is a technology to watch – either for its development in its own right, or for the incorporation of this concept into other XML technologies.

RDF

RDF (**Resource Description Framework**) is, as its full name suggests, a standard that grew out of a requirement to apply descriptions to information resources; it is also intended to facilitate the computer processing of distributed information such as web resources. Although RDF is usually seen in XML, this is not the only possible syntax for RDF.

One of the design goals of RDF is to make it possible to specify semantics for information resources in a standardized, interoperable manner. This is the basic RDF data model, as it appears in the RDF Recommendation (http://www.w3.org/TR/REC-rdf-syntax).

RDF has three object or entity types:

- ❑ **Resources**: All things being described by RDF expressions are called **resources**. A resource may be an entire web page; such as the HTML document "http://www.w3.org/Overview.html" for example. A resource may be a part of a web page; for example, a specific HTML or XML element within the document source. A resource may also be a whole collection of pages; for example, an entire web site. A resource may also be an object that is not directly accessible via the Web; for example, a printed book.

  Resources are always named by URIs plus optional anchor ids (see RFC 2396 at http://www.ietf.org/rfcrfc2396.txt?number=2396). Anything can have a URI; the extensibility of URIs allows the introduction of identifiers for any entity imaginable.

- ❑ **Properties**: A **property** is a specific aspect, characteristic, attribute, or relation used to describe a resource. Each property has a specific meaning, defines its permitted values, the types of resources it can describe, and its relationship with other properties.

  This document does not address how the characteristics of properties are expressed; for such information, refer to the latest revision of the RDF Schema Recommendation at http://www.w3.org/TR/rdf-schema/.

- ❑ **Statements**: A specific resource, together with a named property, plus the value of that property for that resource, is an RDF **statement**. These three individual parts of a statement are called, respectively, the **subject**, the **predicate**, and the **object**. The object of a statement (the property value) can be another resource or it can be a **literal**; a resource (specified by a URI) or a simple string or other primitive datatype defined by XML. In RDF terms, a literal may have content that is XML markup but is not further evaluated by the RDF processor. There are some syntactic restrictions on how markup in literals may be expressed.

For readers who find diagrams easier than words, here is a diagram from the specification showing a property with a structured value. In this type of diagram ovals represent resources, rectangles represent string literals and the lines (known as arcs) represent properties. The empty oval represents a resource that has not yet been assigned a URI:

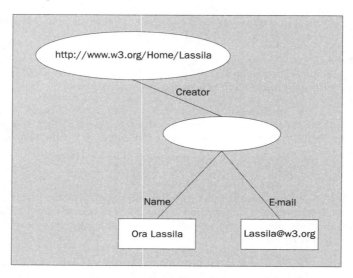

There are several statements of the form [subject][predicate][object] that can be made, such as [http://www.w3.org/Home/Lassila] [has creator] [something] and [something] [has name] [Ora Lassila].

This brief description can only give a rough flavor of RDF; there is a thorough description beginning in Chapter 4. RDF Schemas (covered in Chapter 5) extend the expressive power of the simple resource-property-value "triples" of basic RDF into a network of related descriptions, using types and classes. This is potentially very useful, though it is not yet clear how the version control and configuration management required for large interrelated collections of schemas will be accommodated.

RDF Schema is still formally under development. After being "frozen" at W3C Candidate Recommendation stage since 1999, it is now being taken forward by the RDF Core working group. One reason for this gap is that over the last two to three years, the Web meta data community has got together with the knowledge management community, under the banner of "the Semantic Web", and there is still a lot of work in progress to thrash out good standardized solutions to some of the difficult problems involved. Some of these issues are discussed in the section titled "*Ontologies*" below; you can find much further discussion indexed from the SemanticWeb.org index page (http://www.semanticweb.org), especially concerning the use of RDF together with DAML, which is meta data designed for use by software agents. RDF is also gaining a wide academic following, with several research projects using it in various ways.

Ontologies

Ontologies establish a common terminology, plus consensus on its interpretation, between members of a communicating community. These members can be human or automated agents. Ontology is a well-established field of research in both philosophy and AI, with many representations devised (before XML) with varying expressive power and computational properties. With XML emerging as the standard language for data interchange on the WWW, there was a clear requirement to exchange ontologies using an XML syntax. Examples include Simple HTML Ontology Extensions (SHOE, http://www.cs.umd.edu/projects/plus/SHOE/), Ontology Exchange Language (XOL, http://www.ai.sri.com/~pkarp/xol/), Ontology Markup Language/Conceptual Knowledge Markup Language (OML/CKML, http://www.ontologos.org/OML/CKML-Grammar.html), and Riboweb (http://riboweb.stanford.edu/). All of them use XML syntax, with their different origins reflected in different tag names and structures.

OIL (Ontology Interchange Language) is based on RDF and RDF Schema, and has been combined with DAML (DARPA Agent Markup Language, a framework providing information to web-agents) to give DAML+OIL, which is gaining wide acceptance.

There is comprehensive information on ontologies and ontology representation in XML, including all those mentioned above, indexed from http://www.semanticweb.org.

Topic Maps

Topic maps grew out of an original requirement for mergeable indexes for electronic publications, within the pre-XML SGML community. Driven by the ideal of ubiquitous shared information on the Web, organized by subject (similar to the motivation for RDF, but tending in a different direction), topic maps have grown into a meta data technology with a following cutting right across traditional divisions between publishing, knowledge management, web technology, and others.

As will be discussed in Chapter 7 of this book, the core concept of topic maps is a **topic**, a "dimensionless point" around which related information resources can gather. The underlying idea is that a subject such as "the fall of Rome" or "the rise of atomic power" does not have an existence in itself; it exists purely as a means of organizing information resources such as books, papers, TV documentaries, lectures, discussions, etc., into a related group. Individual resources do not inherently belong to any topic – they are *linked* to topics for particular purposes, or from particular points of view. For example, Gibbon's "Decline and Fall" (an information resource) could be linked to the topic "the fall of Rome" by someone studying the development of historical writing. In topic map terminology, Gibbon's "Decline and Fall" is an **occurrence**, in the **scope** "English Historiography", of the topic "the fall of Rome". Furthermore, the topics "the fall of Rome" and "the rise of atomic power" could be **associated** within this same scope, and also linked to resources discussing changing political attitudes and writing styles.

The strength of topic maps is in the versatility of the multiple filtered viewpoints and associative structures which can be built up using topics, associations, and scoping. However, this same strength is also a grave weakness – large, poorly organized concept structures can easily be built (especially by auto-generation from information prepared for a different purpose) – and will not be very useful. The current enthusiasm for topic maps in some parts of the XML community is reminiscent of the 1970s enthusiasm for Artificial Intelligence (AI) – and possibly has just as hard a fall to come. Perhaps most promising in this area is the involvement of a number of experienced AI people in topic maps, together with strong links to the broader "Semantic Web" community.

Well used, topic maps have great potential – for instance in the representation of ontologies and thesauri as organizing structures for large collections of information resources. There is also work in hand to define the relationship between topic maps and RDF – in principle, anything you can do with one you can do with the other, but they will be much more powerful if used together, in ways which respect their respective strengths and weaknesses. See Chapter 11 and the paper by Graham Moore, presented at XML Europe 2001 (http://www.topicmaps.com/topicmapsrdf.pdf), for an up-to-date discussion (at the time of writing) – more progress is expected to be reported at the Extreme Markup Languages conference in August 2001 (see http://www.gca.org for further information on this conference series).

Dublin Core

Dublin Core is a standard for what you put in meta data, rather than a standard for how meta data is represented. It is included here because it is widely used, and very appropriate (by design) for use with electronic documents in XML which are intended to be used much like print documents. Because of this, the information contained in the Dublin Core elements is very similar to bibliographic information for printed documents. As discussed in Chapter 4, the Core meta data elements include `Title` (a name given to the resource), `Creator` (an entity primarily responsible for making the content of the resource), `Subject` (the topic of the content of the resource), and `Date` (a date associated with an event in the life cycle of the resource).

Although clearly originally inspired by bibliographic requirements for electronic documents, the scope of Dublin Core as stated in the Recommendation (http://www.dublincore.org/documents/dces/) and accompanying documents is very broad: a resource is "anything that has identity"; and the aim is "interoperable online meta data standards". The Dublin Core collection of meta data standards is a lot more than the Core itself: there are reference bindings to programming languages and to RDF, for example, together with a methodology for community-specific extensions.

A big virtue of Dublin Core is its simplicity, and its independence from any representing syntax. You can represent it in simple XML, or in RDF, but it is still Dublin Core no matter how it is represented, and it is designed to be easy for systems to translate from one representation to another. In this respect, it is a model of good practice for standards and specifications concerning the content of meta data.

A Real World Scenario – UK Government Interoperability Framework

Let us take a look at a real world example in the field of meta data technologies – the UK government interoperability framework for delivering new electronic services in the public sector.

The UK Government has initiated a drive throughout the public sector in the UK towards making information-based services and transactions happen electronically, and using a single interoperable set of standards and methods. This activity started formally with the "Modernising Government White Paper" of March 1999, which gave "a new target of all dealings with Government being available electronically by 2008" (since revised to 2005); the objective is to have "joined-up government in action – including a clear commitment for people to be able to notify different parts of government of details such as a change of address simply and electronically in one transaction".

As you might imagine, this is not as simple as it looks. The first substantive step was the definition of the "electronic Government Interoperability Framework", commonly known as e-GIF. Key points of e-GIF are:

❑ Its aim is to aid the seamless flow of information across Government, whilst ensuring that data protection and information security are still respected.

❑ Adherence is mandatory for all new projects and outward facing legacy systems (especially, of course, projects initiated to meet the 2005 deadline).

❑ It includes the provision of guidance and support to related projects regarding best practice, toolkits, and schema development.

❑ It is supported by http://www.govtalk.gov.uk, which holds publicly available documents and project workspaces, and also hosts formal public consultations on individual specifications.

The e-GIF Model

The e-GIF itself is in three sections:

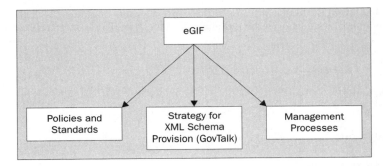

The first part defines the policies and standards to be applied in electronic interactions between the public and private sectors, and within the public sector. The second is described as a strategy for schema provision, although it also includes many aspects of information management and general usage of meta data. The third is the process for maintaining the e-GIF itself.

The interactions covered by the e-GIF fall into in three broad categories: citizen to government (C2G), business to government (B2G), and intra-government (G2G). The account given here concentrates on C2G and G2G, where "government" includes the full public sector, including local government and the National Health Service.

Policies

The policies in e-GIF are based on internet standards and technology as the means of service delivery. The other main policies are the adoption of XML as the core technology for data integration (including meta data), and the adoption of the web browser as the key human computer interface. At a lower level, relating specifically to meta data, Dublin Core has been adopted, with extensions (minimal ones) to cover more specific requirements. See http://www.govtalk.gov.uk for further details.

Although the use of XML required some promotion and justification when the e-GIF was under development in 1998, now that decision just looks obvious. This early decision to use XML is now being refined into working policies regarding XML technologies for specific parts of the architecture, with XML Schema seeing the most action at the present time.

Another significant policy is the use of the browser as the key interface. The core policy is that all information must be available through a browser, although the definition of the browser is sufficiently broad to include WAP devices, digital TV and other delivery channels. However, this is being reviewed as detailed requirements are developed for specific services – for example, when sending payroll information at the end of the tax year, small companies might well wish to complete a web form, while larger companies and payroll bureau would prefer to just press a "submit" button in their payroll system, sending XML data which is not intended or suited for browser use.

Standards

The e-GIF specifies a set of standards selected according to criteria regarding interoperability, openness, market support, and scalability. They cover interconnection, data integration, and information access, and the overall aim is to make support of the e-GIF simple and cheap for implementers. These implementers include IT departments in the public sector, and also independent software vendors such as the manufacturers of accounting systems and farm management systems.

The standards that are of particular interest in the context of this book are the XML technologies selected, all of which in some way involve the use of meta data. The base standards are, from the W3C:

❑   XML.

❑   Namespaces in XML.

❑   XML Schema.

❑   XSL.

❑   XML Signature.

and defined by Government:

❑   Information architecture.

❑   Envelope and other common schemas.

❑   Gateway interoperation standards.

Support

The development of an effective infrastructure for all this, and support for projects wanting to interoperate within that framework, is being managed by a team within the Cabinet Office, responsible to a senior civil servant given the title of e-Envoy (a nice quirky blend of modern terminology and UK civil service tradition). The policies and adoption of external standards are at the time of writing (June 2001) relatively stable; the major work in hand is the development of the next level: the meta data schemas required to turn the concepts and architecture (outlined below) into working systems.

The support being offered by the Office of the e-Envoy includes:

❑   Development of XML Schemas defining core meta data.

❑   Best practices guidelines (for example guidelines on designing XML Schemas for meta data structures).

❑   Facilitating the development of other schemas, for example by holding meetings where departments with similar information requirements can get together to design common data structures, and by managing formal public consultation on draft schemas prior to adoption.

All this is happening under the general name of "GovTalk"; you can see several schemas already developed, on the UK GovTalk web site at http://www.govtalk.gov.uk.

UK Online Infrastructure

The roles played by meta data in this scenario will become very clear when you see the architecture being used. The first diagram shows the overall architecture of UK Online, a collection of services and portals giving a single access point for government information and services:

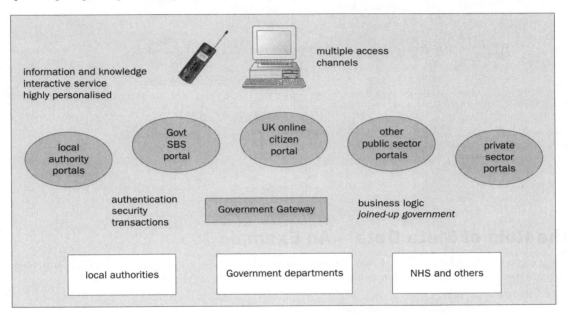

Within this overall architecture, a number of different layers are required, with careful management of security, whilst allowing all the required business relationships (for example, professionals such as accountants and lawyers working on behalf of companies and individuals; companies providing services on contract to local government, etc., etc.).

A key part of the UK Online architecture is the Government Gateway. Its role is to authenticate users, authorize requests for e-services, route transactions to destination organizations, provide retrieval of output communications, provide a payment service, etc., and do it safely and securely, 24x7. The gateway architecture is shown in the following diagram:

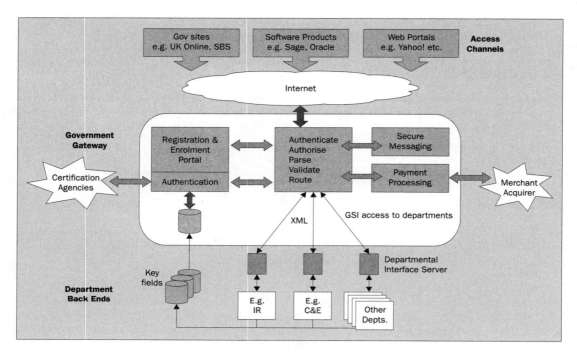

The Role of Meta Data – An Example

To give you an idea of the essential role of meta data in this scenario, consider this model for authentication (of participants in a gateway transaction):

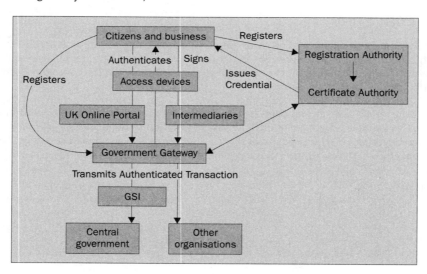

In this diagram, whatever information a citizen or business is sending to central government passes through all these stages unchanged and unread. Everything you can see here is to do with meta data. There are signatures, certificates, protocols, and so on – all using XML meta data technologies. The majority of the meta data implemented so far in this project is using XML Schema to define the structure of the meta data, and also in its own right as meta data identifying the structure of messages, message envelopes, etc., coming through the gateway. XML Signature (http://www.w3.org/Signature/) is also being used for authentication.

The gateway went live on 25 January 2001; transactions started in March: two kinds of tax return and a farm subsidy claim. This is a small beginning, and there is much more work to be done; hopefully a future edition of this book will be able to say much more about its development and implementation, but you have at least seen that meta data technologies are beginning to reach realization.

The Future of XML Meta Data

XML meta data is without doubt here to stay. However, I believe there is something important to be learned here from the fate of the W3C Meta Data Activity. That group defined meta data as "machine understandable information for the web"; it did much useful work, but the key fact in this context is that after issuing the basic RDF Recommendation, and taking RDF Schema through to Candidate Recommendation status, it was wound up, and succeeded as a top-level W3C activity by the W3C Semantic Web Activity. To me, this is a clear indication that the development of data structures in XML is becoming less of an aim in itself, with more emphasis now given to wider concerns based on user needs, and this is a "Good Thing".

However promising all this is, remember that it is not yet a fully developed working technology. What XML meta data lacks so far more than anything is proven, high profile applications. The WWW has moved into mainstream IT; and it is mainstream IT which will be the effective driving force for the next 20 years of the Web, including the XML meta data technologies. One to watch for as an early starter is the UK Government's UK Online development as discussed in the scenario above – this is still in its early stages, but you can watch its progress and see the emerging technical specifications on its technical consultation web site at http://www.govtalk.gov.uk.

Summary

In this introductory chapter we've taken a brief look at some of the meta data terms and technologies that will be covered in much greater detail later in the book. Perhaps more importantly we discussed why these technologies came about, the needs they aim to fulfil, and gave an honest appraisal of current progress. XML meta data is a rapidly evolving and exciting area to be involved in – we'll begin our study of the individual technologies by first learning about the various XML schemas.

DataProfessionalXMLMeta DataProfessionalXMLMeta DataProfessionalXMLMeta

2

XML Schemas

It is frequently stated that knowledge management is a key factor in a business establishing or maintaining its competitive position in our rapidly changing economic environment. Few organizations lack data – most are swamped by huge volumes of it, much of which may be ill understood and inadequately exploited. The problem is one of failing to make effective business use of the large volumes of data that are already available. Such a failure is due, for example, to a lack of awareness that the required data exists, a lack of appropriate or widely understood structure of the data, or the use of several incompatible data structures within an organization. If data cannot be easily and predictably accessed, or its implications or importance understood, or if two or more related pieces of data cannot be easily used together for a business purpose, then inefficiency in knowledge exploitation and wasted business opportunity results.

Increasingly, storing data or documentation in XML, or passing data as XML between business units or business applications, is seen as an effective approach within a knowledge management strategy where data must be interchanged between departments within organizations or between separate organizations. As more and more data is held or passed as XML, it becomes increasingly important to have a grasp of the content and structure of the potentially huge amounts of information held as XML. In all but the smallest business environment it is not possible to examine each and every individual document. Some form of information about the data held – the meta data which is the subject of this book – is essential and is a more practical and manageable asset to understand. **XML schemas**, of several types, can help provide that important information about the content and structure of XML instance documents. Understanding how to use XML schemas efficiently in a knowledge management strategy is of great importance.

There are many aspects to gaining a grasp of and exploiting information, or meta data, about the business data which a corporation holds as XML, and it isn't possible to cover all aspects of that in one chapter. In this chapter we will examine the basics of XML schemas and their use as part of an effective knowledge management strategy to gain meta data, in some usable form, about the data which may already be held by the organization. Where data or documents are held as XML, potentially useful information about the content of documents or XML-based data files may already be held as XML schemas – either as a **document type definition (DTD)** or in a schema written in XML itself. If that meta data held as XML schemas is not exploited then an opportunity is being missed. As an alternative or adjunct to use in the discovery of meta data, XML schemas also provide a prospective way of deciding on or ensuring the structure of business documents or data.

In this chapter I will introduce you to a number of the available flavors of XML schemas and discuss how they can contribute to understanding the knowledge that is already stored in a business context. I cannot hope to cover all issues relating to XML schemas.

More specifically, I will describe the original XML schema, the DTD, which was defined within the original XML 1.0 Recommendation, and discuss how DTDs may be used to provide meta data. More information on DTDs can be found in *Professional XML*, 2nd Edition, Wrox Press, ISBN 1-861005-05-9.

In addition I will describe the recently released XML Schema from the W3C, which is constructed using an XML-based syntax, and which I term **XSD Schema**. For a fuller treatment of XSD Schema, see Wrox's *Professional XML Schemas* (ISBN 1-861005-47-4).

Brief mention will also be made of RELAX NG, the combined proposal of what was formerly TREX and RELAX.

> **Throughout this chapter I will use the term "XSD Schema" to refer to the World Wide Web Consortium's XML schema, simply but potentially confusingly termed "XML Schema".**

So, before looking at the characteristics of each of these available forms of XML schema and discussing their relative merits as sources of meta data, let's look at some general issues which relate, in varying measure, to all schemas.

Introduction to Schemas

In this section I will discuss some general issues that we need to bear in mind when thinking about schemas of any type, although the focus will primarily be on issues that are directly relevant to XML schemas.

> **A schema is a description or definition of the structure of a database or other data source. In our context the term XML schema refers to a definition of the structure of a class of XML documents, whether or not the XML schema is itself written in XML syntax. Thus the broad term "XML schema" includes DTDs, the W3C's XSD Schema, and other XML schemas such as RELAX NG, XDR, Schematron, etc., that will be discussed later.**

What Do Schemas Do?

The key thing that schemas do is to provide us with an overview of the allowable content or structure of data of a variety of types. A schema provides us with an abstract definition of the relationships and characteristics of a class of objects or pieces of data.

Schemas, while they have slightly different meanings in different contexts, are a means of describing or constraining the structure and content of some data. That data may be in the form of structured documents, or may be highly complex relational or other data.

In the context of relational databases, a **database schema** defines the table names and columns, describes the relationships between tables (via keys), and acts as a repository for triggers and stored procedures. In the context of object oriented programming, a **class interface** is in essence a schema that describes the properties and methods of a class of objects.

In XML, an XML schema describes the ordering and inter-relationships of XML elements and attributes in the class of XML documents to which the schema applies. In addition, optionally, an XML schema may provide simple or sophisticated constraints on the data types allowable in parts of or all instance documents of the class to which it applies.

Why Do We Need Schemas?

The Extensible Markup Language provides enormous flexibility in creating structured XML documents or data sets. That flexibility is both an advantage and a potential difficulty. The advantage is that we can create XML documents that can meaningfully reflect an enormous diversity of real-world situations. The disadvantage is that the potential diversity of the detail of document structures is even more daunting, and to process documents efficiently we must have some means of determining the bounds within which the structure and content of a document instance or a class of documents is contained.

XML documents must, according to the specification, be well-formed, having correctly nested elements and balanced start and end tags, for example. In addition to well-formedness, such documents may additionally be checked for validity – that is they must conform to the structure and constraints on content defined in an XML schema.

When we come to exchange XML documents with other users or companies it is essential that the sender and recipient have the same expectations about the content of XML documents. As the volume of XML-based "messages" increases, so the efficient functioning of e-business will depend increasingly on understanding the structure and content of those interchanges, enabling processing in a predictable way. Of course, it is possible to examine the content and structure of every exchanged XML document, but it is much more efficient to use an XML schema to provide meta data about those documents as a class.

The Trustworthiness of a Schema

An important issue in connection with any schema is assurance of whether or not the schema, or other meta data, accurately describes the data or content to which it applies. It is not safe to assume, without appropriate checks, that the schema or meta data necessarily corresponds, as it ought, to the data which it describes.

For example, if you have had any exposure to HTML web pages you will likely be familiar with the <META> tags contained in the <HEAD> tag of an HTML page, which contain a description, supposedly, of the content of the <BODY> tags of the same HTML/XHTML document. The content of such <META> tags is a form of schema that ought to describe the content of the HTML page. In practice the content of the <META> tags can be largely fictional, being made up of information unconnected to the actual content of the page and more concerned with marketing of a web site. This everyday scenario with HTML illustrates the pitfalls which can result from a situation where supposed meta data exists but there is no easy and reproducible way to confirm that the meta data and the content to which it refers correspond fully.

The loose coupling between HTML <META> tags and the HTML content which they purport to describe arises because there is no mechanism for validating the content of the <META> tags as accurately representing the web page content. When we come to XML schemas that problem need not arise since XML schemas for XML instance documents are to a lesser degree marketing documents, rather they are descriptive. XML schemas must correspond to the XML instance documents in the manner described in the W3C Recommendations for XML 1.0 (which describes the rules for Document Type Definitions) and XML Schema (which describes the rules for XSD Schemas). Validating XML parsers provide the necessary checking mechanism to ensure that an XML instance document, and the XML schema that is believed to describe it, do in fact correspond to each other. Thus, in our consideration of XML schemas and their use as meta data, the practical value of validating parsers becomes clear, since without them we cannot conveniently determine whether or not the schema and the instance documents correspond fully, partly or at all.

Schemas as a Basis for Querying

One important use for XML schemas in the discovery of XML meta data is as a basis for querying of document instances. In the absence of a schema we could discover the general structure of a class of XML documents by examining a number of such documents. However, in the absence of a formal schema we would always, to a degree, be guessing at whether we had viewed all possible variants of allowed content. Using an XML schema we can be sure, subject to the document being validated against that schema, that we know the permitted structure for all documents in that class and can therefore design queries appropriately.

Querying of XML data is the subject of Chapter 3, so we will leave any further discussion until then.

Defining the Structure of an XML Document

In defining the structure of a class of XML documents you will want to proceed through some form of information modeling process, such as that described in Chapter 11 of *Professional XML Schemas* (ISBN 1-861005-47-4). In the discussion that follows in the remainder of this chapter, it will be assumed that you have carried out some form of information modeling appropriate to the needs of your own project.

For XML documents and data structures there are two broadly defined alternative types of schema – those written in XML itself, which we will look at later in this chapter, and those written in a non-XML syntax, that is the Document Type Definition (DTD). The syntax and characteristics of the DTD and of XSD Schema will be described. XSD Schema was created because of a realization of the limitations of the DTD, particularly when applied to data-centric rather than document-centric uses of XML.

Document Type Definitions – DTDs

In the strict sense of the term a DTD is an XML schema – it describes the content and structure of a class of XML documents. More narrowly, XML schemas are descriptions *in XML syntax* of the content and structure of such a class of XML document instances. A number of XML schemas exist, some of which will be described later in this chapter, but in this section I will examine the use of DTDs and consider how they perform as sources of meta data.

A class of XML documents that share a common vocabulary and structure is termed a **document type**. Each individual XML document belonging to a particular document type is termed an **instance document**. The XML 1.0 Recommendation provides that a DTD contains the description of the structure and allowed content for a particular document type. Thus the DTD is a schema, admittedly not in XML syntax, which describes the content and structure of a class of XML instance documents. If we understand the structure expressed by a DTD, then assuming that we can be sure that instance documents are genuinely valid against that DTD, we can be sure of the permitted structure within all and any instance documents.

The DTD was a facet of the Extensible Markup Language (XML), which it inherited from the **Standard Generalized Markup Language (SGML)**. The syntax of DTDs, which we will examine in a little more detail later, uses a format that is visibly not XML. For users of XML who had a background in SGML, familiarity with the syntax of DTDs was a given, but for the much larger numbers of programmers who have (or will) come to XML with no background whatsoever in SGML the need to learn two forms of syntax – XML 1.0 and **Extended Backus-Naur Form (EBNF)** – is an additional hurdle, which for some is a significant barrier to early understanding of some topics. Given the increasing importance of schemas in the XML world it would be advantageous if that barrier could be removed.

Creating a Simple DTD

I find that quite a number of people glaze over when first seeing a DTD of any complexity, so in this section I am going to introduce you to the syntax of DTDs at a very gentle pace, using short examples to illustrate how a DTD describes the constraints on the content of a class of XML documents. In a later example we will look at creating and understanding an example DTD which, although substantially simpler than many real-world DTDs, serves to illustrate many practical issues regarding creating and interpreting DTDs.

Linking a DTD to Instance Documents

At its simplest a DTD must be linked in some way to the XML document instance(s) that it is intended to describe. The XML 1.0 Recommendation provides two ways for that to be done. The DTD can be incorporated directly, into the confusingly named **document type declaration** commonly called the DOCTYPE declaration (as the *internal subset* of the DTD), or it can be a wholly separate file which is referenced from the DOCTYPE declaration (the *external subset* of the DTD). Alternatively, both the internal and external subsets may be used to refer to a particular document instance.

Each XML instance document may have only one DOCTYPE declaration. Each DOCTYPE declaration may reference only one DTD. That single DTD may be split into internal and external subsets but for the purposes of validating the instance document there is only one DTD.

For our purpose in discovering meta data, there are significant disadvantages when the internal subset of the DTD is used. The prioritization of element and attribute definitions in the external and internal subsets of the DTD, within the rules of XML 1.0, means that any use of the internal subset will over-ride the definition of any element or attribute already defined in the external subset. When dealing with small numbers of documents, such fine tuning or individualization of the DTD may be useful, but when dealing with information on a large scale any modifications made within the internal subset of allowed structure or content previously defined in the external subset may hamper an accurate understanding of the content and structure of a class of XML documents. Depending on how substantial the modifications made within the internal subset are, it may also cause particular problems in processing modified documents, if no allowance has been made for changes in structure or content. Those documents may be processed correctly by applications aware of any modifications in the internal subset, but may cause a processing error when the criteria of the external subset are applied.

For establishing a sound knowledge of the meta data which applies to a class of XML documents it is advantageous to use solely the external subset of the DTD. In other words, to have all information defining structure and content in a single external file, which applies to all instance documents in the class of documents, rather than have multiple tweaks for each instance document within an internal subset.

The syntax of the DOCTYPE declaration permits the use of PUBLIC and SYSTEM identifiers to reference a file containing the external subset of the DTD. In the examples that follow I will use only the SYSTEM identifier, since that allows you to easily run the examples on your own machine if you wish. For a fuller discussion of DTD syntax and usage see Chapter 5, "Validating XML: DTDs", in *Professional XML 2nd Edition* from Wrox Press (ISBN 1-86100-5-05-9).

The following very simple example instance document, HelloWorld.xml, uses the SYSTEM identifier to delineate the URI at which the DTD is located:

```
<?xml version="1.0"?>
<!DOCTYPE global_greeting SYSTEM "HelloWorld.dtd">
<global_greeting>
Hello, world!
</global_greeting>
```

The DTD (or more strictly the external subset of the DTD), HelloWorld.dtd, looks like this:

```
<!ELEMENT global_greeting (#PCDATA)>
```

The DOCTYPE declaration in the instance document has the **element type name** of the document element as its first parameter, in this case <global_greeting>. If that first parameter does not match the element type name then an error will occur.

The definition of the element <global_greeting> is that it has an element type name of <global_greeting> and its permitted content is **parsed character data**, as indicated by (#PCDATA) in the element type definition.

Element Type Declarations

All well-formed XML documents must contain at least one element; therefore even the very simplest of XML documents, such as the one you saw in the preceding section, must contain an element type declaration in the corresponding DTD. Typically, an XML document will contain many elements, forming a potentially deeply nested hierarchy, with some elements being allowed to contain other elements, while some elements may only be permitted to contain parsed character data. Some will be empty elements and some will contain **mixed content**, consisting of both elements and PCDATA.

If we add a little to our previous simple example to include a couple of nested elements we can see in the XML instance document, `HelloMillenium.xml`:

```
<?xml version="1.0"?>
<!DOCTYPE global_greeting SYSTEM "HelloMillenium.dtd">
<global_greeting>
  <welcome>Hello, world! Welcome to a new Millenium.</welcome>
  <farewell>Have a good century!</farewell>
</global_greeting>
```

and its corresponding DTD, `HelloMillenium.dtd`:

```
<!ELEMENT global_greeting (welcome,farewell) >
<!ELEMENT welcome (#PCDATA)>
<!ELEMENT farewell (#PCDATA)>
```

that expressing the notion that the `<global_greeting>` element contains a `<welcome>` element and a `<farewell>` element in that order is very straightforward. Having established that the `<global_greeting>` element contains one `<welcome>` element, followed by one `<farewell>` element, we then proceed to define the allowed content of the `<welcome>` and `<farewell>` elements.

> *In the example above the location of the DTD is the same directory as the XML instance document. If that is not the case then you must provide an appropriate relative or absolute URI.*

An element may have a **content model** of one of the five categories indicated in the following table:

Content Category	Meaning
ANY	The element can contain content of any structure, provided that it is well-formed XML. Thus while the parser checks for well-formedness, no check is made for validity.
element	The element may have child elements (which may contain content of any of the five categories) but the parent element may not directly contain character data.
EMPTY	The element has no child element or character data content (only attributes are permitted).
mixed	The element may contain either parsed character data or child elements.
PCDATA	The element may contain parsed character data only (but may also additionally have attributes).

The ANY category is totally unhelpful as far as helping to elucidate meta data is concerned, and is also undesirable since it provides no control over content which is well-formed XML. If you wish to be able to include XML comments or processing instructions you would need to use an ANY content model. An element with ANY content can, at least in principle, contain just about anything. Thus it is very difficult to conduct validation of such an element. An element type declaration for this category would look like this:

```
<!ELEMENT AnyWellFormedHere ANY >
```

The element category provides us with two choices – a **sequence list** or a **choice list**. If we want to ensure that child elements are in a particular order, then we would use a sequence list, using a comma as a separator:

```
<!ELEMENT InOrder (FirstChild, SecondChild, ThirdChild) >
```

as here:

```
<InOrder>
  <FirstChild/>
  <SecondChild/>
  <ThirdChild/>
</InOrder>
```

Or, if the child elements could occur in any order, we would use a choice list, using a vertical bar as a separator:

```
<!ELEMENT AnyOrder (FourthChild | SecondChild | ThirdChild | FirstChild)+ >
```

giving us this possibility:

```
<AnyOrder>
  <FourthChild/>
  <SecondChild/>
  <ThirdChild/>
  <FirstChild/>
</AnyOrder>
```

or this one, where not all elements are present:

```
<AnyOrder>
  <SecondChild/>
</AnyOrder>
```

or this one where the order of elements is different:

```
<AnyOrder>
  <FirstChild/>
  <ThirdChild/>
  <FourthChild/>
  <SecondChild/>
</AnyOrder>
```

or one of many other variants. You can see how we have lost control over the precise structure of the document.

Typically, a choice list would be used with a **cardinality operator** indicating how many times the elements in the choice list may be used. In the example above we have one or more occurrences, indicated by the + operator. Notice that not only do we lose control of the ordering of the elements when using a choice list, we also cannot be sure that all four elements will occur, nor that each element will occur any specified number of times. That degree of flexibility is desirable for creation of XML *documents*, but is a very loose framework for many data-centric uses of XML.

The EMPTY category means that there is nothing between the start and end tags of an XML element, but that element will have one or more attributes. An element type declaration for the EMPTY category would look like this:

```
<!ELEMENT NothingInHere EMPTY>
```

The mixed category allows us to have both parsed character data and elements as content. In a DTD we cannot specify a sequence of the parsed character data and elements, and must use a choice list of the type you saw for the element category. However, to use character data with element content the PCDATA must be declared first, as here:

```
<!ELEMENT MixedContent (#PCDATA | SecondElement | ThirdElement |
FirstElement)* >
```

The fact that #PCDATA must appear first in the choice list does not constrain the position of any occurrence of PCDATA within the element which contains mixed content. Again, typically, there would be an indication of how often the content in the choice list could be used. In the above example the * operator indicates that the content of the choice list would be included zero or more times.

In the example later in the DTD section we will see examples of element type declarations that use element, mixed, and PCDATA content.

Attribute Declarations

Defining elements is something that has to be done in every DTD. A DTD other than a trivial one is likely also to contain attributes of many elements.

A simple example of the way in which we can include attributes in a DTD is shown here. An XML instance document, PhoneNumbers.xml, might look something like this:

```
<?xml version='1.0'?>
<!DOCTYPE PhoneNumbers SYSTEM "PhoneNumbers.dtd">
<PhoneNumbers>
  <PhoneNumber type="Home">020 123 456789</PhoneNumber>
  <PhoneNumber type="Office">020 987 65432</PhoneNumber>
  <PhoneNumber type="Mobile">020 098 7654321</PhoneNumber>
</PhoneNumbers>
```

with its DTD, PhoneNumbers.dtd, looking like this:

```
<!ELEMENT PhoneNumbers (PhoneNumber*)>
<!ELEMENT PhoneNumber (#PCDATA)>
<!ATTLIST PhoneNumber type (Home | Office | Mobile) #REQUIRED>
```

The instance document has a simple structure. The document element is the element <PhoneNumbers>, which contains in our example three <PhoneNumber> elements, each of which has a type attribute.

The first line of the DTD indicates that zero or more <PhoneNumber> elements may occur as children of the <PhoneNumbers> element. The * indicates the cardinality of zero or more. Cardinality will be discussed in more detail in the next section.

Each `<PhoneNumber>` element contains parsed character data, the syntax for which you have seen previously.

To indicate that the `<PhoneNumber>` element has an attribute, as in this case, or potentially many attributes, we use the following syntax:

```
<!ATTLIST PhoneNumber type (Home | Office | Mobile) #REQUIRED>
```

The `ATTLIST` is short for "attribute list" – in this case there is only one attribute. The parameter `PhoneNumber` indicates unambiguously that the `ATTLIST` refers to a `<PhoneNumber>` element. The next parameter indicates that the name of the attribute is "`type`". The choice list:

```
(Home | Office | Mobile)
```

indicates that there are three possible values that the `type` attribute is allowed to take: Home, Office, or Mobile. The following keyword:

```
#REQUIRED
```

indicates that the `type` attribute is *required* on each `<PhoneNumber>` element.

Cardinality

Cardinality defines how often an element may occur in a particular position in an XML document. An attribute may, of course, occur only once on any one element so the issue of cardinality doesn't arise for attributes.

DTDs permit us to express the four choices of cardinality listed in the following table:

Cardinality Operator	Meaning
[No operator]	The absence of a cardinality operator indicates that exactly one occurrence of the element is required.
?	The ? operator indicates that zero or one occurrences are allowed.
*	The * operator indicates that zero or more occurrences of an element are allowed.
+	The + operator indicates that one or more occurrences of an element are allowed.

Let's look at a few fragments of DTD code that illustrate these.

The following code snippet:

```
<!ELEMENT PersonalDetails (FirstName, MiddleInitial*, LastName, Street*, City?,
PhoneNumber+, Email+) >
```

would indicate that the `<PersonalDetails>` element must have exactly one `<FirstName>` element child, an optional `<MiddleInitial>` element child (zero or more occurrences), exactly one `<LastName>` child element, zero or more `<Street>` element children, an optional `<City>` element child, a required `<PhoneNumber>` element which may occur more than once, and a required `<Email>` element which may occur more than once.

There are limitations to how precisely a DTD can define cardinality. There is, for example, no way in which a DTD can express the notion that an element must occur "at least twice and up to 7 times". We can only express that the minimum number of occurrences is zero or one, and that the maximum number of occurrences is unbounded.

DTDs – Datatypes

Datatyping in DTDs is very weak. In many situations when we want to ensure that meta data is both precise and accurate we would want to constrain input of information into an individual data item. For example, in an invoice we might want to ensure that what was entered into a `<DatePurchased>` element could only be a valid date, rather than some mistyped information. Unfortunately DTDs do not allow us to provide that useful, indeed necessary, constraint. A DTD can indicate that the element contains parsed character data but is unable to specify that the parsed character data should be a date, a currency value, a product ID in a particular format, etc. Since a DTD cannot express that constraint, a DTD-orientated validating parser is unable to check the content of the element, beyond ensuring that it contains parsed character data. If it does contain parsed character data, even though the particular characters are nonsense in context, a DTD-orientated validating parser will pass that entry as valid. Thus, from a business perspective, additional custom programming will be necessary to validate the content of documents, adding potential delays and additional development costs.

Creating a DTD

Let's move on and analyze how we might create a DTD for a class of XML instance documents that is a little less trivial than the examples you have seen so far. This example is substantially simpler than real world DTDs you are likely to be asked to interpret or create but it will serve to demonstrate some relevant techniques that can be applied to more substantial tasks. It is often said that a company's greatest asset is its people, so it would be natural for a company to wish to know what information it has on file about its employees. Our example will create and analyze a significantly simplified human resources file stored as XML.

First, let's look at a typical instance document which our DTD will be required to describe. This is a simplified human resources file `HRFile01.xml`. In a typical employment situation such a file would contain dozens, hundreds, or even thousands of entries. To save space I have shown it with the entry for only one person.

```xml
<?xml version='1.0'?>
<HRFile>
  <Person>
    <EmployeeNo>12345</EmployeeNo>
    <Name>
      <FirstName>John</FirstName>
      <MiddleInitial>R</MiddleInitial>
      <LastName>Smith</LastName>
    </Name>
    <ContactInformation>
      <HomePhone>020 123 456789</HomePhone>
      <WorkPhone>020 987 654321</WorkPhone>
      <WorkExtension status="current">1234</WorkExtension>
      <WorkExtension status="lapsed">2345</WorkExtension>
      <EmailAddresses>
        <Email>JohnR@xmml.com</Email>
        <Email>JohnR@XSL-T.com</Email>
        <Email>JohnR@FreeEmailAddressesForAnyoneWhoIsInterested.com</Email>
      </EmailAddresses>
    </ContactInformation>
```

```
      <Address>
        <Street>123 Main Street</Street>
        <Street>Old Town</Street>
        <City>London</City>
        <PostalCode>E99 6XX</PostalCode>
        <Country>U.K.</Country>
      </Address>
      <EmploymentHistory>
        <JoiningDate>01/06/1999</JoiningDate>
        <LeavingDate></LeavingDate>
        <Department title="Documentation" site="London">
          <DeptJoinDate>01/06/99</DeptJoinDate>
          <JobTitle>XML Technical Author</JobTitle>
          <ReportsTo>Albert Steptoe</ReportsTo>
          <DeptLeaveDate></DeptLeaveDate>
        </Department>
      </EmploymentHistory>
      <Skills>
        <Skill>XML</Skill>
        <Skill>XSLT</Skill>
        <Skill>XSD Schema</Skill>
      </Skills>
      <AnnualReports access="HROnly">
        <Year>1999
          <Grade></Grade>
          <Comments>John recently joined XMML.com and has made good initial
                                                    progress.

          </Comments>
          <GradingManager>Harold Steptoe</GradingManager>
          <Recommendations></Recommendations>
          <ActionTaken></ActionTaken>
        </Year>
        <Year>2000
          <Grade>2</Grade>
          <Comments>John has continued to make good initial progress in his
                                    role as XML technical author.

          </Comments>
          <GradingManager>Harold Steptoe</GradingManager>
          <Recommendations>He requires some additional XSLT training.
          </Recommendations>
          <ActionTaken></ActionTaken>
        </Year>
      </AnnualReports>
    </Person>

    <!-- Other <Person> elements would be listed here. -->

</HRFile>
```

As I mentioned earlier, before creating a DTD you would work through a process of modeling the information you wanted to collect. The high level view of the desired information would help you to construct the skeleton of a desired instance document something like this:

```
<?xml version='1.0'?>
<HRFile>
  <Person>
    <EmployeeNo></EmployeeNo>
    <Name>

    </Name>
```

```
        <ContactInformation>

        </ContactInformation>
        <Address>

        </Address>
        <EmploymentHistory>

        </EmploymentHistory>

        <Skills>

        </Skills>

        <AnnualReports access="HROnly">

        </AnnualReports>
    </Person>
    <!-- Other <Person> elements would be listed here. -->
</HRFile>
```

The `HRFile` element is the document element and it has `<Person>` elements as its children. A `<Person>` element has seven element children: `<EmployeeNo>`, `<Name>`, `<ContactInformation>`, `<Address>`, `<EmploymentHistory>`, `<Skills>`, and `<AnnualReports>`.

For the skeletal instance document shown above, a skeletal DTD can be readily constructed as follows, in `HRFile00.dtd`:

```
<!ELEMENT HRFile (Person*) >
<!ELEMENT Person (EmployeeNo, Name, ContactInformation,
                  Address, EmploymentHistory, Skills, AnnualReports) >
<!ELEMENT EmployeeNo (#PCDATA) >
<!ELEMENT Name (#PCDATA) >
<!ELEMENT ContactInformation (#PCDATA) >
<!ELEMENT Address (#PCDATA) >
<!ELEMENT EmploymentHistory (#PCDATA) >
<!ELEMENT Skills (Skill+) >
<!ELEMENT AnnualReports (#PCDATA) >
<!ATTLIST AnnualReports access (HROnly | LineManager) #REQUIRED >
```

The skeletal DTD and instance document give us an indication of how to approach the larger task – in a modular way. The element type declaration for the `<Person>` element:

```
<!ELEMENT Person (EmployeeNo, Name, ContactInformation,
                  Address, EmploymentHistory, Skills, AnnualReports) >
```

indicates the natural modules into which our human resources file breaks and which we can develop one step at a time.

Thus, for example, the fully developed part of the DTD for the `<Name>` element reads like this:

```
<!ELEMENT Name (FirstName, MiddleInitial*, LastName) >
<!ELEMENT FirstName (#PCDATA) >
<!ELEMENT MiddleInitial (#PCDATA) >
<!ELEMENT LastName (#PCDATA) >
```

Here is the full DTD for our HR document, `HRFile01.dtd`. Most of it you should be able to work out from the brief introduction that I have given you to DTDs and your general knowledge of how, approximately, a human resources department works. I have formatted it so that you should be able to easily see the modules that make up the DTD – element type declarations of the child elements of the `<Person>` element.

```
<!ELEMENT HRFile (Person*) >
<!ELEMENT Person (EmployeeNo, Name, ContactInformation,
                  Address, EmploymentHistory, Skills, AnnualReports) >

<!ELEMENT EmployeeNo (#PCDATA) >

<!ELEMENT Name (FirstName, MiddleInitial*, LastName) >
<!ELEMENT FirstName (#PCDATA) >
<!ELEMENT MiddleInitial (#PCDATA) >
<!ELEMENT LastName (#PCDATA) >

<!ELEMENT ContactInformation (HomePhone, WorkPhone, WorkExtension+,
                              EmailAddresses) >
<!ELEMENT HomePhone (#PCDATA) >
<!ELEMENT WorkPhone (#PCDATA) >
<!ELEMENT WorkExtension (#PCDATA) >
<!ATTLIST WorkExtension status (current | lapsed) #REQUIRED >
<!ELEMENT EmailAddresses (Email+) >
<!ELEMENT Email (#PCDATA) >

<!ELEMENT Address (Street+, City, PostalCode, Country) >
<!ELEMENT Street (#PCDATA) >
<!ELEMENT City (#PCDATA) >
<!ELEMENT PostalCode (#PCDATA) >
<!ELEMENT Country (#PCDATA) >

<!ELEMENT EmploymentHistory (JoiningDate, LeavingDate, Department+ ) >
<!ELEMENT JoiningDate (#PCDATA) >
<!ELEMENT LeavingDate (#PCDATA) >
<!ELEMENT Department (DeptJoinDate, JobTitle, ReportsTo, DeptLeaveDate) >
<!ELEMENT DeptJoinDate (#PCDATA) >
<!ELEMENT JobTitle (#PCDATA) >
<!ELEMENT ReportsTo (#PCDATA) >
<!ELEMENT DeptLeaveDate (#PCDATA) >
<!ATTLIST Department
          title CDATA #REQUIRED
          site (London | Tokyo | Chicago) #REQUIRED >

<!ELEMENT Skills (Skill+) >
<!ELEMENT Skill (#PCDATA) >

<!ELEMENT AnnualReports (Year*) >
<!ELEMENT Year (#PCDATA | Grade | Comments | GradingManager |
                          Recommendations | ActionTaken)* >

<!ELEMENT Grade (#PCDATA) >
<!ELEMENT Comments (#PCDATA) >
<!ELEMENT GradingManager (#PCDATA) >
<!ELEMENT Recommendations (#PCDATA) >
<!ELEMENT ActionTaken (#PCDATA) >

<!ATTLIST AnnualReports
          access (HROnly | LineManager) #REQUIRED >
```

However, I would like you to look carefully at the following part of the DTD:

```
<!ELEMENT AnnualReports (Year*) >
<!ELEMENT Year (#PCDATA | Grade | Comments | GradingManager |
                              Recommendations | ActionTaken)* >
<!ELEMENT Grade (#PCDATA) >
<!ELEMENT Comments (#PCDATA) >
<!ELEMENT GradingManager (#PCDATA) >
<!ELEMENT Recommendations (#PCDATA) >
<!ELEMENT ActionTaken (#PCDATA) >

<!ATTLIST AnnualReports
          access (HROnly | LineManager) #REQUIRED >
```

Notice that the content model for the <Year> element indicates that PCDATA, as well as the elements <Grade>, <Comments>, <GradingManager>, <Recommendations>, and <ActionTaken>, occurs zero or more times. That is, the <Year> element has mixed content. However, we have no control over the *ordering* of the PCDATA and child elements, since the vertical bar indicates that any of those choices is acceptable in any order, which is not what we want to express. The parsed character data representing the calendar year is intended to occur only immediately after the start tag of the <Year> element and not elsewhere among the following elements. If we want to include parsed character data as part of the content model for the <Year> element, then we lose the ability to specify the ordering of the elements that are also part of the content model of the <Year> element. This gives flexibility in how the content is structured, which may be undesirable in some circumstances.

The point to note is that the DTD is incapable, at least in the version associated with XML 1.0, of specifying a mixed content model and at the same time defining the order in which child elements should occur.

If you have read through the DTD you may have noticed that we repeatedly see lines like this:

```
<!ELEMENT GradingManager (#PCDATA) >
```

indicating that the content of the element is parsed character data. But what if we want to indicate the permitted content of an element more precisely? If, for example, we wanted to ensure that the joining date was not only parsed character data, as expressed here:

```
<!ELEMENT JoiningDate (#PCDATA) >
```

but was also a valid date, we have no way, using a DTD, of enforcing that simple requirement. In part, that limitation of DTDs arises from the historical background to XML and hence DTDs. SGML, which is often said to be XML's parent, was document-centric. It was used, and still is, to allow the production of highly structured documentation. In a document-centric, rather than a data-centric, environment it was acceptable to permit great flexibility in content. But for data-centric use of XML on the Web and elsewhere, with many parts of a transaction perhaps never meeting a human eye, it is essential to ensure that precise data typed data is entered.

Take the simple case of a business to business (B2B) transaction where a company wishes to check for all purchase orders received in a certain month and which haven't yet been fulfilled. If the date on the purchase order is not a valid date then the delivery of the goods requested may not be recognized as being overdue. Similar uncertainty applies to the data typing of other parts of the document. In practice, of course, a company that wants to stay in business will carry out checks on such transactions very carefully.

The inability to specify the data types of character content of an element may also be disadvantageous in other contexts. Suppose we have a catalogue of machinery parts whose elements take the form:

```
<PartNo>ABC-1234</PartNo>
```

A DTD will only allow us to specify this as parsed character data, while we might want to ensure that the content is of the form of three characters, followed by a "-", followed by four digits. A DTD doesn't allow us to specify that.

Let's move on to examine how we might access meta data about a class of XML instance documents by examining the content of the relevant DTD.

Understanding a DTD

If you imagine that there were 100 or 1,000 records stored in the human resources file which we created in the previous section, I am sure you can appreciate that it could be difficult to see the wood for the trees in such a substantial volume of XML data if we examine only the, by then large, instance document. So, examining the instance documents is not a practical approach with large volumes of XML data – although in situations where the XML schema has been corrupted or is non-existent such a tedious process may be necessary. A methodical examination of the DTD is a much more promising approach.

However, if you are unfamiliar with DTDs, it may not be easy at first glance to understand an XML schema expressed as a DTD, since it is easy to "glaze over" when viewing a potentially lengthy document expressed in a not wholly familiar syntax. But it is easy to get an overview understanding of a well-written DTD very quickly. For example, if you concentrate on the first two element type declarations in the DTD which we have just created:

```
<!ELEMENT HRFile (Person*) >
<!ELEMENT Person (EmployeeNo, Name, ContactInformation,
                  Address, EmploymentHistory, Skills, AnnualReports) >
```

you can see that the <HRFile> element contains zero or more <Person> elements. Thus by examining only the first line of the DTD we can see that if we understand the content model of a <Person> element we essentially understand the content model of the whole XML file.

The second line defines the content model for a <Person> element. We can see that a <Person> element must have an <EmployeeNo> element, a <Name> element, a <ContactInformation> element, an <Address> element, an <EmploymentHistory> element, a <Skills> element, and an <AnnualReports> element as element children.

However, be aware that there is no obligation on the writer of a DTD to present the element type definition as the first in a DTD, he could choose to order element type definitions alphabetically which would make it significantly more difficult to follow the modular construction of a DTD.

From a simple overview of a well-written DTD the main aspects of the instance documents quickly become clear. Of course, gaining insight into the meaning of that meta data is crucially dependent on the XML elements having sensible names. Assuming that the element type names are appropriate to their use and are sufficiently long so as to be human readable, it takes very little time to grasp the generality of what the content of an instance document such as HRFile01.xml is about. That overview will allow an appraisal, for example, of whether or not all relevant information is being collected. In our example a human resources person at that stage might spot the obvious omissions of any information about salary, bonuses, and disciplinary record, for example, and want to ensure that such data was collected. Similarly, they may prefer that what I have structured as an <Address> element child of the <Person> element was rather an element child of the <ContactInformation> element.

Having seen what the content model for the `<Person>` element is we now have a fuller understanding of what the DTD is about and, more importantly for our current purposes, we now have a succinct summary of the data contained in the `HRFile01.xml`.

Depending on our needs, we might well proceed to examine in full detail the content model for further layers of the hierarchy expressed in the DTD. As we explore those further layers we will either find further nested content models or an indication that the content of the element concerned is parsed character data.

Documenting DTDs

In a sense I have been providing a running commentary assisting you to understand the DTD we have just looked at. In more realistic settings, where you need to become oriented to an unfamiliar DTD, you will likely be relying on printed documentation or documentation within a DTD itself, if it exists. Where it does exist, it may or may not be up-to-date.

Documentation of DTDs is fairly primitive, making use of the XML comment syntax, inherited from SGML, with which you are likely familiar from using HTML or XML:

```
<!-- This is a comment. -->
```

If you had come to the `HRFile01.xml` without access to a running commentary or in the absence of printed documentation, you might find that a DTD which has each section commented, as in `HRFile01com.dtd`, makes it significantly easier for you to be sure that you have grasped the structure of the DTD:

```
<!-- This is the element type definition for the element root. -->
<!ELEMENT HRFile (Person*) >


<!-- The Person element contains only element content and summarizes an
     employee's employment record. -->
<!ELEMENT Person (EmployeeNo, Name, ContactInformation,
                 Address, EmploymentHistory, Skills, AnnualReports) >

<!-- The EmployeeNo is the unique identifying number which identifies an
     individual employee. -->
<!ELEMENT EmployeeNo (#PCDATA) >


<!-- Each Person has their name recorded as first name, middle initial
(optional),and last name. -->
<!ELEMENT Name (FirstName, MiddleInitial*, LastName) >
<!ELEMENT FirstName (#PCDATA) >
<!ELEMENT MiddleInitial (#PCDATA) >
<!ELEMENT LastName (#PCDATA) >


<!-- The contact information for a person includes phone numbers (home, work, work
extension) and email addresses. -->
<!ELEMENT ContactInformation (HomePhone, WorkPhone, WorkExtension+,
        EmailAddresses) >
<!ELEMENT HomePhone (#PCDATA) >
<!ELEMENT WorkPhone (#PCDATA) >
<!ELEMENT WorkExtension (#PCDATA) >
```

```
<!ATTLIST WorkExtension
        status (current | lapsed) #REQUIRED >
<!ELEMENT EmailAddresses (Email+) >
<!ELEMENT Email (#PCDATA) >

<!-- Mailing address information is held separately. -->
<!ELEMENT Address (Street+, City, PostalCode, Country) >
<!ELEMENT Street (#PCDATA) >
<!ELEMENT City (#PCDATA) >
<!ELEMENT PostalCode (#PCDATA) >
<!ELEMENT Country (#PCDATA) >

<!-- The employment history is held in a separate section which is publicly
accessible. -->
<!ELEMENT EmploymentHistory (JoiningDate, LeavingDate, Department+ ) >
<!ELEMENT JoiningDate (#PCDATA) >
<!ELEMENT LeavingDate (#PCDATA) >
<!ELEMENT Department (DeptJoinDate, JobTitle, ReportsTo, DeptLeaveDate) >
<!ELEMENT DeptJoinDate (#PCDATA) >
<!ELEMENT JobTitle (#PCDATA) >
<!ELEMENT ReportsTo (#PCDATA) >
<!ELEMENT DeptLeaveDate (#PCDATA) >
<!ATTLIST Department
        title CDATA #REQUIRED
        site (London | Tokyo | Chicago) #REQUIRED >
<!ELEMENT Skills (Skill+) >
<!ELEMENT Skill (#PCDATA) >

<!-- Annual reports by a grading manager are accessible only to selected
personnel, for example in the human resources department. -->
<!ELEMENT AnnualReports (Year*) >
<!ELEMENT Year (#PCDATA | Grade | Comments | GradingManager |
        Recommendations | ActionTaken)* >
<!ELEMENT Grade (#PCDATA) >
<!ELEMENT Comments (#PCDATA) >
<!ELEMENT GradingManager (#PCDATA) >
<!ELEMENT Recommendations (#PCDATA) >
<!ELEMENT ActionTaken (#PCDATA) >
<!ATTLIST AnnualReports
        access (HROnly | Line Manager) #REQUIRED >
```

In a DTD such as the above example, which is relatively short and with subject matter which is broadly familiar to all of us, the absence of comments/documentation is no great hindrance, but with DTDs which may be many times the length of the current example, comments may be of significant assistance in understanding what is happening.

Let's move on now to consider the strengths and weaknesses of DTDs.

Pros and Cons of DTDs

Document Type Definitions are essentially creatures of their time. They were, in one sense, a creation of the 1970s when the **Generalized Markup Language (GML)**, the predecessor of SGML, was under development. The focus of SGML was on document production rather than on data. GML and SGML were created before the World Wide Web, thus it is not surprising that DTDs have shortcomings in the current context when large and growing amounts of data are exchanged using XML across the Web.

If you are wondering why XML used a non-XML syntax for its schema, the DTD, the short-term advantage when XML was first announced in early 1998 was that SGML tools could be used to process both XML instance documents, since XML is claimed to be a subset of SGML, and the associated DTDs. The immediate availability of powerful tools is a significant benefit for a new technology.

DTDs provide only three content models (ignoring the ANY and EMPTY categories):

❑ Parsed character data (PCDATA).

❑ Element (only) content.

❑ Mixed content (a mixture of the first two).

This gives us some useful access to meta data but has significant limitations.

For example, we know nothing of the allowed data types which are appropriate, or which exist, within the PCDATA of any particular element. Of course, custom-written applications may be written to impose restrictions or to confirm that desired further restrictions have been correctly implemented, but if the DTD requires PCDATA for the content of an element which clearly should contain a date, an XML validating parser will (technically, correctly) allow text, integers, etc., as content, since the DTD does not define those as being disallowed.

Similarly, if the content model indicates that mixed content is allowed (that is both PCDATA and elements are acceptable) then we lose the ability to validate that elements are present in the correct order. Consider a document-centric use such as a paragraph in an HTML page:

```
<HTML>
  <BODY>
    <P>A DTD has the option of defining <B>PCDATA</B> but cannot control
        the data types of the element content, which is a <I>significant</I>
        disadvantage. The use of <B>element</B> content allows us to control
        the order and cardinality of child elements.
    </P>
  </BODY>
</HTML>
```

It is entirely acceptable, indeed desirable, to allow elements which control presentation attributes to be placed within character data where they make most sense. However, for data-centric applications this is undesirable.

Again, we are left with a choice of either avoiding mixed content or losing the ability to use XML validation to confirm that elements are correctly ordered (and so writing custom validation software).

If we have element content we have precise control over the ordering and cardinality of elements but we are restricted to allowing character data only within child elements which themselves do not have element children.

An XML instance document may be associated with one and only one DTD. Thus, when we come to create more complex schemas, it is not easy to modularize parts of a schema as separate DTD modules. It can be done using external entities, but it is an approach with which many feel uncomfortable or unequipped to implement. Thus if we want to use the same <Address> element in separate human resources and mailing list files we must also have separate DTDs. This has a negative impact on ease of maintenance and implementation of changes in the allowed structure.

DTDs were created as part of the XML 1.0 Recommendation at a time when XML Namespaces, discussed below, had not been defined. Understandably then, DTDs lack the ability to appropriately handle XML namespaces. At the time the XML 1.0 Recommendation was produced it was possible to deal only with "XML" since many of the application languages of XML with which we are now becoming familiar, such as **Extensible Stylesheet Language – Formatting Objects (XSL-FO), Scalable Vector Graphics (SVG), Extensible Hypertext Markup Language (XHTML)** or **Synchronized Multimedia Integration Language (SMIL)**, etc., did not exist. Therefore there was no possibility of mixing elements from several namespaces within one XML document. However, with the beginnings of the emergence of multi-namespace XML browsers, such as the **X-Smiles** processor (see http://www.xsmiles.org for further information) it is already not out of the ordinary for a document to have content which mixes XSL-FO, SMIL, and SVG. Similarly in business to business interchange of XML documents it may necessary, or convenient, to mix elements from several namespaces, a scenario which a DTD is poorly equipped to handle.

DTDs do not provide the facility to create new data types, thus unlike XML itself a DTD is not extensible. Nor can DTDs provide inheritance of the type that you may be familiar with in object-oriented programming languages.

In summary, the DTD has several limitations that led the W3C to begin development of what I call XSD Schema. DTDs lack:

❑ Integration with XML namespaces.

❑ Datatyping.

❑ Inheritance.

And, of course, a DTD is not written in XML syntax, thus making DTDs inaccessible to DOM-based processing and also to many of the tools written to process XML. Wouldn't it be nice to be able to create schemas for XML documents in XML itself?

XML Schemas in XML Syntax

The W3C had precisely that idea and presented the aims for what it terms "XML Schema" in a 1999 requirements document, located at http://www.w3.org/TR/1999/NOTE-xml-schema-req-19990215.

The W3C uses the term "XML Schema" to refer to its own form of XML schema, which reached full Recommendation status on 2nd May 2001. As mentioned earlier, to avoid ambiguity I will refer to the W3C's form of XML schema as XSD Schema. An XSD schema file typically uses a file extension of ".xsd" and also typically uses a namespace prefix of "xsd". The term XSD schema will allow clear distinction of XSD schemas from the XDR (XML-Data Reduced) type and other alternative XML schemas such as TREX-RELAX (recently renamed RELAX NG), which we will discuss briefly later.

In the aforementioned requirements document the XML Schema Working Group stated:

> *"For some uses, applications may need definitions of markup constructs more informative, or constraints on document structure tighter than, looser than, or simply different from those which can be expressed using document type definitions as defined in XML 1.0. "*

In other words a DTD doesn't provide all the answers to the needs of different users to define the allowable structure and content of XML documents.

Among the stated aims of the requirements document was to provide structural schemas and data typing. The structural schemas were envisaged as providing facilities similar to those provided by DTDs, but also to provide:

❑   Integration with XML namespaces.

❑   Integration of structural schemas with data types.

❑   Inheritance.

The primitive data types envisaged included:

❑   Integers.

❑   Dates.

❑   Binary data.

Thus they would provide the basis for XML-based validation of XML documents according to the desired data types of element content, a facility which DTDs did not provide.

The notions underlying the W3C XML schema had, and have, much to do with the notion of the Semantic Web, of structuring information in a more machine-readable way to elucidate "meaning". In other words W3C was, partly, thinking of structuring XML data to elucidate its meaning, an approach which also assists the capture of meta data relating to that same XML data.

Let's go on and look at the final result of the W3C's deliberations on XSD Schema, which was released as a full Recommendation in May 2001.

XSD Schema – the "XML Schema" Recommendation

As with earlier drafts, the final Recommendation from the W3C consisted of three parts, Part 0, Part 1, and Part 2. If you are a newcomer to XSD Schema, I strongly suggest you begin with the primer, Part 0, since the other two parts, particularly Part 1, are more demanding reads.

Part 0, the primer, is located at http://www.w3.org/TR/xmlschema-0/. It provides a relatively readable and friendly introduction to the approach taken in XSD Schema and gives numerous examples of creating some example XSD schemas, building up from some relatively simple schemas to some significantly more complex ones. For many practical purposes Part 0 provides a definitive introduction to XSD Schema but, of course, in W3C terminology it is not normative. The primer recognizes that limitation and includes numerous cross-references to Parts 1 and 2 of the Recommendation.

Part 1, *Structures*, is located at http://www.w3.org/TR/xmlschema-1/. It specifies the XSD Schema definition language, which provides the means to describe the structure and constrain the content of XML documents. It is stated explicitly that XSD Schema reconstructs and extends the functionality provided by DTDs. It also describes the conceptual approach behind XSD Schema and enumerates and details the component parts of an XSD schema, only some of which I will describe in this section.

Part 2, *Datatypes*, is located at http://www.w3.org/TR/xmlschema-2/ and is significantly simpler than Part 1. Part 2 depends on Part 1 and describes a number of built-in data types as well as the means for defining data types using the XSD Schema Definition Language.

XSD Schema has the namespace URI of "http://www.w3.org/2001/XMLSchema". Typically the namespace prefix of "xsd" is used to refer to that URI. The xsd prefix will be used in that way in the following description of XSD Schema.

45

XSD Schema – Element Type Declarations

XSD Schema provides a number of mechanisms for declaring elements depending on the simplicity or complexity of the structure of their content. The simplest element type declaration is when an element contains only an XSD primitive data type. For example:

```
<xsd:element name="comment" type="xsd:string"/>
```

is the XSD element type declaration for an element in a non-XSD namespace whose element type name is "comment" and whose type is "xsd:string". The content type xsd:string is broadly equivalent to #PCDATA in a DTD.

In addition to xsd:string, XSD Schema provides many other data types. Those are discussed a little later in this chapter.

XSD Schema also allows more complex element structures to be expressed. For example, if we wanted to create a generic <Address> element that contained the usual information about the person and location, we could do so in XSD Schema something like this:

```
<xsd:complexType name="Address">
  <xsd:sequence>
    <xsd:element name="Name" type="xsd:string"/>
    <xsd:element name="Street" type="xsd:string"/>
    <xsd:element name="City" type="xsd:string"/>
    <xsd:element name="StateOrRegion" type="xsd:string"/>
    <xsd:element name="PostalCode" type="xsd:string"/>
    <xsd:element name="country" type="xsd:string"/>
  </xsd:sequence>
</xsd:complexType>
```

As you can see, the XSD schema is significantly more verbose than the equivalent DTD. However, XSD Schema allows more control. For example, if you had wished to focus solely on a US address, the type attribute of the PostalCode element could have been replaced by an xsd:positiveInteger type or we could have created a custom data type.

Not only does XSD Schema allow us to easily state the allowed content of an element, but we can also define a more constrained range within the scope of the datatype that is applicable. For example, if we wanted to impose a maximum credit allowance on an individual we could do so by constraining the xsd:positiveInteger type which describes the <MaxCredit> element:

```
<xsd:element name="MaxCredit">
  <xsd:simpleType>
    <xsd:restriction base="xsd:positiveInteger">
      <xsd:maxInclusive value="1000"/>
    </xsd:restriction>
  </xsd:simpleType>
</xsd:element>
```

The <MaxCredit> element has only a simple type content model (no element children and no attributes). Thus to define its content model we use the <xsd:simpleType> element within which we indicate that the simple type is restricted, by using the <xsd:restriction> element, and finally nest within the <xsd:restriction> element the <xsd:maxInclusive> element which defines the maximum allowed credit, which in this case is 1000. It would have been possible to also include a <minInclusive> element but it is not needed here since we know already that the content is a positive integer.

Not only can the `<xsd:restriction>` element be used to define *numerical values* but it is also possible to apply *regular expressions* to elements which are of type `xsd:string`. For example, imagine we had a `<PartNumber>` element that we wished to be constrained to a format like this, with two letters followed by a dash followed by three numerical digits:

```
<PartNumber>XA-321</PartNumber>
```

We could constrain the content of the `<PartNumber>` element in the following manner, using the `<xsd:pattern>` element, whose `value` attribute contains the value of the regular expression which defines the allowable content:

```
<xsd:simpleType name="PartNumber">
  <xsd:restriction base="xsd:string">
    <xsd:pattern value="[A-Z]{2}-\d{3}"/>
  </xsd:restriction>
</xsd:simpleType>
```

Alternatively, it is possible to provide an enumeration of *permitted values* for element content. For example, if a US-based publisher had copyright only in the US and Canada, they would be obliged to restrict shipping of books sold from their web site to those two countries. We can restrict the allowed values for the `<Country>` element as follows:

```
<xsd:complexType name="Address">
  <xsd:sequence>
    <xsd:element name="Name" type="xsd:string"/>
    <xsd:element name="Street" type="xsd:string"/>
    <xsd:element name="City" type="xsd:string"/>
    <xsd:element name="StateOrRegion" type="xsd:string"/>
    <xsd:element name="PostalCode" type="xsd:string"/>
    <xsd:element name="country" type="xsd:string">
      <xsd:simpleType >
        <xsd:restriction base="xsd:string">
          <xsd:enumeration value="USA"/>
          <xsd:enumeration value="Canada"/>
        </xsd:restriction>
      </xsd:simpleType>
    </xsd:element>
  </xsd:sequence>
</xsd:complexType>
```

I hope you can see that with such facilities to constrain the values or the format of element content we have a tool which is both much more precise and more powerful than the DTD. It thus makes it much easier to create meta data of a level of sophistication and precision that is simply not available when using DTDs.

XSD Schema – Attributes Declarations

In XSD Schema we may declare attributes either locally or globally. Elements that contain other elements or have attributes are considered to be of **complex type** in XSD Schema, therefore to declare an element with a *local* attribute we have to use syntax similar to the following:

```
<xsd:element name="SalaryInfo">
  <xsd:complexType>
    <xsd:attribute name="AccessControl"/>
  </xsd:complexType>
</xsd:element>
```

We can add restrictions to permitted values of attributes in a manner similar to that which we used on elements earlier:

```
<xsd:element name="SalaryInfo">
  <xsd:complexType>
    <xsd:attribute name="AccessControl">
     <xsd:simpleType>
      <xsd:restriction base="xsd:string">
        <xsd:enumeration value="HumanResources"/>
        <xsd:enumeration value="LineManagerOnly"/>
      </xsd:restriction>
     </xsd:simpleType>
    <xsd:attribute>
  </xsd:complexType>
</xsd:element>
```

If we planned to use the AccessControl attribute in several places within a document then we would declare it *globally*, which means that we need to declare it as a direct child of the <xsd:schema> element:

```
<xsd:schema xmlns:xsd="http://www.w3.org/2001/XMLSchema">
<!-- Other element or global attribute declarations can go here. -->

<xsd:attribute name="AccessControl">
 <xsd:simpleType>
  <xsd:restriction base="xsd:string">
    <xsd:enumeration value="HumanResources"/>
    <xsd:enumeration value="LineManagerOnly"/>
  </xsd:restriction>
 </xsd:simpleType>
<xsd:attribute>

<!-- Other declarations can follow. -->
</xsd:schema>
```

If, later in the document, we wanted to reference that declaration of the AccessControl attribute, in a particular element we could do so like this:

```
<xsd:element name="SalaryInfo">
  <xsd:complexType>
    <xsd:attribute ref="AccessControl"/>
  </xsd:complexType>
</xsd:element>
```

In complex schemas, which make recurrent use of a particular attribute, the use of a global attribute can aid maintenance of the schema. For example, in the case of the AccessControl attribute a change in security categorization could be implemented so that it cascaded down to various elements defined in the schema.

XSD Schema – Cardinality

XSD Schema provides a significant enhancement to the functionality for defining cardinality present in DTDs. XSD Schema uses the minOccurs and maxOccurs to respectively indicate the permitted minimum and maximum number of occurrences of an element. XSD Schema provides equivalent functionality to the DTD + operator like this:

```
<xsd:element name="Email" minOccurs="1" maxOccurs="unbounded" />
```

and functionality equivalent to the DTD * operator like this:

```
<xsd:element name="Street" minOccurs="0" maxOccurs="unbounded" />
```

XSD schema also provides functionality that goes beyond the scope of a DTD. For example, if we wanted to be able to specify that an <AnnualPurchases> element must occur at least 3 times (perhaps for a mail order book club) but no more than 20, that could be done using this syntax:

```
<xsd:element name="AnnualPurchases" minOccurs="3" maxOccurs="20" />
```

XSD schemas can express essentially any realistic cardinality requirements. The minOccurs attribute defines the minimum number of occurrences. The maxOccurs attribute defines the maximum number of occurrences. The value "unbounded" allows the notion of an unlimited number of occurrences to be expressed, otherwise 0 or a positive integer describes the values of the minOccurs and maxOccurs attributes.

XSD Schema – Datatypes

XSD Schema takes us far beyond the simplistic notion of #PCDATA as the sole data type constraint directly available to us with DTDs. XSD schema has several built-in **primitive datatypes** and a number of built-in **derived datatypes**.

The following table lists and briefly describes the built-in primitive datatypes. For further information on the **value space**, **lexical space**, and **constraining facets** of each primitive datatype consult Chapter 3 of Part 2 of the XSD Schema Recommendation.

Primitive Datatype	Description
xsd:string	strings in XML
xsd:boolean	binary value logic – true and false
xsd:decimal	arbitrary precision decimal numbers
xsd:float	IEEE single-precision floating point type
xsd:double	IEEE double-precision floating point type
xsd:duration	a duration of time
xsd:dateTime	a specific instant in time
xsd:time	an instant of time that recurs every day
xsd:date	a calendar date
xsd:gYearMonth	a specific Gregorian month in a specific Gregorian year
xsd:gYear	a specific Gregorian calendar year
xsd:gMonthDay	a Gregorian date that recurs each year, for example the 29th January

Table continued on following page

Primitive Datatype	Description
xsd:gDay	a Gregorian day which recurs, for example the 6th of each month
xsd:gMonth	a Gregorian month which recurs each year, for example February
xsd:hexBinary	hex-encoded binary data
xsd:base64Binary	Base64-encoded arbitrary binary data
xsd:anyURI	a Uniform Resource Identifier
xsd:QName	an XML Qualified Name
xsd:NOTATION	a NOTATION attribute type of XML 1.0

Detailed discussion of XSD Schema data types is beyond the scope of this chapter, but I am sure you can see that even the built-in primitive datatypes provide many more validation possibilities than were available with DTDs.

XSD Schema also allows new complex data types to be created. For example, to create a datatype that corresponds to a purchase order, the `<PurchaseOrder>` element can be declared to be of a new data type, like so:

```
<xsd:element name="PurchaseOrder" type="PurchaseOrderType"/>
```

Elsewhere in the XSD schema the structure that constitutes a "PurchaseOrderType" can be declared.

If, on a purchase order, we wanted to create an address type specific to United Kingdom addresses, we could do so as follows:

```
<xsd:complexType name="UKAddress">
  <xsd:sequence>
    <xsd:element name="DeliverTo" type="xsd:string"/>
    <xsd:element name="Street" type="xsd:string"/>
    <xsd:element name="City" type="xsd:string"/>
    <xsd:element name="County" type="xsd:string"/>
    <xsd:element name="PostalCode" type="xsd:string"/>
  </xsd:sequence>
  <xsd:attribute name="country" type="xsd:NMTOKEN" fixed="UK"/>
</xsd:complexType>
```

The ability to create new datatypes is a very useful function of XSD Schema. However, XSD Schema as exemplified in an earlier part of this section, also allows regular expressions to be used to further define the content of elements or attributes.

XSD Schema – Namespaces

XSD Schema has its own namespace URI as shown in the following:

```
<xsd:schema xmlns:xsd="http://www.w3.org/2001/XMLSchema">
```

Typically, as you will probably already have surmised, elements in the XSD Schema namespace use the namespace prefix of "xsd", although as you may be aware, any namespace prefix could be used provided it was associated with the appropriate namespace URI.

The increasing use of XML increases the likelihood that element type names in a compound document will collide. Let's suppose that we have a US-based weather bureau which needs to clearly distinguish between a *state*, for instance Alaska, and the *state* of its warning on hurricane alerts. By associating its hurricane alerts with a namespace URI, as shown in the following example, reference to the <state> element can be made unambiguous.

```
<?xml version='1.0'?>
<xsd:schema xmlns:xsd="http://www.w3.org/2001/XMLSchema"
            xmlns:alts="http://www.weatherbureau.com/alerts"
            targetNamespace="http://www.weatherbureau.com/alerts">
<!-- Other definitions would go here. -->
<xsd:element name="alts:state" type="xsd:string">
  <xsd:simpleType >
    <xsd:restriction base="xsd:string">
      <xsd:enumeration value="low"/>
      <xsd:enumeration value="medium"/>
      <xsd:enumeration value="high"/>
    </xsd:restriction>
  </xsd:simpleType>
</xsd:element>
<!-- Other definitions would go here. -->
</xsd:schema>
```

Let's move on and explore how we can use XSD Schema to describe a class of XML instance files.

XSD Schema – Creating a Schema

In this section we will create, step-by-step, an XSD schema that describes the HRFile01.xml human resources file we looked at in the DTD section.

The basic skeleton for an XSD schema is the <xsd:schema> element, with its associated namespace declaration, following an optional XML declaration, as in HRFile001.xsd:

```
<?xml version='1.0'?>
<xsd:schema xmlns:xsd="http://www.w3.org/2001/XMLSchema">

</xsd:schema>
```

As you can see, this skeleton is a well-formed XML document.

The XSD Schema specification provides a straightforward mechanism for adding documentation to an XSD schema, as you can see:

```
<?xml version='1.0'?>
<xsd:schema xmlns:xsd="http://www.w3.org/2001/XMLSchema">
<xsd:annotation>
```

```
    <xsd:documentation xml:lang="en">
      Human resources schema for XMML.com.
      Copyright 2001 XMML.com. All rights reserved.
    </xsd:documentation>
  </xsd:annotation>

  </xsd:schema>
```

At that stage we still haven't added any content to our draft schema. First, we can add the representation of the element root:

```
  <?xml version='1.0'?>
  <xsd:schema xmlns:xsd="http://www.w3.org/2001/XMLSchema">
  <xsd:annotation>
   <xsd:documentation xml:lang="en">
    Human resources schema for XMML.com.
    Copyright 2001 XMML.com. All rights reserved.
   </xsd:documentation>
  </xsd:annotation>

  <xsd:element name="HRFile" type="HRFileType"/>

  </xsd:schema>
```

In the <xsd:element> element we have a name attribute which corresponds to the <HRFile> element, which you are familiar with from HRFile01.xml. In addition we specify, using the type attribute of the <xsd:element> element, that the <HRFile> element is of type "HRFileType".

You may ask what type HRFileType is. We are just about to define it. But first let's define the <EmployeeNo> element:

```
  <xsd:element name="EmployeeNo" type="xsd:decimal"/>
```

since we will reference its definition when we define the <Person> element. As you can see, we again use the <xsd:element> element with the name attribute defining the element type name. The type attribute of the <xsd:element> element is "xsd:decimal". The EmployeeNo is a five digit integer and the designation xsd:decimal takes us significantly further than the DTD could do; we are no longer limited to #PCDATA as our only description of element content.

Our definition of the HRFileType is shown here:

```
  <xsd:element name="HRFile">
    <xsd:complexType>
      <xsd:sequence>
        <xsd:element ref="Person"/>
      </xsd:sequence>
    </xsd:complexType>
  </xsd:element>
```

The definition includes the <xsd:complexType> element, since the content of the <HRFile> element is a sequence of <Person> elements. We haven't yet needed to define the <Person> element, but will do so now:

```
<xsd:element name="Person">
  <xsd:complexType>
    <xsd:sequence>
      <xsd:element ref="EmployeeNo"/>
      <xsd:element ref="Name"/>
      <xsd:element ref="ContactInformation"/>
      <xsd:element ref="Address"/>
      <xsd:element ref="EmploymentHistory"/>
      <xsd:element ref="Skills"/>
      <xsd:element ref="AnnualReports"/>
    </xsd:sequence>
  </xsd:complexType>
</xsd:element>
```

As you can see, this is significantly more verbose than the equivalent element type definition in a DTD. However, we can see that the content of the `<Person>` element consists of a sequence of `<xsd:element>` elements respectively representing the `<EmployeeNo>`, `<Name>`, `<ContactInformation>`, `<Address>`, `<EmploymentHistory>`, `<Skills>`, and `<AnnualReports>` elements of our XML instance documents.

We have already defined what the content of the `<EmployeeNo>` element is – it is an `xsd:decimal`. If you had forgotten that we had already defined it, then rewind a little. We use the `ref` attribute to reference that earlier definition.

We have yet to define the content of the `<Name>` element. Here is its definition:

```
<xsd:element name="Name">
  <xsd:complexType>
    <xsd:sequence>
      <xsd:element ref="FirstName"/>
      <xsd:element ref="MiddleInitial"/>
      <xsd:element ref="LastName"/>
    </xsd:sequence>
  </xsd:complexType>
</xsd:element>
```

together with the definition of the `<FirstName>`, `<MiddleInitial>`, and `<LastName>` elements:

```
<xsd:element name="FirstName" type="xsd:string"/>
<xsd:element name="MiddleInitial" type="xsd:string"/>
<xsd:element name="LastName" type="xsd:string"/>
```

Then we define the `<ContactInformation>` element:

```
<xsd:element name="ContactInformation">
  <xsd:complexType>
    <xsd:sequence>
      <xsd:element ref="HomePhone"/>
      <xsd:element ref="WorkPhone"/>
      <xsd:element ref="WorkExtension" minOccurs="1" maxOccurs="unbounded"/>
      <xsd:element ref="EmailAddresses"/>
    </xsd:sequence>
  </xsd:complexType>
</xsd:element>
```

together with the definitions of its constituent elements:

```
<xsd:element name="HomePhone" type="xsd:string"/>
<xsd:element name="WorkPhone" type="xsd:string"/>
<xsd:element name="WorkExtension">
  <xsd:complexType>
    <xsd:simpleContent>
      <xsd:restriction base="xsd:short">
        <xsd:attribute name="status" use="required">
          <xsd:simpleType>
            <xsd:restriction base="xsd:NMTOKEN">
              <xsd:enumeration value="current"/>
              <xsd:enumeration value="lapsed"/>
            </xsd:restriction>
          </xsd:simpleType>
        </xsd:attribute>
      </xsd:restriction>
    </xsd:simpleContent>
  </xsd:complexType>
</xsd:element>
```

The definitions of the <HomePhone> and <WorkPhone> elements are straightforward. As written they have xsd:string content because of the spaces. If we wished to ensure that only numerical digits were used then we would have to exclude the spaces, and then we could use xsd:int or xsd:long, depending on how many numerical digits were to be allowed within a telephone number. Since the WorkExtension is a four digit number we can use xsd:short, in conjunction with a restriction that the value of the status attribute is an xsd:enumeration, with the only valid values being current or lapsed.

And the <EmailAddresses> element consists of a sequence of <Email> elements. The minimum number of occurrences is 1 and the maximum is unbounded. This corresponds to the DTD + operator.

```
<xsd:element name="EmailAddresses">
  <xsd:complexType>
    <xsd:sequence>
      <xsd:element ref="Email" minOccurs="1" maxOccurs="unbounded"/>
    </xsd:sequence>
  </xsd:complexType>
</xsd:element>
```

The referenced definition of an <Email> element is straightforward:

```
<xsd:element name="Email" type="xsd:string"/>
```

The <Address> element and its content is defined as a sequence of references to the definitions of other elements, the <Street> element may occur more than once:

```
<xsd:element name="Address">
  <xsd:complexType>
    <xsd:sequence>
      <xsd:element ref="Street" minOccurs="1"  maxOccurs="unbounded"/>
      <xsd:element ref="City"/>
      <xsd:element ref="PostalCode"/>
```

```
        <xsd:element ref="Country"/>
      </xsd:sequence>
    </xsd:complexType>
  </xsd:element>
```

These elements are all simply of type `xsd:string`:

```
<xsd:element name="Street" type="xsd:string"/>
<xsd:element name="City" type="xsd:string"/>
<xsd:element name="PostalCode" type="xsd:string"/>
<xsd:element name="Country" type="xsd:string"/>
```

Next we create the definition of the `<EmploymentHistory>` element:

```
<xsd:element name="EmploymentHistory">
  <xsd:complexType>
    <xsd:sequence>
      <xsd:element ref="JoiningDate"/>
      <xsd:element ref="LeavingDate"/>
      <xsd:element ref="Department"/>
    </xsd:sequence>
  </xsd:complexType>
</xsd:element>
```

The definitions of the `<JoiningDate>` and `<LeavingDate>` elements are straightforward:

```
<xsd:element name="JoiningDate" type="xsd:date"/>
<xsd:element name="LeavingDate" type="xsd:date"/>
```

but we have more control over their content than with the DTD since we can define the content of both elements as being of type `xsd:date`.

The definition of the `<Department>` element is more complex, since it has its own child elements and also has `title` and `site` attributes:

```
<xsd:element name="Department">
  <xsd:complexType>
    <xsd:sequence>
      <xsd:element ref="DeptJoinDate"/>
      <xsd:element ref="JobTitle"/>
      <xsd:element ref="ReportsTo"/>
      <xsd:element ref="DeptLeaveDate"/>
    </xsd:sequence>
    <xsd:attribute name="title" type="xsd:string" use="required"/>
    <xsd:attribute name="site" type="xsd:string" use="required"/>
  </xsd:complexType>
</xsd:element>
```

The child elements of the `<Department>` element have straightforward definitions. The `<DeptJoinDate>` and `<DeptLeaveDate>` elements appropriately use the `xsd:date` type, giving us more information than the equivalent "#PCDATA" in a DTD.

```
<xsd:element name="DeptJoinDate" type="xsd:date"/>
<xsd:element name="JobTitle" type="xsd:string"/>
<xsd:element name="ReportsTo" type="xsd:string"/>
<xsd:element name="DeptLeaveDate" type="xsd:date"/>
```

The definition of the `<Skills>` element is straightforward:

```
<xsd:element name="Skills">
  <xsd:complexType>
    <xsd:sequence>
      <xsd:element ref="Skill" maxOccurs="unbounded"/>
    </xsd:sequence>
  </xsd:complexType>
</xsd:element>
<xsd:element name="Skill" type="xsd:string"/>
```

since it consists simply of a sequence of `<Skill>` elements which are of type `xsd:string`.

And, finally, we define the `<AnnualReports>` element:

```
<xsd:element name="AnnualReports">
  <xsd:complexType>
    <xsd:sequence>
      <xsd:element ref="Year" maxOccurs="unbounded"/>
    </xsd:sequence>
    <xsd:attribute name="access" type="xsd:string" use="required"/>
  </xsd:complexType>
</xsd:element>
```

which consists of a sequence of `<Year>` elements which each have their own definition:

```
<xsd:element name="Year">
  <xsd:complexType mixed="true">
    <xsd:choice minOccurs="0" maxOccurs="unbounded">
      <xsd:element ref="ActionTaken"/>
      <xsd:element ref="Comments"/>
      <xsd:element ref="Grade"/>
      <xsd:element ref="GradingManager"/>
      <xsd:element ref="Recommendations"/>
    </xsd:choice>
  </xsd:complexType>
</xsd:element>
```

The `<Year>` element's child elements are defined as follows:

```
<xsd:element name="ActionTaken" type="xsd:string"/>
<xsd:element name="Comments" type="xsd:string"/>
<xsd:element name="Grade" type="xsd:byte"/>
<xsd:element name="GradingManager" type="xsd:string"/>
<xsd:element name="Recommendations" type="xsd:string"/>
```

The `<ActionTaken>`, `<Comments>`, `<GradingManager>`, and `<Recommendations>` elements are of type `xsd:string`, but the numerical grading in the `<Grade>` element is of type `xsd:byte`. Again, we have additional information about the content of an element that a DTD does not give us.

As you can see, an XSD schema for a relatively simple document, such as the one we have used to demonstrate DTDs and XSD Schema, can very quickly become lengthy. However, I hope you can also see that an XSD schema adds further meta data about the class of instance documents to which it relates.

XSD Schema – Understanding a Schema

Let's take a look at how easy you might find it to gain an understanding of the content of an XSD schema. Our completed XSD schema for `HRFile01.xml` is much longer than the equivalent DTD, which you saw earlier. We will not repeat it all again here but it is available in the code download.

With this structure, which starts with the element root and deconstructs the XSD schema into its component modules, I hope that as you read through it you are able to follow what is being described.

But you may come across XSD schemas much longer than this and which may "helpfully" be structured with the definitions in alphabetical order, as produced by some tools that attempt to automatically generate a schema. It then becomes much more difficult to discern the structure of the XSD schema, and hence it is more difficult to gain an understanding of the class of instance documents. For example, if you use XML Spy (http://www.xmlspy.com) to generate an XSD Schema for an instance document, then you will find all the elements in the schema in alphabetical order. This can be a little confusing if you are not aware that it is likely to happen.

Pros and Cons of XSD Schema

I have touched on various comparisons between DTDs and XSD schemas in the last several pages and only want to briefly mention a few here.

One of the basic advantages that XSD Schema has over DTDs is that XSD schemas are written in XML. Programmers or web designers new to XML will have only one syntax to master – the XML syntax – rather than also having to learn the EBNF which underpins DTDs.

XSD Schema provides better documentation facilities using the `<xsd:annotation>` and `<xsd:documentation>` elements. Faced with a lengthy XSD schema you could use the **Extensible Stylesheet Language for Transformations, XSLT,** to pull out any `<xsd:annotation>` and `<xsd:documentation>` elements to quickly gain an overview of what is contained in the schema, assuming the schema authors took advantage of the facilities to document their work within the schema itself.

XSD Schema provides enormously improved control over data typing when compared to DTDs, thus improving the precision of meta data which can be gleaned from an XSD schema in comparison to a DTD. XSD Schema provides methods of restriction, including enumeration and the use of regular expressions, which add greatly to what was previously available with DTDs.

XSD also allows more precision regarding cardinality. If the minimum allowed occurrences is not zero or one, XSD Schema can accommodate that situation, whereas a DTD cannot. Similarly if the maximum number of allowed occurrences is not "unbounded" then a DTD cannot represent that situation, whereas XSD can represent that situation in a wholly flexible manner.

As processing of XML becomes a multi-tiered process it is increasingly likely that it will be a requirement for schemas to be created or processed dynamically. Since XSD schemas are themselves written in XML they can be processed in any way which is appropriate using XSLT, opening up possibilities which may be possible using DTDs but are less straightforward to implement. Using XSLT it is possible to produce an approximation of a schema given a suitable instance document (as is explained in Chapter 14 of *Professional XSL*, Wrox Press, ISBN 1-861003-57-9). Inevitably that skeleton of a schema will require refinement but it does provide a potentially sound basis on which to build more specific constraints.

Other XML Schemas

A number of alternative XML schemas exist or are under active development. Some existed before XSD Schema was finalized. A number, including XML-Data, were submissions to the W3C way back in 1998 as possible bases on which the official W3C version should be built. These alternate schemas will be described here more briefly than were DTDs and XSD Schema.

Let's begin by looking at an XML schema proposal, which is both potentially exciting and potentially confusing, RELAX NG.

RELAX NG – Formerly TREX and RELAX

At the present time an alternative XML schema to XSD Schema is under active development at OASIS – the Organization for Advancement in Structured Information Standards. Formerly, what is now officially termed "**RELAX NG**", existed as two draft proposals for XML schemas:

- ❑ **TREX, Tree Regular Expressions**, proposed by James Clark, the technical lead for the XML 1.0 Recommendation and editor of the XSLT and XPath Recommendations.
- ❑ **RELAX**, proposed by Murata Makoto.

Perhaps the first thing to be informed about is where to locate up-to-date information. The mailing list for the RELAX NG Technical Committee at OASIS is located at http://lists.oasis-open.org/archives/relax-ng/. Be aware that this is a live discussion among the committee members. Do not expect to find pre-digested, pre-summarized material at that URL. The archives of discussions under the previous TREX Technical Committee have also been collated at the URL given, so you can follow the whole process, if you wish.

RELAX NG aims to provide a simpler schema language than that provided in Part 1 of the W3C XSD Schema. RELAX NG seems likely to be combined with some means of datatyping and it may be that Part 2 of the W3C XSD Schema will either be the datatyping framework or something very similar to that will be chosen.

A draft tutorial for RELAX NG is available at http://www.oasis-open.org/committees/relax-ng/tutorial.html. By the time this book appears in print a final version of the tutorial may be available. Check the discussion list mentioned above to determine the URL at which it will be posted.

Stop Press

Immediately prior to this book going to press further information on RELAX NG became available. The following URLs are provided so that you may familiarize yourself with these developments:

The ongoing work of the RELAX NG Technical Committee at OASIS is described at http://www.oasis-open.org/committees/relax-ng/.

A validator for RELAX NG, called Jing, has been made available for download from http://www.thaiopensource.com/relaxng/jing.html. The Jing validator is written in Java and is an adaptation of the previous JTrex processor.

A number of other RELAX NG tools, including schemas and an XSLT stylesheet to convert RELAX CORE (now replaced by RELAX NG) to RELAX NG, are available at http://www.thaiopensource.com/relaxng/.

XML-Data Reduced (XDR)

XDR schemas form the basis for the BizTalk initiative promoted by Microsoft. XDR is a modification of the XML-Data proposal submitted to the W3C in 1998 as a Note. XML-Data has had a significant influence on the development of XSD Schema and also was the basis for XML-Data Reduced, XDR.

The future of XDR is somewhat uncertain. Microsoft has indicated that it intends to replace XDR with XSD Schema once XSD Schema has been adopted, but the precise criteria for deciding when XSD has been "adopted" and by whom are unclear. Therefore it is equally unclear whether Microsoft intends to replace XDR and declare it obsolete, as they did with Microsoft "XSL" when that was replaced by XSLT in MSXML3, or whether it will be some time before XDR will be replaced, if at all.

In any case, XDR does not raise major new issues as a source of meta data when compared with XSD Schema. Detailed syntax and capabilities of XDR does differ from XSD Schema, however. If you propose to use XDR then consult the Microsoft web site (http://www.microsoft.com) for the latest information on the status of XDR.

Summary

In this chapter we have looked at the need for schemas to define the structure and content of XML instance documents, and discussed how meta data contained in such XML schemas can be useful in gaining an overview of the content of the ever growing volume of data held as XML.

We also covered the original XML schema, the Document Type Definition, introducing its syntax, and demonstrating how to create a DTD to provide summary meta data and how to approach a DTD to understand the information which it describes. The limitations of DTDs as a schema for data-centric XML documents were discussed.

We also looked at XSD Schema, a recently released Recommendation from the W3C. Some of the basic features of XSD Schema syntax were demonstrated and it was shown how, by using the improved data typing, more precise meta data is available about the permitted content of a class of XML documents. In addition, XSD Schema has the advantage of being written in XML. It also has improved documentation facilities compared to DTDs. XSD Schema also provides a means to express types of cardinality which a DTD cannot constrain.

Taken together, the features of XSD Schema offer significant advantages over DTDs for the definition of meta data regarding classes of XML documents.

Areas where XSD Schema has significant advantages over DTDs include:

- ❑ It has an XML syntax.
- ❑ It includes better datatyping and the facility to create new data types.
- ❑ It allows the use of regular expressions to constrain data.
- ❑ It has better handling of cardinality.
- ❑ It handles XML namespaces.
- ❑ It provides improved facilities to document schemas.

The advantages of XSD Schema over DTDs are particularly evident for data-centric applications of XML. However, for document-centric uses of XML the DTD may well provide adequate meta data for many uses.

Some programmers have seen XSD Schema as overly complex, leading to the development, for example, of TREX (now subsumed into the combined RELAX NG proposal currently under development at OASIS). Whether RELAX NG will prove to be a viable competitor or alternative to XSD Schema is an open question.

In the next chapter we'll be taking a look at two other W3C initiatives that are just emerging as implemented meta data-related technologies – XML linking and querying.

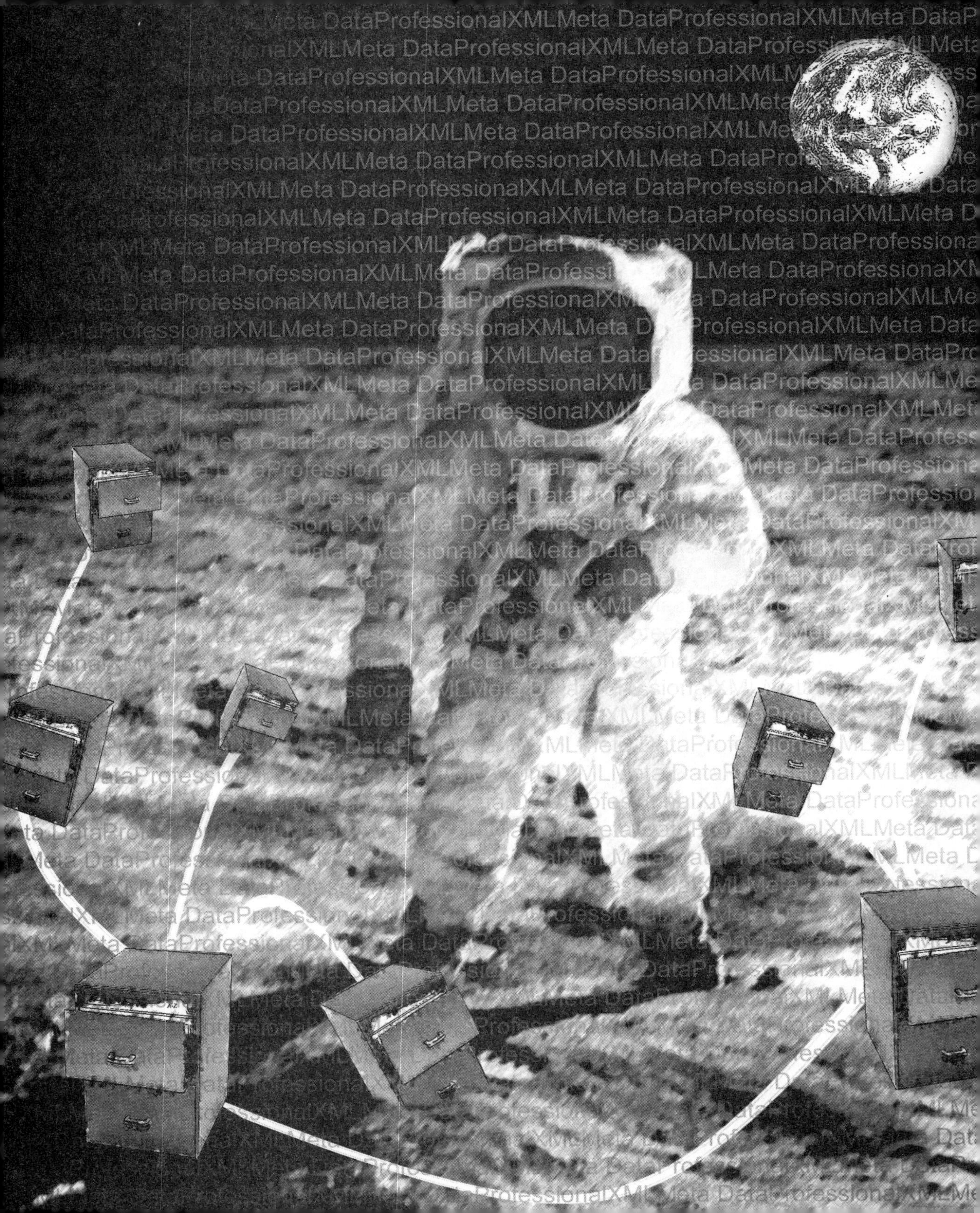

XML Linking and Querying

3

The purpose of this chapter is to provide an overview of the various XML technologies under development at the Word Wide Web Consortium, W3C, which address the need to link or interrogate XML documents, as well as related technologies on which the **linking** and **querying** technologies are based, or with which they inter-operate.

At the time of writing most of these technologies have not yet been finalized as Recommendations by the W3C. Therefore be sure to check the W3C web site for the most up-to-date versions of the specifications mentioned. The current versions of all the specifications can be accessed from http://www.w3.org/TR/.

It might not be immediately obvious that links or queries *are* meta data, yet they both provide data about data, this book's working definition of meta data. The links between XML documents provide information regarding the relationships which one XML data item or data set has with other data. Similarly, querying XML documents or files provides information about what data is there. Understanding the relationships between XML documents and querying such documents to establish what they contain are important aspects of defining XML meta data.

In this chapter we will examine a number of XML technologies that are relevant to the linking or querying of XML resources. As you will see, as more and more W3C XML specifications reach or move towards full Recommendation status, use of one specification will depend on an understanding of one or more other XML-related specifications, or may make use of another specification. Thus in this chapter you will be introduced to a number of W3C specifications that impact on the linking and querying draft specifications.

In particular, with respect to *linking*, you will be introduced to:

- ❑ The XML Linking Language, **XLink**, an XML-based syntax which allows links to be asserted between XML (and non-XML) resources.

- ❑ The XML Pointer Language, **XPointer**, which may be used with XLink to enable linking to fragments of XML documents, and which in turn is built on the XML Path Language, **XPath**.

- ❑ XML Inclusions, **XInclude**, which enables two or more XML documents, or portions thereof, to be merged, or more precisely their information sets (infosets) to be merged. XInclude therefore depends on the **XML Information Set** specification.

With respect to *querying* XML we will look at:

- ❑ The Extensible Stylesheet Language for Transformations, **XSLT**, which also has dependencies on XPath, making use of both XPath expressions and XPath functions.

- ❑ The XML Query Language, **XQuery**, which has dependencies on XSLT and XPath, as they are likely to be developed in XSLT 2.0 and XPath 2.0. As this chapter was being written a new XQuery Working Draft was issued (one of five new XQuery drafts issued within 24 hours). This particular draft is entitled XQuery 1.0 and XPath 2.0 Data Model (located at http://www.w3.org/TR/2001/WD-query-datamodel-20010607/), confirming the future intimate relationship between XQuery and XPath.

Of the W3C specifications discussed in this chapter only XSLT and XPath are full W3C Recommendations at the time of writing. XSLT 1.0 and XPath 1.0 Recommendations were issued in November 1999 and can be located, respectively at http://www.w3.org/TR/1999/REC-xslt-19991116 and http://www.w3.org/TR/1999/REC-xpath-19991116. XLink, XML Information Set, XInclude, XPointer, and XQuery are all under development. The XLink and XML Information Set specifications are respectively a Proposed and a Candidate Recommendation, so although they are not likely to change in a major way, significant change remains possible. XInclude, XPointer, and XQuery are Working Drafts and therefore potentially subject to considerable change. Be aware that details of what is discussed in this chapter and exact syntax may have changed by the time you read this. Check the latest version of each technology at the URLs given later in the chapter.

The Need for Linking

Linking, or asserting relationships between data, is fundamental to database technology and to the use of the World Wide Web. Links provide access to information of various types that are related, in some way, to the data from which the link was made.

In database management systems the relationships established between tables by means of keys define relationships among data items which are fundamental to completely understanding what the data means.

Typically, in HTML pages, the association is created *ad hoc* by human HTML programmers. Whatever type of information is linked to it a link provides, or should provide, additional information that adds in some way to the understanding of the data contained in the referring page.

Any user of the World Wide Web will be familiar with HTML **hyperlinking**. Despite, or perhaps because of, the familiarity of HTML hyperlinking, many users take it for granted and have never thought in detail about its capabilities and limitations. HTML links are immensely useful, as evidenced by the fact that they are everywhere on the Web.

Let's take a closer look at what makes up an HTML link and consider how we might be able to improve on that. Many HTML links serve to link whole web pages, or resources (see http://www.ietf.org/rfc/rfc2396.txt), but in addition there is a facility to create links to portions of resources, by the use of **anchors**.

An HTML hyperlink has the following characteristics:

❑ It uses a **Uniform Resource Identifier** (**URI**) to identify the resource to which a link is made.

❑ The link is expressed at one of its two ends only. If I link from Page 1 to Page 2 there is nothing on Page 2 to indicate that a link from Page 1 exists.

❑ The hyperlink identifies the other end of the link. In other words the value of the `href` attribute identifies where to find the target for the link.

❑ The links are unidirectional – a link can be traversed only in the direction from the end at which the link is expressed to the other end. The link expresses only how to move from Page 1 to Page 2, but says nothing on Page 2 about how to get back to the referring page. (That does not stop a browser collecting information to provide broadly equivalent functionality to that of a bidirectional link. Typically, web browsers provide a `Back` button, but the HTML link itself provides no way to traverse the link in the opposite direction, unless an additional HTML <A> element exists in the page linked to by the first link).

❑ It is necessary to have write access to the file/document from which the link is initiated, in order to create a link.

Both XLink and HTML linking use URIs as the means to identify resources to which links are made. However, an XLink need not be expressed only at one end, nor is an XLink necessarily limited to traversal in one direction. Also it is not necessary to have write access to an XML document in order to create an XLink. Some concepts which may be new to many programmers are introduced in XLink, so, to better understand how these more sophisticated links work, let's take a closer look at the XLink language.

XML Linking Language – XLink

XLink is based on the XML 1.0 Recommendation, the Namespaces in XML Recommendation, and the XML Base specification (currently at Proposed Recommendation status). The XLink specification defines several attributes which belong to the XLink namespace, whose namespace URI is `http://www.w3.org/1999/xlink`.

First I think it is sensible to dispel one possible misunderstanding – that XLink defines any linking elements, in the same sense that, say, XSLT has XSLT elements. The XLink Proposed Recommendation states:

"This specification defines the XML Linking Language (XLink), which allows elements to be inserted into XML documents in order to create and describe links between resources".

In fact, the XLink specification no longer defines any linking elements (although it did in an earlier draft) to be included in an XML document – all XLink functionality is provided by **global attributes**, (described more fully in a later section) which can be attached to elements in other namespaces. When the XLink specification refers to "linking elements" what is meant is elements from namespaces other than the XLink namespace on which XLink global attributes are present.

We will now take a look at some of the XLink terminology. It differs in important respects from the usage of similar terms which you might have intuitively understood for HTML links.

In XLink a **link** is a relationship between two or more resources or portions of resources. Such a link (and by implication the relationship) is made explicit by means of what the specification calls **linking elements**. These are XML elements from any namespace that possesses XML elements (the XLink namespace has no elements, only attributes) on which exist XLink global attributes which define the link. A **resource** is any addressable unit of information or service, including files, images, or query results. The means of addressing a resource, or a portion of a resource, is a Uniform Resource Identifier, URI (see http://www.ietf.org/rfc/rfc2396.txt).

When an XLink link associates resources, the resources are said to **participate** in the link. All XLink links are contained within XML documents, but they may describe links between resources either expressed in XML or some other format. Thus, in a sense, such links provide XML meta data in two possible ways – the links can provide meta data *about* XML data, or they may express meta data *in* XML, which describes data held in some other non-XML format.

In XLink terminology, using or following a link for any purpose is called **traversal**. A link can associate an arbitrary number of resources, but traversal involves a pair of resources (or portions of resources). Traversal takes place from the **starting resource** to the **ending resource**. In this context a "resource" may mean either a whole resource or a portion of a resource.

Information about how to traverse a link, including for example the direction of traversal, is called an **arc**. If two arcs in a link specify the same pair of resources, but switch places as starting resource and ending resource, then the link is *bidirectional*. This is not the same as merely "going back" after traversing a link, as such a multidirectional link is conceptually different from following a unidirectional HTML link then hitting the Back button in a web browser.

As well as the concepts of a starting resource and an ending resource, XLink introduces the concepts of a **local resource** and a **remote resource**. A local resource is an element which participates in a link by means of having a parent which is itself what the XLink specification calls a linking element (defined above). Any resource which participates in an XLink link because it is addressed by means of a URI, is termed a remote resource. A remote resource in this context may be a complete resource or a part of a resource. A remote resource may be in another XML document, it may be in the same XML document, or it may even be within the same linking element as the local resource. The key distinguishing factor of a remote resource from a local resource is that a remote resource is specified by a URI reference and a local resource is specified by value.

In the following simple example, the `<Chapter>` element would be the local resource and the file "Chapter1.xml" (not supplied) is the remote resource, since it is referenced by means of the href attribute from the xlink namespace.

```
<?xml version='1.0'?>
<TableOfContents>
  <Chapter number="1"
    xmlns:xlink="http://www.w3.org/1999/xlink"
```

```
        xlink:type="simple"
        xlink:href="Chapter1.xml"
        xlink:role="to chapter text"
        xlink:title="Go to chapter 1"
        xlink:show="replace"
        xlink:actuate="onRequest">
        Chapter 1 - Why Meta Data Why XML
    </Chapter>
    <!-- Other chapters in the table of contents would appear here. -->
</TableOfContents>
```

An arc that has a local starting resource and a remote ending resource goes **outbound**. Conversely, an arc that has a remote starting resource and a local ending resource goes **inbound**. However, another possibility exists – that neither the starting resource nor the ending resource is a local resource. In that case the arc is termed a **third-party** arc.

Inbound arcs and third-party arcs allow XLink links to be defined in relation to documents to which you may not have write access. An XML document which contains a collection of inbound or third-party links is termed a **link database** or a **linkbase**.

XLink Attributes

As mentioned earlier, XLink provides a number of global attributes which provide its functionality. To use an XLink link it is necessary to declare the XLink namespace on the XML element to which the XLink attributes are to be placed. Thus, using a namespace prefix of xlink, we would declare the XLink namespace like this:

```
<AnyElement xmlns:xlink="http://www.w3.org/1999/xlink">
    <!-- Any content goes here. -->
</AnyElement>
```

The appropriate XLink global attributes, so called because they can be placed on any XML element for which the XLink namespace is in scope, are as follows:

❏   xlink:type – this required attribute specifies what type of link is being created. The value of this attribute determines whether the remaining attributes are required, optional, or not appropriate. We'll see what each of these types is a little later.

❏   xlink:href – this attribute states where a remote resource can be found.

❏   xlink:role – this optional attribute describes, for the benefit of the processing application, the meaning of the link resource.

❏   xlink:arcrole – this is similar to role.

❏   xlink:title – this provides a human readable description of the meaning of the link.

❏   xlink:show – this essentially defines where to display the linked resource.

❏   xlink:actuate – this essentially defines when to display the linked resource.

❏   xlink:label – this can be used to identify an end point of a link.

❏   xlink:from – this can be used to specify an end point of a link.

❏   xlink:to – this can be used to specify the origin of a link.

Any individual XLink need not have all of the attributes present (this depends on the type of link). A typical format is illustrated here for a simple-type XLink, which might appear as part of an XML-based web page on the (fictitious) XMML.com web site.

```
<xmml:consultancy
  xmlns:xmml="http://www.xmml.com/ "
  xmlns:xlink="http://www.w3.org/1999/xlink"
  xlink:type="simple"
  xlink:href="consultancy.xml"
  xlink:role="consultancyinfo"
  xlink:title="Consultancy Information"
  xlink:show="new"
  xlink:actuate="onRequest">
    Consultancy Information and Charges
</xmml:consultancy>
```

Each attribute in the above code can be explained as follows:

❑ The xlink:type attribute value indicates that the XLink is, in this case, of simple-type, which we'll look at in a moment.

❑ The xlink:href attribute value indicates that the ending resource is a file, consultancy.xml, in the same directory.

❑ The xlink:role attribute value indicates that the role is "consultancyinfo".

❑ The xlink:title attribute value provides a title for the link, in this case "Consultancy Information".

❑ The xlink:show attribute value specifies that the referenced file should be displayed in a new window.

❑ The xlink:actuate attribute value indicates that the arc is traversed on request; in practice this would typically mean when the text content of the element on which the XLink attributes are placed is clicked.

The XLink type attribute may have any of the following values:

❑ simple

❑ extended

❑ locator

❑ arc

❑ resource

❑ title

A simple-type XLink may exist on its own. Typically however, elements with the locator-type, arc-type, resource-type, and title-type will be children of an element on which the xlink:type attribute has the value "extended". Additionally, title-type elements may be children of locator-type or arc-type elements.

We will examine more closely the use of these various attributes when we look at XLink simple-type links and extended-type links in more detail next.

To create a valid XLink, as well as ensuring that the XLink namespace is in scope (either by declaration on the element or one of its parent elements), on each attribute it is necessary to use a namespace prefix corresponding to the XLink namespace, and also the xlink:type attribute must be present.

Simple-Type Links

An XLink simple-type link provides functionality very similar to that provided by an HTML hyperlink.

The following example, which you saw earlier, demonstrates a simple-type XLink which behaves much as does a typical HTML hyperlink. In a browser which supports simple-type XLinks, such as Netscape 6, when the text "Chapter 1 – Why Meta Data Why XML" is clicked, the referenced file, Chapter1.xml, replaces the table of contents in the browser window.

```xml
<?xml version='1.0'?>
<TableOfContents>
  <Chapter number="1"
    xmlns:xlink="http://www/w3.org/1999/xlink"
    xlink:type="simple"
    xlink:href="Chapter1.xml"
    xlink:role="to chapter text"
    xlink:title="Go to chapter 1"
    xlink:show="replace"
    xlink:actuate="onRequest">
      Chapter 1 - Why Meta Data Why XML
  </Chapter>
  <!-- Other chapters in the table of contents would appear here. -->
</TableOfContents>
```

As with our previous example we can explain this as follows:

❑　The value of the xlink:type attribute specifies that this XLink is a simple-type link.

❑　The value of the xlink:href attribute specifies the URI of the resource which is the ending resource. If the XLink processor is XPointer-aware then the URI can include XPointers.

❑　The value of the xlink:role attribute specifies that the role is "to chapter text".

❑　The value of the xlink:title attribute specifies that the title of the link is "Go to chapter 1". In some implementations the value of the title attribute may be displayed when the mouse is positioned over the link.

❑　The value of the xlink:show attribute indicates that the referenced resource will replace the current file in the browser.

❑　The value of the xlink:actuate attribute specifies that the content is replaced on request, typically clicking the text of the element content.

To cause the referenced resource to be displayed in a new browser window we can simply alter the value of the xlink:show attribute from "replace" to "new":

```xml
<?xml version='1.0'?>
<TableOfContents>
  <Chapter number="1"
    xmlns:xlink="http://www/w3.org/1999/xlink"
    xlink:type="simple"
```

```
   xlink:href="Chapter1.xml"
   xlink:role="to chapter text"
   xlink:title="Go to chapter 1"
   xlink:show="new"
   xlink:actuate="onRequest">
      Chapter 1 - Why Meta Data Why XML
   </Chapter>
 <!-- Other chapters in the table of contents would appear here. -->
 </TableOfContents>
```

Additionally, if we wanted the referenced resource to be displayed in a separate window which opens when the table of contents is loaded, we could change the value of the xlink:actuate attribute so that it has a value of "onLoad":

```
<?xml version='1.0'?>
<TableOfContents>
  <Chapter number="1"
    xmlns:xlink="http://www.w3.org/1999/xlink"
    xlink:type="simple"
    xlink:href="Chapter1.xml"
    xlink:role="to chapter text"
    xlink:title="Go to chapter 1"
    xlink:show="new"
    xlink:actuate="onLoad">
       Chapter 1 - Why Meta Data Why XML
  </Chapter>
<!-- Other chapters in the table of contents would appear here. -->
</TableOfContents>
```

Then, in an XLink-aware browser, when the main window is loaded a pop-up window will be opened containing the text of Chapter 1.

In an XML-based web browser we might want to embed, for example, Scalable Vector Graphics (SVG) images within XML. The SVG specification uses simple-type XLinks. The following example shows how to do that using the xlink:show attribute:

```
<?xml version='1.0'?>
<TableOfContents>
  <Chapter number="1"
    xmlns:xlink="http://www.w3.org/1999/xlink"
    xlink:type="simple"
    xlink:href="CorporateLogo.svg"
    xlink:role="corportatelogo"
    xlink:title="Our corporate logo"
    xlink:show="embed"
    xlink:actuate="onLoad">
       Chapter 1 - Why Meta Data Why XML
  </Chapter>
  <!-- Other chapters in the table of contents would appear here. -->
</TableOfContents>
```

Unfortunately, embedding using XLinks is not currently supported in the widely available web browsers. The Adobe SVG Viewer, available for download from http://www.adobe.com/svg/, has implemented more XLink functionality (within its own scope of SVG) than Netscape 6 has. At the time of writing Microsoft's Internet Explorer has no XLink functionality in release version browsers. Linking can be implemented in custom applications, for example Java or Visual Basic – an example of which is given in "*Professional Visual Basic 6 XML*" (ISBN 1-861003-32-3), Chapter 11.

It might have struck you that the XLinks shown above are rather verbose. It is possible to define default values for some of the XLink attributes, for example `xlink:show` and `xlink:actuate`, in a DTD or schema, to reduce the amount of code that has to be written for each XLink.

Extended-Type Links

XLink extended-type links can introduce significant complexity, in comparison to HTML hyperlinks. In contrast to simple-type links, which have all attributes on a single XML element, extended-type links may have other elements nested within the element that has the extended-type attribute. These other elements may have values defined for `xlink:locator`, `xlink:resource`, `xlink:arc`, or `xlink:title` attributes. An extended-type link may have an arbitrary number of participating resources. Furthermore, the participating resources may be any combination of local and remote. A simple-type link may be viewed as a special case of an extended-type link – an outbound extended-type link with exactly two participating resources.

Extended-type XLink links may be stored in documents separate from the resources that they associate. Thus extended-type links allow associations to be asserted between resources to which the author of the XLink extended-type link does not have write access. In fact, the resources associated by XLink extended-type links need not be writable at all.

An element which has an `xlink:type` attribute with value of "extended" may have children with further XLink attributes, as follows:

- ❏   `xlink:locator` – these address the resources participating in the link.

- ❏   `xlink:arc` – these provide traversal rules among the link's participating resources.

- ❏   `xlink:title` – these provide human readable titles for the link.

- ❏   `xlink:resource` – these supply local resources which participate in the link.

While extended-type links typically contain at least two participating resources, it is not an error for the number of participating resources to be less than two. That, for example, allows placeholder links to be created whose participants would be defined at a later time.

Local resources of an extended-type link are indicated by means of nested elements which have an `xlink:type` attribute with a value of "resource". Such a resource-type element is, according to the XLink specification, free to have content, but the XLink specification does not define how any such content relates to the resource. However, even if the resource has no content, an XLink processor is expected to generate some (undefined) way to allow the user to initiate traversal of the link.

Remote resources for an extended-type link are indicated by elements which have a value defined for an `xlink:locator` attribute. A locator-type element must have an `xlink:href` attribute, which must have a value which is legal and defines the URI where the resource is located. A locator-type element may have as a child an element which possesses an `xlink:title` attribute. Any other content is permitted by the XLink specification but has no XLink-defined meaning.

Traversal of an extended-type link may be indicated by means of one or more `xlink:arc` attributes. An element with an `xlink:arc` attribute only has an XLink-defined meaning when it has a parent element which has an `xlink:type` attribute with the value of "`extended`". An arc-type element may have the attributes `xlink:from` and `xlink:to`. The `xlink:from` attribute indicates the starting resource and the `xlink:to` attribute indicates the ending resource. The `xlink:show` and `xlink:actuate` attributes indicate behavior similar to that described earlier for simple-type links.

Let's look for a moment at a fairly straightforward use of XLink extended links applied to relationships which we are all familiar with, in one form or another – the human family. Here is an extended link which describes some parent-child relationships within a rather famous family.

```xml
<?xml version='1.0'?>
<family xmlns:xlink="http://www.w3.org/1999/xlink"
        xlink:type="extended"
        xlink:role="family"
        xlink:title="British Royal Family">

<individual
        xlink:type="locator"
        xlink:href="PrincePhilip.xml"
        xlink:label="parent"
        xlink:title="Prince Philip"/>

<individual
        xlink:type="locator"
        xlink:href="QueenElizabeth.xml"
        xlink:label="parent"
        xlink:title="Queen Elizabeth"/>

<individual
        xlink:type="locator"
        xlink:href="Charles.xml"
        xlink:label="child"
        xlink:title="Prince Charles"/>

<individual
        xlink:type="locator"
        xlink:href="Anne.xml"
        xlink:label="child"
        xlink:title="Princess Anne"/>

<individual
        xlink:type="locator"
        xlink:href="Andrew.xml"
        xlink:label="child"
        xlink:title="Prince Andrew"/>

<individual
        xlink:type="locator"
        xlink:href="Edward.xml"
        xlink:label="child"
        xlink:title="Prince Edward"/>

<link   xlink:type="arc"
        xlink:from="parent"
        xlink:to="child"
        xlink:title="Parent to child links"
        xlink:show="replace"
        xlink:actuate="onRequest"/>
</family>
```

Let's take a closer look at how that extended link was constructed. Notice that the start tag of the `<family>` element contains the `xlink:type` attribute with value of "extended" indicating that the element content of the `<family>` element may potentially contain further parts of the extended link.

```
<family xmlns:xlink="http://www.w3.org/1999/xlink"
        xlink:type="extended"
        xlink:role="family"
        xlink:title="British Royal Family">
```

The bulk of the document consists of `<individual>` elements which refer to individual members of the family, either a parent as indicated by the value of the `xlink:label` attribute:

```
<individual
        xlink:type="locator"
        xlink:href="PrincePhilip.xml"
        xlink:label="parent"
        xlink:title="Prince Philip"/>
```

or a child, as here:

```
<individual
        xlink:type="locator"
        xlink:href="Charles.xml"
        xlink:label="child"
        xlink:title="Prince Charles"/>
```

The `<individual>` elements each have an `xlink:type` attribute with the value "locator", indicating the locations that participate in an extended link.

What we might, in HTML terms, think of as the actual link is in XLink specified in this example by the `<link>` element:

```
<link   xlink:type="arc"
        xlink:from="parent"
        xlink:to="child"
        xlink:title="Parent to child links"
        xlink:show="replace"
        xlink:actuate="onRequest"/>
```

It is not the fact that the above element is called a `<link>` element which defines the arcs which may be traversed. That is due to the presence of the `xlink:type` attribute with a value of "arc", indicating that the arc(s) to be traversed are being referred to. The `xlink:from` and `xlink:to` attributes indicate the arcs involved – of which there would be eight in this example. Four from Prince Philip, one to each of his children, and four from Queen Elizabeth, again one to each of her children.

The `xlink:arcrole`, `xlink:role`, and `xlink:title` attributes, the so-called **semantic attributes**, describe the relationship between the starting resource and ending resource. The `xlink:arcrole` attribute corresponds to the RDF notion of a property (see Chapters 1 and 4 for what this means). Thus its meaning takes the form:

```
starting-resource HAS arcrole ending-resource
```

Consequently, if we had an XLink indicating a relationship between Bill and Hillary Clinton, when traversed in one direction the `xlink:arcrole` attribute would correspond in meaning to:

```
Bill Clinton HAS wife Hillary Clinton
```

whereas, when the arc was traversed in the other direction the `xlink:arcrole` attribute would correspond to the meaning:

```
Hillary Clinton HAS husband Bill Clinton
```

The `xlink:title` attribute is used to indicate a human-readable title for a link. In some cases a link may have many `xlink:title` attributes, for example in a situation where there is a multilingual presentation of information.

For an XLink processor to traverse an outbound arc from a starting resource to an ending resource is fairly straightforward, since the linking element is either the linking element itself (that is, the one which has the `xlink:type="extended"` attribute) or a child element of that linking element.

Linkbases

I mentioned earlier that third party arcs exist. That means that the XLink links are contained in an XML document which does not participate in the XLink link, either as a starting resource or as an ending resource. An XML document which provides such linking functionality is called a link database or, more commonly, a linkbase. A linkbase contains one or more extended XLink links. It may link resources which may be XML or have some other content type. For example, a linkbase could specify relationships between an XML catalog and a list of images, perhaps JPEGs, which are not created in XML.

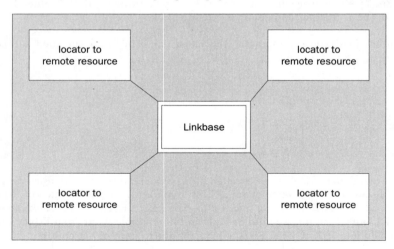

A linkbase stores the linking information needed to associate multiple XLink links. In the diagram four remote resources are linked by means of locator-type elements which are part of one or more extended-type links stored in a linkbase.

Link databases, or linkbases, may be used to bring a number of related links together. XLink provides a way of requiring an XLink processor to access a relevant linkbase by using the `xlink:arcrole` attribute. When the `xlink:arcrole` attribute has the value `"http://www.w3.org/1999/xlink/properties/linkbase"` then the XLink processor will traverse to the specified linkbase. A linkbase may associate resources that can be XML or non-XML, but the linkbase itself must be specified in XML.

Traversal of an arc to a linkbase requires that the links contained within the linkbase are loaded by the XLink processor, or the application using it, for future use. The URI in the `xlink:href` attribute corresponding to traversal of the arc to the linkbase may contain a **fragment identifier**, so that only a portion of the linkbase, for example a range or string range (see the XPointer section later), is extracted for future use by the XLink processor. Traversal of the linkbase arc is controlled by the `xlink:actuate` attribute. If the `xlink:actuate` attribute has the value `"onLoad"` then the linkbase arc will be traversed when the XML document is loaded, and the XLink processor will then extract and make available the contents of the linkbase or, if a fragment identifier is present, the appropriate part of the linkbase.

Since a linkbase may itself serve as the starting resource for a linkbase arc, it is possible to create chains of linkbase arcs, whose behavior may become quite complex to follow.

While you may not have grasped all the aspects of XLink linkbases from this brief summary, I hope you have begun to appreciate that XLink, once the specification progresses to full Recommendation, will provide powerful and potentially sophisticated means to express relationships between resources, which need not necessarily be XML. Further examples of XLink are given in Chapter 5 of "*Professional Visual Basic 6 XML*", ISBN 1-861003-32-3.

XML Pointer Language – XPointer

The XML Pointer Language, XPointer, allows us to specify links to sub-resources within resources identified by a URI. For example, in the preceding section I mentioned that a linkbase arc may reference only a portion of the linkbase. XPointer, once completed and implemented, will allow that facet of XLink to be fully realized.

> *At the time of writing XPointer is at "last call" Working Draft Status, which is located at http://www.w3.org/TR/2001/WD-xptr-20010108. If any changes have taken place since this chapter was written then the January 2001 Working Draft will be replaced at http://www.w3.org/TR/xptr.*

XPointer builds on concepts found in the XML Path Language, XPath, which will be described first, and then the functionality of XPointer will be reviewed.

XML Path Language – XPath – Overview

The XML Path Language, XPath, is not expressed in XML syntax. XPath provides functionality which is the basis of XPointer and also functionality which is extended in XSLT (which is discussed a little later in the chapter).

XPath models an XML document as a hierarchy of nodes. The XPath data model differs from that of the XML Information set (discussed later in this chapter) and the Document Object Model, DOM. However, an XML document can be modeled as a hierarchical tree, with the root node which represents the document entity as the root of the tree.

XPath also provides a number of functions for the manipulation of strings, booleans, numbers, and nodesets.

XPath has the following types of node, which should all be familiar to anyone with basic XML knowledge:

- ❏ Root
- ❏ Element
- ❏ Attribute
- ❏ Namespace
- ❏ Processing Instruction
- ❏ Comment
- ❏ Text

XPath allows the addressing of parts of an XML document. XPath expressions are broadly similar to a set of street directions. You have a defined starting point (in XPath jargon the **context node**), a direction (called in XPath an **axis**), and some description of the final destination which distinguishes it (in XPath a **predicate**).

XPath is expressed in XPath **expressions**.

An XPath expression may yield as a result any of four types of object:

- ❏ A nodeset – an unordered collection of nodes without duplicates.
- ❏ A boolean – true or false.
- ❏ A number – a floating point number.
- ❏ A string – a sequence of Unicode characters.

Typical use of XPath makes use of an important subset of XPath expressions termed **location paths**. A location path consists of one or more **location steps** and, in turn, a location step consists of an axis, a node test, and zero or more predicates. To understand XPath location paths we need to take a slightly closer look at what constitutes an axis, a node test, and a predicate. Let's use a simple example document to illustrate this:

```
<?xml version='1.0'?>
<book>
  <chapter number="1"> Why Meta Data Why XML</chapter>
  <chapter number="2">XML Schemas</chapter>
  <chapter number="3">XML Linking and querying XML</chapter>
  <chapter number="4">RDF Model and Syntax</chapter>
</book>
```

XPath has four types of syntax:

- ❏ Unabbreviated relative location paths.
- ❏ Unabbreviated absolute location paths.
- ❏ Abbreviated relative location paths.
- ❏ Abbreviated absolute location paths.

Relative location paths are constructed with the context node as the starting point for the XPath location path. **Absolute location paths** use as their starting point the root node of the document that contains the context node.

In this initial example we will use the unabbreviated relative location path syntax.

Let's suppose that in our example we wish to define or display the content of the third child element of the <book> element node. To do that we would use the following location path, assuming that the context node is the node representing the <book> element in the above XML document:

```
child::*[position()=3]
```

The `child::` part of the location path indicates that the axis is the child axis. The `*` is the node test of this location path and indicates that *any* child element node matches. The `[position()=3]` is a predicate indicating that the node set which satisfies this location path is a single element node in the third position.

If we had wanted to be more specific we could have used the element type name of the <chapter> element in the location path, as here:

```
child::chapter[position()=3]
```

The axis, node test, and predicate successively filter possible matching nodes in the node hierarchy. The axis means that only nodes which are child nodes of the context node might satisfy the expression. Of those child nodes the node test is that they represent a <chapter> element. Of the child nodes which represent <chapter> elements, only the node in position 3 satisfies the expression.

The abbreviated relative syntax for the above location path is:

```
. chapter[3]
```

As you can see, this is significantly shorter than the unabbreviated syntax. Since XPath location paths can, when using unabbreviated syntax, become quite lengthy, it is more practical to use abbreviated syntax when abbreviated syntax can express the type of filtering which is desired.

In street directions you have four axes (North, South, East, and West). In XPath there is a total of thirteen axes, which begin the process of filtering nodes in the XML document:

- ❑ `Child` – contains all direct children of the context node (not the children's children).
- ❑ `Parent` – contains the direct parent node of the context node.
- ❑ `Descendant` – contains all children of the context node, and their children, children's children etc.
- ❑ `Ancestor` – contains the parent node of the context node, its parent's parent node, etc, up to and including the root node.
- ❑ `Descendant-or-self` – contains the descendant nodes plus the context node.
- ❑ `Ancestor-or-self` – contains the ancestor nodes plus the context node.

- ❑ Following – contains all nodes that come after the context node in document order, only including elements whose opening tag appears after the closing tag of the context node, in other words not descendants of the context node.

- ❑ Preceding – contains all nodes that come before the context node in document order, only including elements that have already been closed, in other words not ancestors of the context node.

- ❑ Following-sibling – contains all sibling nodes that come after the context node in document order.

- ❑ Preceding-sibling – contains all sibling nodes that come before the context node in document order.

- ❑ Attribute – contains all attributes on the context node (if it is an element).

- ❑ Namespace – contains all namespaces on the context node (if it is an element).

- ❑ Self – contains just the context node itself.

By appropriate use of these axes, together with suitable node tests and predicates, many desired expressions can be created. However, limitations existed in the XPath 1.0 Recommendation. Some of these were to be remedied by extensions in the XSLT 1.0 Recommendation and some by extensions in the XPointer specification, which is currently at Working Draft status.

XPointer – Overview

As mentioned earlier, an XPointer allows the addressing of a portion of an XML document. You may already be familiar with fragment identifiers in HTML, as in this example. The <A> elements which have a name attribute, in Fragment01.html, may be linked to from another HTML document.

```
<!DOCTYPE HTML PUBLIC "-//W3C//DTD HTML 4.0 Transitional//EN"
"http://www.w3.org/TR/REC-html40/loose.dtd">
<HTML>
  <HEAD>
    <TITLE>Untitled</TITLE>
  </HEAD>
  <BODY>
    <P>
      <A name="FirstPara">This is the first paragraph.</A>
    </P>
    <P>
      <A name="SecondPara">This is the second paragraph.</A>
    </P>
  </BODY>
</HTML>
```

To link to the second paragraph we could use the following syntax, as in Fragment02.html:

```
<!DOCTYPE HTML PUBLIC "-//W3C//DTD HTML 4.0 Transitional//EN"
"http://www.w3.org/TR/REC-html40/loose.dtd">
<HTML>
  <HEAD>
    <TITLE>Untitled</TITLE>
  </HEAD>
  <BODY>
    <P>
```

```
        <A href="Fragment01.html#FirstPara">Go to First Paragraph</A>
    </P>
    <P>
        <A href="Fragment01.html#SecondPara">Go to Second Paragraph</A>
    </P>
  </BODY>
</HTML>
```

For the linking to be visible to the named `<A>` element in `Fragment01.html`, we need a much longer HTML document than shown, so that the scrolling within the document will be visible in the browser window. As you saw above, in order to link specifically to the first or second paragraphs in `Fragment01.html` it was necessary to insert an `<A>` element with a `name` attribute. Thus in order to use the HTML fragment identifier it is necessary to have write access to the document being linked to. Given the nature of XML it cannot be guaranteed that write access will be possible. Thus a specification which allows addressing of portions of a resource, without assuming that write access is possible, is desirable. XPointer is such a specification.

There are three forms of syntax which may be used in XPointer:

❑   Bare names.

❑   Child sequences.

❑   Full XPointers.

We will illustrate the basic use of these three forms of XPointer using the following simple document, `XPointer01.xml`, as the target of the XPointer:

```
<?xml version='1.0'?>
<book id="MyBook">
  <Chapter id="chapter3">
    <Section type="introduction" id="first">This is the first
                 introductory section.</Section>
    <Section type="text" id="second">This is the second section</Section>
    <Section type="text" id="third">This is the third section</Section>
    <Section type="text" id="fourth">This is the third section</Section>
  </Chapter>
</book>
```

In HTML the # character indicates the beginning of the fragment identifier and XPointer provides a similar syntax using the same character. This type of XPointer is termed a **bare names** XPointer. To reference the `<Chapter>` element we could use the bare names syntax like this:

```
#chapter3
```

Unless we are a little lucky and someone has added `id` attributes to the fragment we want to link to, or we ourselves have write access, the bare names syntax won't allow us to access the desired element using this approach.

Similarly, we could access the second `<section>` element like this:

```
#second
```

Using the **child sequence** syntax we could specify the second `<section>` element like so:

```
#xpointer(/1/1/2)
```

The `#xpointer` part of the child sequence indicates that we are dealing with an XPointer. The first `/` indicates we are starting at the document root. We then choose the first child (the `<book>` element), its first child (the `<Chapter>` element), and its second child (the second `<Section>` element).

Child sequences, used in this way, depend on a knowledge of the structure of a document, perhaps derived from an XML schema, but do not require that any element in the referenced XML document possesses an `id` attribute.

An alternate use of the child sequence syntax would allow us to start from a named node. For example:

```
#xpointer(chapter3/2)
```

It is the `id` attribute on the `<Chapter>` element which is used first, then the second child element of that element is located.

Before we consider the **full XPointer** syntax we need to digress to mention two concepts by which XPointer extends XPath functionality. XPointer adds the concepts of a **point** and a **range**. An XPointer location of type point is defined by a node, called the **container node**, and a non-negative integer, called the **index**. A point can represent the location preceding any individual character, or preceding or following any node in the data set constructed from an XML document. Note that a point is not identical to a node in XPath. A range is defined as the XML structure and content between two XPointer points.

Thus, if we wanted to include both the second and third `<Section>` elements in our sample document we could do so in this way, using the full XPointer syntax:

```
#xpointer(id("second")/range-to(id("third")))
```

We could not have expressed that in XPath. The closest might have been to specify all `<Section>` elements after the first, as here:

```
/book/Chapter/Section[position()>1]
```

Currently it is not easy to find worthwhile implementations of XPointer. To a degree the specification is in some confusion. It recently went backwards from Candidate Recommendation status to Working Draft status, and more recently a former co-chair of the XLink Working Group went on record as supporting an alternative, simpler approach to XPointer. Clearly, there are fundamental divergences of approach within the XLink Working Group as to how the XPointer specification should best be taken forward. The potential of XPointer is significant but progress in the short term is not by any means certain.

XML Inclusions – XInclude

The XInclude specification, at the time of writing a Working Draft of 16th May 2001, describes a processing model and syntax for general purpose inclusion of XML documents. The Working Draft, or any updates to it, may be accessed at http://www.w3.org/TR/xinclude/. Inclusion is achieved by merging a number of XML Infosets into a composite infoset. Therefore, to understand what XInclude is about we need to digress briefly to consider the XML Information Set specification. Both XML Inclusions and the XML Information Set are expressed in XML syntax.

XML Information Set

At the time of writing the current version of the XML Information Set specification is the Candidate Recommendation of 14th May 2001. That Candidate Recommendation or its successor is located at http://www.w3.org/TR/xml-infoset. Since the XML Information Set seems set to be a pivotal part of the W3C's future XML-related specifications, I am going to describe it fairly fully, but be aware that the detail may change before a final Recommendation is approved.

The XML Information Set is defined in the specification as an abstract data set. The purpose of the specification is to define a means for accessing information in well-formed XML documents and the specification is intended to be used by other W3C specifications, such as the XML Inclusions specification that we are now considering. Conveniently, since it avoids some tricky issues, the XML Information Set does not attempt to be exhaustive, but focuses on those information items that are expected to be of the greatest usefulness in future W3C specifications.

An XML document has an information set when it is well-formed and satisfies namespace criteria set out in the XML Information Set specification. An XML document need not be valid in order to have an information set. The namespace criteria which must be satisfied are as follows. First, an XML document must satisfy the criteria set out in the Namespaces in XML Recommendation (see http://www.w3.org/TR/REC-xml-names). Additionally, the namespace URI must not be defined as a relative URI. Thus a namespace name must always refer to an absolute URI, with an optional fragment identifier.

An XML document's information set is made up of one or more **information items**. An information item is an abstract representation of some part of a well-formed XML document. For example, each well-formed XML document has a **document information item** that corresponds to the document entity itself, plus, typically, a number of element and other information items. In all but the simplest XML documents the number of information items can be large.

Each individual information item has a number of associated **properties**.

The XML Information Set specification very deliberately describes an abstract data model, since there is a clear intention not to tie the abstract model to any specific means of implementing it. Broadly, an information set corresponds to the general idea of a **tree** in computing, and an information item broadly corresponds to a **node**. It is important to appreciate that there is no simple one-to-one correspondence between the XML Information Set specification and the Document Object Model specification or the XML Path Language specification. An information item does not directly correspond to a DOM node or an XPath node, nor does the information set correspond to an XPath tree.

An XML information set describes an XML document with its entity references already expanded. However, in practice, it isn't always possible to guarantee that the entities have been expanded. For example, a non-validating XML processor may not read all declarations or may not expand entity references which it has read. Additionally, it may not be possible at any particular point in time to access an external entity for a variety of technical reasons. In circumstances where it is not possible to expand all external entities, an **unexpanded entity reference** information item is used within the infoset to represent the entity reference.

An XML infoset may contain some or all of the following eleven types of information item, all of which are fairly self-explanatory:

- Document
- Element
- Attribute
- Processing instruction
- Unexpanded entity reference
- Character
- Comment
- Document type declaration
- Unparsed entity
- Notation
- Namespace

There is exactly one document information item in an information set, with all other information items in the infoset being accessed from the properties of the document information item, either directly or via the properties of other information items in the infoset.

The XML Infoset Candidate Recommendation makes mention of Document Type Definitions but makes no mention of XML Schema even though it is now, since May 2001, at full Recommendation status. XML Schema adds to the XML Infoset producing the **PSVI**, the **post schema-validation infoset**. For further information see Part 1 of the XML Schema Recommendation located at http://www.w3.org/TR/xmlschema-1/. It seems likely that the XML Information set will in time take account of the XML Schema Recommendation, but it may not be in version 1 of the XML Information Set specification.

XML Information Set – Information Items and their Properties

The XML Information set uses a [square brackets] notation to denote properties of an information item. A document information item has the following properties:

- [children] – an ordered list of child information items in document order. If there is a document type declaration, any comments or processing instructions outside the document element, then there is a corresponding document type declaration information item, comment or processing instruction information item.

- [document element] – this denotes the element information item corresponding to the document element.

- ❑ [notations] – an unordered set of notation information items, one for each notation declared in the document type definition.

- ❑ [unparsed entities] – an unordered set of unparsed entity information items, one for each unparsed entity declared in the document type definition.

- ❑ [base URI] – the base URI for the document entity.

- ❑ [character encoding scheme] – the character encoding scheme in which the document entity is expressed.

- ❑ [standalone] – corresponds to the standalone attribute of an XML declaration, if present. If there is no XML declaration then this property has no value.

- ❑ [version] – corresponds to the version attribute of an XML declaration, if present. If there is no XML declaration then this property has no value.

- ❑ [all declarations processed] – strictly not a property. It is a boolean value which indicates whether or not the processor has read and processed the complete DTD.

An **element information item** exists for each element which appears in an XML document. An element information item may have the following properties:

- ❑ [namespace name] – the namespace name of the element type, if it is in a namespace. If the element type is not in a namespace then this property has no value.

- ❑ [local name] – the local part of the element type name.

- ❑ [prefix] – the namespace prefix of the element type name. If the element has no prefix then this property has no value.

- ❑ [children] – an ordered list, in document order, of child element information items. The children include element, processing instruction, unexpanded entity reference, character, and comment information items.

- ❑ [attributes] – an unordered set of attribute information items, corresponding to each attribute of the element, whether specified directly or derived from default declarations in the DTD.

- ❑ [namespace attributes] – an unordered set of information items, corresponding to each of any namespace declarations for the element.

- ❑ [in-scope namespaces] – an unordered set of namespace information items, one for each of the namespaces in effect for the element.

- ❑ [base URI] – the base URI for the element.

- ❑ [parent] – the document information item or element information item which contains this element information item in its [children] property.

An **attribute information item** exists for each attribute of each element in the document, whether the attribute is specified directly or is declared by default in the document type definition. An attribute information item has the following properties:

- ❑ [namespace name] – the namespace name of the attribute, if it has one. Otherwise this property has no value.

- ❑ [local name] – the local part of the attribute name (excludes any prefix and the following colon).

- ❑ [prefix] – the namespace prefix of the attribute name. If there is no prefix then this property has no value.

- ❑ [normalized value] – the normalized value of the attribute after the algorithm in Chapter 3.3.3 of the XML 1.0 specification has been applied.

- ❑ [specified] – a flag indicating from where this attribute was derived – the start tag of the containing element or a default value in the DTD.

- ❑ [attribute type] – represents the type declared for the attribute in the DTD. Legal values for this property are ID, IDREF, IDREFS, ENTITY, ENTITIES, NMTOKEN, NMTOKENS, NOTATION, CDATA, and ENUMERATION.

- ❑ [references] – if the attribute type is IDREF, IDREFS, ENTITY, ENTITIES, or NOTATION, the value of this property is an ordered list of the element, unparsed entity, or notation information items referred to in the attribute value, in the order that they appear there. If the attribute type is ID, NMTOKEN, NMTOKENS, CDATA, or ENUMERATION, this property has no value. If the attribute type is unknown, the value of this property is unknown.

- ❑ [owner element] – the element information item which contains the present information item in its [attributes] property.

A **processing instruction information item** exists in the infoset for each processing instruction in the corresponding XML document. Remember that the XML declaration is not considered to be a processing instruction. A processing instruction information item has the following properties:

- ❑ [target] – corresponds to the target part of the processing instruction.

- ❑ [content] – a string representing the content of the processing instruction. The value will be an empty string if the processing instruction has no such content.

- ❑ [base URI] – the base URI of the processing instruction.

- ❑ [notation] – the notation information named by the target of the processing instruction. If no declaration is made for a notation with that name then the [notation] property has no value.

- ❑ [parent] – the document, element, or document type declaration information item which contains this processing instruction within its [children] property.

An **unexpanded entity reference information item** is used as a place holder to indicate whether or not an XML processor has expanded a referenced external parsed entity. For each such unexpanded entity which is referenced in a document there will be a corresponding unexpanded entity reference information item. Each such information item has the following properties:

- ❑ [name] – the name of the entity referenced.

- ❑ [system identifier] – the system identifier for the entity. The property has no value if there is no declaration for the entity. The property value is unknown if the [all declarations processed] property of the document information item has the value "false".

- ❑ [public identifier] – the public identifier of the entity, normalized according to the rules in Chapter 4.2.4 of the XML Recommendation.

- ❑ [declaration base URI] – the base URI relative to which the system identifier is to be resolved. The property has no value if there is no declaration for the entity. The property value is unknown if the [all declarations processed] property of the document information item has the value "false".

❑ [parent] – the element information item which contains this information item within its [children] property.

A **character information item** exists for each data character in an XML document whether literally, as a character reference, or in a CDATA section. Each character is considered to be a separate information item but XML applications are free to aggregate character information items. Each character information item has the following properties:

❑ [character code] – the ISO 10646 character code for the character.

❑ [element content whitespace] – a boolean indicating whether or not the character is whitespace contained in an element's content.

❑ [parent] – the element information item which contains this information item within its [children] property.

A **comment information item** is present in the infoset for each comment appearing in the XML document, with the exception of any comments present within the DTD, which are not represented. A comment information item has the following properties:

❑ [content] – the content of the comment as a string.

❑ [parent] – the document information item or element information item which contains this information item within its [children] property.

A **document type declaration information item** is present if the XML document has a document type declaration. Contrary, perhaps, to expectation, entities and notations are properties of the document information item (see above) and not properties of the document type declaration information item. Each document type declaration information item has the following properties:

❑ [system identifier] – if there is an external subset this property consists of its system identifier, otherwise it has no value.

❑ [public identifier] – the public identifier of the external subset of the DTD, normalized according to the requirements of Chapter 4.2.2 of the XML 1.0 Recommendation.

❑ [children] – an ordered list of processing instruction information items representing processing instructions which appear in the document's DTD, in document order. Processing instruction information items from the internal subset are ordered before any in the external subset.

❑ [parent] – the document information item.

An **unparsed entity information item** exists for each unparsed general entity declared in the DTD. Each unparsed entity information item has the following properties:

❑ [name] – the name of the entity.

❑ [system identifier] – the system identifier of the entity.

❑ [public identifier] – the public identifier of the entity, normalized according to the rules in Chapter 4.2.2 of the XML 1.0 Recommendation, if it has a public identifier. If the entity has no public identifier then the property has no value.

❑ [declaration base URI] – the base URI relative to which the system identifier should be resolved.

❑ [notation name] – the notation name associated with the entity.

❑   [notation] – the notation information item indicated by the notation name. If there is no declaration for a notation with that name then the property has no value. If the [all declarations processed] property of the document information item has the value "false" then the value of this property is unknown.

A **notation information item** exists for each notation in the DTD. Each notation information item has the following properties:

❑   [name] – the name of the notation.

❑   [system identifier] – the system identifier of the notation if it has one. Otherwise this property has no value.

❑   [public identifier] – the public identifier of the notation if it has one, normalized according to the rules in Chapter 4.2.2 of the XML 1.0 Recommendation. If the notation has no public identifier then this property has no value.

❑   [declaration base URI] – the base URI of the resource within which the notation declaration occurs.

A **namespace information item** occurs for each element information item for each namespace that is in scope for that element. Each namespace information item has the following properties:

❑   [prefix] – the namespace prefix. If the namespace declaration is simply xmlns= then this property has no value.

❑   [namespace name] – the namespace name to which the prefix is bound.

Having described the information items and their properties which make up the XML Information Set, let's return to our consideration of XML Inclusions.

XInclude – Basics

The namespace URI for XInclude is http://www.w3.org/2001/XInclude. The XInclude namespace contains only one element, with element type name of include. The typical, but non-normative, prefix used to refer to the XInclude namespace URI is xi. Therefore, in typical use the element appears as <xi:include>.

The <xi:include> element has three permitted attributes: href, parse, and encoding. In addition, the <xi:include> element may include its own namespace declaration.

When the document to be included is XML then it is possible to achieve the inclusion using only the href attribute and the namespace declaration, as demonstrated here:

```
<document>
  <xi:include
    href="AnotherDocument.xml"
    xmlns:xi="http//www.w3.org/2001/XInclude"/>
</document>
```

The default value of the parse attribute is "xml". The only other permitted value is "text". When the parse attribute has the value "xml" by default or by specification then the encoding attribute has no effect. When the parse attribute has a value of "text" then the encoding of the text, which must be included as the content of a text node, is carried out as specified in Chapter 4.3.3 of the XML 1.0 Recommendation.

If you grasped the syntax of XSD Schema, presented in Chapter 2, it might help you to understand the XInclude namespace by examining the XSD Schema for it:

```
<xsd:schema xmlns:xsd="http://www.w3.org/2001/XMLSchema"
            xmlns:xi="http://www.w3.org/2001/XInclude"
            targetNamespace="http://www.w3.org/2001/XInclude">
  <xsd:element name="include">
    <xsd:complexType mixed="true">
      <xsd:attribute name="href" type="xsd:anyURI" use="required"/>
      <xsd:attribute name="parse">
        <xsd:simpleType>
          <xsd:restriction base="xsd:string">
            <xsd:enumeration value="xml"/>
            <xsd:enumeration value="text"/>
          </xsd:restriction>
        </xsd:simpleType>
      </xsd:attribute>
      <xsd:attribute name="encoding" type="xsd:string"/>
      <xsd:anyAttribute />
    </xsd:complexType>
  </xsd:element>
</xsd:schema>
```

Note that attributes from other namespaces may be placed on the `<xi:include>` element.

It is important to be clear what XInclude is and what it is not. XInclude has some superficial similarity to the embed-type links of XLink. However, those XLinks simply provide a media-type independent way of embedding a file within an XML document *for display*. The infosets of the two files (assuming the media-type to be embedded is some application of XML) remain distinct. With XInclude the infosets of the including and included document(s) are merged.

XInclude is a specific type of XML Infoset transformation. Having been introduced to the XML Information Set in the previous section you should be able to appreciate what an infoset is. The input for the **inclusion transformation** is termed the **source infoset**. The output is called the **result infoset**. The result infoset is created by merging the source infoset with infosets identified by URI references (the href attribute) in the `<xi:include>` element(s).

Not all well-formed XML documents can be used with the XInclude inclusion process. If, for example, there is an external entity that has more than one top-level element, then its use either as a source infoset or as a result infoset is outside the scope of the XInclude specification, since such an entity does not have a defined information set.

Within the source infoset, inclusion is indicated by the presence of the `<xi:include>` element. The information items referenced by the href attribute of the `<xi:include>` element are called the **included items**. The result infoset is therefore essentially the source infoset but with the `<xi:include>` element in the source infoset replaced by the corresponding included item.

XML is targeted at improving internationalization. The href attribute of the `<xi:include>` element is interpreted as an **Internationalized Uniform Resource Identifier**, an **IURI**. An internationalized URI is one that directly uses Unicode characters. IURI references allow a superset of the characters in URIs to be used, but the % character must always be escaped since the % character is the escaping character in URIs.

If the IURI referenced by the href attribute of the <xi:include> element is a relative IURI then it must be resolved to an absolute IURI. This is done using the base URI for the <xi:include> element, as specified in the **XML Base** specification (see http://www.w3.org/TR/xmlbase). The base URI is an absolute URI relative to which any relative URI is resolved within the scope of the xml:base attribute. The absolute IURI is termed the **include location**.

When the parse attribute of the <xi:include> element has the value of "xml" then the referenced include location is fetched and an infoset is created. This infoset is itself processed to include any further include locations, which may be recursively referenced by any further <xi:include> element to produce an infoset termed the **acquired infoset**.

If any resource at an include location is unavailable, for example due to connection difficulties, then an error results. Similarly, a resource referenced when the parse attribute has the value of "xml" which proves not to be well-formed also results in an error.

When parsing as XML, if the IURI of the include location includes a fragment identifier, then the fragment identifier is interpreted as an XPointer (see the description earlier in this chapter). The presence of an XPointer indicates that a sub-resource is the target for inclusion.

From the acquired infoset a set of included items is derived.

When the include location identifies a document information item (either because the IURI of the include location lacked an XPointer, or because an XPointer was present but pointed at the document entity itself), then the children (as defined in the [children] property) of the acquired infoset's document information item are included, with the exception of the document type declaration information item, if one exists.

An include location which is defined by an XPointer may indicate more than one node for inclusion. In that case the set of included items is the set of information items from the acquired infoset corresponding to the nodes referred to by the XPointer, in the order in which they appear in the acquired infoset. It is possible to have an <xi:include> element as the document element in the source infoset, but if that <xi:include> referenced an XPointer which led to multiple nodes being included an error would occur, since the result infoset would no longer describe a well-formed XML document – since there is no longer a single document element, but multiple top-level nodes.

If an XPointer identifies a location set that includes a **range** (see XPointer section earlier) or set of ranges, then each range corresponds to a set of acquired information items in the acquired infoset.

Thus XInclude allows relationships to be present between XML documents or entities in such a way that their information sets are merged when the documents are processed by an XInclude-aware processor. Applications that seek to determine meta data of such documents will need to be capable of processing XML infosets and carrying out the inclusion process in order to fully document or understand the relationships.

Querying XML

In Chapter 2 we looked at how XML schemas can define what *ought* to be in XML documents. One means to confirm the actual content of an XML document is by validation. Validation, whether based on a DTD or XSD schema, provides information confirming the structure of an XML document, but depending on how constrained (as in an XSD schema) or unconstrained element content may be, it is possible that we derive little information about what the actual content of an element is. We know from the XSD schema and validation that the content is, for example, an `xsd:date` but we do not learn anything about which elements have dates, say, between 1st January 2001 and 15th January 2002. To access data items of that type we need to *query* the XML document.

Querying XML documents provides an alternative view of the content of XML instance documents. In this part of the chapter we will examine how we can establish what is *actually* in XML documents by querying them. Increasingly, XML-based data is being held within relational databases and querying of relational databases is considered in Chapter 12.

W3C Querying Technologies

The area of data models for XML documents is a little fragmented, with the existence of XPath, the DOM, and the XML Information Set. Querying is also a little diverse with XPath, XSLT and, more recently, XML Query emerging as technologies which permit querying of an XML document.

To query an XML document we first need to be able to address selected parts of the document. This is where XPath comes in.

XML Path Language – XPath

XPath 1.0, by means of location paths, can address selected parts of an XML document. The selected parts may be simple or complex. For instance in this simple example we can readily address selected parts of the following document, `Invoice01.xml`:

```xml
<?xml version='1.0'?>
<Invoices>
  <Invoice>
    <Date>2001-07-31</Date>
    <Customer>Acme Engineering</Customer>
    <Amount currency="US">100</Amount>
  </Invoice>
  <Invoice>
    <Date>2002-01-14</Date>
    <Customer>Paradise Engineering</Customer>
    <Amount currency="US">4000</Amount>
  </Invoice>
</Invoices>
```

For example, if we wished to create a list of all customers we could access that using this location path:

```
//Customer
```

This will address every `Customer` node which is a descendant of the root node, in other words every `Customer` node in the document.

Real-life use of XPath identified a number of limitations, in addition to the limitations that were dealt with by means of the extensions to XPath in XPointer and XSLT. For a fuller discussion of the likely future of XPath, including its possible relationship to XSLT 2.0 and XML Query 1.0, see the XPath 2.0 Requirements Working Draft located at http://www.w3.org/TR/xpath20req.

I mentioned earlier the inconsistencies in data modeling among XPath, DOM, and the XML Infoset. That is one issue to be addressed during the development of XPath 2.0 – the ability to express XPath in terms of the XML Infoset. XPath 1.0 boolean expressions are unable to express the notions of "for any" and "for all". That is one deficiency which XPath 2.0 hopes to remedy. The aggregation functions in XPath 1.0 – sum() and count() – must be extended to include min() and max().

I also mentioned earlier node sets as one of the four types of object recognized by XPath 1.0. XPath 1.0 can express the union of two node sets, but XPath 2.0 plans to add difference() and union() functions for node sets.

It is also planned that XPath 2.0 will add further string functions to those already present in XPath 1.0. Possibly the most important proposed addition will be the ability to use regular expressions within XPath expressions. In addition, XPath 2.0 is scheduled to support XSD Schema datatypes.

These planned developments in XPath 2.0 will add significantly to the support for querying functionality available in XPath.

XPath 1.0, in combination for example with XSLT, allows querying of an XML document and display of the results.

Extensible Stylesheet Language for Transformations

At first sight it might seem odd to refer to a transformation language as a potentially useful querying technology. But XSLT had, from the beginning, significant similarities to the Structured Query Language, SQL. XSLT is a declarative language which, using XPath, is able to access selected parts of an XML document and display the results of that query, although we might not always think of the XSLT which produces such visible output as a query. The querying functionality in XSLT 1.0 seems likely to be developed further in XSLT 2.0 as the first Working Draft of the Requirements document for XSLT 2.0 indicates (see http://www.w3.org/TR/xslt20req).

Let's look briefly at a simple example of querying the Invoice01.xml document we mentioned earlier. The following XSLT stylesheet, simpleinvoice.xsl, will display in a very simple HTML page the date, customer name, and amount contained in the first invoice in the above document.

```
<?xml version='1.0'?>
<xsl:stylesheet version="1.0"
   xmlns:xsl="http://www.w3.org/1999/XSL/Transform">
   <xsl:template match="/">
     <HTML>
       <HEAD>
         <TITLE>The first invoice in our XML document</TITLE>
       </HEAD>
       <BODY>
         <BR />
         <xsl:apply-templates/>
         <BR />
         <xsl:value-of select="//Invoice[1]/Date"/>
         <BR />
         <xsl:value-of select="//Invoice[1]/Customer"/>
```

```
            <BR />
            <xsl:value-of select="//Invoice[1]/Amount"/>
            <BR />
        </BODY>
      </HTML>
    </xsl:template>

    <xsl:template match="*">
    </xsl:template>

  </xsl:stylesheet>
```

Much more sophisticated queries can be built using XSLT; however, the broad principle is the same. An XSLT template is applied to selected elements in a source XML document. That selection of elements is defined by a variety of XPath expressions, which may be simple such as `match="/"` in the above example, or may be very lengthy in a deeply nested source document where, for example, conditional display based on the content of an element may be implemented.

XML Query Language – XQuery

The XML Query Language is at an early stage of development, yet its impact on the use of XML is likely to be considerable, as is its likely impact on closely related W3C-specified XML technologies such as XPath and XSLT.

A significant amount of XML-based data may be held in relational databases, but by no means all XML data is ideally suited to the relational data model. In particular, document-centric XML fits only with difficulty into a relational model. In addition a significant, and perhaps increasing, amount of XML is being created dynamically and it is those "virtual documents", as well as static XML files, which the W3C XML Query specification is explicitly targeting.

The W3C XML Query Working Group has produced several Working Drafts which describe the requirements for an XML Query Language, Use Cases which should be achievable, a Data Model, and a Query Algebra, as well as a draft of the XQuery Language itself. Detailed information on each of these topics may be found at the following URLs:

❑   XML Query Requirements – http://www.w3.org/TR/xmlquery-req

❑   XML Query Use Cases – http://www.w3.org/TR/xmlquery-use-cases

❑   XQuery 1.0 and XPath 2.0 Data Model – http://www.w3.org/TR/query-datamodel

❑   XQuery 1.0 Formal Semantics – http://www.w3.org/TR/query-semantics/

❑   XQuery: A Query Language for XML – http://www.w3.org/TR/xquery

❑   XML Syntax for XQuery 1.0 (XQueryX) – http://www.w3.org/TR/xqueryx

The XML Query specification is at an early stage of development, and has significant potential interactions with the prospective specifications for XPath 2.0 and XSLT 2.0, mentioned earlier. As XML Query Language documents may be subject to considerable change, be sure to check the current situation at the URLs given above. A few days before this chapter went to press the XML Query Algebra Working Draft was superceded by the XQuery Formal Semantics Working Draft mentioned above and the XQueryX first Working Draft was released. In addition the XML Query Data Model Working Draft was superceded by the XQuery 1.0 and XPath 2.0 Data Model Working Draft, confirming the intimate relationship which will exist between XPath 2.0 and XQuery 1.0.

The XML Query Requirements Document states that the goal of the XML Query Working Group is to create a **data model** for XML documents, a set of **query operators** on that data model, and a **query language** based on those query operators. The XML Query data model will be based on the XML Information Set. Thus it is likely that some interesting issues may arise in relation to bringing XML Query 1.0, XPath 2.0, and the XML Infoset together. These issues are outlined in the XQuery 1.0 and XPath 2.0 Working Draft mentioned in the list of XQuery Working Drafts above.

XML Query will be able to query single XML documents or collections of XML documents. Such queries will be able to select whole documents or sub-trees of documents based on matching defined conditions. Queries may result in transformation of the results or the creation of entirely new XML documents. In the latter case, there are echoes of the functionality in XSLT where a source tree is transformed into a result tree that is then, typically, serialized into a new XML document. Of course, there are also close parallels with SQL statements.

The XML Query language will be declarative. The draft specification indicates that there will be a form of the XML Query language which can be expressed in XML, while there will be another version of the XML Query language in a non-XML syntax. The version not in XML syntax is termed **XQuery**. The XML-based version of XML Query will be called **XQueryX**.

XML Query queries are declarative. In that respect they are similar to SQL statements and XSLT stylesheets. Thus an XML Query processor will decide the "how" of the individual steps of the query process, whereas the user will decide the relationship between the content of the source and result documents.

Queries must be *closed*. What this means is that the output from one XML Query query can be the input to another XML Query query. In this, XML Query again resembles XSLT, where the result tree of one XSLT transformation can be used in a subsequent transformation. Closure in XML Query can be achieved because the data models of the source and result documents are the same. Interestingly that same feature is the foundation of closure in SQL and XSLT, where the data models are tables and trees respectively.

Some Use Cases

The XML Query Working Drafts outline some use cases which the finished XML Query versions or dialects should be able to carry out. In this section I will outline those use cases, to give you an idea of the scope of uses which XML Query is expected to be able to carry out. For the purposes of this section I have focused on the use cases in the Requirements document, since it is more appropriate for us here to grasp the range of uses of XML Query rather than master the full details of the use cases laid out in the Use Cases Working Draft.

The XML Query Requirements document lists these use cases:

- Human-readable documents
- Data-orientated documents
- Mixed-model documents
- Administrative data
- Filtering streams
- Document Object Model (DOM)
- Native XML repositories and web servers
- Catalog search
- Multiple syntactic environments

The human-readable documents category is intended to perform queries on substantial XML documents, including technical manuals, searching for particular information structures to generate tables of contents or new documents. It might, for example, include queries of the maintenance manuals for an airplane, generating relevant information for a maintenance technician, providing him with meta data which summarizes all the information held in the collection of XML documents relating to a particular, probably specialized topic.

In the data-orientated documents category XML Query will underpin queries of database data, object data, etc., to extract data which meet the query criteria, to generate new XML documents, or to merge data from multiple sources.

In the mixed-model category queries will be both document-orientated and data-orientated on a variety of data sources, such as patient health records, employment records, or business analysis documents. Documents such as patient health records and employment records raise particular issues of confidentiality and security which we have not touched on in this chapter but which are important aspects of the meta data of XML documents or collections of them.

In the administrative data category it is envisaged that queries will be made on user profiles, administrative logs, and configuration files, all of which are increasingly held as XML.

In the filtering streams category it is envisaged that streams of XML data will be queried. This might be used to create e-mail logs, or to process weather data, stock market information, newswire feeds or EDI. Such streams of XML may be filtered, data may be extracted from them or new XML streams may be created.

In the Document Object Model category it is envisaged that queries of the Document Object Model will be carried out, returning sets of nodes that meet specified criteria. As I indicated earlier in the chapter the data model of the DOM and the XML Infoset, on which XML Query is based, do not correspond one-to-one.

The native XML repositories category covers the querying of web servers which use XML natively and repositories of XML data.

The catalog search category covers a broad range of queries. The types of catalog that might be searched could include document servers or XML schemas. It is envisaged that catalogs could be combined to permit queries that could take place in a distributed manner across multiple servers.

XML Query queries are expected to be usable in many environments. For example, a query might be embedded in an XML web page, a JSP page, or an ASP page, or in one of a potentially large number of general purpose programming languages.

General Requirements

The following are several of the requirements for XML Query:

- ❑ May have multiple syntaxes, but at least one should be convenient for humans to read.
- ❑ Must have one syntax expressed in XML.
- ❑ Must be declarative.
- ❑ Must be defined independent of any protocols with which it might be used.
- ❑ Must have defined error conditions.
- ❑ Must permit updates in future versions.
- ❑ Must be defined for finite instances of the data model.

The Data Model

The requirements for the XML Query Data Model include:

❑   Reliance on the XML Information Set.

❑   Must represent XSD Schema datatypes.

❑   Must represent collections of XML documents and collections of simple and complex values.

❑   Must include support for references.

❑   Queries must be possible whether or not a schema (XSD Schema or DTD) is available.

❑   Must be namespace aware.

Query Functionality

The following functionality is expected to be available in a final version of XML Query, whenever that may be produced. XML Query must:

❑   Support operations on all datatypes defined by the data model.

❑   Be able to express conditions on text, including expressing conditions on text which crosses element boundaries.

❑   Include support for universal and existential quantifiers ("for all" and "for any").

❑   Support operations on a hierarchy and sequence of document structures.

❑   Be able to combine information from different parts of one document or from multiple related documents.

❑   Be able to compute summary information from a group of related document elements.

❑   Be able to sort query results.

❑   Support expressions in which operations can be composed, including the use of queries as operands.

❑   Support null values.

❑   Be able to preserve the hierarchy and sequence of input document structures in result documents.

❑   Be able to transform XML structures and create new XML structures.

❑   Be able to traverse intra-document and inter-document references.

❑   Be able to preserve the identity of information items in the XML Query Data Model.

❑   Be able to perform simple operations on names such as element names and attribute names.

❑   Be able to provide access to a schema, if one exists.

❑   Be able to operate on information items produced by the post-schema-validation information set.

❑   Support the use of externally defined functions on all datatypes defined by the XML Query Data Model.

❑   Provide access to information about the environment within which the query is executing, for example date, location, time zone.

❑   Provide closure with respect to the XML Query Data Model.

XQuery Implementations

The syntax of XQuery is not defined in XML, thus an XML-syntax dialect of XML Query now called XQueryX has just been announced and is in its first Working Draft.

An online test bed for experimenting with a version of XML Query has been provided by Microsoft. The syntax provided has been changing with respect to some points, therefore if it is important for your particular use that a query be compliant with the W3C syntax be sure to check carefully that the Microsoft version equates to the W3C version. In the past Microsoft has had a habit of defining its own dialects, such as with Microsoft XSL which it recently abandoned in favor of W3C XLST, and the XDR schema which forms the basis of the BizTalk initiative. The XML Query test bed may be accessed at http://131.107.228.20/. However the version of XML Query available for exploration online is currently based on the February 2001 Working Draft, not the current June 2001 Working Draft. Please check for updates to the prototype application, available at the URL given.

Summary

In this chapter I have looked briefly at several XML-based technologies with the potential to impact on XML meta data. Of the technologies described, only XPath and XSLT have reached a full Recommendation at the W3C, whereas XLink, XInclude, XML Infoset, XPointer, and XML Query are, at the time of writing, still at various draft stages of development. Thus significant changes in detail of how each of these technologies operates may occur. Be sure to check the URLs given to ensure that you are aware of the up to date version.

To fully explore each of these technologies in depth would need at least a chapter for each, and one or two of them merit a book on their own, thus it has been possible only to give you some summary insight into what each of these technologies are and what potential they have.

Understanding relationships between XML documents is an important aspect of XML meta data. The W3C has developed several technologies which impact on this area. XLink allows the creation of simple-type links (similar to HTML hyperlinks) as well as extended-type links and linkbases. The XML Pointer specification, which is designed for use with XLink and is in part based on the XML Path Language, allows addressing of fragments of XML documents and, for example, display of those fragments.

The XML Inclusions specification defines an intimate relationship between XML documents and entities such that their information sets are merged during the inclusion process. To understand XML Inclusions it is necessary to grasp the essentials about the XML Information Set, the infoset, and these were introduced.

Querying XML data may, at a basic level, be carried out using the XML Path Language, XPath, and the Extensible Stylesheet Language for Transformations, XSLT. In addition, the W3C is developing an XML Query Language with ambitious potential capabilities, which were summarized.

Meta DataProfessionalXMLMeta DataProfessionalXMLMeta DataProf

RDF Model and Syntax

The **Resource Description Framework** (**RDF**) is probably the least understood standard to come from the W3C, yet it is perhaps the most powerful and most important if the Web is to achieve its full potential. In many ways RDF helps to deliver what many people seem to think XML will deliver. When XML took off a couple of years ago, there was a great deal of discussion about standardizing on search engine terms, creating documents that could be interchanged, and so on. Yet much of the potential is unrealized, because although we can swap our documents with each other through XML, we still haven't got a clue what they *mean*.

The RDF specification is made up of two W3C documents:

❑ The first, the **RDF Model and Syntax** Specification is currently a W3C Recommendation document, which essentially means that the W3C would like to see people adopting the approach outlined in the document. If you decide to read around the subject you will often see this document referred to as **RDFMS**. It is available at http://www.w3.org/TR/REC-rdf-syntax/.

❑ The second document is the **RDF Schema** Specification 1.0, which sits at Candidate Recommendation stage, meaning it should be treated as "work in progress" – and the W3C would like to see people producing test implementations in order to provide feedback on the proposal. The specification name is often abbreviated to **RDFS**. The Schema Specification document is available at http://www.w3.org/TR/rdf-schema/.

This chapter concentrates on the RDF Model and Syntax whilst the next chapter will look at specifying RDF schemas. In this chapter we will also:

❑ Look at what we mean by data and meta data.

❑ Introduce the idea of the Semantic Web – the notion that the full potential of the Web can be realized only if we can communicate meta data between systems.

❑ Look at how RDF plays a role in realizing this potential.

Data, and Data About Data

Much of the information that we need to be exchanging with each other is not data, but *data about* that data, or meta data. For example, it's not so much the data that makes up a web page that we need to swap, but information concerning what the page is about, who wrote it, what date it was last updated, and so on. The ability to access the page itself is pretty straightforward, but finding it in the first place can be difficult.

XML promised to deliver us from the mass of unstructured information that makes up the Internet, by bringing structure to our data. Rather than pages of information being thrown out onto the Web to fend for themselves, as formatted pages of text, we would use XML to structure our data, enabling it to be extracted and used for many different purposes. XML brought the possibility of separating the appearance of a document – the presentation of information – from the information itself, the underlying data.

So, rather than a web page that shows information within display elements like "bold" or "red", we might have an XML format specifically constructed for musical compositions, like this:

```
<music genre="classical">
    <title>Eine Kleine Nacht Muzik</title>
    <composer>Mozart</composer>
    <key>E Flat</key>
    <tempo>2/4</tempo>
</music>
```

where we indicate the title of a piece, the type of music that it is, its key, its tempo, and, of course, who wrote it. This format gives us many advantages over the old, unstructured form of the Web. For example, we could pick out the keys and tempos of many different pieces of music – perhaps finding all other pieces that are in E flat. This is possible because we are no longer dealing with a load of formatted text, but with a document that has structure.

Let's add another type of XML structure that can be used to convey some of the same information. We might have another XML format that is more general, and use it to describe "documents" of any type, whether they are news stories, poems, films, or music:

```
<document type="classical music">
    <name>Eine Kleine Nacht Muzik</name>
    <author>Mozart</author>
</document>
```

In this case we have an `author` field to indicate who created the document, since the document can be of any type, and the word *composer* is obviously more specific to music.

Once again, this has got to be easier for a machine to process than the same information displayed on a web page. The good old-fashioned web page might have the same information wrapped up in HTML tags, but it is difficult to interpret – of course you know all that, which is why you are using XML. Unfortunately, as I said before, XML doesn't completely solve the problems we have with our information, as I'll try to explain.

What if I wanted to find all pieces of music composed by Mozart? I would first have to search all of the documents of the first type for any document where the `<composer>` element had a value of 'Mozart', and then I would have to search all of the documents of the second type for documents with the `<author>` element set to 'Mozart'. Then if someone devised a further format to hold information about music and its composers, or documents more generally, we would have to search that too. Surely it would be a lot easier if we could just search for any XML documents where "the person who created the document" is called Mozart?

The Semantic Web

In order for this to happen we all have to agree to use the same word to describe "the person who created this document" in any of the documents that we create.

We could also solve this problem by indicating that when one document says "composer" it means the same as when another document says "written by", and another says 'created by', but that is more difficult to implement, although not impossible. It would be a major undertaking to make sure that any set of words – such as "written by" – is mapped to all other possible words with similar meanings, in all languages.

It is this ability to know what each of us is talking about when we use various terms to mean the same thing that is missing from today's Internet, but if we are able to build this layer into the Web it will take information to a fundamentally different level. It is a major component of what the World Wide Web Consortium (W3C), and in particular Tim Berners-Lee, have called the **Semantic Web**. Other aspects of the Semantic Web – such as knowing whether you can rely on the information that you have received – can be implemented with the techniques discussed in the next chapter, and more information is available at the W3C site – see http://www.w3.org/2001/sw/. The W3C is taking the idea of the Semantic Web very seriously, describing it as "phase two of the Internet".

One important step along the road to the Semantic Web was the **Dublin Core initiative**.

Dublin Core

Ironically for the champions of XML, mapping of terms has more widespread usage within good old HTML, largely because of the use of Dublin Core.

At a conference on meta data in 1995, held in Dublin, Ohio, a workshop discussed the issue of semantics and agreed a core set of themes that it was felt were common to most types of document. This set of properties became known as the Dublin Core (DC) initiative, and although it is an important influence on RDF, so far it has its widest application in `<META>` tags within HTML documents.

More information on DC can be found at http://dublincore.org/documents/dces/, but here we will illustrate our points by looking at a small number of the properties.

An HTML document that uses DC might look like this:

```
<HTML>
  <HEAD>
    <TITLE>I will stand says Portillo</TITLE>
    <META NAME="DC.Title" CONTENT="I will stand says Portillo">
    <META NAME="DC.Creator" CONTENT="Craig Hoy">
```

```
        <META NAME="DC.Subject" CONTENT="Tory leadership contest">
    </HEAD>
    <BODY>
        Michael Portillo has announced that he will stand for the leadership
        of the Conservative Party.
    <BR />
        Launching his bid for the Tory crown, Portillo said the Conservative
        Party had to seriously review its approach.
    <BR />
        "Unless the Conservative Party makes huge changes in its style and in
        the issues on which it focuses the party could slip still further in
        public respect," he said.
    </BODY>
</HTML>
```

The meaning of the tags is probably pretty clear, but I'll explain them anyway:

❑   DC.Title contains the title of the document.

❑   DC.Creator is used to indicate the name of the person who was responsible for producing the document.

❑   DC.Subject holds information about what the document is about.

Many web site builders have adopted the DC property set, and so increasingly on search engines you can find all documents "written by" a particular author – although you won't necessarily know that this is going on behind the scenes. In the past, site builders might have described the document's creator using whatever tag name they wanted to, such as this:

```
<META NAME="Author" CONTENT="Craig Hoy">
```

this:

```
<META NAME="Writer" CONTENT="Craig Hoy">
```

or this:

```
<META NAME="Journalist" CONTENT="Craig Hoy">
```

By settling on a common term – in this case Creator – we have made an important step towards our goal of common semantics. And by prefixing this term – using DC. – we take another step, since this ensures that we don't get this definition of Creator mixed up with someone else's.

To illustrate this second point, imagine some HTML page generation software that places a tag in the documents it produces, to indicate what software was used to produce the document:

```
<HTML>
    <HEAD>
        <TITLE>I will stand says Portillo</TITLE>
        <META NAME="DC.Title" CONTENT="I will stand says Portillo">
        <META NAME="DC.Creator" CONTENT="Craig Hoy">
        <META NAME="DC.Subject" CONTENT="Tory leadership contest">
```

```
        <META NAME="Creator" CONTENT="x-port publishing system">
    </HEAD>
    <BODY>
        ...
    </BODY>
</HTML>
```

The prefix removes the ambiguity.

Dublin Core and XML

So how come old-fashioned HTML is a step closer to the Semantic Web than shiny new XML? Well, that's simple to answer – it's not to do with its abilities, but because it is more widely adopted. Let's look at the same problem again, but this time with XML, and we'll see why Dublin Core has not been taken up so readily within XML.

When looked at from the XML standpoint, the problem that we posed earlier becomes how to tell that the <composer> element in this XML:

```
<music genre="classical">
    <title>Eine Kleine Nacht Muzik</title>
    <composer>Mozart</composer>
    <key>E Flat</key>
    <tempo>2/4</tempo>
</music>
```

means the same as the <author> element in this:

```
<document type="classical music">
    <name>Eine Kleine Nacht Muzik</name>
    <author>Mozart</author>
</document>
```

Dublin Core was not designed exclusively for HTML – the 15 core properties that were defined could be used in any context – and the intention is that we should be able to solve our problem of equating data by doing this:

```
<music genre="classical">
    <title>Eine Kleine Nacht Muzik</title>
    <Creator>Mozart</Creator>
    <key>E Flat</key>
    <tempo>2/4</tempo>
</music>
```

and this:

```
<document type="classical music">
    <name>Eine Kleine Nacht Muzik</name>
    <Creator>Mozart</Creator>
</document>
```

Of course we still can't be one hundred per cent certain when we see these two documents that we really are talking about the same concept. As with our HTML example earlier, we don't know that the second document wasn't created using a piece of software called "Mozart", for example. But just as we used the DC prefix earlier – DC.Creator – to remove any ambiguity in the HTML document, XML has an even more precise mechanism through which to do this, and that is **namespaces**. If we expressed our first document like this:

```
<music genre="classical">
    <title>Eine Kleine Nacht Muzik</title>
    <dc:Creator
        xmlns:dc="http://purl.org/dc/elements/1.1/">Mozart</dc:Creator>
    <key>E Flat</key>
    <tempo>2/4</tempo>
</music>
```

and the second like this:

```
<document type="classical music">
    <name>Eine Kleine Nacht Muzik</name>
    <dc:Creator
        xmlns:dc="http://purl.org/dc/elements/1.1/">Mozart</dc:Creator>
</document>
```

then it is clear that these two elements are expressing exactly the same concept, and that is "the person who created this document".

Given that this namespace mechanism within XML looks far more flexible than the facilities available through the use of META in HTML documents, why did I say earlier that XML fairs little better than HTML when specifying meta data? The answer is simply that even using XML, it is not clear that our two documents are both conveying the same information – that Mozart was the "creator" of *Eine Kleine Nacht Muzik*. So, although XML has done an incredible job of giving us structure and ease of manipulation, the move to XML has not given us a way to deal with *meaning*. To put that another way, whilst XML presents us with incredible power at the level of handling *data,* it takes us no further forward than HTML, at the level of *meta data*.

Unique Identifiers

As you're aware from your knowledge of namespaces and XML, the following document is using the same element to describe a song's composer as we used in the previous examples:

```
<music genre="hip hop">
    <title>911</title>
    <x:Creator xmlns:x="http://purl.org/dc/elements/1.1/">
        Wyclef Jean</x:Creator>
    <key>E Flat</key>
    <tempo>2/4</tempo>
</music>
```

Regardless of the prefix used as a placeholder for the namespace, we know that in fact the combination of the namespace and the element name is:

```
http://purl.org/dc/elements/1.1/Creator
```

This is an extremely powerful concept, and provides the foundation for turning the Internet into a giant relational database. I'm going to take a little detour into traditional database programming now, because I want you to see that this idea of using a **unique identifier** to name a property does not have to be confined to XML, but has wide application elsewhere, and is a fundamentally important concept for meta data and the Semantic Web.

A CD Database

Imagine that on your computer you have a little personal database of your favorite CDs. Perhaps you started doing a "teach yourself" course in database design, or perhaps you just need to get out more. Anyway, you have a table in this database, like this:

Primary Key	Album Name	Artist
1	The Ecleftic: Two Sides II a Book?	Wyclef Jean
2	Eine Kleine Nacht Muzik	Mozart
3	Soultrane	John Coltrane
4	The Real	Eminem

Now, let's say that I too need to get out more, and I also have built up a database of CDs. My database looks like this:

Key	Title	Performer
1	Eine Kleine Nacht Muzik	Wolfgang Amadeus Mozart
2	The Ecleftic	Wyclef Jean
3	Kind of Blue	Miles Davis

As you will have noted immediately, the first problem we have if we wanted to exchange any of our information is that I have used different names for the fields in my table from those that you have used. This is the same problem we were looking at earlier with XML but now posed slightly more abstractly – now we can see that not having standard names for fields is not just a problem for XML, but is a problem for any system that wants to exchange data.

This is why the unique identifier idea that we introduced a moment ago becomes so powerful. Let's say that when each of us had designed our databases we had opted for standard names for the columns in our tables. Ignore the issue of whether your database software allows colons and slashes in column names, and imagine that your database table now looks like this:

Primary Key	http://purl.org/dc/elements/1.1/Title	http://purl.org/dc/elements/1.1/ Creator
1	The Ecleftic: Two Sides II a Book?	Wyclef Jean
2	Eine Kleine Nacht Muzik	Mozart
3		John Coltrane
4	The Real	Eminem

while mine looks like this:

Key	http://purl.org/dc/elements/1.1/Title	http://purl.org/dc/elements/1.1/Creator
1	Eine Kleine Nacht Muzik	Wolfgang Amadeus Mozart
2	The Ecleftic	Wyclef Jean
3	A Kind of Blue	Miles Davis

We now have the possibility of exchanging our data, because we know what each of us is talking about. Note that we could have used anything to name the columns – the goal that we are aiming for is commonality, so as long as we both used the same column names we could tell that we mean the same thing by "title". The use of URIs to name the columns is simply that it gives us a way of ensuring the column names that we choose are not going to be used by someone else and so make it unclear as to the meaning of our data.

However, you will probably have noticed two more problems as you looked at the data in the tables. The first is that although we share a couple of CDs in common, we have used a different key to identify them. I have identified Wyclef Jean's album as "2", whilst you have it as "1". This wouldn't be such a big problem if I had typed in the full title, since we could use the title to tell that we are referring to the same thing, but I haven't – I have only called the album *The Ecleftic,* whilst you have used the full title, *The Ecleftic: Two Sides II a Book.* So it obviously would be useful if we had a unique identifier for this album, so we knew that we were both talking about the same thing.

The second problem is that you have not put Mozart's full name into the database, whilst I have. This means that it is difficult to tell if we are both talking about the same person when we swap our data.

Taxonomies

Many of these problems can be solved by defining a **taxonomy** (or controlled vocabulary), which is a set of words – often on a similar subject or from a particular topic area – which we choose from when specifying some property or other. The unique identifier notion that we have been discussing is key to developing taxonomies.

For example, if we were looking to categorize all the CDs in the database, so that we could tell which were jazz and which were hip hop, we might devise a controlled subject list such that a CD's genre could be "jazz", "classical", "soul", "pop", "hip hop", and so on. This would prevent a value of "classic" being used by mistake, so making the job of finding all CDs of a particular genre easier.

A taxonomy could also be devised for the works that we want to refer to. We might have a taxonomy for plays, and one of the values could be "Porgy and Bess", and we might have a taxonomy for albums that also has a value of "Porgy and Bess". If we know which taxonomy a value has come from we would be able to tell if some document is referring to the album or the play. Then if someone was searching for one or the other we would know whether the document in question was relevant to their search or not.

A similar approach could be adopted with any other type of information. If we devised a taxonomy for people, and were able to give any person a unique identifier, then a search for all albums composed by a particular person would be easy to find. But even more than that, any book or article, news story or album review, that mentions one person could be differentiated from a document that referred to another person with the same name.

Many **subject code taxonomies** exist. After all, the Internet did not invent the need to categorize information so that it could be found easily. Systems such as the **Dewey Decimal Classification** (DDC) have been around for years. Although initially used in libraries to group information, it is now being used on the Web to aid classification of sites.

Even with the taxonomies that have been traditionally used, however, we have a similar problem to the semantic discussion that we looked at earlier – two taxonomies may contain the same value. However, if we use identifiers that are unique beyond any particular taxonomy, then this:

```
http://taxonomies.org/Plays/PorgyAndBess
```

is a completely different value to this:

```
http://taxonomies.org/Albums/PorgyAndBess
```

In other words, although two taxonomies may contain the same value – say "PorgyAndBess" – by qualifying that value with a prefix we are able to guarantee the uniqueness of the value for use in many situations.

Let's return to our relational databases. Imagine that there is some authority that keeps track of all CDs that are released. Just as with ISBN book numbers, where each book gets a unique code when it is printed, so too a CD gets an identifier. Let's say that this code is given out by the – fictitious – organization MuzicBiz.org, and they maintain a central database:

Key	http://purl.org/dc/elements/1.1/Title	http://purl.org/dc/elements/1.1/Creator
http://MuzicBiz.org/Albums/1011234	Eine Kleine Nacht Muzik	Amadeus Mozart
http://MuzicBiz.org/Albums/7655432	The Ecleftic	Wyclef Jean
http://MuzicBiz.org/Albums/8997654	A Kind of Blue	Miles Davis

Now, I have a mail order system for selling CDs, and to facilitate this I have a table in my database like this:

Key	http://ebiz.org/Stock	http://ebiz.org/Cost
http://MuzicBiz.org/Albums/1011234	5	£8.00
http://MuzicBiz.org/Albums/7655432	4	£8.50
http://MuzicBiz.org/Albums/8997654	10	£6.00

I have named the columns in my database from the field names specified by a fictitious e-commerce organization called ebiz.org, and I have identified the albums using the identifiers supplied by MuzicBiz.org. Both of these are uses of taxonomies, and as you can imagine, this offers us amazing power. We'll go through some of the things this mechanism allows us to do.

Imagine that your database contains reviews of albums. Perhaps you run a portal web site for gardeners, and you want to sell music to them, using my e-commerce system, but you want the reviews of the music to come from your own writers. Your database might look like this:

Key	http://MuzicBiz.org/Review
http://MuzicBiz.org/Albums/1011234	A relaxing album to prune to.
http://MuzicBiz.org/Albums/7655432	Lively! Perfect when mowing the lawn.
http://MuzicBiz.org/Albums/8997654	Very moody. Great when planning your next planting.

Now, because we are both using the same key to identify the albums, we know exactly which album we are talking about, so your web site can place orders correctly, as well as match your reviews to my price list. Also, since we are using the same key for the album as everyone else you could also retrieve reviews from other web sites, if your readers were interested.

We're not finished yet though. Since we are using standard field names for our tables, if I didn't have a particular CD in stock, you could go to another e-commerce site and find the same album from them. Or you could go and check the price and compare it to mine, so as to get the best deal for your portal users.

Isn't this what the Web should be? Shouldn't we be sharing data among different systems, allowing comparisons to be made, knowing when we are talking about the same item, and knowing when we are not? Shouldn't the Web be one giant relational database, each of us doing joins on other people's tables?

Unfortunately – as I have said already – although many people believe that XML solves all of these problems, it doesn't. However, XML will play a very important part in the solution, but before we get to that, let's dig a little deeper into the very notion of meta data.

What is Meta Data?

Of course we all know what meta data is – it's data about data. You most probably wouldn't be reading this book if you didn't know that. But what does this "data about data" look like? What are the properties of meta data? This probably sounds a bit esoteric, but we need to answer this question if we are going to be able to manipulate meta data. In this section we will try to establish what the common features of all meta data are.

It didn't sound that odd to try and establish what was common to any document. We were happy to say that any document – regardless of whether it was a poem, play, news story, or film script – had common meta information, such as author, length, subject, title, and so on. Now, just as we established what was common to each document, we want to know what all sets of meta data have in common. If we look at different ways of representing meta data, this will help.

So far in this chapter, we have seen three different ways of representing meta data even though they may not all have jumped out at you. The first we saw was using tags in an HTML document. If the document was a news story then we might store the author's names and some categorization information in <META> tags, like so:

```
<HTML>
    <HEAD>
        <TITLE>I will stand says Portillo</TITLE>
        <META NAME="DC.Title" CONTENT="I will stand says Portillo">
        <META NAME="DC.Creator" CONTENT="Craig Hoy">
        <META NAME="DC.Subject" CONTENT="Tory leadership contest">
    </HEAD>
    <BODY>
        Document text
    </BODY>
</HTML>
```

Next we saw that we could use XML to hold similar information, although we recognized that whilst XML is widely used, having standard element names is less common at the moment. Still, one possible document might be:

```
<document type="News Item" xmlns:dc="http://purl.org/dc/elements/1.1/">
    <dc:Title>I will stand says Portillo</dc:Title>
    <dc:Creator>Craig Hoy</dc:Creator>
    <dc:Subject>Tory leadership contest</dc:Subject>
</document>
```

The final way we saw to express meta data was simply through a table in a relational database, using standard column names. The previous document might be expressed like this:

http://purl.org/dc/elements/1.1/Title	http://purl.org/dc/elements/1.1/Creator	http://purl.org/dc/elements/1.1/Subject
I will stand says Portillo	Craig Hoy	Tory leadership contest

What do all of these ways of expressing meta data have in common? Well the first thing is that they use simple **name/value pairs**. It doesn't matter which of these formats you look at, you end up with the following three name/value pairs:

Name	Value
http://purl.org/dc/elements/1.1/Title	I will stand says Portillo
http://purl.org/dc/elements/1.1/Creator	Craig Hoy
http://purl.org/dc/elements/1.1/Subject	Tory leadership contest

However, to fully express this information we need to say what this information is about. We therefore need to add the URI of the document being referred to. With the HTML document this is implicit – the document itself is the document being referred to. The header we have been looking at is from the article http://www.ePolitix.com/Articles/0000005a4787.htm on the ePolitix web site:

```
<HTML>
    <HEAD>
        <TITLE>I will stand says Portillo</TITLE>
        <META NAME="DC.Title" CONTENT="I will stand says Portillo">
```

107

```
                <META NAME="DC.Creator" CONTENT="Craig Hoy">
                <META NAME="DC.Subject" CONTENT="Tory leadership contest">
        </HEAD>
        <BODY>
                Document text
        </BODY>
    </HTML>
```

With the XML example it may also be implicit – the XML document may itself be the document that the meta data is referring to. But here XML has the advantage over HTML, since it could also contain information that refers to a separate document, perhaps like this:

```
<document
   type="News Item"
   url="http://www.ePolitix.com/Articles/0000005a4787.htm"
   xmlns:dc="http://purl.org/dc/elements/1.1/">
       <dc:Title>I will stand says Portillo</dc:Title>
       <dc:Creator>Craig Hoy</dc:Creator>
       <dc:Subject>Tory leadership contest</dc:Subject>
</document>
```

Whichever way we do it, we now have *three* pieces of information for each item of meta data, and that is the name/value pair that contains the actual meta data, plus an indicator of what document this meta data is referring to:

Document	Name	Value
http://www.ePolitix...5a4787.htm	http://purl.org/dc/elements/1.1/ Title	I will stand says Portillo
http://www.ePolitix...5a4787.htm	http://purl.org/dc/elements/1.1/ Creator	Craig Hoy
http://www.ePolitix...5a4787.htm	http://purl.org/dc/elements/1.1/ Subject	Tory leadership contest
http://www.ePolitix...5a4787.htm	Type	News Item

In the meta data literature the lines in this table are called **triples**, and as you have just seen there are a number of ways of expressing triples – as HTML <META> tags, as XML, as relational database tables, and so on. We seem to have reached the core of "what does meta data look like".

A Brief Note on Meta-Meta Data

Of course, since meta data is merely data, we could also establish some **meta-meta data**. Take the example of music on a CD. Let's say you own the single version of Wyclef Jean's song *911*. Your data and meta data could be represented like this:

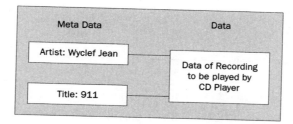

We have the actual data for the track, which in this case is a digital recording, ready for playing on your CD player. We then have data *about* the track – the name of the recording artist and its length – which is of course, the meta data.

But what happens when we put this track on Wyclef Jean's album *The Ecleftic: 2 Sides II a Book*? The track is sixth on the album, so we could represent this as follows (with another track shown):

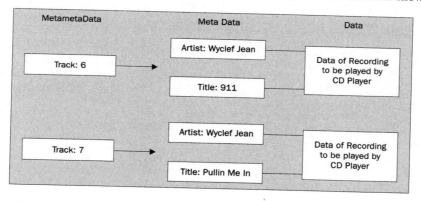

So each song on the album is data, the length of the song and its title is meta data, and the fact that *in this context* one track is "track six" and another is "track seven", could be called meta-meta data. However, before you get too worried about this, we don't generally use the "meta-meta" term. As we said before, data is data is data; what makes a particular piece of data *meta data* is its **context**. So we could say that from the standpoint of an *album*, the data about a track comprises the digitally recorded music (what we were calling the data) *and* the title of the track and its length (what we were calling the meta data). And now the information about which is the sixth track, and which is the seventh, becomes the meta data:

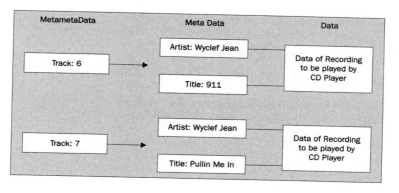

This is even easier to see if we show the information in the form of the triples that we had earlier. Let's assume that MuzicBiz.org has created unique identifiers for every track ever recorded, as well as every album. We might have the following triples for the meta data about the track:

Document	Name	Value
http://MuzicBiz.org/Tracks/1667653	http://purl.org/dc/elements/1.1/Title	911
http://MuzicBiz.org/Tracks/1667653	http://purl.org/dc/elements/1.1/Creator	Wyclef Jean

To place the track into the album we might then have the following triples:

Document	Name	Value
http://MuzicBiz.org/Albums/ 7655432	http://MuzicBiz.org/Prop/ Track	http://MuzicBiz.org/Tracks/ 1667653

As you can see, our meta-meta data has simply become meta data. It's important to not get hung up on the idea of meta-meta data, because we will often want to extend the chain further. For example, suppose the album then appears in a boxed-set, as seems to be the way nowadays. This would give us meta-meta-meta data, and would get us pretty bogged down! With our triple model, and just sticking to meta data, we only need to add this entry:

Document	Name	Value
http://MuzicBiz.org/BoxSets /665	http://MuzicBiz.org/Prop/ Album	http://MuzicBiz.org/Albums/ 7655432

If we add all the triples together, we have the following set of meta data:

The document http://MuzicBiz.org/Tracks/1667653

Has a title of "911", and

Was created by "Wyclef Jean"

The document http://MuzicBiz.org/Albums/7655432

Has a track http://MuzicBiz.org/Tracks/1667653

The document http://MuzicBiz.org/BoxSets/665

Has an album http://MuzicBiz.org/Albums/7655432

As you can see we don't need to complicate things too much with meta-meta-meta data – we can express everything we need to with the concepts of data and meta data.

Transporting Triples

We've now established that meta data can be expressed as a set of triples, and that the key to sharing meta data through the Web is to use URIs to provide unique identifiers. If we are happy that triples give us what we need for expressing meta data then all we need now is some way of exchanging triples. For example, if we return to your gardening portal, I need some way of passing to you the information that I have in my database about stock levels and prices.

Recall that my database contains:

Key	http://ebiz.org/Stock	http://ebiz.org/Cost
http://MuzicBiz.org/Albums/1011234	5	£8.00
http://MuzicBiz.org/Albums/7655432	4	£8.50
http://MuzicBiz.org/Albums/8997654	10	£6.00

For all the reasons we stated earlier, we could store this as a set of triples, which becomes:

Document	Name	Value
http://MuzicBiz.org/Albums/1011234	http://ebiz.org/Stock	5
http://MuzicBiz.org/Albums/1011234	http://ebiz.org/Cost	£8.00
http://MuzicBiz.org/Albums/7655432	http://ebiz.org/Stock	4
http://MuzicBiz.org/Albums/7655432	http://ebiz.org/Cost	£8.50
http://MuzicBiz.org/Albums/8997654	http://ebiz.org/Stock	10
http://MuzicBiz.org/Albums/8997654	http://ebiz.org/Cost	£6.00

We now need some way of conveying this information across the Internet so that it is easy to retrieve and interpret. Of course it will use XML – that goes without saying! The question is rather: what should the XML look like? XML as it stands is quite good at transporting name/value pairs. They can move as elements:

```
<Creator>Craig Hoy</Creator>
```

or attributes:

```
<document Creator="Craig Hoy" />
```

And, as we saw before, by using namespaces we can make the property name unique:

```
<dc:Creator xmlns:dc="http://purl.org/dc/elements/1.1/">
    Craig Hoy</dc:Creator>
```

But while XML is very good at conveying the name/value pair part of our triples, it is not immediately obvious how to specify the third part – the reference to the object that the name/value pair is a property for. One possibility is that the XML document itself is the target for our meta data, but this is very limiting. We couldn't use that technique to transmit the reviews of the albums written by gardeners, for example, since the URLs for the documents are not under our control. Remember that we have the following triples:

Document	Name	Value
http://MuzicBiz.org/Albums/1011234	http://MuzicBiz.org/Review	A relaxing album to prune to.
http://MuzicBiz.org/Albums/~7655 432	http://MuzicBiz.org/Review	Lively! Perfect when mowing the lawn.
http://MuzicBiz.org/Albums/8997654	http://MuzicBiz.org/Review	Very moody. Great when planning your next planting.

We cannot simply send out a document like this:

```
<document xmlns:m="http://MuzicBiz.org/">
    <m:Review>A relaxing album to prune to.</m:Review>
</document>
```

and allow the name/value pair to bind to the document's URL, since the URL will be nothing like http://MuzicBiz.org/Albums/1011234. We need a format more like this:

```
<document
  type="News Item"
  url="http://www.ePolitix.com/Articles/0000005a4787.htm"
  xmlns:dc="http://purl.org/dc/elements/1.1/">
    <dc:Title>I will stand says Portillo</dc:Title>
    <dc:Creator>Craig Hoy</dc:Creator>
    <dc:Subject>Tory leadership contest</dc:Subject>
</document>
```

In this situation we are allowing XML to specify the name/value pair parts of the triples in any way that it wants to – as elements or as attributes. The only thing we need nailed down is some way of expressing the target to which the meta data being conveyed should attach itself.

Summary

We have discovered that storing and manipulating triples is a convenient way to express meta data. We have also seen that XML is pretty good at expressing the name/value pair part of triples, but will need some help when expressing the document to which the meta data is referring. We're now ready to look at the Resource Description Framework – a format for expressing meta data.

RDF: Model and Syntax

We've now covered enough of the general material on meta data to begin to address a standard way of expressing meta data, using RDF. We will be looking in detail at the RDF Model and Syntax specification, which breaks RDF into two parts; the first is a *model* for meta data, and the second is an XML *syntax* for expressing meta data.

The RDF Model

By a model we simply mean the triples that we discussed earlier. The RDFMS document discusses issues relating to triples independently of any mechanism that we might use for storing them, searching on them, transporting them, and so on. As a result of this, RDF is not XML-specific. The second half of the specification does specify an XML format for RDF, but it is made clear that this is only one way that the model might be transported.

Let's look at the terminology used in describing the RDF model.

Statements

The RDF specification uses the term **statement** to describe a triple. You may recall earlier that we laid out some of our meta data in sentences, like this:

> The document http://MuzicBiz.org/Tracks/1667653
>
> > Has a title of "911", and
> >
> > Was created by "Wyclef Jean"

> The document http://MuzicBiz.org/Albums/7655432
>
> > Has a track http://MuzicBiz.org/Tracks/1667653

> The document http://MuzicBiz.org/BoxSets/665
>
> > Has an album http://MuzicBiz.org/Albums/7655432

You can clearly see where the term "statement" arises from – we are making statements about some document, for example that it has a title of *911,* or that it was composed by "Wyclef Jean". Often, discussions on RDF will make these look even more like English language statements, for example:

> http://www.ePolitix.com/Articles/0000005a4787.htm has a creator of Craig Hoy

Triples as Resources with Properties

When we were discussing triples earlier we specified the three parts of a triple as a name/value pair, and then a reference to the document that this meta data referred to. In the RDF specification the name part of the name/value pair is regarded as a **property**, and the subject of the meta data is regarded as a **resource**. A triple then becomes the combination of the three parts – a resource with a property and value:

Resource	Property	Value
http://MuzicBiz.org/Albums/1011234	http://MuzicBiz.org/Review	A relaxing album to prune to.
http://MuzicBiz.org/Albums/7655432	http://MuzicBiz.org/Review	Lively! Perfect when mowing the lawn.
http://MuzicBiz.org/Albums/8997654	http://MuzicBiz.org/Review	Very moody. Great when planning your next planting.

Triples as Relationships between Resources

There is another – more formal – terminology for the parts of a triple, which views a triple not so much as a resource with a property, but as a relationship between two resources. Here are the triples we had earlier when we assigned the track *911* to the album *The Ecleftic*:

Resource	Property	Value
http://MuzicBiz.org/Albums/7655432	http://MuzicBiz.org/Prop/Track	http://MuzicBiz.org/Tracks/1667653

This could be represented diagrammatically like this:

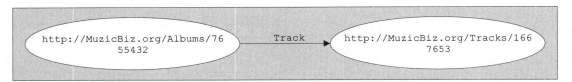

The terminology for this view of the model is that the album is the **subject** of our statement, and the track is the **object**. The two resources are joined by a **predicate** that specifies the nature of the relationship between the two resources.

The fact that there are two ways to express the same thing is a clue to the origins of RDF. The standard has a number of influences on it – some of which are the worlds of knowledge management, databases, object oriented programming, and others. In some contexts meta data is regarded as a set of properties of a resource, and in other contexts meta data is regarded as a set of relationships. Neither view is "right", rather it is a credit to the developers of the standard that they were able to come up with a model that addressed many different needs.

Notation

When people write about RDF it is often handy to be able to show statements or sets of triples for discussion. There are a number of ways of doing this, most of which you have already seen.

The simplest is using English-like statements, such as:

Craig Hoy is the author of http://www.ePolitix.com/Articles/0000005a4787.htm

More generally we could say that:

subject has a **predicate** of **object**

For example:

http://www.ePolitix.com/Articles/0000005a4787.htm has an author of Craig Hoy

Another way of expressing our statements is to use **directed labeled graphs**. These are often used in the relational database world – where they are called **nodes and arcs diagrams** – and would look like this:

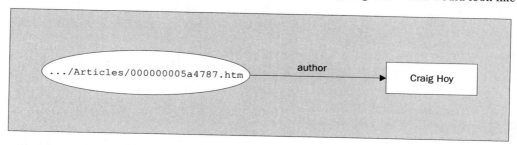

Note that in this diagram the right-hand side is a rectangle rather than an oval – as we saw in the earlier diagram. This indicates that the value is a string literal. The previous diagram had an oval on the right to indicate that the value was another resource.

This next format we haven't seen, but it is very straightforward. In this layout we simply list the three parts of the triple. If one of the items is a string literal then we surround the value with quotation marks, and if it is a resource we put square brackets around it. The entire statement is wrapped in curly brackets:

```
{
    [http://MuzicBiz.org/Review],
    [http://MuzicBiz.org/Albums/1011234],
    "A relaxing album to prune to."
}
{
    [http://MuzicBiz.org/Review],
    [http://MuzicBiz.org/Albums/7655432],
    "Lively! Perfect when mowing the lawn."
}
{
    [http://MuzicBiz.org/Review],
    [http://MuzicBiz.org/Albums/8997654],
    "Very moody. Great when planning your next planting."
}
```

You may have noticed that in this layout the predicate comes first. The curly brace syntax we have just seen reflects this ordering.

With complex sets of meta data, the graphs will often be the most compact means of representation, for example:

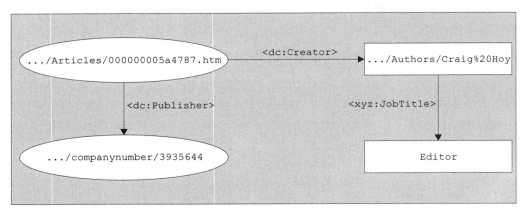

RDF Syntax

We've looked at how RDF models meta data; now we want to see how this information is actually represented in XML. Let's stick with the statement about an article on the ePolitix web site having been created by Craig Hoy. Using the XML syntax of RDF – often referred to as RDF/XML – to express this statement, the XML would look like this:

```
<rdf:Description
 xmlns:rdf="http://www.w3.org/1999/02/22-rdf-syntax-ns#"
 xmlns:dc="http://purl.org/metadata/dublin_core#"
 rdf:about="http://www.ePolitix.com/Articles/0000005a4787.htm">
   <dc:Creator>Craig Hoy</dc:Creator>
</rdf:Description>
```

Look at how a statement is formed:

❑   The statement begins with a reference to the resource that the statement is about; in other words, the subject. This is in the rdf:about attribute of the <rdf:Description> element.

❑   The statement is located inside the <rdf:Description> element, and is saying that there is a property of this resource – dc:Creator – that has a value of "Craig Hoy".

Note that this is as we expected from our earlier discussion. We saw that XML was perfectly adequate for expressing the property values, but needed help identifying the resource that the properties are for. The rdf:about attribute has achieved this.

When there are many namespaces in an RDF document I find it more convenient to group them on an <rdf:RDF> element, so that they stand out:

```
<rdf:RDF
 xmlns:rdf="http://www.w3.org/1999/02/22-rdf-syntax-ns#"
 xmlns:dc="http://purl.org/metadata/dublin_core#"
>
  <rdf:Description
```

```
        rdf:about="http://www.ePolitix.com/Articles/0000005a4787.htm">
            <dc:Creator>Craig Hoy</dc:Creator>
        </rdf:Description>
    </rdf:RDF>
```

This element is optional, and we didn't include it in the first example. If the processor that will deal with your document is expecting an RDF structure then you are free to omit this enclosing element. However, the <rdf:RDF> element is often useful if your XML document only contains RDF, and you want to make more than one statement, as illustrated here:

```
<rdf:RDF
  xmlns:rdf="http://www.w3.org/1999/02/22-rdf-syntax-ns#"
  xmlns:dc="http://purl.org/metadata/dublin_core#"
>
  <rdf:Description
      rdf:about="http://www.ePolitix.com/Articles/0000005a4787.htm">
    <dc:Creator>Craig Hoy</dc:Creator>
  </rdf:Description>

  <rdf:Description
      rdf:about="http://www.ePolitix.com/Articles/0000005a4750.htm">
    <dc:Creator>Craig Hoy</dc:Creator>
  </rdf:Description>
</rdf:RDF>
```

We have now listed two articles that were created by Craig Hoy. I'm sure you could work this out, but for completeness let's show the different meta data models that are represented by this syntax. First, we'll use sentences:

Craig Hoy is the creator of http://www.ePolitix.com/Articles/0000005a4787.htm

Craig Hoy is the creator of http://www.ePolitix.com/Articles/0000005a4750.htm

Secondly, we'll use a labeled graph:

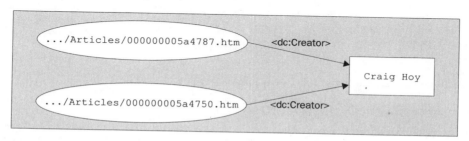

And finally, we'll show the underlying meta data model as a set of triples:

```
{
    [http://purl.org/metadata/dublin_core#Creator],
    [http://www.ePolitix.com/Articles/0000005a4787.htm],
    "Craig Hoy"
```

```
    }
    {
        [http://purl.org/metadata/dublin_core#Creator],
        [http://www.ePolitix.com/Articles/0000005a4750.htm],
        "Craig Hoy"
    }
```

One of the keys to getting the most from RDF is to be able to easily move between these abstract models, and the syntactic representation of that model.

Now that we have introduced the basic RDF syntax, let's look in more detail at the elements that make up the syntax. We have grouped them as:

1. the <rdf:Description> element

2. property elements

3. containers

4. statements about statements

The <rdf:Description> Element

We've seen how the <rdf:Description> element contains within it the URI for the resource that is being described, and we've also seen that a child XML element can be used to describe the properties that are being defined. In terms of triples, the <rdf:Description> element identifies the subject, whilst a child element defines a predicate/object pair. Just as a quick reminder, here's the example we were dealing with earlier:

> Note that I will tend to omit the namespace declarations from now on, unless they are under discussion. This makes the examples a little easier to read.

```
<rdf:RDF>
  <rdf:Description
      rdf:about="http://www.ePolitix.com/Articles/0000005a4787.htm">
    <dc:Creator>Craig Hoy</dc:Creator>
  </rdf:Description>
</rdf:RDF>
```

Now we will go deeper into the <rdf:Description> element, and look at:

❑ Multiple properties for the same resource.

❑ String literals and resource URIs.

❑ Nesting statements.

❑ The rdf:about attribute.

❑ The rdf:ID attribute.

❑ Anonymous resources.

❑ The rdf:type attribute.

Multiple Properties for the Same Resource

You may well have noticed this already, but the `<rdf:Description>` element is actually a container for as many predicate/object pairs as you want. Just as graphically we can show a number of statements being made about the same resource like this:

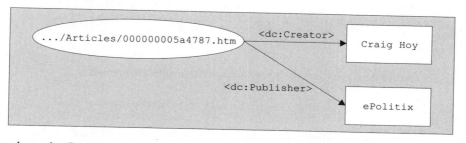

so too we have the flexibility in the syntax to specify a number of properties for the same resource:

```
<rdf:RDF>
  <rdf:Description
     rdf:about="http://www.ePolitix.com/Articles/0000005a4787.htm">
    <dc:Creator>Craig Hoy</dc:Creator>
    <dc:Publisher>ePolitix</dc:Publisher>
  </rdf:Description>
</rdf:RDF>
```

It's also possible to represent the same meta data model using a slightly different syntax, using attributes to take the place of the child elements. The previous example could be represented as follows:

```
<rdf:RDF>
  <rdf:Description
    rdf:about="http://www.ePolitix.com/Articles/0000005a4787.htm"
    dc:Creator="Craig Hoy"
    dc:Publisher="ePolitix"
  />
</rdf:RDF>
```

It is important to keep stressing that the underlying meta data model does not change when we are given flexibility with the syntax. The labeled graph, set of triples, or statements represented by this different syntax are exactly the same as before.

String Literals and Resource URIs

We spoke earlier about the distinction between a string literal and a resource, for the value of a property. Recall that we had the following triples when we said that a particular track appears on a specified album:

```
{
    [http://MuzicBiz.org/Prop/Track],
    [http://MuzicBiz.org/Albums/7655432],
    [http://MuzicBiz.org/Tracks/1667653]
}
```

Let's now look at how we would represent this in RDF/XML, so that a resource is not confused with a string literal:

```
<rdf:RDF>
  <rdf:Description rdf:about="http://MuzicBiz.org/Albums/7655432">
    <m:Track rdf:resource="http://MuzicBiz.org/Tracks/1667653"/>
  </rdf:Description>
</rdf:RDF>
```

As you can see, rather than just placing the resource value inside the element:

```
    <m:Track>http://MuzicBiz.org/Tracks/1667653</m:Track>
```

where it would be indistinguishable from a string literal, we have a special RDF attribute (rdf:resource) that says the value is a resource.

Nesting Statements

The RDF syntax that we have just shown can be expressed in the following nodes and arcs diagram:

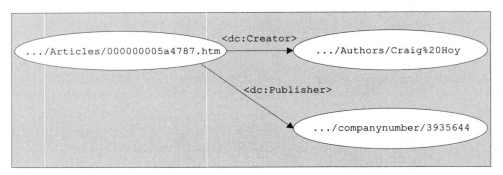

There is nothing to stop us extending this diagram, and making statements about any of these resources, for example:

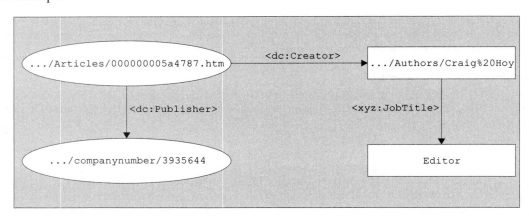

Here, we have added a statement about the author of the article, saying that his job title is "editor". The property "xyz:JobTitle" comes from some schema that we haven't defined, but perhaps the namespace xyz might be a news information format. How should this be represented in RDF? Well, of course we could just add our statement, straight after our other statements, as we saw in the introduction to this section:

```
<rdf:RDF>
  <rdf:Description
   rdf:about="http://www.ePolitix.com/Articles/0000005a4787.htm">
    <dc:Creator rdf:resource="http://www.ePolitix.com/Authors/Craig%20Hoy"/>
    <dc:Publisher
     rdf:resource="http://www.CorpInfo.org/companynumber/3935644"/>
  </rdf:Description>

  <rdf:Description rdf:about="http://www.ePolitix.com/Authors/Craig%20Hoy">
    <xyz:JobTitle>editor</xyz:JobTitle>
  </rdf:Description>
</rdf:RDF>
```

But RDF syntax also allows us to nest <rdf:Description> elements. We could use this approach to represent the same set of statements like this:

```
<rdf:RDF>
  <rdf:Description
   rdf:about="http://www.ePolitix.com/Articles/0000005a4787.htm">
    <dc:Creator>
      <rdf:Description
       rdf:about="http://www.ePolitix.com/Authors/Craig%20Hoy">
        <xyz:JobTitle>editor</xyz:JobTitle>
      </rdf:Description>
    </dc:Creator>
    <dc:Publisher
     rdf:resource="http://www.CorpInfo.org/companynumber/3935644"/>
  </rdf:Description>
</rdf:RDF>
```

Here we are saying that the value in the nested rdf:about attribute is playing a double role. It is the value of the <dc:Creator> property in the first statement, and it is the subject of a further statement.

Exactly which syntax you use will depend on the context, since the model will always be the same. In the example just given, the nested syntax is probably preferable for human readers, since it draws attention to the fact that statements are being made about first the article and then the author. It is less efficient though when there are more articles in our list; we wouldn't want to keep repeating the fact that Craig Hoy's job title was editor if we had a lot of articles:

```
<rdf:RDF>
  <rdf:Description
   rdf:about="http://www.ePolitix.com/Articles/0000005a4787.htm">
    <dc:Creator>
      <rdf:Description
       rdf:about=" http://www.ePolitix.com/Authors/Craig%20Hoy">
        <xyz:JobTitle>editor</xyz:JobTitle>
      </rdf:Description>
    </dc:Creator>

    <dc:Publisher
     rdf:resource="http://www.CorpInfo.org/companynumber/3935644"/>
  </rdf:Description>
```

```
    <rdf:Description
     rdf:about="http://www.ePolitix.com/Articles/0000005a4750.htm">
      <dc:Creator>
        <rdf:Description
         rdf:about="http://www.ePolitix.com/Authors/Craig%20Hoy">
          <xyz:JobTitle>editor</xyz:JobTitle>
        </rdf:Description>
      </dc:Creator>
      <dc:Publisher
       rdf:resource="http://www.CorpInfo.org/companynumber/3935644"/>
    </rdf:Description>
  </rdf:RDF>
```

In such a scenario the following would be more efficient:

```
<rdf:RDF>
  <rdf:Description
   rdf:about="http://www.ePolitix.com/Articles/0000005a4787.htm">
    <dc:Creator rdf:resource="http://www.ePolitix.com/Authors/Craig%20Hoy"/>
    <dc:Publisher
     rdf:resource="http://www.CorpInfo.org/companynumber/3935644"/>
  </rdf:Description>

  <rdf:Description
   rdf:about="http://www.ePolitix.com/Articles/0000005a4750.htm">
    <dc:Creator rdf:resource="http://www.ePolitix.com/Authors/Craig%20Hoy"/>
    <dc:Publisher
     rdf:resource="http://www.CorpInfo.org/companynumber/3935644"/>
  </rdf:Description>

  <rdf:Description rdf:about="http://www.ePolitix.com/Authors/Craig%20Hoy">
    <xyz:JobTitle>editor</xyz:JobTitle>
  </rdf:Description>
</rdf:RDF>
```

This second arrangement is most likely the one you would use if generating an RDF syntax document automatically from some triple storage medium, since you can just throw out information about any resource that you know anything about. Remember though, that no matter which of these syntaxes we use, the meta data model is unchanged, as follows:

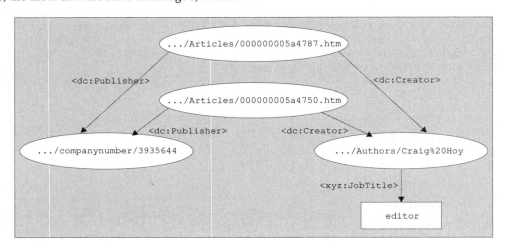

You're probably wondering whether we could make the XML even more efficient, and take out the repetition of having the same author and publisher for both articles. RDF syntax does provide us with an easy way to do this, called **containers**, which we will look at shortly.

The rdf:about Attribute

There are a number of different attributes that can be used with the `<rdf:Description>` element. The one we have seen so far, and probably the one you will see most in the examples you look at, is the `rdf:about` attribute. The contents of the `rdf:about` attribute are a **Uniform Resource Identifier** (URI). Full details of URIs are contained in RFC2396 (see http://www.ietf.org/rfc/rfc2396.txt). As we saw in the first part of this chapter, much of the power of RDF comes from its use of URIs as unique identifiers for resources and properties.

RFC2396 defines a resource as "anything that has identity", before going on to illustrate this point with examples:

> *Familiar examples include an electronic document, an image, a service (for example, "today's weather report for Los Angeles"), and a collection of other resources.*

This is useful since it means that the item referred to need not actually exist, but if it has a URI we can make statements about it. For example, William Shakespeare was not a web page, but if we created a URI such as:

```
uri:playwrights:William%20Shakespeare
```

we could then be sure that we were always talking about *the* William Shakespeare if we added this value to documents. Often what will happen is that people will create URIs by using the domain name of their web server, perhaps like this:

```
http://my.PeopleDatabase.org/WilliamShakespeare
```

but that doesn't mean that anything exists at this location, just because it has a URI.

Note that if the value provided to the `rdf:about` attribute is not a full URI then the RDF syntax allows for it to be converted to a full URI. This may arise if the URI is a relative rather than an absolute URI, or if it uses a fragment identifier. For example, if the document we saw a moment ago was stored at:

http://www.ePolitix.com/RDF/SomeRDF.rdf

then the `rdf:about` attributes may be represented as follows:

```
<rdf:RDF>
  <rdf:Description
   rdf:about="/Articles/0000005a4787.htm">
    <dc:Creator rdf:resource="/Authors/Craig%20Hoy"/>
    <dc:Publisher
     rdf:resource="http://www.CorpInfo.org/companynumber/3935644"/>
  </rdf:Description>

  <rdf:Description
   rdf:about="/Articles/0000005a4750.htm">
    <dc:Creator rdf:resource="/Authors/Craig%20Hoy"/>
    <dc:Publisher
```

```
             rdf:resource="http://www.CorpInfo.org/companynumber/3935644"/>
      </rdf:Description>

    <rdf:Description rdf:about="/Authors/Craig%20Hoy">
      <xyz:JobTitle>editor</xyz:JobTitle>
    </rdf:Description>
  </rdf:RDF>
```

As you can see the URIs for the statements are now relative to the document holding the statements.

It's also possible that the URI uses fragment identifiers on the end of the URI. These URIs are both relative, and use fragment identifiers:

```
<rdf:RDF>
  <rdf:Description
   rdf:about="/Articles#0000005a4787">
     <dc:Creator rdf:resource="/Authors#Craig%20Hoy"/>
     <dc:Publisher
      rdf:resource="http://www.CorpInfo.org/companynumber/3935644"/>
  </rdf:Description>

  <rdf:Description
   rdf:about="/Articles#0000005a4750">
     <dc:Creator rdf:resource="/Authors#Craig%20Hoy"/>
     <dc:Publisher
      rdf:resource="http://www.CorpInfo.org/companynumber/3935644"/>
  </rdf:Description>

    <rdf:Description rdf:about="/Authors#Craig%20Hoy">
      <xyz:JobTitle>editor</xyz:JobTitle>
    </rdf:Description>
</rdf:RDF>
```

As always with URIs, these may not point to any retrievable resource. Whether it uses a fragment identifier, or is absolute or relative, the URI does not need to point to something that can be retrieved from some server – it simply serves as a unique identifier.

The rdf:ID Attribute

Although we just said that the resource identified by the fragment identifier does not need to exist, there is no reason why it can't. RDF provides a way to create a resource inside a document that can be referred to within that document. Let's extend the example we just had:

```
<rdf:RDF>
  <rdf:Description rdf:about="#CraigHoy">
    <v:Email>Craig.Hoy@ePolitix.com</v:Email>
  </rdf:Description>

  <rdf:Description rdf:ID="CraigHoy">
    <v:Name>Craig Hoy</v:Name>
  </rdf:Description>
</rdf:RDF>
```

By using the `rdf:ID` attribute we have created a local resource about which we can make further statements. Note that the `rdf:about` and `rdf:ID` attributes are mutually exclusive – the `<rdf:Description>` element can only have one or other, but not both. (The other permutation is to have neither, as we will see in a moment.)

The fragment identifier isn't only usable in the relative format we have here. Let's say we had a document (`Authors.rdf`) listing the various authors who contribute to the ePolitix web site, along with some of their properties:

```
<rdf:RDF>
  <rdf:Description rdf:ID="CraigHoy">
    <v:Name>Craig Hoy</v:Name>
    <v:Email>Craig.Hoy@ePolitix.com</v:Email>
  </rdf:Description>

  <rdf:Description rdf:ID="BrunoWaterfield">
    <v:Name>Bruno Waterfield</v:Name>
    <v:Email>Bruno.Waterfield@ePolitix.com</v:Email>
  </rdf:Description>

  . . .

  <rdf:Description rdf:ID="ChrisSmith">
    <v:Name>Chris Smith</v:Name>
    <v:Email>Chris.Smith@ePolitix.com</v:Email>
  </rdf:Description>
</rdf:RDF>
```

Let's say this RDF document is located at:

http://www.ePolitix.com/Authors.rdf

We could now refer to any of these authors from other RDF documents within the ePolitix web site, as in the following example:

```
<rdf:RDF>
  <rdf:Description
   rdf:about="http://www.ePolitix.com/Articles/0000005a4787.htm">
    <dc:Creator
     rdf:resource="http://www.ePolitix.com/Authors.rdf#CraigHoy" />
  </rdf:Description>

  <rdf:Description
   rdf:about="http://www.ePolitix.com/Articles/0000005A47F1.htm">
    <dc:Creator
     rdf:resource="http://www.ePolitix.com/Authors.rdf#ChrisSmith" />
  </rdf:Description>

  <rdf:Description
   rdf:about="http://www.ePolitix.com/Articles/0000005A47F6.htm">
    <dc:Creator
     rdf:resource="http://www.ePolitix.com/Authors.rdf#BrunoWaterfield" />
  </rdf:Description>
</rdf:RDF>
```

The difference between `rdf:about` and `rdf:ID` often confuses people, but it really isn't complicated. As far as triples are concerned there is no difference – if you looked in a triple database you would not be able to tell whether a statement was created with an `rdf:ID` attribute or an `rdf:about` attribute. The ability to use `rdf:ID` simply allows for abbreviated syntaxes. I'll illustrate this point.

If we go back to our `Authors.rdf` document that we looked at a moment ago, we said it was located at:

http://www.ePolitix.com/Authors.rdf

This means that we could have expressed the document like this:

```
<rdf:RDF>
  <rdf:Description
   rdf:about="http://www.ePolitix.com/Authors.rdf#Craig%20Hoy">
    <v:Name>Craig Hoy</v:Name>
    <v:Email>Craig.Hoy@ePolitix.com</v:Email>
  </rdf:Description>

  <rdf:Description
   rdf:about="http://www.ePolitix.com/Authors.rdf#Bruno%20Waterfield">
    <v:Name>Bruno Waterfield</v:Name>
    <v:Email>BrunoWaterfield@ePolitix.com</v:Email>
  </rdf:Description>

  ...

  <rdf:Description
   rdf:about="http://www.ePolitix.com/Authors.rdf#Chris%20Smith">
    <v:Name>Chris Smith</v:Name>
    <v:Email>Chris.Smith@ePolitix.com</v:Email>
  </rdf:Description>
</rdf:RDF>
```

and it would have generated exactly the same set of triples as the previous document, which used `rdf:ID` attributes. The easiest way to view the `rdf:ID` attribute is that it allows URIs to be abbreviated if the resource being referred to is the document that contains the meta data.

Anonymous Resources

One more option for the `<rdf:Description>` element would be to not specify an `rdf:about` or `rdf:ID` attribute. It is quite legitimate in the RDF model to have **anonymous resources** – a description element that exists for no other reason than to be given properties. This might be the case if, for example, we wanted to make additional statements about the author of an article, but we had no external resource by which we could refer to the author (using the `rdf:about` attribute) and we weren't interested in making the resource available outside our document (using the `rdf:ID` attribute). The following is a modified version of the example we gave when looking at nesting `<rdf:Description>` statements:

```
<rdf:RDF>
  <rdf:Description
   rdf:about="http://www.ePolitix.com/Articles/0000005a4787.htm">
    <dc:Creator>
      <rdf:Description>
        <v:Name>Craig Hoy</v:Name>
        <v:Email>Craig.Hoy@ePolitix.com</v:Email>
        <xyz:JobTitle>editor</xyz:JobTitle>
      </rdf:Description>
```

```
        </dc:Creator>
        <dc:Publisher
          rdf:resource="http://www.CorpInfo.org/companynumber/3935644"/>
      </rdf:Description>
    </rdf:RDF>
```

It's important to note that how the URI for an anonymous resource is specified when modeling the meta data as triples is undefined. On the one hand we must give the anonymous resource a value so that we can distinguish it from other anonymous resources – a document may have many more than one, though how we actually do that doesn't matter since no external system can query for this resource, *since it's anonymous!* So we could use the following triples:

```
    {
        dc:Creator,
        [http://www.ePolitix.com/Articles/0000005a4787.htm],
        [anon:1]
    }
    { v:Name, [anon:1], "Craig Hoy" }
    { v:Email, [anon:1], "Craig.Hoy@ePolitix.com" }
    { xyz:JobTitle, [anon:1], "editor" }
```

The graphical representation of this RDF is very straightforward, with the oval representing the anonymous resource by simply being left empty:

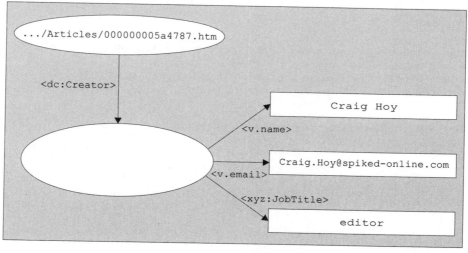

There are many situations where RDF will create anonymous resources automatically or, to be more precise, there are situations where an RDF parser will create anonymous resources in order to correctly represent the meta data that it is processing. This means that in a given meta data model, there may be triples that refer to anonymous resources that have not been explicitly defined by creating an <rdf:Description> element without an rdf:about or rdf:ID attribute. We'll see a number of these later when we look at containers. For now we'll discuss a simple example of when the parser creates an anonymous resource automatically.

Let's go back to Mozart, and assume that some authority on classical music has given the piece "*Eine Kleine Nacht Muzik*" the URL:

http://MuzicBiz.org/233456

Recall also that we mentioned the Dewey Decimal Classification (DDC) system – let's give the piece the DDC code of "781.68", which means classical music. One statement we could make would be:

> `http://MuzicBiz.org/233456` has a `dc:Subject` of 781.68

The RDF for this statement is simply:

```
<rdf:Description rdf:about="http://MuzicBiz.org/233456">
  <dc:Subject>781.68</dc:Subject>
</rdf:Description>
```

However, what if we wanted to indicate that the code "781.68" comes from DDC? The syntax to do this is very straightforward. We haven't met the `<rdf:value>` property before, but it shouldn't cause you any trouble here:

```
<rdf:Description rdf:about="http://MuzicBiz.org/233456">
  <dc:Subject>
    <rdf:Description>
      <rdf:value>781.68</rdf:value>
      <xyz:Classification>DDC</xyz:Classification>
    </rdf:Description>
  </dc:Subject>
</rdf:Description>
```

How would we represent this using nodes and arcs? We have given properties to a resource that has not been explicitly defined, even though we can see its position in the document. We need an extra node as a sort of placeholder for this resource, and then we can attach both the value, and the classification of that value to this node. An RDF parser will create such a resource in just the same way that we might explicitly create an `<rdf:Description>` with no attributes:

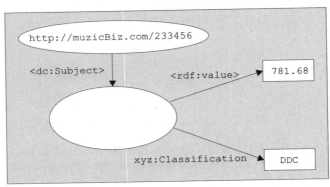

As in our previous example, the node is still a resource just like any other, but, since it is anonymous, other statements outside of this immediate collection of statements cannot refer to it. Another way of saying the same thing is that the only facts you will ever know about this resource are the facts that we have just created.

Finally, a quick look at how the triples might be represented:

```
{ dc:Subject, [http://MuzicBiz.org/233456], [anon:2] }
{ rdf:value, [anon:2], "781.68" }
{ xyz:Classification, [anon:2], "DDC" }
```

It is important to be clear that the name of the anonymous resource really does not matter. The only criteria for it are that it can be differentiated from other anonymous resources in the same document. Although I have made up the format anon:1 to illustrate my points, some parsers are using the prefix genid: in their output, to indicate that the resource is anonymous, and that the URI has therefore been generated.

There is a great deal of discussion on RDF forums about whether there should be an algorithm for generating identifiers for anonymous resources, so that the statements identified within the triple database can be retrieved later. Although this may well happen in the future, I don't at the moment see a need for it. The use of anonymous resources is simply to allow the nesting of statements, as we saw before.

The rdf:type Attribute

Another attribute that can be applied to <rdf:Description> elements is rdf:type. This is a very powerful feature of RDF, linking the worlds of knowledge representation and object orientation. It will be discussed in more detail in the next chapter.

The rdf:type attribute allows us to indicate that the resource being referred to is of a particular class. This will allow parsers that are able to process this information to glean more about the meta data. For instance, a class-aware parser would be able to check whether the statements being made about a certain resource are actually valid. I'll explain this in more detail later, but let's first build up the pieces of the jigsaw that we need.

Let's assume that the organization International Press Telecommunications Council (IPTC) – responsible for the XML format used in the ePolitix articles we have been using – has defined a URI that allows us to indicate that the article being referred to is in their **NITF** format. NITF stands for the News Industry Text Format, and is widely used to transfer news articles between organizations, such as publishers and syndicators. The URL for all object types that belong to the NITF group of objects might be something like this:

http://www.iptc.org/schema/NITF#

We could then enhance one of the statements that we made earlier, as follows:

```
<rdf:RDF>
  <rdf:Description
   rdf:about="http://www.ePolitix.com/Articles/0000005a4787.htm"
   rdf:type="http://www.iptc.org/schema/NITF#NewsArticle"
  >
    <dc:Creator rdf:resource="http://www.ePolitix.com/Authors/Craig%20Hoy"/>
    <dc:Publisher
     rdf:resource="http://www.CorpInfo.org/companynumber/3935644"/>
  </rdf:Description>
</rdf:RDF>
```

Here we are saying that the resource being referred to is not just any resource, but is actually an NITF news article. We have created the full URI for the object type by adding the specific rdf:type – NewsArticle – to the broad grouping of NITF object types. This is because the IPTC have other groups of objects for pictures, video, audio, and so on.

This aspect of RDF is incredibly powerful and is very close to principles of object-oriented programming (OOP). By saying that the resource being pointed to is a news article we create the possibility for checking whether the meta data provided is in fact valid for that resource. For example, it is probably wrong to indicate that a person has a `<dc:Format>` property (the Dublin Core Format property is used to specify the MIME type of documents) as we have done here:

```
<rdf:Description rdf:about="http://www.ePolitix.com/Authors/Craig%20Hoy">
   <dc:Format>text/html</dc:Format>
</rdf:Description>
```

As things stand though, there is no way of knowing anything more about this resource:

http://www.ePolitix.com/Authors/Craig%20Hoy

By specifying a type in the `rdf:type` attribute, we can give an RDF processor more information:

```
<rdf:Description
 rdf:about="http://www.ePolitix.com/Authors/Craig%20Hoy"
 rdf:type="http://www.schemas.org/Schemas#Person"
>
   <dc:Format>text/html</dc:Format>
</rdf:Description>
```

The triples represented by this syntax are:

```
{
    rdf:type,
    [http://www.ePolitix.com/Authors/Craig%20Hoy],
    [http://www.schemas.org/Schemas#Person]
}
{ dc:Format, [http://www.ePolitix.com/Authors/Craig%20Hoy], "text/html" }
```

Whether `<dc:Format>` is an acceptable property to apply to a resource of type Person is something that can be defined using the RDF Schema mechanism, which is discussed in the next chapter. For now we will look at the different ways that type information can be specified in the syntax. This is important to understand for our later discussion on containers.

As we know from previous sections, specifying a value by using an attribute on an `<rdf:Description>` element is the same as specifying the value as an element that is a child of the `<rdf:Description>` element. This is almost the same with a `rdf:type` attribute, except that the contents are a resource, and not a string literal. Our previous example can therefore be expressed using the following syntax, with no loss of meaning at the meta data level:

```
<rdf:Description rdf:about="http://www.ePolitix.com/Authors/Craig%20Hoy">
   <rdf:type rdf:resource="http://www.schemas.org/Schemas#Person" />
   <dc:Format>text/html</dc:Format>
</rdf:Description>
```

Just to remind you – so that you can see the slight difference – since `dc:Format` is a string literal we can express it as an attribute like this:

```
<rdf:Description
 rdf:about="http://www.ePolitix.com/Authors/Craig%20Hoy"
 dc:Format="text/html"
>
    <rdf:type rdf:resource="http://www.schemas.org/Schemas#Person" />
</rdf:Description>
```

Typed Elements

There is another syntax that can be used to express the same type information we have just seen, which is to create what are known as **typed elements**. These are XML elements where the resource that would have been referred to in the rdf:type attribute has been turned into a namespace qualified element. Let's go through this a step at a time.

Remember that we assumed that we had a namespace prefix for objects created by the IPTC for their NITF standard, and we said that this namespace prefix was:

```
http://www.iptc.org/schema/NITF
```

We then said that we could create object types – or references to schemas – by specifying a full URI. In this case we simply appended the class of the object to the prefix, separated by the # delimiter:

```
http://www.iptc.org/schema/NITF#NewsArticle
```

The RDF syntax provides us with a further convenient abbreviation to specify type information, whereby we simply assign the prefix we have just defined to a namespace placeholder, and then use the class name as the name of an element. We then replace the <rdf:Description> element with this whole construction. The previous statements:

```
<rdf:RDF>
  <rdf:Description
   rdf:about="http://www.ePolitix.com/Articles/0000005a4787.htm">
    <rdf:type rdf:resource="http://www.iptc.org/schema/NITF#NewsArticle" />
    <dc:Creator rdf:resource="http://www.ePolitix.com/Authors/Craig%20Hoy"/>
    <dc:Publisher
     rdf:resource="http://www.CorpInfo.org/companynumber/3935644"/>
  </rdf:Description>
</rdf:RDF>
```

could now be represented like this:

```
<rdf:RDF
 xmlns:nitf="http://www.iptc.org/schema/NITF#"
>
  <nitf:NewsArticle
   rdf:about="http://www.ePolitix.com/Articles/0000005a4787.htm">
    <dc:Creator
        rdf:resource="http://www.ePolitix.com/Authors/Craig%20Hoy" />
    <dc:Publisher
        rdf:resource="http://www.CorpInfo.org/companynumber/3935644"/>
  </nitf:NewsArticle>
</rdf:RDF>
```

As far as the model is concerned these two RDFs are exactly the same. Both of them produce this list of triples:

```
{
    [http://www.w3.org/1999/02/22-rdf-syntax-ns#type],
    [http://www.ePolitix.com/Articles/0000005a4787.htm],
    [http://www.iptc.org/schema/NITF#NewsArticle]
}
{
    [http://purl.org/metadata/dublin_core#Creator],
    [http://www.ePolitix.com/Articles/0000005a4787.htm],
    [http://www.ePolitix.com/Authors/Craig%20Hoy]
}
{
    [http://purl.org/metadata/dublin_core#Publisher],
    [http://www.ePolitix.com/Articles/0000005a4787.htm],
    [http://www.CorpInfo.org/companynumber/3935644]
}
```

As you can see, RDF is allowing a namespace-qualified element name to be equivalent to a resource type, simply by concatenating the namespace and the element, so that:

`nitf:NewsArticle`

is effectively:

`http://www.iptc.org/schema/NITF#NewsArticle`

provided of course that the `nitf` namespace was declared as:

`http://www.iptc.org/schema/NITF#`

This is quite an important feature of the RDF syntax so we'll go into it in more detail in a moment. Before we do, there's just one final point to emphasize on the typed node syntax, which is that anything that is valid on an `<rdf:Description>` element is valid when using a typed element. For example, we can use anonymous resources, in the way that the `<v:vCard>` element here contains a made-up vCard syntax (pretend that we have defined the namespace for now):

```
<rdf:RDF>
  <rdf:Description
   rdf:about="http://www.ePolitix.com/Articles/0000005a4787.htm">
    <dc:Creator>
      <v:vCard>
        <v:Name>Craig Hoy</v:Name>
        <v:Email>Craig.Hoy@ePolitix.com</v:Email>
        <xyz:JobTitle>editor</xyz:JobTitle>
      </v:vCard>
    </dc:Creator>
    <dc:Publisher
     rdf:resource="http://www.CorpInfo.org/companynumber/3935644"/>
  </rdf:Description>
</rdf:RDF>
```

We can also turn into attributes some or all of the elements specifying the predicates:

```
<rdf:RDF>
  <rdf:Description
    rdf:about="http://www.ePolitix.com/Articles/0000005a4787.htm">
      <dc:Creator>
        <v:vCard v:Name="Craig Hoy" v:Email="Craig.Hoy@.com">
          <xyz:JobTitle>editor</xyz:JobTitle>
        </v:vCard>
      </dc:Creator>
      <dc:Publisher
          rdf:resource="http://www.CorpInfo.org/companynumber/3935644"/>
  </rdf:Description>
</rdf:RDF>
```

As I said earlier, this last abbreviation is very useful for extracting meta data from your existing XML documents, since it gives us a way of interpreting ordinary XML as a set of triples. Remember from our introduction that if the context allows it you can omit the <rdf:RDF> declaration and go straight into <rdf:Description>. Of course you can only do this if your processor knows that the only document types arriving are RDF, but if it does, you can see that the following document is actually acceptable RDF syntax:

```
<v:vCard xmlns:v="http://www.vCard.org/Schemas#">
  <v:Name>Craig Hoy</v:Name>
  <v:Email>Craig.Hoy@ePolitix.com</v:Email>
</v:vCard>
```

even though it makes no mention of any RDF attributes or elements. Assuming the document was called http://www.ePolitix.com/Authors/CraigHoy.rdf, if you interpreted this as RDF, the triples produced would be:

```
{
    [http://www.w3.org/1999/02/22-rdf-syntax-ns#type],
    [http://www.ePolitix.com/Authors/CraigHoy.rdf],
    [http://www.vCard.org/Schemas#vCard]
}
{
    [http://www.vCard.org/Schemas#Name],
    [http://www.ePolitix.com/Authors/CraigHoy.rdf],
    "Craig Hoy"
}
{
    [http://www.vCard.org/Schemas#Email],
    [http://www.ePolitix.com/Authors/CraigHoy.rdf],
    "Craig.Hoy@ePolitix.com"
}
```

and the labeled graph would be:

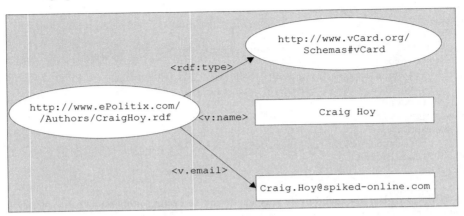

Namespaces in RDF

Let's look a bit more into how namespaces are used in RDF. As things stand with RDF, all we did in the previous examples was to join two strings together – the namespace and the local name of the element. This does raise a problem when trying to re-create the original RDF from a set of triples. Take one of the triples we had earlier:

```
{
    [http://purl.org/metadata/dublin_core#Creator],
    [http://www.ePolitix.com/Articles/0000005a4787.htm],
    [http://www.ePolitix.com/Authors/Craig%20Hoy]
}
```

We know that the RDF that generated this was:

```
<rdf:RDF
  xmlns:rdf="http://www.w3.org/1999/02/22-rdf-syntax-ns#"
  xmlns:dc="http://purl.org/metadata/dublin_core#"
>
  <rdf:Description
      rdf:about="http://www.ePolitix.com/Articles/0000005a4787.htm">
    <dc:Creator rdf:resource="http://www.ePolitix.com/Authors/Craig%20Hoy"/>
  </rdf:Description>
</rdf:RDF>
```

However, given the previous triple, how do we know that the original RDF did not have a namespace of:

```
http://purl.org/metadata/dublin_core#Cre
```

and an element name:

```
ator
```

The source document could well have looked like this:

```
<rdf:RDF
 xmlns:rdf="http://www.w3.org/1999/02/22-rdf-syntax-ns#"
 xmlns:dc="http://purl.org/metadata/dublin_core#Cre"
>
   <rdf:Description
        rdf:about="http://www.ePolitix.com/Articles/0000005a4787.htm">
      <dc:ator rdf:resource="http://www.ePolitix.com/Authors/Craig%20Hoy"/>
   </rdf:Description>
</rdf:RDF>
```

This would have produced exactly the same set of triples as we saw before. This leads to the interesting conclusion that whilst the RDF *syntax* is namespace aware, the *model* is not. This shouldn't surprise you too much, if you have understood the distinction between the model and the syntax, since the syntax is merely an XML mechanism for transporting triples – and triples are the key to RDF. However, it has caused a great deal of discussion in various RDF forums.

Since the XML form of RDF is intended only as a way of conveying the RDF model, then this namespace problem is actually *not* a problem. The RDF model does not provide enough information to round-trip your original XML document anyway, so the best way to deal with this is to treat namespaces as simply a convenient abbreviation, and understand them only at the level of *one possible representation of RDF,* and that is using XML. What I mean by this is that although it is convenient to write this:

```
<dc:Creator>Craig Hoy</dc:Creator>
```

we should always remember that this is merely the XML representation for the predicate/object statement:

```
http://purl.org/metadata/dublin_core#Creator = "Craig Hoy"
```

In other words, the model has no knowledge of namespaces, it only knows about absolute URIs.

When converting back to XML we can do pretty much anything we want as long as we faithfully represent the *model;* we are not required to come up with the original XML. We could therefore transport the triples from our example in the typed nodes discussion earlier:

```
<rdf:RDF
 xmlns:rdf="http://www.w3.org/1999/02/22-rdf-syntax-ns#"
 xmlns:nitf="http://www.iptc.org/schema/NITF#"
 xmlns:dc="http://purl.org/metadata/dublin_core#"
>
   <nitf:NewsArticle
        rdf:about="http://www.ePolitix.com/Articles/0000005a4787.htm">
      <dc:Creator rdf:resource="http://www.ePolitix.com/Authors/Craig%20Hoy" />
      <dc:Publisher
           rdf:resource="http://www.CorpInfo.org/companynumber/3935644"/>
   </nitf:NewsArticle>
</rdf:RDF>
```

in the following format, without any loss of meaning at the model level:

```
<ns1:Description
  xmlns:ns1="http://www.w3.org/1999/02/22-rdf-syntax-ns#"
  xmlns:ns2="http://purl.org/metadata/dublin_core#Cre"
  xmlns:ns3="http://purl.org/metadata/dublin_core#Publi"
  rdf:about="http://www.ePolitix.com/Articles/0000005a4787.htm"
>
  <ns1:type rdf:resource="http://www.iptc.org/schema/NITF#NewsArticle" />
  <ns2:ator rdf:resource="http://www.ePolitix.com/Authors/Craig%20Hoy"/>
  <ns3:sher rdf:resource="http://www.CorpInfo.org/companynumber/3935644"/>
</ns1:Description>
```

Most parsers, however, will work backwards from the end of the URI until they find a character that is not valid in the local part of an element name, and then treat the rest of the URI as the namespace. This approach would have yielded this:

```
<ns1:Description
  xmlns:ns1="http://www.w3.org/1999/02/22-rdf-syntax-ns#"
  xmlns:ns2="http://purl.org/metadata/dublin_core#"
  rdf:about="http://www.ePolitix.com/Articles/0000005a4787.htm"
>
  <ns1:type rdf:resource="http://www.iptc.org/schema/NITF#NewsArticle" />
  <ns2:Creator rdf:resource="http://www.ePolitix.com/Authors/Craig%20Hoy"/>
  <ns2:Publisher
        rdf:resource="http://www.CorpInfo.org/companynumber/3935644"/>
</ns1:Description>
```

This is quite a neat solution, and it's probably advisable for you to adopt the approach that many are already doing and use a "#" suffix to help create a suitable break. It would also cover you should some future version of RDF make the model more aware of namespaces.

However, there is nothing to force you to do this, and if the Dublin Core had decided not to do so, our example would instead look this (sticking with the approach of finding the first non-valid character to turn a URI into a namespace/local name pair):

```
<ns1:Description
  xmlns:ns1="http://www.w3.org/1999/02/22-rdf-syntax-ns#"
  xmlns:ns2="http://purl.org/metadata/"
  rdf:about="http://www.ePolitix.com/Articles/0000005a4787.htm"
>
  <ns1:type rdf:resource="http://www.iptc.org/schema/NITF#NewsArticle" />
  <ns2:dublin_coreCreator
        rdf:resource="http://www.ePolitix.com/Authors/Craig%20Hoy"/>
  <ns2:dublin_corePublisher
        rdf:resource="http://www.CorpInfo.org/companynumber/3935644"/>
</ns1:Description>
```

This would still be perfectly OK from our meta data point of view – the triples that this represents are exactly the same as before.

Summary

The `<rdf:Description>` element can take a number of attributes, although we have still not yet met all of them. The remainder will be looked at later. Those that we have discussed are:

- ❑ `rdf:about`
- ❑ `rdf:ID`
- ❑ `rdf:type`
- ❑ attributes with a namespace prefix (other than `xmlns` and `xml`), which can be used to specify properties

We saw how not specifying an `rdf:ID` or `rdf:about` attribute meant that the resource was anonymous, and we saw how type information could also be provided using namespace-qualified element names. As far as the element itself is concerned, we saw that `<rdf:Description>` can be used to make a number of statements about the same resource, and how the contents of this element would be a number of properties, or name/value pairs.

Let's now look in more detail at what can go inside an `<rdf:Description>` element by looking at the syntax of properties in more detail.

Property Elements

Although in the previous section we discussed the `<rdf:Description>` element, it was inevitable that we'd actually say quite a lot about the properties that this element can contain. We'll recap on what we have seen so far, before looking at other features that are available.

We have already seen three ways that property information can be expressed.

String Literals

The first creates a string literal that is the value for a predicate that is defined by the name of the element containing the literal:

```
<rdf:Description
     rdf:about="http://www.ePolitix.com/Articles/0000005a4787.htm">
  <dc:Creator>Craig Hoy</dc:Creator>
  <dc:Publisher>ePolitix</dc:Publisher>
</rdf:Description>
```

Resources

The second way to express properties for a resource is to say that the value of the predicate is actually another resource, and to use a URI to specify which resource that is:

```
<rdf:Description
     rdf:about="http://www.ePolitix.com/Articles/0000005a4787.htm">
  <dc:Creator rdf:resource="http://www.ePolitix.com/Authors/Craig%20Hoy"/>
  <dc:Publisher
       rdf:resource="http://www.CorpInfo.org/companynumber/3935644"/>
</rdf:Description>
```

Nesting Statements

The third syntax that you have seen, involved nesting RDF statements within other statements. Recall that we are able to do the following:

```
<rdf:Description rdf:about="http://www.ePolitix.com/Articles/0000005a4787.htm">
  <dc:Creator>
    <rdf:Description
         rdf:about="http://www.ePolitix.com/Authors/Craig%20Hoy">
      <xyz:JobTitle>editor</xyz:JobTitle>
    </rdf:Description>
  </dc:Creator>
  <dc:Publisher
       rdf:resource="http://www.CorpInfo.org/companynumber/3935644"/>
</rdf:Description>
```

This is saying that the value of the property <dc:Creator> is itself a resource, and that we have statements to make about that resource. We are also able to specify type information in the content of a property element:

```
<rdf:Description
     rdf:about="http://www.ePolitix.com/Articles/0000005a4787.htm">
  <dc:Creator>
    <rdf:Description>
      <rdf:type rdf:resource="http://www.vcard.org/Schemas#vCard" />
      <v:Name>Craig Hoy</v:Name>
      <v:Email>Craig.Hoy@ePolitix.com</v:Email>
    </rdf:Description>
  </dc:Creator>
</rdf:Description>
```

We also saw before that taking the type of the resource and turning it into a namespace-qualified element name could abbreviate this:

```
<rdf:Description
  rdf:about="http://www.spiked-onlinePolitix.com/Articles/0000005a4787.htm">
  <dc:Creator>
    <v:vCard>
      <v:Name>Craig Hoy</v:Name>
      <v:Email>Craig.Hoy@ePolitix.com</v:Email>
    </v:vCard>
  </dc:Creator>
</rdf:Description>
```

The pattern then, is that an <rdf:Description> element will contain property elements, but those properties can in turn contain <rdf:Description> elements.

parseType="Literal"

But what if that was not our intention? What if the XML inside the <dc:Creator> element was not meant to be interpreted by the RDF parser. Perhaps it was meant to be stored as is. Let's pick a better example to illustrate our point – one of the examples in the RDF Model and Syntax documentation (from Section 7 of RDFMS).

Say we have a mathematical paper whose title is *Ramifications of $(a+b)^2$ to World Peace*. We would like to use MathML (Mathematical Markup Language) to specify this title, since it can help us format the various symbols properly, but if we place the MathML inside a `<dc:Title>` element we need some way of telling an RDF parser not to interpret the XML as RDF. This is achieved using an attribute named `parseType`:

```
<rdf:Description
  xmlns:rdf="http://www.w3.org/1999/02/22-rdf-syntax-ns#"
  xmlns:dc="http://purl.org/metadata/dublin_core#"
  xmlns="http://www.w3.org/TR/REC-mathml"
  rdf:about="http://mycorp.com/papers/NobelPaper1"
>
  <dc:Title rdf:parseType="Literal">
    Ramifications of
    <apply>
      <power/>
      <apply>
        <plus/>
        <ci>a</ci>
        <ci>b</ci>
      </apply>
      <cn>2</cn>
    </apply>
    to World Peace
  </dc:Title>
  <dc:Creator>David Hume</dc:Creator>
</rdf:Description>
```

Note that the contents of this element are not simply a string. For a start the text must be well-formed XML, otherwise the RDF parser will fail. It is not the same as wrapping a CDATA section around everything; and as you can see in the previous example, the XML inside the `dc:Title` element is integral to the structure of the document. In addition to this, the XML requires all its namespace information, since at some point this fragment will need to re-emerge as:

```
Ramifications of
<m:apply>
  <m:power/>
  <m:apply>
    <m:plus/>
    <m:ci>a</m:ci>
    <m:ci>b</m:ci>
  </m:apply>
  <m:cn>2</m:cn>
</m:apply>
to World Peace
```

in order to be displayed correctly.

The `parseType="Literal"` attribute can be applied to any text, so the following would be valid:

```
<rdf:Description>
  <rdf:type rdf:resource="http://www.vcard.org/Schemas#vCard" />
  <v:Name parseType="Literal">Craig Hoy</v:Name>
  <v:Email parseType="Literal">Craig.Hoy@ePolitix.com</v:Email>
</rdf:Description>
```

139

However, the RDF documentation makes clear that anything inside a property element that *does not* contain XML markup will be interpreted as a string literal. We therefore only need to use the "Literal" parse type when we want to prevent the RDF parser from interpreting any XML that it encounters inside an element.

parseType="Resource"

We've seen how we can prevent an RDF parser from interpreting XML inside a property element as if it was RDF, but there is another related situation that can cause problems; when the parser cannot tell the difference between a property value and a resource.

As you know from the previous section we normally have properties inside an <rdf:Description> element, such as this:

```
<rdf:Description rdf:about="http://www.ePolitix.com/Articles/0000005a4787.htm">
  <dc:Creator>Craig Hoy</dc:Creator>
</rdf:Description>
```

or this:

```
<rdf:Description rdf:about="http://www.ePolitix.com/Articles/0000005a4787.htm">
  <dc:Creator rdf:resource="http://www.ePolitix.com/Authors/Craig%20Hoy"/>
</rdf:Description>
```

The RDF syntax allows us to make more statements about the author though, like this:

```
<rdf:Description rdf:about="http://www.ePolitix.com/Articles/0000005a4787.htm">
  <dc:Creator>
    <rdf:Description rdf:about="http://www.ePolitix.com/Authors/Craig%20Hoy">
      <v:Email>Craig.Hoy@ePolitix.com</v:Email>
    </rdf:Description>
  </dc:Creator>
</rdf:Description>
```

However, what if all we wanted to say was that the author had an e-mail address of Craig.Hoy@ePolitix.com, but we weren't bothered about identifying the author? Of course we could remove the resource reference, like this:

```
<rdf:Description rdf:about="http://www.ePolitix.com/Articles/0000005a4787.htm">
  <dc:Creator>
    <rdf:Description>
      <v:Email>Craig.Hoy@ePolitix.com</v:Email>
    </rdf:Description>
  </dc:Creator>
</rdf:Description>
```

but that seems overly elaborate. Surely we should be able to simply do this:

```
<rdf:Description rdf:about="http://www.ePolitix.com/Articles/0000005a4787.htm">
  <dc:Creator>

    <v:Email>Craig.Hoy@www.ePolitix.com</v:Email>
```

```
        </dc:Creator>
    </rdf:Description>
```

This raises an ambiguity, unfortunately. If you started from the inside out, you would say you have an anonymous <dc:Creator> element, which in turn has a <v:Email> property:

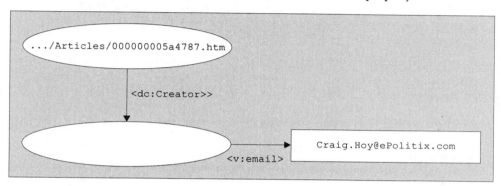

However, if you started from the outside in, you would say you had a resource of a web page, that had a <dc:Creator> property, and that this <dc:Creator> property refers to an anonymous resource of rdf:type v:Email:

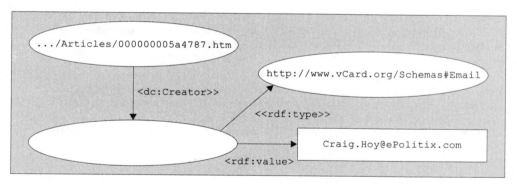

This second diagram is in fact the interpretation of the RDF/XML that we would prefer, but the parser has no way of distinguishing which of these two possible models it should create. The problem is that we need the <dc:Creator> element to be interpreted as both a property of the web page, and also as an anonymous resource in its own right so that properties can be attached to it.

RDF/XML does allow us to force the <dc:Creator> element to be interpreted as if it was both a predicate *and* an anonymous resource. The parseType="Resource" attribute does exactly that – the following RDF syntax gives us just the model we want:

```
<rdf:Description
    rdf:about="http://www.ePolitix.com/Articles/0000005a4787.htm">
  <dc:Creator rdf:parseType="Resource">
    <v:Email>Craig.Hoy@ePolitix.com</v:Email>
```

```
      </dc:Creator>
    </rdf:Description>
```

This is exactly the same as specifying the anonymous resource explicitly:

```
<rdf:Description
      rdf:about="http://www.ePolitix.com/Articles/0000005a4787.htm">
  <dc:Creator>
    <rdf:Description>
       <v:Email>Craig.Hoy@ePolitix.com</v:Email>
    </rdf:Description>
  </dc:Creator>
</rdf:Description>
```

Note that without the `rdf:parseType` attribute the RDF syntax that we used:

```
<rdf:Description
      rdf:about="http://www.ePolitix.com/Articles/0000005a4787.htm">
  <dc:Creator>
    <v:Email>Craig.Hoy@ePolitix.com</v:Email>
  </dc:Creator>
</rdf:Description>
```

would cause an error, since the `<v:Email>` element would be interpreted as a new statement, and so should contain properties, and not a string literal. By indicating that `<dc:Creator>` is both a property and the beginning of a new statement, the `<v:Email>` element gets correctly interpreted as a property, and the string literal can then be correctly seen as the value of that property.

> *Some discussions are taking place on bulletin boards and in discussion papers, suggesting that `parseType="Resource"` is the default behavior for all RDF documents unless otherwise specified. The intention is to be able to interpret meta data that is stored in ordinary XML files as RDF. This would mean that just about any XML file could be interpreted as RDF meta data, by making every single element into an anonymous resource that is connected to its parent element.*

Summary

We have seen a number of different ways of expressing the value of a property:

- ❏ as a string literal
- ❏ as a URI which refers to a resource
- ❏ as well-formed XML
- ❏ as an anonymous resource with its own properties
- ❏ as a typed resource with its own properties

Containers

A **container** is simply a list, or collection, of resources. The collection might be a list of articles that make up a web site, or a list of authors who have contributed to an article. RDF has three different types of container – a bag, a sequence, and an alternative – and they can be used anywhere that the `<rdf:Description>` element can be used.

<rdf:Bag>

The simplest container is a **bag**, and it is used to contain multiple values for a property when there is no significance to the order in which the values are listed. The following shows the RDF syntax for a bag that enables more than one author to be specified for an article on the ePolitix web site:

```
<rdf:RDF>
  <rdf:Description
   rdf:about="http://www.ePolitix.com/Reviews/0000000012.htm">
    <dc:Creator>
      <rdf:Bag>
        <rdf:li
         rdf:resource="http://www.ePolitix.com/Authors/Bruno%20Waterfield"/>
        <rdf:li
         rdf:resource="http://www.ePolitix.com/Authors/Craig%20Hoy"/>
        <rdf:li
         rdf:resource="http://www.ePolitix.com/Authors/Chris%20Smith"/>
      </rdf:Bag>
    </dc:Creator>
  </rdf:Description>
</rdf:RDF>
```

The syntax for a bag is simply the enclosing element – `<rdf:Bag>` – followed by the list of resources in the bag. The members of the container are identified using `<rdf:li>` elements (so named because of the HTML "list item" tag), and although in this example they have resource attributes to indicate their value, they could also be string literals:

```
<rdf:RDF>
  <rdf:Description
   rdf:about="http://www.ePolitix.com/Articles/0000005a4787.htm">
    <dc:Subject>
      <rdf:Bag>
        <rdf:li>democracy</rdf:li>
        <rdf:li>voter apathy</rdf:li>
        <rdf:li>general election</rdf:li>
      </rdf:Bag>
    </dc:Subject>
  </rdf:Description>
</rdf:RDF>
```

Note that as far as the meta data in this example is concerned, the resource being referred to – the article .../Articles/0000005a4787.htm – only has *one* property, but that property (`<dc:Subject>`) is a container, holding three values. This is very different to not using a bag, and giving the resource three values:

```
<rdf:RDF>
  <rdf:Description
   rdf:about="http://www.ePolitix.com/Articles/0000005a4787.htm">
```

```
      <dc:Subject>democracy</dc:Subject>
      <dc:Subject>voter apathy</dc:Subject>
      <dc:Subject>general election</dc:Subject>
   </rdf:Description>
 </rdf:RDF>
```

This repeated properties syntax – in this case we have three occurrences of the same property – is modeled as follows:

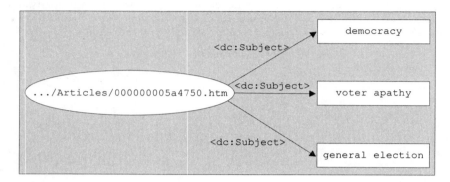

That is straightforward, and we have met it before. But the container syntax requires a resource to represent the bag that holds the values for the subject. This is modeled very differently, as follows:

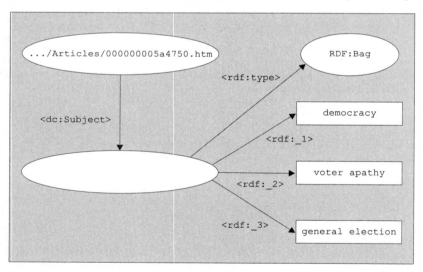

In this scenario – with <rdf:Bag> – we are saying that the resource *article* is connected to another resource *container,* and that this container has three items within it. In the previous diagram we were saying that the resource *article* is connected to three other items (in this case string literals), which are each subject values in their own right.

You may recall, when we were discussing anonymous resources, that I said there were a number of situations where an RDF parser would automatically create anonymous resources in order to correctly model your meta data. The processing of containers is one such situation. As you can see, an anonymous resource has automatically been created as a placeholder onto which the resource type can be added, as well as the string literals that represent the values.

You will have noticed that an RDF parser will also automatically name the predicates for the <rdf:li> values. If this were not the case then the above model would have looked like this, with each arc from the anonymous resource to the string literals labeled with <rdf:li>:

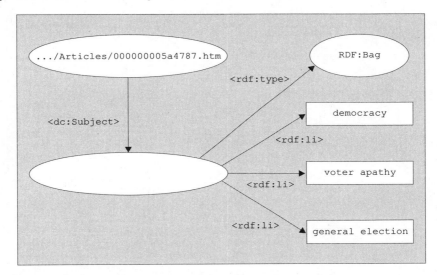

At first sight there seems nothing wrong with this, but recall that properties can be specified with attributes on a resource, just as easily as they can with child elements. This means that the above graph *should* be able to be represented something like this:

```
<rdf:Description
     rdf:about="http://www.ePolitix.com/Articles/0000005a4787.htm">
  <dc:Subject>
    <rdf:Bag
     rdf:li="democracy"
     rdf:li="voter apathy"
     rdf:li="general election"
    />
  </dc:Subject>
</rdf:Description>
```

Of course this is not possible though, since XML does not allow a repeat of an attribute with the same name. RDF/XML therefore allows us to use this syntax:

```
<rdf:Description
     rdf:about="http://www.ePolitix.com/Articles/0000005a4787.htm">
  <dc:Subject>
    <rdf:Bag
     rdf:_1="democracy"
     rdf:_2="voter apathy"
```

```
      rdf:_3="general election"
    />
  </dc:Subject>
</rdf:Description>
```

Whilst we only need to explicitly use these names if we are using the attribute syntax, by making the parser automatically create these names when using the element syntax, we can be sure that whichever format is used the model will be the same. The attribute syntax just used would create the following graph, which is exactly the same as our first example:

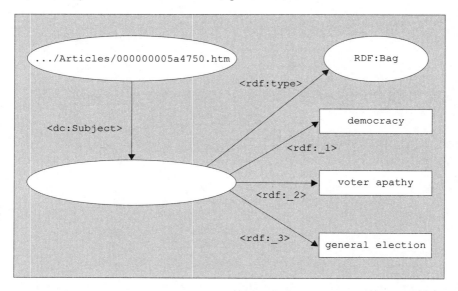

There's yet another way that this model can be expressed syntactically – so far we have used elements as children of an `<rdf:Bag>` element, and we have attached attributes to the `<rdf:Bag>` element – and that is to specify a `<rdf:type>` property on an `<rdf:Description>` element. I'm sure you spotted this possibility when you saw the graph, but we may as well spell this out. In this syntax we explicitly create an anonymous resource onto which we can attach a resource type and the three string literals:

```
<rdf:Description
    rdf:about="http://www.ePolitix.com/Articles/0000005a4787.htm">
  <dc:Subject>
    <rdf:Description>
      <rdf:type
            rdf:resource="http://www.w3.org/1999/02/22-rdf-syntax-ns#Bag" />
      <rdf:li>democracy</rdf:li>
      <rdf:li>voter apathy</rdf:li>
      <rdf:li>general election</rdf:li>
    </rdf:Description>
  </dc:Subject>
</rdf:Description>
```

As a little diversion, I'll just demonstrate that RDF is completely consistent, no matter where you start. Let's put aside all of the previous discussion on `<rdf:Bag>`, and begin with the idea that a container can be an anonymous resource:

```
  <rdf:Description
      rdf:about="http://www.ePolitix.com/Articles/0000005a4787.htm">
    <dc:Subject>
      <rdf:Description>
        ...
      </rdf:Description>
    </dc:Subject>
  </rdf:Description>
```

Let's treat this as a base class onto which we will build. Just as in object-oriented programming you might have an abstract notion of a container that is then refined to produce lists, sequences, arrays, and so on, so too we will give this abstract container a type:

```
<rdf:Description
      rdf:about="http://www.ePolitix.com/Articles/0000005a4787.htm">
  <dc:Subject>
    <rdf:Description>
      <rdf:type
          rdf:resource="http://www.w3.org/1999/02/22-rdf-syntax-ns#Bag" />
      ...
    </rdf:Description>
  </dc:Subject>
</rdf:Description>
```

We'll also throw in the `<rdf:li>` property to allow us to add as many members to the collection as we want:

```
<rdf:Description
      rdf:about="http://www.ePolitix.com/Articles/0000005a4787.htm">
  <dc:Subject>
    <rdf:Description>
      <rdf:type
          rdf:resource="http://www.w3.org/1999/02/22-rdf-syntax-ns#Bag" />
      <rdf:li>democracy</rdf:li>
      <rdf:li>voter apathy</rdf:li>
      <rdf:li>general election</rdf:li>
    </rdf:Description>
  </dc:Subject>
</rdf:Description>
```

Note that this time we have started with the expanded syntax, directly corresponding to the figure that we saw earlier. Now, let's use the abbreviated format where we can create typed nodes by using the type value of an `<rdf:Description>` as the namespace qualified element name:

```
<rdf:Description
      rdf:about="http://www.ePolitix.com/Articles/0000005a4787.htm">
  <dc:Subject>
    <rdf:Bag>
      <rdf:li>democracy</rdf:li>
      <rdf:li>voter apathy</rdf:li>
      <rdf:li>general election</rdf:li>
    </rdf:Bag>
  </dc:Subject>
</rdf:Description>
```

Which is where we came in! Recognizing that containers are essentially typed nodes is not integral to understanding containers, but it does illustrate the consistency within the RDF model and its corresponding syntax. As you can see we can move backwards and forwards from model to syntax, making abbreviations here and adding detail there – with no loss of meaning.

<rdf:Seq>

Whilst the contents of `<rdf:Bags>` are unordered – that is, there is no implied order to the contents and any software processing the list can treat them in whatever order it likes – there will always be a need for ordered lists of resources, or **sequences**. Such lists can be created using the `<rdf:Seq>` element. Let's create a list of the articles that appear in the election section of the ePolitix web site:

```
<rdf:RDF>
  <rdf:Description rdf:about="http://www.ePolitix.com/Sections/election">
    <xyz:Contents>
      <rdf:Seq>
        <rdf:li
         rdf:resource="http://www.ePolitix.com/Articles/0000005A47F1.htm"/>
        <rdf:li
         rdf:resource="http://www.ePolitix.com/Articles/0000005A47F2.htm"/>
        <rdf:li
         rdf:resource="http://www.ePolitix.com/Articles/0000005A47F3.htm"/>
        <rdf:li
         rdf:resource="http://www.ePolitix.com/Articles/0000005A47F4.htm"/>
        <rdf:li
         rdf:resource="http://www.ePolitix.com/Articles/0000005A47F5.htm"/>
        <rdf:li
         rdf:resource="http://www.ePolitix.com/Articles/0000005A47F6.htm"/>
        <rdf:li
         rdf:resource="http://www.ePolitix.com/Articles/0000005A47F7.htm"/>
      </rdf:Seq>
    </xyz:Contents>
  </rdf:Description>
</rdf:RDF>
```

As before, we are simply saying that the `<rdf:type>` of the element `<xyz:Contents>` is `<rdf:Seq>`. However, this time we are saying to any software that processes this RDF, that the order of the articles in the contents container is important.

<rdf:Alt>

Whilst `<rdf:Bag>` and `<rdf:Seq>` provide us with a way of creating lists of resources, it is also useful to be able to provide a selection from which any one resource can be chosen, in other words **alternative** options. The `<rdf:Alt>` container is a means by which a number of resources can be specified which are deemed to be equivalent. A processor of the RDF can then choose one of these based on whatever criteria seem applicable.

For example, the ePolitix web site might have different language versions of the same article. The absolute URL of the article may stay the same – to assist when moving our meta data around – but a container could be created with other articles that could be deemed to be equivalent. Some software engine might then map all hyperlinks within the ePolitix site to the correct language version of the article:

```
<rdf:RDF>
  <rdf:Description
   rdf:about="http://www.ePolitix.com/Articles/0000000054E8.htm">
    <xyz:Translations>
      <rdf:Alt>
        <rdf:li
         rdf:resource="http://www.ePolitix.com/Articles/0000005A47F1.htm"/>
        <rdf:li
         rdf:resource="http://www.ePolitix.com/Articles/Italian/5A47F1.htm"/>
        <rdf:li
         rdf:resource="http://www.ePolitix.com/Articles/French/5A47F1.htm"/>
      </rdf:Alt>
    </xyz:Translations>
  </rdf:Description>
</rdf:RDF>
```

Note that I have included the English version of the article in the `<rdf:Alt>` list. This is because the first item in the list of alternatives is deemed to be the default and preferred selection. If I didn't include it then the default would become the Italian version. As it happens, in this case that is completely application-dependent, and we could just as easily have left the English version out and just not processed the alternatives if we were dealing with English users. I mention it because there is a more significant point, which is that the consequence of the first item in the list being the default means that an `<rdf:Alt>` *must always contain at least one member*.

`<rdf:li>`

So far we have seen two ways that the `<rdf:li>` element is used to identify the items in a container. The first was to simply contain a string literal, whilst the second was to refer to some external resource. Since both of these ways of declaring an item in a container are similar to the syntax alternatives available when specifying property elements, you may well have wondered whether we can use the other syntax alternatives, such as nesting `<rdf:Description>`s or using `parseType="Literal"` attributes.

Well, your intuition was right. We can indeed use any of the forms available to us when specifying property elements, the only difference being that if we want to add further properties to the collection member we either have to use the `parseType="Resource"` attribute that we discussed earlier, or nest an `<rdf:Description>` element. Let's look at a few examples.

The first example shows how we might embed some translated XHTML into our RDF document:

```
<rdf:RDF>
  <rdf:Description rdf:about="http://www.w3.org/Metadata/">
    <xyz:Translations>
      <rdf:Alt>
        <rdf:li parseType="Literal" xmlns:lang="en">
          <h1>Metadata and Resource Description</h1>
        </rdf:li>
        <rdf:li parseType="Literal" xmlns:lang="fr">
          <h1>Metadata et description de resource</h1>
        </rdf:li>
      </rdf:Alt>
    </xyz:Translations>
  </rdf:Description>
</rdf:RDF>
```

Note that I have used the `xml:lang` attribute on the `<rdf:li>` element. However, I tend to avoid doing this since this attribute does not create a triple, and many processors will ignore this attribute. The correct approach, as outlined in the spec, is for the language to be stored as part of the literal – although this is open to a great deal of interpretation, as to what that means. To be safe, if this information were important then you would need to add it to the main meta data.

The next example shows how we might add information to the illustration we had in the `<rdf:Bag>` section – where an article was written by a number of people – by nesting `<rdf:Description>` elements:

```
<rdf:Description rdf:about="/Articles/0000000054C4.htm">
  <dc:Creator>
    <rdf:Bag>
      <rdf:li>
        <rdf:Description rdf:about="/Authors/Bruno%20Waterfield">
          <v:Email>Bruno.Waterfield@ePolitix.com</v:Email>
        </rdf:Description>
      </rdf:li>

      <rdf:li>
        <rdf:Description rdf:about="/Authors/Craig%20Hoy">
          <v:Email>Craig.Hoy@ePolitix.com</v:Email>
        </rdf:Description>
      </rdf:li>

      <rdf:li>
        <rdf:Description rdf:about="/Authors/Chris%20Smith">
          <v:Email>Chris.Smith@ePolitix.com</v:Email>
        </rdf:Description>
      </rdf:li>
    </rdf:Bag>
  </dc:Creator>
</rdf:Description>
```

The final format is to use the `<rdf:li>` element to create a resource, and then add properties to that. Of course the resource will not be accessible from anywhere else, since it will be anonymous. Adding properties to an `<rdf:li>` anonymous resource can be achieved by using the `parseType="Resource"`, as follows:

```
<rdf:Description rdf:about="/Articles/0000000054C4.htm">
  <dc:Creator>
    <rdf:Bag>
      <rdf:li parseType="Resource">
        <v:Email>Bruno.Waterfield@ePolitix.com</v:Email>
      </rdf:li>

      <rdf:li parseType="Resource">
        <v:Email>Craig.Hoy@ePolitix.com</v:Email>
      </rdf:li>

      <rdf:li parseType="Resource">
        <v:Email>Chris.Smith@ePolitix.com</v:Email>
      </rdf:li>
    </rdf:Bag>
  </dc:Creator>
</rdf:Description>
```

> Don't forget that if you don't use the `parseType="Resource"` then the parser will think that it has a typed node, that is, the abbreviated form of an `<rdf:Description>` that has an `rdf:type` attribute set to indicate its type.

The rdf:ID Attribute on Containers

Although we have tended to create anonymous resources for our collections, there will be situations where we want to make statements about the collection in just the same way that we make statements about any other resource. Let's go back to a shortened version of the contents page that we created for the election section of the ePolitix web site:

```
<rdf:Description rdf:about="http://www.ePolitix.com/Sections/election">
  <xyz:Contents>
    <rdf:Seq>
      <rdf:li
        rdf:resource="http://www.ePolitix.com/Articles/0000005A47F1.htm"/>
      <rdf:li
        rdf:resource="http://www.ePolitix.com/Articles/0000005A47F2.htm"/>
      <rdf:li
        rdf:resource="http://www.ePolitix.com/Articles/0000005A47F3.htm"/>
    </rdf:Seq>
  </xyz:Contents>
</rdf:Description>
```

Instead of just specifying one section in this document, let's use it to express all the sections, noting that it is perfectly legitimate to have a container within another container, but that we need to use the `<rdf:li>` element to achieve this nesting:

```
<rdf:Description rdf:about="http://www.ePolitix.com/Sections">
  <xyz:Contents>
    <rdf:Bag>
      <rdf:li>
        <rdf:Seq rdf:ID="election">
          <rdf:li
          rdf:resource="http://www.ePolitix.com/Articles/0000005A47F1.htm"/>
          <rdf:li
          rdf:resource="http://www.ePolitix.com/Articles/0000000054E8.htm"/>
          <rdf:li
          rdf:resource="http://www.ePolitix.com/Articles/0000000054C0.htm"/>
        </rdf:Seq>
      </rdf:li>

      <rdf:li>
        <rdf:Seq rdf:ID="news">
          <rdf:li
          rdf:resource="http://www.ePolitix.com/Articles/000000005527.htm"/>
          <rdf:li
          rdf:resource="http://www.ePolitix.com/Articles/000000005513.htm"/>
          <rdf:li
          rdf:resource="http://www.ePolitix.com/Articles/000000005526.htm"/>
        </rdf:Seq>
      </rdf:li>

      <rdf:li>
        <rdf:Seq rdf:ID="people">
          <rdf:li
            rdf:resource="http://www.ePolitix.com/People/000000005474.htm"/>
```

```
            <rdf:li
              rdf:resource="http://www.ePolitix.com/People/00000000552B.htm"/>
            <rdf:li
              rdf:resource="http://www.ePolitix.com/People/00000000551F.htm"/>
          </rdf:Seq>
        </rdf:li>
      </rdf:Bag>
    </xyz:Contents>
  </rdf:Description>
```

Now that we have added `rdf:ID` attributes to each bag, we can reference the containers just like any other resource. We might indicate what order the sections should appear in when shown inside a menu, for example:

```
<rdf:Description rdf:about="http://www.ePolitix.com/MainMenu">
  <xyz:Menu>
    <rdf:Seq>
      <rdf:li rdf:resource="#people"/>
      <rdf:li rdf:resource="#election"/>
      <rdf:li rdf:resource="#news"/>
    </rdf:Seq>
  </xyz:Menu>
</rdf:Description>
```

We might also indicate the e-mail address for readers' enquiries, which could then be displayed on each contents page:

```
<rdf:RDF>
  <rdf:Description rdf:about="#election">
    <v:Email>election@ePolitix.com</v:Email>
  </rdf:Description>

  <rdf:Description rdf:about="#news">
    <v:Email>news@ePolitix.com</v:Email>
  </rdf:Description>

  <rdf:Description rdf:about="#people">
    <v:Email>people@ePolitix.com</v:Email>
  </rdf:Description>
</rdf:RDF>
```

The aboutEach Attribute

The `rdf:ID` attribute that we have attached to a container has allowed us to make statements about that container. However, there may be situations where we want to make statements not about the container but the *members* of the container.

You may recall that when we were discussing nesting statements in the section on `<rdf:Description>`, we speculated on whether a certain meta data model could be abbreviated further. Let's go back to that example to see how this might be done. The model is as follows:

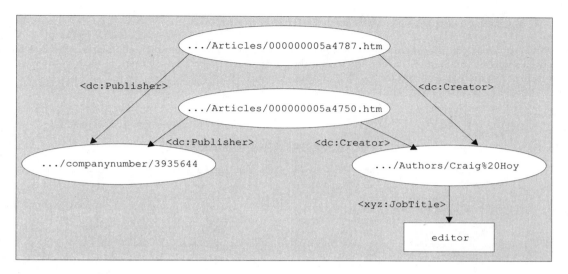

The syntax for this model is this:

```
<rdf:RDF>
  <rdf:Description
   rdf:about="http://www.ePolitix.com/Articles/0000005a4787.htm">
    <dc:Creator rdf:resource="http://www.ePolitix.com/Authors/Craig%20Hoy"/>
    <dc:Publisher
     rdf:resource="http://www.CorpInfo.org/companynumber/3935644"/>
  </rdf:Description>

  <rdf:Description
   rdf:about="http://www.ePolitix.com/Articles/0000005a4750.htm">
    <dc:Creator rdf:resource="http://www.ePolitix.com/Authors/Craig%20Hoy"/>
    <dc:Publisher
     rdf:resource="http://www.CorpInfo.org/companynumber/3935644"/>
  </rdf:Description>

  <rdf:Description rdf:about="http://www.ePolitix.com/Authors/Craig%20Hoy">
    <xyz:JobTitle>editor</xyz:JobTitle>
  </rdf:Description>
</rdf:RDF>
```

Intuitively we felt that we must be able to abbreviate this syntax further, since each article has the same publisher and the same author, and indeed we can. The first step is to create a bag that contains the two articles being referred to and give the bag an identifier so that we can make statements about it:

```
<rdf:RDF>
  <rdf:Bag rdf:ID="articles">
    <rdf:li
        rdf:resource="http://www.ePolitix.com/Articles/0000005a4787.htm" />
    <rdf:li
        rdf:resource="http://www.ePolitix.com/Articles/0000005a4750.htm" />
  </rdf:Bag>
</rdf:RDF>
```

Note that a container is an acceptable top-level element in RDF.

Now we can use a different attribute on the `<rdf:Description>` element, called `aboutEach`, which applies whatever statements are made within the `<rdf:Description>` element to each of the resources in the bag referred to:

```
<rdf:RDF>
  <rdf:Bag rdf:ID="articles">
    <rdf:li
         rdf:resource="http://www.ePolitix.com/Articles/0000005a4787.htm" />
    <rdf:li
         rdf:resource="http://www.ePolitix.com/Articles/0000005a4750.htm" />
  </rdf:Bag>

  <rdf:Description aboutEach="#articles">
    <dc:Creator rdf:resource="http://www.ePolitix.com/Authors/Craig%20Hoy"/>
    <dc:Publisher
     rdf:resource="http://www.CorpInfo.org/companynumber/3935644"/>
  </rdf:Description>
</rdf:RDF>
```

As you can imagine, the real power of this syntax comes when the bag is filled with hundreds – or even thousands – of articles. But bear in mind that the only abbreviation we are getting here is in the syntax. The model is *exactly the same* as if each of the statements about each of the articles had been made separately. The `aboutEach` attribute does not create anything special in the model. Instead it simply acts as if the statements within the `<rdf:Description>` element were applied one at a time across each member of the container referred to. For this reason the `aboutEach` attribute is called a **distributive referent**.

In other words, when you look at the model produced – whether a graph or triples – there would be no indication that `aboutEach` had been used in the source. In our example here, the only difference between the model produced in the earlier scenario and this one is that the latter has a resource for the bag. However, please note that the `<dc:Creator>` and `<dc:Publisher>` properties are not attached to the bag, they are attached to each member individually, so the existence of the bag is irrelevant as far as the model of the meta data is concerned.

This doesn't mean that some RDF processor could not store the fact that the statements created originated with a distributive referent. How triples and other information are stored is not defined in the specification. What we are saying is that if some system comes to query the meta data store, it should be able to query as if the statements were made individually. The fact that there is no clearly defined way to implement the `aboutEach` attribute means that most current parsers don't implement it.

The aboutEachPrefix Attribute

The final attribute that can be applied to an `<rdf:Description>` element is `aboutEachPrefix`. This attribute is also a distributive referent, but this time the distribution takes place across any resource that begins with the specified characters. For example, to indicate that anything that appears on the ePolitix web site is published by Parliamentary Communications Ltd., we could use this syntax:

```
<rdf:Description aboutEachPrefix="http://www.ePolitix.com/">
  <dc:Publisher
   rdf:resource="http://www.CorpInfo.org/companynumber/3935644"/>
</rdf:Description>
```

The model for this is an anonymous bag, which contains all of the resources that begin with the specified prefix. The statements that are in the `<rdf:Description>` element are being made about each of the resources in this anonymous bag.

Summary

In this section we looked at the containers that RDF provides, which are:

- bags
- sequences
- alternatives

We also looked at how the members of a container can contain any of the formats from the RDF syntax that can appear in other parts of an RDF document. Finally, we looked at ways that we can make statements about all resources in a collection, rather than just the collection itself.

Statements about Statements

The final area of the RDF Model and Syntax specification that we need to discuss concerns what we called in our introduction *meta-meta data*. Just as RDF provides us with facilities to make statements about resources it also provides us with a way of making statements about other statements.

Much of what follows may seem largely esoteric, and often seems irrelevant to most real-world uses of meta data after all, most of us are used to dealing with search engines and ratings systems but that may well be the extent of our experience of meta data. Never the less, recall that the aim of RDF is to be a model for meta data in all its forms. Just as much as it provides us with a framework within which we can say that:

> the rating for the ePolitix website is 100

so too it must be able to cope with a statement such as:

> the web ranking service says that:
> the rating for the ePolitix website is 100

This is not the same as chaining together a series of statements. At first sight it looks like we are saying nothing very different to what we have done in the rest of this chapter, where the resource that is the subject of one statement is the object of another statement, but just as in mathematics this:

> $(5 + 7) * 6$

yields a different result to this:

> $5 + (7 * 6)$

so too we have a world of difference between:

> the web ranking service says that
> there is a rating
> which refers to the ePolitix website
> and has a value of 100

and:

> the web ranking service says (X)

with X itself being an entire statement.

Why might you want to make the distinction? Well there are a number of reasons. The first and most obvious is the one that we have just seen, where some information is provided by a third party and we want to record the source of that information. We have a statement about the ePolitix web site – that it has a ranking of 100 – and we want to record who made that statement. We might also want to record when that statement was made and how long it is valid for. We may even want to record the statement for posterity, so that even if next week the ranking of the ePolitix web site changed to 90, we still had a record somewhere that said, that on some particular day, "the web ranking service said that ePolitix had a rank of 100".

The ability to make statements about statements is also important for other fields beyond ranking web sites or creating archives of statements. One obvious example is security. What if we wanted to transport some statements that contained election results? We know from our knowledge of RDF how to encode statements that say "the winner in Great Grimsby is Austin Mitchell" but how does anyone know whether to trust that statement? We need to be able to say that "the originator of this election result is the returning officer, and here is their security ID".

Other areas worth mentioning are those of knowledge management and logic. RDF provides a means to model knowledge as a set of meta data. However, to make that knowledge useful, we may need to qualify that in some way. For example, if you created meta data that reflected someone's beliefs, you would also want some meta data to indicate the status of those beliefs. I may believe that the world is flat or that I am a good dancer – and these statements can be modeled easily in RDF, but your knowledge system wants to store what I *believe* to be true as a belief, not a fact. You don't want to store the statement "the world is flat" or "Mark is a good dancer" – rather you want to store "Mark *believes* the world is flat" and "Mark *believes* that he is a good dancer".

In RDF terms, what all of these examples require is the ability to make statements about statements, and RDF adds some extra features to make this easier.

It would seem at first glance that all we need do is give a statement an identifier, and then we have the facility to make second-level statements about it – it would seem that ordinary RDF syntax is sufficient.

The problem with this, particularly for the world of knowledge representation, is that the statement that you are making statements about may not actually exist. Let's take the example we gave earlier – I want to record that I believe the world is flat, but I don't want to record that the world *is* flat.

We might at first think that I could use the following RDF syntax to express this:

```
<rdf:RDF>
  <rdf:Description rdf:about="#MarkBirbeck">
    <xyz:Believes rdf:resource="#fact" />
  </rdf:Description>

  <rdf:Description rdf:ID="fact">
    <xyz:Belief>
      <rdf:Description rdf:about="#world">
        <xyz:shape>flat</xyz:shape>
```

```
          </rdf:Description>
        </xyz:Belief>
      </rdf:Description>
    </rdf:RDF>
```

Alternatively, I might decide to just group what it is that I believe inside an `<rdf:Bag>`, rather than inventing an element to contain it:

```
<rdf:RDF>
  <rdf:Description rdf:about="#MarkBirbeck">
    <xyz:Believes rdf:resource="#fact" />
  </rdf:Description>

  <rdf:Bag rdf:ID="fact">
    <rdf:li>
      <rdf:Description rdf:about="#world">
        <xyz:shape>flat</xyz:shape>
      </rdf:Description>
    </rdf:li>
  </rdf:Bag>
</rdf:RDF>
```

Whichever approach we take, the problem is we are left at the end with an unfortunate by-product; our meta data model contains the statement that the world is flat, which we know is wrong. That's not to say that we would never model data that is incorrect – RDF is only a human creation, after all – it's just that in our example we never *intended* to say anything about the world, or its shape; we were only trying to store what *I believed*. To make this clear, look at the triples produced by this statement, and note the last triple:

```
{ [#MarkBirbeck], [xyz:Believes], [#fact] }
{
    [http://www.w3.org/1999/02/22-rdf-syntax-ns#type],
    [#fact],
    [http://www.w3.org/1999/02/22-rdf-syntax-ns#Bag]
}
{
    [http://www.w3.org/1999/02/22-rdf-syntax-ns#_1],
    [#fact],
    [#world]
}
{ [#world], [xyz:shape], "flat" }
```

If this example doesn't convince you, imagine that you are using RDF in some publishing system to hold information about processes. I have checked the spelling on my document and the system needs to record this. However, just as storing the statement *believed* by me has the consequence of creating the statement that the person believes, so too in this case – if we try to model that I believe that the document is spelled correctly, we end up with a statement that says that the document *is* spelled correctly.

It's not just this spurious statement that is a problem. If you look at the triples again, you will see that the first is OK, since it simply says that I believe the resource identified by "fact". However, the bag identified by "fact" is actually connected to the resource "world", not the entire statement. What we need is a way of grouping the parts of a statement together as one unit, and then making our statement about that unit. We also need to avoid creating a "real" statement, when all we want is the *model* of the statement.

RDF addresses these problems through a process called **reification**.

Reification

A reified statement is simply a representation of a statement, rather than the statement itself. We can create a model of my mistaken belief, as follows (assuming that "`http://xyz.com#`" is the namespace for xyz):

```
<rdf:RDF>
  <rdf:Description>
    <rdf:subject rdf:resource="#world" />
    <rdf:predicate rdf:resource="http://xyz.com#shape" />
    <rdf:object>flat</rdf:object>
    <rdf:type rdf:resource="http://www.w3.org/1999/02/22-rdf-syntax-
      ns#Statement" />
  </rdf:Description>
</rdf:RDF>
```

As you can see, RDF syntax has given us three more properties that we can use to specify the subject, predicate, and object of a statement. There's also a new type added with which we can indicate the type of the resource, `<rdf:Statement>`. I'm sure I don't need to spell it out, but the type information can also be expressed like this:

```
<rdf:RDF>
  <rdf:Statement>
    <rdf:subject rdf:resource="#world" />
    <rdf:predicate rdf:resource="http://xyz.com#shape" />
    <rdf:object>flat</rdf:object>
  </rdf:Statement>
</rdf:RDF>
```

As you can see from the triples produced, we no longer have a statement about the shape of the world; instead we have a *representation of a statement* about the shape of the world:

```
{
    [local#fact],
    [http://www.w3.org/1999/02/22-rdf-syntax-ns#subject],
    [#world]
}
{
    [local#fact],
    [http://www.w3.org/1999/02/22-rdf-syntax-ns#predicate],
    [http://xyz.com#shape]
}
{
    [local#fact],
    [http://www.w3.org/1999/02/22-rdf-syntax-ns#object],
    "flat"
}
{
    [local#fact],
    [http://www.w3.org/1999/02/22-rdf-syntax-ns#type],
    [http://www.w3.org/1999/02/22-rdf-syntax-ns#Statement]
}
```

Now that we have this statement, we can do with it whatever we can do with any other resource. In particular we want to say that I believe this statement to be true:

```
<rdf:RDF>
  <rdf:Description rdf:about="#MarkBirbeck">
    <xyz:Believes rdf:resource="#fact" />
  </rdf:Description>

  <rdf:Statement rdf:ID="fact">
    <rdf:subject rdf:resource="#world" />
    <rdf:predicate rdf:resource="http://xyz.com#shape" />
    <rdf:object>flat</rdf:object>
  </rdf:Statement>
</rdf:RDF>
```

One new triple is generated:

```
{ [#MarkBirbeck], [xyz:Believes], [#fact] }
```

For completeness here is the graph of our syntax:

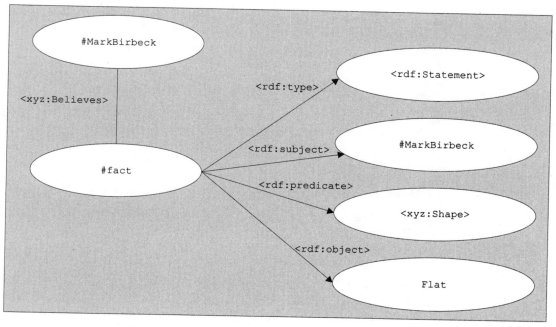

It's all very well dealing with the case of making statements about mistaken beliefs, but what of statements about things we believe are true? In this case we would want both the reified statement, *and* the original statement of fact. Let's develop an example.

When articles are entered into the ePolitix publishing system they are categorized:

```
<rdf:Description rdf:about="http://www.ePolitix.com/Articles/0000005a4787.htm">
  <dc:Creator>Craig Hoy</dc:Creator>
  <dc:Subject rdf:resource="http://www.iptc.org/SubjectCodes#10101010" />
  <dc:Subject rdf:resource="http://www.iptc.org/SubjectCodes#10101011" />
  <dc:Subject rdf:resource="http://www.iptc.org/SubjectCodes#10101012" />
</rdf:Description>
```

However, more than one person can categorize the article, depending on their particular area of expertise. Let's say that we want to keep track of who added which category to an article. The first thing we would need to do is create reified statements that model the statements we have made about the subject codes. This will give us something to refer to:

```
<rdf:RDF>
    <rdf:Description
        about="http://www.ePolitix.com/Articles/0000005a4787.htm">
        <dc:Creator>Craig Hoy</dc:Creator>
        <dc:Subject rdf:resource="http://www.iptc.org/SubjectCodes#10101010" />
        <dc:Subject rdf:resource="http://www.iptc.org/SubjectCodes#10101011" />
        <dc:Subject rdf:resource="http://www.iptc.org/SubjectCodes#10101012" />
    </rdf:Description>

    <rdf:Statement rdf:ID="subject1">
        <rdf:subject
         rdf:resource="http://www.ePolitix.com/Articles/0000005a4787.htm" />
        <rdf:predicate
            rdf:resource="http://purl.org/metadata/dublin_core#Subject" />
        <rdf:object rdf:resource="http://www.iptc.org/SubjectCodes#10101010" />
    </rdf:Statement>

    <rdf:Statement rdf:ID="subject2">
        <rdf:subject
         rdf:resource="http://www.ePolitix.com/Articles/0000005a4787.htm" />
        <rdf:predicate
            rdf:resource="http://purl.org/metadata/dublin_core#Subject" />
        <rdf:object rdf:resource="http://www.iptc.org/SubjectCodes#10101011" />
    </rdf:Statement>

    <rdf:Statement rdf:ID="subject3">
        <rdf:subject
         rdf:resource="http://www.ePolitix.com/Articles/0000005a4787.htm" />
        <rdf:predicate
            rdf:resource="http://purl.org/metadata/dublin_core#Subject" />
        <rdf:object rdf:resource="http://www.iptc.org/SubjectCodes#10101012" />
    </rdf:Statement>
</rdf:RDF>
```

Now we can add our statements *about* these reified statements:

```
<rdf:RDF>
  <rdf:Description
   rdf:about="http://www.ePolitix.com/Articles/0000005a4787.htm">
    <dc:Creator>Craig Hoy</dc:Creator>
    <dc:Subject rdf:resource="http://www.iptc.org/SubjectCodes#10101010" />
    <dc:Subject rdf:resource="http://www.iptc.org/SubjectCodes#10101011" />
    <dc:Subject rdf:resource="http://www.iptc.org/SubjectCodes#10101012" />
  </rdf:Description>

  <rdf:Statement rdf:ID="subject1">
    <rdf:subject
     rdf:resource="http://www.ePolitix.com/Articles/0000005a4787.htm" />
    <rdf:predicate
        rdf:resource="http://purl.org/metadata/dublin_core#Subject" />
```

```
      <rdf:object rdf:resource="http://www.iptc.org/SubjectCodes#10101010" />
    </rdf:Statement>

    <rdf:Statement rdf:ID="subject2">
      <rdf:subject
        rdf:resource="http://www.ePolitix.com/Articles/0000005a4787.htm" />
      <rdf:predicate
          rdf:resource="http://purl.org/metadata/dublin_core#Subject" />
      <rdf:object rdf:resource="http://www.iptc.org/SubjectCodes#10101011" />
    </rdf:Statement>

    <rdf:Statement rdf:ID="subject3">
      <rdf:subject
        rdf:resource="http://www.ePolitix.com/Articles/0000005a4787.htm" />
      <rdf:predicate
          rdf:resource="http://purl.org/metadata/dublin_core#Subject" />
      <rdf:object rdf:resource="http://www.iptc.org/SubjectCodes#10101012" />
    </rdf:Statement>

    <rdf:Description rdf:about="#subject1">
      <dc:Creator>Craig Hoy</dc:Creator>
    </rdf:Description>

    <rdf:Description rdf:about="#subject2">
      <dc:Creator>Craig Hoy</dc:Creator>
    </rdf:Description>

    <rdf:Description rdf:about="#subject3">
      <dc:Creator>Craig Hoy</dc:Creator>
    </rdf:Description>
  </rdf:RDF>
```

We've achieved what we set out to do, which is to attribute various statements about the subject matter to the person who actually set that category. Since the category is valid for the article, regardless of who set it, then we also have the actual statement of fact to sit alongside our reified version.

If you are feeling that this may be a little long-winded, then you are right, but there is also another problem besides verbosity. Notably, there is a direct correlation between each statement of fact and a reified version. Any changes or additions to the subject codes in the first description element would need to be reflected in our reified statements. It is not like our example earlier where the statement that I believed – that the world is flat – did not exist in our version of truth, but the statement that *I believed that statement* was in our world-view. In fact, here the situation is almost the opposite in that for every real statement there must be a matching reified statement, and there must be no reified statements for which there is not a real statement. In other words, we do not want a statement:

Craig Hoy was responsible for the fact that article x has subject code y

if article "x" no longer has subject code "y". Of course, if you were tracking the history of changes to the meta data about a document, then you may well retain the reified statements, even after the subject codes have been changed. This would take us back to our Mark believes scenario – the fact that we have a statement that says:

On Monday Craig Hoy set the subject code of article x to the value y does not imply that the subject code for the article *is* "y", since on Tuesday someone might have deleted it. Anyway, let's stick with the example in which we want there to be a reified statement for every ordinary statement. RDF syntax has a neat way to achieve this using one final attribute on the `<rdf:Description>` element – `bagID`.

The bagID Attribute

The `bagID` attribute does not replace any of the other attributes that can appear on an `<rdf:Description>` element, but sits alongside them. The reason for this is that the `<rdf:Description>` element still needs to do its main job of reflecting statements about a resource – and so still needs the attributes `rdf:ID`, `rdf:about`, `aboutEach`, and so on. Instead, adding a `bagID` effectively says, create an `<rdf:Bag>` element, give it the `rdf:ID` specified, and then fill it with a reification of each of the statements in the `<rdf:Description>` element.

We could therefore create all the statements and reified statements for Craig in one go, with the more convenient syntax that follows:

```
<rdf:Description
 rdf:about="http://www.ePolitix.com/Articles/0000005a4787.htm"
 bagID="reify"
>
   <dc:Subject rdf:resource="http://www.iptc.org/SubjectCodes#10101011" />
   <dc:Subject rdf:resource="http://www.iptc.org/SubjectCodes#10101012" />
</rdf:Description>
```

This is an extremely convenient abbreviation, and you will use it a lot if you enter the world of meta-meta data! So, to make sure that we are completely clear on what is being stated, the shortened form we have just seen is completely equivalent to:

```
<rdf:RDF>
  <rdf:Description
   rdf:about="http://www.ePolitix.com/Articles/0000005a4787.htm"
   bagID="reify"
  >
    <dc:Subject rdf:resource="http://www.iptc.org/SubjectCodes#10101011" />
    <dc:Subject rdf:resource="http://www.iptc.org/SubjectCodes#10101012" />
  </rdf:Description>

  <rdf:Bag rdf:ID="reify">
    <rdf:li>
      <rdf:Statement>
        <rdf:subject
         rdf:resource="http://www.ePolitix.com/Articles/0000005a4787.htm" />
        <rdf:predicate
         rdf:resource="http://purl.org/metadata/dublin_core#Subject" />
        <rdf:object
             rdf:resource="http://www.iptc.org/SubjectCodes#10101011" />
      </rdf:Statement>
    </rdf:li>

    <rdf:li>
      <rdf:Statement>
        <rdf:subject
         rdf:resource="http://www.ePolitix.com/Articles/0000005a4787.htm" />
        <rdf:predicate
         rdf:resource="http://purl.org/metadata/dublin_core#Subject" />
        <rdf:object
```

```
                rdf:resource="http://www.iptc.org/SubjectCodes#10101012" />
          </rdf:Statement>
        </rdf:li>
      </rdf:Bag>
    </rdf:RDF>
```

And if you spotted the other convenience provided by the abbreviation, then you are a fully-qualified RDF master; we can now use aboutEach when making statements about these statements. Recall that Craig was responsible for the two statements about the subject codes of the article in question. We can state this in the following way:

```
<rdf:Description aboutEach="reify">
  <dc:Creator>Craig Hoy</dc:Creator>
</rdf:Description>
```

Since we were only showing the <rdf:Bag> element to make it clear what was happening behind the scenes when we used the bagID, let's finish off by showing the fully abbreviated syntax for the statements that Craig has made about the subject codes of the article:

```
<rdf:RDF>
  <rdf:Description
   rdf:about="http://www.ePolitix.com/Articles/0000005a4787.htm"
   bagID="reify"
  >
    <dc:Subject rdf:resource="http://www.iptc.org/SubjectCodes#10101011" />
    <dc:Subject rdf:resource="http://www.iptc.org/SubjectCodes#10101012" />
  </rdf:Description>

  <rdf:Description aboutEach="reify">
    <dc:Creator>Craig Hoy</dc:Creator>
  </rdf:Description>
</rdf:RDF>
```

Although the bag is implied by the use of the bagID attribute but not explicitly declared, we can still use aboutEach to distribute our statements across the bag. Also, along with the advantages of using this compact syntax, we have the ease of maintaining only the original statements with all reifications being produced "behind the scenes".

Summary

In this section we looked at the facilities RDF provides that allow us to make statements about statements. We looked at:

- ❑ Reification, which creates a model of a statement.
- ❑ The bagID attribute, which automatically causes statements to be reified.

Summary

We have seen how RDF models meta data, using the key concept of triples to represent statements that are made about resources. We also saw how RDF provides a syntax for representing this model in an XML format. Much of the promise of the Web hinges on being able to communicate meta data between systems as well as indicating who is responsible for a particular set of meta data. Both of these requirements can be met through RDF, and so the wider adoption of this standard points towards a more powerful and flexible Internet.

In the next chapter we will look at how schemas can be expressed with RDF, before going on to discuss some of the implementation issues that arise when trying to parse RDF in Chapter 6.

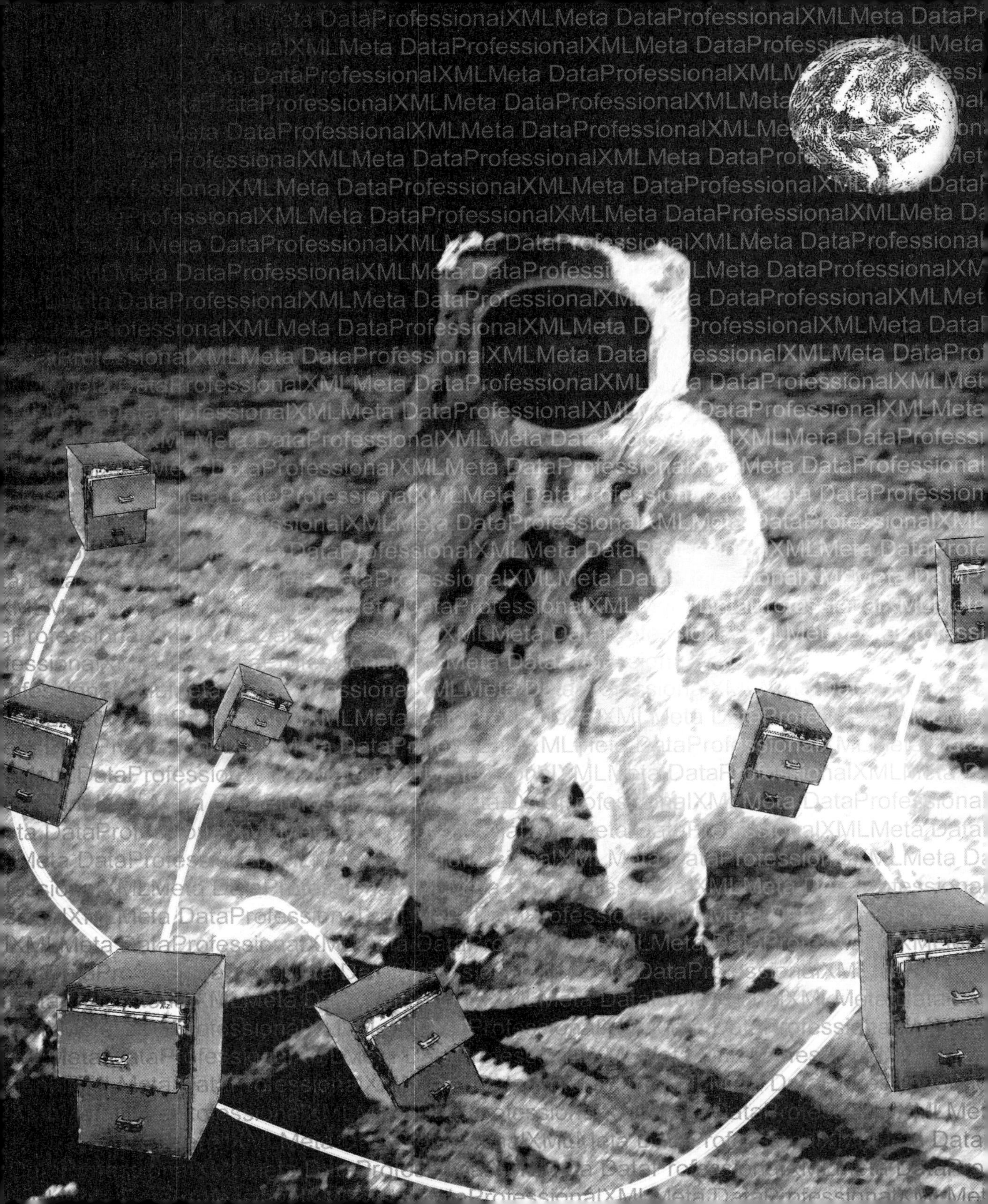
DataProfessionalXMLMeta DataProfessionalXMLMeta

5

RDF Schema

Now that we have got to grips with the XML syntax for conveying meta data as RDF, we can go on to look at how we might check the validity of this data. This is achieved using **RDF Schema,** which is defined by the W3C at http://www.w3.org/TR/2000/CR-rdf-schema-20000327.

> *Note that this document is a Candidate Recommendation, which means that it is to be treated as work in progress. This does not mean that we can't write programs that use this format, but we have to understand that the final version of the documentation could be completely different – the W3C puts out Candidate Recommendation documents to help the process of clarification and to spot problems.*

In that spirit, we'll have a look at RDF Schema in this chapter. We'll also look at extensions to RDF Schema, such as **DAML+OIL** (http://www.daml.org/).

Why Do We Need a Schema for RDF?

In the previous chapter we presented the idea of RDF as a *model* for meta data, alongside RDF/XML as a *syntax* which could be used to transport this model. This allowed us to represent name/value pairs of information and assign them to a resource or URI. We concluded that RDF/XML was an important standard for conveying this type of information.

For many applications RDF/XML is sufficient. The ability to transport triples is such a useful concept, who could want more? But there are many situations where we do want more. For example, there will be times when we need to know additional information about the resource being referred to, such as what it represents. For example, if we have a property that represents an author, then we may require that the value of the property is a reference to a person (and not a car or house). If we have a property that represents a birthday, then we want to check that the value is a date (and not a number or type of animal).

But we may want to check more than just the *validity* of the value – we may also want to *restrict* where certain properties can be applied. It is probably meaningless to allow a birthday property to be applied to a piece of music, for example.

The key to achieving these things is the RDF Schema specification. While the RDF Model and Syntax specification sets down how XML documents can be constructed to convey RDF, the RDF Schema document defines how we can be sure that the structure of some RDF/XML document or other conveys the correct *meaning*.

To understand what we mean by this, let's look at data integrity in a little more detail, to see why we are concerned with it.

Data Integrity

During the course of the recent British General Election the main subjects of interest were the constituencies (the locations in which the elections are taking place) and in the candidates (the people who have put themselves forward for election). Whoever wins the most votes in each constituency becomes the Member of Parliament – or MP – for that constituency. We'll use information from ePolitix.com, an apolitical provider of political news/information, to illustrate some of our points.

Remember that we are using RDF to convey name/value pairs, attached to some resource or other. Let's take a candidate in the Great Grimsby constituency – the Labour Party member Austin Mitchell, who actually won the seat. The UK's national news agency, PA News (www.pa.press.net), has a code for each constituency, and Great Grimsby's is 281. I've made up a URI to represent Grimsby (http://www.pa.press.net/constituencies/281). The meta data that we now have for this candidate is as follows:

```
primary key=http://www.epolitix.com/austin-mitchell
name=Austin Mitchell
candidateFor=http://www.pa.press.net/constituencies/281
memberOf=Labour Party
dob=19 September, 1934
```

As you already know from the first part of Chapter 4, RDF/XML is ideal for conveying this information across computer networks. We might use syntax like this (as in the previous chapter, assume that namespaces have all been defined correctly in the code fragments):

```
<rdf:Description rdf:about="http://www.epolitix.com/austin-mitchell">
    <epx:Name>Austin Mitchell</epx:Name>
    <epx:CandidateFor
        rdf:resource="http://www.pa.press.net/constituencies/281" />
    <epx:MemberOf>Labour Party</epx:MemberOf>
    <epx:DOB>19 September, 1934</epx:DOB>
</rdf:Description>
```

Our first data integrity problem is that we have no way of knowing whether the resource referred to in the rdf:resource property of the <epx:CandidateFor> element actually represents a constituency or not. What if, for example, we had the following:

```
<rdf:Description rdf:about="http://www.epolitix.com/austin-mitchell">
    <epx:Name>Austin Mitchell</epx:Name>
    <epx:CandidateFor rdf:resource="http://www.microsoft.com/" />
    <epx:MemberOf>Labour Party</epx:MemberOf>
    <epx:DOB>19 September, 1934</epx:DOB>
</rdf:Description>
```

As far as an RDF/XML parser is concerned this is perfectly acceptable. As long as the `rdf:resource` property is identified by a URI then everything is fine. But at the level of the meta data, the value that we have here is totally wrong, unless Austin is standing for election against Bill Gates, as the resource `http://www.microsoft.com/` is not a constituency.

Our second data integrity problem is that we might have used a property in an incorrect situation. Imagine that we had some meta data about the constituency that Austin was a candidate for:

```
<rdf:Description rdf:about="http://www.pa.press.net/constituencies/281">
    <epx:Name>Great Grimsby</epx:Name>
    <epx:MainIndustry>Fishing</epx:MainIndustry>
</rdf:Description>
```

This is fine, but what if we then saw this meta data:

```
<rdf:Description rdf:about="http://www.pa.press.net/constituencies/281">
    <epx:Name>Great Grimsby</epx:Name>
    <epx:MainIndustry>Fishing</epx:MainIndustry>
    <epx:DOB>19 September, 1934</epx:DOB>
</rdf:Description>
```

It is obvious that a parliamentary constituency doesn't have a date of birth property, but RDF/XML has no way of spotting this. As far as RDF/XML is concerned there is nothing wrong with this RDF syntax, so while RDF syntax can efficiently *convey* meta data, it is unable to *ensure its integrity*.

> Our schema language must therefore be able to express the relationship between different items of meta data, regardless of the syntax used to express that meta data – that is, it must be able to validate *statements* and not just XML.

Validating Statements

So what does it mean to validate statements? What sort of things should we be able to check for?

As you know from the previous chapter, statements are essentially triples, comprising a name/value pair – the predicate and the object that it refers to – and the resource that the pair refers to – the subject. To ensure the integrity of triples we only actually need to check two things:

❑ That the predicate is suitable for the subject, in other words that the property is acceptable for the resource.

❑ That the object is suitable for the predicate, in other words that the value is acceptable for the specified property.

I haven't included checking the subject since that is implied by RDF/XML anyway – the subject and predicate must both be identified by URIs, while the object can be a URI or a string literal. Here I am concentrating on checks that are beyond RDF/XML.

Checking the Predicate

Checking the predicate part of a statement requires us to check that the property being used is allowable when applied to the particular subject. In other words, is it legitimate to have a triple such as this?

```
{ epx:DOB, [http://www.pa.press.net/constituencies/281], "19 September, 1934" }
```

In this example we would like to prevent this, since we know that the subject of the statement is a constituency and that constituencies don't have birthdays.

Checking the Object

Checking the object part of a statement requires us to check that the value used refers to a resource or literal that is acceptable for the predicate. In other words, is it legitimate to have a triple such as this:

```
{
    epx:CandidateFor,
    [http://www.epolitix.com/austin-mitchell],
    [http://www.microsoft.com/]
}
```

Again, we would like to prevent this, since we know that the correct value should refer to a constituency.

Summary of Why We Need a Schema for RDF

The advantages to defining a schema that can specify how meta data should be structured, rather than how RDF/XML should be structured, mean that we have the ability to check the validity of meta data structures, even if they do not use RDF/XML to convey them. Provided that the meta data can be parsed into a set of triples – that is, into an RDF *model* – then we can validate the information against this schema.

The information we want to check against a schema is that:

❑   Properties applied to a resource make sense.

❑   Values used with properties make sense.

We can now start to look at how we might define a schema that meets these requirements.

Defining the Schema

Now that we have established why we need a way to distinctly specify RDF schemas, over and above the ability to define XML schemas, we can begin to look at how these schemas should be specified. The first question is what should we use to specify these schemas?

If you answered "RDF" you have either read the story's end, or have moved well beyond RDF guru status to a higher plain. The answer is indeed RDF. If we can specify RDF schemas in RDF itself, then we can move our schemas around and store them in a way that pays no regard to the syntax used to transmit those schemas. This means that we can use triples to define a schema, knowing that regardless of whether RDF/XML or some other syntax is used to convey those triples, the underlying meaning of the schema definition will still be understood.

Having said that, since the only widely accepted means of transporting triples is RDF/XML, we will discuss here the RDF/XML syntax for specifying an RDF schema, as defined in the W3C documentation. However, bear in mind that it is not the syntax that is important, but the underlying model.

Now we've established how we can specify the schema, let's look at how we can check properties and their values. Let's begin with the values.

Checking the Object of a Statement

The first area that we want to be able to check is that a resource being referred to by the predicate – the object, in other words – is right for the predicate. Let's return to our previous example of a candidate in the General Election:

```
<rdf:Description rdf:about="http://www.epolitix.com/austin-mitchell">
    <epx:Name>Austin Mitchell</epx:Name>
    <epx:CandidateFor
          rdf:resource="http://www.pa.press.net/constituencies/281" />
    <epx:MemberOf>Labour Party</epx:MemberOf>
    <epx:DOB>19 September, 1934</epx:DOB>
</rdf:Description>
```

Recall that we were concerned that there was no way of indicating that the value of the epx:CandidateFor property must be a constituency. The problem with the syntax as it stands is that we have no way of knowing what the following resource actually refers to:

```
http://www.pa.press.net/constituencies/281
```

The meta data we had for the constituency was as follows:

```
<rdf:Description rdf:about="http://www.pa.press.net/constituencies/281">
    <epx:Name>Great Grimsby</epx:Name>
    <epx:MainIndustry>Fishing</epx:MainIndustry>
</rdf:Description>
```

but there is nothing here to say that this is a constituency. The key to data integrity within RDF is to indicate to the schema processor what the **type** of the resource is.

Typing Resources

You may remember that in the last chapter we introduced the concept of a type property and typed nodes. We didn't go into much detail, but we indicated that it was possible to specify the type of a resource. The ability to specify the type of a resource is crucial to making the leap from RDF Model and Syntax to RDF Schemas.

The type of a resource is specified by making a statement in which the predicate is `rdf:type`, and the object is a URI that refers to the type of the resource. Let's say that ePolitix has defined a set of resource types for this purpose, and that the URI to use with an `rdf:type` property, if you want to indicate that a resource is of type `Constituency`, is this:

```
http://www.ePolitix.com/2001/03/rdf-schema#Constituency
```

Our document could now be specified as follows:

```
<rdf:Description rdf:about="http://www.pa.press.net/constituencies/281">
    <rdf:type
            resource="http://www.ePolitix.com/2001/03/rdf-schema#Constituency" />
    <epx:Name>Great Grimsby</epx:Name>
    <epx:MainIndustry>Fishing</epx:MainIndustry>
</rdf:Description>
```

and our resource has been typed. Don't forget that, provided that the namespace `epx` has been defined as `http://www.ePolitix.com/2001/03/rdf-schema#`, we can also specify the same information using the following syntax:

```
<epx:Constituency rdf:about="http://www.pa.press.net/constituencies/281">
    <epx:Name>Great Grimsby</epx:Name>
    <epx:MainIndustry>Fishing</epx:MainIndustry>
</epx:Constituency>
```

Now that we have indicated that the resource being referred to is of type `epx:Constituency`, we need to indicate that the property `epx:CandidateFor` can only have a value of a resource that has a type of `epx:Constituency`. This is achieved by creating a statement in which the resource is the name of the property – `epx:CandidateFor` – and this resource has a predicate that indicates the type for resources assigned to that property. First we need to indicate that `epx:CandidateFor` is indeed a property.

rdf:Property

A property is specified in an RDF schema by making a statement where the URI referred to identifies the resource which represents the property, and the `rdf:type` of the resource is `rdf:Property`. Our property to indicate which constituency a candidate is standing for election in would be defined like this:

```
<rdf:Description
   rdf:about="http://www.ePolitix.com/2001/03/rdf-schema#CandidateFor"
   xmlns:rdf="http://www.w3.org/1999/02/22-rdf-syntax-ns#"
>
        <rdf:type resource="http://www.w3.org/1999/02/22-rdf-syntax-ns#Property" />
</rdf:Description>
```

As you are of course aware, we can also use the abbreviated syntax:

```
<rdf:Property
   rdf:about="http://www.ePolitix.com/2001/03/rdf-schema#CandidateFor"
   xmlns:rdf="http://www.w3.org/1999/02/22-rdf-syntax-ns#"
/>
```

Using either syntax we have created a property, but we haven't yet indicated in any way that this property can only have a value that is a resource that has a type of `epx:Constituency`. To do this we add a statement to our property URI to indicate what values can be used.

It is not immediately clear why the `rdf:Property` element should be in the `rdf` namespace, instead of the `rdfs` namespace (introduced below). After all, it does seem to be part of the schema. However, since the RDF model can have properties regardless of whether there is a schema to say anything more about those properties, the URI for the property type must exist in the RDF namespace. This means that we can do this, for example:

```
<rdf:RDF>
    <rdf:Description rdf:about="http://www.pa.press.net/constituencies/281">
        <rdf:type
            resource="http://www.ePolitix.com/2001/03/rdf-schema#Constituency" />
        <epx:Name>Great Grimsby</epx:Name>
    </rdf:Description>
    <rdf:Description
        rdf:about="http://www.ePolitix.com/2001/03/rdf-schema#Name">
        <rdf:type
            resource="http://www.w3.org/1999/02/22-rdf-syntax-ns#Property" />
    </rdf:Description>
</rdf:RDF>
```

In this document we have said that the resource `http://www.pa.press.net/constituencies/281` is of type `Constituency`, and that it has a property of `epx:Name`. We then go on to say that `epx:Name` is indeed a property. Although this is not necessary at the RDF Model and Syntax level, `Property` must be in the `rdf` namespace so as to be consistent. Otherwise we could not make the statement we have just made without introducing RDF Schema.

rdfs:range

Just as we had a specific namespace to help identify RDF/XML within an XML document, so we need an RDF Schema namespace. The `rdfs` namespace prefix can be anything we want, but the URI that it evaluates to must be:

```
http://www.w3.org/2000/01/rdf-schema#
```

The statement we need – to indicate that a property can only take on certain values – has a predicate of `rdfs:range`:

```
<rdf:Property
  rdf:about="http://www.ePolitix.com/2001/03/rdf-schema#CandidateFor"
>
    <rdfs:range
        rdf:resource="http://www.ePolitix.com/2001/03/rdf-schema#Constituency" />
</rdf:Property>
```

Now we have defined a predicate that can be used with any set of statements, but when it is used it must have as an object a resource. But that resource cannot be just any resource. That resource must somewhere appear in a triple in which the predicate is `rdf:type`, and the object is the following URI:

```
http://www.ePolitix.com/2001/03/rdf-schema#Constituency
```

As we know from the previous chapter, this long URI will often be made easier to manage through the use of XML namespaces. For example, if a school was to hold pretend – or "mock" – elections to give students experience in running campaigns, they may wish to use our `CandidateFor` property, but use their school schema for the pupil's name and date of birth:

```
<rdf:Description
  rdf:about="http://www.GrangeHill.edu/mark-birbeck"
  xmlns:e="http://www.ePolitix.com/2001/03/rdf-schema#"
  xmlns:gh="http://www.GrangeHill.edu/2001/03/rdf-schema#"
>
    <gh:Name>Mark Birbeck</gh:Name>
    <e:CandidateFor rdf:resource="http://www.pa.press.net/constituencies/281" />
    <gh:Born>28 September, 1964</gh:Born>
    <gh:Comments>A little old for this school.</gh:Comments>
</rdf:Description>
```

As the RDFS spec currently stands there can only be one `rdfs:range` predicate for a property, but there is no requirement that a property *must have* a `range` predicate. In that case the predicate could take any value.

> *There are some further restrictions on the resources that can be referred to with `rdfs:range`, but these will be discussed later in this chapter. They are important, but do not affect your understanding of the concepts so far.*

rdfs:Literal

As we know from the previous chapter, the object of a statement can either be a resource or a literal. The examples we have just given for `rdfs:range` allow us to handle resources that have a type, but we will also want to specify that a value cannot be a resource, but must be a literal. This is achieved using `rdfs:Literal`, as follows:

```
<rdf:Property rdf:about="http://www.ePolitix.com/2001/03/rdf-schema#Name">
    <rdfs:range rdf:resource="http://www.w3.org/2000/01/rdf-schema#Literal" />
</rdf:Property>
```

This indicates that the value of the `epx:Name` property can only be a string literal, and not a resource.

Summary of Object Checking

We have looked at how a predicate can be shared among different meta data models, and also how the type of the resource that the predicate refers to can be restricted. We have seen that the key to this is the ability to specify the type of a resource through the `rdf:type` predicate.

Checking the Predicate of a Statement

We can now look at how RDF schemas allow us to indicate what predicates can appear with which resources. Again the key is to indicate the *type* of the resource, and then indicate whether a property is *legitimate* for that resource.

The `CandidateFor` property that we defined in the previous section required a constituency as its value, but there was no indication of what resources it could be used with. At first sight this worked in our favor, since it allowed the property used on a commercial web site like ePolitix to be the same as the property used in a school mock election web site. Recall that ePolitix used the property like this:

```
<rdf:Description rdf:about="http://www.epolitix.com/austin-mitchell">
    <epx:Name>Austin Mitchell</epx:Name>
    <epx:CandidateFor
        rdf:resource="http://www.pa.press.net/constituencies/281" />
    <epx:MemberOf>Labour Party</epx:MemberOf>
    <epx:DOB>19 September, 1934</epx:DOB>
</rdf:Description>
```

While the school used the same property like this:

```
<rdf:Description rdf:about="http://www.GrangeHill.edu/mark-birbeck">
    <gh:Name>Mark Birbeck</gh:Name>
    <epx:CandidateFor
        rdf:resource="http://www.pa.press.net/constituencies/281" />
    <gh:Born>28 September, 1964</gh:Born>
</rdf:Description>
```

When building up common properties – such as those used in the Dublin Core (which we discussed in Chapter 4) – it will often be the case that the property definition will allow the property to appear with *any* resource. For example, the DC Creator property may be defined like this:

```
<rdf:Property rdf:about="http://purl.org/dc/elements/1.0/Creator" />
```

Just as with our CandidateFor property, the Creator predicate can appear in a statement with any resource. However, while this may work for very broad properties like Creator, it doesn't work for our political properties. It would be nonsensical, for example, if we had the following:

```
<rdf:Description  rdf:about="http://www.conservatives.org.uk/">
    <rdf:type
        resource="http://www.ePolitix.com/2001/03/rdf-schema#PoliticalParty" />
    <epx:CandidateFor
        rdf:resource="http://www.pa.press.net/constituencies/281" />
</rdf:Description>
```

What does it mean for a political party to be a candidate for a constituency? Or a house or car? We need to be able to say that only resources that have been typed with something that indicates that they are a person can have the CandidateFor property. This is achieved through the use of the rdfs:domain predicate.

rdfs:domain

The rdfs:domain property is used to indicate what type of resources can be associated with the subject of a particular property. For example, imagine that we have a widely accepted type value that indicates that a resource represents a human being:

```
http://www.Schemas.org/2001/01/rdf-schema#Person
```

Let's now take our statements about Austin Mitchell being a candidate for Great Grimsby and indicate that the resource that we are making statements about – Austin – represents a person:

```
<rdf:Description rdf:about="http://www.epolitix.com/austin-mitchell">
    <rdf:type resource="http://www.Schemas.org/2001/01/rdf-schema#Person" />
    <epx:Name>Austin Mitchell</epx:Name>
    <epx:CandidateFor
```

```
              rdf:resource="http://www.pa.press.net/constituencies/281" />
      <epx:MemberOf>Labour Party</epx:MemberOf>
      <epx:DOB>19 September, 1934</epx:DOB>
</rdf:Description>
```

We also use the same URI in the `rdfs:domain` predicate of our `CandidateFor` property to indicate that this property (`CandidateFor`) is only acceptable when used with a resource that has been typed as a `Person`:

```
<rdf:Property
      rdf:about="http://www.ePolitix.com/2001/03/rdf-schema#CandidateFor">
    <rdfs:domain
           rdf:resource="http://www.Schemas.org/2001/01/rdf-schema#Person" />
    <rdfs:range
           rdf:resource="http://www.ePolitix.com/2001/03/rdf-schema#Constituency" />
</rdf:Property>
```

So where does this leave the school elections? If the school wants to use the `CandidateFor` property in their meta data then all they have to do is make sure that their resources are also of type `Person`:

```
<rdf:Description rdf:about="http://www.GrangeHill.edu/mark-birbeck">
    <rdf:type resource="http://www.Schemas.org/2001/01/rdf-schema#Person" />
    <gh:Name>Mark Birbeck</gh:Name>
    <epx:CandidateFor
           rdf:resource="http://www.pa.press.net/constituencies/281" />
    <gh:Born>28 September, 1964</gh:Born>
</rdf:Description>
```

Now the `CandidateFor` property is acceptable.

As with the `rdfs:range` predicate there is no limit to the number of domains that a property can be applied to. Taking our previous example of a `Region`, we might say that a `Person` can have a property of a `Region`, and that a `Company` can also have a property of a `Region`:

```
<rdf:Property
  rdf:about="http://www.ePolitix.com/2001/03/rdf-schema#Region"
  xmlns:rdf="http://www.w3.org/1999/02/22-rdf-syntax-ns#"
>
    <rdfs:domain
           rdf:resource="http://www.Schemas.org/2001/01/rdf-schema#Person" />
    <rdfs:domain
           rdf:resource="http://www.Schemas.org/2001/01/rdf-schema#Company" />
</rdf:Property>
```

But note an interesting consequence of the distributed nature of RDF – if we are running an event web site with a database of plays and exhibitions that people might want to go to, we can organize my data by region too. And to help with meta data searches we might use the ePolitix `Region` property within our meta data:

```
<rdf:Property rdf:about="http://www.ePolitix.com/2001/03/rdf-schema#Region">
    <rdfs:domain
           rdf:resource="http://www.WhatsOnWhere.com/2001/01/rdf-schema#Event" />
</rdf:Property>
```

Even though we didn't invent the `Region` property, and we don't own its schema definition, we have been able to use it in my schemas.

The most likely scenario though, is that organizations will define schemas for public use, and then other organizations will adopt the schemas of the most authoritative organization for a particular subject category. So the original ePolitix definition of `Region` would have been similar to the event web site definition, in that they would both have been in reference to another schema:

```
<rdf:Property rdf:about="http://www.Schemas.org/2001/01/rdf-schema#Region">
    <rdfs:domain
            rdf:resource="http://www.Schemas.org/2001/01/rdf-schema#Person" />
    <rdfs:domain
            rdf:resource="http://www.Schemas.org/2001/01/rdf-schema#Company" />
</rdf:Property>
```

(Similarly the event web site would also have taken the more authoritative schema.)

There are some further restrictions on the resources that can be referred with `rdfs:domain`, but these will be discussed later in this chapter. Again, they are important, but do not affect your understanding of the concepts so far.

Summary of Predicate Checking

A property can be linked to one or more resource types through the `rdfs:domain` predicate. This does not prevent properties being shared amongst different schemas, but ensures that when properties are reused, they are placed into meaningful contexts.

Hierarchy of Types

So far we have seen that the typing system is key to specifying what properties are acceptable and what values a property can take. We simply make a statement about a resource that indicates what type that resource is. For example, we saw in the previous section that we could indicate that a resource was a `Person` so that we could then restrict the `CandidateFor` property to only be applicable to resources that were of type `Person`.

Let's refine this a little. It is not the case that *any* `Person` resource might be a candidate in an election. We might have a `Person` resource that represents an author of a book, or an astronaut. Ideally we would want to restrict the `CandidateFor` property to only apply to resources that are of type `Candidate`, so that if we saw this property attached to a resource of type `CircusClown` we could be sure that it was an error.

Of course, if the resource were of type `CircusClown` and of type `Candidate`, then we would allow the property `CandidateFor`.

This doesn't also mean that we don't want to keep the type `Person`, but instead, resources of this type should perhaps have more basic information common to all people, such as a name and date of birth. The `CandidateFor` property should then only apply to resources of type `Candidate`. To create an election candidate we would then create a resource of type `Person`, and a resource of a new type, called `Candidate`. Let's see how this is done.

Resources with Multiple Types

The property definitions for predicates that can be used with resources of type `Person` would be defined by some accepted schema organization, like this:

```
<rdf:RDF>
    <rdf:Property rdf:about="http://www.Schemas.org/2001/01/rdf-schema#Name">
        <rdfs:domain
                rdf:resource="http://www.Schemas.org/2001/01/rdf-schema#Person" />
        <rdfs:range
                rdf:resource="http://www.w3.org/2000/01/rdf-schema#Literal" />
    </rdf:Property>
    <rdf:Property rdf:about="http://www.Schemas.org/2001/01/rdf-schema#DOB">
        <rdfs:domain
                rdf:resource="http://www.Schemas.org/2001/01/rdf-schema#Person" />
        <rdfs:range
                rdf:resource="http://www.w3.org/2000/01/rdf-schema#Literal" />
    </rdf:Property>
</rdf:RDF>
```

This means that we have two string literal properties – `Name` and `DOB` – which can be applied to a resource of type `Person`.

Our ePolitix `CandidateFor` property could now be limited to only be acceptable with resources of type `Candidate`, like this:

```
<rdf:Property
        rdf:about="http://www.ePolitix.com/2001/03/rdf-schema#CandidateFor">
    <rdfs:domain
            rdf:resource="http://www.ePolitix.com/2001/03/rdf-schema#Candidate" />
    <rdfs:range
            rdf:resource="http://www.ePolitix.com/2001/03/rdf-schema#Constituency" />
</rdf:Property>
```

Now all we need to do is give our election candidate two resource types, instead of one:

```
<rdf:Description
  rdf:about="http://www.epolitix.com/austin-mitchell"
  xmlns:rdf="http://www.w3.org/1999/02/22-rdf-syntax-ns#"
  xmlns:s="http://www.Schemas.org/2001/01/rdf-schema#"
  xmlns:epx="http://www.ePolitix.com/2001/03/rdf-schema#"
>
    <rdf:type resource="http://www.Schemas.org/2001/01/rdf-schema#Person" />
    <s:Name>Austin Mitchell</s:Name>
    <s:DOB>19 September, 1934</s:DOB>
    <rdf:type resource="http://www.ePolitix.com/2001/03/rdf-schema#Candidate" />
    <epx:CandidateFor
            rdf:resource="http://www.pa.press.net/constituencies/281" />
    <epx:MemberOf>Labour Party</epx:MemberOf>
</rdf:Description>
```

A number of statements have been made here about the resource `http://www.epolitix.com/austin-mitchell` and all of them are acceptable:

- ❑ The Name and DOB statements are acceptable because the resource is of type Person.

- ❑ The CandidateFor statement is acceptable because the resource is also of type Candidate.

- ❑ The MemberOf statement is acceptable because this particular predicate currently has no restrictions on where it may appear.

However, this still does not feel complete. Just as we said earlier that we do not want the CandidateFor property to be applied to people who are not a Candidate, or to objects such as cars and houses, so too it seems that a Candidate will *always* be a Person. Ideally we'd like to say that any resource that has the type of Candidate automatically acquires the type of Person, and so any properties that are acceptable for a Person resource are fine for a Candidate resource.

In **object-oriented programming** (**OOP**) terminology this is much the same as defining a **class** that has **inherited** from another class. In fact, issues to do with OOP were taken into account when specifying the RDF Schema specification, and the documentation actually uses the term class, so let's look at that now.

Classes

If you are not familiar with OOP then let's have a quick look at some of the concepts. A class is a special kind of template from which to produce things. Remember as a child using a plastic cutter shaped like a little man to cut gingerbread men from a cake mix? Little did you know, all those years ago, that you were creating **instances** of a class. The plastic cutter defines the shape of all objects that are created with it, but it is not itself that object. The cutter is not a gingerbread man, but it is the template that you can use to create instances of gingerbread men. (Apologies for being gender-specific; I don't feel it is the place of this chapter to give voice to the hidden history of gingerbread women!)

We might also build other classes on top of our class. We might start with a template for creating faxes in Microsoft Word, and then modify it to become a template that creates faxes that demand payment on overdue accounts. The more specific fax – the one demanding money – is said to **inherit** features and properties from the more general fax. The more specific class is said to be a **subclass** of the more general one. **Inheritance** is a key concept in OOP.

Any object created using the **class definition** of a class that has inherited from another class is said to be an instance of both classes. A fax demanding money from one of your clients is said to be an object of type "fax payment demand", as well as an object of type "fax".

The template that the class definition specifies lists the properties that an instance of this class will have. Creating an object of type "gingerbread man" will create an object that has arms, legs, a body, and a head. Creating an object of type "fax" will create an object that has a fax number, a subject line, some text, and so on.

Creating an object using a class that inherits from another actually gives the object properties from both classes, or it may hide some properties from the parent class, or it may even set them to specific values. For example, an object of type "fax payment demand", might only have properties of company name and amount owed – the "text" property of "fax" might then be set automatically to contain a message that says "please pay the amount of £[amount owed] now".

Whilst an understanding of classes from the world of OOP may help you in your dealings with RDF Schema, you should be aware that there are two major differences between the notion of class within RDF and in programming.

The first and most obvious is that whilst a class in an object-oriented language would have functions – or methods – associated with it, RDF classes have no such thing. Classes written in Java or C++ might have a method such as `postToAccounts()` on an `Invoice` class, but with RDF classes there are only properties.

The second difference is that whilst a class is defined as a set of properties (and methods) in OOP languages, with RDF a property is defined as being applicable to a class. This makes sense if you think back to what we want to check for – whether the predicate part of a triple is valid for the subject. But it also makes sense in the context of the distributed nature of the Web, in that I can make *my* properties valid for *your* classes.

We'll now go through how each of these concepts is represented in RDF Schema. We'll now look at:

- ❑ Defining a class.
- ❑ Creating subclasses from a class.
- ❑ Creating instances of a class, or instantiating a class.

Defining a Class

Let's return to our General Election candidate example:

```
<rdf:Description
  rdf:about="http://www.epolitix.com/austin-mitchell"
  xmlns:rdf="http://www.w3.org/1999/02/22-rdf-syntax-ns#"
  xmlns:s="http://www.Schemas.org/2001/01/rdf-schema#"
  xmlns:epx="http://www.ePolitix.com/2001/03/rdf-schema#"
>
    <rdf:type resource="http://www.Schemas.org/2001/01/rdf-schema#Person" />
    <s:Name>Austin Mitchell</s:Name>
    <s:DOB>19 September, 1934</s:DOB>
    <rdf:type resource="http://www.ePolitix.com/2001/03/rdf-schema#Candidate" />
    <epx:CandidateFor rdf:resource="http://www.pa.press.net/constituencies/281" />
    <epx:MemberOf>Labour Party</epx:MemberOf>
</rdf:Description>
```

Our candidate resource has been defined as being of type `Person` and `Candidate`. We would now like to say that this resource is only of type `Candidate`, and that in turn any resource of type `Candidate` is a `Person`. This is achieved through the OOP technique of inheritance, or subclassing.

In the world of OOP we can take a class and create a more specific class from it. In our example we need a class to represent resources of type `Person`, which is then used as the basis for a class that represents resources of type `Candidate`. Let's define the class `Person`.

rdfs:Class

RDF Schema allows us to define a class using a resource that has a type of `rdfs:Class`. This definition probably sounds like it won't stand up in court – unless the court is in Alice's Wonderland – since all we have said is that a class is defined as a class of type class! However, we have to assume here that an RDF parser that understands schemas will understand the key concept of the `rdf:type` property. In that case our schema processor will understand that any resource with a type of `rdfs:Class` is a class.

Using the URI for the RDF Schema namespace, the fictitious schema organization we introduced earlier could use the `rdf:type` property to specify a `Person` class:

```
<rdf:Description
 rdf:about="http://www.Schemas.org/2001/01/rdf-schema#Person"
 xmlns:rdf="http://www.w3.org/1999/02/22-rdf-syntax-ns#"
>
    <rdf:type resource="http://www.w3.org/2000/01/rdf-schema#Class" />
</rdf:Description>
```

Alternatively, we can use a typed node to define the class, like this:

```
<rdfs:Class
 rdf:about="http://www.Schemas.org/2001/01/rdf-schema#Person"
 xmlns:rdfs="http://www.w3.org/2000/01/rdf-schema#"
/>
```

We have now "created" a class. In actual fact, all that we have done is created a triple that says that the resource s:Person has an rdf:type predicate with a value of rdfs:Class – but that's good enough! We now have a class from which we can derive others.

Creating Subclasses

We discussed earlier that one of the most powerful features of OOP was the ability to define a class that inherits properties from some other class. If we take our Candidate class, we can see that properties like date of birth and name are not features of the candidate *as a candidate*. A person could still have a birthday and a name even if they didn't stand in an election.

Equally, the fact that the person is a member of a political party is not a feature of being a candidate. Most people who are members of political parties never stand for office.

Inheritance allows us to manage information much more neatly, by designing a class structure that uses inheritance to logically separate properties out. In our example we began with a class of Person, but now we might inherit from that to create a class called Politician, before finally ending with a class called Candidate – based on the Politician class. We could then attach the properties "name" and "date of birth" to the Person class, and then have the "member of" property assigned only to the Politician class.

rdfs:subClassOf

We can use RDF/XML to define these levels of inheritance using the rdfs:subClassOf predicate, as follows:

```
<rdf:RDF
 xmlns:rdf="http://www.w3.org/1999/02/22-rdf-syntax-ns#"
 xmlns:rdfs="http://www.w3.org/2000/01/rdf-schema#"
>
    <rdfs:Class rdf:about="http://www.Schemas.org/2001/01/rdf-schema#Person" />

    <rdfs:Class
        rdf:about="http://www.ePolitix.com/2001/03/rdf-schema#Politician">
        <rdfs:subClassOf
         rdf:resource="http://www.Schemas.org/2001/01/rdf-schema#Person"
        />
    </rdfs:Class>

    <rdfs:Class
```

```
              rdf:about="http://www.ePolitix.com/2001/03/rdf-schema#Candidate">
         <rdfs:subClassOf
          rdf:resource="http://www.ePolitix.com/2001/03/rdf-schema#Politician"
          />
      </rdfs:Class>
   </rdf:RDF>
```

Using this schema we are able to say that the ePolitix `Candidate` class is a subclass of the ePolitix `Politician` class, which in turn is a subclass of the Schemas.org `Person` class. This means that classes of the more specialized type (`Candidate`) are automatically classes of the more general type (`Person`). And the consequence of *that* is that any property that can take a `Politician` class as a value, can also take a `Candidate` class as a value, and any property that can take a `Person` class as its value will accept `Candidates` *and* `Politicians`.

Before we go on, I'm going to make an assumption for my examples that will allow me to abbreviate the text a little. As things stand the name of the file in which all of the above statements have been made is irrelevant, since the `about` attribute is used to identify resources. However, if I was to place all of this RDF/XML into a file called `http://www.ePolitix.com/2001/03/rdf-schema` then we could shorten all of the above URLs, as follows:

```
<rdf:RDF
 xmlns:rdf="http://www.w3.org/1999/02/22-rdf-syntax-ns#"
 xmlns:rdfs="http://www.w3.org/2000/01/rdf-schema#"
>
    <rdfs:Class rdf:about="http://www.Schemas.org/2001/01/rdf-schema#Person" />

    <rdfs:Class rdf:ID="Politician">
        <rdfs:subClassOf
            rdf:resource="http://www.Schemas.org/2001/01/rdf-schema#Person" />
    </rdfs:Class>

    <rdfs:Class rdf:ID="Candidate">
        <rdfs:subClassOf rdf:resource="#Politician" />
    </rdfs:Class>
</rdf:RDF>
```

As you can see, by containing everything within the same file we can use a **fragment identifier** rather than a long URL. It's important to note, however, that `rdf:about` attributes must then become `rdf:ID` attributes.

Getting back to our example, for completeness let's show how the properties are defined. First the properties for a `Person`, which we have already seen:

```
<rdf:RDF>
    <rdf:Property rdf:about="http://www.Schemas.org/2001/01/rdf-schema#Name">
        <rdfs:domain
            rdf:resource="http://www.Schemas.org/2001/01/rdf-schema#Person" />
        <rdfs:range
            rdf:resource="http://www.w3.org/2000/01/rdf-schema#Literal" />
    </rdf:Property>
    <rdf:Property rdf:about="http://www.Schemas.org/2001/01/rdf-schema#DOB">
        <rdfs:domain
            rdf:resource="http://www.Schemas.org/2001/01/rdf-schema#Person" />
        <rdfs:range
            rdf:resource="http://www.w3.org/2000/01/rdf-schema#Literal" />
    </rdf:Property>
</rdf:RDF>
```

Next, resources with a type of `Politician` can have a `MemberOf` predicate:

```
<rdf:Property rdf:ID="MemberOf">
    <rdfs:domain rdf:resource="#Politician" />
    <rdfs:range rdf:resource="#PoliticalParty" />
</rdf:Property>
```

Note that I have made it so that the range of values that are acceptable for the `MemberOf` property are resources that have an `rdf:type` of `epx:PoliticalParty`. I haven't bothered to show that class, but add it here to indicate how the system keeps extending.

Finally, as we saw before, our ePolitix `CandidateFor` property is limited to resources of type `Candidate`, like this:

```
<rdf:Property rdf:ID="CandidateFor">
    <rdfs:domain rdf:resource="#Candidate" />
    <rdfs:range rdf:resource="#Constituency" />
</rdf:Property>
```

Now that we have defined our classes we need only use the `Candidate` class, like this:

```
<rdf:Description
 rdf:about="http://www.epolitix.com/austin-mitchell"
 xmlns:rdf="http://www.w3.org/1999/02/22-rdf-syntax-ns#"
 xmlns:s="http://www.Schemas.org/2001/01/rdf-schema#"
 xmlns:epx="http://www.ePolitix.com/2001/03/rdf-schema#"
 >
        <rdf:type resource="http://www.ePolitix.com/2001/03/rdf-schema#Candidate" />
        <s:Name>Austin Mitchell</s:Name>
        <s:DOB>19 September, 1934</s:DOB>
        <epx:CandidateFor
            rdf:resource="http://www.pa.press.net/constituencies/281" />
        <epx:MemberOf rdf:resource="http://www.ePolitix.com/parties#labour" />
</rdf:Description>
```

Although we are using predicates that are only acceptable with different classes, we no longer need to specify all of those classes, since the resource `http://www.epolitix.com/austin-mitchell` is now of type `Candidate`, `Politician`, and `Person`.

Remote Inheritance

The beauty of using `rdf:resource` to specify the class that we are subclassing from is that it could be a class not under our control. As we just saw, we were able to subclass from the `Person` class, even though it was not within our schema.

And we can take this further. You might want to create and maintain meta data about cabinet ministers – that is, those politicians who are members of the British government, and you might decide to create a class called `Minister` that is a subclass of the ePolitix `Politician` class:

```
<rdf:RDF
 xmlns:rdf="http://www.w3.org/1999/02/22-rdf-syntax-ns#"
 xmlns:rdfs="http://www.w3.org/2000/01/rdf-schema#"
 >
```

```
    <rdfs:Class rdf:about="http://mydata.com/2001/01/rdf-schema#Minister">
        <rdfs:subClassOf
         rdf:resource="http://www.ePolitix.com/2001/03/rdf-schema#Politician"
        />
    </rdfs:Class>
</rdf:RDF>
```

As you can see, you have created a class from one of my classes, which was in turn created from someone else's class. This works in much the same way as you might inherit from someone else's classes if you use a Java or C++ library. But rather than you having to have the library of classes on your computers for the subclassing to work, RDF Schema is using URIs to create a distributed network of classes. This is an incredibly powerful feature.

Multiple Inheritance

If you are familiar with OOP concepts then you will know that a class can be defined as being a subclass of more than one other class – known as **multiple inheritance**. This is not the same as the example we have been using, where `Candidate` is a subclass of `Politician`, which is in turn a subclass of `Person`. Instead, multiple inheritance involves creating a class from two or more other classes at the same time.

An example might be a defending candidate, who is both a candidate in the election but also the previous winner for that constituency. RDF Schema allows a class to be a subclass of as many classes as you like:

```
<rdf:RDF
  xmlns:rdf="http://www.w3.org/1999/02/22-rdf-syntax-ns#"
  xmlns:rdfs="http://www.w3.org/2000/01/rdf-schema#"
>
    <rdfs:Class
      rdf:about="http://www.ePolitix.com/2001/03/rdf-schema#DefendingCandidate">
        <rdfs:subClassOf
         rdf:resource="http://www.ePolitix.com/2001/03/rdf-schema#Candidate"
        />
        <rdfs:subClassOf
         rdf:resource="http://www.ePolitix.com/2001/03/
                                       rdf-schema#ElectedRepresentative"
        />
    </rdfs:Class>
</rdf:RDF>
```

Versioning Schemas

Note the (invented) URLs we have been using for these illustrations, such as `http://mydata.com/2001/01/rdf-schema#Minister` and `http://www.ePolitix.com/2001/03/rdf-schema#Politician`.

They contain a year and month, in much the same way the URIs for the RDF namespaces do. This is not a requirement of your schema URIs, but it certainly helps if you change your schemas over time. You can release a new schema at a new URL safe in the knowledge that anyone who has derived classes from your previous schema will be unaffected. The RDF Schema specification takes this idea further, and suggests that if everyone adopts the approach of freezing the schema at a particular URL, then RDF software could cache the schema model without having to retrieve the RDF/XML every time it needs to use it.

Using techniques that we have seen so far – inheriting classes – we can link a newer schema to an older one. This would mean that rather than creating a brand new class with no relationship to a previous class, you could build a new class with new properties, but derive it from an old class with its old properties. This would mean that the base type of both classes would be the same.

For example, imagine that we want to create a new version of the ePolitix `Candidate` class. We could derive this class from our older class, like this:

```
<rdf:RDF
  xmlns:rdf="http://www.w3.org/1999/02/22-rdf-syntax-ns#"
  xmlns:rdfs="http://www.w3.org/2000/01/rdf-schema#"
>
    <rdfs:Class
           rdf:about="http://www.ePolitix.com/2002/07/rdf-schema#Candidate">
        <rdfs:subClassOf
           rdf:resource="http://www.ePolitix.com/2001/03/rdf-schema#Candidate"
        />
    </rdfs:Class>
</rdf:RDF>
```

Then all ePolitix `Candidate` resources will have a common base class, regardless of whether they use the old or the new schema.

RDF Schema also provides a technique to do the same thing with properties – we can say that one property is based on another property. This allows us to either create a new property based on the existing one in a new schema, or it allows us to create a more specific property from a general one. An example might be a property that holds a value that indicates an organization that a person is a member of:

```
<rdf:Property rdf:ID="MemberOfOrganisation">
    <rdfs:domain rdf:resource="#Person" />
    <rdfs:range rdf:resource="#Organisation" />
</rdf:Property>
```

which is then used to create another property to show the more specific *party* membership of politicians:

```
<rdf:Property rdf:ID="MemberOfParty">
    <rdfs:subPropertyOf rdf:resource="#MemberOfOrganisation" />
</rdf:Property>
```

The `MemberOfParty` property has all of the attributes of the `MemberOfOrganisation` property, but of course it could also have its own features.

The `rdfs:subPropertyOf` property looks like this in the RDF schema:

```
<rdf:Property rdf:ID="subPropertyOf">
  <rdfs:range
         rdf:resource="http://www.w3.org/1999/02/22-rdf-syntax-ns#Property"/>
  <rdfs:domain
         rdf:resource="http://www.w3.org/1999/02/22-rdf-syntax-ns#Property"/>
</rdf:Property>
```

Instantiating a Class

We've already seen how to create instances of a class when we discussed the `rdf:type` property. For completeness let's look at it again, since I want to add a few other comments.

As you've seen, we can say that a resource is an instance of a class by giving it an `rdf:type` property:

```
<rdf:Description rdf:about="http://www.epolitix.com/austin-mitchell">
    <rdf:type resource="http://www.ePolitix.com/2001/03/rdf-schema#Candidate" />
    <s:Name>Austin Mitchell</s:Name>
    <epx:MemberOf>Labour Party</epx:MemberOf>
    <s:DOB>19 September, 1934</s:DOB>
</rdf:Description>
```

However, unlike most OOP languages, we can say that an object is an instance of two classes. This is not the same as creating a class with multiple inheritance – as you can do with some OOP languages – since you would still then create an instance of the new class. With RDF Schema we only have to add more type properties to increase the classes that the object is an instance of:

```
<rdf:Description rdf:about="http://www.epolitix.com/austin-mitchell">
    <rdf:type resource="http://www.ePolitix.com/2001/03/rdf-schema#Candidate" />
    <s:Name>Austin Mitchell</s:Name>
    <epx:MemberOf>Labour Party</epx:MemberOf>
    <s:DOB>19 September, 1934</s:DOB>
    <rdf:type resource="http://www.Schemas.org/2001/01/rdf-schema#Husband" />
    <s:Wife rdf:resource=" http://www.epolitix.com/linda-mcdougall" />
</rdf:Description>
```

Rather than creating a new class that is of type `CandidateWhoIsAlsoAHusband`, we have instead created an object that is an instance of both the `Candidate` and `Husband` classes. When processing software encounters this RDF/XML it will know that the class instance must match the requirements of both classes.

Summary of Classes

We have looked at how the schema definitions used in RDF Schema specify classes. We have seen how we can say that a resource is an instance of one or more classes, and we've begun to look at how we might specify a class. So far we have seen how we can create a hierarchy of classes, but we haven't seen how we indicate the properties of a class. We'll look at that now.

Using the Schema on the Schema

When we were discussing `rdfs:domain` and `rdfs:range` I made a note that there were further restrictions on using these properties, and that I would explain what they were later. These restrictions are that the values referred to by the resource attributes must be resources of type `rdfs:Class` – in other words the values used in defining a schema are themselves determined by the schema. Let's look at this more closely.

Recall that we indicated the type of a `Constituency` as follows:

```
<rdf:Description rdf:about="http://www.pa.press.net/constituencies/281">
    <rdf:type
        resource="http://www.ePolitix.com/2001/03/rdf-schema#Constituency" />
    <epx:Name>Great Grimsby</epx:Name>
    <epx:MainIndustry>Fishing</epx:MainIndustry>
</rdf:Description>
```

We then used the same URI to indicate that values used with the epx:CandidateFor property had to refer to resources that had an rdf:type property set in the same way as the Great Grimsby constituency:

```
<rdf:Property
    rdf:about="http://www.ePolitix.com/2001/03/rdf-schema#CandidateFor">
  <rdfs:domain
        rdf:resource="http://www.Schemas.org/2001/01/rdf-schema#Person" />
  <rdfs:range
      rdf:resource="http://www.ePolitix.com/2001/03/rdf-schema#Constituency" />
</rdf:Property>
```

We can put these two pieces together and use the URI for Great Grimsby in some meta data, like this:

```
<rdf:Description rdf:about="http://www.epolitix.com/austin-mitchell">
    <epx:Name>Austin Mitchell</epx:Name>
    <epx:CandidateFor
          rdf:resource="http://www.pa.press.net/constituencies/281" />
    <epx:MemberOf>Labour Party</epx:MemberOf>
    <epx:DOB>19 September, 1934</epx:DOB>
</rdf:Description>
```

Looking at both fragments of code, we are able to establish:

❑ That the resource referenced in the epx:CandidateFor property must have a type of epx:Constituency.

❑ That http://www.pa.press.net/constituencies/281 does indeed represent a constituency, and not a boat or a book.

However, if we are going to check the type of the resource referred to by the URI of this statement:

```
<epx:CandidateFor
      rdf:resource="http://www.pa.press.net/constituencies/281" />
```

why shouldn't we check the type of the resource referenced by this statement:

```
<rdfs:range
    rdf:resource="http://www.ePolitix.com/2001/03/rdf-schema#Constituency" />
```

Just as we want to differentiate a constituency from boats and books, surely it is even more important to ensure that the resources referred to in rdfs:range – in this case epx:Constituency – do actually exist as types? The same applies to rdfs:domain – it is important that we determine that the resource referred to here is really a class, otherwise it makes no sense to allow it to have properties:

```
<rdfs:domain
      rdf:resource="http://www.Schemas.org/2001/01/rdf-schema#Person" />
```

All of this is achieved by specifying RDF schema restrictions on the components of the RDF schema. We know that there are properties called rdfs:domain and rdfs:range, and that they can only be used inside an rdf:Property definition, so let's specify that:

```
<rdf:RDF
  xmlns:rdf="http://www.w3.org/1999/02/22-rdf-syntax-ns#"
  xmlns:rdfs="http://www.w3.org/2000/01/rdf-schema#"
>
    <rdf:Property rdf:about="http://www.w3.org/2000/01/rdf-schema#domain">
        <rdfs:domain
            rdf:resource="http://www.w3.org/1999/02/22-rdf-syntax-ns#Property" />
    </rdf:Property>
    <rdf:Property rdf:about="http://www.w3.org/2000/01/rdf-schema#range">
        <rdfs:domain
            rdf:resource="http://www.w3.org/1999/02/22-rdf-syntax-ns#Property" />
    </rdf:Property>
</rdf:RDF>
```

We also know that both properties have a value that must be an `rdfs:Class`:

```
<rdf:RDF
  xmlns:rdf="http://www.w3.org/1999/02/22-rdf-syntax-ns#"
  xmlns:rdfs="http://www.w3.org/2000/01/rdf-schema#"
>
    <rdf:Property rdf:about="http://www.w3.org/2000/01/rdf-schema#domain">
        <rdfs:domain
            resource="http://www.w3.org/1999/02/22-rdf-syntax-ns#Property" />
        <rdfs:range resource="http://www.w3.org/2000/01/rdf-schema#Class" />
    </rdf:Property>
    <rdf:Property rdf:about="http://www.w3.org/2000/01/rdf-schema#range">
        <rdfs:domain
            resource="http://www.w3.org/1999/02/22-rdf-syntax-ns#Property" />
        <rdfs:range resource="http://www.w3.org/2000/01/rdf-schema#Class" />
    </rdf:Property>
</rdf:RDF>
```

You'll find in the RDF Schema specification more information on the domain and range values for the elements of the schema. If you will be using RDF schema a lot then it is worth studying the RDF/XML Recommendation at http://www.w3.org/2000/01/rdf-schema to get a handle on the syntax. We'll look at them briefly here.

Other Schema Elements

The most important parts of RDF Schema have now been introduced. For the sake of completeness, in this section we will run quickly through the remaining elements. The following schema excerpts can be found in http://www.w3.org/2000/01/rdf-schema which is why they use the `rdf:ID` attribute, rather than full URIs in `rdf:about` attributes.

Resources

This first group of schema items relates to the definition of resources.

rdfs:Resource

Although we have acted as if any URI that appears in an `rdf:about` or `rdf:ID` attribute identifies a resource, it is possible to more explicitly state that a URI refers to a resource. Although a bit self-referential, `rdfs:Resource` is defined as a class:

```
<rdfs:Class rdf:ID="Resource" />
```

This therefore also gives us the `rdf:type`:

http://www.w3.org/2000/01/rdf-schema#Resource

rdfs:label

In some situations a human-readable version of a URI would be required, perhaps to display on a data entry form or in a report. To achieve this, the schema allows for a label to be attached to a resource. For example:

```
<rdf:RDF
 xmlns:rdf="http://www.w3.org/1999/02/22-rdf-syntax-ns#"
 xmlns:rdfs="http://www.w3.org/2000/01/rdf-schema#"
>
    <rdfs:Class rdf:about="http://mydata.com/2001/01/rdf-schema#Minister">
        <rdfs:label>Government Minister</rdfs:label>
        <rdfs:subClassOf
         rdf:resource="http://www.ePolitix.com/2001/03/rdf-schema#Politician"
         />
    </rdfs:Class>
</rdf:RDF>
```

Note how the RDF schema limits the range of the `rdfs:label` property to a string literal:

```
<rdf:Property rdf:ID="label">
    <rdfs:domain rdf:resource="#Resource"/>
    <rdfs:range rdf:resource="#Literal"/>
</rdf:Property>
```

rdfs:comment

RDF Schema also provides a facility for comments to be added to resources. Again the property can only be used on a resource of type `rdf:Resource` and its value must be a string literal:

```
<rdf:Property rdf:ID="comment">
    <rdfs:domain rdf:resource="#Resource"/>
    <rdfs:range rdf:resource="#Literal"/>
</rdf:Property>
```

Schema Control

This next group of schema items is intended to relate to the use of schemas.

rdfs:seeAlso

The `rdfs:seeAlso` property indicates a resource that may contain more information. Exactly what that information is remains undefined – it will depend on the application. The domain and range of this property are as follows:

```
<rdf:Property rdf:ID="seeAlso">
    <rdfs:range rdf:resource="#Resource"/>
    <rdfs:domain rdf:resource="#Resource"/>
</rdf:Property>
```

rdfs:isDefinedBy

Although the exact workings of `rdfs:seeAlso` are undefined, a sub-property of that property does deal directly with schema. As with `rdf:seeAlso`, this property can be applied to any instance of `rdfs:Resource` and may have as its value any `rdfs:Resource`. The most common anticipated usage is to identify an RDF schema:

```
<rdf:Property rdf:ID="isDefinedBy">
    <rdfs:subPropertyOf rdf:resource="#seeAlso"/>
    <rdfs:range rdf:resource="#Resource"/>
    <rdfs:domain rdf:resource="#Resource"/>
</rdf:Property>
```

The main use of this property will be when it is not obvious what schema should be used for a property or class. We can express our earlier candidate example using a typed node, as follows:

```
<epx:Candidate
 rdf:about="http://www.epolitix.com/austin-mitchell"
 xmlns:rdf="http://www.w3.org/1999/02/22-rdf-syntax-ns#"
 xmlns:s="http://www.Schemas.org/2001/01/rdf-schema#"
 xmlns:epx="http://www.ePolitix.com/2001/03/rdf-schema#"
>
    <s:Name>Austin Mitchell</s:Name>
    <s:DOB>19 September, 1934</s:DOB>
    <epx:CandidateFor
        rdf:resource="http://www.pa.press.net/constituencies/281" />
    <epx:MemberOf rdf:resource="http://www.ePolitix.com/parties#labour" />
</epx:Candidate>
```

Then it is pretty straightforward to see where the schemas are located since they are identified by the XML namespace declarations. However, if we had represented the same information like this, it is not so clear where the schema that defines `epx:Candidate` is located:

```
<rdf:Description
 rdf:about="http://www.epolitix.com/austin-mitchell"
 xmlns:rdf="http://www.w3.org/1999/02/22-rdf-syntax-ns#"
 xmlns:s="http://www.Schemas.org/2001/01/rdf-schema#"
 xmlns:epx="http://www.ePolitix.com/2001/03/rdf-schema#"
>
    <rdf:type resource="http://www.ePolitix.com/2001/03/rdf-schema#Candidate" />
    <s:Name>Austin Mitchell</s:Name>
    <s:DOB>19 September, 1934</s:DOB>
```

```
      <epx:CandidateFor
          rdf:resource="http://www.pa.press.net/constituencies/281" />
      <epx:MemberOf rdf:resource="http://www.ePolitix.com/parties#labour" />
  </rdf:Description>
```

In this case it is useful to indicate where the schema for the type can be located, like this:

```
<rdf:Description
  rdf:about="http://www.ePolitix.com/2001/03/rdf-schema#Candidate"
  xmlns:rdf="http://www.w3.org/1999/02/22-rdf-syntax-ns#"
>
    <rdfs:isDefinedBy
          rdf:resource="http://www.ePolitix.com/2001/03/rdf-schema" />
</rdf:Description>
```

Constraints

We have seen two types of limitation on the relationships that can be described with RDF Schema, and they are `rdfs:domain` and `rdfs:range`. However, RDF Schema has a facility to allow other constraints to be created, although it does not define how those constraints should be handled by a particular RDF processing application.

rdfs:ConstraintResource

The first element in this group is a base class from which other constraint classes can be derived.

```
<rdfs:Class rdf:ID="ConstraintResource">
    <rdfs:subClassOf rdf:resource="#Resource"/>
</rdfs:Class>
```

The purpose is simply that a parser will know that it has a constraint if it encounters a class that is based on this class. As RDF Schema stands at the moment though, there is no way for the parser to then "discover" how it should process that constraint. RDF Schema in its basic form does derive some classes – the `rdfs:domain` and `rdfs:range` constraints – from this class though.

rdfs:ConstraintProperty

The `ConstraintProperty` class is also used as a basis from which to derive other classes – in this case classes that are properties that in some way constrain values in RDF schema. Note that this class is both a constraint resource and a property:

```
<rdfs:Class rdf:ID="ConstraintProperty">
    <rdfs:subClassOf
          rdf:resource="http://www.w3.org/1999/02/22-rdf-syntax-ns#Property"/>
    <rdfs:subClassOf rdf:resource="#ConstraintResource"/>
</rdfs:Class>
```

This class forms the basis for the two constraints that you have already seen – `rdfs:domain` and `rdfs:range`. I'll show their schema definitions here for completeness. First `rdfs:domain`:

```
<rdfs:ConstraintProperty rdf:ID="domain">
    <rdfs:range rdf:resource="#Class" />
    <rdfs:domain
          rdf:resource="http://www.w3.org/1999/02/22-rdf-syntax-ns#Property" />
</rdfs:ConstraintProperty>
```

and then `rdfs:range`:

```
<rdfs:ConstraintProperty rdf:ID="range">
    <rdfs:range rdf:resource="#Class" />
    <rdfs:domain
        rdf:resource="http://www.w3.org/1999/02/22-rdf-syntax-ns#Property" />
</rdfs:ConstraintProperty>
```

RDF Elements

RDF Schema also defines the basic RDF types.

rdf:Property

RDF Schema defines a class for `rdf:Property` as follows:

```
<rdfs:Class rdf:about="http://www.w3.org/1999/02/22-rdf-syntax-ns#Property">
    <rdfs:subClassOf rdf:resource="#Resource"/>
</rdfs:Class>
```

rdf:value

RDF Schema defines the `rdf:value` property as follows:

```
<rdf:Property rdf:about="http://www.w3.org/1999/02/22-rdf-syntax-ns#value" />
```

rdf:Statement, rdf:subject, rdf:predicate, and rdf:object

The elements required to create reified statements, in other words to create representations of the statements, are defined in RDF Schema like this:

```
<rdfs:Class rdf:about="http://www.w3.org/1999/02/22-rdf-syntax-ns#Statement">
    <rdfs:subClassOf rdf:resource="#Resource"/>
</rdfs:Class>

<rdf:Property rdf:about="http://www.w3.org/1999/02/22-rdf-syntax-ns#subject">
    <rdfs:domain
        rdf:resource="http://www.w3.org/1999/02/22-rdf-syntax-ns#Statement"/>
    <rdfs:range rdf:resource="#Resource"/>
</rdf:Property>

<rdf:Property rdf:about="http://www.w3.org/1999/02/22-rdf-syntax-ns#predicate">
    <rdfs:domain
        rdf:resource="http://www.w3.org/1999/02/22-rdf-syntax-ns#Statement"/>
    <rdfs:range
        rdf:resource="http://www.w3.org/1999/02/22-rdf-syntax-ns#Property"/>
</rdf:Property>

<rdf:Property rdf:about="http://www.w3.org/1999/02/22-rdf-syntax-ns#object">
    <rdfs:domain
        rdf:resource="http://www.w3.org/1999/02/22-rdf-syntax-ns#Statement"/>
</rdf:Property>
```

Container Elements

All of the RDF container elements – `rdf:Bag`, `rdf:Seq`, and `rdf:Alt` – are based on a class called `rdfs:Container`. This makes it easier for the parser to spot resources that are of type container, regardless of which type of container is used. The schema therefore defines the base class first:

```
<rdfs:Class rdf:ID="Container">
  <rdfs:subClassOf rdf:resource="#Resource"/>
</rdfs:Class>
```

It then defines the `rdf:Bag`, `rdf:Seq`, and `rdf:Alt` classes:

```
<rdfs:Class rdf:about="http://www.w3.org/1999/02/22-rdf-syntax-ns#Bag">
    <rdfs:subClassOf rdf:resource="#Container"/>
</rdfs:Class>

<rdfs:Class rdf:about="http://www.w3.org/1999/02/22-rdf-syntax-ns#Seq">
    <rdfs:subClassOf rdf:resource="#Container"/>
</rdfs:Class>

<rdfs:Class rdf:about="http://www.w3.org/1999/02/22-rdf-syntax-ns#Alt">
    <rdfs:subClassOf rdf:resource="#Container"/>
</rdfs:Class>
```

There is one more property that relates to the members of a container, which we saw in the previous chapter. As you remember, to specify the following property we can use syntax like this:

```
<rdf:Description rdf:about="http://www.ePolitix.com/Articles/0000001AEA32.htm">
  <dc:Subject>
    <rdf:Bag>
      <rdf:li>foot-and-mouth</rdf:li>
      <rdf:li>agriculture</rdf:li>
    </rdf:Bag>
  </dc:Subject>
</rdf:Description>
```

or this:

```
<rdf:Description rdf:about="http://www.ePolitix.com/Articles/0000001AEA32.htm">
  <dc:Subject>
    <rdf:Bag rdf:_1="foot-and-mouth" rdf:_2="agriculture" />
  </dc:Subject>
</rdf:Description>
```

Either of these two ways of specifying the property amounts to the same set of triples when parsed. RDF Schema calls this property a **container membership property**, and defines it as follows:

```
<rdfs:Class rdf:ID="ContainerMembershipProperty">
    <rdfs:subClassOf
            rdf:resource="http://www.w3.org/1999/02/22-rdf-syntax-ns#Property"/>
</rdfs:Class>
```

Note that the definition does not limit the domain of this property to a class of type rdfs:Container, but it should actually be like this:

```
<rdfs:Class rdf:ID="ContainerMembershipProperty">
    <rdfs:subClassOf rdf:resource="http://www.w3.org/1999/02/22-rdf-syntax-
ns#Property" />
    <rdfs:domain rdf:resource="#Container" />
</rdfs:Class>
```

Of course, as RDF Schema stands, there is no easy way to automatically generate all the triples for the properties that are derived from this class:

```
<rdf:Description rdf:about=" http://www.w3.org/1999/02/22-rdf-syntax-ns#_1">
    <rdf:type resource="http://www.w3.org/1999/02/22-rdf-syntax-ns#Property"/>
    <rdfs:subPropertyOf rdf:resource="#ContainerMembershipProperty"/>
</rdf:Description>
<rdf:Description rdf:about=" http://www.w3.org/1999/02/22-rdf-syntax-ns#_2">
    <rdf:type resource="http://www.w3.org/1999/02/22-rdf-syntax-ns#Property"/>
    <rdfs:subPropertyOf rdf:resource="#ContainerMembershipProperty"/>
</rdf:Description>
<rdf:Description rdf:about=" http://www.w3.org/1999/02/22-rdf-syntax-ns#_3">
    <rdf:type resource="http://www.w3.org/1999/02/22-rdf-syntax-ns#Property"/>
    <rdfs:subPropertyOf rdf:resource="#ContainerMembershipProperty"/>
</rdf:Description>
...
```

The closest we can get would be to use the aboutEachPrefix:

```
<rdf:Description
    rdf:aboutEachPrefix="http://www.w3.org/1999/02/22-rdf-syntax-ns#">
    <rdf:type resource="http://www.w3.org/1999/02/22-rdf-syntax-ns#Property" />
    <rdfs:subPropertyOf rdf:resource="#ContainerMembershipProperty" />
</rdf:Description>
```

but this would allow non-integers as the final part of the fragment identifier:

```
<rdf:Description rdf:about="http://www.ePolitix.com/Articles/0000001AEA32.htm">
  <dc:Subject>
    <rdf:Bag rdf:_yt7ER4="foot-and-mouth" rdf:_ab113zy="agriculture" />
  </dc:Subject>
</rdf:Description>
```

It is highly likely that this type of constraint will be possible in a future version of RDF Schema.

Typing in RDF and RDF Schema

The only remaining item to discuss is rdf:type. RDF Schema defines this as follows:

```
<rdf:Property rdf:about="http://www.w3.org/1999/02/22-rdf-syntax-ns#type">
    <rdfs:range rdf:resource="#Class" />
</rdf:Property>
```

which implies that the only resources that can be used as values for the `rdf:type` predicate are those that are of type `rdfs:Class`.

I've purposefully left this until the end because it points to a glaring gap between RDF syntax and RDF Schema. From this schema constraint it would appear that an RDF/XML document can only use the `rdf:type` property if it is using an RDF schema. This may well be the intention, but it is not referred to at all in the RDF Model and Syntax document. In that document it seems that a resource can be typed, without the type URI itself being checked – in other words you can produce RDF/XML documents that have typed resources but on which you don't want to impose a schema.

At first sight this does not seem to be a problem – give schema to those who want it, and omit if for those who don't. The problem is, what should a schema processor do with a document that uses `rdf:type`, but was intended for a non-schema aware processor? How is it to know that the resource referred to in the type attribute is *not* a schema, but just some made up URI? And what if there *is* a schema at the address referred to by the URI? It may well be the case that some RDF model makes use of types that originate in some schema, but it does not want to be validated against that schema – how is our parser to know?

Inferencing

Anther point worth mentioning about RDF schemas – and currently quite contentious – is that although the most obvious way to use schemas is to validate an RDF model, they could also be used to draw conclusions about an RDF model – or inference.

Take the schema statements that we gave earlier for a party member:

```
<rdf:Property rdf:ID="MemberOf">
    <rdfs:domain rdf:resource="#Politician" />
    <rdfs:range rdf:resource="#PoliticalParty" />
</rdf:Property>
```

Now imagine that our inferencing software was given the following model:

```
<rdf:Description
  rdf:about="http://www.epolitix.com/austin-mitchell"
  xmlns:rdf="http://www.w3.org/1999/02/22-rdf-syntax-ns#"
  xmlns:s="http://www.Schemas.org/2001/01/rdf-schema#"
  xmlns:epx="http://www.ePolitix.com/2001/03/rdf-schema#"
>
    <s:Name>Austin Mitchell</s:Name>
    <s:DOB>19 September, 1934</s:DOB>
    <epx:MemberOf rdf:resource="http://www.ePolitix.com/parties#labour" />
</rdf:Description>
```

Note that there is no type information, but given the presence of the `epx:MemberOf` predicate, we could use the schema statement to infer that:

❑   The resource identified by `http://www.epolitix.com/austin-mitchell` is of type `epx:Politician`.

❑   The resource identified by `http://www.ePolitix.com/parties#labour` is of type `epx:PoliticalParty`.

Although this usage of RDF Schema has obvious uses, there are problems with merging validation and inferencing into one set of definitions. The main problem as far as the current state of RDF Schema is concerned relates to the `rdfs:domain` property. Recall that this property can appear more than once in an `rdf:Property` definition, reflecting the fact that a property can be valid on more than one class:

```
<rdf:Property
  rdf:about="http://www.ePolitix.com/2001/03/rdf-schema#Region"
  xmlns:rdf="http://www.w3.org/1999/02/22-rdf-syntax-ns#"
>
    <rdfs:domain
          rdf:resource="http://www.Schemas.org/2001/01/rdf-schema#Person" />
    <rdfs:domain
          rdf:resource="http://www.Schemas.org/2001/01/rdf-schema#Company" />
</rdf:Property>
```

As far as validation is concerned, this simply means that the `epx:Region` property may appear on a `Person` class or a `Company` class. But what would the same schema mean when performing inferencing? The occurrence of the `epx:Region` property would mean that the resource with this property is either a `Person` or a `Company`, but we cannot conclude which.

There is a proposal with the W3C's working group on RDF to resolve this by saying that if a resource has the `epx:Region` property it is *both* a `Person` and a `Company`. The consequence of this when using the schema for validation would be that the `epx:Region` property would only be applicable to classes which are of type `Person` *and* of type `Company`. This seems to me to actually weaken RDF Schema as a whole, and instead the situation is best resolved by adding a layer of classes to RDF Schema specifically for inferencing. We will look at how further languages can be layered on top of RDF Schema in the next section.

New Layers on RDF Schema

RDF Schema provides a number of useful features that can be used to restrict meta data. We have seen that a limit can be placed on the possible values that can be used with a predicate, and we have also seen that it is possible to specify which predicates can apply to which resource types.

But whilst this is an important layer to build on top of RDF, for many applications it will not be enough. For example, we may want to say that if a person has credit card information in their meta data, then they must also have an address. Restrictions such as this cannot be specified with the current set of constraints used in RDF Schema. RDF Schema was deliberately scaled back to provide a minimum set of features. The idea is to enable the development of a number of ontology languages, but that each such language would have the same basic notions of Class, Property, domain and range.

We may also want to use the schema information for different applications. As we saw in the previous section, we may want to use the schema to say that any resource that has a constituency property is a Member of Parliament. We noted in the previous section that simple inferences such as this could be carried out using RDF Schema as it stands, but more complex derivations could not. What if we want to say that any MP, who won their seat by only 5% more votes than whoever came second, is in a precarious situation come the next election?

That may seem a little long-winded, but there are many situations where the ability to either define a new class from another class with additional restrictions – a `child` is a `person` whose `age` is less than 18 – or to infer something from a combination of values – if you are `male` and your `father` is the same `person` as my `father` then you are my `brother` – will be extremely useful, if not essential.

RDF Schema was designed with extension in mind, and you'll find some extensions at the SemanticWeb.org web site (http://www.semanticweb.org). We will finish this chapter with a brief look at two of these extensions – OIL and DAML.

An Example RDF Schema Extension: OIL

The OIL initiative is funded by the European Union IST program for Information Society Technologies under the On-To-Knowledge project and IBROW. More information can be found at http://www.ontoknowledge.org/oil.

It's not completely clear what OIL stands for – it could be Ontology Inference Layer, or Ontology Interchange Language. Regardless of the exact definition, the concept of **ontologies** is key.

Ontologies

An ontology is a set of agreed terms. For example, we might create an ontology for the animal kingdom that gives us terms such as animal, mammal, fish and carnivore. Similarly, the concepts we have seen for politics – politician, candidate, minister, and so on – could also comprise an ontology, because it is an agreed set of terms. Arranging the terms hierarchically allows us to determine that, for example, mammals are animals, or candidates are politicians.

Within an ontology we can go further than just defining a set of terms – we can also specify how they relate to each other. So we might say, for example, that an animal that is a carnivore cannot also be a herbivore. We might also specify conclusions that can be drawn, for example, if the food source of an animal is only other animals then we can infer that the animal is a carnivore.

Whilst RDF Schema has certain features to allow the building of simple ontologies, OIL has been created with ontologies in mind, and adds more functionality. Let's have a look at some of the features of OIL.

Defining an Ontology

We won't go into OIL in great detail, since the purpose of this chapter is RDF Schema. Instead we'll look at a few features of OIL and then see how they can be implemented by extending RDF Schema.

OIL ontologies do not actually *require* RDF. The language provides a simple English-type syntax to express rules in. However, these sentences are very easily mapped to RDF and the OIL documentation discusses how the English-type syntaxes can be represented with RDF/XML. We'll explore both means of representation as we look at some of the features of OIL.

The first feature to look at is the class definition. At its simplest a class can be defined as a specialisation of another class (words that are part of OIL's semantics get shown in bold in the OIL language):

```
class-def lion
     subclass-of animal
```

You probably didn't have to spend long thinking about that one to see how we might model this using RDF Schema:

```
<rdf:Class rdf:ID="lion">
    <rdf:subClassOf rdf:resource="#animal">
</rdf:Class>
```

Let's look at some more of OIL's features. We said that OIL could define a class as a set of objects that meet certain criteria. Let's say that the class of `herbivores` has as its members all objects that are *not* a member of the class `carnivores`:

```
class-def herbivore
      subclass-of animal
      subclass-of NOT carnivore
```

We could specify this using the OIL RDF Schema, as follows:

```
<rdf:RDF
 xmlns:rdf="http://www.w3.org/1999/02/22-rdf-syntax-ns#"
 xmlns:rdfs="http://www.w3.org/TR/1999/PR-rdf-schema-19990303#"
 xmlns:oil="http://www.ontoknowledge.org/oil/rdf-schema"
>
    <rdfs:Class rdf:ID="herbivore">
        <rdf:type rdf:resource="http://www.ontoknowledge.org/oil/rdf-
schema/#DefinedClass"/>
        <rdfs:subClassOf rdf:resource="#animal"/>
        <rdfs:subClassOf>
            <oil:NOT>
                <oil:hasOperand rdf:resource="#carnivore"/>
            </oil:NOT>
        </rdfs:subClassOf>
    </rdfs:Class>
</rdf:RDF>
```

First we define the class. This class is then made a subclass of two other classes. The first is pretty easy to see, and is the `animal` class. However, note the second – the class is effectively an anonymous resource which represents all objects that are *not* members of the `carnivore` class. The ability to subclass from an anonymous resource is perfectly valid in ordinary RDF Schema – what is new here is the ability to define one set of objects as the negation of some other set of objects. The class `herbivore` is defined as all `animals` that are *not* `carnivores`.

We'll now look at how OIL handles what we would call properties in RDF Schema. The definition of a `carnivore` is any `animal` that eats others:

```
class-def defined carnivore
    subclass-of animal
    slot-constraint eats
        value-type animal
```

The OIL RDF Schema version of this is:

```
<rdfs:Class rdf:ID="carnivore">
    <rdfs:subClassOf rdf:resource="#animal"/>
    <oil:hasSlotConstraint>
        <oil:ValueType>
            <oil:hasProperty rdf:resource="#eats"/>
            <oil:hasClass rdf:resource="#animal"/>
        </oil:ValueType>
    </oil:hasSlotConstraint>
</rdfs:Class>
```

In OIL terminology a slot is basically a property. **Slot constraints** allow the value of a particular property to limited – or in this case inferred. So any class that is derived from the class animal, which has a property of eats and a value of a class that is also derived from the class animal can be concluded to be a carnivore. We merely need to extend our definition of lion as follows, to allow us to infer that lions are carnivores:

```
<rdfs:Class rdf:ID="lion">
    <rdfs:subClassOf rdf:resource="#animal"/>
    <oil:hasSlotConstraint>
        <oil:ValueType>
            <oil:hasProperty rdf:resource="#eats"/>
            <oil:hasClass rdf:resource="#herbivore"/>
        </oil:ValueType>
    </oil:hasSlotConstraint>
</rdfs:Class>
```

Just to reinforce the fact that the OIL elements in this schema are extensions of RDF Schema, let's look at the schema definition for one of the elements in an earlier example. The hasOperand property was used within <oil:NOT> to link the Boolean expression – in this case *not* – with another expression – in this case the class carnivore. The hasOperand property is defined as being allowable on classes of type BooleanExpression, and the values that can be used with hasOperand must be Expressions:

```
<rdf:Property rdf:ID="hasOperand">
    <rdfs:domain rdf:resource="#BooleanExpression" />
    <rdfs:range rdf:resource="#Expression" />
</rdf:Property>
```

The range of features that OIL defines is quite wide, although the plan is that further levels build on top of OIL, as the following diagram from the OIL web site shows:

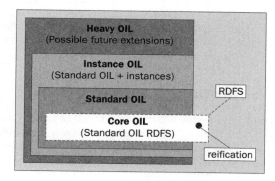

I'll leave you to explore the web site if you want to find out more, but before I do, let's finish on one more example from OIL, which is the very useful ability to define inverse relations. At their simplest these can be used to say things like, if class A eats class B, then class B can be said to be eaten by class A. This is extremely useful in many areas – not just ontologies – and can be expressed in OIL the following way:

```
slot-def eats
    inverse is-eaten-by
```

and using RDFS, like this:

```
<rdf:Property rdf:ID="eats">
    <oil:inverseRelationOf rdf:resource="#is-eaten-by"/>
</rdf:Property>
<rdf:Property rdf:ID="is-eaten-by"/>
```

As you can see we have two properties `eats` and `is-eaten-by`. However, one is defined to be the inverse of the other, so that from our previous example:

```
<rdfs:Class rdf:ID="lion">
    <rdfs:subClassOf rdf:resource="#animal"/>
    <oil:hasSlotConstraint>
        <oil:ValueType>
            <oil:hasProperty rdf:resource="#eats"/>
            <oil:hasClass rdf:resource="#herbivore"/>
        </oil:ValueType>
    </oil:hasSlotConstraint>
</rdfs:Class>
```

we can conclude that `herbivores` are eaten by `lions`.

OIL and RDF Schema

We have said that OIL extends RDF Schema, but be aware that this would require an RDF processor that knew how to handle the OIL extensions. Although an RDF Schema processor would have no problems processing an ontology defined using OIL, there is much that it would miss out.

For example, in our illustrations above, we showed that the `hasOperand` property could be restricted to classes of a certain type. However, that doesn't help the processor when trying to work out what to *do* with such a property. All a simple RDF Schema processor could do would be to say that an OIL model was consistent from an RDF point of view (no properties are assigned to classes that shouldn't be, for example) but it couldn't draw anything more from the document. It certainly couldn't, for example, conclude that some object is an `herbivore`, because it is not a `carnivore`, or that some object is an `animal` because it is eaten by `lions`. A further layer of processing software would be needed.

An Example RDF Schema Extension: DAML

The US Department of Defence has a research department called DARPA – the Defence Advanced Research Projects Agency. In August 2000 they kicked off a program to develop a language that would better describe the relationships between objects. The language was the DARPA Agent Markup Language – or DAML.

Many regard agents as the key software that will make the Semantic Web work. The idea is that one day you should be able to say to your agent software that you need to organize a business meeting with me in New York, and your software would then check availability dates with my diary agent, check flight information with a travel agent, reserve hotel rooms with a hotel agent, and then confirm all of this information with you and me.

As you can imagine, with the web as it stands the biggest barrier to this type of technology is not so much with the reasoning software, but the fact that most information sources are not talking the same language – the very problem that we encountered at the beginning of our discussion on RDF. The DAML project aims to provide a language that can be used to define further languages that enable the communication of agents.

We won't go into the details on DAML here, but if you are interested you can get more information at http://www.daml.org. For the purposes of our discussion on RDF Schema it is worth just pointing out that DAML is simply a thin layer on top of RDF Schema, providing only a small number of features. These features include simple things such as providing the ability to restrict the number of occurrences there are of a particular property, and the addition of XML Schema data types.

DAML is significant not so much for these additions to RDF Schema, but more because it is itself the basis for further extensions. The DAML project provides a number of further languages for different areas that will hopefully all come together to enable agent technology. One example is DAML+S – or DAML Services – which allows a data service to indicate to other services what features it is capable of supporting. Another example is DAML+OIL, which incorporates all of the elements of OIL that we saw in the previous section, but builds them onto DAML, rather than straight onto RDF Schema. These extensions – and many others – are outlined on the DAML web site.

Summary

We have looked in this chapter at how RDF Schema uses RDF to encode schemas that can be used to check the intention of some RDF-encoded meta data, rather than simply its format, as XML Schema might do. We also saw that RDF Schema is intended to be extendable, and that a great deal of work is going on to extend RDF Schema, particularly in the worlds of knowledge representation and logic. We looked at OIL, which is used to define ontologies, and at DAML, which adds a small number of features to RDF Schema to make it easier to define further languages to facilitate agent technologies to communicate.

In the next chapter we will look at some of the issues that arise when processing the RDF/XML documents that carry our meta data. In particular, we will look at parsing.

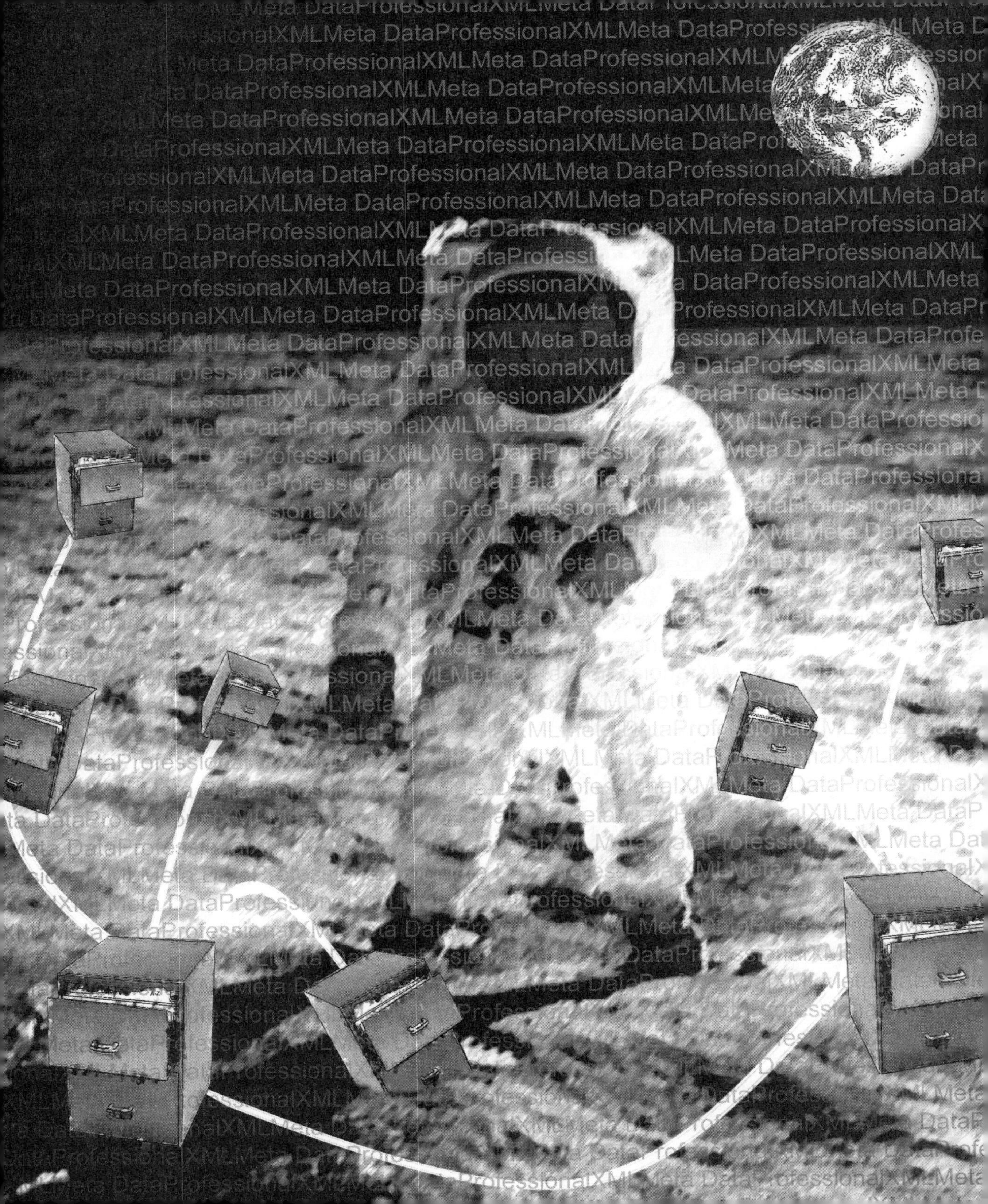

6

Parsing RDF

We have looked in great detail in the last two chapters at how we can represent the RDF model – triples and statements – using XML. We've also looked at how schemas can be used to check the validity of different parts of a triple.

As we said right at the beginning, crucial to understanding RDF is to appreciate that it is the *model* of meta data that we are concerned with, and that RDF/XML is merely one representation of that model using XML. Similarly, RDF Schema uses RDF/XML to represent some rules for checking the integrity of model data, but it is the underlying model of the schema that is important, not its XML representation.

Now that we are familiar with RDF – and I would not recommend this chapter unless you are – the issue is how to make use of it. How do we build applications on top of RDF, which make use of it? In the later chapters of this book, you will see a number of applications that make use of meta information in various forms, and all of these would be suitable candidates to be built on RDF.

However, to build an application that makes use of RDF means that we need to be able to manipulate statements and triples. Whilst we have stressed the importance of triples, and constantly drawn a distinction between the model and the syntax, we haven't said anything about how we get from the syntax to the model, and back again. To achieve this we need a parser – the foundation of any application that will use RDF.

In this chapter we will show how to create an RDF parser. Part of creating the parser will be the creation of an RDF framework. Although you may not want to write your own framework or parser, by the end of this chapter you should be in a position to understand how to integrate RDF parsers into your applications. Let's now look at what a parser is.

Parsers

You will probably be familiar with parsers from a number of computing environments, but most likely from the world of XML. You will not have been able to do much with XML without using a parser, which converts text documents that use the familiar XML syntax into a series of nodes, modeling the logical hierarchy of that text document. Parsers are also available to model the document as a series of events. More information on both types of parser is available in *Professional XML*, 2nd Edition, Wrox Press, ISBN 1-861005-05-9.

Just as XML requires a parser that can translate a text file into something more abstract, so too the world of RDF needs a parser to move from RDF/XML syntax to the RDF model.

RDF Parsers

One of the many confusions for those new to RDF is why you should even need an RDF parser at all. After all, RDF is XML, so why can't we just use a standard XML parser? The simple answer is that the two parsers produce very different abstract models. An XML parser has the task of producing a hierarchical node set, where each node corresponds to one of the XML elements – or attributes, text, comments, and so on – in the original document. The parser can ensure that the XML document conforms to some DTD or schema, but beyond that infers no meaning to the document.

However, the underlying abstraction behind RDF – as we saw in Chapter 4 – is very different. Now, we are dealing with meta data, or the properties of a particular resource rather than simple data types as with DTD and schema. One implication of this is that the two very different XML documents that follow – with their correspondingly varied node hierarchies – would yield exactly the same RDF model. In the first document we say that there is some article that has two pieces of meta data – an author who is identified as Craig Hoy, and a publisher, which is Parliamentary Communications Ltd. In addition we have a piece of meta data about Craig, which indicates that he is an editor:

```
<rdf:RDF>
  <rdf:Description
      about="http://www.ePolitix.com/Articles/0000001AEA32.htm">
    <dc:Creator rdf:resource="http://www.ePolitix.com/Authors/Craig%20Hoy"/>
    <dc:Publisher
        rdf:resource="http://www.CorpInfo.org/companynumber/01262354"/>
  </rdf:Description>

  <rdf:Description about=" http://www.ePolitix.com/Authors/Craig%20Hoy">
    <xyz:JobTitle>editor</xyz:JobTitle>
  </rdf:Description>
</rdf:RDF>
```

The second document also refers to the same article. It has a piece of meta data that says that its author is called Craig Hoy, and that in turn Craig is an editor. There is also another piece of meta data for the article, which is that the publisher is PCL:

```
<rdf:RDF>
  <rdf:Description
      about="http://www.ePolitix.com/Articles/0000001AEA32.htm">
    <dc:Creator>
```

```
     <rdf:Description about=" http://www.ePolitix.com/Authors/Craig%20Hoy">
        <xyz:JobTitle>editor</xyz:JobTitle>
      </rdf:Description>
    </dc:Creator>
    <dc:Publisher
        rdf:resource="http://www.CorpInfo.org/companynumber/01262354"/>
  </rdf:Description>
</rdf:RDF>
```

Since you are a human being with sophisticated parsing abilities, you will have noticed that the two sentences describing the meta data about the article amount to the same thing. Whether we say that:

> A has properties of B and C, and B has a property of D

Or:

> A has a property of B, which has a property of D. A also has a property of C

makes no difference. And indeed you can establish this to be the case since both of these RDF/XML documents amount to the same graph:

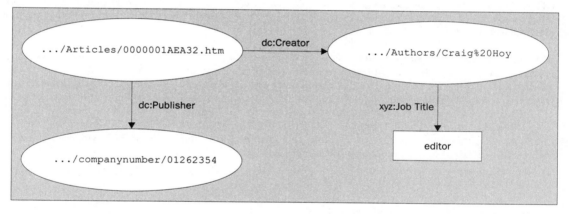

Manipulating this meta data at the level of the RDF *model* is fairly straightforward – we could establish what role Craig plays, or who the publisher of the article is. It wouldn't be so easy if we tried it at the level of XML though. Although we *could* write lots of code to walk through the node hierarchy and then process the RDF however we wanted, we'd find that no sooner had we written some code to navigate through the XML node hierarchy to establish the role of the author, than the meta data would change and we would need to establish the subject of the article. It would be a lot easier to convert the RDF/XML to the model first, and then manipulate the model.

For this reason we need to have a distinct processor for RDF documents. As RDF/XML documents must be valid XML, we can build this processor on top of an XML parser, but then we will need to add functionality so that our RDF parser understands documents as collections of meta data.

So what is the output of an RDF parser to be? If an XML parser produces a hierarchical tree of nodes, what will the RDF parser produce?

Parser Output

An RDF parser must generate statements in the form of triples. Note that there is nothing in the RDF specification that says this is *all* that can be produced. Just as the XML 1.0 specification does not rule out producing a series of "events" when processing an XML document (as is the case with SAX) so the RDF Model and Syntax specification (http://www.w3.org/TR/REC-rdf-syntax/) is not prescriptive about how the underlying model should be represented.

We could mirror the node structure of XML DOM and represent triples as a series of "objects", or we could mirror SAX and represent triples as a series of events – we'll look at both approaches here.

The number of RDF parsers available is growing – although not large. There is enough code out there for you to have a play and see what is possible, and as more and more people get interested in RDF the range of tools will surely grow. The simplest group of tools that you can use to play with RDF makes use of an XSLT stylesheet to convert RDF into a set of triples.

XSLT Stylesheets

It may have already occurred to you that one way of creating a collection of triples would be to run an RDF/XML document through a stylesheet that generates a list of the subject/predicate/object tuples. This is indeed a good way to proceed, and is especially useful to those who are new to RDF, since it makes use of all the tools with which you are familiar.

Although the approach is simple and does not involve writing a parser "proper", the XSLT stylesheets produced are very complex. A number of people have designed very thorough XSLT stylesheets to transform RDF into a list of the triples that would represent the underlying data model. The stylesheet from Jason Diamond (available at http://injektilo.org/rdf/rdft.xsl) is a good place to start, since it covers most parts of RDF, as well as being used by others inside stylesheets that have different purposes. An example of the latter is Jonathan Borden's RDF Extractor (http://www.openhealth.org/RDF/rdf_Syntax_and_Names.htm), which takes HTML with embedded RDF and produces RDF from it (or more exactly, extracts RDF from XHTML).

Typical output from Jason's stylesheet is:

```
<?xml version="1.0" encoding="UTF-16"?>
<model>
  <statement>
    <subject>http://www.ePolitix.com/Articles/0000001AEA32.htm</subject>
    <predicate>http://purl.org/dc/elements/1.0/Creator</predicate>
    <object
       type="resource">http://www.ePolitix.com/Authors/Craig%20Hoy</object>
  </statement>

  <statement>
<subject>http://www.ePolitix.com/Articles/0000001AEA32.htm</subject>
    <predicate>http://purl.org/dc/elements/1.0/Publisher</predicate>
    <object
       type="resource">http://www.CorpInfo.org/companynumber/01262354
    </object>
  </statement>

  <statement>
```

```
        <subject>http://www.ePolitix.com/Authors/Craig%20Hoy</subject>
        <predicate>http://www.xyz.com/Schema/JobTitle</predicate>
        <object type="literal">editor</object>
    </statement>
  </model>
```

This format is much easier to handle than RDF/XML. Navigating through these nodes with the XML DOM would make it easy to use this output for other purposes, such as creating database entries.

For small documents, using stylesheets like Jason's is fine – and indeed is a good way to get to grips with RDF without having to install new software. However, bear in mind that XML DOM needs to read the entire source document before it can style it, which is not a problem for short documents, but becomes very expensive in processing terms when the source document is much larger.

Take WordNet for example. WordNet is a project at Princeton University, which aims to provide an interconnected network of words in English and other languages (see http://www.cogsci.princeton.edu/~wn/). The idea is to provide a hierarchy of words (so that a human is a type of mammal, or a shark is a type of fish), along with their meanings and synonyms. The data is constantly being updated, but what is most exciting for us is that the data is available in RDF. The following section from the "nouns" information shows some different words for the different types of cat:

```
<rdf:RDF
 xmlns:rdf="http://www.w3.org/1999/02/22-rdf-syntax-ns#"
 xmlns:a="http://www.cogsci.princeton.edu/~wn/concept#"
 xmlns:b="http://www.cogsci.princeton.edu/~wn/schema/">
    ...
    <b:Noun
       rdf:about="http://www.cogsci.princeton.edu/~wn/concept#101630921">
        <b:wordForm>Felis catus</b:wordForm>
        <b:wordForm>Felis domesticus</b:wordForm>
        <b:wordForm>domestic cat</b:wordForm>
        <b:wordForm>house cat</b:wordForm>
    </b:Noun>
    <b:Noun
       rdf:about="http://www.cogsci.princeton.edu/~wn/concept#101631393"
     b:wordForm="pussycat"
    >
        <b:wordForm>kitty</b:wordForm>
        <b:wordForm>kitty-cat</b:wordForm>
        <b:wordForm>puss</b:wordForm>
        <b:wordForm>pussy</b:wordForm>
    </b:Noun>
    <b:Noun
       rdf:about="http://www.cogsci.princeton.edu/~wn/concept#101631497"
     b:wordForm="mouser"
    />
    <b:Noun
       rdf:about="http://www.cogsci.princeton.edu/~wn/concept#101631577">
        <b:wordForm>alley cat</b:wordForm>
        <b:wordForm>stray</b:wordForm>
    </b:Noun>
    <b:Noun
       rdf:about="http://www.cogsci.princeton.edu/~wn/concept#101631653">
        <b:wordForm>tom</b:wordForm>
        <b:wordForm>tomcat</b:wordForm>
    </b:Noun>
    ...
</rdf:RDF>
```

207

The problem here is that the document that this excerpt comes from is 9Mb. Using Microsoft Internet Explorer 5 as a very rough test it seems to take over 60Mb of memory, at peak, to run this document through an XSLT stylesheet. But worse – the document takes an age to transform, even if only using Internet Explorer's default stylesheet. And before XSLT can get to work on the document it must be fully loaded. Yet if you look at the structure of the document it is very *flat*; there is no reason why we couldn't be performing some action on the meta data for word alternatives held near the start of the file, while the remainder of the file continues to load.

It is problems like these that SAX addresses for XML, so it makes sense that we can do the same if we build RDF parsers on SAX.

Event-driven RDF Parsers

The most widely used RDF parser is **SiRPAC**, which stands for the Simple RDF Parser and Compiler. Written in Java, the parser is available from http://www.w3.org/RDF/Implementations/SiRPAC/. The parser can also be accessed remotely at this URL, so that you can cut and paste some RDF into a form and get the results back as a set of triples or as a graph. This is very useful when we are experimenting with our own RDF.

As well as the XSLT solution offered earlier, Jason Diamond is also responsible for **repat**, a C version of the Java-based **RDF Filter** by David Megginson, creator of SAX. repat is available at http://injektilo.org/rdf/repat.html, whilst RDF Filter is available at http://www.megginson.com/Software/.

There are a few other parsers –a good starting place if you wish to look for further resources is http://www.w3.org/RDF/ – but I won't list more here since they all rely on much the same principles. Instead we will look at some of the issues that must be addressed in order to write an RDF parser. By understanding these issues we should be well placed to build applications on top of someone else's parser, or to write our own.

SAX

SAX is an event-driven API, firing events whenever the processor encounters some fundamental XML unit. (More detailed information on SAX is available in Chapter 12 of *Professional XML*, 2nd Edition, Wrox Press, ISBN 1-861005-05-9.) For example, if a SAX processor operated on the following XML document:

```
<x>text</x>
```

software built on top of SAX would receive an event for the beginning of the element when the <x> tag was processed, then another event for the text, and lastly an event triggered by the closing <x> tag. SAX has distinct callback functions for each of these events, so with the appropriate processing code, we would get function calls something like this:

```
startElement("x");
characters("text");
endElement("x");
```

To build an RDF parser on top of SAX we would want to process these events as our input and then fire our own set of events as the output. We may want to get very detailed and fire an event like this:

```
    startSubject(s);
```

and this:

```
    startPredicate(p);
```

Or we may be less detailed and fire an event such as:

```
    AddStatement(s, p, o);
```

when all the parts of a triple have been found in a document.

Although it is clear that to process large RDF/XML documents, we need to build our parser on SAX, it's not immediately obvious how exactly to go about this. We could just process the `startElement` event, watch for elements like `<rdf:Description>` and attributes like `rdf:about`, and store the relevant subjects, objects, and predicates, and then each time we have a triple, fire an event. This approach has been taken by some of the parsers that you will see.

There is another approach, however. Imagine that we finished writing our parser and someone wanted to hook the `AddStatement` event up to a database. The way I have described the structure of the parser, this would be pretty straightforward – just add some database specific code to act on the event, but what exactly are the parameters for this `AddStatement` method? Obviously we need a subject, object and predicate, but what should they look like? Of course we know that they are resources and literals, but how should we implement a resource? Should it be an object made up of a string, or perhaps two strings – the namespace and the local name? In some situations we might want to make a resource into a pointer that references an entry in a table of resources, so that duplication of URIs is avoided – multiple references to the same resource would refer to the same entry. We might even want to specify a resource as being a database record ready for insertion into the database when the entire triple is ready.

You can see from this example that although we might be able to define the concepts involved quite clearly – a statement is made up of resources and literals – we don't want to be overly prescriptive about the detail, that is, how they are implemented. We can achieve this flexibility by developing our parser within a generalized framework – an **RDF API**. This is the approach taken by SiRPAC.

RDF API

We have seen that a general-purpose RDF/XML parser is best built on top of SAX, and we want to make it as flexible as possible so that it can be applied to as wide a range of situations as possible. We will now look at how we might achieve this.

Flexibility is achieved by making the parser as modular as possible. For example, while we will obviously want to have a part of the parser that understands RDF/XML, we will also want to allow for the fact that we might want to process the XML created by Jason Diamond's stylesheets. In addition, we might want a module to display the resulting triples on screen as strings, yet we may also need the parser to be able to send the triples to a database or display a labeled graph. In fact, we may even want to change the way that we represent resources – as strings or as references to a dictionary of resources, for example. Firstly, therefore, we need to define what the *concepts* are, in order that we can plan our modules, even if we don't want to say what the detail is.

There are a few such APIs that specify these concepts:

❑ The W3C has the **RDF API,** which is maintained as Stanford University by Sergey Melnik. More information is available online at http://www-db.stanford.edu/~melnik/rdf/api.html. Sergey is also currently working on a more ambitious framework, called the **Generic Interoperability Framework**, which accommodates schemas, and provides means to expand the processing to cope with other schema features (as would be required, say, for OIL).

❑ **Redland** is an RDF application framework built in C, and available at http://www.redland.opensource.ac.uk/. (The author, Dave Beckett, also maintains an excellent list of RDF resources at http://www.ilrt.bris.ac.uk/discovery/rdf/resources/.)

❑ **Jena** is a Java API for RDF that allows RDF models to be manipulated as triples. The software is open source, and is available at http://www-uk.hpl.hp.com/people/bwm/rdf/jena/index.htm. One interesting aspect is support for some DAML+OIL features (see the previous chapter). This API is used and further described in Chapter 12 of this book.

In this chapter we will build our own RDF API, but closely model it on the Stanford API, which has W3C involvement. This API is written in Java, which reflects the involvement of the academic community in the development of much of the software in this area. However, we will use C++ for a couple of reasons:

❑ Little is currently available in this language for RDF.

❑ We want the parser to be as fast as possible so that we can use it inside other applications.

The finished framework can be downloaded from http://www.wrox.com/, as part of the code download for this book.

The API in Brief

Many of the concepts of the API will be discussed in detail in the next section on implementing an RDF parser framework, but here I shall just touch briefly on the main elements that are required. As you may expect, Stanford University's API is somewhat more comprehensive than this brief outline:

❑ During the processing of the XML source document the parser needs to track predicates, subjects, and objects, regardless of the form that the document takes.

❑ Tracking these predicates, subjects, and objects requires the creation and deletion of resources, literals, and statements.

❑ Once a triple has been completely found an event is fired.

The framework therefore needs – at a minimum – to provide the following:

❑ A module to control the generation of RDF from XML. In the RDF API this is called `GenericXML2RDF`.

❑ A module to create resources, literals, and statements with the structure that is specific for a particular application. In the RDF API this is called a **node factory**.

❑ A module to process the events fired when triples are found.

In the following section we will show one way to implement an RDF parser framework, and by the end we will also have produced one variety of RDF parser. By deciding to build a framework, rather than just one specific parser, we will facilitate the creation of other types of parser.

Implementing the RDF Parser Framework

The first set of modules that we will create will allow us to handle SAX more efficiently. These are:

- ❑   A default event handler.
- ❑   A default parser application.

Once we have these modules we can then implement others that provide:

- ❑   A *generic* XML to RDF processor.
- ❑   A *specific* XML to RDF processor. We will build one that understands RDF/XML.
- ❑   A node factory.
- ❑   A *generic* triple event consumer.
- ❑   A *specific* triple event consumer. We will build one that simply writes to the standard output stream so that we can see the results of our parsing.

In the following diagrams, single line rectangles indicate classes in the code, whilst boxes with double lines represent interfaces – that is, classes that are a basis for other classes, but are never themselves used. An arrow between two classes indicates that one class inherits from the other, in the direction of the arrow so, for example, in the first diagram DefaultHandler, the class inherits from the GenericParser class. A dotted arrow indicates that one class has a reference to the other class.

The naming convention I have adopted in the code that follows is that a class will begin with "C" (for example, CGenericParser, or CDefaultHandler) whilst an interface will begin with "I" (for example, IRDFParser).

The resulting framework will be as follows. We have a generic parser that takes XML input of some sort – not necessarily RDF/XML – and onto that we build a specific RDF/XML processor:

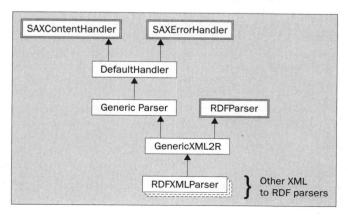

CRDFXMLParser is specific to RDF/XML, whilst CGenericXML2RDF provides the core functionality for parsing XML to RDF. This core functionality will use whatever node factory it is provided with to create resources, literals and statements, and whatever consumer it is provided with to build its model:

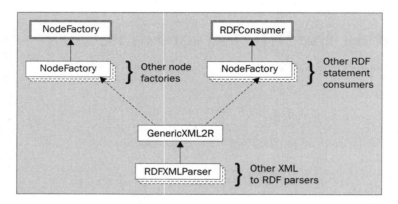

Preparation

In the following code I will be using Microsoft's XML COM objects as the SAX parser, but the principles we will discuss will apply to any SAX parser. In order to run the parser application we are discussing (for which the code is available in the code download for this book), you will need to be running or install Microsoft's XML Parser (MSXML) 3.0. If you are already running it you will have SAX2 available to you. If not, MSXML3 can be downloaded from http://msdn.microsoft.com/xml/.

To program on top of SAX we just need some way of registering our callback functions to receive events, but it does not matter what SAX implementation you use to provide you with the events in the first place. The following code could work on any SAX parser that can provide C/C++ style events.

Creating a Default Event Handler Module

The first module we can place over SAX is the DefaultHandler module. This makes implementation of a SAX application quick and easy. To see how useful this can be, let's first think about how we would normally implement a simple SAX application in C++.

First, we check that a URL to process has been supplied as a command line parameter – if not, we display usage syntax and terminate:

```
int main(int argc, char* argv[])
{
    if (argc < 2) {
        printf("\nUsage:");
        printf("\n\tMySaxApp file:///drive:/path/file.xml\n");
        printf("\n\tMySaxApp http://url\n");
        return 0;
    }
}
```

The next step is to create a SAX XMLReader object. The following code is very specific to the Microsoft SAX implementation, but any application built on SAX would need to create an XMLReader object at this point, using code specific to that parser:

```
CoInitialize(NULL);

ISAXXMLReader* pRdr = NULL;

HRESULT hr = CoCreateInstance(
    __uuidof(SAXXMLReader),
        NULL,
        CLSCTX_ALL,
    __uuidof(ISAXXMLReader),
        (void **)&pRdr);
```

XMLReader is an object that acts as a bridge between SAX and our event handlers. We create functions to handle events such as "start element" and "end element", and then we tell the XMLReader object where it can find these functions. When SAX then processes the XML source document, it calls the events referred to by the XMLReader object as necessary. Our next step, therefore, is to tell the XMLReader object, instantiated by the CoCreateInstance function above, where to find our event-processing functions:

```
if (FAILED(hr))
    printf("\nFailed to create SAX parser (%08X)\n\n", hr);
else
{
    CSAXContentHandler * pCH = new CSAXContentHandler();
    CSAXDTDHandler * pDH = new CSAXDTDHandler();
    CSAXEntityResolver * pER = new CSAXEntityResolver();
    CSAXErrorHandler * pEH = new CSAXErrorHandler();

    pRdr->putContentHandler(pCH);
    pRdr->putDTDHandler(pDH);
    pRdr->putEntityResolver(pER);
    pRdr->putErrorHandler(pEH);
```

You'll see that we haven't actually given the XMLReader a series of event functions, but rather given it a series of objects, which in turn contain the event functions as methods. This allows us to group the events together by the type of situation in which they occur. The advantage of this in normal SAX programming is that you don't have to implement all of the objects listed above. SAX will continue processing if you have no error handling functions, no DTD handling functions, and even no content handling functions. Should an error be encountered, however, the result is unpredictable. It is wise therefore for any SAX application to define all the handler objects specified, even if the functions are empty and do nothing except return.

This approach of creating classes containing the callback functions is key to SAX programming, and is the same whether you use a Java SAX parser or the C++ SAX parser that we are using here. In a moment we will look at how these various classes are implemented, but first let's finish off the typical 'standard' application. Our next step is to get a copy of the URL passed on the command line, and indicate that we are about to begin parsing it:

```
int iLen = strlen(argv[1]) + 1;
wchar_t * pURL = new wchar_t [iLen];
mbstowcs(pURL, argv[1], iLen);
wprintf(L"\nParsing document: %s\n", pURL);
```

Next we actually do the parsing, and echo the result code:

```
hr = pRdr->parseURL(pURL);
```

As you can see, we haven't called the functions that we created in the various handler classes, above. That is because the SAX parser does all of that. We give the parser the address of some functions and then we give program control to SAX. SAX then calls our functions when it has some information for us – such as having found an element or some text – and when it has run out of XML to process, SAX gives program control back to us. The result of the parsing is then available, so that we can determine if the whole process went successfully, so in our typical program we'll print the result:

```
printf("\nParse result code: %08x\n\n",hr);
```

Before we finish the program, we must free up any objects we have created and release the COM object created by Microsoft's XML parser object. This will probably need doing in some form or another, whichever SAX implementation you use:

```
    delete [] pURL;
    pRdr->Release();
    delete pEH;
    delete pER;
    delete pDH;
    delete pCH;
}
```

Finally tidy up and exit:

```
    CoUninitialize();
    return 0;
}
```

When we told XMLReader where to find the event handling functions we could have just passed the address of each function we wanted to implement. However, by passing the address of an object, we can give the XML reader a whole group of functions in one go. We'll now have a look at how classes like CSAXContentHandler and CSAXErrorHandler – which provide the methods that XMLReader will call – are implemented.

Interfaces

Both SAX and the RDF API were defined in Java. This language makes much use of interfaces, which effectively provide templates for further class definitions.

Say we wanted to define in advance what it means to be a television. We might say that to be a television you need to be able to be turned on and off, to change channels, to adjust your brightness, and so on. We wouldn't necessarily say to Sony or Phillips *how* they should implement volume control, or whatever, but we would say that if it didn't have all of these features, we wouldn't call it a television, and of course there is nothing to stop a television from having *more* features, such as a sleep feature, or an alarm clock.

Another example might be a washing machine. A washing machine is not a washing machine if it doesn't have an opening into which laundry can be placed but we wouldn't insist on the hole being on the front or on the top for a machine to earn the title "washing machine". Over the years the position of the hole has changed, without affecting the "washing machineness" of a washing machine.

In object-oriented programming (OOP) the same applies. We have "machines", which in the world of OOP are pieces of software that do a job – **objects**. Objects are always created from classes which essentially specify how the object should look, that is, what features it should have. We might define a class for a person that has properties for the name and age of the person. Then, every time we create an instance of that class – say an object to represent each of the members of the British government – we know that every object would have the same features as the class definition.

As with all of these examples – washing machines, televisions, and people – so too an object must have certain features if it wants to call itself a SAX ContentHandler class. The specification of these features is defined by an **interface** in Java, and an **abstract base class** in C++.

Let's have a look at the definition for ISAXContentHandler, which is the interface definition for ContentHandler in Microsoft's implementation of SAX. Don't worry about the uuid numbers or the fact that the class is derived from IUnknown – these elements relate to bridging between the worlds of COM and C++, and won't concern us until later:

```cpp
struct __declspec(uuid("1545cdfa-9e4e-4497-a8a4-2bf7d0112c44"))
ISAXContentHandler : IUnknown
{
    //
    // Raw methods provided by interface
    //

    virtual HRESULT __stdcall putDocumentLocator (
        struct ISAXLocator * pLocator ) = 0;
    virtual HRESULT __stdcall startDocument ( ) = 0;
    virtual HRESULT __stdcall endDocument ( ) = 0;
    virtual HRESULT __stdcall startPrefixMapping (
        unsigned short * pwchPrefix,
        int cchPrefix,
        unsigned short * pwchUri,
        int cchUri ) = 0;
    virtual HRESULT __stdcall endPrefixMapping (
        unsigned short * pwchPrefix,
        int cchPrefix ) = 0;
    virtual HRESULT __stdcall startElement (
        unsigned short * pwchNamespaceUri,
        int cchNamespaceUri,
        unsigned short * pwchLocalName,
        int cchLocalName,
        unsigned short * pwchQName,
        int cchQName,
        struct ISAXAttributes * pAttributes ) = 0;
    virtual HRESULT __stdcall endElement (
        unsigned short * pwchNamespaceUri,
        int cchNamespaceUri,
        unsigned short * pwchLocalName,
        int cchLocalName,
        unsigned short * pwchQName,
        int cchQName ) = 0;
    virtual HRESULT __stdcall characters (
        unsigned short * pwchChars,
        int cchChars ) = 0;
    virtual HRESULT __stdcall ignorableWhitespace (
```

```
        unsigned short * pwchChars,
        int cchChars ) = 0;
    virtual HRESULT __stdcall processingInstruction (
        unsigned short * pwchTarget,
        int cchTarget,
        unsigned short * pwchData,
        int cchData ) = 0;
    virtual HRESULT __stdcall skippedEntity (
        unsigned short * pwchName,
        int cchName ) = 0;
};
```

The main thing to note is that the function declarations have "= 0" after them. This is how C++ says that the functionality of this method is not defined here, but any class that inherits from this class *must* implement this method.

To recap – this is an interface, more properly an abstract base class as this is C++, which means you cannot actually create an object of type ISAXContentHandler, but you can derive other classes from it. This is lucky, because if we did create such an object and then gave it to the XMLReader object we met earlier, SAX would be trying to call our event handlers, such as "start of element", "end of element", and so on. Also, since we haven't defined any of these handlers, the parser would crash. ISAXContentHandler is an interface that tells us what our ContentHandler should *look like*, but doesn't actually implement any code.

This is how we implement the "modules" that we were discussing when we introduced the idea of an RDF API or parser framework. One of the modules we said we needed, for example, was to provide generic XML to RDF processing instructions. Although we won't say how someone must implement that module, we can use interfaces to say what that module must look like, by specifying its input/output requirements. We can define the methods it must expose, what parameters they should take, and the values each should return.

So what does an implementation of a ContentHandler object look like? We start by declaring that the class inherits the above interface, in other words that this new class is a type of SAXContentHandler:

```
class CSAXContentHandler : public ISAXContentHandler
{
public:
    CSAXContentHandler();
    virtual ~CSAXContentHandler();
```

We then have to provide a proper implementation for each of the 'template' methods:

```
virtual HRESULT STDMETHODCALLTYPE putDocumentLocator(
    /* [in] */ ISAXLocator __RPC_FAR *pLocator);

virtual HRESULT STDMETHODCALLTYPE startDocument(void);

virtual HRESULT STDMETHODCALLTYPE endDocument(void);

...
```

Note that we have now dropped the '= 0' from the end of each method's declaration, which means that we are going to actually implement their functionality in this class. Also noteworthy is that we have still declared the function as virtual, which means that a class that bases itself on this class can define alternative methods to employ when SAX events are fired. This will be important when we come to actually implement a particular parser, since it will be necessary to overload the empty handler methods that do nothing.

One quick point before we move on – recall that ISAXContentHandler itself was based on IUnknown. This allows it to be a COM interface if necessary – more later – which means the following three functions must be implemented too:

```
    long __stdcall QueryInterface(const struct _GUID &,void **);
    unsigned long __stdcall AddRef(void);
    unsigned long __stdcall Release(void);
};
```

Now back to our SAX events. The actual implementations of each of the methods can be as simple as this:

```
HRESULT STDMETHODCALLTYPE CSAXContentHandler::startElement(
        /* [in] */ wchar_t __RPC_FAR *pwchNamespaceUri,
        /* [in] */ int cchNamespaceUri,
        /* [in] */ wchar_t __RPC_FAR *pwchLocalName,
        /* [in] */ int cchLocalName,
        /* [in] */ wchar_t __RPC_FAR *pwchRawName,
        /* [in] */ int cchRawName,
        /* [in] */ ISAXAttributes __RPC_FAR *pAttributes)
{
    return S_OK;
}
```

Remember that SAX is firing events whenever it has some information to tell our program about. The startElement event is called when an element is found, and SAX passes four parameters to the event:

❑   the namespace of the element

❑   the actual name of the element without the namespace – called the local name

❑   the raw source name

❑   the attributes for the element

These parameters are passed regardless of the SAX implementation that you are using.

> *Note that the Microsoft implementation does not use null terminated strings for the parameters so it provides an additional three parameters to indicate the length of the namespace, local and raw name strings.*

The function we have shown may not do anything, but it at least gives SAX something to call each time it finds the beginning of an XML element. In fact, the function doesn't do anything except return, but it must be implemented if the class is to be created as an instance of a ContentHandler interface.

You may recall that one of the advantages that SAX has over XML DOM is that it doesn't need to read the entire source document before it can act on the nodes, so it's quite possible that a SAX application might do nothing more than wait for a certain element to appear and then process it:

```
HRESULT STDMETHODCALLTYPE CSAXContentHandler::startElement(
        /* [in] */ wchar_t __RPC_FAR *pwchNamespaceUri,
        /* [in] */ int cchNamespaceUri,
        /* [in] */ wchar_t __RPC_FAR *pwchLocalName,
        /* [in] */ int cchLocalName,
        /* [in] */ wchar_t __RPC_FAR *pwchRawName,
```

```
                    /* [in] */ int cchRawName,
                    /* [in] */ ISAXAttributes __RPC_FAR *pAttributes)
    {
        if (!wcsncmp(pwchLocalName, L"element", cchLocalName))
            printf("Found the element, 'element'!!");
        return S_OK;
    }
```

Whether there is a large or small amount of processing involved in the method, the principle that each method must be implemented still applies – and this goes for the error handling, DTD, and entity resolving classes too.

The DefaultHandler Class

Since these classes and their methods need implementing – even if they just return "OK"– for each SAX application we write, it would be much more convenient to introduce another class that provides minimal implementations for all of the methods. This class could then be used as a foundation for all our SAX projects. With this basic class in place we would then only need to implement the specific functions required for our SAX application.

In this chapter, I'll only be showing you the SAX RDF parser application, so we could get by just fine without this intermediary class. I will introduce it, however, because it is referred to in Sergey Melnik's RDF API and is fairly standard procedure for SAX developers. Seeing the procedure will have the added effect of making it easier for you to follow any discussions you might read on the API – although they will generally refer to Java code.

To make things easier to maintain, the DefaultHandler class inherits from *all four* of the interfaces that are needed by an XMLReader object, as follows:

```
class CDefaultHandler :
    public ISAXContentHandler
    public ISAXDTDHandler,
    public ISAXEntityResolver,
    public ISAXErrorHandler
{
public:
    CDefaultHandler();
    virtual ~CDefultHandler();

    /*
     * From ISAXContentHandler
     */

public:
        virtual HRESULT STDMETHODCALLTYPE putDocumentLocator(
            /* [in] */ ISAXLocator __RPC_FAR *pLocator);

        virtual HRESULT STDMETHODCALLTYPE startDocument(void);

        virtual HRESULT STDMETHODCALLTYPE endDocument(void);

        ...
```

```
      /*
       * From ISAXErrorHandler
       */

public:
    virtual HRESULT STDMETHODCALLTYPE error(
        /* [in] */ ISAXLocator __RPC_FAR *pLocator,
        /* [in] */ unsigned short * pwchErrorMessage,
        /* [in] */ HRESULT errCode);

    virtual HRESULT STDMETHODCALLTYPE fatalError(
        /* [in] */ ISAXLocator __RPC_FAR *pLocator,
        /* [in] */ unsigned short * pwchErrorMessage,
        /* [in] */ HRESULT errCode);

    /*
     * ... and so on for each of the content handlers
     */

    ...
};
```

Now, I could have derived a separate handler class from each of the implementations, but I will stick with the approach shown here since it is convenient, and it reflects the RDF API as currently implemented by Sergey. Our "standard" SAX application now looks like this:

```
if (!FAILED(hr))
{
    CDefaultHandler * pDH = new CDefaultHandler();

    pRdr->putContentHandler(pDH);
    pRdr->putDTDHandler(pDH);
    pRdr->putEntityResolver(pDH);
    pRdr->putErrorHandler(pDH);
    int iLen = strlen(argv[1]) + 1;
    wchar_t * pURL = new wchar_t [iLen];
    mbstowcs(pURL, argv[1], iLen);
    wprintf(L"\nParsing document: %s\n", pURL);
    hr = pRdr->parseURL(pURL);
    printf ("\nParse result code: %08x\n\n",hr);
    delete [] pURL;
    pRdr->Release();
    delete pDH;
}
```

It's not a great deal different from before, except that we only have one handler class to worry about. And of course it still does absolutely nothing! However, the advantage of using the DefaultHandler class should be clear when we come to use our classes to create a SAX application. Let's write a SAX program that simply echoes the names of the elements as they pass through SAX.

The definition of our handler class looks like this:

```
class MyHandler : public CDefaultHandler
{
public:
    MyHandler();
    virtual ~MyHandler();
```

```
    virtual HRESULT STDMETHODCALLTYPE startElement(
        /* [in] */ wchar_t __RPC_FAR *pwchNamespaceUri,
        /* [in] */ int cchNamespaceUri,
        /* [in] */ wchar_t __RPC_FAR *pwchLocalName,
        /* [in] */ int cchLocalName,
        /* [in] */ wchar_t __RPC_FAR *pwchRawName,
        /* [in] */ int cchRawName,
        /* [in] */ ISAXAttributes __RPC_FAR *pAttributes);
};
```

We have only declared the `startElement` event, but since our class is derived from `CDefaultHandler` we know that every other method at least has a default implementation. The `startElement` event could then be implemented like this:

```
HRESULT STDMETHODCALLTYPE CMyHandler::startElement(
            /* [in] */ wchar_t __RPC_FAR *pwchNamespaceUri,
            /* [in] */ int cchNamespaceUri,
            /* [in] */ wchar_t __RPC_FAR *pwchLocalName,
            /* [in] */ int cchLocalName,
            /* [in] */ wchar_t __RPC_FAR *pwchRawName,
            /* [in] */ int cchRawName,
            /* [in] */ ISAXAttributes __RPC_FAR *pAttributes)
{
    wprintf(L"Start Element: %.*s\n", cchLocalName, pwchLocalName);
    return S_OK;
}
```

Every time we encounter an event that indicates the start of an element, we just take the local name of the element and write it to standard output.

> *If you're C/C++ is a little rusty, the "%.*s" part of the format string, used in the printf family of functions means write out a string, but limit the length of the string to the number of characters defined by the specified parameter. We need to do this here because in the Microsoft implementation strings are not null terminated.*

To round off, let's see the changes that need to be made to the main program to make use of our revised SAX interface:

```
    if (!FAILED(hr))
    {
        CMyHandler * pMH = new CMyHandler();

        pRdr->putContentHandler(pMH);
        pRdr->putDTDHandler(pMH);
        pRdr->putEntityResolver(pMH);
        pRdr->putErrorHandler(pMH);
        int iLen = strlen(argv[1]) + 1;
        wchar_t * pURL = new wchar_t [iLen];
        mbstowcs(pURL, argv[1], iLen);
        wprintf(L"\nParsing document: %s\n", pURL);
        hr = pRdr->parseURL(pURL);
```

```
        printf("\nParse result code: %08x\n\n",hr);
        delete [] pURL;
        pRdr->Release();
        delete pMH;
    }
```

We now have a complete SAX application and we have only had to create one class and declare one method.

The GenericParser Class

You may say, rightly, that much of the functionality I have just placed into the `main` routine is also common to any SAX application. For this reason the RDF API also makes use of another helper class called `GenericParser`. By "generic parser" we mean a generic SAX parser, not an RDF one. We'll get to RDF soon enough, don't worry.

The `GenericParser` class inherits from `DefaultHandler`, so that it provides all of the default content, DTD, entity, and error handling methods that we have just seen, and then extends this class to provide features such as creating `XMLReader` objects and handling **QNames** (the definition of an element name using a namespace, a colon and the local name).

The full implementation of `GenericParser` is quite large, so here I shall only implement the features we need to improve the speed with which we can generate a SAX application. The first function we will define creates an `XMLReader` object:

```
HRESULT CGenericParser::createXMLReader(wchar_t * pwchClassName,
    ISAXXMLReader** pXMLReader)
{
    *pXMLReader = NULL;

    HRESULT hr = CoCreateInstance(
        __uuidof(SAXXMLReader),
            NULL,
            CLSCTX_ALL,
        __uuidof(ISAXXMLReader),
            (void **)pXMLReader);
    return hr;
}
```

As you can see, this is exactly the same as the code that we had in `main()`, but one of the many advantages of this approach is that we hide the fact that `XMLReader` is implemented through COM. This means that we could take other code that has been written to run on the class `GenericParser` and it should still work, even if the specific `GenericParser` class implementation used a different SAX parser, and therefore a different `XMLReader` class. The following revised version of `main()` demonstrates this point:

```
    ...

    HRESULT hr;
    CGenericParser * pGP = new CGenericParser();
    ISAXXMLReader* pRdr = NULL;

    hr = pGP->createXMLReader(L"Parser", &pRdr);
    if(!FAILED(hr))
```

```
    {
        pRdr->putContentHandler(pGP);
        pRdr->putDTDHandler(pGP);

        ...
        pRdr->Release();
        delete pGP;
    }
```

...

As you can see, there is no reference to anything specific to Microsoft's SAX parser, except the release of the ISAXXMLReader COM object – but even that could be hidden inside the delete code for the reader.

If you wanted to use the simple element handler that we wrote earlier – the event that echoes the name of an element when the startElement event is received – the only change you would need to make would be to derive the class from CGenericParser rather than CDefaultHandler:

```
class MyParser : public CGenericParser
{
public:
    MyParser();
    virtual ~MyParser();

    virtual HRESULT STDMETHODCALLTYPE startElement(
        /* [in] */ wchar_t __RPC_FAR *pwchNamespaceUri,
        /* [in] */ int cchNamespaceUri,
        /* [in] */ wchar_t __RPC_FAR *pwchLocalName,
        /* [in] */ int cchLocalName,
        /* [in] */ wchar_t __RPC_FAR *pwchRawName,
        /* [in] */ int cchRawName,
        /* [in] */ ISAXAttributes __RPC_FAR *pAttributes);
};
```

and then create an object of type CMyParser rather than CGenericParser:

```
    CMyParser * pGP = new CMyParser();
    ISAXXMLReader* pRdr = NULL;
```

We now have the same application as before, echoing the names of elements, but built on the generic parsing class.

Up until now, all of the classes and interfaces we have devised have simply served to make generating SAX applications quicker and easier. We could have lived without the classes, but since the RDF API uses them, we've used them too for the sake of consistency.

The GenericXML2RDF Class

So now we have enough building blocks to start building our generic RDF parser class. Why a generic class? Surely an RDF parser is just that – an RDF parser? In one sense this is true, but recall that we wanted to create a parser that could fire events in the same way that SAX fires events. The reason for this was so that we could attach one processor to these events that, for example, stores triples in a database, and we might attach another processor to these events that outputs the statements as a graph. By building a number of intermediate classes that can be overridden as required, we are creating a very flexible and extensible parser framework that will make a powerful addition to our code library.

The GenericXML2RDF class is based on the GenericParser class that we saw earlier. It is also based on an interface called RDFParser, which contains the function needed to initiate parsing. This parse method takes two parameters, the first being the location of the XML to parse, and the second being the address of an object that will "consume" the RDF events, based on the interface RDFConsumer. The GenericXML2RDF class declaration is shown below:

```
class CGenericXML2RDF :
    public CGenericParser,
    public IRDFParser
{
public:
    CGenericXML2RDF();
    virtual ~CGenericXML2RDF();

protected:
    ILiteral *createLiteral(LPCTSTR lpstrStr);
    IResource *createResource(CQName &name);
    IResource *createResource(LPCTSTR lpstrStr);
    IResource *createResource(LPCTSTR pstrNamespace, LPCTSTR pstrLocalName);
    IStatement *createStatement(IResource *pSubject, IResource *pPredicate,
        IRDFNode *pObject);

    ISAXXMLReader *m_pXMLReader;
    INodeFactory *m_pNodeFactory;
    IRDFConsumer *m_pRDFConsumer;

    /*
        * From IRDFParser
    */

public:
    virtual HRESULT parse(LPCTSTR pwchSource, IRDFConsumer *pConsumer);
};
```

Since our generic RDF parser class is derived from the GenericParser class, it automatically inherits default implementations for all of the events that SAX can fire, as well as a function for creating an XML reader. This means that when we create an object of type GenericXML2RDF, all we need do is create an XMLReader and attach the class itself to it. The constructor would, therefore, look like this:

```
CGenericXML2RDF::CGenericXML2RDF()
{
    HRESULT hr = createXMLReader(L"CXMLParser", &m_pXMLReader);

    if (!FAILED(hr))
```

```
    {
        m_pXMLReader->putContentHandler(this);
        m_pXMLReader->putDTDHandler(this);
        m_pXMLReader->putEntityResolver(this);
        m_pXMLReader->putErrorHandler(this);
    }
    else
        m_pXMLReader = NULL;
}
```

Note the parameters to the content handler assignment functions are this, *which means that all of the callback functions are going to be provided by this object. This is a very convenient way of wrapping all of the functionality of a class up in one package.*

When we destroy the parser we must release the XMLReader COM object (this is specific to the Microsoft SAX parser, since it uses COM):

```
CGenericXML2RDF::~CGenericXML2RDF()
{
    if (m_pXMLReader)
        m_pXMLReader->Release();
}
```

As noted previously, the GenericXML2RDF class also uses the RDFParser interface, which consists of the single public parse() method:

```
class IRDFParser
{
public:
    virtual HRESULT parse(LPCTSTR pSource, IRDFConsumer *pConsumer) = 0;
};
```

Remember that the "=0" appended to the method declaration means that this interface requires any class based on it to implement a function that initiates parsing. The parsing function takes as its input a URI to identify the document to parse, and it transfers events to the object pointed to by pConsumer. We'll look in more detail at what RDF consumers are, but for now it is enough to say that the document referred to by pSource will be parsed according to whatever rules are encoded in the consumer. Recall that one of the main advantages of using a framework like the RDF API was so that different rules could be laid down for different RDF formats. Now you can see that this is achieved by 'plugging in' different consumer classes.

The parse function of GenericXML2RDF is defined like this:

```
HRESULT CGenericXML2RDF::parse(LPCTSTR pwchSource, IRDFConsumer *pConsumer)
{
    HRESULT hr = !S_OK;
```

The first step is to save the address of the consumer object that will be notified of events when statements are ready, and the address of the node factory that is responsible for creating the various objects that we need – such as literals, resources and statements:

```
    m_pRDFConsumer = pConsumer;
    m_pNodeFactory = pConsumer->getNodeFactory();
```

Next we convert the source URL to the right format for the parser (it saves us having to define this in `main`):

```
if (m_pXMLReader)
{
    int iLen = strlen(pwchSource) + 1;
    wchar_t * pURL = new wchar_t [iLen];
    mbstowcs(pURL, pwchSource, iLen);
```

Finally, we ask the XML reader to do the parsing:

```
hr = m_pXMLReader->parseURL(pURL);
```

As you can see, no matter how many layers we add to our framework, at some point we still have to ask SX to do the parsing,

After SAX has returned control to the framework, we need to tidy up and return from our routine:

```
    delete [] pURL;
    }
    return hr;
}
```

We'll see later what an `RDFConsumer` looks like. Imagine for now that we have created one that simply writes out the names of the elements as they are found by the SAX parser. If we include this "dump consumer" in our `main` routine, our code drops down to pretty much four lines:

```
int main(int argc, char* argv[])
{
    if (argc < 2)
    {
        printf("\nUsage:");
        printf("\n\trdfparser file:///drive:/path/file.rdf\n");
        printf("\n\trdfparser http://url\n");
        return 0;
    }

    CGenericXML2RDF * pGX2R = new CRDFXMLParser();
    CDumpConsumer RDFConsumer;
    pGX2R->parse(argv[1], &RDFConsumer);
    delete pGX2R;

    return 0;
}
```

Note that by building the framework in this way, we have essentially reduced the SAX program to the four lines highlighted above.

Resources, Literals, and Statements

The `GenericXML2RDF` class provides a number of methods of its own, beyond those that it implements for the `IRDFParser` interface, or the `GenericParser` class. These methods are used to create objects such as literals, resources, and statements as we work our way through the RDF/XML. It won't surprise you though, to learn that in the RDF API, even this can be generalized! We can say that to implement the interface "volume control" our television can have a volume control knob, and still not say what exactly a volume control knob should be like. The same goes for our parser; we know what a statement should look like – it needs a subject, object, and predicate – but how it is stored is entirely up to the person implementing the parser. Rather than limiting the use of the parsing structure that we have been building to one specific way of storing resources and literals, say, as strings, the RDF API we've created allows us to plug in our own implementations.

As the parser steps through the source document it makes calls such as "create a literal and initialize it with this value", or "create a statement using these three values". These calls are made to an object we must provide, called a **node factory**. This does the job of creating the nuts and bolts that make up the RDF model. By providing this extra interface, we allow for the possibility that these elements – literals, resources, and statements – can be stored in many different ways without affecting the functionality of our parser, although for the purposes of this sample, we will show a simple node factory.

The following is an abbreviated version of the interface for the node factory:

```
class INodeFactory
{
public:
    virtual ILiteral *createLiteral(LPCTSTR lpstrStr) = 0;

    ...

    virtual IResource *createResource(LPCTSTR lpstrStr) = 0;
    virtual IResource *createResource(LPCTSTR pstrNamespace,
        LPCTSTR pstrLocalName) = 0;
    virtual IStatement *createStatement(IResource *pSubject,
        IResource *pPredicate, IRDFNode *pObject) = 0;
};
```

The `GenericXML2RDF` class has methods to create resources, literals, and so on, which look similar to the ones just defined. However, the generic XML to RDF parsing class simply passes our calls on to the specific node factory that has been defined. For example, if we wanted to create a literal value whilst parsing, we would call the `GenericXML2RDF` method `createLiteral()`, like this:

```
CLiteral *pLiteral = (CLiteral *) createLiteral("A literal");
```

This simply says at some point in our program, create an object of type literal – but we don't know what that object looks like. The implementation of that function in the generic parser would simply pass the call on to whatever node factory has been connected, as follows:

```
ILiteral *CGenericXML2RDF::createLiteral(LPCTSTR lpstrStr)
{
    return m_pNodeFactory->createLiteral(lpstrStr);
}
```

As we said, the node factory is free to implement an object of type literal in whatever way it wants, provided that it has certain features, such as the ability to modify and retrieve the value of the literal. How the node factory implements the literal should be completely hidden from GenericXML2RDF. The programmer may have decided to remove duplications and only store unique strings, or that the literal value can go straight into a database. Whatever the details – and they really can be anything – our framework can cope. In *our* NodeFactory we will implement the createLiteral method like this:

```
ILiteral *CNodeFactory::createLiteral(LPCTSTR lpstrStr)
{
    return new CLiteral(lpstrStr);
}
```

In other words we just return a pointer to a CLiteral object. The constructor for this object looks like this:

```
CLiteral::CLiteral(CString sStr)
{
    m_sContent = sStr;
}
```

I'll show the template for a resource here, and you can find all the other classes, such as those for statement and literal, in the download files Impl.cpp and Impl.h:

```
class IResource : public IRDFNode
{
public:
    virtual CString getLocalName(void) = 0;
    virtual CString getNamespace(void) = 0;
    virtual CString getURI(void) = 0;
};
```

I really want to hammer the notion of interfaces home – all this declaration says is that no matter how you implement your resource class (based on this interface, of course), it must provide the methods getLocalName, getNamespace, and getURI. Our particular implementation looks like this:

```
CResource::CResource(LPCTSTR pstrNamespace, LPCTSTR pstrLocalName)
{
    m_sNamespace = pstrNamespace;
    m_sLocalName = pstrLocalName;
}

CResource::CResource(LPCTSTR pstrLocalName)
{
    m_sNamespace = _T("");
    m_sLocalName = pstrLocalName;
}

CResource::~CResource()
{

}

CString CResource::getURI(void)
{
```

```
      return m_sNamespace + m_sLocalName;
}

CString CResource::getLocalName(void)
{
   return m_sLocalName;
}

CString CResource::getNamespace(void)
{
   return m_sNamespace;
}

CString CResource::getLabel (void)
{
   return getURI();
}
```

Another developer could implement a completely different class, and although that wouldn't change the way the parsing proceeds, it would change the actual objects created during the process.

Of course, we haven't got a consumer object to call with our RDF events, and our parser still doesn't parse RDF! But we are now in a position to add these parts of our application.

Extending GenericXML2RDF

Let's just summarize where we are. We have created a structure of classes such that an RDF parser can be built from a series of predefined interfaces. By defining the classes in a modular fashion, different parts of the parser can be assembled using different objects. For example, one implementation might place triples into a database, another might display the triples in a graphical user interface. Equally, one implementation might process only the model part of the RDF syntax, whilst another implementation might handle schemas.

Surely now we are ready to implement the actual parser? Shouldn't we just place the code to handle the parsing of RDF/XML in `GenericXML2RDF` and fire events when we receive statements?

Unfortunately, if we did that our parser would only be able to understand RDF in the RDF/XML format, but it wouldn't understand it in any other format. Although this seems like a limitation we can live with, if you think back to the discussion on the RDF model in Chapter 4 – that RDF/XML is *simply a means to transport triples* – then we realize that RDF/XML may not be the *only* way that triples are transported.

I'm not saying that we don't want to parse RDF/XML – far from it, and in the next section we will show how we can build a module that will "consume" RDF/XML. What I am saying is that I don't want to build the framework in such a way that we can *only* parse RDF/XML. We want to be able to plug in parsers for other styles.

Take the output from Jason Diamond's XSLT stylesheet, which we saw earlier:

```
<?xml version="1.0" encoding="UTF-16"?>
<model>
  <statement>
    <subject>http://www.ePolitix.com/Articles/0000001AEA32.htm</subject>
    <predicate>http://purl.org/dc/elements/1.0/Creator</predicate>
    <object
```

```
        type="resource">http://www.ePolitix.com/Authors/Craig%20Hoy</object>
  </statement>

  <statement>
    <subject>http://www.ePolitix.com/Articles/0000001AEA32.htm</subject>
    <predicate>http://purl.org/dc/elements/1.0/Publisher</predicate>
    <object
     type="resource">http://www.CorpInfo.org/companynumber/01262354</object>
  </statement>

  <statement>
    <subject>http://www.ePolitix.com/Authors/Craig%20Hoy</subject>
    <predicate>http://www.xyz.coom/Schema/JobTitle</predicate>
    <object type="literal">editor</object>
  </statement>
</model>
```

Wouldn't it be handy if we also had a parser that could convert this XML document to a set of triples? If anything, this syntax would be easier to parse than RDF/XML since everything is much more regular. By deriving our parsers from GenericXML2RDF we allow for just this type of scenario. GenericXML2RDF provides us with as much of the generalized functionality as possible – creating resources, literals, statements, and so on – which is required no matter what the original XML format is. But this class is then extended and overloaded where necessary to cope with the specifics of parsing a particular format.

And at last, we can write a class that understands RDF/XML – it's been a long journey – thanks for your patience!

The RDF/XML Parser

So let's build an RDF/XML parser class. As we have said, the class is derived from GenericXML2RDF to gain the methods that create units such as literals and statements, but we still need to implement the methods that were provided way back in the DefaultHandler class, which we looked at in the early stages of our discussion – the methods for events such as startElement and startDocument.

These events will be fired at various stages as we step through the RDF/XML document, and we need to keep track of our progress through the document with resources, literals, and statements provided by the node factory. Recall that the RDFConsumer class creates the node factory, and pointers to both the consumer and the node factory are stored in the GenericXML2RDF class from which our specific RDF/XML parser is derived:

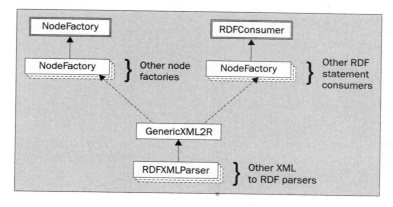

A Simple Consumer

We're going to build a class called RDFXMLParser, which will *only* parse RDF/XML. It will fire events at any consumer, and use any node factory to do this parsing, but the only XML that it will understand will be the XML dialect of the RDF Model and Syntax specification.

However, although it will work with any consumer, we still need to devise one for our application so that we can see the events that are being fired to it. The interface for an RDFConsumer looks like this:

```
class IRDFConsumer
{
public:
    virtual void startModel(void) = 0;
    virtual void endModel(void) = 0;
    virtual void addStatement(IStatement *pStatement) = 0;
    virtual INodeFactory *getNodeFactory(void) = 0;
};
```

This means that any consumer of our RDF must provide an event handler for:

❑ The beginning of a model, which means that we have found some RDF.

❑ The end of a model.

❑ Each statement.

❑ A node factory to create literals, resources, and statements.

Note that the addStatement method takes a parameter that is the interface for a statement, so that any object based on IStatement will constitute a valid parameter.

The DumpConsumer Class

Our simple consumer is called DumpConsumer, since it will simply echo every event to the standard output. It implements the required methods from the RDFConsumer interface and is coded like this:

```
CDumpConsumer::CDumpConsumer()
{
    m_pNodeFactory = new CNodeFactory();
}

CDumpConsumer::~CDumpConsumer()
{
    delete m_pNodeFactory;
}

void CDumpConsumer::startModel(void)
{
    printf("Start Model\n");
}

void CDumpConsumer::endModel(void)
{
    printf("End Model\n");
}
```

```
void CDumpConsumer::addStatement(IStatement *pStatement)
{
    printf(
        "{ %s, %s, %s }\n",
        (LPCTSTR) pStatement->predicate()->getLabel(),
        (LPCTSTR) pStatement->subject()->getLabel(),
        (LPCTSTR) pStatement->object()->getLabel()
    );
}


INodeFactory *STDMETHODCALLTYPE CDumpConsumer::getNodeFactory(void)
{
    return m_pNodeFactory;
}
```

Hopefully you are now starting to see the value of using a framework – the events for the beginning and end of the model could just as easily have been used to open and close a database connection, and the events for each statement could then have been used to add triples to that database.

Now that we have a way of seeing the output from the parsing process, we can build the actual code that understands RDF/XML.

Start and End of the Model

Much of the current RDF literature uses the term "model" to describe a collection of RDF statements. Two of the events that an RDFConsumer requires are notification of the start and end of a model, so we will first of all implement these methods. Note that this is not the same as the start and end of a document, since one document may contain zero, one or more RDF models.

Let's remind ourselves of the simplest way to define an RDF model with the XML syntax:

```
<rdf:RDF
 xmlns:rdf="http://www.w3.org/1999/02/22-rdf-syntax-ns#"
 xmlns:b="http://www.cogsci.princeton.edu/~wn/schema/">
    <b:Noun
        rdf:about="http://www.cogsci.princeton.edu/~wn/concept#101631577">
        <b:wordForm>alley cat</b:wordForm>
        <b:wordForm>stray</b:wordForm>
    </b:Noun>
</rdf:RDF>
```

As you'll remember from Chapter 4, an RDF document can begin with `<rdf:RDF>`. It doesn't have to, however, and may just go straight into a typed node:

```
<b:Noun
 rdf:about="http://www.cogsci.princeton.edu/~wn/concept#101631577"
 xmlns:rdf="http://www.w3.org/1999/02/22-rdf-syntax-ns#"
 xmlns:b="http://www.cogsci.princeton.edu/~wn/schema/">
    <b:wordForm>alley cat</b:wordForm>
    <b:wordForm>stray</b:wordForm>
</b:Noun>
```

or a description element:

```
<rdf:Description
  rdf:about="http://www.cogsci.princeton.edu/~wn/concept#101631577"
  xmlns:rdf="http://www.w3.org/1999/02/22-rdf-syntax-ns#"
  xmlns:b="http://www.cogsci.princeton.edu/~wn/schema/">
  rdf:type="http://www.cogsci.princeton.edu/~wn/schema/Noun">
    <b:wordForm>alley cat</b:wordForm>
    <b:wordForm>stray</b:wordForm>
</rdf:Description>
```

To begin with, though, we'll write the parsing code to spot an `<rdf:RDF>` element and fire the `startModel` event. We'll also be looking out for the close of the `<rdf:RDF>` element so that we can fire the `endModel` event. You may be wondering why we should bother looking for these specific elements at all, when we could just use the `startDocument` and `endDocument` events that SAX gives us – like SiRPAC does in fact.

There are two reasons why I have gone for a solution that looks for an `<rdf:RDF>` element rather than just firing at the beginning and end of a document. The first is that we may want to nest the RDF/XML within another type of document. This may be for embedding RDF inside HTML, as discussed in the W3C's RDF Model and Syntax specification, but it may also be the case that some transport envelope is used to carry the RDF/XML – perhaps SOAP – or that some other XML standard – such as news articles with embedded meta data – may contain RDF/XML as a component. We should therefore only fire the `startModel` and `endModel` events if we really do find some RDF – and it's possible the document might not contain any.

This scenario of embedding meta data inside other XML standards leads to my second reason for looking for RDF elements rather than just firing on the start and end of the document, which is that a document may carry more than one model. There is nothing in the RDF syntax specification to prevent documents that contain two "parallel" RDF blocks such as this:

```
<Envelope xmlns:rdf="http://www.w3.org/1999/02/22-rdf-syntax-ns#">
    <rdf:RDF xmlns:b="http://www.cogsci.princeton.edu/~wn/schema/">
        <b:Noun
            rdf:about="http://www.cogsci.princeton.edu/~wn/concept#101631577">
            <b:wordForm>alley cat</b:wordForm>
            <b:wordForm>stray</b:wordForm>
        </b:Noun>
    </rdf:RDF>
    <rdf:RDF xmlns:b="http://www.cogsci.princeton.edu/~wn/schema/">
        <b:Noun
            rdf:about="http://www.cogsci.princeton.edu/~wn/concept#101631497"
            b:wordForm="mouser"
        />
    </rdf:RDF>
</Envelope>
```

In this situation, I would prefer to receive two `startModel` events, rather than one, and so our parser has been coded to achieve that.

The startElement Event

Triggering our `startModel` event on seeing `<rdf:RDF>` is pretty straightforward, but as you'll see from the code, I have added a few other features to the `startElement` event to prepare us for processing the other elements that we will see. Let's go through the `startElement` code, beginning with the function declaration:

```
HRESULT STDMETHODCALLTYPE CRDFXMLParser::startElement(
    /* [in] */ wchar_t __RPC_FAR *pwchNamespaceUri,
    /* [in] */ int cchNamespaceUri,
    /* [in] */ wchar_t __RPC_FAR *pwchLocalName,
    /* [in] */ int cchLocalName,
    /* [in] */ wchar_t __RPC_FAR *pwchRawName,
    /* [in] */ int cchRawName,
    /* [in] */ ISAXAttributes __RPC_FAR *pAttributes)
{
```

The first thing to do is call the generic parser's `start element` function. This is useful because one of the things that it does is create a copy of the element that we are processing, complete with attributes:

```
_startElement(pwchNamespaceUri, cchNamespaceUri, pwchLocalName,
                                        cchLocalName, pAttributes);
```

Now that we have the current element, we have to create a QName to hold the namespace and local name:

```
HRESULT hr = S_OK;
CQName *pName = m_pCurrent->getName();
```

Next set a flag to indicate whether we have an element that is in the RDF namespace. This is useful later because, as we saw in the previous chapter, many RDF documents specify attributes like `about` without the specifying the namespace:

```
BOOL bInRDFNamespace = (pName->getNamespace() == RDF_NS);
```

Next, we save the current parse state. We'll look at the parser state and its stack in a little more detail in a moment, but for now we just need to know that we must save the state of the parser in order to keep track of where we are as we receive new events. An element like `<b:WordForm>` might be a typed node if received when we are looking for a description element, or it might be a predicate if we have found a description element and are looking for a property element:

```
CParseItem::parseState parseStateNew = m_parseStateCurrent;
```

The only state that we have implemented here is the `Ready` state, which means we haven't encountered anything yet. Also, the only valid element that we have in the `Ready` state is `<rdf:RDF>` – anything else sets the parser into an "unknown" state. As you can see, if we come across an `<rdf:RDF>` element, we fire the `startModel` event, and set the value for the next state that the parser should enter, namely the RDF state:

```
switch (m_parseStateCurrent)
{
    case CParseItem::Ready:
        if (bInRDFNamespace)
        {
            if (pName->getLocalName() == RDF_RDF)
            {
                parseStateNew = CParseItem::RDF;
                m_pRDFConsumer->startModel();
            }
        }
```

```
        break;

    default:
        parseStateNew = CParseItem::Unknown;
        break;
    }
```

The only thing left to do is save the state that we are in to the stack, and set our current state to the new state. Note that even if we haven't actually *changed* the state we still push it, because when we get to the `endElement` event, we are going to pop the states back off again, and we have to make sure they balance:

```
    CParseItem *pParseItem = new CParseItem(m_parseStateCurrent);
    m_ParseItemStack.Push(pParseItem);
    m_parseStateCurrent = parseStateNew;
    return hr;
}
```

The Parse State Stack

One of the difficulties in writing any parser is working out what an element means when it is valid in different contexts. Although it might be easy to spot elements that use the RDF namespace, we need more information when we are differentiating elements in situations like this:

```
<b:Noun
  rdf:about="http://www.cogsci.princeton.edu/~wn/concept#101631577"
  xmlns:rdf="http://www.w3.org/1999/02/22-rdf-syntax-ns#"
  xmlns:b="http://www.cogsci.princeton.edu/~wn/schema/">
    <b:wordForm>alley cat</b:wordForm>
    <b:wordForm>stray</b:wordForm>
</b:Noun>
```

As far as our SAX events are concerned, there is no difference between `b:Noun` and `b:wordForm`, but as far as the RDF model is concerned there is – one is a typed node, and the other is a property of the resource referred to by that typed node. The situation is complicated further when the children elements are not actually RDF but the literal value of the property:

```
<b:Noun
  rdf:about="http://www.cogsci.princeton.edu/~wn/concept#101631577"
  xmlns:rdf="http://www.w3.org/1999/02/22-rdf-syntax-ns#"
  xmlns:b="http://www.cogsci.princeton.edu/~wn/schema/">
    <b:wordForm parseType="literal"><i>alley cat</i></b:wordForm>
    <b:wordForm>stray</b:wordForm>
</b:Noun>
```

Perhaps the most natural way to differentiate these states is through a stack, as it is well suited to the nested nature of RDF/XML. When we receive an event triggered by the next element, we push our current state on to the stack, and then pop that state back off the stack when we encounter the closing element. The states that will be needed are given in the following enumeration:

```
class CParseItem : public CObject
{
public:
    enum parseState
    {
```

```
        Unknown = 0,
        Ready,
        RDF,
        Description,
        PropertyElt,
        Type,
        TypedNode,
        Value,
        String
    };
    CParseItem(parseState ParseState);
    virtual ~CParseItem();

public:
    parseState m_ParseState;
};
```

The enumeration allows us to make statements to change state of the following form:

```
parseStateNew = CParseItem::PropertyElt;
```

Note that the names of the enumerations correspond to the names of the productions in the EBNF for RDF. This should help you match the code to the specification if you want to go through it in detail. There's more about productions in the RDF/XML Syntax section later in this chapter.

The stack that the items are saved to is a pretty standard implementation, and you'll find the code for that in the RDFXMLParser.cpp source file in the code download for this chapter.

The endStatement Event

Now that you have seen how the stack works, we can look at how to implement the endStatement method. All we do – for the time being – is pop off the states that have been pushed onto the stack, and when we come to pop off the RDF state, we can fire the endModel event:

```
HRESULT STDMETHODCALLTYPE CRDFXMLParser::endElement(
    /* [in] */ wchar_t __RPC_FAR *pwchNamespaceUri,
    /* [in] */ int cchNamespaceUri,
    /* [in] */ wchar_t __RPC_FAR *pwchLocalName,
    /* [in] */ int cchLocalName,
    /* [in] */ wchar_t __RPC_FAR *pwchRawName,
    /* [in] */ int cchRawName)
{
    _endElement(pwchNamespaceUri, cchNamespaceUri, pwchLocalName,
    cchLocalName);

    HRESULT hr = S_OK;

    switch (m_parseStateCurrent)
    {
        case CParseItem::RDF:
            {
                m_pRDFConsumer->endModel();
            }
            break;
```

```
      default:
         break;
   }

   CParseItem *pParseItem = m_ParseItemStack.Pop();
   m_parseStateCurrent = pParseItem->m_ParseState;
   delete pParseItem;

   return hr;
}
```

We've now got enough to start parsing some real live RDF! Firstly, you'll need to compile the application. The source files are available to download, and if you are using Microsoft Visual C++ all you need to do is load the workspace, which is RDFParser.dsw. Once you have the workspace loaded, you will see a number of projects. The project we are dealing with here is Step1, so set this project to be the current project – on the Project menu choose Set Active Project and then choose Step1 – and then from the Build menu choose Build Step1.exe.

> **Note, you will not be able to build or run the .exe if you do not have MSXML 3 available on your PC, as we mentioned earlier.**

You will now have Step1.exe in the Step1/debug directory, underneath the location that you unpacked the sample files to. There are some test files in the TestFiles directory. Run the first one, as follows:

Step1 ../../TestFiles/example1.rdf

This test file looks like the following and should tell us if we are spotting the model correctly:

```
<rdf:RDF
  xmlns:rdf="http://www.w3.org/1999/02/22-rdf-syntax-ns#"
  xmlns:epx="http://www.ePolitix.com/RDFschema/">
    <rdf:Description
      ID="TonyBlair"
      type="http://www.ePolitix.com/RDFschema/Politician"
      epx:MemberOf="Labour Party"
    />
    <rdf:Description
      ID="WilliamHague"
      type="http://www.ePolitix.com/RDFschema/Politician"
      epx:MemberOf="Conservative Party"
    />
</rdf:RDF>
```

Executing the command line above should give you the following output:

Start Model
End Model

Exciting? Not really, but it's a start. Before we move on to the guts of our parsing, it's worth running a few more documents through to ensure that everything is working as it should. The next document (which you'll find as `example1a.rdf`) illustrates that SAX2 is doing a lot of namespace handling for us. The document that we just saw could be represented like this:

```
<rdf:RDF
 xmlns="http://www.w3.org/1999/02/22-rdf-syntax-ns#"
 xmlns:epx="http://www.ePolitix.com/RDFschema/">
    <rdf:Description
     ID="TonyBlair"
     type="http://www.ePolitix.com/RDFschema/Politician"
     epx:MemberOf="Labour Party"
    />
    <rdf:Description
     ID="WilliamHague"
     type="http://www.ePolitix.com/RDFschema/Politician"
     epx:MemberOf="Conservative Party"
    />
</rdf:RDF>
```

As you can see we are using the default namespace for RDF, but the parser output is still the same – SAX2 is supplying our `startElement` and `endElement` methods with the namespaces automatically.

The next document (`example1b.htm`) illustrates embedding the RDF inside another document, to show that we can still fire the model events:

```
<?xml version="1.0"?>
<html>
   <head>
      <title>An embedded RDF test</title>
      <rdf:RDF
       xmlns="http://www.w3.org/1999/02/22-rdf-syntax-ns#"
       xmlns:epx="http://www.ePolitix.com/RDFschema/">
         <rdf:Description
          ID="TonyBlair"
          type="http://www.ePolitix.com/RDFschema/Politician"
          epx:MemberOf="Labour Party"
         />
         <rdf:Description
          ID="WilliamHague"
          type="http://www.ePolitix.com/RDFschema/Politician"
          epx:MemberOf="Conservative Party"
         />
      </rdf:RDF>
   </head>
   <body>
      <p>
         This page is about Tony Blair and William Hague,
         and it has meta data about them. Splendid!
      </p>
   </body>
</html>
```

The next one (`example1c.htm`) checks that we get multiple model events, by splitting our two statements into two different RDF "documents":

```
<?xml version="1.0"?>
<html>
   <head>
      <title>An embedded RDF test</title>
      <rdf:RDF
       xmlns="http://www.w3.org/1999/02/22-rdf-syntax-ns#"
       xmlns:epx="http://www.ePolitix.com/RDFschema/">
         <rdf:Description
          about="TonyBlair"
          type="http://www.ePolitix.com/RDFschema/Politician"
          epx:MemberOf="Labour"
          />
      </rdf:RDF>
      <meta name="keyword" description="politics" />
      <rdf:RDF
       xmlns="http://www.w3.org/1999/02/22-rdf-syntax-ns#"
       xmlns:epx="http://www.ePolitix.com/RDFschema/">
         <rdf:Description
          about="WilliamHague"
          type="http://www.ePolitix.com/RDFschema/Politician"
          epx:MemberOf="Conservative"
          />
      </rdf:RDF>
   </head>
   <body>
      <p>
         This page is about Tony Blair and William Hague,
         and it has meta data about them. Splendid!
      </p>
   </body>
</html>
```

As you'd expect, our output is:

Start Model
End Model
Start Model
End Model

Let's also check that we get no events (`example1d.htm`):

```
<?xml version="1.0"?>
<html>
   <head>
      <title>An embedded RDF test ... with no RDF!</title>
      <meta name="keyword" description="politics" />
   </head>
   <body>
      <p>
         This page is about Tony Blair and William Hague,
         and it has no meta data about them. Excellent!
      </p>
   </body>
</html>
```

RDF/XML Syntax

We now have a pretty solid basis from which to examine the rest of the RDF/XML syntax. In this sample code we are not going to show the parsing code in its entirety, but rather show a few steps so that the principles can be grasped, and then the interested reader can examine the source code.

Let's look at RDF/XML syntax in more detail to see what we should implement next.

RDF

In the RDF Model and Syntax documentation is a formal definition of the XML syntax that represents RDF. This is specified using a particular type of notation, called **EBNF**, or **Extended Backus-Naur Format**. Each item within the EBNF definition is called a production, and these productions are numbered. Since they are in section 6 of RDFMS, their numbers begin at 6.1. I have retained this numbering so that you can cross-reference the following text with the spec.

We have already created code for the first production:

```
[6.1]     RDF                ::= ['<rdf:RDF>'] obj* ['</rdf:RDF>']
```

This EBNF syntax simply means that an RDF/XML document can optionally begin with <rdf:RDF> before being followed by one or more items (the asterisk) which conform to the production of obj. We therefore need to look next at what an obj is.

obj

If we look at the next production we will see that an obj is actually a description object:

```
[6.2]     obj                ::= description
```

and a description object is made up of either an <rdf:Description> element or a typed node:

```
[6.3] description            ::= '<rdf:description' idAboutAttr? propAttr* '/>'
                               | '<rdf:description' idAboutAttr? propAttr* '>'
                                 propertyElt* '</rdf:description>'
                               | typedNode
```

We can therefore expand our startElement function to cope with this. The start of the function is the same as for step 1:

```
HRESULT STDMETHODCALLTYPE CRDFXMLParser::startElement(
    /* [in] */ wchar_t __RPC_FAR *pwchNamespaceUri,
    /* [in] */ int cchNamespaceUri,
    /* [in] */ wchar_t __RPC_FAR *pwchLocalName,
    /* [in] */ int cchLocalName,
    /* [in] */ wchar_t __RPC_FAR *pwchRawName,
    /* [in] */ int cchRawName,
    /* [in] */ ISAXAttributes __RPC_FAR *pAttributes)
{
    _startElement(pwchNamespaceUri, cchNamespaceUri, pwchLocalName,
      cchLocalName, pAttributes);

    HRESULT hr = S_OK;
```

```
CQName *pName = m_pCurrent->getName();
CParseItem::parseState parseStateNew = m_parseStateCurrent;

switch (m_parseStateCurrent)
{
```

As before, the `Ready` state is essentially the root – a bit like being in the (imaginary) production 6.0, waiting for 6.1. If we have an element with the RDF namespace, then we can allow either `RDF` or `Description` as the local name values. Either of these causes us to kick off our model, and change the parsing state to another level:

```
case CParseItem::Ready:
    if (((CRDFElement*) m_pCurrent)->m_bInRDFNamespace)
    {
        if (pName->getLocalName() == RDF_RDF)
        {
            parseStateNew = CParseItem::RDF;
            m_pRDFConsumer->startModel();
            m_bInModel = true;
        }
        else if (pName->getLocalName() == RDF_DESCRIPTION)
        {
            parseStateNew = CParseItem::Description;
            m_pRDFConsumer->startModel();
            m_bInModel = true;
        }
```

For now, any other element in the RDF namespace is invalid. Of course, this code will need to be expanded to allow containers to be top-level elements:

```
        else
        {
            hr = fatalError((ISAXLocator *) NULL,
            L"\nErr: RDF tag '%.*s' is invalid at top-level", 0);
        }
    }
```

If we didn't get `<rdf:RDF>` or `<rdf:Description>` then we assume everything else is a typed node. According to production 6.13, a typed node is an XML element:

```
[6.13] typedNode        ::= '<' typeName idAboutAttr? bagIdAttr? propAttr* '/>'
                          | '<' typeName idAboutAttr? bagIdAttr? propAttr* '>'
                            propertyElt* '</' typeName '>'
```

The element name may or may not be namespace qualified:

```
[6.15] typeName         ::= Qname
[6.19] Qname            ::= [ NSprefix ':' ] name
```

For the purposes of this parser, however, I have said that any typed node *must be* namespace qualified. This allows us to handle RDF/XML embedded inside HTML, when the RDF/XML begins with a typed node. Otherwise we would just have to parse the HTML as if it was RDF. The code looks like this:

```
        else
        {
           if (cchNamespaceUri)
           {
              parseStateNew = CParseItem::TypedNode;
              m_pRDFConsumer->startModel();
              m_bInModel = true;
           }
        }
        break;
```

The preceding code spotted `obj` items when they were at the top level, but we also need to spot `<rdf:Description>` and typed nodes when they are inside `<rdf:RDF>`. The next piece of code does this:

```
     case CParseItem::RDF:
        if (((CRDFElement*) m_pCurrent)->m_bInRDFNamespace)
        {
           if (pName->getLocalName() == RDF_DESCRIPTION)
              parseStateNew = CParseItem::Description;
           else
           {
              hr = fatalError((ISAXLocator *) NULL,
              L"\nErr: Expected 'obj', but found RDF tag '%.*s'", 0);
           }
        }
        else
           parseStateNew = CParseItem::TypedNode;
        break;
```

Note the error code this time indicates that the parser was expecting an item that conformed to the `obj` production, but found some other element in the RDF namespace instead.

As before, if we cannot understand the RDF/XML we enter the `Unknown` state:

```
     default:
        parseStateNew = CParseItem::Unknown;
        break;
  }
```

Finally, the code that saves the parser state is as in step 1:

```
  CParseItem *pParseItem = new CParseItem(m_parseStateCurrent);
  m_ParseItemStack.Push(pParseItem);
  m_parseStateCurrent = parseStateNew;
  return hr;
}
```

Let's check that all this code handles RDF/XML files as we'd expect. If you're using Microsoft Visual C++ you'll need to set the active project to **Step 2** and build the executable. You can then run `example2a.rdf` through the parser, as follows:

Step2 ../../TestFiles/example2a.rdf

This document looks like this:

```
<rdf:Description
 xmlns:rdf="http://www.w3.org/1999/02/22-rdf-syntax-ns#"
 xmlns:epx="http://www.ePolitix.com/RDFschema/"
 ID="TonyBlair"
 type="http://www.ePolitix.com/RDFschema/Politician"
>
 <epx:MemberOf>Labour Party</epx:MemberOf>
</rdf:Description>
```

and illustrates how we don't need an RDF/XML document to begin with `<rdf:RDF>`. In this case the model begins with the `<rdf:Description>` element, and gives the following output:

Start Model
End Model

We also added code for typed nodes, so let's check this as well. `example2b.rdf` looks like this:

```
<epx:Politician
 xmlns:rdf="http://www.w3.org/1999/02/22-rdf-syntax-ns#"
 xmlns:epx="http://www.ePolitix.com/RDFschema/"
 rdf:ID="TonyBlair"
>
 <epx:MemberOf>Labour Party</epx:MemberOf>
</epx:Politician>
```

and should deliver the following output:

Start Model
End Model

One final check is that we can spot these alternative ways of beginning a model when they are embedded inside HTML. `example2c.htm` checks that typed nodes can be embedded:

```
<html>
  <head>
    <title>An embedded RDF test</title>
    <epx:Politician
     xmlns="http://www.w3.org/1999/02/22-rdf-syntax-ns#"
     xmlns:epx="http://www.ePolitix.com/RDFschema/"
     ID="TonyBlair"
     epx:Party="Labour Party"
    />
    <meta name="keyword" description="politics" />
    <epx:Politician
     xmlns="http://www.w3.org/1999/02/22-rdf-syntax-ns#"
     xmlns:epx="http://www.ePolitix.com/RDFschema/"
     ID="WilliamHague"
     epx:Party="Conservative Party"
    />
```

```
    </head>
    <body>
       <p>
          This page is about Tony Blair and William Hague,
          and it has meta data about them.
       </p>
    </body>
 </html>
```

The output should be:

Start Model
End Model
Start Model
End Model

idAboutAttr

You will have noticed that all the different ways of beginning a statement have an optional idAboutAttr item. The production for this is:

```
[6.5] idAboutAttr    ::= idAttr | aboutAttr | aboutEachAttr
```

meaning that an idAboutAttr item can be either an idAttr, an aboutAttr or an aboutEachAttr – but it cannot be more than one of them. The productions for these are as follows:

```
[6.6] idAttr           ::= ' ID="' IDsymbol '"'
[6.7] aboutAttr        ::= ' about="' URI-reference '"'
[6.8] aboutEachAttr    ::= ' aboutEach="' URI-reference '"'
                        | ' aboutEachPrefix="' string '"'
```

To process these productions we have a routine called getResource. This function scans through the attributes on an obj to see what resource the statements will be referring to. If the resource is in one of the about attributes, then the full URI is used. If the resource is in an ID attribute then the URI is the combination of the document URI and the ID value. Note that in this sample code no tests are carried out on ID or URI values to see if they are valid.

Let's declare the function and set up the variables we will need. (If you are following this with a C++ compiler, we are now using the **Step 3** project.) The function takes as parameters:

❑   The attributes from the element.

❑   A pointer to a resource which will hold the resulting URI.

❑   A flag to indicate if the element that these attributes are attached to is in the RDF namespace. This copes with the fact that some RDF/XML documents will use about, ID, etc., without fully qualifying the namespace.

```
HRESULT CRDFXMLParser::getResource(
   ISAXAttributes __RPC_FAR *pAttributes,
   CResource **ppResource,
   BOOL bInRDF)
{
```

```
HRESULT hr = S_OK;

int l;
wchar_t *ns, *ln, *qn, *v;
int ins, iln, iqn, iv;
BOOL bGotidAboutAttr = false;
```

Next set up a loop to step through each of the attributes:

```
pAttributes->getLength(&l);
for (int i = 0; i < l; i++)
{
```

For each attribute we can get its namespace, its local name and the original name with its namespace prefix:

```
pAttributes->getName(i, &ns, &ins, &ln, &iln, &qn, &iqn);
```

Now we are ready to read the value of the attribute. Note that some XML attributes (like xmlns) have an original – or raw – value, but no namespace or local name. We're not interested in these attributes because SAX has already handled namespaces for us, so step over any attribute that hasn't got either a namespace or a local name:

```
if (ins || iln)
{
    pAttributes->getValue(i, &v, &iv);
```

Now we have the value of the attribute and all the information we need about its name, we can start checking how we should process everything. We regard the attribute as in the RDF namespace, if either it is explicitly in the RDF namespace, or it is in the null namespace *and* the element that the attribute is attached to is in the RDF namespace:

```
if ((!wcsncmp(ns, RDF_NS, ins) || (!ins && bInRDF)))
{
```

If we have an ID attribute then we need to get the URL of the document that we are processing. We then create a resource with this URL and the local name of the ID value:

```
if (!wcsncmp(ln, RDF_IDATTR, __max((int) wcslen(RDF_IDATTR),
    iln)))
{
    if (bGotidAboutAttr)
    {
        printf("\nOnly zero or one idAboutAttr allowed");
        hr = E_FAIL;
    }
    wchar_t *pwchBaseURL;
    m_pXMLReader->getBaseURL(&pwchBaseURL);
    *ppResource = (CResource *) createResource(pwchBaseURL, v);
    bGotidAboutAttr = true;
}
```

An `about` attribute simply uses the value as the resource:

```
if (!wcsncmp(ln, RDF_ABOUTATTR, __max((int) wcslen(RDF_ABOUTATTR),
    iln)))
{
    if (bGotidAboutAttr)
    {
        printf("\nOnly zero or one idAboutAttr allowed");
        hr = E_FAIL;
    }
    *ppResource = (CResource *) createResource(v);
    bGotidAboutAttr = true;
}
```

`aboutEach` and `aboutEachPrefix` do the same, but we put the resource in the distributant namespace for now. In a fully working parser we would need to decide how to handle these attributes, although there is talk of removing them from the next draft of RDF:

```
if (!wcsncmp(ln, RDF_ABOUTEACHATTR, __max((int)
    wcslen(RDF_ABOUTEACHATTR), iln)))
{
    if (bGotidAboutAttr)
    {
        printf("\nOnly zero or one idAboutAttr allowed");
        hr = E_FAIL;
    }
    *ppResource = (CResource *) createResource(L"distributant:", v);
    bGotidAboutAttr = true;
}

if (!wcsncmp(ln, RDF_ABOUTEACHPREFIXATTR, __max((int)
    wcslen(RDF_ABOUTEACHPREFIXATTR), iln)))
{
    if (bGotidAboutAttr)
    {
        printf("\nOnly zero or one idAboutAttr allowed");
        hr = E_FAIL;
    }
    *ppResource = (CResource *) createResource(L"distributant:", v);
    bGotidAboutAttr = true;
}
}
} // if ( either the namespace or local name are set )
} // for ( each attribute on this element )
```

It is perfectly valid for a statement to have no `ID` or `about` attributes. If it is the root of a statement then this should be treated as having an `about` attribute that is the same value as the document's URL. Otherwise we should regard this resource as anonymous:

```
if (!bGotidAboutAttr)
{
    *ppResource = (CResource *) createResource(L"anon:");
}
return hr;
}
```

So, now we have a function that can tell us what resource is used for a set of statements. Note that we used the function `createResource()` to get our resource. The `Resource` object is actually created by the `NodeFactory` that we have devised. The advantage of using a framework to create the parser is that the implementation of `Resource` objects can be changed. In our case the `createResource` functions look like this:

```
IResource *CGenericXML2RDF::createResource(CQName &name)
{
    return m_pNodeFactory->createResource(name.getNamespace(),
    name.getLocalName());
}

IResource *CGenericXML2RDF::createResource(wchar_t *lpstrStr)
{
    return m_pNodeFactory->createResource(lpstrStr);
}

IResource *CGenericXML2RDF::createResource(LPCTSTR lpstrStr)
{
    return m_pNodeFactory->createResource(lpstrStr);
}

IResource *CGenericXML2RDF::createResource(wchar_t *pstrNamespace,
 wchar_t *pstrLocalName)
{
    return m_pNodeFactory->createResource(pstrNamespace, pstrLocalName);
}

IResource *CGenericXML2RDF::createResource(LPCTSTR pstrNamespace,
 LPCTSTR pstrLocalName)
{
    return m_pNodeFactory->createResource(pstrNamespace, pstrLocalName);
}
```

In other words, whatever `NodeFactory` implementation of `createResource` we provide will be used when we need a `Resource` creating. Note also that these functions are attached to the `GenericXML2RDF` class, and not the class that we are building which specifically deals with RDF/XML.

The next step is to use the `createResource` function to ascertain which resource a set of statements is going to refer to. We need to make the call to `getResource` at any point where a statement is beginning. The first place is in our `Ready` state in the `startElement` event, after we have found either an `<rdf:Description>` or a typed node:

```
case CParseItem::Ready:
    if (((CRDFElement*) m_pCurrent)->m_bInRDFNamespace)
    {
        if (pName->getLocalName() == RDF_RDF)
        {
            parseStateNew = CParseItem::RDF;
            m_pRDFConsumer->startModel();
            m_bInModel = true;
        }
        else if (pName->getLocalName() == RDF_DESCRIPTION)
        {
```

```
            parseStateNew = CParseItem::Description;
            m_pRDFConsumer->startModel();
            m_bInModel = true;
            CResource *pResource;
            hr = getResource(pAttributes, &pResource,
              ((CRDFElement*) m_pCurrent)->m_bInRDFNamespace);
            m_SubjectStack.Push(pResource);
        }
        else
        {
            hr = fatalError((ISAXLocator *) NULL,
             L"\nErr: RDF tag '%.*s' is invalid at top-level", 0);
        }
    }
    else
    {
        if (cchNamespaceUri)
        {
            parseStateNew = CParseItem::TypedNode;
            m_pRDFConsumer->startModel();
            m_bInModel = true;

            CResource *pResource;
            hr = getResource(pAttributes, &pResource,
              ((CRDFElement*) m_pCurrent)->m_bInRDFNamespace);
            m_SubjectStack.Push(pResource);
        }
    }
    break;
```

We also need to do the same thing if we find an `<rdf:Description>` element or typed node inside `<rdf:RDF>` – the code will be exactly the same as the code we have just seen.

You will have noticed though, that not only did we create a `Resource` object to hold the URI, but we also pushed it onto a stack. The reason for this is that any XML elements that we see after this resource are effectively predicate/object pairs that are for this resource. In other words, they are the statements about the resource that we have just received. Since it's possible to nest statements within objects, then it seems to make sense to save the resource value to a stack, and then whenever we get a predicate/value pair we can fire an event to say we have a full statement.

If you look back at productions 6.3 and 6.13, you'll see that our predicate/object pairs can come either from attributes (`propAttr`) or elements (`<propertyElt>`). We won't show the code for these productions here, but it is pretty easy to deduce once you have seen how to fire an event when a statement is complete. The full code is available in the download.

Statement Events

If we have a typed node, then we have enough information to fire a triple event. For example, if you look at `example3.rdf`:

```
<epx:Politician
 xmlns:rdf="http://www.w3.org/1999/02/22-rdf-syntax-ns#"
 xmlns:epx="http://www.ePolitix.com/RDFschema/"
 rdf:about="http://www.ePolitix.com/People/TonyBlair"
```

```
>
    <epx:MemberOf>Labour Party</epx:MemberOf>
</epx:Politician>
```

we should fire a triple like this:

```
{
    [http://www.w3.org/1999/02/22-rdf-syntax-ns#type],
    [http://www.ePolitix.com/People/TonyBlair],
    [http://www.ePolitix.com/RDFschema/Politician]
}
```

In other words, the resource referred to by http://www.ePolitix.com/People/TonyBlair is of type epx:Politician. We achieve this by checking the new parse state for a typed node, as follows:

```
switch (parseStateNew)
{
    case CParseItem::TypedNode:
        CResource *subject = m_SubjectStack.Peek();
        CResource predicate(RDF_NS, RDF_TYPEATTR);
        CResource object(pName->getNamespace(), pName->getLocalName());
        CStatement *statement = (CStatement*) createStatement(subject,
         &predicate, &object);
        m_pRDFConsumer->addStatement(statement);
        delete statement;
        break;
}
```

You can see that we are creating a statement by first creating three resources – the subject, predicate and object. Once we have those three then we can invoke the addStatement event on the defined consumer. We don't care what it does, we are simply passing the event on. As it happens, the event simply writes the triple out, but it could have saved it in a database or drawn a graph:

```
void CDumpConsumer::addStatement(IStatement *pStatement)
{
    printf(
        "{ %s, %s, %s }\n",
        pStatement->predicate()->getLabel(),
        pStatement->subject()->getLabel(),
        pStatement->object()->getLabel()
    );
}
```

Now that we have seen how to fire an event, we have all the components we need to build the rest of the parser. We won't do that here, but the sample code is available if you want to dig more deeply.

Summary

We have looked at how RDF parsing can be implemented using XSLT transformations on the XML source, but we also saw that processing large sources of meta data is best done using an RDF parser built on SAX.

We therefore looked at how we might go about building a structured parser that would enable different modules to be replaced as desired, without altering the overall workings of the parser. This was achieved by creating a parsing framework in C++.

You should now be able to make use of some of the RDF frameworks that are available to layer your applications on to, or even write your own framework if the need arises.

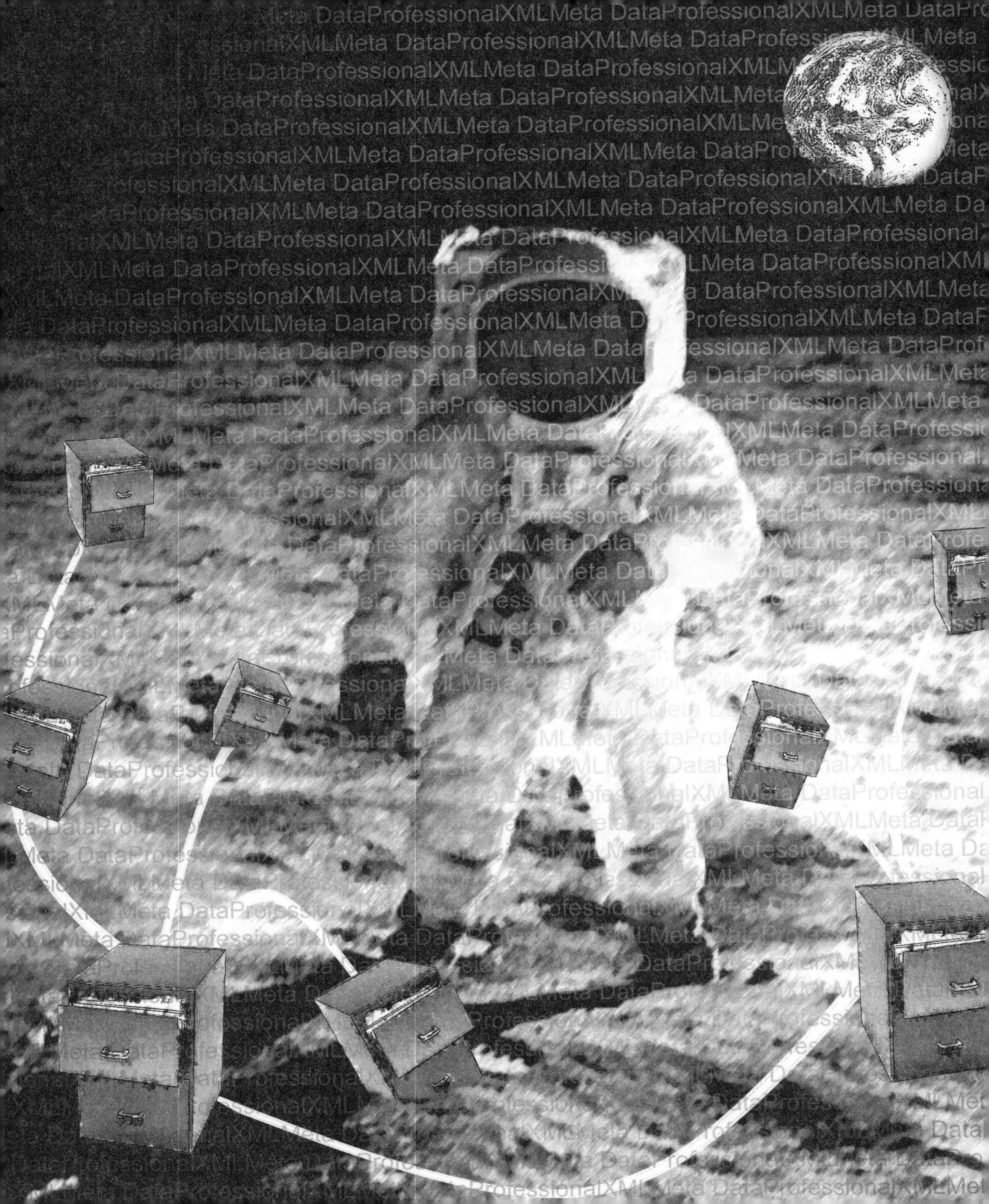

7

Topic Maps and XTM

Topic maps are designed to facilitate the management and navigation of large quantities of information. They achieve this by providing a "navigation layer" over a set of information resources that is independent of the form and format of the resources themselves. A topic map consists of **topics** (which are information objects representing specific subjects of interest), **associations** (which represent relationships among those subjects), and **occurrences** (information resources that are relevant to those subjects in any way). Through these simple constructs, the topic map enables the navigation of information resources based on their subject matter, and the relationships between various subjects, rather than on their format, structure, or even specific content.

A topic map may be a virtual object, existing in memory within a topic map application, or it may be made persistent for the purposes of storage or exchange. The persistent form of a topic map can be an XML document conforming to the **XTM** (**XML Topic Maps**) document type definition. Because the topics, associations, and occurrence information are carried in a document that is external to the resources themselves, the topic map can be constructed without editing or touching the resources in any way. This means that anybody can create a topic map, without requiring read-write access to the files that carry the information the topic map relates to. It is the topic map author who determines what are the subjects and relationships that are of interest, and which specific resources are occurrences of each topic. In this sense, a topic map expresses someone's conceptualization and categorization of an information set.

Any number of different topic maps can be created for a single set of resources. Furthermore, topic maps can be merged, which means that responsibility for developing a topic map can be delegated to several different people, each of whom produces a partial topic map and makes a contribution to the composite world view that the merged topic map represents. In this way, topic maps can be used as an invaluable repository of "corporate knowledge". Topic maps thus provide a powerful bridge between knowledge representation and information management. They enable the information carried by a set of information resources to be categorized and structured, and also enriched by the implicit knowledge that went into the identification of the topics themselves and the relationships between them.

If the primary purpose of topic maps is to facilitate the management, organization, navigation, and retrieval of information from large pools of disparate interconnected resources, a number of subsidiary purposes can be identified, including:

❑ Supporting diversity of language, terminology and viewpoint, while still allowing the common meaning of information to be traceable.

❑ Breaking down barriers to information access by enabling information retrieval across information resources independently of format.

❑ Providing a robust but flexible underpinning for the creation of indexes and thesauri, in order to help users find the information they need.

❑ Allowing information from different sources to be meaningfully brought together and merged, while making sense of the relationships between the information contained therein.

In this chapter we will look at:

❑ What topic maps are and how they can be used.

❑ The XML topic map syntax, XTM.

❑ Creating, processing, and merging topic maps.

Let's begin by considering the basic concepts that make up a topic map.

How Topic Maps Achieve their Purpose

In order to provide examples of some of the concepts we will be considering in this chapter, we shall draw on a short passage from a newspaper article (from the English newspaper, *The Sunday Times* of 6 May 2001). The passage is as follows:

> *"Newly unearthed drawings have shown that Charles Rennie Mackintosh, one of Britain's greatest architects of the early 20th century, made plans for a dome in Glasgow resembling the ill-fated attraction in Greenwich that closed at the end of last year. The designs by Mackintosh, who died in 1928, lay neglected in an archive at Glasgow University until they were rediscovered earlier this year. They have surprised the Millennium Dome's architects."*

Suppose that the article from which this passage is drawn is to be added to a large archive of news stories that we wish to make available for use by readers and researchers. How will we make it accessible in ways that help these readers and researchers find it when they are pursuing a particular line of enquiry or researching some area of interest to them?

There are a number of approaches that have traditionally been applied to this situation. One is the provision of a **full-text** search engine, allowing users to find the article based on the words it contains. Another is to categorize the article according to its principal themes and build a **subject index** in which we will find this article referenced from each of those themes. A third approach is to attach **meta data tags** to the article itself, and build a search engine that queries the content of those tags.

The topic map approach is to identify the subjects of interest within the passage, and to build a map containing a topic representing each of those subjects of interest. The map is then enriched with further objects, known as associations, representing relationships between the subjects. The article itself is considered to be an occurrence of each of the topics drawn from it. When the same subject occurs in several articles, there need only be one topic object representing that subject, and all the relevant articles will be identified as occurrences of that one topic.

This mechanism makes it possible to travel from a particular article to any of the topics of which it is an occurrence, then via associations involving that topic to other topics that are related to it in any way, and then to other articles that are occurrences of those topics. As an example of such navigation, suppose a reader notes from the article above that the Millennium Dome (referred to above as the "ill-fated attraction") is in Greenwich. They might then discover an association in the topic map indicating that Greenwich is a borough within London, and look for articles that are occurrences of the London topic. Or they might go further and look for associations involving architecture and London, and this might take them to the topic for the British Library, and then to occurrences of that topic, which will be articles about the British Library. This navigation scenario does not rely on there being any words in common between the original article and the one about the British Library, nor on there being any hyperlinks between the two articles, nor on the articles having been categorized in the same way in any index. It is sufficient that there is a chain of relationships, captured in association objects within the topic map, that connects from the Millennium Dome to the British Library (in this case via Greenwich, London, and architecture).

Reification

We have said that a topic is an **information object** that represents a subject. The topic exists within the computer. It can be manipulated and interpreted by software that is designed to handle information objects of that type. But what the topic represents will in many cases not be accessible to the computer at all. It is a subject of interest, such as Charles Rennie Mackintosh, the University of Glasgow, the recently discovered drawings of a design for a dome, or the year 1928 (in which, we are told in our sample article, Charles Rennie Mackintosh died).

If the drawings of the dome design had been produced in 1998, they might well have been in an electronic form, and then they would indeed be directly accessible to a computer system, and software designed to handle information objects of that type would be able to manipulate and interpret them. A set of drawings in electronic form is directly accessible to, and addressable by, a computer system. However, a set of drawings on paper, a person, a building, or a calendar year, is not directly accessible to the computer. Things that are directly accessible to a computer system are known as **resources**. Everything else in the world – people, places, physical objects, organizations, abstract concepts, and so on, are known in the language of topic maps as **non-addressable subjects**. There is a world of difference between resources and non-addressable subjects, but these two worlds – the computable and the non-computable – are bridged within the topic map by the fact that both may be represented by the same kind of information object – the *topic*.

The topic is said to **reify** (make real) its subject. It makes the subject accessible to the computer and thus enables the computer system to manipulate it in various ways. Once we have created a topic object to reify a subject, we can associate additional information with the topic object, linking it with other such objects in the complex pool of information that constitutes our topic map, and whose structure reflects the structure of those aspects of the world we wish our topic map to convey.

There are five things we can add to a topic object in order to allow it to be used and manipulated in useful ways:

❏   We can assign one or more **names** to it.

❏   We can identify resources that are its occurrences.

❏   We can identify the relationships that it has with other topics, and the **role** that it plays in these relationships.

❏   In the special case where the topic's subject is a resource, we can identify the resource that is the subject of the topic.

❏   Whether the topic has a resource as its subject, or in the more usual situation where the topic has a non-addressable subject, we can identify one or more resources that act as **subject indicators** for the topic. A subject indicator is defined as a resource (an object directly accessible to the computer) whose content indicates what the subject of the topic is.

The first three items in the above list deal with what are collectively known as **topic characteristics** – names, occurrences, and roles in associations. These are what constitute the *structure* of the topic map, and are the basis for topic map navigation and querying. It is the topic characteristics that make the topic intelligible to the topic map system.

The last two items in the above list deal with the **topic identity**. They provide the *bridge* between the topic map and the subjects that the topics represent. It is these that make the topics intelligible to human beings, or to computer systems beyond the topic map system itself.

Topic Characteristics

In the sections that follow we shall look at each kind of topic characteristic in more detail but first we need to introduce another important concept – that of **scope**.

Scope

One of the strengths of topic maps is that they can be used to capture and formalize multiple viewpoints on the same set of information. This is made possible by the fact that characteristics are always considered to be assigned to a topic within a given scope. The scope is defined as "the context within which the assignment of the characteristic is valid". In the case of a name, for example, the scope might be a language, a community, or a formal vocabulary or naming scheme. Within different communities, languages, or naming schemes, the same things are given different names. This diversity can be captured formally in the topic map by explicitly assigning each of the names to the topic, but at the same time specifying the context within which that particular name assignment is applicable.

The scope itself is represented by a set of topics. Therefore, to specify a language or community as a scope for a name assignment, a topic needs to be created that has as its subject that language or that community. This means that it is then also possible to assign characteristics to the topic representing the language or the community, and so the web of information and knowledge captured by the topic map is progressively built up.

The scope of assignment of a characteristic may or may not be stated explicitly. If it is not, then the scope is deemed to be the **unconstrained scope**, meaning that the assignment is valid in *all* contexts within that topic map. When several topic maps are merged to create a composite topic map, there is the option to specify topics that are added to the scope of every assignment within any given topic map that is being included within the merge, in order to avoid the implicit context of validity being broadened to the entire, merged topic map unintentionally. We shall discuss this more fully in the section on merging topic maps later in this chapter.

As we proceed, we shall see how the notion of scope applies in each kind of topic characteristic assignment.

Names

The first kind of characteristic that may be assigned to a topic is known as a **base name**. The notion of base name is somewhat stricter than the general notion of naming because, in combination with its scope, a base name is guaranteed to refer to only one topic.

In general, a name is a word, or a string of characters, that may be used to refer to an object. The key question is whether the name is usable as an unambiguous reference. The notions of a "namespace" and "controlled vocabulary" refer to situations in which a formal context is set within which no two objects have the same name. Within such a context, a name may be used to provide a reliable and unambiguous indication of which object is being referred to. Without the specification of a precise context, however, it is normally not possible to be certain that a name will have a unique referent.

As with any topic characteristic, a base name is always assigned to the topic within a given scope. In the case of base names, this means that a particular string of characters (the name) can be used to uniquely identify that topic within a certain context (the scope).

The name "Charles Rennie Mackintosh" in our sample passage is sufficiently unusual that it may well identify a single human being, regardless of context. The name "John Smith", on the other hand, does not identify a single human being unless we limit the context within which we are working to one in which there is only one person of that name. We could use the name "Charles", or the name "Mackintosh", to uniquely identify the famous architect, provided we narrowed the context sufficiently. Indeed, in the second sentence of our passage, the name 'Mackintosh' is used to refer to Charles Rennie Mackintosh the architect, and no ambiguity results, because a very specific context has been set. If we take as our scope the set of topics representing architecture, Britain, and the early 20th century, then perhaps the name Mackintosh would identify a unique person.

In the example below, we use the XTM (XML Topic Maps) syntax to illustrate this (we'll be discussing this specification in more detail later in the chapter). We see a `<topic>` element, which is a representation in XTM syntax that reifies Charles Rennie Mackintosh. Mackintosh himself is a real person, no longer living, and certainly not accessible to our computer system. He is therefore a non-addressable subject. It is the creation of the topic reifying this non-addressable subject that allows us to say things about Charles Rennie Mackintosh within our topic map. We do this by assigning characteristics to the topic:

```
<topic id="charles-rennie-mackintosh">
  <baseName>
    <baseNameString>Charles Rennie Mackintosh</baseNameString>
  </baseName>
  <baseName>
    <scope>
      <topicRef xlink:href="#architecture"/>
      <topicRef xlink:href="#britain"/>
```

```
        <topicRef xlink:href="#early-20th-century"/>
     </scope>
     <baseNameString>Mackintosh</baseNameString>
   </baseName>
 </topic>
```

Every `<topic>` element has a unique `id` attribute, which allows it to be referenced from elsewhere in the topic map. This attribute must comply with the rules for XML ID attributes – that is to say, it must consist only of permitted characters (letters, digits and a limited number of symbols defined by the XML specification), and must not begin with a numeric character. For convenience, in the examples given in this chapter, we have made the values of the `id` attributes in our examples human-readable (the first one, for example, has the value `charles-rennie-mackintosh`), but this only serves as a hint to readers and has no particular significance within the system. What begins to give the topic meaning within the topic map system is the assignment of the two base names in our example. The first base name, `Charles Rennie Mackintosh`, has no scope specified, and so is assigned within the unconstrained scope. The second base name, `Mackintosh`, is assigned within the scope of three additional topics, assumed to exist elsewhere in the topic map, whose `id`s are `architecture`, `britain`, and `early-20th-century`. These topics are referenced using `<topicRef>` elements containing a simple form of the **XLink** mechanism (http://www.w3.org/TR/xlink), comprising an attribute whose value consists of a # character, followed by the value of the `id` attribute of the element that is being referenced.

Now, there is a rule called the **topic naming constraint**, which states that when two topics have the same base name in the same scope, they are to be considered identical, and merged into one. It is the responsibility of the topic map author to ensure that the topic naming constraint is met within the topic map. Later, in the section on merging topic maps, we will discuss the issues that arise when topic maps created by different authors are merged, and how the implications of the topic naming constraint should be handled in this case.

Occurrences

The second kind of characteristic that may be assigned to a topic within a topic map is known as an **occurrence**, which is a resource that is relevant to the topic in some way. In the scenario of our news archive, the individual articles in the archive will be occurrences of all the topics representing subjects that are mentioned in them. There may, however, be additional resources, such as definitions, biographies, or other information relevant to these subjects in all kinds of different ways.

A large part of the value of topic maps is to allow users to find additional resources that are relevant to topics that are of interest. In doing this, it is very important for the user to be given an indication of just what is the nature of the relevance of the resource to the topic. To meet this requirement, topic maps include the notion of an **occurrence type**.

In our example, the newspaper article about the design for the Glasgow dome mentions Charles Rennie Mackintosh. There may be several other articles in the archive that also mention him. Perhaps there is also an article that provides a biography of him, and another that is an obituary. We might choose to create special topics representing the notions of "mention", "biography", and "obituary", and use these to provide typing information about the different occurrences.

In the example below we have added several `<occurrence>` elements to our topic, each of which has an `<instanceOf>` sub-element referring to the type of which that particular occurrence is an instance. As with the topics used to scope the second base name, we assume that topics representing these occurrence types have been created elsewhere in the topic map, and it is the values of the `id` attributes of those topics that are used to refer to them, using the `xlink:href` attribute of the `<topicRef>` elements.

```
<topic id="charles-rennie-mackintosh">
  <baseName>
    <baseNameString>Charles Rennie Mackintosh</baseNameString>
  </baseName>
  <baseName>
    <scope>
      <topicRef xlink:href="#architecture"/>
      <topicRef xlink:href="#britain"/>
      <topicRef xlink:href="#early-20th-century"/>
    </scope>
    <baseNameString>Mackintosh</baseNameString>
  </baseName>
  <occurrence>
    <instanceOf>
      <topicRef xlink:href="#mention"/>
    </instanceOf>
    <resourceRef xlink:href="... URL of our newspaper article ..."/>
  </occurrence>
  <occurrence>
    <instanceOf>
      <topicRef xlink:href="#mention"/>
    </instanceOf>
    <resourceRef xlink:href="... URL of another article that also mentions
                Charles Rennie Mackintosh..."/>
  </occurrence>
  <occurrence>
    <instanceOf>
      <topicRef xlink:href="#biography"/>
    </instanceOf>
    <resourceRef xlink:href="... URL of a biography of Charles Rennie
                Mackintosh ..."/>
  </occurrence>
  <occurrence>
    <instanceOf>
      <topicRef xlink:href="#obituary"/>
    </instanceOf>
    <resourceRef xlink:href="... URL of an obituary of Charles Rennie
                Mackintosh ..."/>
  </occurrence>
</topic>
```

Scopes on Occurrences

We can add yet further richness to this structure by including the notion of scope. We have said that a scope can be specified to provide context within which the assignment of a topic characteristic is deemed to be valid. We can therefore specify a context of validity for the assignment of an occurrence to a topic, just as we can for the assignment of a name.

When might we want to do this? Suppose that we have within our information archive not only factual accounts such as newspaper articles, but also pieces of fiction or imaginative writing. Someone may have written a humorous or fantasy piece in which Charles Rennie Mackintosh appears. It would be important in this case to distinguish between factual and fictional occurrences of our topic. This can be done by creating additional topics for each of the contexts in which a mention may be deemed valid – for example, a topic representing fact, and a topic representing fiction. Or we might consider that factual mentions are always valid and can therefore use the unconstrained scope, but create a topic representing the notion of fiction and use it to provide a context within which a certain resource is considered as a valid mention of Charles Rennie Mackintosh. This approach is illustrated in the example overleaf:

```
<topic id="charles-rennie-mackintosh">
  ...
  <occurrence>
    <instanceOf>
      <topicRef xlink:href="#mention"/>
    </instanceOf>
    <resourceRef xlink:href="... URL of our newspaper article ..."/>
  </occurrence>
  ...
  <occurrence>
    <instanceOf>
      <topicRef xlink:href="#mention"/>
    </instanceOf>
    <scope>
      <topicRef xlink:href="#fiction"/>
    </scope>
    <resourceRef xlink:href="... URL of a piece of fiction in which Charles
                 Rennie Mackintosh appears ..."/>
  </occurrence>
  ...
</topic>
```

We can see here how the notion of different viewpoints on our information can be developed within a single topic map. A user might wish to view and navigate the topic map while systematically ignoring all occurrences that have the fiction topic within their scope. In this way they will only be presented with factual mentions of the various topics in the map. Or they may want to see factual and fictional mentions, but have the fictional ones highlighted in some way. Or they may wish simply to read the occurrences, be they factual or fictional, and make their own judgments as to the veracity or the reliability of the information contained therein. The topic map formally captures the various characteristics assigned to each topic, and states the scope of validity of those assignments. Topic map-aware software applications can then be built that allow users to navigate the information conveyed by these assignments in ways that take account of those contexts in any number of ways.

Associations and Roles

The third kind of characteristic that may be assigned to a topic within a topic map relates topics not to strings that act as their names, nor to resources that are relevant to them, but to each other. An **association** is a defined relationship between topics, in which each topic plays a specified **role**. The role played by the topic in the association is a characteristic that can be explicitly assigned to the topic. Once again, the notion of scope applies, meaning that the topic is deemed to play that role within that association, but only within the context represented by the scope.

Let us consider how this plays out in our example. We have so far only created one topic that has our article as an occurrence, and that is the topic that reifies Charles Rennie Mackintosh. There are, however, several other subjects that occur in the article. Here are a few of them:

❑   The dome designed by Charles Rennie Mackintosh.

❑   The plans for that dome.

❑   The recently discovered drawings.

❑   The unnamed group of architects that designed the Millennium Dome.

❑   The Millennium Dome.

- ❑ Greenwich.
- ❑ Glasgow.

Note that the first four items in the list above have not been given any convenient names in the article we are working with. For convenience, we shall refer to them in what follows as "the Mackintosh dome", "the Mackintosh plans", "the Mackintosh drawings", and "the Millennium architects", respectively.

The subjects in the list above, and Charles Rennie Mackintosh himself, are clearly related to one another in various ways. Topic maps can include explicit information about the relationships between the subjects reified by the topics they contain. If we create a topic for each of the subjects listed above, we can then also create associations in the topic map and assign roles in those associations to the various topics. Just as occurrences can be classified by occurrence type, associations can be classified by association type. The type of an association or occurrence is itself a topic within the topic map. Typically an association of a particular type will involve particular roles, and topics of particular types will play those roles. We shall have more to say about this later in the chapter, in the section on association templates.

Let us now begin listing some of the relationships we might identify between the subjects we have identified. Here are a few:

- ❑ The Mackintosh dome was designed by Charles Rennie Mackintosh.
- ❑ The Millennium Dome was designed by the Millennium architects.
- ❑ Charles Rennie Mackintosh devised the Mackintosh plans.
- ❑ Charles Rennie Mackintosh created the Mackintosh drawings.
- ❑ The Mackintosh drawings depict the Mackintosh dome.
- ❑ The Millennium Dome is in Greenwich.
- ❑ The Mackintosh plans place the Mackintosh dome in Glasgow (though it was never built).
- ❑ Glasgow is to the north of Greenwich.

Note that some of these relationships are explicitly stated in the original newspaper article. Others can be inferred from it on the basis of our general understanding and broader knowledge (for example, that the drawings depict the dome, or that Charles Rennie Mackintosh created the drawings – neither of which is explicitly stated in the article). The last relationship (that Glasgow is to the north of Greenwich) cannot be inferred on the basis of the article, but may be known to us through other sources, some of which may exist elsewhere in the topic map.

Looking at this list of relationships we can see certain patterns. The first two are clearly of the same type, since each relates a building (real or planned) to the person or people that designed it. Most of the relationships relate just two things to one another. The second from last is particularly interesting. It would appear to relate three things to one another, and indeed it does. But it relates in an interesting way to the one before it, with an additional statement of scope. The Millennium Dome is in Greenwich and, *within the context of the plans,* the Mackintosh dome is in Glasgow (despite the fact that within the context of buildings in the real world, it is nowhere since it was never built). We shall see shortly how we can use the notion of scope to indicate this rather subtle relationship.

We shall build up the structure involved here piece by piece, concentrating on just a few of the relationships in the above list. Starting with the first association, we can say that this is a relationship between Charles Rennie Mackintosh and the Mackintosh dome. We already have a topic that reifies Charles Rennie Mackintosh. So if we simply create another topic to reify the Mackintosh dome, we can then create an association representing the relationship between them. In XTM syntax, this will give us the following:

```
<topic id="charles-rennie-mackintosh"> ... </topic>
<topic id="mackintosh-dome"/>
<association>
  <member>
    <topicRef xlink:href="#mackintosh-dome"/>
  </member>
  <member>
    <topicRef xlink:href="#charles-rennie-mackintosh"/>
  </member>
</association>
```

This tells us simply that there exists a relationship between the Mackintosh dome and Charles Rennie Mackintosh. Nothing is said about the nature of the relationship or the roles that the two members play in it. To add the information about the roles, we need topics representing those roles. So we shall create a topic for the role of building in a building-designer relationship, and another for the role of designer in that relationship. Having done this, we can specify the role played by each member in the association. The result will be as follows:

```
<topic id="charles-rennie-mackintosh"> ... </topic>
<topic id="mackintosh-dome"/>
<topic id="designed-building"/>
<topic id="building-designer"/>
<association>
  <member>
    <roleSpec>
      <topicRef xlink:href="#designed-building"/>
    </roleSpec>
    <topicRef xlink:href="#mackintosh-dome"/>
  </member>
  <member>
    <roleSpec>
      <topicRef xlink:href="#building-designer"/>
    </roleSpec>
    <topicRef xlink:href="#charles-rennie-mackintosh"/>
  </member>
</association>
```

The next step is to note that there may be other associations of the same type, each representing the relationship between a building and its designer. We can create a topic reifying a class of all associations of this type. That will allow us to specify that this particular association is an instance of that general class of associations. The class is then known as the association type of this particular association.

Here is the complete structure that results when we have done this:

```
<topic id="charles-rennie-mackintosh"> ... </topic>
<topic id="mackintosh-dome"/>
<topic id="designed-building"/>
<topic id="building-designer"/>
<topic id="building-designed-by-designer"/>
<association>
  <instanceOf>
    <topicRef xlink:href="#building-designed-by-designer"/>
  </instanceOf>
  <member>
    <roleSpec>
      <topicRef xlink:href="#designed-building"/>
    </roleSpec>
    <topicRef xlink:href="#mackintosh-dome"/>
  </member>
  <member>
    <roleSpec>
      <topicRef xlink:href="#building-designer"/>
    </roleSpec>
    <topicRef xlink:href="#charles-rennie-mackintosh"/>
  </member>
</association>
```

If we apply this same approach to the case of the Millennium Dome, we come across the interesting fact that, on the basis of the information we currently have at our disposal, we do not know who designed the Millennium Dome. We do, however, know that someone designed it, and that the relationship between that unspecified person or group of people and the Millennium Dome is of the same type as that between Mackintosh and his dome. We can express all this (including the incompleteness of our knowledge) in the following way:

```
<topic id="millennium-dome"/>
<association>
  <instanceOf>
    <topicRef xlink:href="#building-designed-by-designer"/>
  </instanceOf>
  <member>
    <roleSpec>
      <topicRef xlink:href="#designed-building"/>
    </roleSpec>
    <topicRef xlink:href="#millennium-dome"/>
  </member>
  <member>
    <roleSpec>
      <topicRef xlink:href="#building-designer"/>
    </roleSpec>
  </member>
</association>
```

This structure tells us that there is an association of the type reified by the `building-designed-by-designer` topic, involving the Millennium Dome in the role of designed building, and involving a member in the role of building designer, but with no topic being specified to reify the player of the building designer role. This expression of incomplete knowledge is perfectly legitimate. In fact, our knowledge is always incomplete in some way, and we can express within a topic map as much or as little of our knowledge as we please.

Having said that, we do know that the Millennium Dome architects (whoever they may be) were surprised by the Mackintosh drawings, since this fact is explicitly stated in the article. If we wanted to capture that fact in our topic map, we could do so by creating a topic for the association of "person surprised by thing", with the roles of "surprised person" and "surprising thing", and create an association between the drawings and the unspecified people who were surprised by them:

```
<topic id="mackintosh-drawings"/>
<association>
  <instanceOf>
    <topicRef xlink:href="#person-surprised-by-thing"/>
  </instanceOf>
  <member>
    <roleSpec>
      <topicRef xlink:href="#surprising-thing"/>
    </roleSpec>
    <topicRef xlink:href="#mackintosh-drawings"/>
  </member>
  <member>
    <roleSpec>
      <topicRef xlink:href="#surprised-person"/>
    </roleSpec>
  </member>
</association>
```

This structure represents incomplete knowledge in precisely the same way as the one representing the relationship between the Millennium Dome and its unknown designers. However, we do in fact know something more. Despite not knowing who designed the Millennium Dome, or who was surprised by the Mackintosh drawings, we do know they were the same people, and this fact is missing from our topic map. There would be good reason therefore to create a topic reifying these unknown people, and place references to it in the two relevant <member> slots in these association structures. We would end up with something like this:

```
<topic id="millennium-dome"/>
<topic id="mackintosh-drawings"/>
<topic id="x"/>
<association>
  <instanceOf>
    <topicRef xlink:href="#building-designed-by-designer"/>
  </instanceOf>
  <member>
    <roleSpec>
      <topicRef xlink:href="#designed-building"/>
    </roleSpec>
    <topicRef xlink:href="#millennium-dome"/>
  </member>
  <member>
    <roleSpec>
      <topicRef xlink:href="#building-designer"/>
    </roleSpec>
    <topicRef xlink:href="#x"/>
  </member>
</association>
<association>
  <instanceOf>
    <topicRef xlink:href="#person-surprised-by-thing"/>
```

```
      </instanceOf>
      <member>
        <roleSpec>
          <topicRef xlink:href="#surprising-thing"/>
        </roleSpec>
        <topicRef xlink:href="#mackintosh-drawings"/>
      </member>
      <member>
        <roleSpec>
          <topicRef xlink:href="#surprised-person"/>
        </roleSpec>
        <topicRef xlink:href="#x"/>
      </member>
    </association>
```

We see here that our empty <topic> element with the id attribute of x is not as empty of information as at first appeared. It has been assigned a role in each of the associations that follow. We therefore know that whoever designed the Millennium Dome was surprised by the Mackintosh drawings. That is a fact of considerable interest – indeed, it is the main thrust of the brief newspaper article we are capturing – despite the fact that at present we do not know who these people are. If, as we build our news archive, we come across information in subsequent articles telling us more about the designers of the Millennium Dome, we can assign additional characteristics to our topic x, thereby building up our web of knowledge and, incidentally, making connections between other articles that speak of those designers, and this one.

The way in which we build progressively on incomplete knowledge of things is an important part of how we actually build our understanding of the world. Perhaps at first we know only the name of something, or we do not know its name but we know some role it plays, or we know neither, but simply know that it is mentioned in some document. Any and all of these pieces of knowledge are expressible as characteristics of the topic that reifies this at first unknown, but progressively better and better known subject of interest within our topic map.

Scopes on Associations

Before we leave this discussion of associations and roles, let us consider how the notion of scope applies here. We have said that a scope is a set of topics that represents the context of validity of a topic characteristic assignment. In the case of the assignment of roles in associations, this allows us to say the topics play particular roles in particular associations within a specific context.

Consider the association of a building to its location. In our article, we have two buildings, each related to a location. However, there is a difference in the contexts within which these associations apply. If you ask what topic plays the role of location for the Mackintosh dome, the answer is clearly Glasgow. Yet the dome was never built, and if you visit Glasgow you will not see it. In the case of the Millennium Dome, the dome is physically located in Greenwich, and you will see it if you go there. In the case of the Mackintosh dome, it is only located in Glasgow within the context of the imagined world projected by the plans, and hence the scope of the association between the Mackintosh dome and the city of Glasgow is the Mackintosh plans.

We can therefore create associations of the very same type for these two situations, but impose a scope on one of them, saying that it is only valid in the context of the Mackintosh plans. The resulting structure, expressed in XTM syntax, is illustrated overleaf:

```
<topic id="building-in-location"/>
<topic id="located-building"/>
<topic id="building-location"/>
<topic id="greenwich"/>
<topic id="glasgow"/>
<topic id="mackintosh-plans"/>
<association>
  <instanceOf>
    <topicRef xlink:href="#building-in-location"/>
  </instanceOf>
  <member>
    <roleSpec>
      <topicRef xlink:href="#located-building"/>
    </roleSpec>
    <topicRef xlink:href="#millennium-dome"/>
  </member>
  <member>
    <roleSpec>
      <topicRef xlink:href="#building-location"/>
    </roleSpec>
    <topicRef xlink:href="#greenwich"/>
  </member>
</association>
<association>
  <instanceOf>
    <topicRef xlink:href="#building-in-location"/>
  </instanceOf>
  <scope>
    <topicRef xlink:href="mackintosh-plans"/>
  </scope>
  <member>
    <roleSpec>
      <topicRef xlink:href="#located-building"/>
    </roleSpec>
    <topicRef xlink:href="#mackintosh-dome"/>
  </member>
  <member>
    <roleSpec>
      <topicRef xlink:href="#building-location"/>
    </roleSpec>
    <topicRef xlink:href="#glasgow"/>
  </member>
</association>
```

Note that the two members of the above association, namely the Mackintosh dome and Glasgow, play their respective roles in the association in precisely the same context. The <scope> element is therefore provided once only, as a direct child of the <association> element, rather than being redundantly repeated within each <member> element. Indeed, the XTM syntax does not allow <scope> elements as children of <member> elements, so it is a requirement of the syntax that the different roles in the association are applicable within the same context. This is not a limitation in practice, since it is difficult to see what would be meant by an association in which the context of applicability of the different roles was not the same.

Topic Identity

The identity of a topic is determined by its subject. Two `<topic>` elements in the same or different topic maps that have the same subject should be considered to be the very same topic. Suppose you have a topic map covering a library of information resources about the history of British architecture, and I have my topic map covering the newspaper archive I have been working with. Your topic map will no doubt contain a topic that reifies Charles Rennie Mackintosh. So does mine. If we bring your topic map and mine together to build a composite map, the real benefit to doing that is only realized if we can identify that your topic and mine are in fact the same because they have the same subject. If we merge the two topics on the basis of the identity of their subject, then we can navigate freely in the composite topic map between the occurrences of Charles Rennie Mackintosh that my topic map identifies, and those identified by your topic map. We can combine the associations in which your topic plays a role with those in which mine plays an equivalent role, and thus we can glean a richer (and more accurate) set of information than if we treated them as separate entities.

The topic map paradigm provides three ways of explicitly indicating the subject of a topic:

❑ In the special case where the subject is a resource, which by definition is an object addressable by the computer system, we can make an explicit reference to that resource and say "that resource is the subject of this topic". This method is reliable and unambiguous, but is *only* available in the minority of cases where the subject is indeed directly addressable.

❑ We can make an explicit reference to a topic in the same or a different topic map and say "this topic has the same subject as that one". This method is also reliable. It establishes the identity of these two topics and allows the system to merge them, but it does not tell us what the subject of these topics actually is, or enable the system to see whether they should be merged with other topics that may share the same subject.

❑ Finally, we can point to a resource and say "that resource provides an explicit indication of what the subject of this topic is". It is this last option that provides a bridge between the world of resources (objects that are directly addressable by computers) and the wider world of non-addressable subjects (comprising everything else, including physical objects, abstractions and concepts). The bridge is made because the resource has to be *understood* in order to communicate what the subject is, and that process of understanding takes us out of the world of the computable, and into the world of knowledge. Yet, despite the fact that the topic-map system cannot understand the meaning of the resource, it does know its identity. Thus if two topics both identify the same resource, saying "that resource provides an explicit indication of what the subject of this topic is", the system can infer that the subjects of the two topics, though non-addressable, are the same, and therefore the topics themselves should be merged into one.

It is possible to use all three of these methods on the same topic, and the second and third can be repeated multiple times. In other words, we can point to more than one resource that provides an explicit indication of the subject of the topic, and more than one other topic that has the same subject. The exception is the first of the three methods, which can only be used to point to a single resource, because the topic can only have one subject, and pointing to two different resources and saying of each that it is the subject would therefore be an error.

Subject Indicators

A **subject indicator** is a resource that is specified within a topic map (using a `<subjectIndicatorRef>` element) as being an explicit indication of the subject of a topic. This is the third method of providing an identity for a topic that we have just discussed. Subject indicators are a crucial aspect of the topic map paradigm.

The way in which the subject indicator does its indicating is not limited in any way. Typically, the subject indicator will be a document, or a part of a document, that is readable and understandable by a human being. But if it is to be effective in communicating the subject, it must be of a very particular kind. It could be a definition in a dictionary, for example. That would certainly be a clear and unambiguous indication of a subject. It could also be an item in a formal vocabulary, such as the list of country codes provided by the **International Organization for Standardization (ISO –** http://www.iso.ch). A pointer to the item "FR" in the list of ISO 2-letter country codes would be a very clear indication that the subject intended is France, since it is France that the code FR designates within this system.

Since one of the purposes of specifying subject indicators is to facilitate reliable and appropriate merging of topics drawn from different topic maps, it is desirable that they be well chosen. Subject indicators drawn from widely known and accepted standards, where there is common agreement on their exact meaning, are the best ones to use, since they will be both more reliable and more likely to be used by authors of different topic maps than any other kind.

It may be that a resource identified as a subject indicator for a topic is one that is not human-readable at all, but is interpretable by some computer system. This too can be very powerful and very useful. For example, we could imagine a topic map that is developed and used within a computer environment that includes a geographical information system. Within this system, there may be a **data dictionary** containing data objects, interpretable by the system, though not directly to humans, that represent the various countries of the world. Pointing to an item in this data dictionary that stands for the country France, and stating that this is a subject indicator for my topic, would enable the system to make inferences about my topic based on its internal knowledge of geographical entities.

For example, if my topic map had another topic that uses as a subject indicator the item in the data dictionary standing for Germany, the geographical information system would be able to infer that there is a specific relationship between the two topics – namely that the two countries that are their subjects share a common border, and are therefore neighbors. We could create an integration between the geographical information system and the topic map system that would then create an additional association within the topic map, explicitly stating the neighbor relationship between these two topics.

There is very little logical difference between the behavior of the geographical information system described above and that of a human being, acting as author of an extension to the topic map, interpreting the subject indicators in the topic map, thereby identifying the subjects of the topics, and populating the topic map with additional information based on their knowledge about the subjects in question.

Reifying an Association by Using it as a Subject Indicator

A very particular case of the use of a resource as the subject indicator of a topic is in the reification of an association. If we want to assign characteristics to an association – for example, in order to specify that the association itself is part of the subject matter of a particular resource, which is therefore an occurrence of the association – then we need to reify the association as a topic. The way this is done is to create a topic and point to the relevant <association> element as being its subject indicator. This means, in effect, "the subject of this topic is indicated by that <association> element", or to put it another way, what the <association> element *means* is what this topic *reifies*. In the example below, we use this technique to state that the Millennium Dome being in Greenwich is mentioned in our sample newspaper article:

```
<association id="millennium-dome-in-greenwich-association">
  <instanceOf>
    <topicRef xlink:href="#building-in-location"/>
  </instanceOf>
```

```
    <member>
      <roleSpec>
        <topicRef xlink:href="#located-building"/>
      </roleSpec>
      <topicRef xlink:href="#millennium-dome"/>
    </member>
    <member>
      <roleSpec>
        <topicRef xlink:href="#building-location"/>
      </roleSpec>
      <topicRef xlink:href="#greenwich"/>
    </member>
  </association>
  <topic id="millennium-dome-in-greenwich-topic">
    <subjectIdentity>
      <subjectIndicatorRef xlink:href="#millennium-dome-in-greenwich-association"/>
    </subjectIdentity>
    <occurrence>
      <instanceOf>
        <topicRef xlink:href="#mention"/>
      </instanceOf>
      <resourceRef xlink:href="... URL of our newspaper article ..."/>
    </occurrence>
  </topic>
```

Note that to make it easy to reference the <association> element from the <subjectIndicatorRef> element's xlink:href attribute, we have given the <association> element an id attribute. It is good practice to always provide an id attribute for <association> elements, because it makes it easy to reify them in this way later on. However, if this has not been done, it is possible simply to create a new <association> element with the same contents as the original one, and give this duplicate element an id attribute. The merging rules for topic maps state that any two associations with the same topics playing the same roles, that are instances of the same association type, are merged into one. The creation of the second <association> element therefore does not create a second association object when the topic map system interprets the XTM document.

Published Subject Indicators

A special kind of subject indicator is a **published subject indicator** (sometimes referred to as a **PSI**). This is a subject indicator that is explicitly made available at a known address so it can reliably be addressed using a stable URL or other referencing mechanism, for the purposes of being used by the authors of multiple topic maps. This makes the exchange and interchange of topic maps and appropriate merging of the topics they contain easier to achieve.

The XTM specification includes a number of published subject indicators for key topics that are integral to the logic of the topic map paradigm itself, and **TopicMaps.Org** (http://www.topicmaps.org), the group that developed the XTM specification, intends to make other published subject indicators available. These will in many cases be drawn from existing work by standards bodies or other organizations developing shared ontologies, taxonomies, controlled vocabularies, and the like.

Class-Instance Associations and Topic Types

There is a particular kind of association between topics that is of prime importance in the management and organization of knowledge. This is the association between a kind of thing (a **class**), and individual things of that kind (**instances** of the class).

If I want to state, for example, that Charles Rennie Mackintosh was an architect, I can create a topic that reifies the architect class, then create topics for the class-instance association type, and for the roles of class and instance within class-instance associations. Finally, I can create an association of type class-instance in which Charles Rennie Mackintosh plays the role of instance and architect plays the role of class. However, I am spared the trouble of creating special topics for class-instance, class, and instance, because published subject indicators for these core notions have been provided with the XTM specification. Instead of creating my own topics for them and using `<topicRef>` elements to reference them, I instead use `<subjectIndicatorRef>` elements to reference these published subject indicators through their specific URLs. The result is as follows:

```
<topic id="charles-rennie-mackintosh"/>
<topic id="architect"/>
<association>
  <instanceOf>
    <subjectIndicatorRef
      xlink:href="http://www.topicmaps.org/xtm/1.0/core.xtm#class-instance"/>
  </instanceOf>
  <member>
    <roleSpec>
      <subjectIndicatorRef
        xlink:href="http://www.topicmaps.org/xtm/1.0/core.xtm#class"/>
    </roleSpec>
    <topicRef xlink:href="#architect"/>
  </member>
  <member>
    <roleSpec>
      <subjectIndicatorRef
        xlink:href="http://www.topicmaps.org/xtm/1.0/core.xtm#instance"/>
    </roleSpec>
  </member>
  <topicRef xlink:href="#charles-rennie-mackintosh"/>
</association>
```

Though this use of published subject indicators ensures that the nature of this association is clearly specified, in a standard and public way that is not dependent on the interpretation of the meaning of topics I create myself for the notions of class and instance, this construct is nevertheless quite verbose. Such is the importance of the notion of class-instance associations between topics that XTM provides a much more concise syntax for expressing the same thing. This involves the use of an `<instanceOf>` child of a `<topic>` element that directly references a topic that reifies the class of which the current topic's subject is an instance. Note also that the topic's subject may be the instance of many classes.

For example, Charles Rennie Mackintosh was a man as well as being an architect. Some men are not architects; some architects are not men; Charles Rennie Mackintosh was both. Using the short syntactic form of the `<instanceOf>` child of `<topic>`, I can express this extremely concisely, and in a way that is very easy to read and understand, as shown below:

```
<topic id="architect"/>
<topic id="man"/>
<topic id="charles-rennie-mackintosh">
  <instanceOf>
    <topicRef xlink:href="#man"/>
  </instanceOf>
  <instanceOf>
    <topicRef xlink:href="#architect"/>
  </instanceOf>
</topic>
```

Historical Development – from Topic Navigation Maps to XTM

In the examples we have given above, we have been using the XML syntax defined by the XML Topic Maps (XTM) specification (http://www.topicmaps.org/xtm/1.0/). This specification was developed during 2000 and early 2001 by a group that came together under the name TopicMaps.Org, with the express purpose of bringing the topic map paradigm into the world of XML and the World Wide Web. However, the topic map paradigm itself was under development for many years before that. Its development came from the world of SGML (the structured information standard on which XML is based), and in particular the application of SGML to multimedia and hyper-documents, known as HyTime.

Both SGML and HyTime are international standards, approved by the International Organization for Standardization (ISO) and the International Electrotechnical Commission (IEC), through their Joint Technical Committee responsible for document description languages. The same committee developed the standard that was finally ratified in early 2000, under the name Topic Navigation Maps, with the official standard number ISO/IEC 13250.

This standard describes the general concepts underlying topic maps, and defines an interchange syntax for topic maps through an SGML Document Type Definition (DTD) that conforms with the "architectural form definition requirements" specified by the HyTime standard. HyTime is concerned with the specification of hyper-documents, and has extremely robust and complete methods for addressing resources and specifying links between them. The Topic Navigation Map specification makes full use of one of HyTime's linking models (known as "varlink"). Each topic is represented as a link that binds together its various characteristics (names, occurrences, and roles in associations).

By the time the Topic Navigation Map standard had been approved by the ISO/IEC Joint Technical Committee, it had become clear that the SGML and HyTime standards were being used only by a fairly small minority of those potentially interested in the topic map paradigm. XML had emerged as a simplified form of SGML, well suited to use on the World Wide Web. Also the XPointer and XLink specifications had arrived, which took many of the addressing and linking notions included in the HyTime specification and simplified them too, making them XML-compliant and suitable for use by lightweight web-based applications.

In order to make the power and capabilities of topic maps accessible to the XML web community, it was clear that an XML-compliant version of the topic map standard needed to be developed. To this end, at the beginning of 2000, immediately after the ratification of the ISO/IEC 13250 Topic Navigation Maps standard, Steve Newcomb and Michel Biezunski, two of the three co-editors of that standard, created a new organization known as TopicMaps.Org with the express purpose of fast-tracking the development of an XML-compliant, web-compatible topic maps specification, to be known as XTM (XML Topic Maps). Many of the members of the ISO committee were also members of TopicMaps.Org, and a number of new participants joined them to carry out this task.

Model and Syntax

Many specifications begin by defining a syntax for a certain category of information. This syntax is defined formally and rigorously, but what the syntax is intended to signify is explained less formally, in prose descriptions accompanying the syntax definitions. Later, it is often found necessary to develop a more formal specification of the semantics that are represented by the syntax – either at the level of the data objects that should be created within a computer system that has processed a document written in the specified syntax, or at the higher level of the concepts those data objects are intended to represent.

Examples of this pattern are numerous. SGML defined a syntax very fully and formally, but in order to then provide rigorous ways of defining structural transformations on SGML documents, or creating hyperlinks between elements within those documents, a formal model of the objects held in memory once an SGML document has been parsed needed to be created. This model (known as the **grove model**) was a key part of the HyTime specification we have already mentioned. Similarly, XML defines a syntax very fully and formally, but as numerous other specifications have been developed that surround and enhance XML, it has been necessary to define first the **DOM (Document Object Model)**, and then what is known as the **XML Infoset**, in order to give a formal definition of what the XML syntax represents in terms of data objects that can be manipulated in memory once the XML document has been parsed (the DOM), and to define the meaningful information structures that are represented by the syntactic structures of XML itself (XML Infoset).

Like XML and SGML, the Topic Navigation Maps standard (ISO/IEC 13250) provided a formal definition of a syntax, but only a semi-formal, prose definition of what the syntax represents. TopicMaps.Org took the decision that in developing the XTM specification it would be preferable to provide a specification, not only of a syntax that could be used for interchanging topic maps, but also of a conceptual model of what that syntax represents.

By early December 2000, a first draft of the core of the XTM specification was published, and in February 2001 the full XTM 1.0 specification, including a conceptual model, an interchange syntax, a small set of published subject indicators, and a set of processing constraints, was formally approved and published by the TopicMaps.Org authoring group.

Since that time, work has continued, both inside and outside TopicMaps.Org, on enhancing and further developing the capabilities of XTM. This includes work on a formal processing model for topic maps (http://www.topicmaps.net), and on a Topic Map query language.

A number of introductory tutorials, white papers, etc., are available at the web sites of topic map tool vendors: empolis (http://www.empolis.co.uk/technology/tech_tmo.asp), Infoloom (http://www.infoloom.com), Mondéca (http://www.mondeca.com), and Ontopia (http://www.ontopia.net/topicmaps/index.html).

The XTM Conceptual Model

The conceptual model, developed by TopicMaps.Org and included in the XTM specification, uses the **Unified Modeling Language** (**UML**) to describe the conceptual framework of topic maps. The entire model comprises just nine diagrams with accompanying explanatory comments. It is a compact formal structure which shows clearly the relationships between the concepts that make up the topic map paradigm, including those that are directly accessible to the computer (resources, including strings, XML elements, topics, associations held in memory by the computer once an XTM document has been processed, and so on), and those that are not (non-addressable subjects, including classes).

The first diagram in the XTM conceptual model shows a **class hierarchy**:

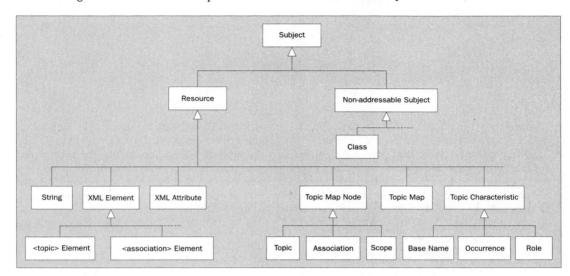

This diagram uses the conventions of UML to show a hierarchy of classes and subclasses, starting from the notion of subject, of which everything else is a subclass. The XTM specification provides the following description of this diagram:

> "A Subject is anything that can be spoken about or conceived of by a human being. A Resource is a Subject that has identity within the bounds of a computer system. Any other Subject is known as a Non-addressable Subject. There are many types of Non-addressable Subject. A Class is a Non-addressable Subject. Types of Resource include String, XML Element and XML Attribute, as well as Topic Map, Topic Map Node and Topic Characteristic, and many others. Types of XML Element include <topic> Element and <association> Element, and many others. There are just three types of Topic Map Node: Topic, Association, and Scope. There are just three types of Topic Characteristic: Base Name, Occurrence, and Role."

The second diagram in the conceptual model is a very simple one, and simply shows that any subject can be an instance of zero or more classes. This is the concept that underpins the notion of topic types, occurrence types, and association types. In each case, the type is a class, and the topic, occurrence or association is an instance of that class.

Now, when we come to express this in XTM syntax, we can do this by creating an <association> element representing our association, and giving it an <instanceOf> child with a <topicRef> child that references a <topic> element whose subject is the class:

```
<topic id="my-class">
  <subjectIdentity>
    <subjectIdentityRef xlink:href="... URL of a resource indicating the nature of
this class of associations ..."/>
  </subjectIdentity>
</topic>
<association id="my-association">
  <instanceOf>
```

```
          <topicRef xlink:href="my-class"/>
      </instanceOf>
      <member>
        ...
      </member>
      <member>
        ...
      </member>
  </association>
```

Alternatively, we could create our <association> element, then create a <topic> element whose <subjectIdentity> child has a <resourceRef> child that references the <association> element, meaning that the <association> element *indicates* the subject of the topic, or that the association represented by that association *is* the subject of the topic or, more succinctly, that the topic *reifies* the association. Now I can create a further <association> element that explicitly represents the class-instance association between the original association and the class of associations (using the published subject indicators for the class-instance association and its constituent roles):

```
<topic id="my-class">
  <subjectIdentity>
    <subjectIdentityRef xlink:href="... URL of a resource indicating the nature of
this class of associations ..."/>
  </subjectIdentity>
</topic>
<association id="my-association">

  <member>
    ...
  </member>
  <member>
    ...
  </member>
</association>
<topic id="topic-reifying-my-association">
  <subjectIdentity>
    <resourceRef xlink:href="#my-association"/>
  </subjectIdentity>
</topic>
<association id="my-association-instance-of-my-class">
  <instanceOf>
    <subjectIndicatorRef
xlink:href="http://www.topicmaps.org/xtm/1.0/core.xtm#class-instance"/>
  </instanceOf>
  <member>
    <roleSpec>
      <subjectIndicatorRef
xlink:href="http://www.topicmaps.org/xtm/1.0/core.xtm#class"/>
    </roleSpec>
    <topicRef xlink:href="#my-class"/>
  </member>
  <member>
    <roleSpec>
      <subjectIndicatorRef
xlink:href="http://www.topicmaps.org/xtm/1.0/core.xtm#instance"/>
    </roleSpec>
  </member>
  <topicRef xlink:href="#my-association"/>
</association>
```

The meaning of these two structures is the same. They are different syntactic expressions of the same conceptual structure. The relationships between the syntax and the concepts are quite subtle and so it is important that the specification provides both an explicit syntax and an explicit conceptual model showing what that syntax is intended to express.

The third diagram in the conceptual model shows the relationships between subjects, which may be resources or non-addressable subjects, topics, and subject indicators. This takes us to the heart of the relationship between the computable world of resources and the non-computable world of subjects which may be non-addressable. We see here how a topic can reify a subject but can only reference it directly if the subject happens to be a resource. Otherwise it can only indicate the subject through the use of subject indicators, which are themselves resources:

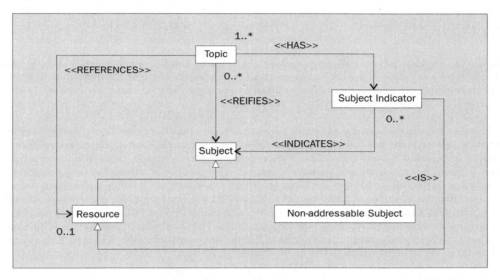

As in the first diagram, the conventions of UML are being used here. The triangular arrow-heads represent class-subclass relationships, as in the previous diagram. The simple arrows represent other kinds of relationships between objects of the types represented by the rectangles, where the nature of the relationship is indicated by the word between double angle brackets that labels the arrow. The numbers beside the arrows represent the number of objects that may be involved in the relationship. If there is no number, the meaning is "exactly one". Thus, the central downward arrow means "*Every Topic reifies exactly one Subject, and every Subject may be reified by zero or more Topics*". The XTM specification provides the following description of this diagram:

> "*A Topic can have any number of Subject Indicators. A Subject Indicator is a Resource that indicates what Subject is reified by the Topic. If the Subject is itself a Resource, there can be a direct reference from the Topic to that Resource in addition to any references there may be to Subject Indicators.*"

Note that this diagram says nothing about syntax. It shows the conceptual structure that the syntax represents. The arrow from topic to resource in the above diagram finds its syntactic expression in XTM syntax in the <resourceRef> element within the <subjectIdentity> child of the <topic> element:

```
<topic id="my-topic">
  <subjectIdentity>
```

```
    <resourceRef xlink:href="... URL of the resource that is the subject of my
 topic .../>
   </subjectIdentity>
 </topic>
```

Similarly, the arrow from topic to subject indicator is expressed syntactically in the
<subjectIndicatorRef> element within the <subjectIdentity> child of the <topic> element:

```
 <topic id="my-topic">
   <subjectIdentity>
     <subjectIndicatorRef xlink:href="... URL of a resource that indicates the
 subject of my topic .../>
   </subjectIdentity>
 </topic>
```

The rest of the diagram is not directly visible in the syntax, but is implicit whenever the syntax is used.
If I reference a resource using the <subjectIndicatorRef> element, then the meaning of this is that
that resource indicates the subject that is reified by the topic. The syntax does not need to spell this out
explicitly.

In the case of the class-instance associations, we have seen that the syntactic expression can be quite
elaborate and verbose, but the concept itself is very simple. In the case of the current diagram, the
syntactic expression is quite simple, but the conceptual structure quite subtle and involved. The two
serve different purposes, but are intimately related. The purpose of the syntax is to provide reliable
interchange of the information in the topic map between computer systems without any information
loss. The purpose of the conceptual model is to provide a formal structure representing the concepts
underlying that information, clear enough to be understood by humans, and to serve as a basis for
defining implementation and processing requirements. The third part of the picture is an explicit
statement of those processing requirements. All three are essential to the full topic map specification,
and all three are present within XTM version 1.0.

The XTM conceptual model goes on to provide diagrams depicting the notions of scope, the various
kinds of topic characteristics, and the notion of a "consistent" topic map, that is one in which all topics
that can be determined to have the same subject have been merged. We shall not provide a detailed
description of these parts of the model, since the purpose of this section has been to give an indication
of the nature and importance of the conceptual model rather than a full account of every detail of it. For
details of the full model, take a look at Annex B of the XTM 1.0 specification.

The XTM Syntax

In this section we will walk through the XTM syntax defined in the XTM 1.0 DTD, commenting on any
aspects that have not been covered in the earlier sections of this chapter.

The <topicMap> Element

The root element of a topic map document is the <topicMap> element. It can contain any number of
<topic>, <association>, and <mergeMap> elements, in any order.

The <topicMap> element has four attributes:

❑   The optional id attribute may be used to provide an identifier that can be used to reference
this element specifically from within or from outside the document.

❑ The xmlns attribute specifies the default namespace for the XTM document. The value of this attribute (http://www.topicmaps.org/xtm/1.0/) is fixed within the DTD, and the attribute does not need to be present within instance documents.

❑ The xmlns:xlink attribute is also fixed, (with a value of http://www.w3.org/1999/xlink/), and specifies that attributes having the xlink: prefix are drawn from the XLink namespace. This is needed so that XLink processors are able to correctly interpret the xlink:href attributes that are used to reference topics and resources. Though the value of this attribute is fixed within the DTD, some applications will require it to be explicitly present within the instance document in order to be able to recognize the xlink: prefix when it occurs.

❑ Finally, the optional xml:base attribute may be used to specify a URI from which all relative URIs in the document are interpreted. If the xml:base is not present, then all relative URIs are interpreted starting from the root element of the XTM document itself.

```
<!ELEMENT topicMap ( topic | association | mergeMap )*>
<!ATTLIST topicMap id          ID     #IMPLIED
                   xmlns       CDATA  #FIXED http://www.topicmaps.org/xtm/1.0/'
                   xmlns:xlink CDATA  #FIXED 'http://www.w3.org/1999/xlink/'
                   xml:base    CDATA  # IMPLIED >
```

The <topic> Element

The <topic> element may contain any number of <instanceOf> elements, followed by an optional <subjectIdentity> element, and any number of <baseName> and/or <occurrence> elements.

The id attribute is required and is used to reference the topic from elsewhere in this or any other document.

```
<!ELEMENT topic ( instanceOf* , subjectIdentity? , ( baseName |occurrence ) )*>
<!ATTLIST topic id ID #REQUIRED >
```

The <instanceOf> Element

The <instanceOf> element can occur within <topic>, <occurrence>, or <association> elements. It indicates a topic whose subject is a class to which the topic, occurrence, or association represented by the parent of the <instanceOf> element belongs. In other words, it indicates the topic type, occurrence type, or association type respectively.

The indication of the topic whose subject is the relevant class is either through a <topicRef> element that directly references a <topic> element representing a topic whose subject is that class, or through a <subjectIndicatorRef> element that references a resource indicating what that class is (either to a human being or to a computer system, or both).

The optional id attribute may be used to provide an identifier that can be used to reference this element specifically from within or from outside the document.

```
<!ELEMENT instanceOf ( topicRef | subjectIndicatorRef )>
<!ATTLIST instanceOf id ID #IMPLIED >
```

The `<topicRef>` Element

The `<topicRef>` element is an `EMPTY` element used to reference a `<topic>`, using the XLink mechanism.

The `xlink:type` attribute has the value `simple`. This value is fixed within the DTD, and the attribute does not need to be present within the instance document. It is used by XLink processors to enable them to correctly interpret the nature of the link. The value of the required `xlink:href` attribute is a relative or absolute URI pointing to the `<topic>` element being referenced. If it is a relative URI, it is interpreted relative to the current document, unless the `<topicMap>` element has an `xml:base` providing a base URI from which all relative URIs in the document are to be interpreted. The optional `id` attribute may be used to provide an identifier that can be used to reference this element specifically from within or from outside the document.

```
<!ELEMENT topicRef EMPTY >
<!ATTLIST topicRef id          ID       #IMPLIED
                   xlink:type NMTOKEN #FIXED 'simple'
                   xlink:href CDATA    #REQUIRED >
```

The `<subjectIndicatorRef>` Element

The `<subjectIndicatorRef>` element is an `EMPTY` element used to reference a resource that indicates the subject of a topic, using the XLink mechanism.

The `<subjectIndicatorRef>` element has three attributes. They are exactly the same as those on the `<topicRef>` element, and are used in the same way:

```
<!ELEMENT subjectIndicatorRef EMPTY >
<!ATTLIST subjectIndicatorRef id          ID       #IMPLIED
                              xlink:type NMTOKEN #FIXED 'simple'
                              xlink:href CDATA    #REQUIRED >
```

The `<subjectIdentity>` Element

The `<subjectIdentity>` element is used to identify the subject that is reified by the topic represented by the parent `<topic>` element. It may contain an optional `<resourceRef>` element referencing a resource that is the subject of the topic (but only if the subject of the topic *is* a resource). Whether the subject of the topic is a resource or a non-addressable subject, the `<subjectIdentity>` element may also contain any number of `<topicRef>` elements referencing `<topic>` elements that represent topics with the same subject as this one, and any number of `<subjectIndicatorRef>` elements referencing resources that indicate what the subject of the topic is (either to a human being or to a computer system, or both).

The optional `id` attribute may be used to provide an identifier that can be used to reference this element specifically from within or from outside the document:

```
<!ELEMENT subjectIdentity ( resourceRef? , ( topicRef | subjectIndicatorRef)* ) >
<!ATTLIST subjectIdentity id ID #IMPLIED >
```

The `<resourceRef>` Element

The `<resourceRef>` element is an `EMPTY` element used to reference a resource, using the XLink mechanism.

The `<resourceRef>` element has three attributes. They are exactly the same as those on the `<topicRef>` element, and are used in the same way:

```
<!ELEMENT resourceRef EMPTY >
<!ATTLIST resourceRef id          ID       #IMPLIED
                      xlink:type NMTOKEN #FIXED 'simple'
                      xlink:href CDATA   #REQUIRED >
```

The `<baseName>` Element

The `<baseName>` element is used to specify a base name for a topic. It consists of an optional `<scope>` element, a `<baseNameString>` element, and any number of `<variant>` elements.

The optional id attribute may be used to provide an identifier that can be used to reference this element specifically from within or from outside the document.

```
<!ELEMENT baseName ( scope? , baseNameString , variant* ) >
<!ATTLIST baseName id          ID       #IMPLIED >
```

The `<scope>` Element

The `<scope>` element can occur within `<baseName>`, `<occurrence>`, or `<association>` elements. It can contain any number of `<topicRef>`, `<resourceRef>`, and `<subjectIndicatorRef>` elements. Each `<topicRef>` element references a `<topic>` element representing a topic included within the scope. Each `<resourceRef>` element references a resource that is the subject of a topic included within the scope. Each `<subjectIndicatorRef>` element references a resource that indicates the subject of a topic included within the scope. Together, all these topics constitute the scope itself, and specify the context within which the topic characteristic assignment represented by the `<baseName>`, `<occurrence>`, or `<association>` parent of the `<scope>` element is valid.

The optional id attribute may be used to provide an identifier that can be used to reference this element specifically from within or from outside the document.

```
<!ELEMENT scope ( topicRef | resourceRef | subjectIndicatorRef )+ >
<!ATTLIST scope id          ID       #IMPLIED >
```

The `<baseNameString>` Element

The `<baseNameString>` element is a container for the character string that is being assigned as base name to a topic.

The optional id attribute may be used to provide an identifier that can be used to reference this element specifically from within or from outside the document.

```
<!ELEMENT baseNameString ( #PCDATA ) >
<!ATTLIST baseNameString id          ID       #IMPLIED >
```

The `<variant>` Element

The `<variant>` element is used to express an alternative name for a topic. Given that the purpose of a base name is to uniquely identify the topic within a given scope, it may be that the base name is not the most appropriate name to be used in various processing contexts. For example, it may be preferable to use a shorter form of the name (which may or may not be unique within the scope) for display purposes, or to use another variant for the purposes of alphabetical sorting.

A given <baseName> element can contain any number of <variant> children. Each <variant> element must contain a <parameters> element indicating the context within which that variant is used. It may also contain a <variantName> element, and/or any number of further <variant> elements. Where there are nested <variant> elements, the contents of the <parameters> elements of all the variants within the tree are brought together to provide a composite context for the applicability of the <variantName> that appears at the end of the series.

The optional id attribute may be used to provide an identifier that can be used to reference this element specifically from within or from outside the document.

```
<!ELEMENT variant ( parameters , variantName?, variant* ) >
<!ATTLIST variant id         ID       #IMPLIED >
```

The <parameters> Element

The <parameters> element only occurs as a child of <variant> element, which in turn is either nested within other <variant> elements, or included directly within a <baseName> element. The <parameters> element contains any number of <topicRef> and/or <subjectIndicatorRef> elements, each of which identifies a topic, either directly in the case of <topicRef> or through a resource that indicates the subject of the topic in the case of <subjectIndicatorRef>. Together, the topics identified by the sub-elements of all the <parameters> elements within the <variant> ancestors of a <variantName> element specify the context within which the <variantName> element is applicable as an alternative to the <baseNameString> that is a sibling to the topmost <variant> element in the nested series.

The optional id attribute may be used to provide an identifier that can be used to reference this element specifically from within or from outside the document.

```
<!ELEMENT parameters ( topicRef | subjectIndicatorRef )+ >
<!ATTLIST parameters id         ID       #IMPLIED >
```

The <variantName> Element

The <variantName> element contains either a <resourceRef> indicating a resource that acts as the variant name, or a <resourceData> element that contains the variant name directly as a string. The <resourceRef> element references a resource that may itself be a string, or may be an object of some other kind. It might, for example, reference a graphic, such as a company logo representing the name, or an audio file containing an audible representation of the name. It is the <parameters> elements associated with the variant name that determine the processing contexts in which the resource identified by the <variantName> element are to be used.

The optional id attribute may be used to provide an identifier that can be used to reference this element specifically from within or from outside the document.

```
<!ELEMENT variantName ( resourceRef | resourceData ) >
<!ATTLIST variantName id         ID       #IMPLIED >
```

The <resourceData> Element

The <resourceData> element is a container for a character string that is an occurrence of a topic or the variant form of a base name for a <topic> element.

The optional id attribute may be used to provide an identifier that can be used to reference this element specifically from within or from outside the document.

```
<!ELEMENT resourceData ( #PCDATA ) >
<!ATTLIST resourceData id        ID       #IMPLIED >
```

The <occurrence> Element

The <occurrence> element is used to identify a resource that is relevant to the topic represented by the <topic> element that is the parent of the <occurrence> element. The <occurrence> element contains an optional <instanceOf> element identifying the occurrence type, an optional <scope> element indicating the context of validity of the assignment of this occurrence to the topic, and a <resourceRef> element referencing the resource that is the occurrence, or a <resourceData> element containing the actual resource inline in the form of a string.

The optional id attribute may be used to provide an identifier that can be used to reference this element specifically from within or from outside the document.

```
<!ELEMENT occurrence ( instanceOf? , scope? , ( resourceRef | resourceData ) ) >
<!ATTLIST occurrence id ID #IMPLIED >
```

The <association> Element

The <association> element is used to specify a relationship between topics. It contains an optional <instanceOf> element indicating the association type, an optional <scope> element indicating the context within which the association is valid, and a <member> element for each distinct role in the association.

The optional id attribute may be used to provide an identifier that can be used to reference this element specifically from within or from outside the document.

```
<!ELEMENT association ( instanceOf? , scope? , member+ ) >
<!ATTLIST association id ID #IMPLIED >
```

The <member> Element

The <member> element is used to indicate the topic or topics playing a given role in the association represented by the <association> parent of the <member> element. The <member> element may contain an optional <roleSpec> element, and a may contain any number of <topicRef>, <resourceRef>, and <subjectIndicatorRef> elements, in any order.

Each <topicRef>, <resourceRef>, and <subjectIndicatorRef> element identifies a topic, either directly in the case of <topicRef>, or through a resource that is the subject of the topic in the case of <resourceRef>, or through a resource that indicates the subject of the topic in the case of <subjectIndicatorRef>. All the topics identified by the children of a given member element are involved in the association in the same way (that is, they play the same role in the association). The <roleSpec> element, if present, identifies a topic whose subject is that role.

The optional id attribute may be used to provide an identifier that can be used to reference this element specifically from within or from outside the document.

```
<!ELEMENT member ( roleSpec? , ( topicRef | resourceRef | subjectIndicatorRef )* )
>
<!ATTLIST member id ID #IMPLIED >
```

The *<roleSpec>* Element

The <roleSpec> element contains either a <topicRef> or a <subjectIndicatorRef> element that indicates a topic, either directly in the case of <topicRef>, or through a resource that indicates the subject of the topic in the case of <subjectIndicatorRef>. The subject of the topic thus indicated is the role played by all the topics identified by the direct children of the <member> element parent of the <roleSpec> element.

The optional id attribute may be used to provide an identifier that can be used to reference this element specifically from within or from outside the document.

```
<!ELEMENT roleSpec ( topicRef | subjectIndicatorRef ) >
<!ATTLIST roleSpec id ID #IMPLIED >
```

The *<mergeMap>* Element

The <mergeMap> element is used to reference another topic map document that is to be merged with this one in order to create a composite topic map.

The <mergeMap> element has three attributes. They are exactly the same as those on the <topicRef> element, and are used in the same way, invoking the XLink mechanism to point to the document containing the topic map that is to be merged.

The <mergeMap> element may contain any number of <topicRef>, <resourceRef>, and <subjectIndicatorRef> elements, in any order. Each of these identifies a topic, either directly in the case of <topicRef>, or through a resource that is the subject of the topic in the case of <resourceRef>, or through a resource that indicates the subject of the topic in the case of <subjectIndicatorRef>. The topics thus identified are added to the scope of every base name, occurrence, or association in the topic map being merged. The reasons for this are discussed later in the chapter, in the section on topic map merging.

```
<!ELEMENT mergeMap ( topicRef | resourceRef | subjectIndicatorRef )* >
<!ATTLIST mergeMap id ID #IMPLIED
                   xlink:type NMTOKEN #FIXED 'simple'
                   xlink:href CDATA   #REQUIRED >
```

XTM Processing

In order to be sure that XTM documents can be used effectively to ensure interoperable interchange of topic map information between different systems, some aspects of how the information is to be processed have to be specified. There are various schools of thought as to how prescriptive it is necessary to be in order to ensure interoperability. The XTM specification takes the view that since topic maps are designed to allow the sharing of knowledge and information between widely differing applications and environments, the restrictions on how the information must be processed should be kept to an absolute minimum. However, there is a necessary minimum required in order to ensure that the syntax is interpreted in a way that is consistent with the conceptual model that accompanies it, and to ensure that the meaning intended by topic map authors in creating XTM instance documents is preserved.

The result of this dual consideration is that the XTM specification does not specify *how* XTM documents should be processed, but it does specify certain minimal constraints that must be met by any conformant processor; these constraints are specified in Annex F of the XTM 1.0 specification. Essentially they provide formal statements of what different syntactic constructions must be treated by processors as being equivalent to one another, and when topics or associations must be merged into one because they are found to be equivalent in relevant ways. We have said that any two topics that have the same base name in the same scope must be the same. We have also said that topics are the same if they have the same subject. Given that there are several ways of indicating what is the subject of a topic, it is necessary to be precise about the nature of these equivalence rules. This is what Annex F of the specification sets out.

There is also work being done, both within and outside TopicMaps.Org, to go somewhat further than this, and to identify a specific formal processing model, which complies with the constraints given in Annex F, and which can provide a basis for different implementers to build systems that are certain to be interoperable, because they do follow the same processing model. This work is still in progress at the time of writing, and it remains to be seen whether the processing model or models that emerge from it will be considered sufficiently general-purpose to be able to be specified as normative – that is to say that software that claims to conform to the topic maps specification *must* also conform to a given processing model – or whether they will simply serve as a useful "reference model" that implementers can use for guidance in developing their own topic map processors, but which need not be followed in every respect, provided the constraints laid out in Annex F of XTM 1.0 are complied with.

These are highly technical issues, and a lot of high-powered thinking is going into them. Whatever the outcome, we can be sure that there will be a strong basis for the development of powerful topic map processing software based on the XTM specification, its conceptual model, and its XML-based interchange syntax.

Topic Maps in Practice

Topic Map Creation

It will be clear from the discussion of the topics and associations that can be drawn out of the very short sample article we have been discussing within this chapter, that the development of a topic map covering a large body of information is a sizeable task. The benefit that can be gained from a rich topic map is considerable, but so is the amount of work and thought that has to go into its creation.

It is somewhat like the creation of an index for a book, but with much broader implications. A good index for a book is an extremely valuable resource and makes the book a great deal more useful as a research or knowledge communication tool. However, the writing of a good index is no small undertaking, and is generally best carried out by a combination of manual and software-aided processes.

The task does get progressively easier as the topic map grows however, because once we have created topics for frequently recurring subjects, associations, or association types, we can use this information bank as a basis for our analysis of further information resources, looking in them for recurrences of topics that are already known about, as well as seeking new ones that have to be created from scratch.

Techniques for developing a topic map out of a set of information resources include:

- ❑ Extraction of topics and topic associations based on the textual content of documents in the information set, using a combination of natural language processing software and the judgment of a human editor.

❑   Using existing standard vocabularies (such as the ISO country codes) or taxonomies (such as the library of core concepts that have been developed by the Cyc initiative, http://www.cyc.com) as the source for a base set of topics.

❑   Derivation of topics and topic associations from the content of structured databases or documents, with association types based on the structure of the database or document schemas.

These approaches are mentioned here simply to provide initial food for thought. A much fuller treatment of how to approach the automatic generation of topic maps is given in Chapter 11.

Topic Map Merging

A very important way of building up a sizeable topic map is by merging existing ones to build a composite map. Because of the nature of the interconnections between topics based on the associations between them, the topic map becomes more and more useful the larger it gets, so merging topic maps together can be a very powerful and useful technique.

However, there does need to be a word of caution, based on the fact that a name chosen as the base name for a topic in one topic map, which the author knew to refer to only one topic in that map, might have been used by the author of another topic map to designate some other topic. It is important when merging maps to take a look at how the author of the other map has used base names. If they have only used base names scoped on standard and universally applicable vocabularies then there is no danger, because that scope does provide a sound guarantee of the uniqueness of the application of the name.

However, if there are many base names used in the unconstrained scope, or if the scopes used for base names are extremely general (such as names scoped on "English", or "architecture", for example), then care needs to be taken. Within the context of the English language, and even within the context of a specific discipline such as architecture, the same name may be used with more than one meaning, and if the authors of two topic maps have used the same name as the base name for topics that were intended to reify different subjects, then we will not want these topics to be merged in the composite topic map on the basis of the topic naming constraint alone.

This is the reason why the <mergeMap> element in XTM syntax may need to be given child elements that specify additional topics that are to be added to the scopes of all topic characteristic assignments in a topic map to be merged. We can create a special topic whose subject is the topic map being merged (let us call it "topic map B") and have this topic be added to all the scopes from that map:

```
<topic id="topic-map-b">
  <subjectIdentity>
    <resourceRef xlink:href="http://somesite.org/topicmapb.xtm"/>
  </subjectIdentity>
</topic>
<mergeMap xlink:href="http://somesite.org/topicmapb.xtm">
  <topicRef xlink:href="#topic-map-b"/>
</mergeMap>
```

Now, what was scoped on "architecture" in topic map B will, in the composite topic map, be scoped on "architecture" and "topic map B", and characteristics that were assigned in topic map B within the unconstrained scope (having no scope specified), will in the composite topic map be scoped on "topic map B". This will prevent automatic and inappropriate merging of topics based solely on the topic naming constraint. It will not prevent appropriate automatic merging based on other considerations, such as the use of identical subject indicators for topics in the two maps. Thus we achieve a safe though still powerful merging process. If we wish, we can then perform searches for topics in the composite map that have not been automatically merged but which did have matching base names within equivalent scopes in the two source topic maps. Studying the results of this search, we can then make a human judgment as to whether any of these topics should now be made to merge, by deleting from the scope of the base name assignments the topics that were added through being specified in the `<mergeMap>` element.

Association Templates

Much thought was given during the development of XTM to the notion of **association templates**. An association template would be a specification of a set of constraints on associations of a given type. Such constraints might be the roles that exist within associations of that type, the number of players permitted for each role, the topic types (classes of which the topics are instances) that must apply to topics playing each of the roles, and so on.

In our example topic map, we have identified some specific association types, of which the first was given the `id` attribute `building-designed-by-designer`. We could imagine specifying that any association of this type must involve precisely two roles, namely `designed-building` and `building-designer`. We could further specify that the `designed-building` role must be played by precisely one topic, and that the topic must be of type "building", and that the `building-designer` role must be played by one or more topics, and that these topics must be of type "person|".

If we were to create such a set of constraints, then in order to conform to them, our association for Charles Rennie Mackintosh designing the Mackintosh dome would not, in its current form, comply. To make it comply, we would need to create a `building` topic and a `person` topic, add an `<instanceOf>` child to the `mackintosh-dome` topic referencing the `building` topic, and add an `<instanceOf>` child to the `charles-rennie-mackintosh` topic referencing the `person` topic (in addition to the two `<instanceOf>` children it already has, for `man` and `architect`).

The XTM Authoring Group finally decided not to include a specific association template mechanism within XTM 1.0. There were different opinions as to how rich and constraining it should be, and the key requirement was to have a specification agreed and in use as quickly as possible. Resolving all the issues surrounding association templates would simply have taken too long. What the specification does provide is simply the association typing mechanism we have already discussed, whereby an association can be stated to be of a given class through its own `<instanceOf>` child element.

This minimal solution is extremely powerful, however, and leaves the door open for developing various constraint definition mechanisms for associations, not necessarily limited to the kinds of constraints suggested above. The `<instanceOf>` child identifies a topic that is the class to which the association belongs. It can do this through a resource that is a subject indicator for that topic. If that resource indicates the class through a formal statement of criteria for membership of the class, written in whatever formalism is desired, then we can use software that understands that formalism to infer the nature of the constraints on the association that being a member of that class implies.

In the code sample below, we have added a `<subjectIndicatorRef>` child to the `<topic>` element that is referenced as the association type for our association.

```
<topic id="building-designed-by-designer">
  <subjectIdentity>
    <subjectIndicatorRef link:href="http://www.mysite.com/constraints.txt"/>
  </subjectIdentity>
</topic>
<association>
```

```
<instanceOf>
  <topicRef xlink:href="#building-designed-by-designer"/>
</instanceOf>
<member>
  <roleSpec>
    <topicRef xlink:href="#designed-building"/>
  </roleSpec>
  <topicRef xlink:href="#mackintosh-dome"/>
</member>
<member>
  <roleSpec>
    <topicRef xlink:href="#building-designer"/>
  </roleSpec>
  <topicRef xlink:href="#charles-rennie-mackintosh"/>
</member>
</association>
```

The subject is a file called `constraints.txt` at `http://www.mysite.com`. In the minimal case, the `constraints.txt` file might contain an English-language description of the constraints that all associations of my designated type must comply with. A subject indicator of this sort indicates the subject to a human being who understands the meaning of the English. Such a human being could then check the association for compliance with the rules of the association type. In due course, when a Topic Map query language (TMQL) has been developed, we could replace the text file with a formal expression of a topic map query that checks for the existence of the relevant structures within the association. This depends on there being a formal TMQL, and my system incorporating a TMQL processor. But there are other formalisms that are designed for expressing constraints on information sets. One, currently under development within ISO, is known as **EXIST** (**Expression of Information based on Logic and Set Theory**). This includes the notions of class-instance, class-subclass, quantification, and other mechanisms, which relate well with the constructs already in existence within the topic maps paradigm, and could extend it into a way of formally expressing constraints on association types.

The XTM specification provides a starting point that is open to extensions that will increase its capabilities. Some of these extensions may build on other standards that already exist or are in development. It will be very interesting to see how this work will develop over the coming period.

NewsML and Topic Maps

We have seen that XTM includes a conceptual model, a set of processing requirements, and an interchange syntax. All are important, and none alone is sufficient to define what topic maps are. The specification explicitly recognizes that the XTM interchange syntax is not the only possible syntax for describing topic maps. Indeed it states in its definition of a topic map document that it "*may be serialized for the purpose of storage or interchange in a syntax governed by this or some other specification*".

During the time that XTM was being developed, the **International Press Telecommunications Council (IPTC** – http://www.iptc.org), which develops standards for the news industry worldwide, was developing a standard called **NewsML** for the management and delivery of multimedia news items (http://www.newsml.org). This specification can handle structured collections of news objects in various media, the relationships between them, and rich meta data associated with each. The requirements that had to be met within the specification included the controlled extensibility of meta data vocabularies, and keeping track of the subjects of interest that occur within various news stories, pictures, media files, and so on.

There is clearly much in common between these requirements and those that the topic maps paradigm aims to meet. The NewsML 1.0 specification was approved in October 2000, a few months before the completion of the XTM 1.0 specification. There was no way, therefore, that the IPTC could make explicit use of the XTM specification within its own standards. However, it was aware of the topic map work and the core concepts that underlie it, and built into its own syntax a number of constructs that, though using different element names and structures, nonetheless share some key features. For example, NewsML includes the notion of a Topic, and of a TopicOccurrence. It also states that two Topics in a TopicSet that have the same FormalName within the same Scheme are to be merged. This is highly analogous to the topic naming constraint, with FormalName substituted for base name, and Scheme substituted for scope.

It may be that a NewsML processor could be developed that would process NewsML documents in ways that comply both with the NewsML specification itself, and with the topic map processing requirements stated in Annex F of XTM 1.0. If this were achieved, then it would become the case that the NewsML documents (or at least certain structures within them) could be considered as topic map documents in conformity with the XTM specification, and we would be close to an environment in which the NewsML documents that are being delivered out of the news agencies and newspapers of the world would be able to feed directly into a huge knowledge repository, navigable through the topic associations between the topics of which the various news stories are seen as occurrences.

Knowledge and the Semantic Web

As information passes through its life, it will be carried and presented in multiple forms depending on context and purpose. Something common is needed to maintain object identity through its life cycle. Topic maps can provide a conceptual framework for this. Each object is a topic, and each way in which it occurs is an occurrence of that topic. XTM allows the topics themselves to be accessed and navigated. This can be the foundation for the "Semantic Web" (the Web of meaning). The World Wide Web Consortium (W3C) sees RDF (Resource Description Framework) as central to the Semantic Web but the Semantic Web Activity Statement (http://www.w3.org/2001/sw) states:

> *"The ISO Topic Map (XTM) community has been finding increasing synergy with the RDF data model. We are hopeful that the markup language background of the Topic Map community will suggest syntax alternatives for graph-oriented data that can be considered for incorporation into RDF and that RDF will be seen to be usable for Topic Map data as well."*

The work that is currently underway to develop a topic map processing model, querying language, templating mechanism, and constraint specification language, will all feed into the work on the Semantic Web. These initiatives will without doubt cross-fertilize to build a basis for rich knowledge navigation and management on the Web that will shape the development of our information systems over the coming few years. It will be interesting indeed to see how it all unfolds, but however things go forward, there is likely to be a strong place for topic maps within the eventual picture.

Summary

In this chapter we have taken a look at how topic maps can be used to build a navigable map of collections of information resources, based on their subject matter and the relationships between the subjects they cover. We have worked through the constructs made available by the topic map paradigm, with worked examples expressed in XTM (XML Topic Maps) syntax. We have described the XTM syntax in some detail, and explained how other syntaxes, such as NewsML can in principle provide alternative representations for topic map structures. We spoke briefly of ongoing work on topic map processing models, querying language and association templates, and ended with a look forward to future work on integrating topic maps into the Semantic Web activity at the World Wide Web Consortium, which aims to lay the foundation for the next generation of semantically aware Web applications.

Another initiative concerned with semantics is the focus of the next chapter. Meaning Definition Language is a schema adjunct designed to bridge the gap between an XML document's structure and its actual meaning.

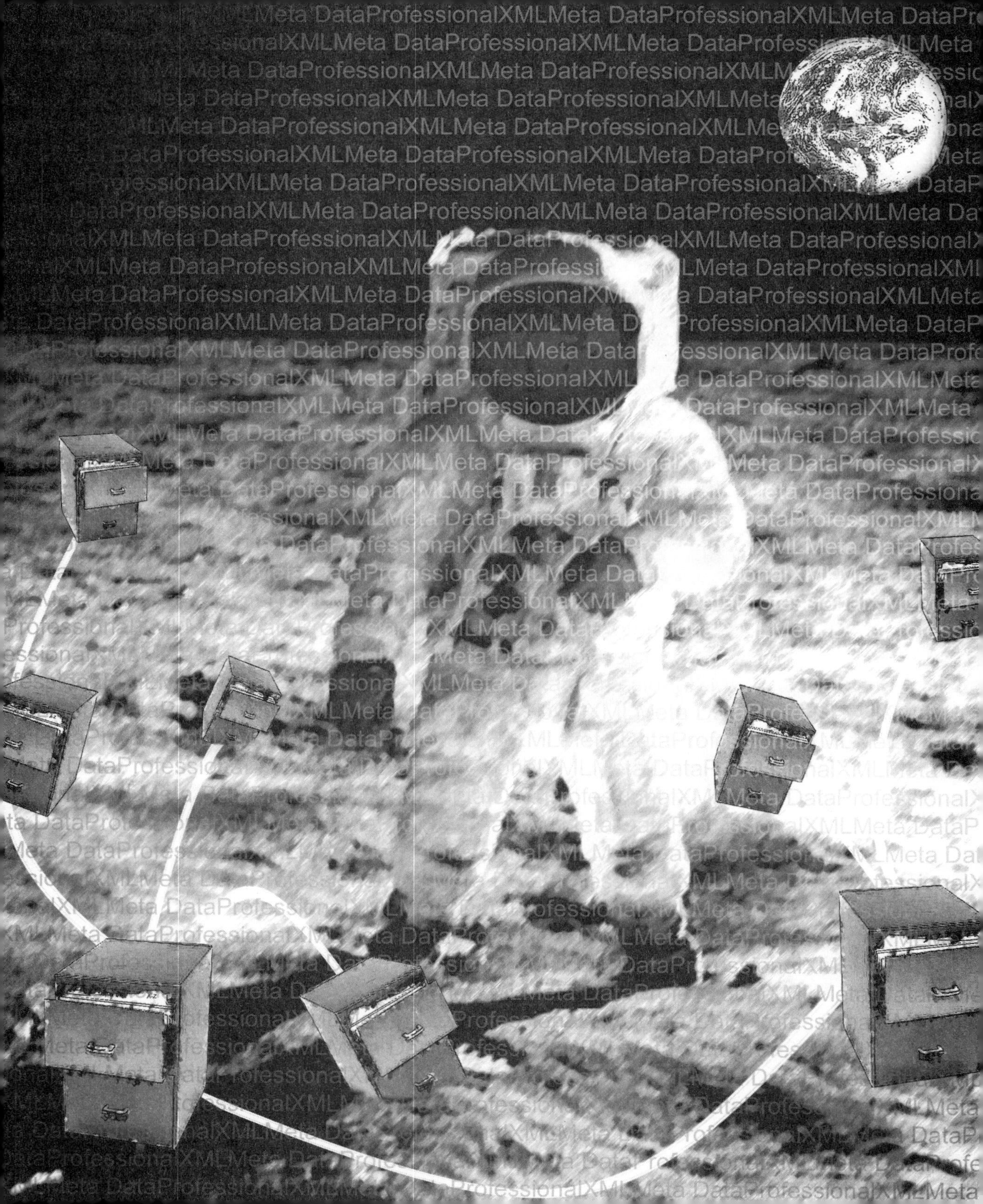

Meaning Definition Language

8

XML is designed to make meanings explicit in the structure of XML languages. However, when we build XML applications today, we interface to XML at the level of structure, not meaning. We navigate document structure by interfaces such as DOM, XPath, and XQuery, which all refer explicitly to the structure of XML documents. Therefore every developer or user has to re-discover for himself "how the structure conveys meaning" for each XML language he uses. This is wasteful and error-prone. We need to develop tools so that XML developers and users can work at the level of meaning, not structure – with the tools providing the bridge between the two.

Schema languages such as XSD Schema and RELAX NG are concerned with the structure of XML documents. UML, RDF Schema, and DAML+OIL are concerned with meaning. None of these notations provide the link between structure and meaning.

> **Meaning Definition Language (MDL) is the bridge between XML structure and meaning – expressed precisely, in XML. The draft specification for MDL is available from http://www.charteris.com/mdl/.**

Using MDL, the language designer can express how the structure of an XML language conveys its meaning. From then on, MDL-based tools allow users and developers to interface to that language at the level of meaning. The tools can automatically convert a meaning-based request into a structure-based provision of the answer. This chapter explains how, by introducing MDL and then describing three working applications of MDL:

- ❑ **A meaning-level Java API for XML**: allowing developers to build applications with Java classes that reflect XML meaning, not structure; then to interface those applications automatically to any XML language which expresses that meaning.

❑ **A meaning-level XML query language**: allowing users to express queries in terms of meaning, without reference to XML structure; to run the same query against any XML language that expresses that meaning, and to see the answer expressed in meaning-level terms.

❑ **Automated XML translation, based on meaning**: allowing precise, automatic generation of XSLT (Extensible Stylesheet Language Transformations) to translate messages between any two XML languages that have a common MDL model.

We then go on to look at MDL in the context of the Semantic Web and topic maps, and briefly examine MDL documentation and validation before closing the chapter with a final discussion of the possible impact of a meaning-level approach to XML using MDL.

What MDL Does

As we have already said, MDL acts as the bridge between XML structure and meaning. The benefits of the meaning-level approach to XML are far-reaching:

❑ Users and developers can work at the level of meaning – which they understand – rather than grappling with XML structures, where they may poorly understand the language designer's intention or make mistakes in the detail (particularly for large complex languages).

❑ Applications, XML queries, and presentations of XML information can be developed *once* at the meaning level, and then applied to any XML language whose MDL exists, without further changes.

So whenever a new XML language comes along – as will frequently happen – all you need do is find (or if need be, write down) the MDL definition of that language. Then all your systems and users, using that MDL, will be immediately adapted to the new language, without any further effort. As XML usage grows and languages proliferate, the cost-savings from this easy adaptation could be huge.

The W3C Semantic Web initiative (http://www.w3.org/2001/sw/) aims to make web-based information usable by automated agents. Currently, such automated agents are not able to use information from most XML documents, because of the diverse ways in which XML expresses meanings. So the Semantic Web depends on RDF, which expresses meanings in a more uniform manner than XML. MDL enables agents on the Web to extract information from XML documents, as long as their MDL is known – thus extending the scope of the Semantic Web from the RDF world to the larger world of XML documents on the Web.

Brief Examples

In this chapter we shall need to spend some time talking about what MDL is, before we can describe what MDL does more fully. So that readers know where they are going, here are two samples of what MDL does. Suppose you have XML documents in one or more XML languages for purchase orders, which convey information about purchase order lines, quantities of items, products, unit prices and so on.

First, imagine you could query these XML documents using query language statements such as:

```
Display orderLine.quantity, product.name, product.unitPrice
where product.unitPrice > 30.0
and orderLine isFor product
```

Second, imagine you could write Java applications to access the same XML documents with code such as:

```
XFactory xf = new Xfactory(root,mdl);
Vector allProducts = xf.every_product();
For (int i = 0; i < allProducts.size(); i++)
{
    product p = (product) allProducts.elementAt(i);
    orderLine ol = p.orderLine_isFor();
    if (p.unitPrice() > 30.0)
      System.out.println(ol.quantity() + ", "
        + p.name()+ ", " + p.unitPrice());
}
```

Both of these examples could be run using the code download available with the book. The latter sample is not in the download; we are just saying it could work. In fact it would need a minor modification to convert the string value returned by p.unitPrice() *to a number, for comparison with 30.*

What is special about these fragments of code? They are directly concerned with the objects of the application domain (in this case products and order lines) and their properties (quantity, name, unit price). Unlike, say, DOM-based coding, they are not about physical XML structures such as elements, child nodes or XPaths. The code refers to XML meaning, not structure. An MDL module then converts these meaning-based requests into structural operations to get the information from the XML – shielding the user or developer from all structural details of the XML.

This means the code is much simpler to write and maintain, and it will run unchanged against documents in many different XML languages that express the same meaning. Let's look at how MDL does this.

XML – Meaning and Structure

In this section we will introduce the Meaning Definition Language and show how it provides a precise bridge between XML structure and XML meaning – defining how XML structures convey meanings. Before we build the bridge, we need first to describe the two pillars that MDL spans – *meaning* and *structure*.

Defining What XML Documents Mean

Since the Meaning Definition Language is all about meanings of XML documents, we need first of all to explain clearly our definition of "meaning" in this context, and what sort of XML documents we intend it to apply to.

We can do this quite concisely:

> **MDL defines the link between the meanings of data-centric XML documents and their structure. Here "meaning" is used in the same sense as in ontology formalisms such as DAML+OIL, as in UML class models, and as in the W3C Semantic Web Initiative.**

However, that is more a statement of allegiance than an explanation. For those who are not familiar with ontology formalisms, UML, or the Semantic Web Initiative, we need to spell out explicitly what this concept of meaning is.

Note first that we are not addressing document-centric XML applications. XML applications span a spectrum between document-centric applications – which basically wrap XML structures around long stretches of text – and data-centric applications, which convey small data items within XML structures. This chapter has little to say about document-centric XML documents or their meaning. To analyze the meaning of document-centric XML requires natural language understanding, which is not our concern here. We are discussing the meanings conveyed by data-centric XML documents.

Addressing these, we (and ontology formalisms like DAML+OIL) are using at heart a very simple definition of "meaning". If you ask about an XML document "What does it mean?" then by this definition you are asking: "What **things** is it about? What **properties** and **associations** of those things is it about?" Once you have defined what types of things, properties and associations the XML is about, you have defined what it is capable of meaning. Things, properties and associations are the building blocks of DAML+OIL ontologies, of UML class models, and of RDF-Schema (used in the Semantic Web).

To some, this concept of meaning is too simple. They believe that to talk of meaning only in terms of things, properties and associations must inevitably miss out some part of our intuitions about meaning. So I will try briefly to explain how we came to this apparently sparse definition of meaning.

Researchers in AI (by which I mean "Good Old-Fashioned 'symbolic' AI", known as GOFAI, not neural nets) have long had practical motives to articulate what a computer program can "mean" for tasks such as automated reasoning, planning, learning or natural language understanding. These are deep problems and have forced researchers to think hard about what the data in a computer can mean, and what meaning means. GOFAI researchers developed a rich armory of meaning-related concepts such as frames, semantic nets, constraints, possible worlds, intensions, procedural knowledge, defaults, and more logics than you can count. Any of these might reasonably be pressed into a model of what computer programs (or XML documents) can mean.

However, as these rich models of meaning were applied over the years, two things were realized:

❑ All the different facets of meaning (such as rules and procedures) are built on things, properties and associations. Rules are about how things are or how they behave. Behavior consists of changes to things, properties, and associations over time; and so on. You just cannot talk about rules, constraints, procedures or anything else, without talking about things. Things are characterized by their properties and associations to other things. So things, properties, and associations are the building blocks for all meaning.

❑ When building computer programs, simplicity counts for a lot. If you can get away with a minimal model of meaning, then you should do so. Don't introduce elaborations on top of it unless you really have to for the problem in hand.

That is why the rich ferment of AI research into meaning over twenty years has now converged on a few ontology formalisms, such as DAML+OIL which – while having some elaborations such as constraints – are firmly grounded on the basic triad of things, properties, and associations. "Ontology" means "about things". In that, they have converged with UML, the leading analysis notation for building software systems. UML has many specialized notations within it, but they are all grounded on class models – which again are about things, properties, and associations. In UML, things are called objects, and we will follow that convention.

In developing the Meaning Definition Language, Charteris have started with a minimal model of meaning – defining meaning purely in terms of things, properties, and associations – to see how far this model will go, intending to expand our model only if the applications of MDL require it. We are saying in effect: "Here are the 'elements' of meaning. Build up your own 'chemical compounds' of meaning from the elements, as you need them for particular applications. If certain compounds are always useful, maybe we will add them to the toolkit later."

For instance, consider the XML representation of a purchase order, an example we use in several places in this chapter. Many would say that a purchase order is just one part of an extended process – a process in which one party buys things from another – and that any purchase order message gets much of its meaning from this fact. We agree. But the whole purchasing process is an object; the individual process steps are objects; they all have properties and there are associations between them (such as sequence); the participants in the process are objects, and so on. In this way, we could build a DAML+OIL ontology (or a UML class model) of the whole purchasing process, and embed any purchase order within it, to as much detail as we need. We can then give each purchase order its full process-embedded meaning. However, for many purposes the full ontology (or object model) of the whole process is in the background, and we can concentrate on those objects directly involved in a single process step. It all depends on the application.

Our minimal model of XML meanings assumes that any XML document can express meanings of three kinds:

- About **objects** in classes: information of the form "there is a product" or "there are three purchase order lines".

- About the simple **properties** of the objects: "the product type is 'video camera'" or "the product price is $31.50".

- About **associations** between the objects: "the goods recipient has this address" or "this manufacturer made that product".

Associations are often referred to as "relations", but we will use the UML term "association" for uniformity. It is hard to see how much meaning can be expressed at all without using all three of the core meaning types. Inspection of any data-centric XML document shows that it expresses meanings of all three types: about objects, simple properties, and associations. In other words, data-centric XML documents identify objects in classes, and describe their properties and associations.

The three concepts outlined above are the building blocks of **UML class diagrams**. They have a successful track record of application in modeling of information and knowledge – for instance, in Entity-Relation Diagrams and AI frames. If you need to find out more about UML, try the Wrox book *"Instant UML"*, by Pierre-Alain Muller, ISBN 1-861000-87-1.

For instance, there are many XML message formats for purchase orders in e-commerce. We can draw a class diagram showing the core object classes, properties, and associations expressed by typical purchase order messages:

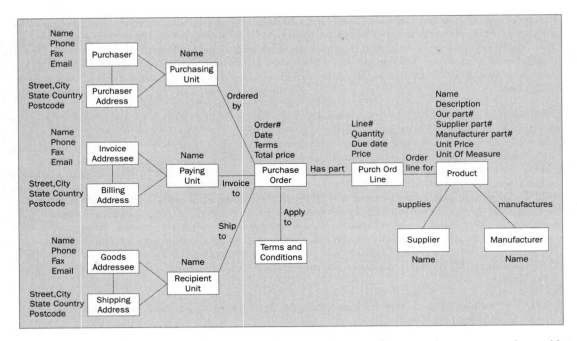

Here, classes of object are denoted by boxes, and associations by lines. Simple properties are denoted by words next to the boxes. To summarize a central part of the diagram in words: "Several purchase order lines can be part of a purchase order. Each order line has a line number and a quantity, and is an order line for a product".

If necessary, we could draw a much richer object model showing the place of the individual purchase order in the whole purchasing process. But this is unnecessary for many applications, and there is not space to do it in this chapter.

Most XML purchase order message formats convey a large part (if not all) of the information on this diagram – while some convey extra information not on the diagram. For instance, you can easily spot the equivalences between some of the properties of this diagram with nodes of the Exel XML purchase order message tree diagram shown later, in the *"Defining XML Structure"* section.

The MDL for any XML language is defined relative to some ontology/object model such as the one above. The applications of MDL are most powerful when many different XML languages (which may differ in their tag names and structure) can be referenced to the same ontology/object model. Then the ontology becomes a basis for interoperability of the XML languages. So a company may develop one ontology of its own business – for use in all its XML applications – or there may be ontologies made available by standards bodies or repository initiatives such as ebXML (http://www.ebxml.org). Our hope is that these public "reference" ontologies will not proliferate in the same way that XML languages have proliferated – so that the ontologies are a useful basis for XML interoperability. Alternatively, since ontologies (unlike XML languages) do not embody implementation decisions, we hope that it will be relatively easy to map one ontology onto another, even if they do proliferate. The W3C Semantic Web initiative requires the same non-proliferation or interoperability of ontologies, because ontologies expressed in RDF-Schema or DAML+OIL are the basis of many of its important applications (for example, see the example later in this chapter).

In any case, for many applications of MDL we need an XML notation in which to express the ontology/object model itself. This notation is not MDL; an MDL document only defines the links between the ontology and the structure of one XML language. There are several publicly available XML languages for expressing ontologies.

As an ontology is closely equivalent to a UML class model, it can be expressed in any notation for class models. One such notation is **XML Metadata Interchange** (**XMI**), an XML language designed for interchange of meta data, for instance between CASE tools. However, XMI is a highly generic language designed to support many types of meta data, and in practice is rather verbose. We shall not consider it further here but you can read more about it at http://www.omg.org.

RDF Schema, proposed as a foundation for defining the meanings of web resources in RDF, embodies the same three concepts of classes, properties, and associations (as we saw in Chapters 4, *"RDF Model and Syntax"* and 5, *"RDF Schema"*, the term "property" encompasses both what we here call "simple properties" and "associations"). The close equivalence between RDF Schema and UML class models has often been noted. XML encodings of RDF Schema are more concise than XMI, and more readable. The ontology formalism **DAML+OIL** is a modest extension of RDF Schema, which retains its readability while adding a few extra useful concepts, and has well-defined semantics, as we saw in Chapter 5.

For use in association with MDL, we use DAML+OIL (March 2001 version, see http://www.daml.org/2001/03/daml+oil-index) as our preferred way to encode in XML the model of classes, associations, and properties needed to define the meanings of XML documents.

A fragment of DAML+OIL describing the purchase order class model in the diagram has the form:

```
<daml:Class rdf:ID = "purchaseOrder">
    <rdfs:label>purchaseOrder</rdfs:label>
    <rdfs:comment>document committing one organization
                  to purchase goods from another</rdfs:comment>
    <rdfs:subClassOf ID = "purchaseOrderPart" />
</daml:Class>

<daml:Class rdf:ID = "orderItem">
    <rdfs:label>orderItem</rdfs:label>
    <rdfs:comment>one line of a purchase order, specifying a
                  quantity of one item</rdfs:comment>
    <rdfs:subClassOf ID = "purchaseOrderPart" />
</daml:Class>

<daml:ObjectProperty ID = "[orderItem]isPartOf[purchaseOrder]">
    <rdfs:label>isPartOf</rdfs:label>
    <rdfs:domain rdf:resource = "#orderItem"/>
    <rdfs:range rdf:resource = "#purchaseOrder"/>
</daml:ObjectProperty >

<daml:DatatypeProperty ID = "orderItem:quantity">
    <rdfs:label>quantity</rdfs:label>
    <rdfs:domain rdf:resource = "#orderItem"/>
    <rdfs:range rdf:resource =
              "http://www.w3.org/2000/10/XMLSchema#nonNegativeInteger"/>
</daml:DatatypeProperty >
```

Note the use of three different namespaces – with prefixes `daml:`, `rdf:`, and `rdfs:` – because DAML+OIL is an extension of RDF Schema incorporating concepts from both RDF and RDF Schema.

The `<daml:Class>` elements define a class inheritance hierarchy in a fairly straightforward way; properties and associations are inherited down this taxonomy. `<daml:DatatypeProperty>` elements define simple properties of objects in classes. The resource name (`ID`) of these properties must be unique across the model, but property labels such as `quantity` may occur several times in different classes, with different meanings for the properties. The XML schema data type of any simple property is defined. `<daml:ObjectProperty>` elements define associations, using `<rdfs:domain>` and `<rdfs:range>` elements to identify the two classes involved in each association.

A class model, as expressed in DAML+OIL or XMI, generally defines a space of possible meanings, and its coverage is made wide enough to encompass a set of XML languages. Any one XML language typically only expresses a subset of the possible objects, associations, and properties in the class model.

DAML+OIL is the notation we use to define what meaning an XML language conveys; next we consider XML structure and how XML structures convey meaning.

Defining XML Structure

There is a proliferation of ways to define XML structures. In spite of W3C support for XSD Schema (www.w3.org/xml/schema), the proliferation shows little sign of abating, with other candidates such as TREX (http://www.thaiopensource.com/trex/) and RELAX (http://www.xml.gr.jp/relax/) supported by many, and the combination of both into RELAX NG. We will have to learn to live with a diversity of schema-defining languages. Despite this diversity, two points remain true:

❑ **Schema languages are mainly about structure, not meaning**. For all the work that has gone on to define data types in XSD Schema and other schema languages, *type* is only a small part of meaning. It is of little use to know that some element has type "date" if I do not know what the date relates to, or how it relates to it. Is it the date of a purchase order, or someone's birthday? Is it the date the order was sent, or approved, or received? Data type, on its own, tells you none of these things.

❑ **The most important structure information remains "what XML trees are allowed"**. All schema languages basically define allowed nesting structures of elements. Even the elaborate apparatus in XSD Schema for deriving complex types by extension or restriction serves only to define what nodes can be nested inside other nodes, and their sequence restrictions.

Note that schema languages (like XML itself) allow the language designer to use element and attribute names that are suggestive of meaning. However, interpreting the language designer's intentions from tag names is notoriously tricky – like trying to understand undocumented code from the variable names. It is far better to look at some proper documentation. In our case, the "proper documentation" for meaning is a DAML+OIL ontology, and MDL will link the XML to that.

The most important tool for understanding XML structure is a **tree diagram**, showing the possible nesting structure of elements (without repetition of the repeatable elements). A typical tree diagram, for one of the many published purchase order formats, is shown in the following figure:

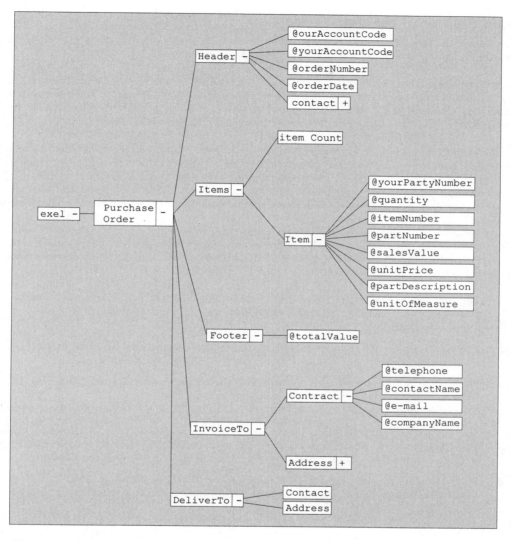

This XML purchase order structure, from Exel Ltd (http://www.exel.com/), is one of the simpler purchase order structures available. It shows most of the core purchase order meaning components in a fairly self-evident way. For instance, the <Header> element contains information about the whole purchase order, such as the order date. Each order line is represented by an <Item> element, which gives the quantity, unit price, and so on of the order line.

Attribute nodes are marked with @. The number of distinct nodes in this tree diagram (with repeatable nodes not repeated) is 55. Not all of these are shown in the diagram; the '+' boxes show where sub-trees for <Address> and <Contact> have not been expanded in the diagram.

Other purchase order message formats can be much more complex – having hundreds or even thousands of distinct nodes, even without repeating any repeatable nodes. To fully understand even a few of these formats is a non-trivial exercise.

Example Problem – Purchase Orders

As we will use the example of XML purchase orders in several places to illustrate the use of MDL, we give a little more background on XML purchase order message formats here.

e-Commerce is one of the "killer apps" which has propelled XML to fame over the past three years. Central to the conduct of much e-commerce is the electronic exchange of purchase orders. Consequently, a large number of XML message formats for purchase orders have been developed. Many of these can be found at the main XML repositories such as http://www.xml.org/ and http://www.biztalk.org/.

The core meaning of a purchase order is fairly simple. A buying organization sends an order to a selling organization, committing to buy certain quantities of goods or products. There is usually one order line for each distinct type of goods, specifying the product and the amount required. The purchase order may also define who authorized or initiated the purchase, to whom the goods are to be delivered, and who will pay. Many other pieces of information may be given in specific purchase orders, but that is the basic framework.

The core meaning of a purchase order encompasses the classes, properties and associations shown in the class diagram given above. Many different XML languages have been published which convey more or less the same "core purchase order" meaning in different XML structures. Typical of the purchase order XML formats that have been analyzed with MDL are:

❏ The Business & Accounting Software Developer's association (BASDA) purchase order message format, part of the BASDA eBIS-XML suite of schemas available from http://www.basda.org/.

❏ The cXML protocol (http://www.cxml.org/) and data formats, used by Ariba in their e-commerce platform.

❏ Purchase order messages generated from an Oracle database by Oracle's XML SQL Utility (known as XSU, more details can be found at http://technet.oracle.com/tech/xml/oracle_xsu/); these have a relatively flat structure that mirrors the database structure directly.

❏ The Navision purchase order message format from Navision Software a/s in Denmark, (http://www.navision.com/), a part of the Navision WebShop e-commerce solution.

❏ Purchase order message formats from the Open Applications Group (OAG, http://www.openapplications.org/) in the OAGIS framework for application integration.

Now imagine you are setting up to sell goods by XML-based e-commerce, and your clients tell you what purchase order message formats they use. They are the customers, and you cannot tell them to use your own favorite XML format, so your systems must be able to accept all these formats – and others, as new e-commerce frameworks emerge. Suppose for example that there are thirteen different formats you must deal with. That is the test problem used for the examples in this chapter.

MDL – Defining How XML Expresses Meaning

There follows an outline description of MDL, intended to give enough of the flavor of MDL to understand the sample applications introduced later in this chapter. This outline does not cover all aspects of MDL – for that see the full description at http://www.charteris.com/mdl.

If an XML language expresses meanings in a UML (or DAML+OIL) class model, then an MDL file can define how the XML expresses that meaning. The MDL defines how the XML represents every object, simple property, or association that it describes.

Generally, particular nodes in the XML structure express particular types of meaning; for instance each element with some tag name may represent an object of some class, or each XML attribute may represent some property of an object. However, there is more to it than that.

To define how an XML language represents information, you need to define not only what nodes carry the information, but also the *paths* to get to those nodes. The best way to define such paths is to use the W3C-recommended **XPath** language. For more information, see www.w3.org/TR/xpath, Chapters 3 and 13 of this book, Chapter 5 of the Wrox Press book *"XSLT Programmer's Reference, 2nd Edition"*, ISBN 1-861005-06-7), or Chapter 2 of *"Professional XSL"* (ISBN 1-861003-57-9). For instance, you need to define what XPaths to follow to get from a node representing an object to the nodes representing all of its properties. This leads to the core principle of MDL:

> **For every type of meaning expressed by an XML language, MDL defines which nodes carry the information, and what XPaths are needed to get to those nodes.**

MDL is designed to be the simplest possible way to define this node and path information in XML. It turns out that the nodes and paths you need in order to define how XML represents information follow a simple **1-2-3-Node Rule**:

- ❑ To define how XML represents *objects* of some class, you need to specify one node type and the path to it from the root node.

- ❑ To define how XML represents a simple *property* of objects of some class, you need to specify two node types and a path between them.

- ❑ To define how XML represents some *association* between classes, you need to specify three node types and some of the paths between them.

We shall see how this works out in the examples that follow.

Structure of MDL

The primary form of an MDL document is a **schema adjunct**. Schema adjuncts are a recent proposal for a simple XML file to contain meta data about documents in any XML language, which goes beyond the meta data expressed in typical schema languages (in any way thought useful by the person defining the adjunct) and may be useful when processing documents. Schema adjuncts have a wide range of potential uses, described at http://www.extensibility.com/resources/saf.htm.

An MDL document is an adjunct to a schema (for example, an XSD Schema) that defines the structure of a class of documents. The MDL defines the meanings of the same class of documents. An MDL document has a form such as:

```
<schema-adjunct  target=http://www.myco.com/myschema.xsd
xmlns:me="http://www.myCo/dmodel.daml"  >

<document>
```

```
...
</document>

<element context = "product">
...
</element>

<element context = "product/manufacturer">
...
</element>

<attribute context = "product/@price">
...
</attribute>

</schema-adjunct>
```

The `target` attribute of the top `<schema-adjunct>` element is the URL of the schema of the XML language that this MDL describes, when there is a unique schema. The namespace in the `<schema-adjunct>` element (in this example with prefix me) has a namespace URI for the semantic model (for example in DAML+OIL) to which this meaning description is referenced. This could be an RDDL URI, enabling access to the DAML+OIL model (RDDL is discussed briefly in Chapter 9). Thus the top `<schema-adjunct>` element gives the means for an MDL processor to access both the schema and the semantic model, and to check the MDL against each of them individually or together.

The XPath expressions used in MDL must have namespace prefixes to distinguish elements from different namespaces in the same document. The `<document>` element is used to declare all those namespaces, so that an MDL processor can correctly resolve multiple namespaces in documents processed. The `<element>` and `<attribute>` elements each define what meaning is carried by various elements and attributes in the XML language. For each `<element>` element, the `context` attribute defines the XPath needed to get from the root of the document to the element in question (and similarly for attributes). The contents of the `<element>` element define what meaning that element carries (and similarly for attributes). The ways in which they do this are illustrated by the examples below.

How XML Encodes Objects

Objects are almost always denoted by XML elements. There is typically a 1:1 correspondence between element instances and objects in a class. Therefore the MDL for an element may typically say "all elements of this tag name, reached by this path, represent objects of that class". A typical piece of MDL to do this is:

```
<element context="/NavisionPO">
   <me:object class="purchaseOrder"/>
</element>
```

This simply says "every element reached from the document root by the XPath '/NavisionPO' represents one object of class 'purchaseOrder'". The me: prefix refers to the namespace for elements such as `<object>` and `<property>` that are part of the MDL language itself.

Thus, in accordance with the 1-2-3 Node Rule, the MDL to define how XML represents an object defines one node type, and the path to it from the document root. This is shown in the following diagram:

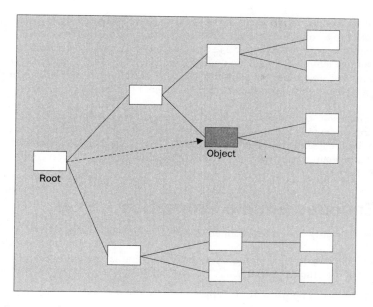

There are cases where one element simultaneously represents two or more objects of different classes. In that case, in the MDL there may be several `<me:object>` elements nested inside the same `<element>` element.

MDL may provide two further pieces of information about how elements represent objects:

❑ An element may represent an object of a class only *conditionally* – only when certain other conditions (in the XML document) apply. MDL lets you define what those conditions are – in other words, to define just which elements represent objects of some class.

❑ When an XML document represents objects of a class, it will usually not represent all objects of the class, but only those objects that satisfy certain *inclusion conditions* (in the semantic model). MDL lets you define what the inclusion conditions are – in other words which objects within the class are represented in the document.

An example of an element representing an object only conditionally can be found where there are several individuals involved in a purchase transaction. One XML language may represent these individuals by different element types – `<authoriser>`, `<recipient>`, `<payer>` and so on. Another language may represent them all by the same element type `<participant>`, with an attribute role = "authorizer", "recipient" and so on. In the second language, the element `<participant>` represents objects of class recipient only conditionally – when the attribute role has value recipient. MDL lets you define these conditions. The MDL for the second language looks like:

```
<element context="/participant">
   <me:object class="recipient">
   <me:when objectToLeftValue="@role"
            rightValue = "recipient">
   </me:object>
</element>
```

The condition for the element to represent the object is stated in the <me:when> element. <me:when> elements always refer to a condition that has a left-hand side, a right-hand-side, and a test (=, contains, etc.). The test defaults to '='. The attribute objectToLeftValue says "to get from the node representing the object to the node representing the value on the left-hand side of the test, follow this XPath". The attribute rightValue defines the constant value on the right-hand side of the condition. So the <participant> element only represents a recipient when it has an attribute role = "recipient".

As an example of inclusion conditions, an XML document about a university may have <student> elements describing students. It is implicit that the document does not describe all students living or dead; it only describes students currently enrolled at the college. That is the inclusion condition, and MDL gives you a way to state it. Since many applications of MDL work without using inclusion conditions, we do not give the relevant MDL here.

How XML Encodes Simple Properties

Simple properties are nearly always represented in XML in one of two ways:

❑ A simple property is represented by an attribute (that is, the value of the attribute represents the value of the simple property).

❑ The value of a simple property is represented by the text value of an element.

Other ways of representing properties are conceivable in principle, but rarely used in practice. In either of the two ways described above, you need to tie together the property with the object of which it is a property – the object instance that owns the property instance. This is done in MDL by defining the XPath to get from a node representing an object to the node representing its property.

The following piece of MDL, based on our purchase chain model, defines how XML represents a property:

```
<element context="/NavisionPO/Line/Unit_of_Measure">
    <me:property class="product" property="unitOfMeasure">
        <me:find objectToProperty="Unit_of_Measure"/>
    </me:property>
</element>
```

The <me:property> element defines what property the element represents; it defines the property name (unitOfMeasure) and the class (product) of which it is a property.

In this case, the MDL for objects of class product is:

```
<element context="/NavisionPO/Line">
    <me:object class="product"/>
</element>
```

Therefore each <Line> element represents a product, and each <Unit_of_Measure> element represents the <unitOfMeasure> property of the product – as defined by the <me:property> element in the MDL. The objectToProperty attribute states that to get from an element representing a product object to the element representing its unit of measure, you have to follow the XPath Unit_of_measure – that is, find the immediate child element with that name.

The `objectToProperty` attribute serves the important purpose of tying up each object instance with the actual properties of that object instance. Without it, an XML document might represent many objects, and many property values, but you might not be able to link them together correctly. XPath is the general way to define the linkages.

Again in accordance with the 1-2-3 Node Rule, the MDL to define how XML represents some property depends on two node types (nodes representing objects, and nodes representing the property) and the XPath between them. This is shown in the following diagram:

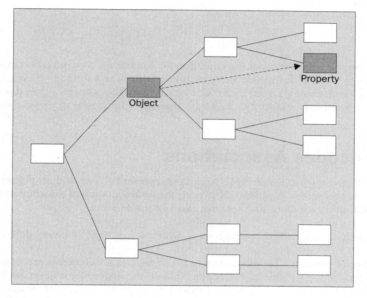

MDL can describe other aspects of how XML represents properties:

❑ It may be that not all elements of given tag name, reached by a given XPath, represent a property; sometimes certain other conditions may need to be satisfied. MDL lets you define what these conditions are. See the example below.

❑ The XML may represent the value of a property in a particular format, which may need conversion to a "central" format defined in the semantic model. MDL lets you define format conversion methods, for example in Java or XSLT.

As an example of conditional representation of properties, some XML languages adopt an "uncommitted" style in which the language itself does not define what properties can be represented. For instance:

```
<person pid = "1234">
    <personAttribute att = "name" value = "Fred" />
    <personAttribute att = "age" value = "37" />
    <personAttribute att = "employed" value = "yes" />
</person>
```

Here the language designer has allowed users of the language to describe whatever they want to describe about a person, if they provide the appropriate att-value pairs. The element `<personAttribute>` can represent many properties, depending on its `att` attribute. In this case, the relevant MDL is:

```
<element context="/person/personAttribute">
    <me:property class="person" property = "name">
        <me:find objectToProperty = "personAttribute"/>
        <me:when propertyToLeftValue="@att"
                rightValue = "name"/>
    </me:property>
    <me:property class="person" property = "age">
        <me:find objectToProperty = "personAttribute"/>
        <me:when propertyToLeftValue="@att"
                rightValue = "age"/>
    </me:property>
</element>
```

Here, the `<me:when>` element encodes the condition for conditional representation much as it did for objects: the condition has a left-hand side and a right-hand side. The left-hand side is got by following the XPath specified in the attribute `propertyToLeftValue` from the property node; the right-hand side is the constant given by the attribute `rightValue`. Only when this condition is true does the element represent the property.

How XML Encodes Associations

As described above, the ways in which XML languages represent objects and properties are generally straightforward, and present few problems. However, the representation of associations (sometimes called relations) in XML is more complex, and requires careful consideration.

XML can represent associations in three main ways, which at first sight look very different from one another:

❑ By **nesting of elements**: for example when `<orderLine>` elements are nested inside a `<purchaseOrder>` element, this means that all the order line objects are part of the purchase order – representing the association [order line] is part of [purchase order] by element nesting.

❑ By **overloading of elements**: for example where the same `<line>` element represents an order line, the product that the order line is for, and the association [order line] is for [product]; the one element is "overloaded" to represent objects of several classes and their associations.

❑ By **shared values**: where elements representing the two associated objects are remote from one another in the XML, but their association is indicated by the fact that they share common values of some elements or attributes.

Each one of these three methods occurs commonly in practice, and cannot be neglected. Fortunately, the three methods all share some common underlying principles, which means that the same XPath-based form of description can be used to define all of them. We can define a common **three-node model** of representing associations, which covers all these cases.

In any XML representation of an association [E]A[F] between objects of class E and class F, nodes of some type denote instances of the association. We call these **association nodes**. Therefore each instance of an association in a document involves just three nodes – the two elements representing the objects at either end of the association instance, and the association node itself. To define how XML represents the association, we need to define how to tie together the three nodes of each instance of the association. If we can tie together these three nodes, we have in so doing tied together the two object-representing nodes – and can thus find out which object instances are linked in an association instance. That is all the information carried in an association, so it defines fully how XML represents the association.

In many cases, the three-node model will be "degenerate", in that two or more of the three nodes will be identical; a two-node model, or even a one-node model, would have been adequate. Nevertheless, the three-node model is adequate for *all* cases; the fact that it is more than adequate for some cases does not matter. Using the three-node model for all associations means that MDL-based tools (described below) can treat all associations in a uniform and simple manner.

MDL defines how the three nodes are linked using XPath expressions, and supplementary conditions which the nodes must satisfy (these are necessary to describe the "shared value" representation of associations). MDL provides the means to define the XPaths both from the object-representing elements to the association node, and in the reverse direction. When extracting association information from a document, paths in either direction may be needed – either to go from E => A => F, or to go in the reverse direction.

The three-node model of associations is shown:

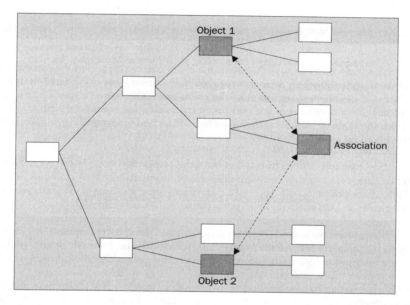

In cases where the three-node model is an overkill, and two or more of the nodes of any association instance are identical, then the XPaths between the identical nodes are just the trivial " . " path which means "stay where you are". Therefore the full MDL definition of an association has a path from the root to define the set of association nodes, and it has relative paths between the association nodes and the elements representing objects at the two ends of the association.

For instance, an important part of the meaning of any purchase order is the association [orderLine]inOrder[purchaseOrder], which means that the order line is part of the purchase order. In many XML purchase order message formats, this association is represented by nesting the elements for each order line inside the one element for the purchase order, as in the XML sample:

```
<PO poNumber = "1234">
    <POLine partNo = "245" qty = "10" />
    <POLine partNo = "246" qty = "5" />
    <POLine partNo = "247" qty = "8" />
</PO>
```

In this case, the MDL for the element <orderLine> states that it represents both an order line and its association to its purchase order:

```
<element context="/PO/POLine">
    <me:object class="orderLine"/>
    <me:association assocName="inOrder">
        <me:object1 class="orderLine"
                    objectToAssociation ="."
                    associationToObject="."/>
            <me:object2 class="purchaseOrder"
                    objectToAssociation ="POLine"
                    associationToObject="parent::PO"/>
    </me:association>
</element>
```

The <me:object> element says that elements of tag name <POLine> represent objects of class orderLine.

The <me:association> element says that the same elements also represent the association [orderLine]inOrder[purchaseOrder]. So in this case, the association node is the same as one of the object-representing nodes (that is, the one representing the order line). The objectToAssociation and associationToObject attributes of the <me:object1> element are both trivial "stay here" paths; they mean, "to get from the node representing the order line to the node representing its association, or back again, just stay where you are".

The <me:object2> element defines how to get from the association node to the purchaseOrder node, or back again. In this case it is clear that recipient units are represented by <PO> elements, which are parent nodes to the <POLine> nodes. So the associationToObject attribute says "go to your parent node" and the objectToAssociation attribute says "go to your <POLine> child node".

All this says that the association [orderLine]inOrder[purchaseOrder] is represented by element nesting. But because it does so by using general XPath expressions, which can also be used for any other representation of an association, the association information can be extracted by general XPath-following mechanisms.

As an example of representing an association by overloading, in many XML purchase order messages, the same element represents both an order line ("deliver 4 widgets") and details about the product itself ("a widget is perishable"). The product is related to the order line by the association [orderLine]forProduct[product] – so the same element represents the order line, the product, and the association between them. A typical XML fragment doing this is:

```
<pOrder>
    <oLine qty = "20" pName = "widget" unPrice = "2" />
    <oLine qty = "40" pName = "gasket" unPrice = "10" />
</pOrder>
```

Here the MDL describing the element <oLine> would be:

```
<element context="/POrder/oLine">
    <me:object class="orderLine"/>
    <me:object class="product"/>
    <me:association assocName="forProduct">
        <me:object1 class="orderLine"
```

```
                              objectToAssociation ="."
                              associationToObject="."/>
           <me:object2  class="product"
                              objectToAssociation ="."
                              associationToObject="."/>
       </me:association>
    </element>
```

Here, because the same node is representing both objects and the association between them, all the paths between the association node and the object nodes are the trivial "stay here" path denoted by ".".

Finally, associations can be represented by having no obvious nesting or identity relation between the nodes representing the associated objects, but by some shared value. A typical example, in XML representing students attending courses, might be:

```
<college>
    <course cid="124" name = "English"/>
    <course cid="101" name = "French"/>
    <course cid="102" name = "Latin"/>
    <student name = "Fred" attends = "101 124" />
    <student name = "Fred" attends = "101 102" />
</college>
```

Here the XML denotes the association [student]attends[course] by a shared value; we know that Fred attends English because of the shared value '124'. In this case we say that the association is represented by the attribute attends, and we state this in MDL as follows:

```
<element context = "/college/course" >
    <me:object class = "course" />
</element>

<element context = "/college/student" >
    <me:object class = "student" />
</element>

<attribute context = "/college/student/@attends" >
    <me:association assocName = "attends">
        <me:object1 class = "student"
                    objectToAssociation = "@attends"
                    associationToObject = "parent::student" />
        <me:object2 class = "course"
                    objectToAssociation = "ancestor::college/student/@attends"
                    associationToObject = "ancestor::college/course" />
            <me:when test = "contains"
                    associationToLeftValue = "."
                    objectToRightValue = "@cid" />
        </me:object2>
    </me:association>
</attribute>
```

This piece of MDL says that:

- ❑ <course> elements represent courses.

- ❑ <student> elements represent students.

- ❑ attends attributes are association nodes representing the association [student]attends[course].

- ❑ To get from an association node to its "student-representing node" you follow a path up to its parent.

- ❑ To get from a student-representing node to the association node you go to the descendant attends attribute.

- ❑ To get from an association node to its course-representing node, you go all the way up to the <college> node and down to a <course> node.

- ❑ To get from a college-representing node to one of its association nodes, you go up to the <college> node and down to an attends attribute.

- ❑ These paths link many <course> elements to many attends attributes. But to be part of an association instance, a pair of such nodes must also satisfy the shared value condition.

- ❑ The shared value condition is denoted by the <me:when> element. This applies a text-string contains test. To get the value for the left-hand side, you go from the association node to itself. To get from the node representing the <course> object to the value for the right-hand side, you find its cid attribute.

You can check that a triad of nodes {student node, association node, course node} only represents an instance of the association [student]attends[course] if the three nodes are linked by the paths as specified in the MDL, and if they satisfy the <me:when> condition which defines the shared value.

In accordance with the 1-2-3 Node rule, the MDL to define how XML represents some association depends on three node types (two for the objects linked by the association, and one for the association node) and some XPaths between them. Sometimes two or more of the three nodes coincide; but the three-node model seems capable of capturing the vast majority of the representations of associations in XML documents.

Summary – What MDL Defines

We can summarize the information defined by MDL in the following table:

Meaning Component	Nodes Defined	XPaths Defined	Conditions Evaluated At
Object	Object Node	Root => Object	Object Node
Property	Object Node	Root => Property	Property Node
	Property Node	Object => Property	
Association	Object 1 Node	Root => Association	Association Node and Object 1 or 2 Node
	Object 2 Node	Association <=> Object 1	
	Association Node	Association <=> Object 2	

The first column gives the three different types of meaning the XML document may convey. The second column states, for each type, what XML nodes you need to specify to define how the XML conveys meanings of that type. The third column gives the XPaths you need to specify, and the fourth column states where any conditions (for conditional representation of the information) may be evaluated. Conditions are evaluated by navigating an XPath from the specified node, getting a value from the end node, and comparing it with a constant (or in the case of associations, a value got by navigating an XPath from the other start node of the condition). For a more detailed explanation of how this works, with examples, see the preceding sections.

A Simplification – Shortest Paths

MDL requires the specification of XPaths for both simple properties and associations in order to define how you get from a node representing an object to the nodes representing its properties and associations.

Specifying all of these paths might be a lot of work, unless you have an automatic tool to help you do it. Fortunately, in the vast majority of cases, the required path, for instance the path from a node representing an object to a node representing one of its simple properties, obeys a "shortest path" heuristic; it is the shortest possible path from the one node to the other. Similarly, nearly all paths from object-representing nodes to their association nodes are shortest paths.

In the examples so far, we have always used full-form MDL, but in practice the language can be written more tersely without most of the paths. We can therefore simplify the language by defining that the default XPath is always the simplest path; we only need to define the XPath explicitly when it is some different path. This means that the great majority of XPaths need not be provided explicitly, but can be simply computed by MDL-based tools.

In the code fragments you have seen so far, every path between an object-representing node and a property-representing node or association node has been the shortest possible path. In order to show what a path that is not the shortest path looks like, here is an example. Suppose we have an XML language about people and their relationships, in which a sample document extract looks like:

```
<people>
    <person id = "1234" name = "fred"
            wifeId="1270" />
    <person id = "1270" name = "wilma"
            husbandId = "1234" />
    <person id = "1291" name = "joe"
            fatherId = "1234" motherId = "1270" />
</people>
```

Here, the attribute `wifeId` represents an association "hasWife", and other family relationships are similarly represented. The MDL defining how this language represents the association "hasWife" is:

```
<attribute context = "/people/person/@wifeId">
    <me:association assocName = "hasWife">
        <me:object1 class = "person"
                    objectToAssociation = "@hasWife"
                    associationToObject = "parent::person" />
        <me:object2 class = "person"
                    objectToAssociation = "ancestor::people/person/@wifeId"
                    associationToObject = "ancestor::people/person" >
```

```
        <me:when test = "contains"
                associationToLeftValue = "."
                objectToRightValue = "@id" />
    </me:object2>
  </me:association>
</attribute>
```

Here the association [person]hasWife[person] is represented by a shared value – between the `wifeId` attribute of one person and the `id` attribute of another. This value sharing is captured in the `<me:when>` element, as in the previous example of a shared-value association. However, consider the XPaths between the association node and the wife-representing node. These paths are in the attributes `objectToAssociation` and `AssociationToObject` of the `<me:object2>` element, and they both involve going up to the root `<people>` element and coming down again. This is not the shortest path between a `<person>` element and a `wifeId` attribute; that shortest path is just a parent-child path – which would only allow one specific person to have a particular wife. So XPaths are not always the shortest possible path; but they are so 90% of the time.

How to Use MDL

In summary, MDL defines "how information is encoded in XML" in a rather uniform manner for the three main types of information, about objects, properties, and associations. For each type of information, the MDL says "to extract the information from an XML document, follow these XPaths".

MDL-based tools are given a definition at the level of meaning – in the semantic model – of what is required, and then they use the information in the MDL to convert this automatically to a structural description of how to navigate (or construct) the XML to do this.

This means that both users and developers can state what they want from an XML document (in meaning terms) and an MDL-based tool can find (in the MDL) the XPaths to be navigated to get that information. For instance, a user or developer can say "I want information about the association [person]hasFather[person]". The MDL for a language says "to get that information, you need to follow these XPaths". So an MDL-based tool can follow those paths for the user or developer, without the user/developer ever having to know what the paths are. MDL can give users and developers what they want from XML, without their having to understand XML structure. This can work both ways – getting information from XML documents, and putting it into them.

To do so, builders of MDL-based tools need to solve two problems – the input problem and the output problem:

❑   The **input problem** is to extract the information from an "incoming" XML document and view that information directly in terms of the classes, simple properties, and associations of the semantic model. From the nature of MDL, this problem is fairly simple to solve. MDL defines the XPaths you need to follow in order to extract from a document a given object, or any of its simple properties, or any of its associations. So to find the value of any simple property or association of some object, you simply need to follow the relevant XPaths in the document, as defined in the MDL. This is easily done if you have an implementation of XPath, such as Apache Xalan (from http://xml.apache.org/).

❑ The **output problem** is to "package" the information in an instance of the semantic model into an "outgoing" XML document which conveys that information. It is not quite so obvious how to do this from the definition of MDL, but in fact it is fairly straightforward. You need to construct the document from its root "downwards". For this, you use a definition of the XML structure from some schema language such as XSD Schema. Generally you will come to nodes representing objects before you come to nodes representing their properties and associations. As you come to each node type, you check in the MDL what type of information the node type represents (such as what class of object, or what property), and you check what instances of that type of information exist in the semantic model instance. You then construct node instances to reflect these information model instances.

To construct structurally correct output XML, the MDL-based tools need knowledge of the allowed XML structures. In fact MDL itself contains, within the XPaths, almost all the information required to construct valid output XML. However, there are structural constraints, such as allowed orders of siblings, not captured in MDL. If these constraints are important, an MDL-based XML output tool can use, for instance, the XSD Schema for the output document to apply the constraints.

We will illustrate this by describing three MDL-based tools which allow users and developers to view XML at the level of its meaning. The first and second of these – a Java API to XML, and a meaning-level query language – only require a solution to the input problem; while the third (automated XML translation) requires a solution of both the input problem *and* the output problem.

We know of no other tools or techniques which today deliver any of these three capabilities – on a meaning-level API to XML, a structure-independent XML query language, or automated, meaning-preserving transformation.

The Generic MDL API to XML

Before describing the three main applications of MDL, we shall describe the API to XML documents which MDL makes possible, and which underlies all three applications. This is a Java API, and if you understand the functionality provided by this API, that is one way to see clearly the power of MDL for building XML applications.

Two of the three MDL applications described below (the meaning-level Java API, and the meaning-level query language) are made available in the code download for this book in Java source and executable form, so you can try them out, modify them or extend them. To do so, you will use the generic MDL API described here. Full Javadoc documentation and a .jar implementation of this API is provided.

The API consists of a single class mdl that sits on top of the W3C DOM and XPath APIs (as implemented in the Apache Xalan and Xerces implementations). An object of class mdl first reads an MDL file (of the form described above) and an XML document in the language described by the MDL.

As we have discussed, the XML document represents a set of objects, properties and associations in a UML class model (or a DAML+OIL ontology). The way it does so (that is, the XPaths you need to follow in the XML to get this information out of it) is described in the MDL file. The MDL API then provides three core methods:

❑ **Vector getAllObjectNodes(String className, Node root)** is given the name of a class (such as product or student) and the root node of the XML document (Node is a class in the DOM interface, representing any node in an XML document). It returns a vector of every node in the document that represents an object of the named class.

❑ **String getPropertyValue(String className, String propertyName, Node objectNode, boolean warn)** is given the name of a class (such as `student`), the name of a property of that class (such as `age`), and a node in the XML document which represents an object of that class (for example,.a node in the vector returned by the method above). It returns (as a string) the value of the property. The flag `warn` is true if the property has multiple values for the object (which it should not; but this depends on the XML document).

❑ **Vector getAssociatedObjectNodes(String class1Name, String associationName, String class2Name, Node obj12, int oneOrTwo)**. `oneOrTwo` can be 1 or 2. When it is 1, `obj12` is a node in the document representing an object of class `class1Name`. The method returns a vector of nodes representing all the objects of class `class2Name` which are related to the first object by the association [class1Name]associationName[class2Name]. When `oneOrTwo = 2`, an object of class `class2Name` is the starting point, and objects of class `class1Name` are the result.

That is it. Using these three methods, you can retrieve from an XML document all objects of any class, find the values of all their properties, and navigate their association links to find the objects related to them by any association. You can do this with no knowledge of the structure on the XML (check this – no argument of any method mentions XML structure such as child nodes, XPaths, etc). That is because the MDL file contains all this structure information, and the MDL interface uses it, hiding it from the user of this API.

Using the MDL API, therefore, you can write Java XML applications with no knowledge of XML structure. The same application will run unchanged against different XML languages, provided that each language represents the classes, properties and associations you refer to, and its MDL defines how it does so.

Compare this with programming using the W3C DOM API, described below. The benefits of the MDL API are:

❑ It is much simpler.

❑ It works at a higher level – in terms of the classes, properties and association used for analysis and design of the application.

❑ It does not require any knowledge of XML document structure.

❑ The same application will work unchanged against many different XML languages.

❑ Applications are much easier to maintain as XML languages evolve through different versions.

If you have experienced some of difficulties of DOM implementation, and understand how MDL avoids them, then you have understood the core message of this chapter.

The meaning-level Java API can be packaged up in a form that is slightly more convenient for some applications. This is described next.

Meaning-Level API to XML

When we write applications to use XML in a language such as Java, we generally interface between the application and the XML via some standardized API, such as the W3C-recommended Document Object Model (DOM – find out more at http://www.w3.org/DOM/). Several XML parsers provide high-quality implementations of the DOM API, and many XML applications are built on top of them.

The way this works, for a read-only application that consumes XML but does not create it, is illustrated in the following diagram:

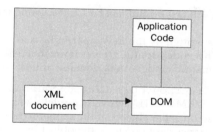

Here, the XML document is read in by the parser, which makes available the DOM interface to the resulting document tree, for use by the application code.

However, the DOM interfaces are defined entirely in terms of document structure – giving facilities to construct and navigate the document tree in memory. Therefore interfacing to XML via the DOM has two drawbacks:

❑ Developers are interested in getting the meaning out of an XML document (or putting it in). To do this via the DOM, they need to understand the XML document structure, and how it conveys meanings, quite precisely. For large and complex XML languages, this is costly and error-prone, and also very hard to maintain or change later.

❑ Applications need to be written with one document structure in mind, "hard-wiring" that document structure into the code. If the application is to be re-used with another XML language that conveys the same meanings, that application needs to be rewritten.

Using MDL, we can write applications which interface to the XML at the level of its meaning, not its structure – and so avoid the two drawbacks above. The way this works (again for a read-only application which consumes XML but does not create it) is shown in the following diagram:

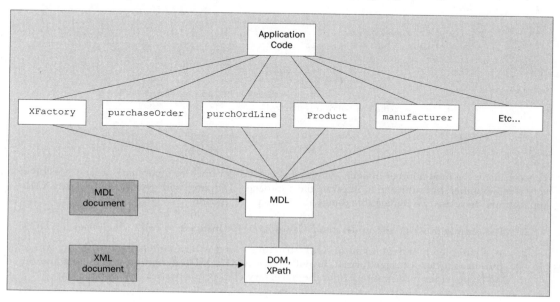

The components of this diagram will first be outlined before discussing some of them in more detail:

❑ The **application code** is written by the developer in Java to accomplish whatever the application is about. This code uses the classes immediately below it in the diagram – classes that reflect only the semantic model of the domain, and are independent of XML structure.

❑ The classes `purchaseOrder`, `purchOrdLine`, `product`, `manufacturer` and so on are the classes of the UML (or DAML+OIL) semantic model. Each instance represents one purchase order, order line, and so on – the objects of the semantic model that supports the application. The available object instances are precisely the object instances represented in the input XML. Their instance methods return the values of an object's properties, or sets of other objects linked to that object by the associations of the semantic model.

❑ The class `XFactory` is a factory class that can return all the `purchaseOrder` objects, or all the `purchOrdLine` objects, or all objects of any class represented in the XML.

❑ The class `MDL` reads in the MDL file for a particular XML language and stores all its information in internal form. It then makes available methods used by the classes of the semantic model, and by the factory class, to return values that reflect information in the XML document.

❑ The XPath and DOM APIs are an implementation of these W3C standard interfaces – for instance, as provided by the Apache Xalan XPath/XSLT implementation with the Apache Xerces XML parser.

A typical sample of Java application code, using the purchase order XML languages described earlier, looks like this:

```
// compute the total quantity of all items in a PO
int totQuant(Node root, MDL mdl)
    {
        int total = 0;
        XFactory xf = new XFactory(root,mdl);
        Vector oLines = xf.everyOrderLine();
        if (oLines != null)
            for (int i = 0; i < oLines.size(); i++)
            {
                purchOrdLine ord = (purchOrdLine) oLines.elementAt(i);
                total = total + ord.quantity();
            }
        return total;
    }
```

This calculates the total number of items, summed over all order lines for a purchase order – possibly not a very useful number, but sufficient to illustrate the approach. Compared with typical DOM-based XML applications, there are two remarkable things about this piece of code:

❑ It is simple to write and understand – compared for instance to code which uses the DOM.

❑ It is completely independent of XML structure – so it will run unchanged with any XML purchase order message format, provided that XML's MDL definition is available and the XML provides information about the necessary classes, properties and associations.

The MDL instance mdl has previously been initialized and has an internal representation of the MDL file. First the method above creates an XFactory instance, and uses that instance to create a vector, oLines, of all purchOrdLine objects represented in the XML message. It then inspects the individual purchOrdLine objects, and for each one adds its quantity to the total. The supporting classes do all the work of navigating the XML document to find this information.

The next layer of classes in the diagram above (XFactory and all the domain classes such as purchaseOrder) is generated automatically from the DAML+OIL definition of the semantic model.

The class XFactory has one method for each class in the semantic model – to return a vector of all the objects of the class represented in the XML document. The generated code for one of these methods looks like this:

```
/* return a vector of all 'purchOrdLine' objects represented in the document; or
null if the language does not represent objects of this class. */

public Vector every_purchOrdLine()
{
    int i;
    Vector res = null;
    Vector nl = mdl.getAllObjectNodes("purchOrdLine", root);
    if (nl != null) {
        res = new Vector();
        for (i = 0; i < nl.size(); i++)
            {res.addElement(new purchOrdLine((Node)nl.elementAt(i),mdl));}
    }
    return res;
}
```

As can be seen, just substituting the class name at several places into a standard template can generate this code.

The source code for each class of the semantic model is also generated automatically. A typical generated class has the following source code:

```
import org.w3c.dom.*;
import java.util.*;

public class orderLine
{
    private Node objectNode;
    private MDL mdl;

    public purchOrdLine(Node n, MDL m)
        {objectNode = n; mdl = m;}

// String value of 'quantity' property
    public String quantity()
    {return mdl.getPropertyValue("purchOrdLine","quantity",objectNode,false);}

/* Single 'purchaseOrder' object related by[purchOrdLine]isPartOf[purchaseOrder]*/
    public purchaseOrder isPartOf_purchaseOrder()
    {
```

```
    purchaseOrder res = null;
    Vector nl = mdl.getAssociatedObjectNodes("purchOrdLine","isPartOf",
                                              "purchaseOrder",objectNode,1);

    if ((nl != null) && (nl.size() > 0))
    {res = new purchaseOrder((Node)nl.elementAt(0),mdl);}
    return res;
  }
}
```

*For reasons of space, only one or two of the property and association methods are shown. Typically a class
has many properties and associations, each with its own method.*

Note that the generated code depends on the semantic model, but not at all on the XML structure or MDL.
The same generated code can be used unchanged with many different XML languages. For each different
language, the MDL captures all that needs to be known about document structure context, and hides it from
the programmer using this API.

These classes use lazy evaluation of their properties and associations. When an instance is created, its only
internal state consists of the node in the XML document that represents the object. Whenever the value of a
property or association is required, the value is computed by calling the MDL class instance, which navigates
the XML to retrieve the values. It would of course be possible to cache values in each instance, so that
repeated evaluation did not cause repeated traversal of the DOM tree, but the current implementation of the
mdl class does not do this.

Again, you can see that substituting various class names, property names, and association names into
standard code templates generates this source code.

All the semantic-level generated classes rely on the class mdl to get information from the XML document. It
is here that the real work is done, but it is not difficult work. The API presented by the mdl class has been
described in the previous section.

The code of the mdl class is completely independent of the application, being driven by the data from the
MDL file. The implementation of the three core methods is fairly straightforward, since the class mdl knows
all the XPaths to be traversed in the document to retrieve the relevant information. Currently the mdl class
makes use of the following XPath interfaces provided by the XPathAPI class of Apache Xalan:

❑   selectNodeList(Node n, String xPath) returns a NodeList of all nodes reachable by
    following the path xPath from the node n.

❑   selectSingleNode(Node n, String xPath) returns a single node, in cases where you
    know only a single node can be returned.

These interfaces make the job of the mdl class very simple. Therefore by using the XPath interface to XML
documents, and using a few simple intermediate classes (some generated, and others independent of the
application) we are able to insulate the Java application completely from the details of XML document
structure. With this interface, developers can work at the level of semantic model classes that they
understand. They do not have to learn the intricacies of XML document structure and their applications will
work unchanged with many different XML document formats. For instance, the sample purchase order
application fragment works unchanged with any of the thirteen different XML purchase order message
formats Charteris has analyzed with MDL. Applications can even switch dynamically to handle messages in
different XML languages at the same time.

In the API we have just described, there are separate (generated) Java classes for all of the classes of object represented in the XML, as defined in a DAML+OIL ontology or class model for the domain. This matches naturally with typical styles of OO development, where there are classes modeling the classes of object in the domain. The generated classes may be sub-classed to do things specific to the application. This style of development is different from the generic API described in the previous section, where one mdl class gives methods to navigate the whole class model and inspect the properties of any object. Both styles of programming have their uses, but we would expect the generated-class approach to be used more widely.

In the code download available with the book are the generator program that creates the Java class definitions, and a sample application developed with this API. These programs require the Apache Xerces XML parser and Xalan XPath implementation (available from Apache at http://xml.apache.org/) and an implementation of the mdl class. With these you can extend or modify the demonstration applications against XML sample documents provided with the download. These include sample purchase order documents in thirteen different XML languages, and two sample documents in a domain of students, lecturers and courses. Alternatively you can generate Java classes and use the API with any XML documents of your choice, if you write a DAML+OIL class model for the domain and the MDL for the XML language.

Here we have only discussed "read-only" applications that read XML but do not write it. The application of these techniques to read/write applications is a bit more complex, but very feasible. In order to be able to create XML documents with given structure, the API layer needs to know what the allowed structures are – that is, to know the schema. For this, it can use information from an XSD schema, DTD, or XDR (XML Data Reduced) document, to define allowed language structures. This is the approach taken to output valid XML in the automated translation application, described below.

As XML languages continue to proliferate, the benefits of this meaning-level style of application development – in quality, development costs, and maintenance costs – will be overwhelming. There is no reason not to start doing it now.

Meaning-Level XML Query Language

The current state of XML query languages is similar to the current state of programming APIs to XML, in that XML query languages, like APIs, are tightly coupled to XML document structures. To use an XML query language, such as the current W3C Working Draft XQuery, you need to understand the structure of the XML document being queried and to navigate around it, retrieving the information that interests you.

This has the same drawbacks for query users as the structure-level APIs have for developers. Users need to understand the structure of XML languages – which for large languages may be costly and error-prone – and queries are not transportable across XML languages.

Using MDL, we can build XML query tools that operate at the level of meaning rather than structure. In such a language, the query is expressed in terms independent of XML structure – so users can formulate queries without knowledge of XML language structures, and the same query can be re-used across many XML languages that express the same meaning.

The diagram that follows describes a small demonstrator of a meaning-level XML query language:

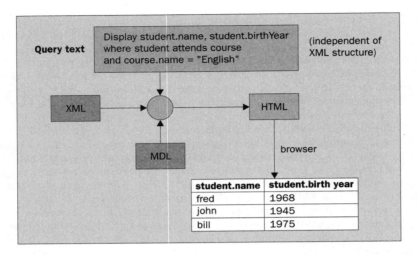

This demonstrator is available in Java source form and executable form in the code download for the book. It is a batch program that accepts as input:

- ❑ A text file containing the text of the query.
- ❑ The XML document that the query is to run against.
- ❑ The MDL file for the language being queried against.

The program does not display an answer to the query, but outputs an HTML file. When the HTML is displayed on a browser it shows the answer to the query against the document – as in the diagram.

The queries that are input to this tool are expressed in a simple language of the form:

```
Display class.property, class.property … where condition and condition and …
```

Names of classes and properties are taken from the semantic model. Each condition is either of the form class.property = value (possibly using other relations such as 'contains', 'startsWith', '>') or of the form 'className association className'. Despite its limited nature, this simple language can express a wide range of useful queries, linking together information about objects of several related classes. Most important, it expresses these queries entirely in terms of the semantic model, and independent of XML structure.

Typical queries in this language are:

```
Display orderLine.quantity, product.name where orderLine isPartOf purchaseOrder
and orderLine isFor product.
```

```
Display address.city, address.zip where purchasingUnit hasAddress address
```

It is evident that you do not have to know about XML document structure to write these queries.

The demonstration program parses and validates queries of this form, and devises a query strategy. This strategy defines the order of classes involved in visiting and filtering the objects of the classes mentioned in the query, using the query conditions to filter objects. The query strategy is then executed against an XML document, using the `mdl` class described in previous sections to find the XPaths needed to navigate the document tree to get the required information.

For everyday use, you would probably not use the query program as a batch program taking a text query file as input and delivering HTML output; you would probably prefer an interactive program where queries could be typed in, and answers displayed immediately. Since the source of the query program is included in the download, you could easily create such an interactive version for yourself.

Again, you can run the query demonstrator either against the sample XML documents provided in the download for the book, or against XML documents in any language, provided you write the MDL for that language.

In summary, this style of meaning-level query language has two key benefits over other existing XML query languages:

❑ Users can write queries without knowing the structure of XML documents.

❑ The same query can be freely re-used across documents in several different XML languages, provided their MDL is known.

Automated XML Translation

A core application of XSLT is to translate documents from one XML language to another. It is implicit, although rarely stated, that the intention of such translations is to preserve the meaning in the documents. Therefore we would expect a Meaning Definition Language to be very relevant to XML translation.

It is only possible to translate documents between XML languages if their meanings overlap. If one language is about cookery and another about astronomy, we could not translate at all from one to the other. At the simplest level, we can test the overlap in meaning between two languages by comparing their MDL – as long as both MDL definitions are made against the same DAML+OIL ontology, or UML class model. We can test which components of meaning (which classes, properties and associations) are represented in both languages. It is only these "overlap" components or meaning that can be translated (in principle). So the MDL overlap acts as a specification of the translation.

However, we can do much more than this. Since MDL defines not only *what* information is expressed by each XML language, but also *how* it is expressed by the XML structure, the MDL can tell us how to extract each component of meaning from the input document, and how to package it in the output document. Therefore the MDL for the two languages (together with their structure definitions) is sufficient to create automatically the complete XSLT translation from one to the other. Charteris have developed a translation tool, **XMuLator**, which does just this. XMuLator is available for licence from Charteris, at http://www.charteris.com/mdl/. The way XMuLator operates is shown in the following diagram:

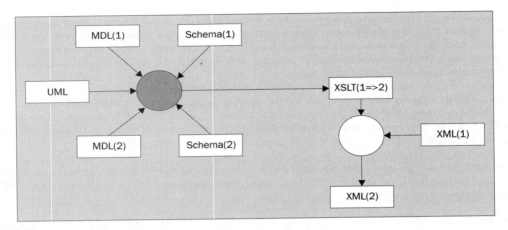

The shaded circle represents the XMuLator translator generator. It takes as input:

❑ The UML (or DAML+OIL) semantic model of classes, properties, and associations.

❑ The structure definition (XML Schema or XDR) for the input language – here denoted as language (1).

❑ The MDL definition for the input language.

❑ The structure definition for the output language – here called language (2).

❑ The MDL definition of the output language.

As output, it generates a complete XSLT translation between the two languages. This can be used by any standards-conformant XSLT processor (such as xt, Saxon, or Xalan) to translate documents from language 1 to language 2.

Charteris have used XMuLator to generate and test all 13*12 translations between the thirteen purchase order message formats available in the download for this book. We have verified that the output documents have the required structure for their languages, and correctly represent all the information that can in principle be conveyed in the translation – in other words all the information conveyed by both the languages involved in a translation.

We have also carried out a stringent "round trip" test of the translations. In this, we verify that when a document is translated through some cycle of languages (such as A=>B=>A or A=>B=>C=>D=>A) the output document is a strict subset of the input document – so that any information that survives the round trip survives it undistorted. In general, not all the information in the input document will survive a round trip, because the languages do not overlap perfectly in the information they convey. However, the XMuLator-generated translations preserved all the information that could in principle be preserved in the round trip (that is, that information which was represented in all languages in the round trip) and delivered it undistorted to the final output document.

Among the thirteen different purchase order languages we have translated are some deeply nested languages, and some very shallow languages, such as those resulting from the use of the Oracle XML SQL Utility (XSU – http://technet.oracle.com/tech/xml/oracle_xsu/). Therefore the translations have involved major structural changes to the XML – not just a few changes in tag names. These major structural transformations have all passed the stringent round trip test.

There are currently two alternatives to this meaning-based generation of XSLT translations. The first is to write XSLT by hand, and the second is to generate translations by some XML-to-XML mapping tool such as Microsoft's BizTalk Mapper. The meaning-based approach has major advantages over both of these.

Compared with the meaning-driven approach, writing and debugging of XSLT is much more expensive and error-prone. Even to write one XSLT translation is, we believe, more costly than to write down the MDL for the two languages involved. The XSLT is generally a much larger and more complex document than the two MDL files; and in many cases you will already have the MDL files available.

However, it is when there are several different languages that the advantages of the MDL approach become overwhelming. With N different languages, you may require as many as $N*(N-1)$ distinct translations among them. Using MDL, the cost of creating all these translations grows only as N (this is the cost of writing all the MDL files). This can rapidly amount to a huge cost difference – especially as each different language may go through a series of versions.

We believe that in practice the MDL-based approach is much more reliable than hand writing XSLT. Using MDL-based translation, as long as the meaning of each language has been captured accurately, then the translation will be accurate – accurate enough to pass the stringent round-trip tests. For complex languages, debugging XSLT to that level of accuracy would be very time-consuming.

XML mapping tools, such as BizTalk Mapper, display two tree diagrams side by side, showing the element nesting structures of two XML languages. The user can then drag-and-drop from one tree to the other, to define "mappings" between the two languages, and these mappings are used to generate an XSLT translation between them. However, this simple node-to-node mapping technique does not capture all the ways in which the two XML languages may represent associations; therefore it is not capable of translating association information correctly. For instance, if one language represents an association by shared values, while the other represents the same association by element nesting, tools like BizTalk Mapper cannot do faithful translations in both directions. Since association information is a vital part of XML content, and XML languages represent associations in a wide variety of ways, this means that XML-to-XML mapping tools will fail for many important translation tasks. Furthermore, since these tools require mappings to be defined afresh for each pair of languages, the cost of creating all possible translations between N languages grows as $N*(N-1)$, rather than N.

Therefore the meaning-based automatic translation method, which is enabled by MDL, has major advantages over other available methods of XML translation.

MDL and the Semantic Web

The vision of the Semantic Web is that the information content of web resources should be described in machine-usable terms, so that automatic agents can do useful tasks of finding information, logical inference, and negotiating transactions. Therefore work on the Semantic Web has emphasized tools for describing meanings, such as RDF Schema and DAML +OIL.

The Resource Description Framework (RDF) was developed to describe resources on the web – such as web pages and XML databases. It was designed to say things about what these resources mean – thus the term "semantic" web. It was also designed to say these things in a way that is semantically transparent – so that an automated agent can extract and use information from any RDF document, provided the agent has knowledge of the RDF Schemas used by the RDF. For RDF documents, therefore, access by automated agents is a realizable goal.

However, RDF is designed primarily to represent meta data – information about information resources on the Web. This is how RDF tends to be used, so the semantic transparency and automated processing extends only to meta data in RDF. It is widely recognized (for example, by Tim Berners-Lee in 1999) that XML itself does not have this semantic transparency – precisely because XML can represent meaning in many different ways.

Therefore as it stands, automated agents cannot access the information in (non-RDF) XML documents. They cannot step outside the RDF world to access the information in the bulk of XML documents on the Web. This severely limits the ability of automated agents to access the information they need.
MDL can remove the restriction. If the authors of an XML language define its meaning in MDL, then (as described in previous sections) an automated software agent can access the information in any document in the language – greatly extending the power of automated agents.

We can illustrate this by a typical usage scenario for the Semantic Web. I hear from a friend about some Norwegian ski boots, but do not know the name of the manufacturer. I want to buy them over the Web. My software agent finds the leading ontologies (RDF Schema based) used to describe WWW retail sites. From these ontologies it learns that ski boots are a subclass of footwear and of sports gear; that to buy footwear you need to specify a shoe size. It then inspects the RDF descriptions (meta data) of several online catalogues. The catalogues themselves are accessible in XML, whose MDL definitions are all referenced to the same RDF Schema. From the RDF, my agent identifies those catalogues that contain information about the kind of goods I want.

The agent then needs to retrieve information of the form "footwear from manufacturer based in Norway who makes sports gear" – applying the same retrieval criteria to several XML-based catalogues, which use different XML languages, and very different representations of the associations [manufacturer]makes[product], [manufacturer]based in[country] and so on. The only automated way to make these retrievals is to know the XPaths needed to retrieve the associations from the different XML languages. The MDL definitions of the languages provide just this information, enabling my software agent to retrieve and compare what it needs from the different catalogues.

Thus the agent uses a two-stage process of:

1. Access RDF meta data to find out which catalogues are relevant.

2. Using MDL, access the XML catalogues themselves and extract the required information.

This two-stage process offers much more power than the first enabled by RDF on its own.

In considering the relation of MDL to the semantic web initiative, we should be clear that the relation between MDL and RDF itself is at present a rather remote one. RDF is a notation for describing meta data about the meanings of information resources on the web. RDF-based tools make this information available to human readers in accessible forms, and to automated agents so they can reason about it. In contrast, MDL defines in a formal manner how XML structure conveys meaning. What MDL and RDF share is the need to talk precisely about meaning, and for this they both use ontology formalisms such as RDF Schema and DAML+OIL. There the resemblance ends – as the current applications of RDF are very different from the applications of MDL. Nobody has (to our knowledge) ever used RDF to support a meaning-level query of general data-centric XML documents, or a meaning-level API to XML, or automated translation of XML documents. We have proposed some powerful hybrid applications of RDF and MDL together, but until these are done, the overlap of RDF and MDL in applications is minimal. In summary, realizing the Semantic Web will require not only semantics, but also a bridge between semantics and XML structure. MDL provides that bridge.

MDL and Topic Maps

Readers familiar with topic maps may suppose that there are possible links between MDL and topic maps (see Chapter 7 for more on these). After all, they are both in some sense about meanings. However, as with RDF, the relation between MDL and topic maps (as currently applied) is a remote one.

The dominant use-case of topic maps is to enable people to navigate more effectively around large-scale information resources on the Web – which is completely different from the use-case of MDL, to provide meaning-level, structure-independent access to individual data-centric XML documents. Thus a recent description of topic maps (*"Topic Maps: Introduction and Allegro"* by Dr Hans Holger Rath and Steve Pepper, available from http://www.topicmaps.com/content/resources/mt99/hhr-stp.pdf) has stated:

> *"A topic map annotates and provides organising principles for large-scale information resources. It builds a structured semantic link network above those resources. Topic maps are the GPS of the information universe."*

In their goal of enhanced navigation of large-scale information resources on the web, topic maps overlap strongly with RDF. This high degree of overlap has been frequently remarked upon. The fact that topic maps and RDF are both expressing very similar things with similar purposes, but different syntax, has caused confusion amongst users. Commentators have urged the two technologies to seek convergence, and mappings between the two notations have now been developed to the point that automated translation between RDF and topic maps can be envisaged. If so, users may not need to make a choice.

In their earlier applications, topic maps were not linked to any formal semantics to the same extent as RDF was so linked (through its link to RDF Schema). The emphasis was on making topics useful for people, rather than defining them formally. In the words of a recent presentation on topic maps "a topic can be anything you like". Thus topic maps did not in the first instance use any equivalent of RDF Schema or DAML+OIL to define any formal semantics for the resources they "hover above" and point down to. Given the present convergence between topic maps and RDF, topic map applications can now of course use semantic underpinnings such as RDF Schema if they wish.

To that extent, topic maps and MDL may both use the same semantic underpinnings; but in their use cases, topic maps are far closer to RDF than to MDL. To the author's knowledge, none of the MDL applications described in this chapter have been attempted with topic maps; and it is hard to see how they could be.

Documentation and Validation

There are two other important applications of MDL that we have not described in this chapter, but will briefly mention:

- ❏ The MDL for an XML language serves as a precise form of **documentation** of what the language authors intend it to mean, and how it is intended to convey that meaning. Since the language authors' intentions are not always clear from the schema and associated documentation, this extra documentation can be very useful.

- ❏ Since MDL forms a bridge between meaning and structure, an MDL file can be **validated** against the definition of possible meanings (for example, a DAML+OIL class model), against the definition of XML structure (such as an XSD Schema), or against both together. This validation forms a very useful check that the XML is capable of conveying the meanings that the language authors intended. We have found that in many cases, the XML structure does not match up precisely with the intended meanings; these validation checks will frequently produce useful warnings.

Summary

We can summarize the potential impact of MDL as follows:

> **MDL will enable both applications and users to interface to XML at the level of its meaning, rather than its structure.**

Using MDL, users and application designers need not be concerned with the details of XML structure – with elements, attributes, nesting structure, and paths through a document. They can think purely in terms of the meaning of the document (the objects, properties, and associations it represents) and leave it to MDL-based tools to deal with document structure. These tools will automatically navigate the XPaths necessary to extract meaning from structure.

This meaning-level approach to XML has tremendous advantages – allowing users and developers to think at the level of meaning, which they understand; freeing them from the need to understand XML document structures, which may be extremely complex; and allowing them to develop any application once and then adapt it automatically, via MDL, to new XML languages in its domain.

We believe that as XML languages continue to proliferate, the benefits of the meaning-level approach will become overwhelming. In time, all access to XML documents will move to the level of meaning rather than structure. There are many precedents for this move in the history of programming. There is an almost inevitable tendency to move up from structural, implementation-level tools to application-level, meaning-level development tools. The whole progress from assembler languages to high-level languages, then to "fourth generation" languages, is an example of this trend. Another example comes from databases.

In the 1970s databases were based on a Codasyl navigational model, which exposed a pointer-based database structure to users and application developers. To get at information you had to grapple with database structure, following the pointers. Relational databases and SQL removed this tight structure-dependence of data, enabling us to view data in more structure-independent ways. This was such an advance that it swept the Codasyl database model into history.

In the next few years, we will make similar advances in how we regard XML documents, seeing them in terms of their information content rather than structure. Structure-centric views of XML may become history, just as Codasyl databases are now history. MDL can be the key tool to enable this meaning-level view of XML.

Demonstration programs for the MDL-based meaning-level API to XML, and the meaning-level query language are available (as Java source code and `.jar` files, with sample XML and MDL files) in the code download for this book, and can be run using software freely available from http://xml.apache.org/. Try it out now!

Meta DataProfessionalXMLMeta DataProfessionalXMLMeta DataProfessionalXML

Meta Data Architectures

This chapter introduces some of the architectures of meta data and the techniques for its implementation. As there can be as many different meta data uses as there are schemas, this chapter cannot and does not attempt to provide an exhaustive list of implementation techniques. Instead, we will explore the different ways in which meta data manifests itself "in the wild", and then look at ways in which each of these different manifestations may be required to be put to use, and what kinds of techniques can be used to turn "wild" meta data into productive, "domesticated" meta data.

By the end of this chapter you will have a good grasp of:

❑   The architecture of meta data from the client prospective.

❑   The architecture of meta data from the resource prospective.

❑   The concepts involved in ensuring meta data consistency.

Meta Data Forms

The form of the meta data which is processed by a particular application may be broadly categorized along two different axes. The first of these axes specifies the relationship of the meta data to the resource that it describes – the meta data may be **embedded** within the resource or it may be **external** to the resource. The second axis specifies the relationship of the meta data to the application itself. An application may only be required to deal with a single, **centralized** source of meta data, or it may be required to deal with multiple, **distributed** meta data sources.

Embedded meta data is contained within the body of the resource that it describes. The classic web example of embedded meta data involves the <META> and <TITLE> tags in HTML. In many applications, embedded meta data has the advantage of being extremely simple to create, as the creation of the meta data is often supported by the same tool that is used to create the rest of the resource. For a service, "embedded" means that the service must be contacted directly in order to retrieve the meta data.

External meta data is contained in a data store which is separate from the resource that it describes. The data store for external meta data may be a database application, a flat file, or a structured file format (such as XML). External meta data can be easier to maintain in applications which make use of the meta data for establishing relationships between, or the organization of, a large set of resources. As the meta data can be manipulated and indexed separately from the content, it allows the creation of multiple "views" of the same set of resources without the need to modify the resources themselves. External meta data is also an empowering tool for the consumer of information as it allows them the opportunity to create their own annotations or navigation structures across many different information sources, effectively integrating diverse resources to which they themselves may have no editorial access.

Centralized meta data is retrieved by the application from a single source. Typically this will be some data store which the application will be capable of querying to determine which resources match a particular set of criteria. For example, a document management system may be used to maintain meta data regarding all of the documents stored within it. From the perspective of a client application of that document management system, the meta data is centralized because, to find all documents written by a specific user, say, the client application needs to query just one data store. Another example of centralized meta data would be a **UDDI registry**, which stores "yellow pages", "white pages" that enable a client to locate a service by the service type or service address, and "green pages" which describe the interface of the service. From a client application's viewpoint, a centralized data store is simple to deal with – it is merely a question of knowing how to issue a query and how to interpret the results. In some applications, such as the document management system, meta data is centralized naturally, as the domain to which the meta data applies is also centralized. However, in other situations, in order to provide the client with the convenience of a centralized meta data store, it is necessary for the provider of that store to aggregate meta data from a distributed set of stores. For example, a web search engine provides the user with a single interface from which she may query some large number of web pages to determine which of those web pages have meta data which match her search criteria. A centralized meta data store such as a web search engine means that individual web browsers do not need to attempt to query every page on the Web for matches, but this functionality comes at a cost – the search engine provider must extract and aggregate the meta data from many millions of web pages.

From the client application's viewpoint, meta data is distributed if it is retrieved from multiple data stores. Working with multiple stores places an extra workload on the client, which must be capable of establishing multiple query sessions with the data stores and also must be able to combine the results from each of the data stores it queries before presenting the results to the user. This additional overhead may seem unnecessary if it is possible to aggregate all of the meta data in a single store, but this is not always possible – for example if the domains of the data are sufficiently different, it may not be possible for one data store to completely index meta data from both domains. For example, a company would not index its sensitive internal documents on a publicly accessible Internet search engine – but neither would such a company be likely to provide the resources for a private index of the Web, so an application wishing to search both the local intranet and the Internet must work with distributed meta data sources.

When considering these two axes together, it is clear that embedded meta data must, by its nature, be distributed from the point of view of the client application, as the meta data will be contained within a set of resources which themselves are distributed with respect to the client application. Combining centralized and embedded meta data would mean that the application only ever has access to a single resource providing both content and meta data in a single stream – it is unlikely that any processing application will deal with a single data resource with embedded meta data. External meta data may be either distributed across multiple resources, for example multiple **RDF Site Summary (RSS)** channels, or centralized within a single data store, which may have been generated, for example, as the result of aggregating distributed meta data channels.

Assuming that centralized, embedded meta data is an outside case of little interest we can therefore identify three forms of meta data that may be of interest to a processing application:

❑ Embedded meta data (for example, the <META> tags in HTML pages, or **Resource Directory Description Language (RDDL)** links contained within XHTML documents).

❑ Distributed, external meta data (for example, RSS, RDF annotations for web pages).

❑ Centralized, external meta data (for example, a UDDI registry).

These classifications are shown in the figure below:

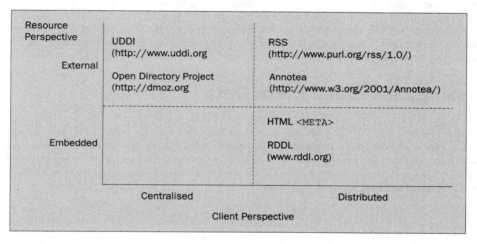

The rest of this chapter will use the three-way classification developed here to present some of the challenges in building meta data applications and some possible approaches to dealing with those challenges.

Embedded Meta Data

Due to its co-location with the resource, embedded meta data is most easily put to use in the presentation of content or the description of services. For an application that is already capable of accessing and processing the content of a resource, making use of the embedded meta data should be a relatively easy task, as the format is recognized and parse-able. However, to be able to provide navigation or search capabilities, an application must be capable of relating the meta data of the resource being processed to the meta data of the other resources available. In other words, the application needs access to some form of meta data index. What this means in practice is that an application which only has access to meta data embedded in a single resource is restricted to one of the following activities:

❑ Modifying the presentation of the resource based on the embedded meta data, for example by hiding content which is not relevant to the user.

❑ Retrieving additional resources indicated by the meta data, such as a schema against which the content can be validated.

❑ Storing the meta data into an index for later retrieval.

Creating Embedded Meta Data

For manually created or resource-specific meta data, a distributed, embedded meta data structure is usually the easiest to create and maintain – applications can be tailored to prompt the user to supply meta data values or could even be used to extract meta data values from the content automatically. By embedding the meta data within the content, the meta data becomes independent of location and so less liable to being broken by a physical reorganization of content files than external meta data.

The benefit of having the meta data embedded within the resource it describes can also be a liability. The principle difficulty with embedded meta data is that it is not possible to modify the meta data without having access to modify the content. Additionally, the embedded meta data vocabulary tends to be inextricably intertwined with the format of the content – the notable exception to this being the case of an application of XML that makes use of XML namespaces. Because the content and meta data formats are linked in this way, it may be difficult or impossible to add new meta data fields or modify the data types in existing fields without breaking the applications that read and write the content format.

Processing Embedded Meta Data

Despite such restrictions, the processing of embedded meta data can still enable a wide range of application features, such as the filtering of content based on user preferences or device capabilities. A very simple form of embedded meta data is provided in HTML by the <META> tag. The <META> tag has two attributes: name, which is typically used to define the meta data property being assigned, and content, which is typically used to define the value of that meta data property. For example a keyword list for a web page may be defined as follows:

```
<HTML>
  <HEAD>
    <META name="keywords" content="topic maps, rdf, meta data"/>
    ...
  </HEAD>
  ...
</HTML>
```

The value of the name attribute specifies an element of a shared vocabulary for HTML processing applications – to a processing application, the content attribute of a <META> tag with a name attribute of "keywords" specifies a list of words and phrases which may be used to index the content of the page. The keyword list on its own is of little use to a local processing application because, taken in isolation, the keywords are only a (very rough) guide to the content of the page. However, if the application has access to an aggregated index of keyword values for a set of other resources, the keywords embedded in any one HTML page could easily be used to create a query for other pages which have keywords in common with it. In contrast, the <META> tag may also be used to convey information such as the character encoding used in the file – this is vital information that enables the application to correctly present the page content.

The HTML <META> tag can also be used as a simple mechanism for embedding more complex RDF meta data within the content of the HTML file. The following example shows the use of the <META> tag to store some Dublin Core meta data within an HTML page:

```
<HTML>
  <HEAD>
    <LINK REL="schema.DC" href="http://purl.org/DC/elements/1.1/">
```

```
        <META NAME="DC.creator" content="Smith, John"/>
        <META NAME="DC.title" content="Financial Results 1999-2000"/>
        <META NAME="DC.description" content="Financial results of MyCorp
                for the fiscal year 1999-2000"/>
        <META NAME="DC.date" content="2001-01-03"/>
    </HEAD>
    ...
</HTML>
```

If the HTML page has the URL http://www.mycorp.com/financials.html, then the equivalent RDF in its XML interchange syntax would be as follows:

```
<?xml version="1.0"?>
<rdf:RDF xmlns:rdf="http://www.w3.org/1999/02/22-rdf-syntax-ns#"
         xmlns:dc="http://purl.org/dc/elements/1.1/">

  <rdf:description about="http://www.mycorp.com/financials.html">
    <dc:creator>Smith, John</dc:creator>
    <dc:title>Financial Results 1999-2000</dc:title>
    <dc:description>Financial results of MyCorp for the fiscal year
                1999-2000</dc:description>
    <dc:date>2001-01-03</dc:date>
  </rdf:description>
</rdf:RDF>
```

Another example of the use of meta data embedded within document content can be found in the Resource Directory Description Language (RDDL, see http://www.rddl.org). RDDL is a modular extension to the XHTML specification that enables hyperlinks within a document to be supplemented with meta data regarding the resource being linked to. Because an RDDL description is associated with a hyperlink, it is possible to use RDDL as a form of external meta data (after all, it is providing information regarding the resource at the other end of the link). In fact, if a document consisted entirely of RDDL links it could be seen as a data store of external meta data. However, there are aspects to RDDL that enable it to be used for modifying the presentation of the hyperlink within the source document, and so the RDDL description acts as embedded meta data.

RDDL defines a meta data vocabulary, which enables the description of both the nature and the purpose of a hyperlink. The **nature** of the RDDL link is defined using the xlink:role attribute of the link. This attribute value provides a machine-readable description of what the resource at the other end of the link actually is. The value of this attribute must be a URI that describes the resource type so that it can give some clue to a processing application as to the kind of resource being linked to. If the resource is an XML resource using a vocabulary for which a namespace is defined, then the namespace URI should be used. For other, non-XML, resources that can be adequately defined by their MIME type, the MIME type may be encoded as a URI and used to describe the resource nature. If the link is provided for some form of identification purposes, then the nature attribute may be used to define the kind of entity being identified.

The **purpose** of the RDDL link is specified using the xlink:arcrole attribute of the RDDL link. Again, the value of this attribute must be a URI, which defines the purpose of the link. The RDDL specification contains links to a set of well-known natures and purposes, which a processing application may be expected to recognize. The following example shows an XHTML document containing three RDDL links:

```
<html
  xmlns:rddl="http://www.rddl.org/"
  xmlns:xlink="http://www.w3.org/1999/xlink">
  <body>
    <p>The
      <!-- Link to the XTM specification -->
      <rddl:resource
          xlink:role="http://www.w3.org/TR/xhtml1/DTD/xhtml1-transitional"
          xlink:arcrole="http://www.rddl.org/purposes#normative-reference"
          xlink:href="http://www.topicmaps.org/xtm/1.0/"
          xlink:title="XTM 1.0 Specification"
          xlink:type="simple">
        XTM 1.0 specification
      </rddl:resource>
      and
      <!-- Link to the XTM DTD -->
      <rddl:resource
          xlink:role="http://www.isi.edu/in-notes/iana/assignments/media-
types/application/xml-dtd"
          xlink:arcrole="http://www.rddl.org/purposes#validation"
          xlink:href="http://www.topicmaps.org/xtm/1.0/#dtd"
          xlink:title="XTM 1.0 DTD"
          xlink:type="simple">
        DTD
      </rddl:resource>
      are defined by
      <!-- Reference to TopicMaps.Org -->
      <rddl:resource
          xlink:role="http://www.myontology.org/organization"
          xlink:arcrole="http://www.myontology.org/organization#homepage"
          xlink:href="http://www.topicmaps.org/"
          xlink:title="Topicmaps.Org"
          xlink:type="simple">
        TopicMaps.Org
      </rddl:resource>
    </p>
  </body>
</html>
```

The first RDDL resource in this fragment is identified as being an HTML page which conforms to the XHTML transitional DTD (xlink:role="http://www.w3.org/TR/xhtml1/DTD/xhtml1-transitional") and which provides a normative reference – asserting that it is a link to the text of a standard (xlink:arcrole="http://www.rddl.org/purposes#normative-reference").

The second resource is identified as being an XML DTD by using the MIME type "application/xml-dtd" encoded into the xlink:role URL (xlink:role="http://www.isi.edu/in-notes/iana/assignments/media-types/application/xml-dtd"). The xlink:arcrole attribute uses another URI defined by RDDL.org to specify that the resource may be used for validation purposes (xlink:arcrole="http://www.rddl.org/purposes#validation").

The final resource uses another ontology to define that the reference is used to identify a specific organization (xlink:role="http://www.myontology.org/organization") and that the link can be traversed to retrieve the homepage of that organization (xlink:arcrole="http://www.myontology.org/organization#homepage").

An RDDL-aware application may make use of the embedded meta data provided by the above example to categorize the referenced resources (for example making it easy to pick out all links which are to an organization) or to provide additional processing based on the resource nature or purpose (for example by opening the DTD in a different application).

Aggregating Embedded Meta Data

The usefulness of embedded meta data in isolation is very much restricted to a modification of either the way in which the application behaves (by causing it to retrieve additional resources) or the way in which the application presents the resource. Other application features such as enhanced search and navigation capability require that the meta data of all resources to be searched or navigated be accessible to the user agent, and typically that means that the meta data needs to be aggregated into a centralized meta data repository which is external to the resource itself. The process of converting the embedded meta data within a set of resources into a meta data repository involves four steps:

- ❑ Discovery (location of a resource with embedded meta data).
- ❑ Extraction (teasing out the meta data from the content).
- ❑ Conversion (combining diverse vocabularies into a single consistent vocabulary).
- ❑ Output (creating the data store in the form required).

Discovery is the process by which resources containing embedded meta data are located. The discovery process may be guided by an external agent that knows the location of such a resource (for example a user browsing the file system) or it may require an automated trawl of a set of resources by techniques such as a recursive walk through directories in a file-system or a set of web pages.

Extraction is the process of filtering out the meta data from the resource content. As the meta data is embedded within the resource content, extraction requires some knowledge of the content format – so there are at least as many potential extraction processes as there are file formats. Structured information formats such as XML make easier targets for extraction than most, as the format is standardized; the markup contained within the document can specify the semantics of the content; and parsers for the format are freely and widely available. However, the nature of the XML format means that without knowledge of the resource document's definition (its DTD or schema), determining which tags are meta data and which are content is a guessing game. So for XML we are faced with the need to create as many extraction processes as there are DTDs or schemas; although with the common data format of XML, the extraction processes for each schema may in fact be implemented using the same set of tools based on standard XML querying and access technologies, such as XPath.

When dealing with resources of multiple forms, the chances are that the meta data vocabularies used by the different resource formats will not correlate either with each other or with the requirements of the processing application. For example, one format may provide a single field for the author's name whereas a different format has separate fields for forename and surname. If this is the case, then two options are open to the application designer. The first option is to store the meta data values in their original vocabularies and to use run-time processing to infer equivalence between different vocabularies. However, if the application designer chooses instead to map all of the different meta data vocabularies to a single common vocabulary, then a **conversion** stage is required. A conversion stage may also be required if the meta data specified on the processed resources is not consistently defined – for example if one user has specified their name as "Smith, John" and another as "Joan Smithers". The conversion stage of the aggregation process attempts to turn the raw meta data into quality meta data by enforcing a degree of consistency amongst possibly diverse meta data vocabularies and meta data instances. Conversion can include simple lexical tasks such as splitting single values into multiple values on some separator string, forcing string values to a single case, or formatting real numbers to a specific precision.

However, conversion can also require far more complex tasks such as recognizing multiple forms of the same name, date format conversions, and extraction of multiple meta data values from a single structured meta data value such as an address. It should be noted here that the issue of dealing with meta data in multiple forms is not a new one; these are issues that need to be addressed in the integration of data sources for data warehousing or online analytical processing (OLAP) applications.

Output is the process of adding the extracted meta data to a repository. If storing the extracted meta data using a single common vocabulary, then at this stage, the equivalences between the vocabularies must be correctly mapped into the common vocabulary, for example mapping a `"zip code"` property from one set of meta data to the `"postal code"` property in another set; and when common subject identity for different resources must also be established, for example, determining when two different documents are about the same subject. If, on the other hand, the application is to perform this kind of inference at run-time then it is sufficient that the output stage of the process simply concerns itself with correctly storing the meta data into whatever repository is being used. The meta data repository may be an XML meta data format such as RDF or XTM, a simple text file, or an application such as a relational database or a spreadsheet application.

Each stage of the process of aggregation can be done independently of the preceding and following steps – a software module capable of extracting meta data from a particular graphics file format should be able to feed a process which will eventually create an RDF file, just as well as a process which generates an XTM file or one which populates a relational database. The extraction process should not be concerned with the final format of the meta data repository, nor should the conversion process necessarily be concerned with the source of meta data – forcing a string to a single case, reformatting dates and numbers, and extracting multiple values from single fields can all be done irrespective of the format of the original data. And for all of these processes, whether the resource was discovered by web crawling, directory recursion or a user-specified file name is irrelevant to the remainder of the process as long as the resource address is made available to later stages for the purpose of assigning processed meta data properties to it. In other words, by decoupling the stages of discovery, extraction, conversion and output we can focus on creating reusable software components with which we can build an unlimited number of meta data processing utilities. However, for all of these components to interconnect, what is required is a framework within which the interface between the components is defined. An example of this is the **Meta Data Processing Framework** (**MDF** – see http://www.techquila.com/mdf.html for more information), which is described in Chapter 10.

Centralized External Meta Data

As discussed in the previous section, with access only to the embedded meta data in a single resource, the kinds of processing that can be performed with that meta data are limited to either modifying the presentation of the resource or retrieving related resources. To apply meta data to the tasks of locating a resource or service, or to the navigation of a set of resources, the overhead of visiting each potential resource in turn and extracting and processing the meta data within it would make an application based solely on embedded meta data non-scalable. To address these requirements, the meta data from a set of resources must be extracted and aggregated into a collection, where it becomes possible to query the collection to locate resources by their meta data properties and also to establish relationships between resources that might otherwise have no reference to each other, based on commonalities in their meta data.

Meta Data Centralization Architectures

The process of meta data aggregation has been described above. This section addresses the means by which we can aggregate the meta data and the ways in which the aggregated meta data can be stored.

XML meta data applications may be designed and implemented in much the same way as meta data applications that deal with meta data in a non-XML form. It is instructive when considering a centralized approach to meta data applications to consider the existing data warehousing application architectures.

The approach taken by a **data warehousing** application is to physically centralize the data in a single data store. Data is extracted from a set of distributed meta data sources and cleaned to make it consistent with the vocabulary and datatyping used by the data warehouse before it is inserted. A user wishing to query the meta data then makes a query directly against this centralized store. A modular approach to aggregating meta data as described above could be applied in building the data warehouse from a wide variety of meta data sources.

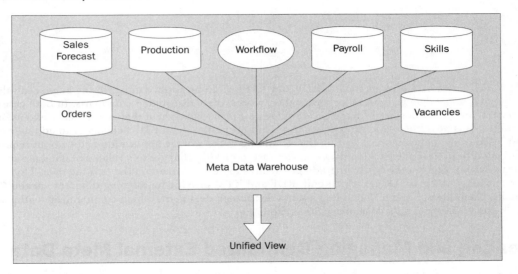

A **data mart** is a smaller, more localized version of a data warehouse, which provides its users with a view over a subset of all available meta data. Data warehouses tend to be large both in terms of their use of physical resources and the time and effort required to successfully implement them. A useful data mart, on the other hand, may be constructed by integrating far fewer distributed sources of meta data and yet still provide value to a group of users in one particular functional area of the business. For example, the technical documentation department may want to see project schedules and statuses, outstanding development tasks such as bug fixes, lead times from suppliers such as translation houses and so on, but would be far less concerned with sales figures or forecasts or payroll information. A data mart for these users would provide them with an integrated view of the information they need to do their work without the overhead of a much larger data warehouse.

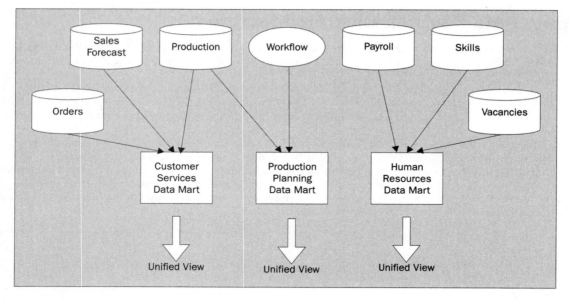

The XML meta data formats such as RDF and XTM could be applied either to the huge, centralized approach of the data warehouse or the smaller, more widely distributed data marts. In both cases, constructing the data store is made easier by using a meta data format that enables easy extension of the schema. It is possible to add or extend classes and properties in an RDF Schema or to add new topics to an XTM topic map without requiring the rebuilding of the storage application and without requiring any modification to the existing data – in contrast to making changes to a relational database schema which may require some costly upgrade procedures to be performed on the existing data. This extensibility and the facilities which both RDF and XTM provide for aligning different vocabularies makes them ideally suited to building a set of distributed data marts which communicate with clients using an XML meta data vocabulary (or vocabularies).

Creating and Managing Centralized External Meta Data

Centralizing the meta data from a set of distributed resources may be done by one of two processes.

- ❑ Aggregation of distributed meta data.
- ❑ Centralized querying of distributed meta data.

Creating and Managing Meta Data by Aggregation

Aggregation of distributed meta data is best applied when the meta data to be aggregated is embedded within the contents it describes or when the meta data is centralized already but not query-able by client applications. The process of aggregation has already been described in the section *Aggregating Embedded Meta Data*, above.

In creating centralized meta data, whether that may be in the form of a single data warehouse-style meta data store or a set of distributed data mart-style stores, the principal problem is maintaining the link between the meta data and the resource that it describes. In some environments (such as a document management system), it may be possible to assign some persistent unique identifier to the resources described which are immutable even if the document changes its location within the repository, although resolving the persistent identifier to the actual resource may involve additional lookups. In other cases, such as a file-system, a document's location is the only form of unique identification that can be provided by the underlying repository. In either case, the location of the resource is not the only property that a centralized system must be concerned with – changes to the resource content could require that changes to the meta data be made and deletion of the resource may require the associated meta data to be deleted or modified to indicate that the resource is no longer available.

When the centralized meta data store is aggregating meta data from multiple, distributed repositories, the use of formal update processes and/or workflow applications can provide the structure for ensuring that meta data is updated if resource content is altered. Alternatively, a distributed messaging infrastructure could be applied to ensure that the meta data repository is notified of changes in resource repositories – although how the meta data repository makes use of this notification may be constrained by the processing or interaction required to update the meta data. In the absence of workflow or messaging systems, a centralized solution may have to rely on the periodic update of the centralized meta data by a process of locating and extracting up-to-date embedded meta data from resources.

When aggregating meta data into a central location, the way in which that meta data will be stored must be addressed. Options for storing centralized meta data include:

- ❏ Meta data-specific schema in a database.
- ❏ RDF or XTM in an XML file.
- ❏ An RDF or XTM database.

Let's look at the pros and cons of each of these approaches in turn.

Meta Data-Specific Database Schema

The traditional way of storing meta data has been to create a schema for the meta data vocabulary in the relational or object-oriented database of choice. This approach is attractive because it is a well-understood, tried-and-trusted approach to meta data management. Additionally it is relatively easy to define a mapping from a given RDF schema into a database schema and to create interfaces for loading and extracting data in RDF format. However, each time the RDF schema is altered or a new RDF schema is introduced, the database schema will need to be updated and any existing data migrated to the new schema.

In a closed environment in which the modification of existing vocabularies and the overall rate of change in the vocabularies is slow, creating database schemas which are specific to particular meta data vocabularies may continue to provide the desired functionality. However, this approach is becoming less viable in a world of rapidly evolving meta data vocabularies and will continue to be less viable as the Semantic Web, upon which automated agents will freely interchange meta data in a wide variety of vocabularies, augments the World Wide Web.

What is needed instead is an extensible data model for the definition of vocabularies and the storage of meta data using those vocabularies. Such a data model would enable a wide range of different vocabularies to be stored using the same underlying database schema. It is this data model which is provided by both RDF and XTM.

RDF or XTM In an XML File

Both RDF and XTM provide a more flexible means of defining meta data vocabularies – these standards define a data model for creating meta data vocabularies (RDF in terms of subject-predicate-object triples and XTM in terms of topics, occurrences and associations) and they define an interchange syntax for that data model which enables both the vocabulary definition and instance of the vocabulary to be serialized into XML syntax. As querying and transformation facilities for XML either already exist or are in preparation in the form of XQuery and XSLT, it is tempting to believe that it would be possible to create a searchable meta data repository simply by storing RDF or XTM in its XML form and then using standard XML query or transformation tools to extract meta data from it. In practice such an approach is non-trivial to implement and non-scalable. While both RDF and XTM can be serialized into an XML file, both standards define a data model based upon a mathematical graph and both standards also define a degree of additional semantics beyond that of the graph concepts of nodes and arcs. The data models defined by RDF and XTM are not easily processed directly from their XML representations, nor are the XML representations of them easily queried with standard XML tools such as XPath processors or XSLT transforms.

As an example of the difficulty in querying the data model of a meta data standard, consider the case of the XTM standard. A processing application providing query operations on data in the XML serialization of XTM must also be capable of determining which topics in the topic map need to be merged when they represent the same subject, according to the rules laid out by the XTM specification. This constraint is not enforced by the XML syntax (it is perfectly allowable, and indeed sometimes desirable, to have two or more <topic> elements which represent the same subject), and so to query an XML representation of the topic map directly, the query must be encoded in such a way that it not only locates the topic which matches the query constraints, but that it also locates all topics which would be merged with that topic (and ideally it should also perform the merge).

A case can be made for creating an application that reads an XML serialization of RDF or XTM to build a data model in memory, which may then be queried through the application, although to do this leaves the problems of safely updating the data model and of ensuring that updates are eventually written back to the file. An architecture such as this would be suitable for a single-user application but would not be applicable to a multi-user environment.

RDF or XTM Schema in a Database

As already stated, both RDF and XTM define a data model within which vocabularies may be constructed and meta data instances using those vocabularies can be defined. Either of these data models may be implemented as a schema for a relational or object-oriented database. The advantage of defining a schema for either the RDF or XTM data model is that a database using such a schema will be able to store any meta data expressed using the supported data model. In addition, applications built on a DBMS will be able to make use of support for transaction control, data integrity and support in a multi-user environment, which the underlying database provides.

Databases for storing and managing both RDF and XTM are already available both commercially and from open-source projects and any developer considering building a large or multi-user application for the processing and persistent storage of centralized meta data should consider using a specialized RDF or XTM database such as RDFDB (http://web1.guha.com/rdfdb/) or the persistent storage backend of TM4J (http://tm4j.sourceforge.net).

Creating and Managing Meta Data by Centralized Querying

If the distributed meta data sources to be centralized are query-able (for example, if the meta data exists in a collection of database or content management applications), then an alternative approach to aggregating the meta data into yet another data store is to provide a unified query interface to those meta data stores. Such an interface would be responsible for reflecting the meta data of each of the underlying stores in a single unified model of all of the resources described by those stores. This "data hub" interface (shown in the figure below) would be required to translate from queries made against that model into queries against the underlying data stores; and then to translate the results received from those stores into a unified query result expressed in the XML meta data syntax expected by the client. With a wide variety of potential meta data sources, a data hub may use a modular system of wrappers for each of the data sources it integrates, which serve to isolate the data hub application from the differences in access to the different data sources.

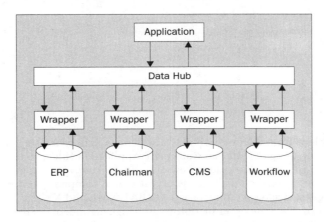

This architecture has the advantage of eliminating the problem of maintaining an up-to-date correspondence between the centralized meta data and the distributed resources that the meta data describes. The cost of such an architecture is firstly in the additional time required to design and implement such a system or to upgrade it when a new data system is introduced or an existing one is modified; and secondly there is a runtime cost in performing queries against multiple systems plus the overhead of combining the results – all of which must be borne by the data hub and client application, rather than being delegated to an off-line batch process as is possible when aggregating the meta data to a separate store. However, by careful design of the wrapper functions to be as configurable as possible and to provide caching or other forms of performance enhancements it is possible to reduce the size of these overheads.

Distributed External Meta Data

As with centralized meta data, a distributed external meta data model may be used to provide querying, navigation and service access functionality. The extent of the distribution will affect the ways in which some of these additional features may be exploited. A distributed meta data system that maintains a one-to-one relationship between meta data sources and the resources described may be no easier to manage than distributed embedded meta data. However, as we are considering distribution from the point of view of an application, it can be said that any application which deals with more than one source of meta data is dealing with "distributed" meta data – it is this situation where there are a number of meta data sources each storing meta data regarding a number of (possibly overlapping) resources, which we will primarily deal with in this section.

The difference between a centralized meta data store which deals with multiple, distributed meta data repositories and a distributed external meta data application is shown in the following diagram. Put simply, if a meta data repository aggregates content from multiple meta data stores, then the meta data repository treats the data as distributed, external meta data. However, a client accessing that server has a single service to query for meta data, so to the client, the meta data repository is a centralized external meta data repository.

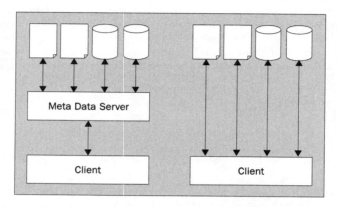

Once again taking a lead from the established world of meta data processing, a distributed XML meta data application may be designed after an **Enterprise Application Integration (EAI)** architecture. A key goal of EAI is to develop a new, integrated view of business data. This is typically achieved without aggregating the data but instead by making use of distributed computing technologies such as the **Common Object Request Broker Architecture (CORBA)**. XML and XML schema play strongly in the field of EAI as they provide a means of platform- and language-independent message encoding. Both RDF and topic maps can be used to encode an additional level of integration to an EAI architecture by allowing individual database schemas to be directly related to each other or to be related to a common business model which describes the business in terms of entities and relationships which are separate from the data systems that describe them.

By enabling applications to deal with distributed meta data stores, we can increase the diversity of sources from which meta data may be received. We may, for example, choose to receive meta data from sources that are not under our own control and combine it with our own meta data, thus enlarging and enriching our world-view. Alternatively, distribution of meta data sources might be applied to reduce the amount of distributed embedded meta data that any single meta data source must aggregate. The issues relating to the creation and management of distributed external meta data are similar to those for the creation of centralized meta data. A highly distributed meta data system may enable each meta data store in that system to have much closer control over the resources about which it maintains the meta data. For example, a client application which is capable of querying a set of distributed data mart-style meta data stores could construct its own "virtual" data warehouse by a process of combining the meta data from the distributed sources (see the figure below).

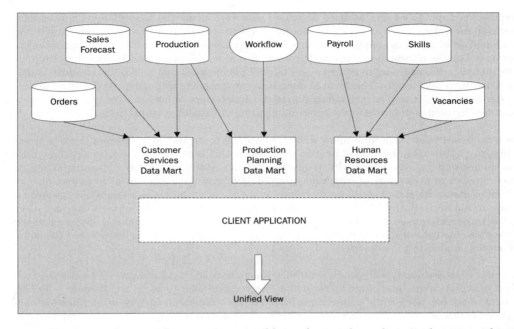

Unified View

However, distributing the meta data stores raises additional issues for a client application wishing to read or query the meta data. The main issues are:

❑   Locating sources of meta data.

❑   Combining query results.

Locating Sources of Meta Data

Distributed meta data architectures may embrace distribution of many different forms. The most common form of distributed architecture is simple client-server architecture. Most client applications will interact with a meta data source by issuing queries to a single source and receiving responses from it. With this type of architecture, standard forms of server location may be used, such as defining a static list of servers on the client, by using a broker architecture such as CORBA to locate a meta data source, or by using a central registry to lookup available sources.

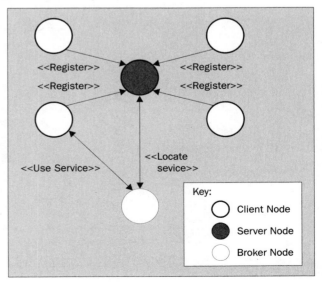

Client-server approaches such as those described above are all appropriate when the number of potential sources of meta data which a client may require access to at any one time are relatively small (such as a distributed set of data mart applications) or when an application knows which meta data source will provide it with the information it needs. However, in a more distributed environment, it is more likely that a client application will want to issue a query to multiple meta data sources simultaneously and to aggregate the results locally. This form of querying is an integral part of peer-to-peer applications such as Napster and Gnutella, and so an examination of the architecture of peer-to-peer systems may prove instructive in the design of meta data applications using distributed external meta data.

The term peer-to-peer is used in many different contexts to mean many different types of system architecture. However, the type of peer-to-peer system that is of interest to us for distributed external meta data systems is a system in which individual clients issue a query that is disseminated across an entire network of nodes, any of which may provide a response. In this way a client may query a very rich set of meta data sources without the need for the client to know the address of each and every source on the network. In this sense, such an architecture is very similar to the broker architecture of CORBA, the difference being that in a peer-to-peer system, even if a client does have a single point of contact into the network, it is not necessary that the node which serves as the point of contact knows all of the other nodes on the network.

An application architecture in which centralized meta data sources pass queries from server to server on behalf of a particular client could be termed a "hierarchical peer-to-peer" architecture – there is an element of peer-to-peer in the connections between the servers, but each client application connects to a single server as its point of contact into the network of meta data sources. Such an architecture combines the convenience for the client of needing to contact and communicate with only one server with the convenience of distributing the task of meta data aggregation across a number of servers. Note that in this architecture, any given client node must know the address of the server node which forms its point of contact for the network, but that server node does not need to be connected to every other node in the network as queries are disseminated amongst the peer nodes in the network.

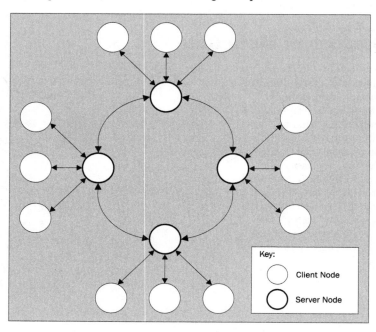

A true peer-to-peer architecture, such as that shown in the figure below, may also be applied to radically reduce the degree of centralization in a meta data application architecture by making each networked client a server of the meta data that it has aggregated from the local machine. While such application architectures are relatively new and not yet widely implemented in commercial applications, the current interest in peer-to-peer architectures and in meta data processing promises to result in this form of distributed meta data architecture becoming more prevalent. The diagram below shows the architectural difference between a hierarchical peer-to-peer system and a true peer-to-peer system. In this system there is no distinction between nodes which generate queries and nodes which provide answers – any node may be a source of both queries and results sets. Additionally, each node need not be aware of every other node in the network – as long as queries are passed from node to node, a query will eventually travel to all parts of the network to seek its results set.

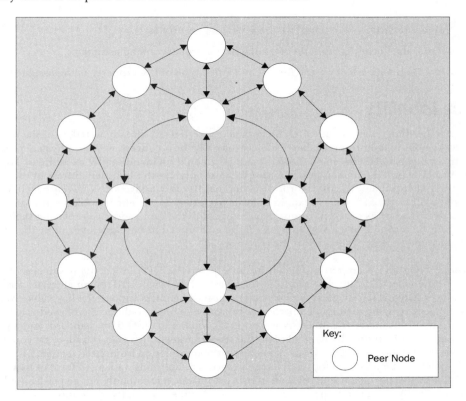

Implementing efficient distributed query systems is still an area of active research in the peer-to-peer community. Issues such as result caching, minimizing the bandwidth used, and minimizing the number of nodes contacted to complete a query are still to be resolved for this form of architecture. Additionally, if a query is issued to multiple sources, it is quite possible that different results will be received from each source, based on the meta data that has been aggregated at that source.

The ability of the client application to intelligently combine the results depends on a number of factors including the correct determination of subject identity and the combination of diverse vocabularies. These issues are covered in the next section.

Consistency in Meta Data Applications

Meta data is commonly defined as "data about data" – that is, meta data defines the properties of resources, which we typically consider to be data files such as word processor documents, web pages, graphics files, MP3 music files, and so on. However, a more accurate definition of meta data would be "*All data and knowledge providing information about processes, data and entities*". We are used to referring to file resources by URIs, but the Semantic Web will require us to unambiguously identify not only files, but also services, processes and non-electronic entities such as people and organizations.

To enable our applications to behave consistently with this wide diversity of resources, we need to be consistent about three things:

❑ **Subject Identity** – the 'thing' we are giving a property to.

❑ **Meta Data Vocabularies** – the meaning of the property being assigned.

❑ **Meta Data Consistency** – the format and value type of the property being assigned.

Subject Identity

A subject is anything at all about which meta data is asserted. As already noted, subjects may be digital resources or non-digital resources, but a subject may also be a concept with no physical presence (such as a company). A subject that is retrievable via a URI could be identified by its address. To talk about a specific machine or a document on a web site, I can simply use the Internet address of the machine or document in question and the rules for formatting that Internet address as a URI are well-known. Address-based resource identifiers can, in themselves, cause consistency problems as a resource is modified over time or as different resources are copied to the same address (replacing the original resource). If the resource at a given address can be guaranteed to be stable over time, then the address is a suitable candidate for the identity of the resource.

However, not all subjects are retrievable via a stable, persistent URI. In fact many subjects of interest cannot be stored electronically and so will never be retrievable via a URI. So an alternate approach to determining identity is to rely on an authoritative registry of entities and use the key value from that registry. For example the identity of a particular imprint of a book could be established using its ISBN number, a country could be identified by its two-letter code in the ISO 3166 standard, and a public company could be identified by its symbol on the stock-market on which it is traded. Of course, to be able to use such information, a standard way of encoding the information from these registries is required. In practice a URI can be used, but for interchange purposes establishing an agreed form of that URI is critical. While this may be a useful solution in many domains, it is certainly not generally applicable for two reasons. Firstly, not everything has such a unique identifier. Secondly, the entity may have a number of these unique properties, which means that there is the potential for one entity to have multiple identifiers and an application should be able to map multiple identifiers to a single entity correctly.

Another way to identify a subject is to simply describe it – this is the means by which humans have always communicated subjects to other humans and is a natural way to identify a subject when the final interpreter of that subject is intended to be another person. Of course, what constitutes an unambiguous description of a subject will vary from one application context to another. To my bank I am probably best described by my account details, whereas to members of my family a photograph would probably be sufficient to establish my identity.

In summary, a subject may be identified in one of three ways:

❑ If the subject is a retrievable resource and the address of that resource is stable, use the resource address.

❑ Use a URI that identifies the subject (but does not necessarily resolve to any resource).

❑ Use the address of a retrievable resource that unambiguously describes the subject.

In some applications it may be necessary to combine multiple identifiers of different types in order to establish an identity that is portable across multiple systems. In this case, the question of determining when two identifiers indicate the same subject arises.

Determining Subject Equality

Whatever the form of subject identification we use, we must also determine what rules will be used to establish when two identifiers indicate the same subject. In XTM, rules are already provided in the specification for doing this (and are covered elsewhere in this book); however, in general we can break down the different approaches to determining subject equality as follows:

❑ Identifier equality.

❑ Identifier equivalence.

❑ Subject description equivalence.

Identifier Equality

Resolution of subject identity based on formal identifiers can be most easily done by simple lexical comparison – if two URIs are identical, then they indicate the same subject. This approach is disarmingly simple, but must be used with care as it conceals two major problems.

The first problem is that this approach requires that every individual creating an identifier for a specific subject choose the same identifier. However, if we allow a single subject to be indicated by multiple identifiers, then we introduce the possibility of creating "mediating" representations of the subject which aggregate multiple identifiers for the subject – this means that if one person chooses identifier A for a subject and another person chooses identifier B for the same subject, then a third party can indicate that equivalence by simply creating a representation of that subject with both identities.

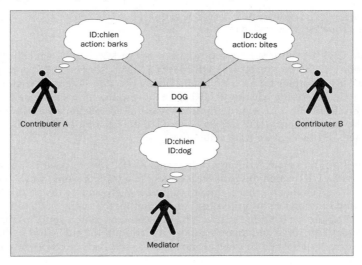

The second problem with this approach is that when a URI is used to signify something other than the real source it resolves to, such as a concept which is described by the resource, then there is always a possibility that the same URI can be used by different people to indicate different things. For example, Alice uses the URI http://www.w3.org/TR/REC-xml as the identifier for the subject "The XML Recommendation", but Bob uses the same URI to identify the subject "XML" and Charlie uses the same one again to represent the concept "Markup Languages". Each user can claim that the URI does indicate their chosen subject. All of this is not to say that using a URI to indicate a subject is wrong – in fact, in a closed domain with an agreed interpretation for the URIs, this approach is valid and useful.

Identifier Equivalence

Moving beyond simple lexical comparison of identifiers, some identifiers may be computable as being equivalent. For example, both an International Standard Book Number (ISBN) and a Library of Congress Catalog Card Number can be assigned to the same book. An application with access to a registry of the mapping between ISBN and Library of Congress identifiers could determine that two identifiers indicate the same book, even if they are expressed in terms of different cataloging systems.

Subject Description Equivalence

When a subject is described by a resource (for example in prose text or a picture), the final arbiter of equivalence between two subjects can only be the human being who is the end user of the information. As with all forms of communication, it is important that the creator of the subject description gauges the level of the audience and creates or chose a subject descriptor that is as unambiguous as possible in order to minimize the possibility of being misinterpreted.

Subject Identity in RDF and XTM

Both RDF and XTM use URIs to identify subjects, which are addressable and retrievable via current Internet technologies. In RDF the URI may be the subject or object in an RDF statement and in XTM the URI may be used to define the subject of the topic. The difference between RDF and XTM is in the way in which non-addressable subjects (those which cannot be retrieved by a URI) are specified.

In RDF, there is no distinction made between a URI that resolves to the resource being described and a URI which cannot be resolved to a resource but is instead a unique label for the subject. So a statement such as:

```
http://www.techquila.com/index.html written-by
http://www.techquila.com/people/kal
```

mixes a resolvable URI (`http://www.techquila.com/index.html`), which is the resource to which the meta data applies, and a non-resolvable URI (`http://www.techquila.com/people/kal`), which is simply a URI identifier for an individual. Taking this one statement in isolation, an RDF process has no way to determine whether a URI is a real resource or a surrogate for an entity, which cannot be retrieved. RDF also provides no built-in means of establishing that two or more identifiers actually specify the same subject. RDF has no concept of the use of a URI to indicate a resource, which describes the subject or object of an RDF statement.

The XTM specification does mark a difference between a URI which specifies a resource which is the subject of a topic and a URI which describes the subject of a topic in some way. The former is achieved by the `<resourceRef>` element – this element references the resource that is the subject of the containing topic; and only one `<resourceRef>` may identify the subject of a topic. The latter form of identity is achieved by the `<subjectIndicatorRef>` element, which specifies the URI of some resource that provides a positive and unambiguous indication of the subject of a topic. XTM allows the identity of a topic to be established by zero or more `<subjectIndicatorRef>` elements.

A subject indicator may be a human-readable resource and an XTM processing application may choose to present the subject indicator resource to the user to clarify the subject represented by the topic. Alternatively a subject indicator may be specified by a URI that does not resolve to a resource but instead is some encoded form of the subject description (for example by encoding the ISBN number of a book into a URI string). For example, in the following topic map, the topic with the id "cia-map-france" uses a URI as a resource ref, and the topic itself represents a particular graphical representation of the country; whereas the topic with the id "france" represents the entire country of France and uses the same resource as a subject indicator.

```
<?xml version="1.0"?>
<topicMap xmlns="http://www.topicmaps.org/xtm/1.0"
          xmlns:xlink="http://www.w3.org/1999/xlink">

  <!-- This topic represents the CIA World Factbook's map of France -->
  <topic id="cia-map-france">
    <subjectIdentity>

      <resourceRef
xlink:href="http://www.cia.gov/cia/publications/factbook/maps/fr-map.jpg"/>
    </subjectIdentity>
    <baseName>
      <baseNameString>Map of France from the CIA World Fact book
      </baseNameString>
    </baseName>
  </topic>

  <!-- This topic represents France, using the CIA World Factbook's map
       as a subject indicating resource. -->
  <topic id="france">
    <subjectIdentity>
      <subjectIndicatorRef
xlink:href="http://www.cia.gov/cia/publications/factbook/maps/fr-map.jpg"/>
    </subjectIdentity>
    <baseName>
      <baseNameString>France</baseNameString>
    </baseName>
  </topic>
</topicMap>
```

The resource or form of URI encoding chosen by the creator of the topic is not constrained by the XTM specification – the creator is free to select any resource or use any form of URI that she thinks will invoke the correct concept in the mind of the reader or that will unambiguously identify the subject of the topic to a processing application. The only constraint that the XTM specification imposes on the subject indicator is that when two topics have one or more subject indicators in common, then those two topics are assumed to be about the same subject and are merged (for more on this see Chapter 7, *Topic Maps and XTM*). This merging rule allows the creator of a topic to assign it multiple subject indicators for the purpose of establishing an identity in a wider range of contexts. For example a topic representing the imprint of a book could have an ISBN-based subject indicator and a subject indicator based on its Library of Congress catalog entry, that topic would then be merged with any topic which uses either one of these identifiers as a subject indicator. This approach also enables the creation of sets of topics purely for the purposes of establishing that two or more identifiers specify the same subject, so allowing the creation of topic maps to facilitate interoperability between two or more other topic maps by establishing common subjects within them.

In addition to providing ways of using a URI to establish the subject identity of a topic, the XTM specification also provides a means of using the name of a topic to define its subject identity. This feature applies to the <baseName> element. In fact it is a combination of the string value of the <baseName> element and the scope that is applied to that element which together determine the subject identity. Two topics with the same <baseName> in the same scope are regarded as referring to the same subject and so are merged.

In some applications, this is a powerful feature, as it maps directly to the human convention of determining the identity of a thing by labelling it, but as with the human form of labelling, can lead to confusion when two people use the same word to mean two different things. Consider the following example:

```
<?xml version="1.0"?>
<topicMap xmlns="http://www.topicmaps.org/xtm/1.0"
          xmlns:xlink="http://www.w3.org/1999/xlink">
  <topic id="ab12345">
    <baseName>
      <baseNameString>Paris</baseNameString>
    </baseName>
    <occurrence>
      <instanceOf>
        <topicRef xlink:href="#streetplan"/>
      </instanceOf>
      <resourceRef xlink:href="http://www.paris-france.org/Carto/carto.htm"/>
    </occurrence>
  </topic>
  ...
  <topic id="fg6789">
    <baseName>
      <baseNameString>Paris</baseNameString>
    </baseName>
    <occurrence>
      <instanceOf>
        <topicRef xlink:href="#streetplan"/>
      </instanceOf>
      <resourceRef xlink:href="http://www.paristexas.com/map1.html"/>
    </occurrence>
  </topic>
</topicMap>
```

Since both topics have the same name "Paris" in the same scope (it is unspecified and so defaults to the unconstrained scope), a conformant XTM processor must treat these topics as representing the same subject and so merge them. This means that the topics shown in the topic map above are equivalent to a single topic as shown below:

```
<?xml version="1.0"?>
<topicMap xmlns="http://www.topicmaps.org/xtm/1.0"
          xmlns:xlink="http://www.w3.org/1999/xlink">
  <topic id="de0987">
    <baseName>
      <baseNameString>Paris</baseNameString>
    </baseName>
    <occurrence>
      <instanceOf>
        <topicRef xlink:href="#streetplan"/>
      </instanceOf>
      <resourceRef xlink:href="http://www.paris-france.org/Carto/carto.htm"/>
    </occurrence>
    <occurrence>
      <instanceOf>
```

```
            <topicRef xlink:href="#streetplan"/>
          </instanceOf>
          <resourceRef xlink:href="http://www.paristexas.com/map1.html"/>
        </occurrence>
      </topic>
      ...
    </topicMap>
```

The first of these two topic maps provides no information to a processing application that the first Paris is in France and the second is in the USA. The concept of scope provides some means for disambiguating such name clashes – although to apply and use name-based identification of topics in a distributed application would require first establishing a common vocabulary or naming scheme not only for the classes of topics, but also for the instances of those topics.

Using a naming scheme to disambiguate our example topic map we could end up with a topic map such as:

```
<?xml version="1.0"?>
<topicMap xmlns="http://www.topicmaps.org/xtm/1.0"
          xmlns:xlink="http://www.w3.org/1999/xlink">
  <topic id="ab12345">
    <baseName>
      <baseNameString>Paris, Ile-de-France, France</baseNameString>
    </baseName>
    <occurrence>
      <instanceOf>
        <topicRef xlink:href="#streetplan"/>
      </instanceOf>
      <resourceRef xlink:href="http://www.paris-france.org/Carto/carto.htm"/>
    </occurrence>
  </topic>
  ...
  <topic id="fg6789">
    <baseName>
      <baseNameString>Paris, Texas, USA</baseNameString>
    </baseName>
    <occurrence>
      <instanceOf>
        <topicRef xlink:href="#streetplan"/>
      </instanceOf>
      <resourceRef xlink:href="http://www.paristexas.com/map1.html"/>
    </occurrence>
  </topic>
</topicMap>
```

Alternatively we can apply scope to the base names to indicate their different contexts:

```
<?xml version="1.0"?>
<topicMap xmlns="http://www.topicmaps.org/xtm/1.0"
          xmlns:xlink="http://www.w3.org/1999/xlink">

<!-- Topics for regions or states -->
  <topic id="iledf">
    <baseName>
      <baseNameString>Ile-de-France</baseNameString>
    </baseName>
```

```
    </topic>

    <topic id="texas">
      <baseName>
        <baseNameString>Texas</baseNameString>
      </baseName>
    </topic>
    <topic id="ab12345">
      <baseName>
        <scope>
          <topicRef xlink:href="#iledf"/>
        </scope>
        <baseNameString>Paris</baseNameString>
      </baseName>
      <occurrence>
        <instanceOf>
          <topicRef xlink:href="#streetplan"/>
        </instanceOf>
        <resourceRef xlink:href="http://www.paris-france.org/Carto/carto.htm"/>
      </occurrence>
    </topic>
    ...
    <topic id="fg6789">
      <baseName>
        <scope>
          <topicRef xlink:href="#texas"/>
        </scope>
        <baseNameString>Paris, Texas, USA</baseNameString>
      </baseName>
      <occurrence>
        <instanceOf>
          <topicRef xlink:href="#streetplan"/>
        </instanceOf>
        <resourceRef xlink:href="http://www.paristexas.com/map1.html"/>
      </occurrence>
    </topic>
  </topicMap>
```

Meta Data Vocabularies

The vocabulary of a meta data application defines the properties that the application processes and what the relevance of those properties are to the resource described. When two or more applications share a meta data vocabulary, they are able to exchange information with relative ease. If the applications attempting to share information use different vocabularies, some mapping between the two vocabularies must be either defined by an application designed or inferred by the applications themselves. To successfully share a given vocabulary, both applications must agree on not only the set of meta data properties that constitute the vocabulary but also the rules for specifying values such as typing information (for example, "price" must be a fixed point integer with two decimal places) and semantic information (for example, "price" must be the price of the goods before any local sales tax or shipping costs are added). Without both typing and semantic information, the likelihood of two separate applications using a set of property definitions in the same manner is extremely small.

Shared vocabularies can come from many sources. Specifications for horizontal applications, such as specifying the capabilities of Internet devices or a set of standard country codes, tend to be created and standardized under the auspices of bodies such as the W3C or ISO. Specifications for vertical industry applications may be defined either by companies that operate in the vertical industry or by service providers to the industry.

Sharing Vocabularies in RDF and XTM

An RDF document in its XML serialization may make use of XML Schema's datatyping facilities to provide additional typing information for the values assigned to resources. The typing information may be included transparently to the RDF processor because the datatyping information is in a separate XML namespace.

Additionally, multiple RDF schemas may be arbitrarily intermingled. A single collection of RDF statements may assign properties from any number of separate schemas to the same set of resources. The use of XML namespaces enables a processing application to determine which vocabulary a particular property is defined in, thus enabling a schema-specific application to locate just those properties that it is capable of processing.

RDF Schema also allows one RDF vocabulary to be built on another by extending the classes and properties of the base schema. The RDF Schema language also provides a facility for declaring constraints on a schema such as the class of resources to which a specific class of property may be assigned. Vocabularies that are defined using RDF schema may be extended by defining additional subclasses, superclasses or constraints. For more information on RDF Schema, see Chapter 5.

Sharing Vocabularies in XTM

XTM is less data-centric than RDF and the ability to embed XML Schema within an XTM file is not provided for by the XTM specification. However, individual data occurrences associated with topics in a topic map may be typed, with the typing information being represented by a topic.

Because the entire vocabulary of a topic map is defined in terms of topics which are used to declare classes of topics, associations, occurrences and roles in associations, using an external topic map vocabulary is simply a matter of merging in the topic map which defines the vocabulary to be used. In XTM, topic maps can merged either by using the `<mergeMap>` element to reference the topic map to be merged or simply by referencing a topic from the external vocabulary topic map directly (using the full URI of the topic). In either case, a topic map processing application must retrieve the topic map containing the referenced topic and merge it into the topic map that makes the reference.

Unlike RDF Schema, the XTM specification does not define a constraint mechanism. A number of different approaches to encoding constraint information within a topic map have been suggested by the community but at the time of writing, no standard approach exists. The lack of such a standard mechanism means that it is up to individual topic map applications to determine what constraints are applied on the occurrences which may be assigned to a topic or the kinds of associations a topic may be a member of and what roles it may play in that association. However, the specification does define a set of core topics, which includes the topics necessary to create subtype/supertype associations. These associations may be used to extend the topic type hierarchy specified in an external vocabulary.

The following table summarizes the comparison of RDF and XTM for creating vocabularies:

Concept	RDF Implementation	XTM Implementation
Typing	Can use XML Schema's datatyping facility to assert the type of the objects in RDF statements. RDF Schema allows the definition of classes and properties and their constraints.	Topics are used to determine typing for both topic-related data (occurrences) and topics themselves.

Table continued on following page

Concept	RDF Implementation	XTM Implementation
Referencing External Vocabularies	XML namespacing allows intermingling of RDF vocabularies.	`<mergeMap>` or reference to a resource in an external topic map can be used to force the merge of that topic map.
Extending External Vocabularies	RDF Schema enables superclassing and subclassing of externally defined classes and properties and the modification of their constraints.	Can use the standard subtype/supertype association to create topics representing the subclasses and superclasses. No constraint mechanism.

Meta Data Consistency

To be useful to processing applications and to be consistently query-able, it is important that meta data values be created and applied in a consistent manner. For example, if the "Author" property of a document is expected to be the full name of the creator of that document, then values such as "J Smith", "jsmith@xyzcorp.com" and "john", while they might all specify the same individual, would be inconsistent and the document would not be findable against a query for the expected value of "John Smith". As another example a "Price" property for shares in a company traded on the London Stock Exchange could be specified in pounds sterling (£25.25) or, more commonly, in pence (2525p). If prices are entered into a meta data store without regard to a consistent use of a single unit, some very expensive mistakes could be made!

To some extent, the issues of consistency in meta data values can be addressed by the degree to which the semantics of the vocabulary are described and the degree of automated validation of meta data values that can be performed. Some vocabularies may have strongly defined semantics, such as a Library of Congress record for a book. Other vocabularies may be more weakly defined, such as the keyword list placed in the `<META>` tag of HTML pages. Note here that it is not just the definition of the vocabulary that is important; it is that the practical use of that vocabulary be consistent with the definition. In practice, it is no use having a meta data property called "price" which specifies that the prices should be in US dollars and should be exclusive of all sales taxes and shipping costs if the creators of meta data values do not follow these guidelines. The issue of meta data quality is sufficiently complex to be worthy of a book in itself – meta data quality is not guaranteed by strong datatyping (such as is provided by XML Schema), but also requires the consistent creation and application of meta data and it is important to note that the none of the proposed XML meta data formats can address these issues directly – they must be addressed by the applications.

As an application designer, it is important to always be aware of the possibility of inconsistently created meta data and seek to limit this possibility as much as possible. Techniques for avoiding or reducing inconsistent meta data are:

- ❑ Using public vocabularies.
- ❑ Using/creating tools to validate meta data.
- ❑ Creating a meta data catalog.

The use of public vocabularies assists application development in a number of ways. Firstly, adopting a public vocabulary improves the ease of interchange of meta data with other organizations. Secondly, a well-defined public vocabulary should be accompanied by not only clear documentation but, potentially, also applications for easing the creation and/or validation of meta data. Where no public vocabulary is entirely suitable for use in your application, starting with a public vocabulary as a basis for extension and careful modification will at least provide your application with a migration path back to the public vocabulary for later sharing of the meta data.

Tools that enable the creation and validation of meta data enormously assist the meta data creator. It is probably unreasonable to expect every user to manually create a complete and consistent description of every word processor document that they create and yet pervasive meta data is the key to a successful organization-wide application. However, the chances of getting a large quantity of meta data would be increased if that meta data were derived automatically or were solicited from the user during the course of their normal work processes. In addition to improving the quantity of meta data provided by the creators of information, good tools can also improve the meta data quality by ensuring that only valid values are provided.

In all meta data integration work, a key part of the project will be to document all of the meta data currently in use in the organization. As well as documenting what the meta data is, it is also important to catalog how the meta data is accessed, what the type of the meta data value is, what business information that meta data represents, and how and from what source the meta data was derived. There are many sources of information about meta data in the organization, such as existing database schemas, policy documents, and even the organization of documents in the file system. Such a catalog of the meta data in use within an organization is an invaluable starting point in designing and implementing any meta data processing application. A thoroughly researched meta data catalog should enable the application designer to see where there are commonalities between different existing schemas and allow her to determine the kinds of conversion and aggregation tools that would be needed by a given application in order to make use of the meta data which is already available. The principles for gathering and compiling this information into a complete meta data catalog are beyond the scope of this section, but you can find more information on data warehousing at http://www.dwinfocenter.org/ and on Enterprise Application Integration at http://eai.ittoolbox.com/.

Summary

Unlike the more traditional database approach to storing meta data, XML meta data formats are extensible. This extensibility provides a broad range of opportunities for integrating information from multiple sources with ease. However, this flexibility comes at a price – the price of maintaining consistency. The use of standard vocabularies, with clearly defined semantics and with typing and formatting controls on allowed values, greatly enhances the ability to share meta data. In addition, applications must also be aware of the need to consistently and unambiguously identify the subjects to which the meta data applies – this may be done by addressing the subject directly, by describing the subject by a unique identifier, or by addressing a resource which describes the subject. Whereas humans may make use of all three of these forms of identification, applications will typically only be able to use one of the first two.

XML meta data may be located inside the resource it describes – in which case we need a way to extract the meta data in order to do anything other than use it for personalized presentation of the resource – or it may be separate from the described resource. When meta data for collections of resources are aggregated externally from those resources, we can process the meta data to infer relationships between the resources that may further enhance search and navigation facilities. An application making use of aggregated meta data may choose to use a single source for that meta data, or to use a source, which hides the details of distributing the query across multiple resources. Alternatively the application may distribute its query across multiple meta data sources, in which case it must be capable of consistently merging the results. Both XTM and RDF provide some core facilities for merging query results, but in many cases the precise algorithm for doing this will be application-specific.

As we may be dealing with a wide variety of resource formats, a modular approach to resource discovery, extraction and aggregation enables a high degree of code reuse.

In the next chapter we'll be building on what we've covered so far in the book, and taking a look at ways of processing the meta data representations, for the purposes of enhancing search and navigation capabilities, personalizing content delivery and providing a means of describing the location of and interface to services.

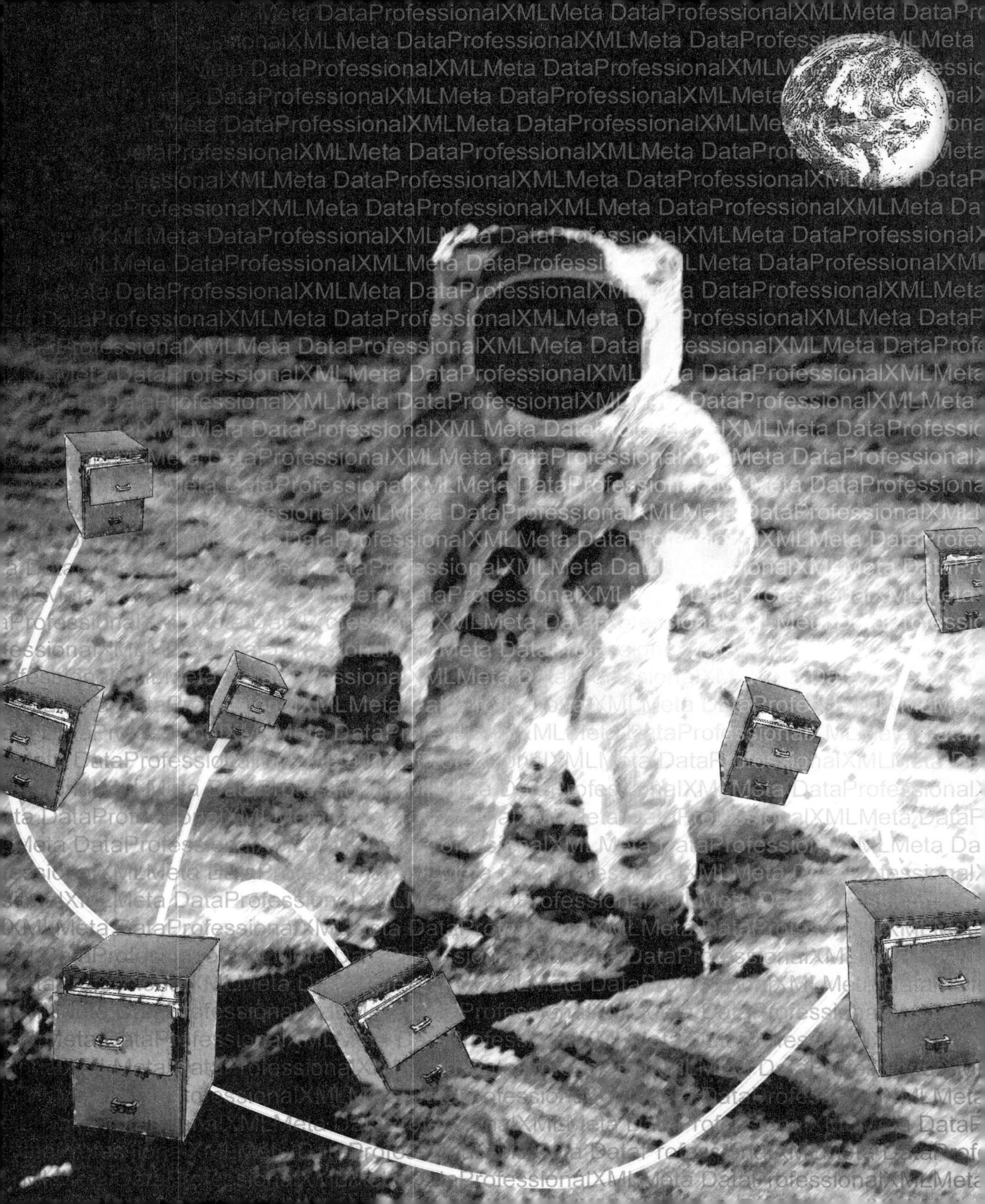

10

Processing Techniques for Meta Data

This chapter builds on what we learned about meta data architecture in the previous chapter by introducing some of the practical applications of meta data and the techniques for implementation. We will examine how meta data processing can be used to query meta data, for inferencing and to establish context. We will introduce the **Meta Data Processing Framework (MDF)** as an application framework used to create modular meta data processing utilities.

We begin by discussing how meta data processing applications may be used to perform one or more of the following functions:

- ❑ Enhancing search capabilities
- ❑ Enhancing navigation capabilities
- ❑ Personalization of content delivery
- ❑ Describing the location of and interface to services

Introduction

Before we begin looking at the actual processing techniques, we need to clarify what we mean by each of the applications above, and describe the ways in which they involve meta data.

Searching

Meta data values are always associated with a vocabulary. The vocabulary describes the meaning behind the value being assigned. For example, the vocabulary for the Dublin Core meta data standard describes the `"Creator"` property in their vocabulary as follows (see http://www.dublincore.org/documents/dces/ for the full vocabulary description):

Element	Creator
Name	Creator
Identifier	Creator
Version	1.1
Registration Authority	Dublin Core Meta data Initiative
Language	en
Definition	An entity primarily responsible for making the content of the resource
Obligation	Optional
Datatype	Character String
Maximum Occurrence	Unlimited
Comment	Examples of a Creator include a person, an organization, or a service; typically, the name of a Creator should be used to indicate the entity

With the semantic information provided by a meta data vocabulary and the availability of meta data using this vocabulary, it is possible to enable an application to provide a more "intelligent" querying service than one based purely on an index of content or keywords and so enable more rapid location of resources. For example, a search which can be expressed as "find all documents *created by* 'John Smith'" rather than as "find all documents *containing* the phrase 'John Smith'" is able to return a smaller, more targeted result set by querying the meta data of the documents as opposed to the content.

For the query given in the example above, every document that was written by John Smith would need to be identified as such by a meta data property that the application performing the query can recognize as asserting authorship of the document. Not only that, but the application may also need to be able to recognize 'Smith, John' or 'J. Smith' as potential matches. Furthermore, if the user issuing the query has in mind one particular John Smith, the name alone may not be a sufficiently unique identifier (unless the domain being searched contains only one John Smith who creates documents). These problems touch on three major issues for the use of meta data in an open environment such as the Semantic Web:

- ❑ **Sharing Vocabularies**. When two applications share the same meta data vocabulary, it is a relatively straightforward task for those applications to exchange or compare the meta data they have access to. Of course, it never has been (and probably never will be) the case that a single standard vocabulary can be used in place of all of the individual vocabularies developed over time by individuals and organizations. Rather, it has become necessary for those developing Semantic Web applications to explore the ways in which the mapping between two or more different vocabularies may be automated.

- ❑ **Meta Data Consistency**. Even with a clearly defined meaning for a meta data property, it is still possible to create confusion for a processing application if the values are not assigned in a consistent manner across all resources described by the property.

❏ **Subject Identity**. All meta data property/value pairs are assigned to some entity or set of entities – these may be digital resources, people, places, organizations or concepts. It is therefore necessary for interoperability between meta data processing applications that those applications be able to unambiguously identify such entities and communicate that identification not only with other processing applications, but also with any human being interacting with the application.

We will return to each of these issues, and ways of addressing them in the design of applications using XML meta data, later in this chapter.

Navigation

For most people, navigation around resources on a computer system means one of three things – either browsing a file-system; browsing a compiled categorization system (such as a table of contents or index); or following references embedded in content (such as links on a web page). However, meta data may be employed to develop additional forms of information navigation and organization.

One way in which this may be achieved is by applying meta data searching to determine commonalities among resources, for example a web page may contain a set of keywords as part of its meta data. Using that keyword information, a browser application can "suggest" other pages which may be of interest, by consulting a database (which itself may have been created by extracting the same meta data from many pages across the Web).

A second application of meta data to navigation would be to use the meta data to determine when one resource is dependent on another, or when two resources are otherwise complementary. For example, the meta data for one resource may indicate that it is a commentary on another resource (such as the review of a movie or the critique of a piece of art). As well as explicitly encoded relationships between resources, additional relationships may be determined by inference, and typically such inferencing requires domain-specific knowledge and domain-specific rules. Determining the inferencing rules can be complex and requires deep insight into the meta data vocabularies, and the data or work processes being described. There are, however some simple rules-of-thumb that can be used to derive inferencing rules for a set of meta data, which we will investigate later.

Meta data need not be kept as part of the resource it describes, however, and navigation by meta data external to the resource is interesting for two reasons: for the producer, external meta data can be easier to maintain and to modify than embedded links; and for the consumer, external meta data enables the user to modify or augment the meta data of a set of resources with their own additional meta data. When meta data is kept external to the resources described, it is possible for the creator of the resources to easily determine relationships between resources by querying the external meta data store, rather than having to query the resource content – this is even the case when the resources themselves are indexed, as meta data indexes tend to be smaller, and more efficiently query-able than content indexes. And storing the relationship between resources externally to those resources enables a number of different "views" of the resources to be created without the need to alter the content for each individual view. As a user of published resources, meta data that is external to the resource may be easier to modify or to augment with additional external meta data. The ability to augment existing navigation structures or even to create personal navigation structures without the need to access or modify the content itself is empowering, enabling users to reorganize and reclassify content to suit their requirements and to share that content organization and classification with others.

Personalization

In some respects, personalization may be seen as a simple extension of querying – by using elements of a user's profile, or meta data describing the user's context, to locate the content most likely to be of interest to the user. Of course, such querying would be impossible without consistent, high-quality meta data about both the individual and the content. But personalization need not stop at the location of content. With the wide variety of formats in which content may be produced and the increasing number of ways in which that content may be required for consumption, meta data becomes increasingly important in providing the information needed to convert data from its source representation into some representation which is accessible to the consumer. Such applications involve a third parameter – the device. We will come back to the issue of device-, personal-, and task-context meta data later.

Service Access

The use of meta data is not restricted to the definition of static documents but is equally applicable to the description of services. Meta data may be used to provide information about the *static* qualities of a service (such as the type of service provided, the interfaces supported, the service location, and so on) and *dynamic* qualities (such as current processing delay time or lead time from order to fulfillment). Initiatives in this area show the application of meta data to both service discovery, for instance **Universal Description, Discovery, and Integration (UDDI)** and **Electronic Business XML (ebXML)**, and the description of service interfaces such as **Web Services Description Language (WSDL)**.

This chapter does not discuss the use of meta data for service description and access separately from document description and access, as the principles are almost entirely the same. It is important, therefore, that you keep in mind that a resource could be a service just as easily as a document, graphic, or music file.

Meta Data Processing

Now that we understand the kinds of meta data that exist, we can look at how we might go about using that meta data in our applications, for each of the purposes outlined above – search and navigation, personalization, and interfacing with services.

Querying Meta Data

The simplest use of external meta data is to provide enhanced search capabilities, which allow clients to express their queries in terms of values of specific meta data properties. For example, if a client is allowed to express a query such as "find all documents where the 'Author' property contains the string 'John Smith'", the potential set of results would be much smaller, and more targeted at the clients requirements, than the results of a query such as "find all documents containing the string 'John Smith'".

In the field of database technology, querying is a well-understood and standardized capability – SQL provides a standard language for querying relational databases; and OQL is the standard language for object-oriented databases. These standard languages make it exceedingly simple to query meta data stored in a database if the database schema matches the schema of the meta data that is stored in the database. In the XML family of standards, however, standards for querying are, at the time of writing, somewhat undefined and especially so for the XML meta data standards.

Work on RDF query languages includes **SQUISH** (http://swordfish.rdfweb.org:8085/rdfquery/squish.html) and **RQL** (http://139.91.183.30:9090/RDF/RQL/). In SQUISH queries are expressed in terms of selecting statements according to matches on the object and subject of a predicate. The following code shows a simple query expressed in SQUISH:

```
SELECT ?sal, ?t, ?x
  FROM  http://ilrt.org/discovery/2000/11/rss-query/jobs-rss.rdf,
        http://ilrt.org/discovery/2000/11/rss-query/jobs.rss
  WHERE
     (job::advertises ?x ?y)
     (job::salary ?y ?sal)
     (job::title ?y ?t)
  AND ?sal > 55000
  USING job for
        http://ilrt.org/discovery/2000/11/rss-query/jobvocab.rdf#
```

This example locates all job advert resources and extracts the job advertised, the salary, and the title. If the salary value is over 55000, then the salary, title, and address of the job advert resource are added to the resultset.

In RQL, the equivalent query would be expressed as:

```
select S,T,X from {X}advertises.salary{S}, {W}advertises.title{T}, S > 55000
```

What both SQUISH and RQL share is the ability to combine constraints on both the *structure* of the data ("find a job resource that has a title" for instance) and the *value* of the data ("salary > 55000") in a single query. However, RQL goes further than SQUISH in that it provides operators for dealing with the structure of the data vocabulary, such as the hierarchy of classes of objects and properties that can be specified in RDF Schema.

The following example will find all resources (X) which created some work (Y) where the class of X (Z) is more specific than "Painter" and more general than "Flemish":

```
select X, Y from {X:$Z}creates{Y} where $Z<=Painter and $Z >=Flemish
```

Work on a **Topic Map Query Language (TMQL)** has been started, and is being carried out under the auspices of ISO. TMQL is intended to provide a language not only for querying but also for modifying topic maps. Information about TMQL can be found at the TMQL mailing list and archives on http://groups.yahoo.com/group/tmql-wg. Currently there is no formal specification of the query language syntax, although as with SQUISH and RQL, the proposed syntaxes bear a strong similarity to the syntax of SQL and OQL.

Meta Data-Based Inference

By virtue of the meta data for a collection of resources being co-located, it is a relatively easy task to inter-relate different resources according to their meta data. The task of analyzing meta data according to some set of rules in order to establish relationships between the resources is a form of **inference**. There are already a number of efforts under way to establish a way to create and exchange inference rules using XML, such as **RDF Inference Language** (RIL, see http://rdfinference.org/ril/about.html) and **RuleML** (see http://www.dfki.uni-kl.de/ruleml/).

Once the types of relationships in the meta data set have been identified and expressed as rules, an inference engine may then apply these rules to the meta data set. The new relationships found by the inference engine may then be encoded in the meta data store. In XTM the discovered relationships would be stored as associations between the topics that represent the related resources. In RDF, additional statements may be created which assert the relationship between the resources. Of course, once written back to the meta data store, these new relationships may be used for further inferencing, leading to a step-wise enrichment of the meta data store in which relationships identified at one stage of the enrichment process may be used as the predicates for determining additional relationships at the next stage.

RIL

A RIL **script** consists of a collection of **rules** each of which contain **queries** and **actions**. Queries are expressed in terms of the predicates in the RDF being processed by the RIL script. Actions are used to modify the rule-base. The final result of processing with a RIL script is a set of RDF triples which contain the statements derived by applying the rules. The following code shows a simple RIL script:

```xml
<?xml version = "1.0"?>
<ril:expression xmlns:ril="http://namespaces.rdfinference.org/ril"
                xmlns:book="http://myontology.com/book"
                xmlns:person="http://myontology.com/person">
  <ril:rule>
    <ril:premise>
      <book:author>
        <ril:variable name="X"/>
        <ril:variable name="Y"/>
      </book:author>
      <book:publisher>
        <ril:variable name="X"/>
        <ril:variable name="Z"/>
      </book:publisher>
      <person:name>
        <ril:variable name="P"/>
        <ril:variable name="Y"/>
      </person:name>
    </ril:premise>
    <ril:conclusion>
      <ril:assert>
        <person:published-by>
          <ril:variable name="P"/>
          <ril:variable name="Z"/>
        </person:published-by>
      </ril:assert>
    </ril:conclusion>
  </ril:rule>
</ril:expression>
```

The effect of this script is to find all cases where the value of the "!book:author" property assigned to a resource matches the value of a "person:name" property assigned to a resource. In that case, the value of the "book:publisher" property of the first resource is used as the value of a "person:published-by" property of the second resource. In English, this rule can be expressed as "*If a book B is authored by a person named N and the book is published by a publisher P, then the person named N is published by the publisher P*". As an aside, it is interesting to note here the two different forms of the English phrase "published by" – in one case it means that a particular written work was produced under the auspices of an organization and in the other it means that a particular author has had one or more of his or her works produced under the auspices of an organization. In the RDF model we use two different properties (book:publisher and person:published-by) for the two different meanings of the same English phrase.

So, given the following input:

```xml
<?xml version="1.0"?>
<rdf:RDF
  xmlns:rdf="http://www.w3.org/1999/02/22-rdf-syntax-ns#"
  xmlns:book="http://myontology.com/book"
  xmlns:person="http://myontology.com/person">

  <rdf:Description rdf:about="http://shakespeare.org/hamlet">
    <book:publisher>Arden</book:publisher>
    <book:author>William Shakespeare</book:author>
  </rdf:Description>

  <rdf:Description rdf:about="http://shakespeare.org/will.html">
    <person:name>William Shakespeare</person:name>
  </rdf:Description>

</rdf:RDF>
```

The RIL processor infers an additional RDF triple that can be expressed in XML as:

```xml
<rdf:Description rdf:about="http://shakespeare.org/will.html">
  <person:published-by>Arden</person:published-by>
</rdf:Description>
```

RuleML

RuleML's markup language is quite similar to that of RIL. A RuleML document defines a "**rulebase**" consisting of both **rules** and **facts**, which are constructed out of **"atoms"**. An atom in the rule base is a constant, a variable, or a predicate (which expresses a relationship between constants or variables). The core construct of the rules base is the `<if>` tag which specifies a **conclusion** as an atom, followed by the conditions (**premises**) which lead to that conclusion. A statement of fact may be asserted by having an `<if>` tag with a conclusion atom but no premises.

A RuleML equivalent to the RIL script and the RDF input above would be:

```xml
<?xml version="1.0"?>
<!DOCTYPE rulebase SYSTEM "http://www.dfki.de/ruleml/dtd/ruleml-datalog-
standalone.dtd">

<rulebase>

  <!-- First the rule: person is published-by pub if the book is
       published by pub and the author of the book is authname and
       the name of person is authname.
  -->
  <if>
    <atom>
      <rel>published-by</rel>
      <var>person</var>
      <var>pub</var>
    </atom>
    <and>
      <atom>
```

```
            <rel>publisher</rel>
            <var>book</var>
            <var>pub</var>
          </atom>
          <atom>
            <rel>author</rel>
            <var>book</var>
            <var>authname</var>
          </atom>
          <atom>
            <rel>name</rel>
            <var>person</var>
            <var>authname</var>
          </atom>
        </and>
      </if>

      <!-- FACT: Publisher of Hamlet is Arden -->
      <if>
        <atom>
          <rel>publisher</rel>
          <ind>http://shakespeare.org/hamlet</ind>
          <ind>Arden</ind>
        </atom>
        <!-- No conditions, hence always true -->
        <and/>
      </if>

      <!-- FACT: Author of Hamlet is Shakespeare -->
      <if>
        <atom>
          <rel>author</rel>
          <ind>http://shakespeare.org/hamlet</ind>
          <ind>William Shakespeare</ind>
        </atom>
        <and/>
      </if>

      <!-- FACT: Name of Shakespeare -->
      <if>
        <atom>
          <rel>name</rel>
          <ind>http://www.shakespeare.org/will.html</ind>
          <ind>William Shakespeare</ind>
        </atom>
        <and/>
      </if>

    </rulebase>
```

Types of Inference

Whether using RIL, RuleML, or some other means of expressing the inference rules for a set of meta data, the initial step in enriching meta data by inference is to identify what kinds of relationships can be inferred from the data. In some cases, the relationships may be intuitive ones – based not so much upon the meta data vocabularies but upon some deeper understanding of the context within which the meta data was created. However, there are some basic forms of meta data relationship, which can be described in general terms as either explicit or implicit resource relationships.

Explicit resource relationships are encountered when a meta data property of one resource has a value that is a reference to (or is) another resource. Typically, the name or documentation of the meta data property will express what the nature of the relationship is; and the relationship is between the resource which has the meta data property assigned to it and the resource which is referenced by the meta data property. For example, a book may have an "authors" property which is a list of names of the contributors to the book. This property establishes a relationship between each individual resource in the list (each author) and the book to which the "authors" property is assigned. The important thing to note here is that the value of the "authors" property is a name string, but it is used as an identifier to establish a relationship between the book resource and a third resource (the author) which is identified by the name string.

Implicit resource relationships can be of two types, common value relationships or common resource relationships. A common value relationship may exist between two or more resources when they share a common value for a particular meta data property. For example two children have a relationship of siblings when they share a common value for a parent property. Many common value relationships may also be represented by associating the resources that share the common value with a resource that represents the value shared. For example, the two children in our example both have a "child-of" relationship with the common parent. Common resource relationships may occur where a single resource references two or more different resources from separate meta data properties. The fact that one resource references two other resources from different meta data properties does not always establish a common resource relationship – especially if the two properties are not semantically related. As an example of this, consider the meta data for this book. This may include an "authors" property (which would be a list of individuals), the year of publication, the publisher, and the title. The "authors" property and the "publisher" property together establish a common resource relationship between each author and the publisher – the authors are published by the publisher. However, there is really no semantic relationship between a title such as "Professional XML Meta Data" and a year "2001" so these two meta data properties cannot be said to establish a common resource relationship.

By looking for explicit and implicit resource relationships in the meta data for a set of resources, we can establish some core rules for locating those resources participating in a specific relationship with a given resource. These rules may then be encoded in a rule-language such as RIL or RuleML, or they can be used to create queries to interrogate the meta data store and return resources related to a specific resource.

Making Use of Resource Relationships

In practical client-server applications, the relationship between resources that we can determine from the meta data for those resources can be used to provide a rich navigation structure for those resources. That navigation structure may be presented in a number of different ways: as an external index of the resources, as embedded links to queries for related resources, as embedded links to related resources, or as embedded content from related resources.

An external index of resources is the easiest to construct. The index itself is a separate resource, which simply presents the aggregated meta data in a browse-able format. That index includes links to the resources described by the meta data and to the resources, which are the values of meta data properties. The user is then able to browse the index and jump to resources of interest. Resource relationships are expressed by grouping all of the related resources together in some way so that from any given resource, the user may easily locate all the related resources. External indexes are already widely used in portals of all types, such as the **Open Directory Project** (http://dmoz.org).

Embedding links within the resources requires that the meta data and the resources are served through the same application. Such an application would examine the meta data for the resource being served and apply the rules, which determine the relationships to other resources for that set of meta data values. The result of applying those rules would be a set of queries that may then be executed against the meta data store. An application may embed those queries within the resource in the form of a link which, when followed, executes the query and displays the results. Alternatively, the application may choose to execute those queries when the original resource is retrieved and rather than embed the queries in the content, embed the results of executing those queries. Taking the processing of the resource relationship one step further, an application may determine that particular related resources are important enough to be retrieved and embedded within the resource originally requested.

Using Meta Data to Establish Context

If by a process of meta data analysis we can establish relationships of many different kinds among resources of many different forms and with many different purposes, the issue of information overload becomes important. However, meta data may also be brought to bear on the task of filtering a set of resources to include only those that are most relevant to the user. Meta data has two roles to play in this process. Firstly, the meta data can be used to unambiguously describe the resource – reducing ambiguity regarding the resource itself enables an application to make more intelligent decisions about when the resource is relevant and when it is not. Secondly, meta data about the user can be applied to determine what kinds of resources are relevant – this meta data may include meta data about the device being used to access the resources, meta data regarding the user such as their language preference or preferred subject matter, or meta data regarding the task that the user is performing or the resource that the user is currently accessing. All of these things together can be thought of as the user's context.

Device Profile

Device profile meta data may be used to describe limitations such as the types of resource that the device can handle; the maximum size of resource that can be displayed by the device; the kind of interaction that the device can provide between a resource and the user. So, device context is most useful in processing a set of resources to adapt them for display on the user's device.

In practice a device profile would be received by the server from the client which submitted the original request – such device information need only be transmitted once per session and may include information regarding intervening proxy devices which may introduce limitations of their own on what kinds of data may be transmitted between client and server.

An example of the definition of device profile meta data is the **Composite Capabilities/Preference Profiles Specification** (**CC/PP**, see http://www.w3.org/Mobile/CCPP/), which defines a vocabulary for describing both device profiles and user preferences. CC/PP is RDF-based, and uses a hierarchical tree to enable the specification of attributes for the different components of a device such as the hardware platform, software platform, or browser environment. The CC/PP specification defines a base vocabulary which is primarily concerned with the hardware and software platform; however, the vocabulary is extensible to allow the definition of other kinds of components that may include user profile information. A profile expressed in CC/PP may then be transmitted from the client to the server to express a context within which the client's request should be processed. The CC/PP standard also allows a server to make use of default values for information not received from the client – this allows a client to transmit a minimal amount of data (such as the device type and any differences that the device has from the standard profile for that type). In the course of that transmission, the profile may cross several other machines (proxies) which may introduce further restrictions on the kind of content which may be transmitted back to the client – CC/PP allows proxies to introduce their own requirements into the profile. The server can determine from the CC/PP profile the most appropriate content and content format to deliver to the client.

Personal Profile

Personal profile meta data covers a wide range of properties, such as the language preference of the user, the user's interests, or geographic location.

Some of the elements of a user's profile may be provided by the device – for example the user's language preference could default to the language of the operating system in use, or a mobile device may be able to provide information on the user's current geographic location. Other pieces of information may need to be specified by the user more explicitly. One current example of the use of meta data standards for compiling a personal profile is the W3C's **Platform for Privacy Preferences** (**P3P,** see http://www.w3.org/P3P/), which enables a browser to compare a web site's privacy policy (expressed in RDF) against the user's preferences and to take appropriate actions when that site is visited. P3P is a *passive* profile in the sense that the server is not notified of the user's preferences; instead action is taken locally by the client. However, we are all used to providing personal information to web sites in return for services such as access to e-mail accounts or free software, and it is only a matter of time before the vocabularies for both privacy and personal information combine to allow client software to negotiate directly with a server for a trade of personal meta data for personalized services.

Task and Resource Context

The user's task or resource context defines what the user is trying to achieve or the context from which the current request was issued. The way in which a task context is defined must be application-specific but techniques for determining a task context may be as simple as allowing the user to specify a context – for example, letting the user choose whether they are looking for a flight for business or for pleasure provides a task context which can be used to filter what kinds of accommodation or services might be offered in conjunction with the travel. However, whereas both device and personal profiles consist overwhelmingly of static meta data (with the possible exception of geographic location for mobile devices), the task context is far more dynamic and, in some cases, the best option may be to attempt to determine the user's task context based on their browse history. The browse history maintained may be a long-term history with statistical weighting regarding the types of information the user tends to be most interested in (such as is gathered by web-tracking software), or it may be a more immediate and session-based history, perhaps being as short as just looking at the resource from which the user has traversed.

As a simple example of the application of this short-term, session-based history, consider a hierarchical classification of technical articles. The top level of the hierarchy might include high-level subject areas such as "Administration", "Security", and "Development", but may also include separate subject areas for different operating systems such as "Windows 2000", "Linux", "Solaris", and so on. Within "Administration" there may be sub-topics such as "User Management" and "Network Management", but it would also make sense for those operating system subject areas to be repeated at this level and for the sub-topics of "User Management" and "Network Management" to appear within the lower one. In fact what the hierarchy is trying to represent is a multi-faceted index – that is, an index that has more than one categorization strategy. This leads to a complex hierarchy such as this:

```
Administration
    User Management
        Linux
        Windows 2000
    Network Management
    Linux
        User Management
    Windows 2000
        User Management
```

```
Development
Security
Linux
      Administration
            User Management
Windows 2000
      Administration
            User Management
```

While this hierarchy may be relatively stable and straightforward to update as new categories are added, to classify individual documents within this hierarchy would be a headache. For example a document about the `groupadd` command in Linux would need to be inserted in three separate places in the hierarchy, whereas a more general document about how to make less easily guessable passwords relates both to the "User Management" topic and the "Security" topic, but may not necessarily be related to any one specific operating system.

However, by applying the concepts of scope and a user context based only on the current position of the user in the hierarchy, it is possible to present the documents in the correct places in the hierarchy. To do this, we first subdivide the hierarchical categories by the type of categorization that they represent. So the categories "Linux" and "Windows 2000" are "operating system" categories and the other categories such as "Administration" and "User Management" are "subject area" categories. We can then define the scope of a document by the subject area and operating system topics to which the document is related. The user's context may be defined as the current subject area and operating system topic being browsed. For example, at the bottom of the Linux/Administration/User Management branch, the user's context would be {Linux, User Management}. Finally, the rule for determining whether or not a resource is in scope is that the resource is in scope only when one of the "subject area" topics which are in its scope is also in the user's context, and one of the "operating system" topics in its scope (if it has any such topics in its scope) is also in the user's context. This means that the document about the `groupadd` command has a scope of {Linux, User Management} and that the passwords article has a scope of {Security, User Management}. By applying our in-scope rule, the `groupadd` documentation will appear only on a branch which contains both "Linux" and "User Management" whereas the passwords article would appear at any node which is either "Security" or "User Management", regardless of the position of that node in the hierarchy. By applying these rules to the hierarchy, we get the following (names in curly braces denote the user's context at that position in the hierarchy):

```
Administration {Administration}
      User Management    {User Management}
            passwords.txt
            Linux {User Management, Linux}
                  groupadd.html
            Windows 2000 {User Management, Windows 2000}
      Network Management {Network Management}
      Linux
            User Management
                  passwords.txt
                  groupadd.html
      Windows 2000
            User Management
                  passwords.txt
Development
Security
      passwords.txt
Linux
      Administration
            User Management
```

```
            passwords.txt
            groupadd.html
   Windows 2000
       Administration
           User Management
               passwords.txt
```

By using the meta data of the documents to define their position in the hierarchy, it is now possible to generate the listing for each branch of the tree dynamically by performing a query, which means that when a new piece of content is created, it can be added to all the relevant parts of the hierarchy without requiring any modification to the hierarchy itself.

Context in RDF

The RDF specification itself includes no concept of context – assertions made in RDF are always true, and it requires an additional vocabulary and additional processing to apply modifiers to those statements that restrict the context within which the statement is true. We have already seen how P3P allows a client to specify their "privacy context" and how that context may be applied by the browser application to determine what information may be shared with a server. We have also shown how CC/PP provides a way for a client application to specify its preferences and capabilities to a server as a form of advanced content negotiation. Both of these uses of RDF are application-specific, as there is no underlying concept of the use of RDF statements to define a limited context within which an RDF statement applies.

Context in Topic Maps

The topic map standard addresses the issue of context more directly than RDF. Topic names, occurrences, and the roles played by topics in an association (collectively known as the topic characteristics) are all defined within a context called a scope. The scope specifies the context within which a particular characteristic assignment is valid and is defined as a collection of topics. The use of scope enables a topic map application to filter out all resources connected to the topic map that are not relevant to the context of the user.

How an application uses the scope of topic characteristic assignments to filter them is not constrained by the XTM specification nor is the means by which an application determines a user's context. However, the most obvious way to specify a user's context in a topic map application is to define the context as a collection of topics. The most obvious forms of filtering are to either filter out any characteristic assignments for which the scope defined for that assignment is not a subset of the context of the user (in other words, an assignment is not filtered out if every one of the topics in its scope is also in the user's context), or to filter out only characteristic assignments for which the scope does not overlap with the user context (in other words, an assignment is not filtered out if its scope contains at least one topic in the user's context).

Using Meta Data for Personalized Classification

Where meta data properties take on a discrete set of values within a given application, it is possible to create personalized hierarchical classifications based on them. A user could be allowed to specify the order in which each property is evaluated to produce a hierarchy of classification. For example, one online CD catalog user may choose to view recordings classified first by performer and then by title, without any regard to the record label or recording date, whereas another user may choose to view the same catalog classified first by composer, then by conductor, and finally by title. Such a dynamic classification system is a powerful navigation tool, especially across multi-faceted data such as library indices.

MDF – the Meta Data Processing Framework

The **Meta Data Processing Framework** (**MDF**, see http://www.techquila.com/mdf.html) is an application framework that enables the modular creation of meta data processing utilities. MDF attempts to address the problems of handling multiple input data formats, multiple output meta data repository formats and the myriad of meta data conversion and cleaning processes. It does this by enabling each process to be neatly encapsulated in a module with a simple interface which enables it to be interconnected with any other module with the same interface.

The key concepts in MDF are the meta data set, the processing module, and the processing chain.

A **meta data set** is a set of name/value pairs which are accessible using the name as the key. A key must be a string, and while MDF makes no requirement regarding what format the value must take, for ease of interconnection a string value is preferred.

A **processing module** is a single MDF software component that performs some processing task using a single meta data set as an input and producing one or more meta data sets as output.

A **processing chain** is constructed by connecting the output of one processing module to the input of another. If the output of module A is connected to the input of module B, module B is said to be the "downstream module" of module A and module A is said to be the "upstream module" of module B.

The following diagram shows a simple MDF processing chain consisting of four modules and the meta data set as it is passed from one module to the next during a processing run.

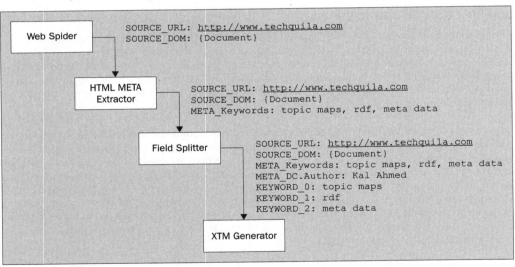

The first module in the chain, **Web Spider**, generates a single meta data set for each URL that it visits, it stores the URL and the DOM document representing the resource (assuming the resource is an (X)HTML document) in the meta data set which is passed to the downstream module, the **HTML META Extractor**. The HTML META Extractor looks in the DOM document for <META> tags and for each tag found generates an entry in the output meta data set. The **Field Splitter** module is configured to split the value of the META_Keywords field on the comma and so generates an additional set of property/value pairs in its output set which together form the final input for the **XTM Generator** which writes the extracted and cleaned meta data into an XTM file.

MDFModule

The interface `com.techquila.mdf.framework.MDFModule` must be implemented by any class intended to be used as a module in an MDF processing chain. The interface for a module is very simple, consisting of only three methods, `init()`, `rcv()`, and `chain()`.

The `init()` method is invoked once for each processing session and has a single parameter which specifies the meta data set for the purpose of module initialization. The `rcv()` method is invoked by the upstream module when it has a meta data set ready for processing by this module and its downstream modules. The `rcv()` method also has a single parameter which specifies the meta data map for processing. The `chain()` method takes as a parameter the module which is to become the new downstream module for this module. In Java code, this interface is defined as follows:

```java
package com.techquila.mdf.framework

import java.util.*;

/**
 * The basic interface for a processing element in an MDF processing
 * chain. Modules are chained together by calling the chain() function
 * to set the next downstream processing module.
 * The element receives information from the upstream processing
module via the rcv() function.
 * Modules should pass information to downstream modules by calling the
 * downstream module's rcv() function.
 */
public interface MDFModule
{
    /**
     * The init() function for a module should be invoked once before a
     * processing session begins. Initialization information may be passed
     * to this function via the <code>initInfo</code> parameter.
     * The module should chain the initialization to the next downstream
     * module (if there is one) by invoking the init() function on that
     * module.
     * As the same initialization information is passed to all modules in
     * the chain, care should be taken in modifying the input map.
     *
     * @param initInfo The map containing initialization information for the
     *                 processing session.
     *
     * @return false if a fatal error has prevented initialization of this
     *         module. Otherwise the module must return the value returned
     *         by the init() function of the downstream module.
     */
    public boolean init(Hashtable initInfo);

    /**
     * The rcv() function for a module is invoked by the upstream module to
     * provide a map of data to be processed by this module and/or any
     * downstream modules in the chain. The module invoked is free to
     * modify this map in any way and to pass one or more maps to the
     * downstream modules in the chain.
     *
     * @param info The information map to be processed by this module.
     */
    public void rcv(Hashtable info);

    /**
```

```
 * The chain() function is called to set the downstream module for
 * this module.
 * Typically modules will support only one downstream module, so
 * calling chain() will replace the current downstream module with the
 * specified module.
 *
 * @param next The module to become the downstream module for
 * this module.
 */
public void chain(MDFModule next);
}
```

A module which implements this interface is required to maintain the chain correctly by ensuring that the meta data set passed into the `init()` method is passed to the `init()` method of the downstream module, and that each meta data set passed into the `rcv()` method results in one or more meta data sets being passed on to any downstream modules.

MDFModuleAdapter

As it was envisaged that many MDF modules will be simple modules that receive a meta data set, modify it and pass it on, all of this basic plumbing is provided in the class `MDFModuleAdapter`. This adapter class provides default implementations of the `init()`, `rcv()`, and `chain()` methods and adds three new interface methods. These new methods are:

❑ The `initialise()` method is called from the `init()` method and should be overridden by a derived class to provide class-specific initialization. The `initialise()` method receives the meta data set which was passed into the `init()` method.

❑ The `process()` method is called from the `rcv()` method and should be overridden to provide class-specific processing operations. The `process()` method receives the meta data set which was passed into the `rcv()` method.

❑ Finally, the `notify()` method is provided to enable the derived class to pass additional meta data sets to the downstream modules.

By overriding `initialise()` and `process()`, a processing module may be implemented without the code overhead of the making and maintaining connections to other modules.

MDF Module Patterns

There are four categories of MDF module, each of which exhibit a specific pattern in the usage of the `init()` and `rcv()` methods: producers, pass-through processors, generators, and consumers.

A **producer** module is responsible for generating all of the initial meta data sets in a processing run. Almost all MDF processing chains will start with a producer. A producer module does not receive any calls into its `rcv()` method, instead when the `init()` method is called, the producer will pass the initialization information down the chain (by invoking the `init()` method of the downstream module) and then begin generating meta data sets based on the initialization information received. Each of these meta data sets is passed down the chain by invoking the `rcv()` method of the downstream module.

A **pass-through processor** receives a meta data set from an upstream module, performs some processing, updates the meta data set, and then passes it on to the downstream module. This is the most common type of MDF processing module and a default implementation is provided in the framework (`com.techquila.mdf.framework.MDFModuleAdapter`) which enables a developer to create a new module by simply overriding the `process()` and/or `inititalise()` methods of that class.

A **generator** receives a meta data set from an upstream module and performs some processing on the module, which causes multiple meta data sets to be created and passed to the downstream module. A generator module may be created by overriding the `rcv()` method of the `MDFModuleAdapter` class to perform the class-specific processing without passing the received meta data set on to the downstream module, and then to pass the meta data sets created as a result of processing to the downstream module directly, by calling the `notify()` method. The classes `com.techquila.mdf.impl.html.SpiderModule` and `com.techquila.mdf.impl.xml.XPathExtractor` are examples of generator modules.

A **consumer** is a specialized form of pass-through processor. The consumer module receives a meta data set from an upstream module and uses it to change the state of some meta data repository, but does not alter the meta data set in any way. Typically a consumer module will only ever occur at the end of an MDF processing chain. A more extreme form of consumer module could be created by making a module which never passes on the received meta data sets, but to do so would be an unnecessary constraint, limiting the reuse potential of the module. A consumer module can be derived from the `MDFModuleAdapter` class as the code in that class will handle the module being placed at the end of the chain gracefully.

These four patterns are shown in the following figure:

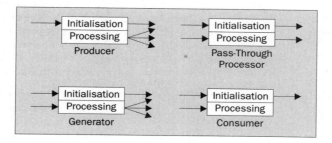

Existing MDF Modules

The Java implementation of the MDF framework is available for download from http://www.techquila.com/mdf.html. The implementation consists of the framework plus a number of modules. The number of implemented modules is increasing all the time. The following table shows some of the modules that are currently part of the MDF package:

Module	Type	Description
impl.BasicPrinterModule	Consumer	Writes the key/value pairs in the received map to the standard output.
impl.SplitterModule	Pass-through processor	Splits the value in one key of the input map into multiple values in the output map. Each value is mapped to outputkeyname_N where N is an integer starting from 0.

Table continued on following page

Module	Type	Description
xml.XPathExtractor	Generator	Creates a number of meta data sets from a DOM document received in the input map. This module is configured with a set of XPath statements, which define the elements which trigger the creation of a new meta data set and the elements or attributes which provide values for those meta data sets.
xml.ConfigurableXPath Extractor	Generator	A derived version of the XPathExtractor class which is capable of reading its configuration information from an XML file.
html.MetaExtractor	Pass-through processor	Receives a DOM document representing the HTML document to be processed and adds an entry to the meta data set for each <META> tag found in the <HEAD> of the document. The key name of each generated entry is HTML_META_x where x is the value of the name attribute of the <META> tag, and the value is the string value of the content attribute of the tag.
html.SpiderModule	Generator	Retrieves a resource specified by a URL provided in the input meta data set. If the resource is an (X)HTML document, it is parsed and the URL of that document and its DOM representation are passed to the downstream module. The SpiderModule then proceeds in a depth-first traversal of all links contained in anchor (<A>) elements, passing the URL and parsed DOM tree of each linked page to the downstream module.
rdf.SimpleRDFMapper	Consumer	Creates an RDF model of the received meta data sets. This module is configured to recognize certain meta data set entries as specifying the resource of an RDF statement and other entries as specifying the predicate and value of the statement. This module is also capable of recognizing key names of the form generated by the SplitterModule and creating RDF Alt, Bag, or Seq statements to represent the multiple values.

Module	Type	Description
rdf.ConfigurableRDFMapper	Consumer	A derived version of the SimpleRDFMapper that is capable of reading the mapping of meta data set properties to RDF statements from an XML file.
xtm.SimpleXTMMapper	Consumer	Creates an XTM model of the received meta data sets. This module may be configured to recognize particular meta data set entries as specifying topics and other entries as specifying occurrences of topics. In addition, the occurrence of particular meta data set values may be used to infer the creation of associations between topics.

Sample Application: Harvesting Web Meta Data with MDF

To show how simple it is to combine MDF modules into a working application, we will use the MDF framework to construct a web-spider application to extract meta data from a web site. This application will be aggregating meta data from the pages on the site into a local meta data store.

> Note that there may be connectivity problems if you access the Internet via a proxy server. If this is the case then try accessing a site located on a local web server such as Microsoft's IIS.

To start with we need to identify what meta data will be extracted and how it will be represented in the meta data store. Web pages tend to contain little in the way of explicit meta data. The only mechanism for explicitly defining meta data in HTML is the <META> tag, which has name and content attributes. Common uses of the <META> tag are to define keywords or to define HTTP header information such as page-redirects or character encoding information. For this application, we choose to extract just keywords encoded in <META> tags in the HTML. The content attribute of the keywords <META> tag is a comma-separated list of keywords for that web page.

In our application we will map this keyword information into RDF. As we are only dealing with a single meta data property, we need to define just one RDF statement. That statement asserts that the topic of the resource may be expressed by the keyword. This concept maps neatly to the <Subject> element of the Dublin Core element set (see Chapter 4 for more details on the Dublin Core), so we will reuse that vocabulary in our mapping.

We can now define the steps in harvesting the keyword meta data from a set of resources. To do this we need to:

- ❑ Spider over the web pages.
- ❑ Extract the content attribute of all <META> tags where the name attribute is "keywords".
- ❑ Split the content attribute value into multiple keyword entries, treating a comma as the separator character.

❏ Map each keyword entry to an RDF statement in which the subject is the page being processed, the predicate is "Subject" as defined by the Dublin Core element set, and the object is the keyword.

In MDF, each of these steps maps to a single module's processing. The SpiderModule will generate meta data sets for each page that it spiders; the MetaExtractor module can be used to extract the value of the content attribute of the <META> tags found in the HTML; the SplitterModule can divide up the content string using the comma character as a separator; and finally the SimpleRDFMapper module can be used to create statements in an RDF model which we can finally write to a file. This processing chain is the same as the one shown in our earlier figure, repeated here:

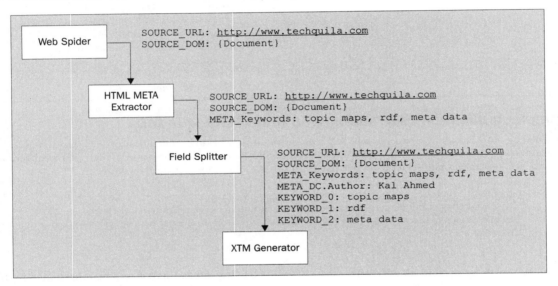

The following code shows how this is achieved:

```
package com.wrox.proxmlmetadata.chapter10;

import com.hp.hpl.mesa.rdf.jena.mem.*;
import com.hp.hpl.mesa.rdf.jena.model.*;
import com.techquila.mdf.impl.basic.*;
import com.techquila.mdf.impl.html.*;
import com.techquila.mdf.impl.rdf.*;
import com.techquila.mdf.impl.xml.*;
import java.io.*;
import java.net.*;
import java.util.*;

public class HTMLKeywordExtractor
{
    protected File rdfFile;
    protected URL  spiderSource;
    protected int  spiderHops = 3;
    protected boolean spiderNonLocal = false;

    public static void main(String args[])
```

```
{
    HTMLKeywordExtractor app = new HTMLKeywordExtractor();
    app.run(args);
}

protected void run(String args[])
{
    SpiderModule spider = new SpiderModule();
    MetaExtractor extractor = new MetaExtractor();
    SplitterModule splitter = new SplitterModule();
    SimpleRDFMapper mapper = new SimpleRDFMapper();

    if (!parseArgs(args))
    {
        usage();
        System.exit(-1);
    }

    // Initialize the RDF Mapper:
    mapper.addProperty("subject", "http://purl.org/dc/elements/1.1/",
                       SpiderModule.SRC_URL, false,
                       "KEYWORD", true, SimpleRDFMapper.COLLECTION_BAG);
    mapper.setModel(new ModelMem());

    // Create initialization meta data set
    Hashtable initInfo = new Hashtable();
    // Add initialization info for the spider module
    initInfo.put(SpiderModule.PARSERSTRATEGY,
                 "com.techquila.mdf.impl.html.JTidyParserStrategy");
    initInfo.put(SpiderModule.SPIDER_NONLOCAL,
                 String.valueOf(spiderNonLocal));
    initInfo.put(SpiderModule.MAXHOPS, String.valueOf(spiderHops));

    // Add initialization info for the SplitterModule
    initInfo.put(SplitterModule.SPLIT_FIELD,
                 MetaExtractor.META_PREFIX + "KEYWORDS");
    initInfo.put(SplitterModule.SPLIT_CHARS, ",");
    initInfo.put(SplitterModule.OUTPUT_FIELD, "KEYWORD");

    // Create the processing chain
    spider.chain(extractor);
    extractor.chain(splitter);
    splitter.chain(mapper);

    // Initialize the chain
    spider.init(initInfo);

    // Create the initial meta data set to be processed.
    Hashtable runInfo = new Hashtable();
    runInfo.put(SpiderModule.SRC_URL, spiderSource.toString());

    // Run processing
    spider.rcv(runInfo);

    // Write out the complete RDF model
    try
```

```
    {
        mapper.write(rdfFile);
    }
    catch(IOException ex)
    {
        System.out.println("Error writing RDF model to file:\n"
                            + ex.toString());
    }
    catch(RDFException ex)
    {
        System.out.println("Error while writing RDF model:\n"
                            + ex.toString());
    }
    }
    // code for parseArgs() and usage() omitted for brevity.
}
```

Implementing an MDF Chain with No Code

The simple chain we coded in the example above can actually be generated without the need to write any code. The framework for doing this is provided by the class com.techquila.mdf.impl.basic.MDFApp. This class is an application that creates, initializes, and runs an MDF processing chain from information contained in an XML configuration file. The configuration file for the application above, HTMLKeywordExtractor.xml, looks like this:

```xml
<?xml version="1.0" ?>

<mdf:chain xmlns:mdf="http://www.techquila.com/mdfapp/1.0"
            xmlns:map="http://www.techquila.com/mdf/simplerdfmapper/1.0">

    <!-- Modules are declared in the order they appear in the chain -->
    <mdf:module>com.techquila.mdf.impl.html.SpiderModule</mdf:module>
    <mdf:module>com.techquila.mdf.impl.html.MetaExtractor</mdf:module>
    <mdf:module>com.techquila.mdf.impl.basic.SplitterModule</mdf:module>
    <mdf:module>com.techquila.mdf.impl.rdf.ConfigurableRDFMapper</mdf:module>

    <!-- Declares the initialization meta data set -->
    <mdf:initialise>
      <mdf:property
          key="com.techquila.mdf.impl.html.SpiderModule.SPIDER_MAX_HOPS">
        3
      </mdf:property>
      <mdf:property
          key="com.techquila.mdf.impl.html.SpiderModule.SPIDER_PARSER">
        com.techquila.mdf.impl.html.JTidyParserStrategy
      </mdf:property>
      <mdf:property
          key="com.techquila.mdf.impl.html.SpiderModule.SPIDER_NON_LOCAL">
        false
      </mdf:property>
      <mdf:property
          key="com.techquila.mdf.impl.basic.SplitterModule.SPLIT_FIELD">
        HTML_META_KEYWORDS
      </mdf:property>
      <mdf:property
```

```
            key="com.techquila.mdf.impl.basic.SplitterModule.OUTPUT_FIELD">
        KEYWORD
    </mdf:property>
    <mdf:property
            key="com.techquila.mdf.impl.basic.SplitterModule.SPLIT_CHARS">,
    </mdf:property>
    <!-- The following value gets replaced by the path name of
            the configuration file -->
    <mdf:property key="com.techquila.mdf.framework.XML_CONFIG">
        _CFG_SRC_
    </mdf:property>
</mdf:initialise>

<!-- This run will spider the specified resource and generate
        an RDF model from the meta data found in the spidered pages -->
<mdf:run>
    <mdf:property key="SOURCE_URL">http://www.w3c.org</mdf:property>
</mdf:run>

<!-- This run will write the generated RDF model to a file -->
<mdf:run>
    <mdf:property
            key="com.techquila.mdf.impl.rdf.ConfigurableRDFMapper.WRITE_MODEL">
        output.rdf
    </mdf:property>
</mdf:run>

<!-- Configuration of the RDF mapper -->
<map:statement
        namespace="http://purl.org/dc/elements/1.1"
        localname="subject">
    <map:resourceProperty>SOURCE_URL</map:resourceProperty>
    <map:objectProperty
            multi="true" collection="seq">
        KEYWORD
    </map:objectProperty>
</map:statement>
</mdf:chain>
```

You may have noticed that the class used at the end of the chain for creating and writing the RDF model is not the same as in the coded application. Instead we use the class com.techquila.mdf.impl.rdf.ConfigurableRDFMapper, which extends the SimpleRDFMapper class to add the ability to read the mapping of meta data set entries to RDF statements from an XML configuration file. Because this configuration information is in a separate namespace from the configuration information read by MDFApp, we can combine both sets of configuration information into the same file. To pass the file name through the initialization chain, we can specify a special property value _CFG_SRC_, which will be replaced with the full pathname of the configuration file read by MDFApp. This same file can then be read and parsed by the ConfigurableRDFMapper class. In fact, to avoid the overhead of parsing the XML twice, the special value _CFG_DOM_ may be used to pass the DOM document created by MDFApp through to the initialization of other modules (although the ConfigurableRDFMapper does not currently support such initialization). The other difference between the ConfigurableRDFMapper and the SimpleRDFMapper is that the former recognizes an additional property key in the processing step – if a property with the key com.techquila.mdf.impl.rdf.ConfigurableRDFMapper.WRITE_MODEL is found in a meta data set, then the value of that property is treated as the name of a file to be opened and written to with the XML serialization of the RDF model.

Extracting Dublin Core Meta Data with MDF

Our simple example above only maps values extracted from <META> tags where the name attribute is "keywords". However, the <LINK> tag mechanism has also been adopted as one mechanism for the specification of RDF meta data in HTML (see http://www.ietf.org/rfc/rfc2731.txt). To achieve this, the <LINK> tag's name attribute is used to contain the namespace of the RDF schema being used and the name of the property being assigned, and the content attribute is used to specify the value of the property. For example:

```
<META name="DC.Creator" content="Kal Ahmed"/>
```

The namespace prefix is mapped to a namespace URI by using a <LINK> tag. The rel attribute of the tag contains the fixed string "schema." followed by the namespace prefix for the schema and the href attribute of the tag specifies the namespace URI of the prefix. For example:

```
<LINK rel="schema.DC" href="http://purl.org/DC/elements/1.1">
```

The Dublin Core standard defines a set of meta data properties which may be assigned to a resource and which may be specified by using the <META> and <LINK> tag as described above. The vocabulary of this standard includes concepts such as the creator of the resource, the resource title, copyright statement, and so on. A complete listing of the element set can be found on the Dublin Core site (http://www.dublincore.org). To extend our MDF application to recognize this form of embedded meta data we need to add the ability to parse the <LINK> tag for schema information and to re-map the prefixed meta data names to a form, which can then be recognized by the RDFMapper downstream. The MDF processing chain for this application would look like this:

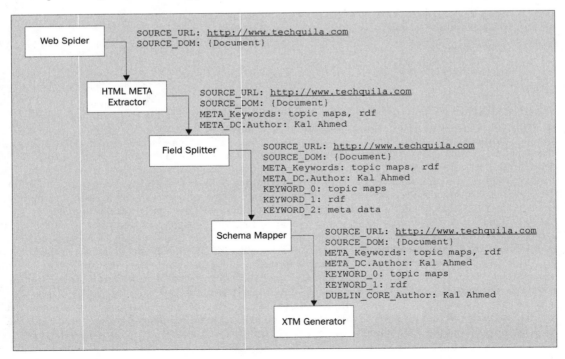

The new module, `SchemaMapper`, will parse the DOM tree of the HTML document received from the upstream `MetaExtractor` module looking for `<LINK>` tags with the `"schema."` prefix in their `rel` attribute. The `SchemaMapper` module will be initialized with the URI of the schema or `schemata` of interest and a prefix for each schema. If a URI is found in the `href` of a schema-specification `<LINK>` tag which matches one of the `schemata` of interest, then a mapping will be registered between the prefix declared in the `<LINK>` tag and the prefix specified in the initialization of the `SchemaMapper`. This mapping will then be used to look for extracted `<META>` tags, which will appear as properties in the form `HTML_META_LINKPREFIX.ELEMENTNAME`; where `LINKPREFIX` is the schema prefix specified in the `<LINK>` tag and `ELEMENTNAME` is the name of the RDF property being assigned. This value of this property can then be copied to a new property with a key `RDF_MAPPEDPREFIX_ELEMENTNAME` where `MAPPEDPREFIX` is the fixed schema prefix defined for the schema's URI in the initialization of the `SchemaMapper` module.

The `SchemaMapper` module is a pass-through module and can be most easily implemented by deriving a new class from the `BasicMDFModuleAdapter` class. The `SchemaMapper` module needs only to override the `initialise()` and `process()` methods of the base class.

Inside the initialise() method, the input meta data set is checked for properties with the keys "com.wrox.proxmlmeta data.chapter10.SchemaMapper.MAP_URI" and "com.wrox.proxmlmeta data.chapter10.SchemaMapper.MAP_PREFIX". If these two properties are found, then the values are entered in an internal map. This map will be consulted when processing `<LINK>` tags in the HTML documents we process. This implementation also allows multiple such mappings, so that for each "....MAP_URI_n" property (where n is an integer starting from 0), a "....MAP_PREFIX_n" property is sought and if both are present a mapping is added. The URI_PREFIX specifies the schema URI and the MAP_PREFIX property specifies the prefix to be given to the new entry in the meta data set which will be created by the SchemaMapper for that schema.

```
package com.wrox.proxmlmetadata.chapter10;

import com.techquila.mdf.framework.*;
import com.techquila.mdf.impl.html.*;
import java.util.*;
import org.w3c.dom.*;

public class SchemaMapper extends BasicMDFModuleAdapter
{
    protected Hashtable prefixMap = new Hashtable();
    protected Hashtable currMap;
    public String MAP_URI =
            "com.wrox.proxmlmeta data.chapter10.SchemaMapper.MAP_URI";
    public String MAP_PREFIX =
            "com.wrox.proxmlmeta data.chapter10.SchemaMapper.MAP_PREFIX";

    /**
     * Set up the SchemaMapper to process one or more prefix to URI
     * mappings.
     * Processed keys:
     *    com.wrox.proxmlmeta data.chapter10.SchemaMapper.MAP_URI
     *        This key is used to specify the URI which the mapper should
     *        look for in a <LINK rel="schema"> tag. If the URI is found,
     *        then a mapping will be registered between the prefix declared
     *        in the source document and the prefix specified in the MAP_PREFIX
     *        property.
```

```
 *          This property may be multivalued - each value specified under the
 *          com.wrox.proxmlmeta data.chapter10.SchemaMapper.MAP_URI<i>_n</i>
 *          where <i>n</i> is an integer value starting from 0.
 *
 *       com.wrox.proxmlmeta data.chapter10.SchemaMapper.MAP_PREFIX
 *          This key is used to specify the prefix string to be used
 *          for meta data values which are found to belong to the schema
 *          with the URI specified by the MAP_URI key.
 *          This property may be multivalued - each value specified under the
 *          com.wrox.proxmlmeta
 *          data.chapter10.SchemaMapper.MAP_PREFIX<i>_n</i>
 *          where <i>n</i> is an integer value starting from 0.
 *
 * This method records the mappings internally for use during
 * processing.
 */
public boolean initialise(Hashtable initInfo)
{
    // Look for the key without any integer suffix
    if (initInfo.containsKey(MAP_URI))
    {
        String prefixURI = (String)initInfo.get(MAP_URI);
        if (initInfo.containsKey(MAP_PREFIX))
        {
            prefixMap.put(prefixURI, (String)initInfo.get(MAP_PREFIX));
        }
    }

    // Look for the keys with an integer suffix. A MAP_URI_n
    // key must be partnered by a MAP_PREFIX_n key.
    for (int i = 0;
            initInfo.containsKey(MAP_URI + "_" + String.valueOf(i));
            i++)
    {
        String prefixURI = (String)initInfo.get(MAP_URI + "_"
                                        + String.valueOf(i));
        if (initInfo.containsKey(MAP_PREFIX + "_" + String.valueOf(i)))
        {
            prefixMap.put(prefixURI,
                    initInfo.get(MAP_PREFIX + "_" + String.valueOf(i)));
        }
    }
    return true;
}

// Rest of class methods here
}
```

When the process() method is invoked, this module will expect to find the DOM tree of the HTML document to be processed under the key specified by the constant SRC_DOM in the class com.techquila.mdf.impl.html.SpiderModule. If it is found, then all elements named "link" are extracted from it to be processed. For each <LINK> tag, the rel attribute is checked to see if it starts with the string "schema." – if so, then the rest of the value of that attribute is treated as the prefix which will be found in the name attribute of <META> tags defining values under that schema, and the href prefix is treated as the schema URI. If the schema URI matches one of the URIs that a prefix mapping has been defined for, then a mapping is created from the string "HTML_META_pre" (where pre is the prefix defined by the <LINK> tag) to the prefix defined for the schema URI during module initialization. This new mapping is stored in the internal hashtable called currMap.

Once the `<LINK>` tags have been processed, all of the keys in the input meta data set are enumerated. For each key which contains a period character, the string up to the period is used as a key into `currMap`, if an entry is found in `currMap` then a new entry will be created in the meta data set – the key of this new entry is the value found in `currMap` followed by the sub-string of the key which follows the period. So, given an initialization mapping of "http://purl.org/DC/elements/1.1" to "DUBLIN_CORE_", if a `<LINK>` tag such as:

```
<LINK name="schema.DC" href="http://purl.org/DC/elements/1.1"/>
```

is encountered, `currMap` will contain a mapping from "HTML_META_DC" to "DUBLIN_CORE_".

If that same file contains an element such as:

```
<META name="DC.Creator" content="John Smith"/>
```

then the `MetaExtractor` will have created an entry in the input meta data set with key "HTML_META_DC.CREATOR" and value "John Smith". When the `SchemaMapper` module then processes this meta data set, a new entry will be created with the key "DUBLIN_CORE_CREATOR" and content "John Smith".

The code for the `process()` method is:

```java
/**
 * Processes a meta data set for keys of the form
 * HTML_META_<i>PREFIX</i>.<i>PROPERTY</i>.
 * For each key of this form found, this method will determine the
 * schema URI from the prefix by using the values specified in the
 * <LINK rel="schema"> tags and will insert a new property of the form
 * <i>MAPPED_PREFIX</i>.<i>PROPERTY</i> into the meta data set with
 * the same value as the processed property.
 *
 */
public void process(Hashtable info)
{
    if (info.containsKey(SpiderModule.SRC_DOM))
    {
        // currMap = new Hashtable(prefixMap);
        // Process the LINK elements of the source document
        // to work out how the prefixes used in the document
        // map to prefixes in our prefixMap.
        currMap = new Hashtable();
        Document d = (Document)info.get(SpiderModule.SRC_DOM);
        NodeList links = d.getElementsByTagName("link");
        for (int i = 0; i < links.getLength(); i++)
        {
            processLink((Element)links.item(i));
        }

        // Now process the keys looking for the prefixes
        // we determined by processing the links.
        Enumeration keys = info.keys();
        while (keys.hasMoreElements())
        {
```

```
                    String k = (String)keys.nextElement();
                    int ix = k.indexOf(".");
                    if (ix != -1)
                    {
                        String newPrefix = (String)currMap.get(k.substring(0, ix));
                        if (newPrefix != null)
                        {
                            String newKey = newPrefix + k.substring(ix+1);
                            info.put(newKey, info.get(k));
                        }
                    }
                }
            }
        }


/**
 * Processes a <LINK> element to determine the mapping between
 * any schema prefix specified by that element and prefixes
 * specified for the schema URI.
 *
 * If the URI in the <code>href</code> attribute of the LINK
 * matches a URI in out prefixMap, then a new mapping of
 * property key names is created which maps the
 * the string "HTML_META_<i>pre</i>" to the prefix specified
 * for that URI in prefixMap. Where <i>pre</i> is the string
 * found in the <code>rel</code> attribute without the "schema." prefix.
 */
public void processLink(Element link)
{
    String rel = link.getAttribute("rel");
    String pre = null;
    String href = null;
    if ((rel != null) && (rel.startsWith("schema.")))
    {
        // This link specifies a schema prefix to URI mapping
        pre = rel.substring(7);
        href = link.getAttribute("href");
        if (href != null)
        {
            if (prefixMap.containsKey(href))
            {
                // Store the property mapping for later use.
                currMap.put("HTML_META_" + pre,
                        prefixMap.get(href));
            }
        }
    }
}
```

Summary

In this chapter we explored how XML meta data can be applied to provide enhanced search, navigation, personalization, and access to both data and services. We introduced RIL and RuleML as languages under development to create and exchange inference rules using XML. We then saw how RDF can be applied when creating modular meta data processing utilities.

In the next chapter we're going to look at a couple of ideas which will take RDF and topic maps into the next stage of development, the automatic construction of topic map code and the possibilities for combining topic maps with RDF representations.

Meta DataProfessionalXMLMeta DataProfessionalXMLMeta DataPro

11

Further Topic Map/RDF Developments

In this chapter we're going to discuss possible future developments of RDF and topic maps. We'll be looking at:

- ❑ Automatic topic map construction, and one possible way to go about it
- ❑ *Combining RDF and topic maps*

Automatic Topic Map Construction

As we saw in Chapter 7, traditionally topic maps have been created manually, using either straightforward text editors or, more recently, topic map-oriented editing systems. In both of these cases the topic map file is created by human hand, which can often be a laborious task. It is, of course, very desirable to be able to create topic maps by means of an *automated* process. The reason for doing so is fairly obvious; creating topic maps by an automated process will reduce the overall cost of production, by reducing the amount of time it takes, and minimizing the risk of errors and omissions.

This chapter discusses one approach to automatically constructing a topic map. I say "one" because there are many ways in which the construction of an XTM topic map can be automated. The method discussed here is not a universal approach – in this chapter a particular kind of topic map is built, and it is built from particular data sources.

Broadly speaking, automatic topic map construction can mean two things – *automated* construction and *automatic* construction – we'll explore the difference between these two next. The discussion presented here focuses on automatic construction (the XTM output is constructed from pre-existing electronically represented data; we do not see an example of an XTM topic map that is created solely by a person making up all of the topics and associations from his head).

Automated Topic Map Construction

There are several approaches that could be taken when constructing topic maps:

- ❏ Manual construction, the traditional approach used to create topic maps.
- ❏ Combination of manual and automated construction.
- ❏ Use of an XTM-aware visual construction tool.

Manual Construction

Traditionally, the topic map author types all of the code statements required to create a topic map into a text editor, like Notepad. They must spell everything perfectly, use the exact proper syntax for the topic map statements, and place the statements in the correct order. All of the content for that map comes from the author's own knowledge; it is not obtained from any pre-existing electronic source.

I have built a couple of very small topic maps this way. Most of the topic maps that are on the Internet were originally built this way too. It is very tedious process, error prone, and takes an interminable amount of time.

Combination of Manual and Automated Construction

With this method, the user manually creates the various necessary code snippets with the aid of a construction tool. The topic map author is responsible for providing the information placed into the map he is creating, as well as the placement of the appropriate code segments in the correct order or location in the program.

This should seem familiar to anyone who has created a web page using an HTML editing tool such as Allaire's HomeSite or Microsoft's FrontPage. HomeSite is "HTML aware" in that it can perform HTML syntax checking and be helpful to an HTML author by providing the markup tags to perform various functions without the need for the author to laboriously type them in.

In the same way that an editing program like HomeSite has some useful, functional awareness of the syntax of HTML elements, an automated topic map construction program would have similar limited awareness of the syntax of various XTM syntactical elements. For example, one might choose XTM syntax elements from a drop-down list in the automated XTM constructor program. There might be a symbolic tool bar at the top of the screen as a short-cut to the same XTM syntactical markup. This markup would be "boiler-plate" text appropriate to the particular XTM construct it represents.

For example, it might produce a fixed template like the following:

```
<baseName>
    <baseNameString>?!value</baseNameString>
</baseName>
```

where "?!value" is just a placeholder which shows the user that he needs to provide some text to place at that location. Everything around the marker "?!value" is "boiler-plate" code.

There are number of occasions in topic map code writing where this sort of thing is handy, saving time and reducing the risk of typing errors. There are also places where one needs to insert boiler-code from another construct inside the construct one is creating. This sort of coding assistance is well known to HTML, Java, VB, etc., developers.

While this kind of editor can help with the writing of the required markup and even color-code a page of code to make it clearer to the user (a process sometimes known as syntax highlighting), this kind of editor cannot write the whole program for you, nor can it place snippets of code together by itself to make a complete and correct program.

Similarly, an automated topic map constructor is a kind of editing power tool, but you still have to guide it at every step to create the final result. The author still needs to have fairly detailed knowledge about topic maps somewhat before they can use this kind of editor. This is true of tools like HomeSite, too. If you have no knowledge of HTML then all the cleverness and syntax awareness in HomeSite will not get a functional web page built.

Use of an XTM-Aware Visual Construction Tool

The next level in editing or creating topic map code is to use a visual editor. Instead of typing in the code directly, as you would have to if you were using a text editor, a visual editor would allow you to concentrate on the higher level relationships between the topics and the associations connected with those topics. These would be shown visually on your editor screen. Each topic would be a node in a connected graph structure. Lines would run from them to nodes that were associations for those topic nodes. The whole thing would be color-coded; topics would be one color, and associations another, while the connecting lines would be yet another color, similar to the functionality in UML development tools.

Now instead of typing the code for each node topic or association or whatever, you simply point at a node type icon, drag and drop it into the diagram, and put in the text details required for it using its message box.

Even with this visual system of editing though you still have to have a certain level of knowledge to build a (functional) topic map.

In the future, it might be possible to use a tool like this, but with additional capabilities; it watches your activities as you input information from your own knowledge or point at sources of electronic data to "import" and offers to put them into the right places in the visual map it maintains for you.

> *There was no such automated topic map construction tool available when this chapter was written, but it is probable that some of the more powerful and extensible text editors available (for example, EMACS) could be extended with script or code to make it possible to do many of the things just described. (EMACS is a powerful editor that has long existed in the UNIX world. It is extensible in functionality by the user by means of writing EMACS script or code. The traditional text editing capabilities of EMACS could be extended, using such user-written EMACS scripts, in such a way that EMACS could be made to perform for XTM documents what HomeSite does for HTML documents.)*

Automatic Topic Map Construction

Automatic topic map construction is a somewhat different proposition from *automated* construction. The key difference is that automatic construction is performed by software that "knows more about topic maps" than an editing-level program does.

An automatic topic map constructor can obtain its input information from two types of source:

❑ Input from a person.

❑ Reuse of information already available in some electronic form.

In the case of the example in this chapter the person is the topic map author. The information already available in electronic form is:

- ❑ An RDF Schema, called DAXSVG.
- ❑ An SVG file that contains RDF meta data.

An automatic topic map constructor would be able to use the DTD of XTM 1.0 to verify the syntax of an XTM file. It would also have programming built-in to check the XTM being built for completeness. A given topic map might be syntactically correct but it might also have some necessary topic map elements missing. The completeness checking code would basically run a checklist of things against the code being built to see if essential items are indeed present, and report those that aren't.

Originally topic maps used a different syntax, and the technologies required to handle them are still at the early stages of development. In particular, automatic construction of topic maps is still a very new endeavor. Neither automatic nor automated XTM constructors exist yet. Hence, this chapter is limited in scope to describing an approach that could be taken to automatically generate a topic map representation from another format. We will discuss ways in which this can actually be implemented, and although it is a feasible project for a professional programmer to accomplish, due to space considerations, a complete working topic map builder application will not be demonstrated in this chapter. This chapter does explain how such a system would work, what it needs to do to build an XTM topic map and how the XTM topic map in this chapter was created.

Benefits of Automatic Construction

A primary reason for wanting to be able to produce topic maps is for capturing information from some other, existing, form of representation into a topic map format. We would want to do this when there is a representational benefit to be gained from transforming the source information into a topic map.

An example of where such a gain might be made is part of this chapter's example. Specifically, the source information for the topic map being built here is obtained from an XML file (in this case, a Scalable Vector Graphics (SVG) file of a circuit diagram that also contains RDF). What I refer to as the representational benefit, a gain obtained by trading representations (in this case SVG and RDF to XML topic map), is the opportunity to add information that wasn't present in the original data file.

In the SVG/RDF XML code that was the data source of the topic map there was no indication of these contexts. By adding the <scope> information to each schematic component's picture representation the computer (via the topic map representation) is now able to perceive that each picture component in our example is a kind of circuit-design, and simultaneously a kind of line-drawing, and also a kind of picture. The three things are conceptual contexts, each of these contexts a topic in its own right in the map. This is exciting and powerful. Now the representation can show that not only is a "capacitor" a kind of line-drawing, but it is also a kind of picture.

Some of the hand-made topic maps are just that, information in another form of representation that has been painstakingly coded by hand into a topic map representation. The process of extracting the content from the first representation is called **recognition** and generating a topic map rendition of the same is called **casting**. (The latter is sometimes called re-casting or, according to IBM's terminology, **transcoding,** although some people insist on the term transforming.) In this chapter we will see one approach to how a topic map may be automatically transcoded or transformed (from one representation into topic map representation).

We will be using XTM 1.0 syntax in this chapter so if you are not already familiar with it, you might wish to read Chapter 7 first. We will also be using basic RDF Schema syntax, as covered in Chapter 5.

Transcoding (or Transforming) Example

There are, of course, many different ways that a topic map may be expressed in a computer-based system. There are *graph-based* maps, where lines connect nodes in pictures or diagrams, and there are *serialized* forms of these same graph structures, which occur as text based statements. For the example topic map in this chapter we will use a serialized form. The subject of the example topic map that we'll develop in this chapter is shown here in picture form:

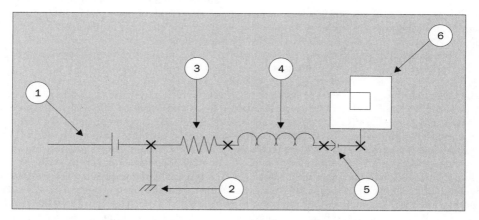

It's an electronic circuit diagram – the device depicted is a *Gravitic Anomalizer*. (This is a futuristic device used in the British science fiction series "Dr. Who", used to perform various amazing tasks, such as picking locks.)

The circuit diagram is made up of several visual objects, with each visual object representing one of the components in the circuit. So, reading from left to right we have visual objects such as battery (labeled as 1 in the figure), ground (2), variable resistor (3), inductor (4), capacitor (5), and antenna (6).

Note that there are crosses ("x"s) located at several points on the diagram. These points designate connection or connectivity. In a real circuit the physical components would have their leads (wires) soldered together to make an electrical connection. In the diagram where the leads of two of the schematic diagram objects are touching signifies that the objects are connected.

The visual objects are defined via both SVG source code (file `circuit.svg`), which is rendered to make the picture, and also by RDF statements used to describe spatial co-location information (file `contentschema`).

SVG is the Scalable Vector Graphics language defined by the W3C for specifying graphics on the Web. It is designed to draw vectors (lines, circles, etc.,) and can also include bitmaps. Its specification is at www.w3.org/TR/SVG.

The SVG code in this example contains RDF meta data which gives spatial information about objects in the SVG coded picture. The RDF was placed there when the SVG was coded to make the picture. This spatial co-location information tells us, for example, that the inductor is to the right of the variable resistor, and that they are also touching (in other words connected in the electronic sense). The meta data vocabulary used to describe the spatial co-locations comes from the **DAXSVG RDF Schema**, which I designed (based on Guillaume Lovet's AXSVG – http://www.w3.org/WAI/ER/ASVG/) to be a taxonomy for visual terminology. It was constructed to be used in examples such as this and is not a standard schema per se. It may be referenced on the Web at http://www.openmeta.org. The SVG code, which uses XML, contains the RDF statements, and the DAXSVG vocabulary will be discussed in further detail shortly. We won't discuss SVG in detail.

The topic map that will be generated consists of a collection of **topics**, each having **names**, **resources**, and **associations**. As we will see, the *topic* items are derived from the **nominal objects** constituting the source diagram. In other words, the XTM topics are obtained by selecting all of the visual/graphic objects present in the diagram and using them as subjects. So we will have `<topic>` elements for the battery, the inductor, the antenna, etc. The topic map *associations* are derived by transcoding the spatial co-location RDF statements into topic map association statement representation form. So we might, for example, have a topic map association representing the fact that "inductor is connected to variable resistor".

What the topic map provides is a set of pointers to objects or resources that are in other files; that is what topic maps are for. They sit above the resources they refer to and organize subjects about those resources. In this case the resources are SVG graphics objects, with names like "capacitor" and "inductor". These names are defined in the SVG markup as the values of `id` attributes. The topic map is not part of the SVG file; it is a separate file. In a sense it sits above the SVG file and allows relationships to be defined between the parts of the XML file pointed at by the topic map. The topic map concept allows you to do things like relate this schematic diagram instance to other schematic diagram instances, perhaps one in a 9 inch thick book at The Boeing Company, which shows the schematic circuit for the 777 aircraft's ILS transponder. The topic map allows the computer to perceive that the schematic shown here in this book is the same kind of "thing" as in the Boeing manual and the same kind of "thing" as the schematic in the manual for your VCR. In the case of this particular topic map it was created to demonstrate that topic map technology could be used to permit the computer to have perception of semantic equivalency. For example, this schematic is a picture, just like the bar chart used in the one of the use cases in Chapter 16 is also a picture. They don't have the same visual contents; they have the same topic map `<scope>` ("context" in regular English). The map created in this section also allows the computer to perceive that all of the individual visual objects (capacitor, inductor, antenna, battery, etc.) are each and collectively a kind of line drawing "thing" as well as a kind of circuit-design "thing". A rich topic map system would have many topics and associations about both categories of "thing", and would therefore be able to perceive that there is a semantic or meaningful relationship between "things" that are in a circuit-design and "things" that are in line drawings! By the way, "thing" is the root level of nearly all taxonomies, and all the other classes are children of it. An ontology or a taxonomy is an organization of terms which provide the semantics of vocabulary in a domain.

The complete topic map generated for this chapter is too long to print in its entirety, but has been provided in the download file, `circuittm.xml`. Subsections of the code are discussed in the body of this chapter to illustrate how the topic map builder application would work.

The Subject of the Topic Map

As we have seen, the picture we are going to generate a topic map for is a diagram of an electronic schematic. Note that the device depicted by the schematic does not physically exist, just as the #mackintosh-dome in Chapter 7 did not exist! That dome was a planned or diagrammed thing. Even so, it can be discussed functionally in a topic map, metaphorically in a sense, without the need for a concrete instance of it existing in the real world. The circuit does not physically exist – we simply have a plan for how to build it. Topic maps have this added value, allowing concepts and plans themselves to be represented in topic maps, and not just the things that result from the execution of those plans. This is the important concept of **reification** as discussed in Chapter 4.

In this example you see that the topic map contains semantic information about the *visual appearance of the content* of the picture. In other words, a blind person could have a topic map scanning program to describe the contents of the picture to them. This topic map also contains some extra information, provided by the topic map author, which the RDF meta data accompanying the SVG drawing code did not have.

The visually distinct constituents of the picture above are the schematic representation of electronic components that would be in an actual electronic circuit. The visual constituents conform to the standard electronic symbols used to depict the equivalent real devices. Standard software such as CAD-CAM (computer aided design and manufacturing) would have a library of such components in visual graphics form. The illustration above shows such components touching each other (that is, "the ends of their leads touch"), using the implicit convention for connectivity in standardized circuit diagrams.

Meta Data Resources Associated with the Diagrammed Objects

Each of the electronic components that make up our circuit diagram has meta data about it – this is contained in the RDF Schema file contentschema.

The RDF below (also part of the circuit.svg file) uses the vocabularies from both the contentschema and the DAXSVG RDF Schema. These vocabularies are used to recognize that there are circuit components in the picture to begin with, and also to recognize the visual relationships they have with each other, the most important of which is that they are connected pair-wise with each other.

DAXSVG is a vocabulary for defining visual spatial relationships, such as "IsNear", "AtRight", "Below", etc.

The first section of code contains all of the required namespace declarations:

```
<?xml version="1.0"?>
<rdf:RDF
    xmlns:rdf="http://www.w3.org/1999/02/22-rdf-syntax-ns#"
    xmlns:DC="http://purl.oclc.org/dc/documents/rec-dces-199809.htm#"
    xmlns:Circuit="http://www.openmeta.org/2000/PhotoRDF/circuit-1-0#"
    xmlns:daxsvg="http://www.openmeta.org/2001/daxsvg#">
```

Next we have an <rdf:Description> element containing several different kinds of Dublin Core, (DC), meta data. As was discussed in Chapter 4, Dublin Core is the most widely used of the standardized meta data systems. The description element also contains circuit references.

```
<rdf:Description about="">
  <DC:Coverage>Circuit 25 revision 7</DC:Coverage>
  <DC:Source>Photo</DC:Source>
```

```
      <DC:Relation>Circuit 25</DC:Relation>
      <DC:Date>2000-04-01</DC:Date>
      <DC:Description>
          A schematic diagram of a GA circuit is shown.
      </DC:Description>
      <DC:Publisher rdf:resource="http://www.openmeta.org/People/David/"/>
      <DC:Title>Gravitic Anomalizer Circuit 25 Revision 7</DC:Title>
      <DC:Type>image</DC:Type>
      <DC:Format>image/jpeg</DC:Format>
      <DC:Identifier>000401</DC:Identifier>
      <DC:Creator rdf:resource="http://www.openmeta.org/People/David"/>
      <Circuit:inductor
rdf:resource="http://www.openmeta.org/People/David/Circuit25v7#inductor" />

      <Circuit:variableresistor
rdf:resource="http://www.openmeta.org/People/David/Circuit25v7#variableresistor"
      />
      <Circuit:capacitor
rdf:resource="http://www.openmeta.org/People/David/Circuit25v7#capacitor" />
      <Circuit:battery
rdf:resource="http://www.openmeta.org/People/David/Circuit25v7#battery" />
      <Circuit:antenna
rdf:resource="http://www.openmeta.org/People/David/Circuit25v7#antenna" />
   </rdf:Description>
...
```

Not all of the objects are shown in the code fragment above, but there are elements for each object in the diagram in the file.

Next we see the first of a series of RDF meta data statements contained in the SVG code file that define the nominals, or objects, such as battery and ground in the schema – here two meta data objects are defined as having the relationship Touching:

```
<rdf:Description about="battery">
   <daxsvg:Touching resource="ground"/>
</rdf:Description>
```

This is the second RDF statement. Here two meta data objects, ground and variableresistor, are also defined as having the relationship Touching:

```
<rdf:Description about=" ground ">
   <daxsvg:Touching resource="variableresistor"/>
</rdf:Description>
```

In these next two RDF statements the nominals battery and ground are defined as having the relationship AtRight (the ground is to the right of the battery), and the nominals variableresistor and inductor are also defined as having the relationship AtRight (the inductor is to the right of the variableresistor):

```
<rdf:Description about="battery">
   <daxsvg:AtRight resource="ground"/>
</rdf:Description>
```

```
<rdf:Description about="variableresistor">
   <daxsvg:AtRight resource="inductor"/>
</rdf:Description>
```

We have several more RDF statements, each describing various other relationships between the components in our electronic circuit:

```
<rdf:Description about="variableresistor">
   <daxsvg:Touching resource="inductor"/>
</rdf:Description>

<rdf:Description about="inductor">
   <daxsvg:Touching resource="capacitor"/>
</rdf:Description>

<rdf:Description about="inductor">
   <daxsvg:AtRight resource="capacitor"/>
</rdf:Description>

<rdf:Description about="capacitor">
   <daxsvg:AtRight resource="antenna"/>
</rdf:Description>

<rdf:Description about="capacitor">
   <daxsvg:Touching resource="antenna"/>
</rdf:Description>

</rdf:RDF>
```

This brings to an end the RDF description code block. The following sections discuss how these RDF concepts are used to create a topic map.

Topic Map Code

The first thing that our automatic topic map generator has to create is an XML document shell to house the topic map code that is to be made – these are typical lines of code required for any topic map document. As you can see from the code below, the XML document shell has a DOCTYPE statement that declares what DTD should be used, and a namespace declaration. This gives the URL of the XTM Topic Map, a W3C XLink namespace statement, and an (optional) xml:base URI. Except for the xml:base attribute, all of that information is stored as a single boilerplate text file which the constructor would simply copy and insert as the start of the text file that will house the topic map code being built.

```
<?xml version="1.0"?>
   <!DOCTYPE topicMap
            PUBLIC "-//TopicMaps.Org//DTD XML Topic Map (XTM) 1.0//EN"
                   "file://usr/local/home/gromit/xml/xtm/xtm1.dtd">
   <topicMap xmlns='http://www.topicmaps.org/xtm/1.0/'
             xmlns:xlink='http://www.w3.org/1999/xlink'
             xml:base='http://www.openmeta.org/People/David/Circuit25v7'>
    <!-- topics, associations, and merge map directives go here -->

   </topicMap>
```

We are more interested in the comment section (which currently holds the comment "topics ... go here"). Now that we have identified the container to place that code into, let's discuss what will be contained within it.

Creating Topic Map: Named-Topics, Scope, and BaseName

The first thing that must be generated is the collection of topics that constitutes the topic map. In an earlier section we saw how the object names occurred in RDF statements – these names, such as battery and ground, are to be used as `<topic>` elements. In order to build our topic map we therefore need to determine the object names from the RDF statements used to describe the diagram we are considering, for example:

```
<rdf:Description about="battery">
    <daxsvg:Touching resource="ground"/>
</rdf:Description>
```

The topic map builder simply takes the string contents of the about= and the resource= parts of the statement and uses this text as the `<topic>` names.

Also found in the description of the diagram is one RDF statement used as the name of the entire collection of circuit components, and given the ID "Circuit":

```
<content:Keywords rdf:ID="Circuit">
    <label xml:lang="en">Circuit</label>
</content:Keywords>
```

Let's take a look at how the Circuit object is represented in the topic map:

```
<topic id="Gravitic-Anomalizer-circuit">
    <baseName>
        <baseNameString>Electronic Circuit Schematic</baseNameString>
    </baseName>
    <baseName>
        <scope>
            <topicRef xlink:href="#circuit-design"/>
            <topicRef xlink:href="#electronic-circuit"/>
            <topicRef xlink:href="#line-drawing"/>
            <topicRef xlink:href="#picture"/>
        </scope>
        <baseNameString>circuit</baseNameString>
    </baseName>
</topic>
```

In a similar fashion, each of the components within the circuit is addressed as a topic in this topic map, starting with our battery component:

```
<topic id="battery">
    <baseName>
        <baseNameString>Electric Circuit Battery</baseNameString>
    </baseName>
    <baseName>
        <scope>
            <topicRef xlink:href="#electrical-power-source"/>
```

```
        <topicRef xlink:href="#circuit-design"/>
        <topicRef xlink:href="#electronic-circuit"/>
        <topicRef xlink:href="#line-drawing"/>
        <topicRef xlink:href="#picture"/>
    </scope>
    <baseNameString>battery</baseNameString>
  </baseName>
</topic>
```

Note that in the battery topic shown above four of the topics used as references in the scope of the topic are shared with the circuit topic, that is, they have four scope items in common (#circuit-design, #electronic-circuit, #line-drawing, and #picture). However, the first scope item of the battery topic, #electrical-power-source, is a *unique* topic in this topic map – it is not shared with any other scopes. The reason for this is that the battery object conceptually is the only object in the circuit that can be a source of electrical power; all the other circuit parts use electricity, they do not generate it. As the <scope> is the "place" in the topic map where conceptual categories are named as contexts, the battery as electrical power source is unique in this map. No other circuit object is a source of electrical power. We'll return to the concept of unique scope later.

```
<topic id="ground">
    <baseName>
        <baseNameString>Electric Circuit Ground</baseNameString>
    </baseName>
    <baseName>
        <scope>
            <topicRef xlink:href="#electrical-ground"/>
            <topicRef xlink:href="#circuit-design"/>
            <topicRef xlink:href="#electronic-circuit"/>
            <topicRef xlink:href="#line-drawing"/>
            <topicRef xlink:href="#picture"/>
        </scope>
        <baseNameString>ground</baseNameString>
    </baseName>
</topic>
```

In the ground topic (above) four of the topics used as references in the scope of the topic are shared with the circuit topic (and three of those are shared with the battery topic). That is, ground topics have four scope items in common. The first scope item of the ground topic, #electrical-ground, is a unique topic in this topic map.

```
<topic id="variableresistor">
    <baseName>
        <baseNameString>Electronic Circuit Variableresistor</baseNameString>
    </baseName>
    <baseName>
        <scope>
            <topicRef xlink:href="#electrical-resistance"/>
            <topicRef xlink:href="#circuit-design"/>
            <topicRef xlink:href="#electronic-circuit"/>
            <topicRef xlink:href="#line-drawing"/>
            <topicRef xlink:href="#picture"/>
        </scope>
        <baseNameString>variableresistor</baseNameString>
    </baseName>
</topic>
```

In the `variableresistor` topic (above) four of the topics used as references in the `scope` of the topic are shared with other topics. That is, there are four `scope` items in common. Only the first `scope` item of the `variableresistor` topic, `#electrical-resistance`, is a unique topic in this topic map.

```
<topic id="inductor">
   <baseName>
      <baseNameString>Electronic Circuit Inductor</baseNameString>
   </baseName>
   <baseName>
      <scope>
         <topicRef xlink:href="#electrical-inductance"/>
         <topicRef xlink:href="#circuit-design"/>
         <topicRef xlink:href="#electronic-circuit"/>
         <topicRef xlink:href="#line-drawing"/>
         <topicRef xlink:href="#picture"/>
      </scope>
      <baseNameString>inductor</baseNameString>
   </baseName>
</topic>
```

The other topics are defined in a similar way:

```
<topic id="capacitor">
   <baseName>
      <baseNameString>Electronic Circuit Capacitor</baseNameString>
   </baseName>
   <baseName>
      <scope>
         <topicRef xlink:href="#electrical-capacitance"/>
         <topicRef xlink:href="#circuit-design"/>
         <topicRef xlink:href="#electronic-circuit"/>
         <topicRef xlink:href="#line-drawing"/>
         <topicRef xlink:href="#picture"/>
      </scope>
      <baseNameString>capacitor</baseNameString>
   </baseName>
</topic>

<topic id="antenna">
   <baseName>
      <baseNameString>Electronic Circuit Antenna</baseNameString>
   </baseName>
   <baseName>
      <scope>
         <topicRef xlink:href="#electrical-antenna"/>
         <topicRef xlink:href="#circuit-design"/>
         <topicRef xlink:href="#electronic-circuit"/>
         <topicRef xlink:href="#line-drawing"/>
         <topicRef xlink:href="#picture"/>
      </scope>
      <baseNameString>antenna</baseNameString>
   </baseName>
</topic>
```

To recap some salient points from the above code:

❑ There are some topics in common, such as "#circuit-design", "#electronic-circuit", "#line-drawing", "#picture", etc. This means that all of the topics having these <scope> topics in common have a *shared* meaning or semantics.

❑ Each of the components also has a <scope> topic that is unique to it. Notice that this topic describes the nature of what the component is, by means of what it does or how it works. For example, our battery component's unique scope is #electrical-power-source, which adequately describes that the purpose of the battery in the circuit is to provide the electrical power.

These unique topics could be used, in conjunction with SYRUP or SPICE programs for example, to specify an equation that computes the behavior of the electrical component in a circuit. SYRUP and SPICE are applications to simulate the functioning of electrical and logic circuits. While it would be very interesting to pursue the details of these unique topic items, it's outside the scope of this chapter.

Adding Topic Occurrences to the Topic Map Code

Another thing that is of value in topic maps is indicating occurrences of any information that is the subject of the various topics in the map. Another way of saying that is that topic maps reference instances of information that are outside of the map itself. The information may be text, a picture or it may be a physical thing. In the example topic map we are building the topics are about visual information that is represented using SVG code in an XML file. Those instances are known as occurrences in topic map terminology. The topic map <occurrence> elements in the map we create here have references to the occurrences or instances of the topics (battery, capacitor, inductor, etc.) that are in the SVG document.

We'll see how that is done next. The following example shows the addition of occurrence information (to the existing topic and scope information) for the single topic capacitor. The constructor has access to both the SVG document, which is the source of the topic map information, and also the DAXSVG schema. In the SVG file there is an instance of SVG code which has an id="capacitor" attribute. There is also a collection of RDF statements in the same file, meta data after all, which have capacitor in both resource and about attributes. This is true for all the other parts of the circuit as well. These id, resource and about attributes are where the constructor gets the names to plug into its <topic id=".."> statements:

```
<topic id="capacitor">
    <baseName>
        <baseNameString>Electronic Circuit Capacitor</baseNameString>
    </baseName>
    <baseName>
        <scope>
            <topicRef xlink:href="#electric-capacitance"/>
            <topicRef xlink:href="#circuit-design"/>
            <topicRef xlink:href="#electronic-circuit"/>
            <topicRef xlink:href="#line-drawing"/>
            <topicRef xlink:href="#picture"/>
        </scope>
        <baseNameString>circuit</baseNameString>
    </baseName>
    <occurrence>
        <instanceOf>
            <topicRef xlink:href="#mention"/>
        </instanceOf>
        <resourceRef xlink:href="www.openmeta.org/2001/contentschema ..."/>
```

```
    </occurrence>
    <occurrence>
       <instanceOf>
          <topicRef xlink:href="#appears-in"/>
       </instanceOf>
       <resourceRef xlink:href="www.openmeta.org/2001/svgpicture.svg ..."/>
    </occurrence>
    <occurrence>
       <instanceOf>
          <topicRef xlink:href="#book"/>
       </instanceOf>
       <resourceRef xlink:href=" URL of this WROX Pro Meta Data book ..."/>
    </occurrence>
```

```
</topic>
```

The topic map author has to provide the information in the `<resourceRef>` statements above, because the constructor would not have enough information to obtain this information by itself.

Notice that there were three topics used to depict occurrence information, to illustrate that there are (at least) three different ways that the information exists: as text in a file, as a picture, and as part of a book.

❑   `#mention` is a topic which refers to the presence of *textual* information in a resource or file, relating to the topic.

❑   `#appears-in` is a topic which refers to the presence of *graphical* information in a resource or file, relating to the topic.

❑   `#book` is a topic which refers to the presence of (paper) "bound" information in a resource relating to the topic. It might be a book or a journal.

In the code above, `#mention` refers to the occurrence of one or more passages of text relating to the `capacitor` topic, in one or more text files. The resource linked to in this case is the `contentschema` file, where there would be at least a single occurrence of the vocabulary term `capacitor` (because that is where `capacitor` is defined to begin with).

Also in the code above, `#appears-in` refers to the occurrence of a visual or graphical object named `capacitor`, in the diagram or "picture". Hence the resource being linked to is the SVG file that represents the graphical image.

> As all of the components appear in the same diagram (in other words they are generated from the same SVG source), they all exist in the same file (`contentschema`), and they are all in this book, each one of the topics that are component subjects have identical occurrence information in this case. Since the exact same occurrence information is placed into each of the component topic code blocks, only this first one was shown. It should sufficiently demonstrate the pattern, so we won't exhaustively list occurrence information for all of the component topics. If you are interested you can view the complete topic map in the code download.

Associations in Topic Map Code

This RDF statement below, found in the SVG meta data section of the SVG source code which renders the circuit diagram picture, is an example of where our topic map-creating program gets its information from for the next bit of topic map code generation.

```
<rdf:Description about="battery">
   <daxsvg:Connects resource="ground"/>
</rdf:Description>
```

It references the DAXSVG vocabulary namespace:

```
<rdf:Property ID="Connects">
<rdfs:comment>has a degree of same location (by value). some same location as
focus object's SVG x,y coords. ie Shares at least one coord point on
{or within} its periphery with another object. This point is not its x,y origin.
Touches is an "at" version of "near". Compute with sorted-extreme-points.
 (uses context)    g14(z)   </rdfs:comment>
<rdfs:range rdf:resource="#SvgEntity" />
<rdfs:domain rdf:resource="#SvgEntity" />
</rdf:Property>
```

The topic map builder simply takes the string contents of the about and the resource attributes of the RDF statement, and takes (from the right hand side of the DAXSVG namespace prefix, daxsvg:) the word Connects. The topics derived from this particular <rdf:Description> meta data statement are battery and ground, and the relationship (in other words the <association>) is connects.

So this SVG meta data says that the battery object is *connected* to the ground object.

Topic Map Code Showing Connectivity of Components

This next bit of topic map code shows how to represent this information, for example, that the battery in the diagram is *connected* to the ground in the diagram. This block of code shows the use of a built-in XTM capability known as **class-instance associations**. The idea behind this code block is that there is a general **class** (defined here as connected-pairs) and that class has **instances**, in this case two of them – battery and ground. The representation in English would be "*A battery topic is connected, in this case, to a ground topic*".

First we have a set of topic references to other parts of the same topic map where the topics battery, ground, variable-resistor, inductor, capacitor, and antenna are defined. These are shown here only for convenience and completeness; in a full topic map they would appear somewhere else in the topic map code and not be repeated.

```
<topic id="battery"/>
<topic id="ground"/>
<topic id="variable-resistor"/>
<topic id="inductor"/>
<topic id="capacitor"/>
<topic id="antenna"/>
<topic id="connected-pairs"/>
```

Next we have an <association> that uses the XTM special class-instance association. The *class* is a *kind* of thing, and the *instance* is an *occurrence* of that thing.

```
<association>
  <instanceOf>
    <subjectIndicatorRef
        xlink:href="http://www.topicmaps.org/xtm/1.0/core.xtm#class-instance"/>
  </instanceOf>
```

The `<scope>` of the relationships in this association are shown next, such that the *context* for the scope is `battery-ground-connection`. Notice that the context or scope for this `<association>` is itself another topic.

```
<scope>
  <topicRef xlink:href="battery-ground-connection"/>
</scope>
```

Notice also the use of a `subjectIndicatorRef` to specify that the `member` in the association has the role of `class`:

```
<member>
  <roleSpec>
    <subjectIndicatorRef
        xlink:href="http://www.topicmaps.org/xtm/1.0/core.xtm#class"/>
  </roleSpec>
```

`connected-pairs` (shown below) is the name of the topic which specifies the type of class. Basically this means the same as "*class of thingA connected-to thingB*".

```
    <topicRef xlink:href="#connected-pairs"/>
  </member>
```

The instance subject indicator in the role specification signals the start of a list of topics that are instances or occurrences of the connected-pairs class. In this case we have `battery` and `ground` as topics, each an instance of a thing in the connected pair relationship:

```
    <member>
      <roleSpec>
        <subjectIndicatorRef
            xlink:href="http://www.topicmaps.org/xtm/1.0/core.xtm#instance"/>
      </roleSpec>
      <topicRef xlink:href="#battery"/>
      <topicRef xlink:href="#ground"/>
    </member>
  </association>
```

The `<scope>` statement was placed there for a reason, which we'll discuss next:

```
<scope>
  <topicRef xlink:href="battery-ground-connection"/>
</scope>
```

You might be wondering what happened to the other components in the diagram. Well, here's where they come in. This next bit of code shows the topic map representation of the following concept: "the `battery` in the diagram is *connected* to the `ground` in the diagram, and the `ground` in the diagram is connected to the `variableresistor` in the diagram". That is what is actually represented in the topic map.

```
<topic id="battery"/>
<topic id="ground"/>
<topic id="variable-resistor"/>
```

```
<topic id="inductor"/>
<topic id="capacitor"/>
<topic id="antenna"/>
<topic id="connected-pairs"/>
<association>
   <instanceOf>
      <subjectIndicatorRef
         xlink:href="http://www.topicmaps.org/xtm/1.0/core.xtm#class-instance"/>
   </instanceOf>
   <scope>
      <topicRef xlink:href="battery-ground-connection"/>
   </scope>
   <member>
      <roleSpec>
         <subjectIndicatorRef
            xlink:href="http://www.topicmaps.org/xtm/1.0/core.xtm#class"/>
      </roleSpec>
      <topicRef xlink:href="#connected-pairs"/>
   </member>
   <member>
      <roleSpec>
         <subjectIndicatorRef
            xlink:href="http://www.topicmaps.org/xtm/1.0/core.xtm#instance"/>
      </roleSpec>
      <topicRef xlink:href="#battery"/>
      <topicRef xlink:href="#ground"/>
   </member>
</association>
<association>
   <instanceOf>
      <subjectIndicatorRef
         xlink:href="http://www.topicmaps.org/xtm/1.0/core.xtm#class-instance"/>
   </instanceOf>
   <scope>
      <topicRef xlink:href="ground-variable-resistor-connection"/>
   </scope>
   <member>
      <roleSpec>
         <subjectIndicatorRef
            xlink:href="http://www.topicmaps.org/xtm/1.0/core.xtm#class"/>
      </roleSpec>
      <topicRef xlink:href="#connected-pairs"/>
   </member>
   <member>
      <roleSpec>
         <subjectIndicatorRef
            xlink:href="http://www.topicmaps.org/xtm/1.0/core.xtm#instance"/>
      </roleSpec>
      <topicRef xlink:href="#ground"/>
      <topicRef xlink:href="#variable-resistor"/>
   </member>
</association>
```

If you compare this block of code with `<association>` code preceding it you will see that the second block simply repeats (twice) the same association pattern of the first. However, the second time the `scope` topic is different from the first, as are the topics in the instances part. What this means is that the second part says, "*The ground is connected to the variable resistor*".

The important difference between the two <associations> is that they have different scope topics: battery-ground-connection and ground-variable-resistor-connection. This prevents a topic map processor from treating the two associations as equivalent because they share the same role specifications; connected-pairs. Otherwise there would be a tangle of connections and we would no longer have a pair-wise connectivity, we would then have everything pretty well connected to everything else! This is not what we mean or want so the <scope> elements in the associations keep things organized logically.

You can see that even the components-connectivity subset of the entire topic map we are creating, if explicitly shown here, would take a couple of pages to list, let alone listing the entire topic map. By looking at the two previous code blocks, you can see that each pair of components that are connected in this circuit is added as an association, which has a unique scope. This ensures that the association refers only to those two components. For the sake of brevity, suffice it to say that the connectivity of all the pair-wise circuit components are put into the topic map using the same method as shown in the two previous code blocks.

> *If you are still having difficulties visualizing what this long piece of topic map code looks like then refer to the complete topic map (*circuittm.xml*) in the code download.*

Topic Map Contains Information on Spatial Relationships in Picture

Having just looked at how the *connectivity* of the circuit components is achieved in the topic map, let us now turn to seeing how the *spatial relationships* are depicted. If you guessed that the same mechanism that was used for connectivity is used for spatiality you'd be right. That is because the spatial relationships are again *instances* of a predefined *class*.

The spatial relationships between the schematic components are specified in RDF statements, as we described above, in the section *"Meta Data Resources Associated with the Diagrammed Objects"*. These RDF statements themselves are part of the content of the SVG <metadata> statement in the SVG document.

It so happens that in this case the RDF description of the spatial co-location relationships of the picture occurred sequentially (pretty much), in the code. This sequence is not something that can be counted on as necessarily occurring in the typical RDF-based description. This means that the entire RDF (or other meta data) description set must be scanned for context-based saliency. By this I mean that relevant bits of RDF may be scattered around the description set in no special order and it is up to the topic map building software to make a prudent search of the set for all usable statements, regardless of the order or sequence of those RDF statements. Putting the semantic content of each RDF statement into a table makes quick work of sorting and so on in a later step.

It doesn't take a particularly sharp eye to notice that this RDF statement:

```
<rdf:Description about="battery">
   <daxsvg:AtRight resource="ground"/>
</rdf:Description>
```

is remarkably similar to the following RDF statement:

```
<rdf:Description about="battery">
   <daxsvg:Connects resource="ground"/>
</rdf:Description>
```

which we just looked at.

This is because the usage is the same for both statements. They are both RDF statements that convey a named relationship between two objects (or "resources" in RDF parlance). In this case the two resources or objects in the diagram are the same, what is different is the name of the relationship between them. Resources can have a countless number of relationships between them, requiring a "sea" of RDF statements to assert them.

In this case our current focus is on identifying all of the RDF statements in the diagram description found in the SVG code, `circuit.svg`, (and also occurring, for this example, in `contentschema`). That is because we wish to know all of the spatial descriptions for our diagram, the diagram that we are transcoding into a topic map.

The DAXSVG schema has the vocabulary items that define which terms are spatial co-location terms. Spatial co-location may be a new term to some; it means the relative location in space between two (or possibly more) objects or points. Examples of such terms are `AtRight`, `AtLeft`, `Below`, `Near`.

```
<rdf:RDF xml:lang="en"
    xmlns:rdf="http://www.w3.org/1999/02/22-rdf-syntax-ns#"
    xmlns:rdfs="http://www.w3.org/2000/01/rdf-schema#">

    <rdfs:Class rdf:ID="SvgEntity">
        <rdfs:comment>The class of SVG entities, referenced by their id in
the SVG code. THIS schema is modeled on the schema at
http://www.w3.org/2000/01/rdf-schema#Resource. It is intended for use in
tandem with it. It is called daxsvg-schema-rdf.xml</rdfs:comment>
        <rdfs:subClassOf
            rdf:resource="http://www.openmeta.org/2001/04/rdf-schema#Resource" />
    </rdfs:Class>

    <rdf:Property ID="IsNear">
        <rdfs:comment>has a degree of nearness (by value). g1(x)</rdfs:comment>
        <rdfs:range rdf:resource="#SvgEntity" />
        <rdfs:domain rdf:resource="#SvgEntity" />
    </rdf:Property>

    <rdf:Property ID="IsFar">
        <rdfs:comment>has a degree of farness (by value). complement of near,
                1 - g1(x)</rdfs:comment>
        <rdfs:range rdf:resource="#SvgEntity" />
        <rdfs:domain rdf:resource="#SvgEntity" />
    </rdf:Property>

    <rdf:Property ID="Touches">
        <rdfs:comment>has a degree of same location (by value). some same
        location as focus object's SVG x,y coords. ie Shares at least one coord
        point on {or within} its periphery with another object. This point is not
        necessarily its x,y origin. Touches is an "at" version of "near".   (uses
        context)   g14(z)   </rdfs:comment>
        <rdfs:range rdf:resource="#SvgEntity" />
        <rdfs:domain rdf:resource="#SvgEntity" />
    </rdf:Property>

    <rdf:Property ID="AtRight">
        <rdfs:comment>has a degree of to the right (by value).  (uses context)
                g15(x)</rdfs:comment>
        <rdfs:range rdf:resource="#SvgEntity" />
```

```
               <rdfs:domain rdf:resource="#SvgEntity" />
      </rdf:Property>

      <rdf:Property ID="AtLeft">
            <rdfs:comment>has a degree of to the left (by value). (uses context)
                         g16(x)</rdfs:comment>
            <rdfs:range rdf:resource="#SvgEntity" />
            <rdfs:domain rdf:resource="#SvgEntity" />
      </rdf:Property>

      <rdf:Property ID="Center">
            <rdfs:comment>has a degree of [at the] centerness (by value).
                         g8(x)</rdfs:comment>
            <rdfs:range rdf:resource="#SvgEntity" />
            <rdfs:domain rdf:resource="#SvgEntity" />
      </rdf:Property>

      <rdf:Property ID="Periphery">
            <rdfs:comment>has a degree of outerness (by value). complement of
                         center, 1 - g8(x) </rdfs:comment>
            <rdfs:range rdf:resource="#SvgEntity" />
            <rdfs:domain rdf:resource="#SvgEntity" />
      </rdf:Property>

      <rdf:Property ID="Connects">
            <rdfs:comment>has a degree of same location (by value). some same
            location as focus object's SVG x,y coords. Shares at least one coord
            point on {or within} its periphery with another object. This point is not
            necessarily its x,y origin. Touches is an "at" version of "near".  (uses
            context)    g14(z)  </rdfs:comment>
            <rdfs:range rdf:resource="#SvgEntity" />
            <rdfs:domain rdf:resource="#SvgEntity" />
      </rdf:Property>

      <rdf:Property ID="Contains">
            <rdfs:comment>has a degree of containingness (by value).
                         uses center g8(x). </rdfs:comment>
            <rdfs:range rdf:resource="#SvgEntity" />
            <rdfs:domain rdf:resource="#SvgEntity" />
      </rdf:Property>

</rdf:RDF>
```

For example, one of these terms, AtRight, is found in the DAXSVG vocabulary as a spatial term and hence all occurrences of RDF descriptions bearing this term are of interest during the "search for spatial terms" phase. We saw earlier that there are five occurrences of AtRight descriptions in our circuit diagram meta data. Now we see the topic map creation using that material. For sake of brevity we will only examine the first two association codes developed from these five statements. The remaining three are developed in exactly the same way that the successive connected-pairs were made, as was described in detail earlier.

```
<topic id="atright-pairs"/>
<association>
 <instanceOf>
  <subjectIndicatorRef
       xlink:href="http://www.topicmaps.org/xtm/1.0/core.xtm#class-instance"/>
 </instanceOf>
 <scope>
  <topicRef xlink:href="#battery-atright-ground"/>
 </scope>
```

```
       <member>
        <roleSpec>
         <subjectIndicatorRef
              xlink:href="http://www.topicmaps.org/xtm/1.0/core.xtm#class"/>
        </roleSpec>
        <topicRef xlink:href="#atright-pairs"/>
       </member>
       <member>
        <roleSpec>
         <subjectIndicatorRef
              xlink:href="http://www.topicmaps.org/xtm/1.0/core.xtm#instance"/>
        </roleSpec>
        <topicRef xlink:href="#battery"/>
        <topicRef xlink:href="#ground"/>
       </member>
      </association>
      <association>
       <instanceOf>
        <subjectIndicatorRef
              xlink:href="http://www.topicmaps.org/xtm/1.0/core.xtm#class-instance"/>
       </instanceOf>
       <scope>
        <topicRef xlink:href="ground-atright-variable-resistor"/>
       </scope>
       <member>
        <roleSpec>
         <subjectIndicatorRef
              xlink:href="http://www.topicmaps.org/xtm/1.0/core.xtm#class"/>
        </roleSpec>
        <topicRef xlink:href="#atright-pairs"/>
       </member>
       <member>
        <roleSpec>
         <subjectIndicatorRef
              xlink:href="http://www.topicmaps.org/xtm/1.0/core.xtm#instance"/>
        </roleSpec>
        <topicRef xlink:href="#ground"/>
        <topicRef xlink:href="#variable-resistor"/>
       </member>
      </association>
```

After transcoding the RDF AtRight description statements into topic map topics and associations, we can scan the remaining descriptions for other spatial terms, as found in DAXSVG. In this case there were no other spatial descriptions and hence we have finished the transcoding of this diagram's RDF-based description.

We've discussed a means to create a topic map from pre-existing (electronic) resources and input from the topic map author. It is likely that there will always be some information that adds to the value of a topic map, which cannot be obtained from pre-existing electronic resources themselves and are only obtainable from a human. This is because, for the foreseeable future at least, humans will have more knowledge and greater breadth of knowledge than all of the world's computer repositories contain. For this reason, automatic construction of topic maps will, for the next few years, create maps with chequered or uneven "coverage" (as in code coverage) of the knowledge or information of a domain. For the time being this doesn't matter too much as no one is expecting or trying to attain complete semantic coverage of any domain. Computer programs are designed to be a tool for people to use to accomplish their desired goals whether it be some aspect of e-business, writing and editing a document or adding to the internet's collective base of data, meta data, information, and knowledge.

Automatic topic map constructors may work algorithmically (that is without "knowledge" or the computer equivalent of "thinking") to transform one or more electronic data sets into a topic map (or number of topic maps, as needed).

One of the means of achieving algorithmically-based automatic topic map construction is to define one's own DTD or schema which declares the syntax or structure of the topic map being built. It would be better to use a DTD available through a standard, such as XTM 1.0, because topic maps constructed with that DTD can be used with standard XTM tools (whereas one might have difficulty finding and using tools to work with topic maps built with arbitrary, non-standard, DTDs).

If, as a practice, you use the XTM DTD to define the structure of your topic map and also obtain your source information from an XML file whose DTD you also have, then it would seem reasonable to use MDL (described in Chapter 8) as a mapping tool, or agent, which maps the source information from its XML into the XML syntax described by XTM's DTD. This source information is the data content that is placed into the topic map being constructed, and it is obtained from one or more electronic files. If these files were XML files it would be possible to use a DTD or schema to read the file and to locate items of interest in it that you want to put into your topic map. If, on the other hand, the files that you were sourcing from were not XML files, then you would need a reliable means of identifying, finding, and extracting the information from them that you want to put into your topic map.

If there is some kind of organization to the source files then you could create a program that would use that organization to locate and extract the information that you want to put into your topic map. One way of doing this is to write a program that does the extraction and then stores the extracted material in a normalized form. The content, now expressed as a normalized form could then be placed into a topic map by a fairly straightforward transfer program.

If the source file is one that is not regular (consistent) in some sense, and not a database, then it is necessary to determine how to locate the information you want to put into the topic map. This can be very daunting. Building topic maps from free text is very demanding. The text needs to be parsed, a difficult enough task in itself. The semantics, or meaning, of the text needs to be perceived after that, and then the material found as a result of both these steps needs to be transformed in some way to be placed into your topic map. Getting useful content from a collection of free text is still more of an art than a science, and is the subject of quite a lot of research. Only simple, short, and rather stylized texts would be achievable at the present time. There are a number of précis or summarization programs available which could automatically obtain some of the gist of the free text and this summary material could be put into a topic map without undue difficulty.

For certain kinds of XML-based source information files it would be possible to write a topic map constructor in XSLT. It would not be a light undertaking.

Within a year or two you should expect to see topic map construction programs that use information and knowledge bases to augment algorithmically-based constructors. For example, it's likely there will be software agents that can write the XSLT required to map an example XML file (used as a topic map source file) into the XML syntax of XTM. There will soon be distributed bases of electronic knowledge available on the topics in various domains.

RDF (meta data representation) is being expanded by means of technologies such as DAML+OIL and this means that ontologies and taxonomies can be exchanged and intermixed to provide greater and greater levels of "construction skill" to automatic topic map constructors. What that means is that progressively you will have constructor tools that are capable of "examining" an XML file and constructing a topic map from it.

With the availability of means to create topic maps from non-topic map sources and also to merge other topic maps into your topic maps you end up with many topics and associations, which could easily number into the thousands or even tens of thousands.

Once you have created all of this topic map material what do you do with it? How can you use it? The next section discusses work I am involved in which provides answers to these questions.

Future Work

At the time of writing I am working in collaboration with Benedicte Le Grande on the visualization of topic maps using SVG and meta data. Our work will provide:

- ❑ A means of clustering topic map topics by name, associations, and their frequencies of occurrence.

- ❑ A means of visually changing those clusters, based on mouse selection and/or sorting and/or hiding/showing of topic map information.

- ❑ A means of displaying topic map content as navigable three-dimensional cities, à la Virtual Reality.

- ❑ A means of using meta data-defined vocabulary in the topic maps themselves to help perform such functions as determining the relevance, saliency, contribution, and context of topic map information, and displaying topic maps appropriately.

Benedicte Le Grande's work can be found at http://www-rp.lip6.fr/~blegrand/indexEng.html. At this site you will find links to her papers and references to others, which are not yet online.

We are developing ideas, and code to implement, which allow a user who comes across a large and or complex topic map to gain an understanding of its contents. While it may at first seem obvious that you "just open the topic map file in a text editor and eyeball the code", this rough and ready approach isn't practical when dealing with typical real-world topic maps. This is because the typical real-world topic map may have between 1000 and as many as 10,000 topics and associations in it. Even a 1000 member topic map would overwhelm the most ardent "seat of the pants" text editor-using topic map enthusiast. There are just too many elements to view to make sense of a typical real-world topic map by looking directly at the text of its constituent code.

There is the second problem that most topic map users don't want to have to be steeped in the knowledge of what topic map constructs, such as topics and association, look like, syntactically, in XTM. Without that kind of knowledge it is pointless to open a 1000 member topic map in a text editor.

What was the strongest negative factor in the text editor approach? It was that there were too many individual things there to look at. Benedicte LeGrande has published some studies whereby aggregation was used to reduce the number of "things" (to reduce the overwhelming by numbers and complexity).

She designed and programmed a clustering algorithm, using topic map topics and associations as the objects of focus. These topics and association clusters were ordered by frequency of occurrence. Those items with high frequency (a threshold applied to select that group) were called general, as in general topics or general focus. This provided a list of topic names and associations that occurred most often in the topic map being considered with that approach. One could then choose to look at those topics that occurred most often by applying text filters to the topic map and obtaining the text content that was "in" (in other words, data of) the most frequent topics. See her papers if you want details on the algorithm and the results of running her clustering programs.

While clustering of "same" topic or "same" association (which assumes consistency of term usage in the construction phase of the topic map) substantially reduces the count of individual topic map "things" (such as topics and associations) you would then need to look at for a large topic map, it still potentially leaves a non-trivially large set of clustered topics and associations.

In the case of a topic map which clusters to fewer than a dozen items, that is a dozen different clusters, then it is reasonable that you may understand the whole map by investigating a filtered (for content) view of each cluster with a text editor or something slightly more sophisticated: a program which extracts the contents of the tags and values of the attributes and displays these in a useable way. When you do this you remember each of the cluster's information and build an "intercluster" relationship in your head.

Usually, unfortunately, a topic map will "cluster" to an unmanageable number of distinct clusters so far as the previous method of seeing their intercluster relationships is concerned. It would not be meaningful to you to have the program simply list or tabularize all the relationships; there would be too many entries to make sense of.

In order to permit the topic map surfer to visualize his topic map Benedicte Le Grande decided to use a graphical depiction of the interrelationships of the clusters found by her program. By using a visual approach that most people would understand intuitively she avoided the problem of a steep training curve. Cleverly, she used three-dimensional graphic modeling of cityscapes; a kind of simplified New York City skyscraper, streets, parks, neighbourhoods visual model. By using virtual reality software to make the scene she could use that same virtual reality software to provide the user with the ability to literally move and navigate through the topic map.

The point of this visualization method is that the huge amount of detail found in a topic map can be distilled by a computer program and displayed succinctly in a visual which (metaphorically) shows the relationships of these (now clustered) myriad occurrences of information. It is even possible to "walk around in the data" to see differing views of it, thanks to the virtual reality software display of the cluster information.

The benefit of clustering topic map topics by name and associations is the reduction of the apparent complexity of the map. People would rather perceive a forest than thousands of individual trees. By grouping topics according to their names and associations we can also see the relative number of occurrences (frequency) of each. The clusters that occur most often are likely those that represent the main topics of the topic map.

Specifically, the work consists of looking at ways of computationally specifying similarity of topics so that they can be clustered based on being similar to each other without having to be the same as each other. I am also working on ways of programming software that can perceive the relative contribution, relevance, and utility of various bits of topic map data so that they can be clustered based on those merits, in addition to, only similarity of topic and/or topic associations.

Automatic Topic Map Construction Summary

In this section we have described a process by which an XTM topic map could be automatically constructed by a program, with some input by a human. Human input will likely be required for such construction for the next few years because there is information, general knowledge, and background information that may be put into a given map, and which does not exist in any of the source data files, nor in any schema or database that the user of the constructor has access to.

One day there will be many knowledge bases covering many domains of knowledge that the constructor program can use to obtain part or all of this general knowledge. That day hadn't arrived when this section was written. It seems quite possible that the OpenCYC / Upper Ontology effort, which uses DAML, will be the kind of tool which begins the period when such domain-specific knowledge bases appear on the web.

This particular approach used:

❑   Pre-existing RDF Schema vocabulary entries (DAXSVG).

❑   A pre-existing RDF Schema based description (`contentschema`) of the semantics of the XML file being transformed to a topic map.

The simulation obtained the topic elements from the meta data objects stated in the mentioned schemas, and obtained the association elements from the namespace information in the schemas. Information provided by me was also used where it was needed but not available to a program from the files mentioned above.

RDF meta data occurring in the XML file was used to determine the topics (their names), and also the relationships between those names, and those were used as associations in the topic map. The occurrence information is simply where instances of the things the topics reference occur. The topic map author typed in the occurrence information, the text strings in the occurrence section of the map code. If the topic map construction tool had access to an artificial intelligence program that could "look at" the text in the RDF meta data, visual information in the picture, and instances of the occurrence of the schematic components in this book, then perhaps that program could infer the category names used in the topic map occurrence code section. Perhaps that AI program could infer, having looked at the text in the RDF meta data, visual information in the picture, and instances of the occurrence of the schematic components in this book, that they should be entered into the topic map code as `#mention`, `#appears-in`, and `#book`, along with the URL where the data is stored.

Combining RDF and Topic Maps

In this section we discuss two ways of dealing with using both topic maps and RDF:

❑   How to use XML's namespacing mechanism to allow the use of the two vocabularies in one document.

❑   How to map between the graphs (the graph structures) of the topic maps and RDF languages.

We've already looked in detail at two information representation technologies – RDF and topic maps – independently. As originally designed, the two systems were addressing different specific needs, as discussed in Chapters 4 and 7. Each of these techniques brings its own processing strengths to the user. However, we might expect that the simultaneous usage of each type of information structure could open up opportunities of data representation not made possible by using each alone. We're now going to discuss ways in which the information presented in topic maps and RDF may be combined, and one way in which they can be safely simultaneously present but not combined.

By combining data sets or files of topic map based information, represented in XML, and of RDF meta data information, coded in RDF syntax, we can obtain the combined capabilities of each. But there is an important caveat to this assertion. The caveat is this: when one of the languages is cast, that is transformed, into the other there are features or capabilities in the one being transformed that do not exist at all in the language being transformed into. Unless specific new programming code is added to the receiving language to add the missing features or capabilities to it, the transformation will lose information. That is, the transformation from language A to language B will not completely transfer all of the features and capabilities in language A. To the extent the topic maps and RDF have a common set of capabilities they can be transformed from one to the other successfully by a program.

If you are not familiar with topic maps or RDF technology it would be best if you read the earlier chapters on topic maps and RDF before you examine the material here, as no review of either of these technologies is given in this section. Those earlier chapters also contain references where you can find more information on each of the technologies.

Comparison of the Features of Topic Maps and RDF

This section describes the similarities and differences in the two technologies. We see what features of topic maps have not appeared in RDF.

The two technologies are similar:

❑   in that they have a common goal.

❑   and that goal is to allow you to find information.

They each do that in a different way, but they both:

❑   Annotate information resources.

❑   Define an abstract model and an SGML/XML based interchange syntax.

❑   Provide a typing system.

❑   Provide entity relationships.

Advantages of Combining Topic Maps with RDF

In a discussion below we will see why would we want to combine them, and what benefits it brings about. There are also problems, such as the lack of a practical way to represent the <scope> or "context" topic map feature when using RDF to model topic maps.

RDF might be seen as a technique for representing simple semantic relationships between resources, their descriptions, and other such triples. For example, a resource is something referred to by a URI, the URI being explicit and providing a unique location of the resource. We can think of a resource being like a subject or concept. The URI is in effect a kind of name, and it relates only things that can be pointed to via URI mechanism. This is an important distinction to remember.

Topic maps may be thought of as being on a higher semantic level than RDF. Another way of saying that is that topic maps have a richer built-in semantic expression capability than does RDF. RDF is almost semantically austere in comparison, but RDF also has the capacity to represent much topic map structure by piecewise transformation and representation of the higher level topic map features that are not yet part of the definition of RDF. The DAML+OIL version of RDF, which is on the horizon, will extend the basic set of semantic representations so that DAML+OIL will be much closer, semantic capability for semantic capability, to present day XTM (XML Topic Maps).

Piecewise transformation is a means of taking apart or disassembling a topic map structure and reformulating or transforming the pieces into the syntax and structure that RDF can handle. This is a lossy transformation; things like context get lost or are, at least, not well transferred into RDF-coded concepts. This kind of transformation, potentially at least, should be achievable by means of using a transformation specifying language such as MDL. Where there are semantic items in one language that are not in the other loss occurs. Unless you know of an adequate way to represent the concept of <scope> from the topic map world in RDF terms, any scope-defined context in a topic map is lost, for example.

We would want to combine topic maps and RDF in order to bring both the common capabilities of each together but particularly so that we can exploit the features of each technology.

The most important difference is that topic maps have a mechanism for referencing not only things on the web (through a URI), but also have a reification mechanism which allows referencing to be made to things that are physical, that are not part of the web, and to subjects (topics) which don't exist physically at all, like ideas in your head or mine. Topic maps also allow for one subject to be another or higher-level topic in a different part of the same topic map. For example, a topic in a map might be the architectural plans for a building. Another topic in the same topic map might treat the plans themselves as a topic, not the content of the plans as the first topic did. This is very important because topic maps can be used to represent and operate on plans of things and not just concrete instances of the results of building or executing those plans. That means the topic map structure can be used to talk about diagrams of things that haven't been built yet, or how the diagrams of one thing relate to or differ from the same kind of plans for another thing, where the second plan has different actual content, so we are not talking about trivial equality here. It allows a computer to perform what might be called recognition of semantic similarity, the ability to perceive that a picture of the Mona Lisa is the same kind of thing a as picture of you and they are both the same kind of thing as a picture of your sports car.

Multiple Namespaces in One File

Probably the easiest way to combine XTM and RDF representations is to employ a **container representation** capable of expressing them both. XML is an example of such a container representation; it enables the use of namespaces to combine the contents of several vocabularies together Since XML supports the namespace capability it is possible to have several different representations present in one XML file. The key factor is that all of those representations must be expressible using XML.

Let's look at how this is done. A namespace is a declaration of a URI such as this:

```
xmlns:dc="http://purl.org/metadata/dublin_core#"
```

and a namespace prefix (in this case dc) is assigned in that declaration.

Several namespaces can be declared in one file, as seen in this fragment:

```
<rdf:RDF
    xmlns:rdf="http://www.w3.org/1999/02/22-rdf-syntax-ns#"
    xmlns:rdfs="http://www.w3.org/TR/. ..-schema#"
    xmlns:dc="http://purl.org/metadata/dublin_core#"
    xmlns:s="http://description.org/schema/">
    xmlns:daxsvg="http://www.openmeta.org/daxschema/">
<rdf:Description
```

The namespace name prefixes obtained via these declarations are rdf, rdfs, dc, s, and daxsvg. These names occur later in the code in statements like this:

```
<rdf:Description rdf:about="#circle4">
```

Using the namespace prefix just gives us a convenient shortcut, so that we don't have to type in the namespace declaration for each XML element. The URI named rdf references a set of terms (sometimes called a *vocabulary*, sometimes called the *schema*) which are used as referents. In this case the schema has vocabulary items, which have meanings. Usually the meaning represents a usage, that is, how a term is *used*. In this case our statement contains the term Description – the usage for Description is to firstly recognize the particular vocabulary term used (Description) in view of all the many possible vocabulary terms available at the RDF schema URI, and to secondly recognize that the term Description can take any namespace qualified attribute. In our example you can see that there is one attribute, about.

So by having one schema (or vocabulary) for RDF and another one for XTM, we can put a mixture of these two kinds of statements into the same XML file. Of course, these statements can't be intermingled in such a way that parts of one kind of element occur in sequence with parts of another kind of element. One still has to follow the rules of XML.

So, the use of the XML namespace mechanism allows us to mix together the various representations, like RDF, XTM, and MathML, in one XML file. It does not create the vocabulary, nor does it provide their meanings – it only serves to connect the existence of the vocabulary and the terms in it to actual files on the Web, which have XML namespace declarations referencing that namespace. It is, of course, necessary to separately define the vocabulary and put it in place – the namespace mechanism does not do that for you.

Using Graph Manipulation to Transform RDF to Topic Map

Because both topic maps and RDF use a graph-based representation, it should be possible to transform between them using the Graph Data Description Language, GDDL (a language for processing the serialized form of complex graph based semantic systems) or another language that has similar functionality. Let's look at why we would want to use it and what such languages do.

First a quick background review. The topic map and RDF standards were developed independently. At the same time they are both paradigms for the representation and interchange of meta data. Because they were developed separately they have their own following, their own user community. Both use a graph-based conceptual framework.

The graph structure, also known as a network or network structure, consists of nodes that are connected by lines, called edges. The edges are labelled, that is they have text assigned to them that states what they are.

An example of such edge label text is "color". A very simple graph would be one consisting of two nodes connected by an edge. Let us label that edge "color" and say that the first node is (labeled) "sky" and the second node is (labeled) "blue".

Here we then have a simple graph structure, consisting of two nodes "sky" and "blue" and an edge labelled "color". This very simple graph structure is a representation of a tiny semantic network. If we were to "read this network in English" we would say that it says: "The sky is colored blue". That sentence is an interpretation of the graph structure. The structure itself just has two nodes and a connector between them, the nodes are labelled "sky", "blue", and the edge is labeled "color".

RDF uses the concept of graph triples, three-member graph structures. There is a resource node and it has a URI that identifies a network resource as its "name". The resource node is connected by an edge to two other nodes that act as attribute-value pairs.

A very simple RDF triple (in other words, a simple RDF graph structure) is one that has three nodes, labeled "John","age","5", resource, attribute and value nodes respectively. We "read" the little structure as saying "John is 5 years old".

A simple corporation topic map graph structure contains a `<topicMap>` node as the root of the topic map structure. It can have any number of topic or association elements. Let's start with just one topic element. Let us also say that this `<topicMap>` node has an id attribute. What the graph structure for such a scenario looks like is: a node `<topicMap>` has an edge connecting it with a node labelled "`samuel clemens`", and the edge is labeled "id". There is another edge connecting that same `<topicMap>` node with a node labelled "`person`" and the edge is labeled "`topic`".

Graph manipulation tools, like GDDL, allow you to point at a node and perform some graph manipulation on it, such as connecting it to some other node that you point at, or changing the labelling on the node (which amounts to changing its contents).

Comparing the graph structures described above, it can be seen that while they both consist of nodes with connecting edges, and that those nodes and edges have labels, the way the nodes and edges are used in the RDF graph structure are not the same as those in the topic map structure. The solution is to define a neutral graph representation that can be used to represent either the RDF graphs or the topic map graphs. Once one has defined that neutral structure then one can use standard graph manipulation techniques, which are part of tools like GDDL, to change the labeling on the edges and nodes of the RDF type graph structure to be consonant with the usage of the nodes and edges in the topic map graph structure. By transforming the connectivity of the edges and the labelling on the nodes and the edges of the RDF graph, it can be expressed (transformed) into a topic map graph structure, and vice versa.

By formally defining the meaning, that is the semantics, of each node-usage type and each edge-usage type in the graph structure for representations of RDF, and similarly defining the same usages for topic maps graph structures a mapping technique like MDL can be used to perform the changes in the graph structures automatically. The problems occur when one or more nodes or edges exist in one of the languages but not in the other. Where there are such nodes usage or edges usage that are not common to both RDF and topic map graphs, then those particular aspects of one language do not get mapped into (and hence don't appear in) the other language.

There is work underway at the W3C and TopicMaps.Org to bring RDF and XML topic maps together through standards to become an officially cooperating means of processing meaning representations on the Web. The W3C RDF progress can be seen at http://www.w3.org/rdf and the XTM progress at http://www.topicmaps.org. Both groups have been in communication and discussions about what changes may be made to each of these systems, what changes are desirable and which are achievable in the near future. An important consideration in the RDF world is that of DAML+OIL, which uses RDF as a kind of base but substantially extends its ability to express.

Summary

In this chapter we've taken a look at some future developments that are likely to be the next stage in the evolution of topic map and RDF technologies into mainstream use. We saw that automatically creating topic maps from existing representations is a useful and labor-saving procedure, and can be done for topic maps which have all of the data already in them which the constructor software needs to populate (place into) the topic map being built.

This kind of construction is a mapping of input files to output file (the topic map), the simplest version of this being only a change in syntax of the elements and structure of the elements in the input files to the syntax of the elements and structure of the elements in the target file (the topic map).

We also considered why and how we might combine topic map representations with RDF representations, and the potential benefits that can be realized when compared to using the techniques individually.

We recognized that both areas are still in the early days of implementation, but that there are clear advantages associated to each.

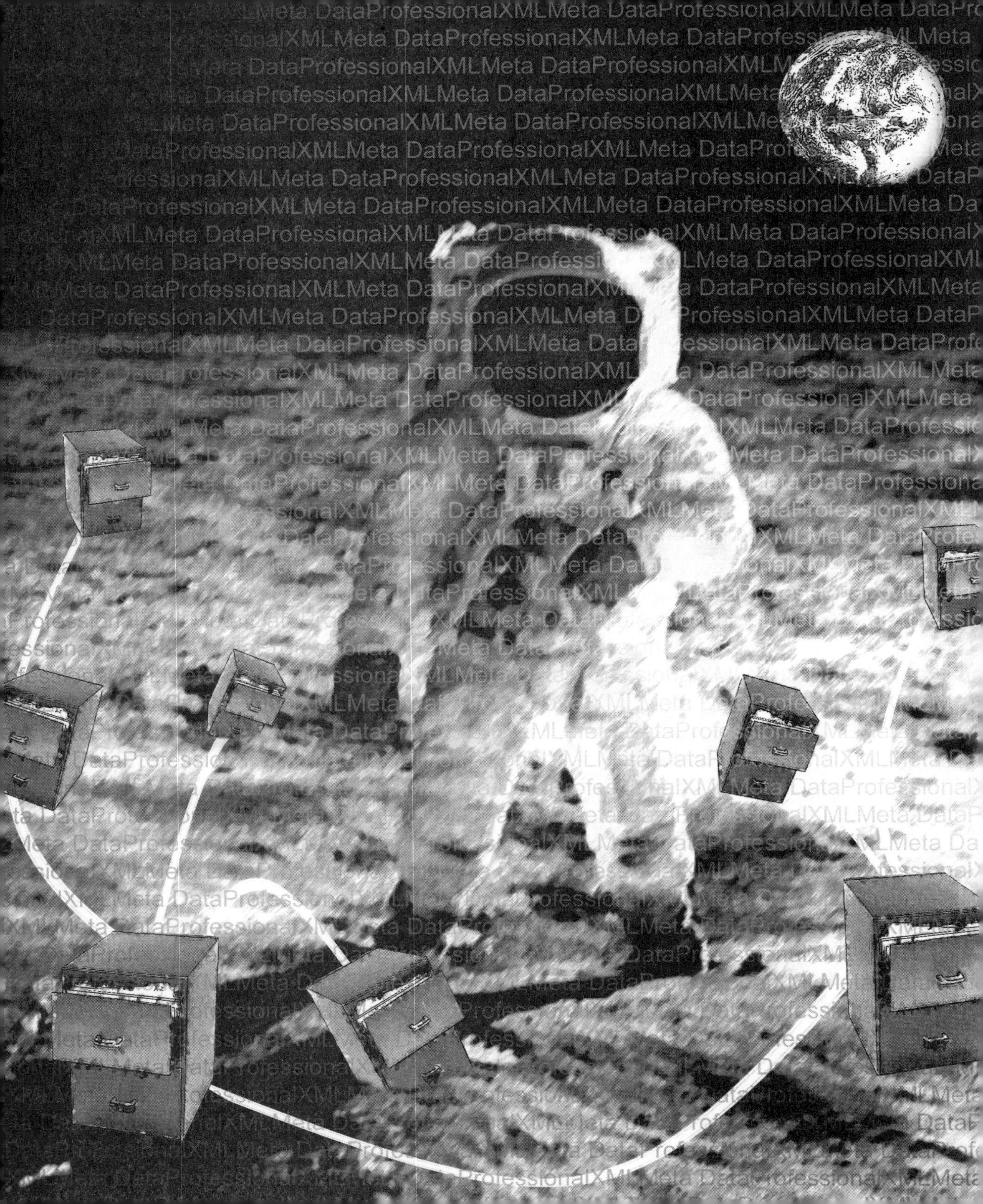

12

Exposing Relational Databases

In this chapter we will be considering extracting meta data from **relational databases**. (The storing of meta data in a database is a rather different problem, which is discussed in an article by Sergey Melnik at http://www-db.stanford.edu/~melnik/rdf/db.html.)

To most IT practitioners, a database is merely a way of persisting and manipulating data in a more efficient manner than using file storage. Those who work with relational databases regularly will be aware of the techniques used with these systems, from theoretical aspects such as table normalization to the practicalities of the Structured Query Language (SQL) dialect used by their database. Before the Web, a relational database management system (RDBMS) was to be found in most enterprises. This is still true – in fact most commercial web sites will be backed by a relational database. Of course, there has been some small encroachment of object-oriented databases (OODBMS), and on occasion XML-only tools might be used where an RDBMS might have previously been the first choice. This use of XML is, however, the exception, as generally speaking this technology can *complement* that of traditional databases, as evinced by the incorporation of XML features into the products of the big database vendors such as Oracle, IBM, and Microsoft.

Relational databases are everywhere and are here to stay, at least for the foreseeable future. A major factor in the ubiquity of relational databases is the ease of use of today's database tools, though this has had a side effect: there is little correlation between practical knowledge of database implementations and the theory that underlies RDBMS. With all the current talk of semantics on the Web, it's a good time to re-examine the fundamentals and take a look at the semantics of relational databases. We will start this chapter by doing just that, and then will have a look at what meta data is available in a database and why we might want to expose it.

In this chapter we will see:

- ❑ A brief overview of relational databases and SQL.
- ❑ A basic ontology for relational database meta data.
- ❑ How to model the ontology in Java.
- ❑ How to use JDBC to extract the meta data and output it as RDF.
- ❑ A prototype application constructed using the above elements.

The main tools used to develop the code in this chapter were:

❑	Java SDK 1.3	http://www.java.sun.com
❑	NetBeans Java IDE	http://www.netbeans.org
❑	Jena RDF Java API	http://www-uk.hpl.hp.com/people/bwm/rdf/jena
❑	Protégé KB	http://smi-web.stanford.edu/projects/protege/
❑	Ontoviz tab for Protégé	http://protege.stanford.edu/plugins/ontoviz/ontoviz.html
❑	Graphviz (needed for Ontoviz)	http://www.research.att.com/sw/tools/graphviz
❑	Microsoft SQL Server	http://www.microsoft.com
❑	Opta2000 JDBC Driver	http://www.inetsoftware.de

Versions of all these tools are available without charge for a variety of platforms, with the exception of SQL Server and the driver, but it should be possible to use any database for which there is a JDBC driver (nearly all of them). Note that the breadth of meta data available will depend both on the RDBMS and the driver implementation – for example the MySQL database with the MM driver will supply slightly less meta data than the i-net/SQL Server combination, whereas the JDBC-ODBC bridge driver tested produced no meta data at all.

Similar results could have been achieved with variations on the list above – the Java SDK 1.2 should be fine, and with a little modification it should be possible to use the Stanford RDF API (available from http://www-db.stanford.edu/~melnik/rdf/api.html*) instead of Jena. The use of a Java IDE is a matter of personal preference, and the Protégé knowledge base modeling tool was primarily used to provide a visual check of the RDF(S) structure (and to generate the diagrams), very nice but by no means essential. As usual the developer may prefer to rely on a good text editor and a keen eye, though often this approach also calls for a ready supply of headache pills.*

All of the code presented in this chapter is contained in the book's download file available from http://www.wrox.com.

Setting the Scene

To be able to access data from RDBMS over the Web, the are two basic requirements: the ability to interact with the database, and the ability to find the database in the first place. The common approach to the first requirement is to provide a browser interface to the database using forms and server-side processing, familiar in the form of publishers' online catalogs and so on. The second requirement is rather less clear-cut at present – the site that contains the database might be found through a web search engine, a link from another page, a television advertisement or whatever. It is proposed that the value of the Web could be increased by the use of meta data together with "intelligent" user agents, which may be local applications or web-based services. Either way, agents and meta data could play key roles in accessing a database over the Web. The interaction with the database could be done through the agent, so the interaction is on the user's terms, rather than through a fixed web interface provided by the database owner. In addition, by the use of **registries** containing meta data, the discovery of the database in the first place can be made a much more efficient operation. A registry would fulfil a function not unlike that of the search engine – a query is made and the URLs that match the query are returned. The difference would be that a non-human agent would make the query and the results of the query would be returned in machine-understandable meta data, rather than a human-readable form. Such an approach would allow improved targeting, firstly so that the user wouldn't have to think quite so carefully about the wording of a query (the agent would formulate this for the user), and secondly the user wouldn't have to wade through partial matches to a query to get to the information they required (the use of meta data would ensure accurate "hits").

The following diagram shows one such way in which the data contained in a relational database could be utilized on the Web. In this scenario the client is communicating with the Web through a personal agent. Located somewhere on the Web, accessible to the agent, is a registry which contains details of various web-based resources.

Our database system has at some point in advance made itself known or been discovered by the registry (0). When the client makes a query (1) the agent chooses a potential source of the information requested, in this case the registry, and queries this in turn (2) to see if it is aware of (that is, has meta data for) any information generally related to the client's request. In this case, the registry knows about the database on the right and so relays the meta data about this resource back to the agent (3). The agent is now in a position to make a specific query of the database (4), the result of which it will receive as data from the database (5), and convey to the client in a suitable form (6).

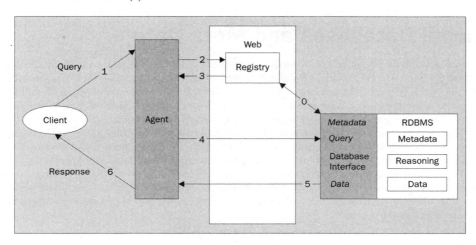

To summarize:

0. Database meta data is made known to a registry on the Web.

1. Client requests information.

2. Agent queries registry.

3. Registry responds with meta data including location of database.

4. Agent makes specific query of database.

5. Database returns data.

6. Agent presents data to client.

In this chapter we will be looking at a possible approach to generating meta data from the RDBMS in a way that could be used in a system such as this. In the diagram on the previous page this merely corresponds to '0', but in many respects this is the most important part of such a system.

There is considerable skipping of details above, where the scenario says the agent is provided with the location of the database. This will be implementation-dependent, for example the agent might be provided with URLs where queries can be made of the database, or simply pages that feature comma separated value lists of table contents. If we can provide identifiers for the various parts of the database, then these can be tailored and interpreted within the implementation to give the kind of access required. We are talking about web resources, so of course the identifiers here are URIs.

> **The aim in this chapter will be to show how it is possible to facilitate the generation of URIs identifying various parts of a database. How these URIs are used is beyond the scope of this chapter.**

Relational Databases and Meta Data

A little surprise for the self-taught SQL wizards – a relational database is actually a mathematical logic system. The seminal paper by Dr. E.F Codd, *A Relational Model for Large Shared Data Banks* (1970), describes this logic in a straightforward fashion. To paraphrase, a mathematical relation can be defined thus: if we have sets $S_1...S_n$, a relation on these sets is a set of n-tuples each of which has its first element from S_1, its second from S_2, and so on. In this definition we have a series of **rows**, each of which is an n-tuple of the relation, the order of which is irrelevant. The order of these sets, which we may call **columns**, is significant in a relation. Codd realized that the user of data wouldn't really want to be bothered with the order of the columns, so he suggested that in practice the columns (or *fields*) are given uniquely identifiable names instead. The resulting structure is what we call a **table** in a relational database. Each row will represent a proposition, usually about something in the real world. An alternative view is that a table represents a collection of **entities** of a particular type, the rows corresponding to the individual entities. We will be returning to this notion when we look at mapping tables to objects.

Relation
(tuples unordered, sets ordered)

	S_1	S_2	S_3
tuple 1	.	.	.
tuple 2	.	.	.
tuple 3	.	.	.

Table
(rows unordered, columns ordered)

	columnA	columnB	columnC
row 1	.	.	.
row 2	.	.	.
row 3	.	.	.

The columns in a table will each be defined on a particular **domain**, in other words the set of possible values that each individual item might take so for instance in an address book one column might have the domain of names, another of addresses, and a third telephone numbers. In practical databases the domain consideration is often just that of data type – in the Name column below all the values would be strings of characters, rather than integers or dates.

Name	Address	Telephone	Email
.	.	.	.
.	.	.	.
.	.	.	.

In such a table one column will uniquely identify each row – here the Name will identify each individual person. The Name domain may then be referred to as the **primary key**. In reality, in a given group of people it is not uncommon for some individuals to share the same name. In a case such as this it is common practice to add another column containing a value that will not be repeated (the ID column in the table below), and use this as the primary key:

ID	Name	Address	Telephone	Email
1	Dan	Bristol	123	d&j@bris.com
2	Jan	Bristol	234	d&j@bris.com
3	Dan	Boston	345	dan@bost.com
...	...	...	...	

The use of key fields is one way of enforcing **integrity** on the database to ensure the quality of the data – we will come to this shortly. Having key fields also allows us to cross-reference between different tables, so if we had a second table, again with a primary key ID:

ID	Email
1	d&j@bris.com
2	dan@bost.com
3	...

the first table can be modified to reduce the amount of redundant data:

ID	Name	Address	Telephone	EmailID
1	Dan	Bristol	123	1
2	Jan	Bristol	234	1
3	Dan	Boston	345	2
...	...	...	...	

The EmailID column refers to a primary key in the first table, and such a column is known as a **foreign key**.

Making sure each row in the table is unique is known as **entity integrity** (each row as an entity). There is also **domain integrity**, which ensures that the values in a column are appropriate (in other words, making sure that they are the correct type), and **referential integrity**, where the relationships between tables are kept valid – if a row in one table refers to an entity in another table it should not be possible to remove the entity without first removing the reference to it. This idea of integrity was one of the main motivations behind relational databases, and by following a few simple rules it is possible to guarantee the quality of the data. To the chagrin of the theoreticians, RDBMS vendors generally allow relatively unconstrained data in their implementations, and popular beliefs about efficiency (for example, putting all the columns in one table makes for faster queries) have moved practice away from the theoretical roots.

SQL

The **Structured Query Language** (**SQL**) is the de facto standard for working with RDBMS. It dates back to the 1970's, though there have been several revisions over the years, and is the prevailing database standard. One thing that can be said in favor of SQL is that for many simple tasks it is very easy to use. For instance, let's say we were building a database of animals' eating habits. We can have one table for a particular animal, bears in this example, and another listing the types of food. We will give each table an identifier field (ID) that will be the primary key in each case, and we will have a secondary key field in the bears table that will point to the primary key of the food table:

'bears'

id (integer)	name (characters)	food (integer)
1	pooh	2
2	teddy	1
3	grizzly	3

'food'

id (integer)	foodtype (characters)
1	kapoc
2	honey
3	campers

This data is used purely for example in the real world a different table structure would have to be used to reflect the possibility of the grizzly bear also eating honey, or even dining on pooh and teddy.

We need to create the food table first, as the bears table refers to it. Many RDBMS offer graphical tools for the creation of databases, tables and so on, but such operations all have SQL counterparts that may be entered into an interactive command-line style client interface. The SQL for creating the 'food' table is as follows:

```
CREATE TABLE food (id INT PRIMARY KEY, foodtype VARCHAR(10));
INSERT INTO food VALUES (1,'kapok');
INSERT INTO food VALUES (2,'honey');
INSERT INTO food VALUES (3,'campers');
```

It has been assumed that we already have a database in which we will create our tables. The first line creates a table with the name specified and with the field characteristics given in parentheses. The first field will be called 'id' and will be of type integer (INT keyword). It will be the primary key, so these keywords are stated too. The second field will be called 'foodtype' and will comprise a series of characters, the maximum number of which will be 10 (VARCHAR keyword). The subsequent three lines use the INSERT keyword to populate the table, with the values simply given as a list in parentheses.

The RDBMS used throughout this chapter is Microsoft's SQL Server. Note that database facilities offered by different vendors can vary, and the SQL dialect varies between products. If a different database system is used then its documentation should be consulted.

The bears table is created in the same way; note the foreign key definition referring to the id field in the food table:

```
CREATE TABLE bears (id INT PRIMARY KEY, name VARCHAR(10), food INT FOREIGN KEY
REFERENCES food(id));
INSERT INTO bears VALUES (1,'pooh', 2);
INSERT INTO bears VALUES (2,'teddy', 1);
INSERT INTO bears VALUES (3,'grizzly', 3);
```

The code for these and all the other listings in this chapter can be found in the code download for this book. The listing above is saved as inthewoods.sql. Instructions for creating a database and populating it using the SQL shown above are given later in this chapter, in the "Running the Application" section.

Now that we have built the tables we can use SQL to query them, again this is very straightforward. For instance, if we wish to find the name of the bear whose id number is 2 from the bears table, in the SQL client we simply have to enter:

```
SELECT bears.name FROM bears WHERE bears.id = '2'
```

and the result will be:

```
name
----------
teddy
```

Database Schema

An RDBMS may be used to manage one enterprise-wide database or any number of smaller task-specific databases. Typically the database will be accessed over a local or wide area network by an enterprise, or made available through a browser over the Web. The overall structure of a database can be referred to as its **schema**, though the terminology gets a little confused as sometimes the list of column names for a table is referred to as a schema, using the same idea of structure. Also, in SQL terms a schema is commonly a subset of the database (subschema) that is accessible to a particular user.

As with any networked resource, it is usual to protect an RDBMS with some form of user authentication system, and this is usually done in the regular fashion using login names and passwords. Most systems allow quite fine-grained control of the rights a user has to view and manipulate data, and as a result the database may look entirely different from one user to the next. For instance, here is what one user might see of a SQL Server database:

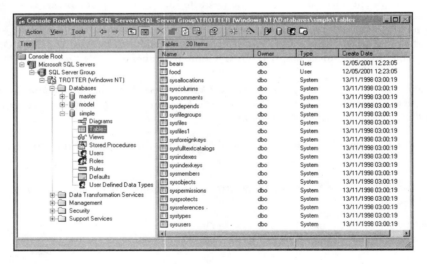

This visual display (SQL Server Enterprise Manager) has been accessed by someone with system administrator's rights, and so in addition to the two tables we created above, there are also a number of system tables visible. This visibility issue is very important when thinking about exposing a database, as we will want to allow access to some data and not others. We may want to allow some of the data to be modifiable, and some to be read only. If we look at the components of a database in a fairly sophisticated RDBMS like this we see that the tables are only one type amongst many, despite being the central feature of the system. A facility of higher-end databases that helps with controlling visibility is the ability to create **views**. These are a kind of virtual tables, the contents of which are taken from a real table or tables but may be tightly restricted, right down to specifying the rows that are visible.

When creating a system such as this it is advantageous to make it reasonably portable, so that it may be plugged in to existing frameworks with ease, and the frameworks may be changed without completely breaking the system. In an ideal world it would probably be best to expose only database views to the outside world, but the prototype application described in this chapter is intended to provide more basic functionality and has been created with less concern about individual database implementation, so the tables of the database will be described directly.

We will, however, make a major gesture towards interoperability by using the platform-independent Java language for our system. We will also allow use with a wide range of databases by only looking at a cut-down set of database components, which we will model in quite a simplistic manner. In terms of meta data we will consider an RDBMS to contain one or more databases with the following hierarchical structure:

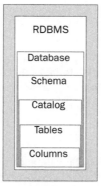

At the top level we have the *database*, which will contain one of more *schemas* (we will be using the "user's view" definition of this term), each of which will contain one or more *catalogs*. A catalog in database terms usually refers to the structural definition of the database (sometimes called the data dictionary), but from our point of view we can see this as being a container for objects from the next level down in the hierarchy, *tables*. The lowest level is the set of *columns*, and this will be the granularity of our meta data – anything lower than a column description we'll consider just plain data.

The aim is to provide enough information about the database (to be more accurate, one specific view of the database) so that items described in the structure above may be located by external agents. We will shortly be looking at how to model the structure in our system, and later how to extract the information from a database and provide URIs for the different parts of the database.

XML and Relational Databases

In paradise it may be possible to communicate directly between disparate entities despite, for example, the different languages of relational databases and object-oriented reasoning systems. Here in purgatory we might have a moderately miraculous infrastructure of HTTP over TCP/IP, but lacking any direct means of crossing language barriers we have to use a common language, and the prevalent language is XML. We do still have to cross a small barrier though – that of the mismatch between the structure of relational data (flat tables, cross-referenced) and that of XML (hierarchical).

As we are in a way looking at things from a high level, this might, however, be a good place to include a couple of precautionary notes for any developer planning to implement an RDBMS <=> XML system. Without extreme care (and quite a lot of work), implementing an XML "wrapper" for a relational database can compromise two of the key reasons for using a relational database in the first place: integrity enforcement and optimization. If all the data processing is simply taken out of the hands of dedicated handling systems (RDBMS) and passed to file-based applications, then we are likely to see serious inefficiency as a result. When the data is held in memory and streamed across networks this shouldn't be a problem, though care should be taken. Integrity is at risk the moment the data leaves the RDBMS – an XML document on its own can easily be compromised, so this risk should be reduced by at least the use of low-level validation using DTDs or XML schemas, and higher level integrity enforcement can be applied at the application level, based on meta data such as that we will be extracting here using our example application.

Exposing Meta Data

The following sections describe the design and implementation of an application that exposes the meta data in a particular database and converts it to RDF. We take this process stage by stage, including in the final section instructions on how to run the application produced and how to view the outputted RDF file graphically, using the Protégé tool.

Modeling the Database

To create meta data in a standard format (RDF) it will be necessary to firstly extract the information from the database and then transform this into a model that can be serialized into XML. The Java programming language is an ideal tool for this process. Being an object-oriented language, it allows hierarchical structures (such as that contained in our database) to be modelled with relative ease. The **JDBC** (**Java Database Connectivity**) **API** contains straightforward methods for getting meta data out of virtually any database, and there are also APIs available for building and serializing RDF models. The diagram below shows how we can achieve the process. The "reality" of the database is examined using JDBC and the information obtained is used to build a model using Java objects. In addition to mapping to the database entities, these objects are also mapped to an RDF Schema that will allow creation of a model in this domain, which can then be serialized out to XML-format RDF.

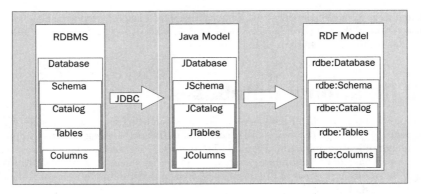

Though the process actually transforms the meta data from the relational system to the RDF system, it is easiest to start by getting an idea of where we want to go, roughing out how our (cut-down) database model may be expressed in an RDF Schema.

An RDBMS Ontology

To be able to express our database meta data in RDF we need to take the concepts of our domain and describe these in a vocabulary. What we are aiming for is coverage of all these concepts in RDF Schema, and at this stage we're only concerned with the model – the syntax will follow later. The first thing to do at this stage is check to see that no-one has done it before – if an ontology that covers all or even just a large proportion of our domain has already been published, then the best course of action is to use it. The match may be imperfect, but even so, using terms from existing models wherever possible is the preferred course of action as one of the primary reasons, if not *the* primary reason for using RDF is to allow interoperability between systems. Occasionally it may be deemed more appropriate to construct a new, cohesive vocabulary where the alternative would involve referring to many diverse namespaces where the semantics might potentially become diluted. This latter approach should be considered the exception – if the available bicycle parts don't fit together, then create new ones, otherwise avoid reinventing the wheel. In the case at hand a fairly thorough web search yielded nothing that offered useful overlap with our requirements, so we'll start from scratch.

We have most of the names (classes) we'll need, in the simple diagram above, though one important item is missing. To communicate with databases it is necessary to establish a connection of some kind, so we will add the name (class) Connection to the above list. Our database domain has a simple hierarchical structure, so it is convenient to develop a model of this now and incorporate the main terms in our ontology.

To encapsulate all our objects in the database model we will have a top-level class, which we will call DBResource (this will be a direct subclass of the Resource object in the rdfs: namespace). To distinguish this and other parts of our model, from now on we will give these items a namespace prefix – **rdbe:** (for "relational database exposed"). The use of rdbe:DBResource at the top level will enable the creation of properties available to all our classes; for example we will be giving everything a name property, which will be looked after by this superclass. Most of the classes we wish to model (catalog, table, etc.) have a lot in common – they are all collections of data. For this reason we will create a common superclass for all the collection types, called rdbe:Dataset. This will be a subclass of the rdbe:DBResource class. There is an exception – we have a class, rdbe:Connection, that will contain details of how to connect to a database – this doesn't fall into the rdbe:Dataset class so we will subclass this directly from rdbe:DBResource.

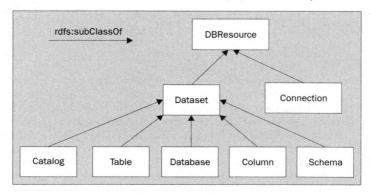

Now we have the classes to which our database objects can belong, the next step is to decide on the properties these objects may have. Although the chosen properties are presented here as a magician pulls a rabbit out of a hat, the decision on which properties were needed was made after a few iterations of approximating these and then making a rough sketch of code (both RDF and Java) to see what would be feasible and desirable.

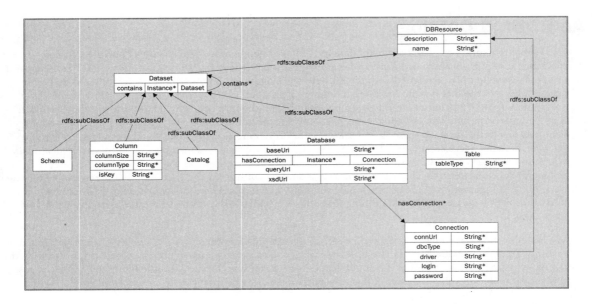

It seemed reasonable to provide the facility for a "human-friendly" name and textual descriptions for any of the database entities that may require them, so the local rdbe:DBResource class has name and description properties, which are inherited by all classes. The hierarchy of the database components can be easily expressed using the rdbe:contains property of rdbe:Dataset, which can be used between any two Dataset (sub)classes to express this relationship. The rdbe:Database class includes the rdbe:hasConnection property, and the instance of a rdbe:Connection to which this points will have all the values (as property values) needed to connect to the database.

> *All we are really saying here within the RDF schema is that the* rdbe:Database *resource has an attribute or relation* rdbe:Connection *, the (Object-Oriented) interpretation of this lies outside of the RDF model.*

The database has been provided with three properties, which will refer to the location of aspects of the database (these will be discussed below). The rdbe:Table class only has one extra property, that of rdbe:tableType, which will be used later to narrow down what the database might call tables (for example, "TABLE", "VIEW", "SYSTEM TABLE", "GLOBAL TEMPORARY", "LOCAL TEMPORARY", "ALIAS", "SYNONYM") into what we want to consider a table for our purposes ("TABLE"). The rdbe:Column class has three properties: rdbe:columnType refers to the SQL data type of the values in the column; if the column type is textual (for example, VARCHAR) then rdbe:columnSize will give the number of characters; if the column type is numeric then rdbe:columnSize will instead give the type's precision. The source of the meta data we will be using (JDBC) has this overloading, so for simplicity's sake we have continued it through into our prototype model, though this ought to be revaluated for a live implementation (an alternative way of modeling this would be to use a resource, and split off the type and other properties, so use could be made of range constraints). The rdbe:isKey property will be used to either hold 'primary' (if the column is the containing table's primary key), 'none' if the column has no key significance, or an identifier for the table and column that this column points to as a foreign key.

RDF Schema

The schema we have just described containing the items with the `rdbe:` prefix is specified in RDF-XML below (`rdbe.rdfs`). The classes and properties correspond directly with the diagram above (the original diagram was generated from this code using the Ontoviz tab of the Protégé knowledge base editor). Comments as found in the RDFS namespace add a little extra human-comprehensible information.

```
<?xml version="1.0"?>

<rdf:RDF   xmlns:rdf = "http://www.w3.org/1999/02/22-rdf-syntax-ns#"
           xmlns:rdfs = "http://www.w3.org/2000/01/rdf-schema#"  >
```

The schema uses definitions from two namespaces, those found in the RDF Model and Syntax and RDF Schema specifications. First we define our top level `rdbe:DBResource` and its two `rdfs:Literal` properties, `rdbe:name` and `rdbe:description`:

```
<rdfs:Class rdf:ID="DBResource">
  <rdfs:label>
    RDB-Exposed Resource
  </rdfs:label>
  <rdfs:subClassOf
          rdf:resource="http://www.w3.org/2000/01/rdfschema#Resource"/>
  <rdfs:comment>
   This is a common base class for all resources in RDB-Exposed.
  </rdfs:comment>
</rdfs:Class>

<rdf:Property rdf:ID="name">
  <rdfs:comment>A short (unqualified) name.</rdfs:comment>
  <rdfs:domain rdf:resource="#DBResource"/>
  <rdfs:range rdf:resource="http://www.w3.org/2000/01/rdf-schema#Literal"/>
</rdf:Property>

<rdf:Property rdf:ID="description">
  <rdfs:comment>A description of the resource.</rdfs:comment>
  <rdfs:domain rdf:resource="#DBResource"/>
  <rdfs:range rdf:resource="http://www.w3.org/2000/01/rdf-schema#Literal"/>
</rdf:Property>
```

An instance of the `rdbe:Database` class will represent the database being described, and this will have properties which are provided to locate the database's contents:

```
<rdfs:Class rdf:ID="Database">
  <rdfs:label>Database</rdfs:label>
  <rdfs:subClassOf rdf:resource="#Dataset" />
  <rdfs:comment>A relational database.</rdfs:comment>
</rdfs:Class>
```

The `rdbe:hasConnection` property of `rdbe:Database` points to resources (instances of `rdbe:Connection`) that will describe the characteristics of possible connections to the database :

```
<rdf:Property rdf:ID="hasConnection">
  <rdfs:comment>Interface.</rdfs:comment>
  <rdfs:domain rdf:resource="#Database"/>
  <rdfs:range rdf:resource="#Connection"/>
</rdf:Property>
```

```
<rdfs:Class rdf:ID="Connection">
  <rdfs:label>Connection</rdfs:label>
  <rdfs:subClassOf rdf:resource="#DBResource" />
  <rdfs:comment>A connection to the database.</rdfs:comment>
</rdfs:Class>

<rdf:Property rdf:ID="dbcType">
  <rdfs:comment>Type of interface.</rdfs:comment>
  <rdfs:domain rdf:resource="#Connection"/>
  <rdfs:range rdf:resource="http://www.w3.org/2000/01/rdf-schema#Literal"/>
</rdf:Property>

<rdf:Property rdf:ID="driver">
  <rdfs:comment>Driver for connection.</rdfs:comment>
  <rdfs:domain rdf:resource="#Connection"/>
  <rdfs:range rdf:resource="http://www.w3.org/2000/01/rdf-schema#Literal"/>
</rdf:Property>

<rdf:Property rdf:ID="login">
  <rdfs:comment>Login name for connection.</rdfs:comment>
  <rdfs:domain rdf:resource="#Connection"/>
  <rdfs:range rdf:resource="http://www.w3.org/2000/01/rdf-schema#Literal"/>
</rdf:Property>

<rdf:Property rdf:ID="password">
  <rdfs:comment>User name for connection.</rdfs:comment>
  <rdfs:domain rdf:resource="#Connection"/>
  <rdfs:range rdf:resource="http://www.w3.org/2000/01/rdf-schema#Literal"/>
</rdf:Property>

<rdf:Property rdf:ID="connUrl">
  <rdfs:comment>URL for connection.</rdfs:comment>
  <rdfs:domain rdf:resource="#Connection"/>
  <rdfs:range rdf:resource="http://www.w3.org/2000/01/rdf-schema#Literal"/>
</rdf:Property>
```

As mentioned earlier, all we are trying to achieve here is to generate URIs to identify the various parts of the database. The baseUri property below is used within the system as a common root URI from which the URIs of the details are constructed, and this and the properties that follow should assist in interfacing the system. We will return to this issue in a moment.

```
<rdf:Property rdf:ID="baseUri">
  <rdfs:comment>The Uri on which all others are based.</rdfs:comment>
  <rdfs:domain rdf:resource="#Database"/>
  <rdfs:range rdf:resource="http://www.w3.org/2000/01/rdf-schema#Literal"/>
</rdf:Property>

<rdf:Property rdf:ID="xsdUrl">
  <rdfs:comment>The location of XML Schemas describing database
                constraints.</rdfs:comment>
  <rdfs:domain rdf:resource="#Database"/>
  <rdfs:range rdf:resource="http://www.w3.org/2000/01/rdf-schema#Literal"/>
</rdf:Property>
```

```
<rdf:Property rdf:ID="queryUrl">
  <rdfs:comment>The location at which the database may be
               queried.</rdfs:comment>
  <rdfs:domain rdf:resource="#Database"/>
  <rdfs:range rdf:resource="http://www.w3.org/2000/01/rdf-schema#Literal"/>
</rdf:Property>
```

Though the order within the schema file doesn't matter, we will continue with the next class down our tree, rdbe:Dataset, which has the property of containership, which will allow us to model the "nesting" of our database elements:

```
<rdfs:Class rdf:ID="Dataset">
  <rdfs:label>Set of data</rdfs:label>
  <rdfs:subClassOf rdf:resource="#DBResource" />
  <rdfs:comment>Base class for different blocks of data.</rdfs:comment>
</rdfs:Class>

<rdf:Property rdf:ID="contains">
  <rdfs:comment>containership</rdfs:comment>
  <rdfs:domain rdf:resource="#Dataset"/>
  <rdfs:range rdf:resource="#Dataset"/>
</rdf:Property>
```

We now continue with the other subclasses of rdbe:Dataset, which correspond to the levels of containership in the database:

```
<rdfs:Class rdf:ID="Schema">
  <rdfs:label>Schema</rdfs:label>
  <rdfs:subClassOf rdf:resource="#Dataset" />
  <rdfs:comment>Defines a database schema.</rdfs:comment>
</rdfs:Class>

<rdfs:Class rdf:ID="Catalog">
  <rdfs:label>Catalog</rdfs:label>
  <rdfs:subClassOf rdf:resource="#Dataset" />
  <rdfs:comment>Defines a database catalog.</rdfs:comment>
</rdfs:Class>

<rdfs:Class rdf:ID="Table">
  <rdfs:label>Table</rdfs:label>
  <rdfs:subClassOf rdf:resource="#Dataset" />
  <rdfs:comment>Defines a database table.</rdfs:comment>
</rdfs:Class>

<rdf:Property rdf:ID="tableType">
  <rdfs:comment>Type of table</rdfs:comment>
  <rdfs:domain rdf:resource="#Table"/>
  <rdfs:range rdf:resource="http://www.w3.org/2000/01/rdf-schema#Literal"/>
</rdf:Property>
```

At the lowest level of our hierarchical model we have the `rdbe:Column` class, with its particular properties:

```
<rdfs:Class rdf:ID="Column">
  <rdfs:label>Column</rdfs:label>
  <rdfs:subClassOf rdf:resource="#Dataset" />
  <rdfs:comment>Individual columns of a table.</rdfs:comment>
</rdfs:Class>

<rdf:Property rdf:ID="isKey">
  <rdfs:comment>Key field in table</rdfs:comment>
  <rdfs:domain rdf:resource="#Column"/>
  <rdfs:range rdf:resource="http://www.w3.org/2000/01/rdf-schema#Literal"/>
</rdf:Property>

<rdf:Property rdf:ID="columnType">
  <rdfs:comment>Type of column</rdfs:comment>
  <rdfs:domain rdf:resource="#Column"/>
  <rdfs:range rdf:resource="http://www.w3.org/2000/01/rdf-schema#Literal"/>
</rdf:Property>

<rdf:Property rdf:ID="columnSize">
  <rdfs:comment>Precision/number of chars</rdfs:comment>
  <rdfs:domain rdf:resource="#Column"/>
  <rdfs:range rdf:resource="http://www.w3.org/2000/01/rdf-schema#Literal"/>
</rdf:Property>
</rdf:RDF>
```

Architectural Suggestions

In the scenario given at the start of this chapter, no detail was given of the nature of the meta data and data that the database would offer to the outside world. In this text we will only describe the construction of the parts of the system needed to generate the RDF, though we can briefly consider other aspects of a possible architecture. To be able to get at the data-level XML over the Web, a URL is required, and for this the `Database` class has been provided with a `queryUrl` property. The suggestion is that queries made to this URL (as HTTP POSTs or GETs) will be passed through an interface to the database, which will return the requested data. The query facility could take many forms, for example a simple servlet setup could pass on a SQL query verbatim to the RDBMS and return the results, perhaps in a browser-viewable format. A solution in keeping with web developments would be to use the XQuery language (http://www.w3.org/XML/Query) to formulate these queries. As an alternative to the query approach, the `baseUri` property is available, which might allow other forms of interfacing, perhaps through a directory services system. The third property we have given the `Database` class is `xsdUrl`. Once the data leaves the RDBMS, it will lose any kind of integrity guarantees the system offered. We can however pass on some of these details in the RDF meta data (such as references between tables and the data types).

The XML technologies provide an additional layer at which we can convey some of the constraints that apply to the data – XML Schemas (or XSD Schemas as we are referring to it in this book). To make a schema available over the Web a URL is required, hence `xsdUrl`. This is only really skeleton provision – a different XSD Schema would be required by each view of the data, so in practice these would also probably have to be dynamically delivered. The essential suggestion here is that by supplying data through three layers, RDF meta data, XSD Schema meta data, and XML data, we could maintain the same kind of control over the data as we had within the RDBMS. Implementations of these parts of a system are beyond the scope of this book, and further discussion of the techniques involved can be found in the Wrox books *Professional XML, 2nd Edition* (ISBN 1-861005-05-9) and *Professional Java XML* (ISBN 1-86100-401-X).

A Problem (and a Cunning Plan)

Now we have an idea of the kind of architecture into which our meta data-generating system might fit, and we have an ontological model into which we will place the meta data we extract from the database. We will shortly start to model the ontology in Java code, and look at the code required to extract the meta data from the database. Before we go any further though, we have a problem. In the model, our database has several characteristics that cannot be programmatically determined from the database. At some point we are going to have to specify properties manually, such as `queryUrl`, `baseUri`, and even the name of the database. To be able to connect to the database in the first place we will need to specify the connection parameters. All this information is meta data, so here is the cunning plan – specify these in RDF at the start.

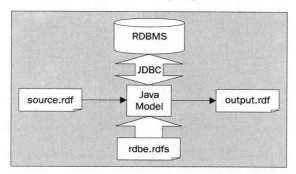

The system will take as its input an RDF-XML file, `source.rdf`, containing details of the connection parameters and any other meta data that isn't machine-readable from the database. The system reads this information, which will put the model in a thinly populated state. The RDF Schema, specified in `rdbe.rdfs`, determines the way in which the information is stored. The system will then query the database (through JDBC) to further populate the model with information regarding the database tables, columns, and so on. Finally the system will spit out the populated model as an RDF-XML file, `output.rdf`.

In the discussion of what terms to use in our meta data, it was mentioned that the best approach is to use existing vocabularies wherever possible. To demonstrate how this can be done, and to add a little extra information we will include some administrative details.

A proposal for a "MetaVocab" vocabulary may be found at http://webns.net/mvcb/. This vocabulary contains just three properties:

- **errorReportsTo** – points to the URI (usually a mailto) of the person who should receive errors about the document.

- **generatorAgent** – points to the URI of the software (if any) used to create the RDF.

- **prefix** – the short prefix or abbreviation used to represent this vocabulary.

The first two of these properties provide additional paths from the user of the data back to the provider, potentially extremely important facilities, though the third is really stylistic sugar. We will see shortly how this information is included in our source file.

The source data file can be looked upon in two different ways – as a configuration properties file and as a means of manually providing meta data. Note that the assumption is being made here that it is acceptable to expose the login details specified for the connection along with the rest of the meta data. This isn't an unreasonable assumption as all the data that can be seen using this login may potentially be exposed, though for additional security it would be straightforward to delete these entries from the RDF model in the Java code after the configuration information had been extracted.

RDF Model in Java – the Jena API

The Jena API was developed in September 2000 by Brian McBride and contains improvements on previous APIs. The API closely mirrors the RDF model, and for a Java programmer this potentially confusing model becomes a set of familiarly specified classes and methods. Even for a novice programmer the API is straightforward to use, and Brian has provided a very helpful tutorial (see http://www-uk.hpl.hp.com/people/bwm/rdf/jena). The core of the model is to be found in the `com.hp.hpl.mesa.rdf.jena.model.*` part of the package, where we find a set of interfaces including the following (amongst others):

```
Model
Resource
Property
Literal
Statement
```

These names are taken directly from the RDF(S) model, and provide a one-to-one mapping between the RDF model and a Java class structure. The developer is free to create their own class implementations, though a perfectly functional set of sample implementations are included in the package. The most notable of these classes is the `ModelMem` class, which can be used to build an in-memory representation of an RDF model.

The RDF Schemas a developer wishes to use with Jena have to be hard-coded in a static class. The classes and properties of RDF and RDFS are specified this way, and looking at these files (`RDF.java` and `RDFS.java`, in the `vocabulary` branch of the package) it is clear how one's own schema should be specified. Here are the three properties of the `MetaVocab` vocabulary coded into a class called `Admin`:

```java
// start of Admin.java
package com.wrapper.vocabulary;

import com.hp.hpl.mesa.rdf.jena.model.Model;
import com.hp.hpl.mesa.rdf.jena.model.Resource;
import com.hp.hpl.mesa.rdf.jena.model.Property;
import com.hp.hpl.mesa.rdf.jena.model.RDFException;

import com.hp.hpl.mesa.rdf.jena.common.ErrorHelper;
import com.hp.hpl.mesa.rdf.jena.common.PropertyImpl;
import com.hp.hpl.mesa.rdf.jena.common.ResourceImpl;
```

The first block of imports are the interfaces used, and the second block are class implementations. Next we have a block of named `Property` fields, as defined in the `MetaVocab` namespace, each initialized to null:

```java
public class Admin {

    public static Property errorReportsTo = null;
    public static Property generatorAgent = null;
    public static Property prefix = null;
```

The vocabulary needs a namespace to unambiguously identify its terms:

```
    // namespace of this vocabulary
    protected final static String uri = "http://webns.net/mvcb#";
```

Now we create (`String`) names, which will shortly be attached to the corresponding field classes:

```
    // Properties
    final static String nerrorReportsTo = "errorReportsTo";
    final static String ngeneratorAgent = "generatorAgent";
    final static String nprefix = "prefix";

    public static String getURI() {
      return uri;
    }
```

Now we have the construction of the static classes themselves, from the implementation class `PropertyImpl`:

```
    static {
      try {
        errorReportsTo = new PropertyImpl(uri, nerrorReportsTo);
        generatorAgent = new PropertyImpl(uri, ngeneratorAgent);
        prefix = new PropertyImpl(uri, nprefix);
      } catch (RDFException e) {
        e.printStackTrace();
      }
    }
}// end of Admin.java
```

Before looking at how we will use these objects, here is the file specifying the model we have developed for our database meta data, contained in the file `RDBE.java`. The class follows the same structure as the file above. You may wish to refer back to the diagram showing the structure of the ontology.

```
// start of RDBE.java
package com.wrapper.vocabulary;

import com.hp.hpl.mesa.rdf.jena.model.Model;
import com.hp.hpl.mesa.rdf.jena.model.Resource;
import com.hp.hpl.mesa.rdf.jena.model.Property;
import com.hp.hpl.mesa.rdf.jena.model.RDFException;

import com.hp.hpl.mesa.rdf.jena.common.ErrorHelper;
import com.hp.hpl.mesa.rdf.jena.common.PropertyImpl;
import com.hp.hpl.mesa.rdf.jena.common.ResourceImpl;
```

Our model has resources as well as properties :

```
public class RDBE {

  // resources
  public static Resource DBResource = null;
  public static Resource Database = null;
  public static Resource Dataset = null;
```

```
    public static Resource Connection = null;
    public static Resource DBCParameter = null;
    public static Resource Catalog = null;
    public static Resource Schema = null;
    public static Resource Table = null;
    public static Resource Column = null;
    public static Resource Key = null;

    // properties
    public static Property name = null;
    public static Property description = null;

    // Dataset property
    public static Property contains = null;

    // Connection properties
    public static Property driver = null;
    public static Property connUrl = null;
    public static Property login = null;
    public static Property password = null;

    // Database properties
    public static Property baseUri = null;
    public static Property xsdUrl = null;
    public static Property queryUrl = null;

    // Table property
    public static Property tableType = null;

    // Column properties
    public static Property isKey = null;
    public static Property columnType = null;
    public static Property columnSize = null;
```

Our vocabulary needs a namespace to unambiguously identify its terms:

```
    // namespace of this vocabulary
    protected final static String uri =
      "http://www.isacat.net/ns/rdbe#";
```

Now we create the names, which again will be attached to the corresponding field classes:

```
    // Resources
    final static String nDBResource = "DBResource";
    final static String nDatabase = "Database";
    final static String nDataset = "Dataset";
    final static String nConnection = "Connection";
    final static String nDBCParameter = "DBCParameter";
    final static String nCatalog = "Catalog";
    final static String nSchema = "Schema";
    final static String nTable = "Table";
    final static String nColumn = "Column";
    final static String nKey = "Key";
```

```
// Properties
final static String nname = "name";
final static String ndescription = "description";

final static String ndriver = "driver";
final static String nconnUrl = "connUrl";
final static String nlogin = "login";
final static String npassword = "password";

final static String nbaseUri = "baseUri";
final static String nxsdUrl = "xsdUrl";
final static String nqueryUrl = "queryUrl";
final static String ntableType = "tableType";

final static String ncontains = "contains";
final static String nisKey = "isKey";
final static String ncolumnType = "columnType";
final static String ncolumnSize = "columnSize";
```

Next we have the URI accessor, which is:

```
public static String getURI() {
  return uri;
}
```

Then we come to the definition of the resource classes, which are constructed using the fully-qualified name of the Resource; for example our Dataset class is defined using http://www.isacat.net/ns/rdbe#Dataset:

```
static {
try {
  DBResource = new ResourceImpl(uri + nDBResource);
  Database = new ResourceImpl(uri + nDatabase);
  Dataset = new ResourceImpl(uri + nDataset);
  Connection = new ResourceImpl(uri + nConnection);
  DBCParameter = new ResourceImpl(uri + nDBCParameter);
  Table = new ResourceImpl(uri + nTable);
  Catalog = new ResourceImpl(uri + nCatalog);
  Schema = new ResourceImpl(uri + nSchema);
  Column = new ResourceImpl(uri + nColumn);
  Key = new ResourceImpl(uri + nKey);
```

Again we have property implementations:

```
  name = new PropertyImpl(uri, nname);
  description = new PropertyImpl(uri, ndescription);

  driver = new PropertyImpl(uri, ndriver);
  connUrl = new PropertyImpl(uri, nconnUrl);
  login = new PropertyImpl(uri, nlogin);
  password = new PropertyImpl(uri, npassword);

  baseUri = new PropertyImpl(uri, nbaseUri);

  xsdUrl = new PropertyImpl(uri, nxsdUrl);
  queryUrl = new PropertyImpl(uri, nqueryUrl);

  tableType = new PropertyImpl(uri, ntableType);
```

```
        contains = new PropertyImpl(uri, ncontains);

        columnSize = new PropertyImpl(uri, ncolumnSize);
        columnType = new PropertyImpl(uri, ncolumnType);
        isKey = new PropertyImpl(uri, nisKey);
    } catch (RDFException e) {
        e.printStackTrace();
    }
  }
}// end of RDBE.java
```

Now that we have defined the vocabulary class, building an RDF model with Jena involving our terms is very straightforward – firstly we need a model object to contain our information:

```
Model model = new ModelMem();
```

Now we can create whatever `Resource` objects we like using one of the various factory methods of `Model`; in this case we are specifying the name of the resource as we create it:

```
Resource demoResource = model.createResource("aTable");
```

To these objects we may add whatever properties we like. Our resources will need to have a type, and this is easy to specify:

```
demoResource.addProperty(RDF.type, RDBE.Table);
```

The type of a resource is specified in the RDF namespace, so here we have simply used the static field type of the class `RDF`. Similarly, to say what that type will be we have given a class from our `RDBE` class, which parallels the objects in our ontology described in the `http://www.isacat.net/ns/rdb-exposed` namespace. We can of course add properties specified in our namespace; here, for example, we give a literal value for a property:

```
demoResource.addProperty(RDBE.tableType, "SYSTEM");
```

As we will see later, reading and writing RDF-XML serial syntax are trivial operations with Jena. We have covered all we really need to know of the Jena API for our application in the last couple of pages (which says rather a lot for the design of the API). We will now move on to seeing how our database entities will be modeled as Java objects.

Wrapping the Database

The technique of wrapping a relational database with an object-oriented representation is well documented, and in recent years there has been a boom in the application of this interfacing between the database and XML. In our application most of the problems normally encountered with object-relational mapping will be largely avoided, as the meta data view we have of the database is hierarchical and so maps to objects easily. We shall see shortly that we do have to do a little impedance matching, as we receive the meta data from JDBC in a row-based form, but the mismatch is such that the mapping can be achieved without difficulty. The Java class structure we will use follows the mapping shown in the following diagram that we saw earlier:

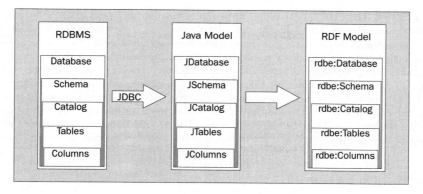

So a `Table` entity in the RDBMS is modeled by a `JTable` class in Java, which in turn maps to a `Table` resource in the RDF model. The Java model is contained in the `com.wrapper.dbmodel` part of the `RDBExposed` package, and we will now look at each of the files here in turn. These are all relatively simple, with the exception of `JDatabase`, which incorporates the JDBC code that extracts the meta data from the database, so we'll save that description until last. We will start with a class not shown in the earlier diagram, which is `JDataset`. This corresponds to the `Dataset` class in our ontology, and similarly acts as a superclass of the other data-containing class of the model.

```
// start of JDataset.java
package com.wrapper.dbmodel;

abstract class JDataset {

  protected JDatabase database = null;
  protected String name = null;

  public JDataset(JDatabase database, String name) {
    this.database = database;
    this.name = name;
  }

  private JDataset() {
  }

  public String getName() {
    return name;
  }

  public String toString() {
    return name;
  }
}// end of JDataset.java
```

There's not a lot to it. The class is declared as `abstract`, as we do not want to allow the instantiation of this class itself, only its subclasses. The fields that are common to our subclasses are the database object in question and the name of this instance of a dataset, and these are given protected access, as we don't want these to be directly accessible outside of our package. The empty constructor is defined as `private` – this little idiom makes it impossible to construct any of the subclasses without supplying arguments. The reason for this is that all our database entities (catalogs, tables, columns, etc.) are going to be referred to a database object which will contain the methods for obtaining the meta data, and the object instances of these entities will not be valid without access to the database object. This object is supplied in the other constructor, along with a name for the instance. The `JDataset` class only has two methods, one to retrieve the name of the instance and one to provide a `String` representation of the instance (overriding the `toString()` method of the `Object` class). Each of these simply returns the value of the `name` field.

Next we have the `JSchema` class:

```
// start of JSchema.java
package com.wrapper.dbmodel;

import com.hp.hpl.mesa.rdf.jena.model.Model;
import com.hp.hpl.mesa.rdf.jena.model.Resource;

import com.hp.hpl.mesa.rdf.jena.vocabulary.RDF;

import com.wrapper.vocabulary.RDBE;
```

This class has a method for representing itself as an RDF resource, so we need to import a couple of Jena classes. In this representation we need terms from both the RDF and RDBE namespaces, which are mirrored in the corresponding static classes, so we also import these. The class extends `JDataset` and so inherits all the characteristics of the class listed above:

```
public class JSchema extends JDataset {

  Resource resource = null;

  public JSchema(JDatabase database, String name) {
    super(database, name);
  }

  public Resource asResource(Model model) {
    if (resource != null) {
      return resource;
    }

    try {
      resource = model.createResource(database.getBaseUri()+"schema." +
                                                            name);
      resource.addProperty(RDF.type, RDBE.Schema);
      resource.addProperty(RDBE.name, name);
    } catch (Exception e) {
      e.printStackTrace();
    }
    return resource;
  }
}// end of JSchema.java
```

The constructor takes the same arguments as the constructor of the JDataset superclass, and in fact all it does is call that constructor with those arguments. The Resource that will be the RDF model representation of this class is initially set to null, so the first time the asResource() method is called the Resource object will be created, whereas subsequent calls will return this pre-fabricated object. The resource that is created is given the URI <baseUri>schema.*name*, where *name* is the name of this object. The dot notation was chosen arbitrarily, though some form of identification is required to avoid different resources being given the same RDF name. The property type of the resource is added (Schema, as defined in our vocabulary), and the name of the resource.

The JCatalog class follows exactly the same pattern as the JSchema class:

```java
// start of JCatalog.java
package com.wrapper.dbmodel;

import com.hp.hpl.mesa.rdf.jena.model.Model;
import com.hp.hpl.mesa.rdf.jena.model.Resource;

import com.hp.hpl.mesa.rdf.jena.vocabulary.RDF;

import com.wrapper.vocabulary.RDBE;

public class JCatalog extends JDataset {
  Resource resource = null;

  public JCatalog(JDatabase database, String name) {
    super(database, name);
  }

  public Resource asResource(Model model) {
    if (resource != null) {
      return resource;
    }

    try {
      resource = model.createResource(database.getBaseUri()+"catalog." +
                                                          name);
      resource.addProperty(RDF.type, RDBE.Catalog);
      resource.addProperty(RDBE.name, name);
    } catch (Exception e) {
      e.printStackTrace();
    }
    return resource;
  }
}// start of JCatalog.java
```

The only difference here is in the object and resource naming. The skeleton of the JTable class is the same again, once more with the names changed. This class has some additional methods and fields to allow retrieval of the columns that are contained in a table.

```java
// start of JTable.java

package com.wrapper.dbmodel;

import java.util.List;
```

```
import com.hp.hpl.mesa.rdf.jena.model.Model;
import com.hp.hpl.mesa.rdf.jena.model.Resource;

import com.hp.hpl.mesa.rdf.jena.vocabulary.RDF;

import com.wrapper.vocabulary.RDBE;

public class JTable extends JDataset {

    Resource resource = null;
    String catalogName = "%";
    String schemaName = "%";
    String type = null;
```

The catalog and schema names will be used shortly in handling the contained columns. The % value is the SQL wildcard, and any queries using these default values are effectively saying "any" catalog or schema. The String type corresponds to the tableType class in our vocabulary. After the constructor we have a getter and setter method for each of the class members:

```
    public JTable(JDatabase database, String name) {
    super(database, name);
}

public void setCatalogName(String catalogName) {
    this.catalogName = catalogName;
}

public void setSchemaName(String schemaName) {
    this.schemaName = schemaName;
}

public void setType(String type) {
    this.type = type;
}

public String getCatalogName() {
    return catalogName;
}

public String getSchemaName() {
    return schemaName;
}

public String getType() {
    return type;
}
```

The next method forwards a call to the getColumns() method of the JDatabase class. To be able to specify a set of columns a String for the schema, table, and column name patterns must be provided. If no value for these has been set by the methods above, then the wildcard default will be used. The object returned will implement the List interface, which is a generic interface for various collections of objects.

```
    public List getColumns() {
      // String catalog, String schemaPattern, String tablePattern,
      //   String columnPattern
      return database.getColumns(catalogName, schemaName, name, "%");
    }
```

Last in this class we have the `asResource()` method. This is very similar to those above, with the addition of a statement to add the `tableType` property to the resource in the RDF model.

```
    public Resource asResource(Model model) {
      if (resource != null) {
        return resource;
      }

      try {
        resource = model.createResource(database.getBaseUri()+"table." +
                                                                       name);
        resource.addProperty(RDF.type, RDBE.Table);
        resource.addProperty(RDBE.name, name);
        resource.addProperty(RDBE.tableType, type);
      } catch (Exception e) {
        e.printStackTrace();
      }
      return resource;
    }
}// end of JTable.java
```

The `JColumn` class is again similar to those above:

```
// start of JColumn.java
package com.wrapper.dbmodel;

import com.hp.hpl.mesa.rdf.jena.model.Model;
import com.hp.hpl.mesa.rdf.jena.model.Resource;

import com.hp.hpl.mesa.rdf.jena.vocabulary.RDF;

import com.wrapper.vocabulary.RDBE;

public class JColumn extends JDataset {

  Resource resource = null;
  private String key = "none";
  private String type = "unknown";
  private int size = -1;
  private String tableName = "unknown";
```

The properties of a column in our ontology are reflected in the middle three member variables above, and the `tableName` is used as part of the identifier of this column as a resource. Once more we have the constructor followed by get/set methods:

```
    public JColumn(JDatabase database, String name) {
      super(database, name);
  }

  public void setTableName(String tableName) {
    this.tableName = tableName;
```

```
    }

    public void setKey(String key) {
        this.key = key;
    }

    public void setType(String type) {
        this.type = type;
    }

    public void setColumnSize(int size) {
        this.size = size;
    }

    public String getTableName() {
        return tableName;
    }

    public String getKey() {
        return key;
    }

    public String getType() {
        return type;
    }

    public int getColumnSize() {
        return size;
    }
```

The name given to a column resource will be of the form <baseUri>column.*tablename*.*columnname* where column is just a literal identifier of the resource type, *tablename* is the name of the table in which this column may be found, and *columnname* is the name of this column itself.

```
    public Resource asResource(Model model) {
        if (resource != null) {
            return resource;
        }
        try {
            resource = model.createResource(database.getBaseUri()+"column."
                    + tableName + "." + name);
            resource.addProperty(RDF.type, RDBE.Column);
            resource.addProperty(RDBE.name, name);
            resource.addProperty(RDBE.columnType, type);
            resource.addProperty(RDBE.columnSize, size);
        } catch (Exception e) {
            e.printStackTrace();
        }
        return resource;
    }
}// end of JColumn.java
```

The next listing is that of the `JConnection` class, which retrieves the JDBC connection parameters from the RDF model (which will be initially populated from a file) and from these create a connection to the database that JDBC can use. The `Connection` object itself is obtained through the `DriverManager` class, and this operation may throw a `SQLException`. These three classes are found in the `java.sql` part of Java 2, and `import` statements for these appear below.

```java
// start of JConnection.java
package com.wrapper.dbmodel;

import java.util.Map;
import java.util.Hashtable;
import java.sql.DriverManager;
import java.sql.Connection;
import java.sql.SQLException;

import com.hp.hpl.mesa.rdf.jena.model.Model;
import com.hp.hpl.mesa.rdf.jena.model.Statement;
import com.hp.hpl.mesa.rdf.jena.model.Resource;
import com.hp.hpl.mesa.rdf.jena.model.StmtIterator;

import com.wrapper.vocabulary.RDBE;

public class JConnection {

  public JConnection() {
  }

public Connection getConnection(Model model, String connectionName) {
      String driver = null;
      String connUrl = null;
      String login = null;
      String password = null;

    try{
      Resource connResource = model.getResource(connectionName);
      driver = connResource.getProperty(RDBE.driver).getString();
      connUrl = connResource.getProperty(RDBE.connUrl).getString();
      login = connResource.getProperty(RDBE.login).getString();
      password = connResource.getProperty(RDBE.password).getString();
    }catch(Exception e){
        e.printStackTrace();
    }

    Connection connection = null;
    try {
      Class.forName(driver);
      connection = DriverManager.getConnection(connUrl, login, password);
    } catch (SQLException sqle) {
      sqle.printStackTrace();
    } catch (ClassNotFoundException cnfe) {
      cnfe.printStackTrace();
    }
    return connection;
  }
}// end of JConnection.java
```

Extracting the Meta Data with JDBC

The usual way of using JDBC involves obtaining a connection, creating `Statement` objects that are Java wrappers for SQL code, and executing these over the database connection. The data is returned in the form of a `ResultSet`, which is a wrapper for a table of data. The way of obtaining individual values in the table is to take the `ResultSet` row by row using a loop of the form `while(resultSet.next())`, and call a typed `getXXX()` method, specifying a particular column name or number; for example `resultSet.getInt(1)` will return the value in column 1 of the present row as an `int`, if such a value exists (if the wrong type is requested an exception will be thrown). There is some provision here for extracting meta data, as the `ResultSet` class has a method `getMetaData()`. Though this gives access to most features relating to a table and its columns, a far richer seam of meta data can be mined by calling the `getMetaData()` method of a `Connection` object. This method returns a `DatabaseMetaData` object, which in turn has literally dozens of methods that can be used for extracting different aspects of the database's meta data. There is no guarantee that a given database and JDBC driver will support all these methods, but fortunately the kind of information we are interested in is that which the driver and database are most likely to be capable of providing. In this application, all the methods that deal with the meta data extraction through JDBC are found in the `JDatabase` class.

Before we look at the code for this, here is part of the source of a utility class that `JDatabase` uses. Within the Java SQL classes the SQL types are normally referenced using a static field of the class `java.sql.Types`, for example `Types.CHAR`. The type of these fields themselves is `int`, which is fine for working within the code as we can name the field. We, however, wish to export the names of the fields outside of Java, and the following class contains a single method to return the name of a SQL type as a `String`, given its `java.sql.Types` value:

```java
// start of (reduced) TypesUtil.java
package com.wrapper.util;

import java.sql.Types;

public class TypesUtil {

  public static String getTypeAsString(int type) {
    switch (type) {
      case Types.ARRAY:
        return "ARRAY";
      case Types.BIGINT:
        return "BIGINT";
      case Types.BINARY:
        return "BINARY";
      ... // cut
      case Types.INTEGER:
        return "INTEGER";
      ... // cut
      case Types.VARCHAR:
        return "VARCHAR";
    }
    return "UNKNOWN";
  }
} // end of (reduced) TypesUtil.java
```

The list of types is quite lengthy, so a couple of long sections have been excised from this listing. The pattern should be clear from the above – each of the cases corresponds to one of the fields in the `java.sql.Types` class (see the `Javadoc` entry). The full listing is included in the code download for this book, in `TypesUtil.java`.

> The type strings will be used as literals in the RDF output, but an alternative would be to use URIs here corresponding to universal definitions of the data types. This would improve the chances of a different system being able to make sense of the data, (assuming the other system was also aware of the type definition URIs). This approach would incur considerable cost in terms of complexity, so for this prototype system the simpler, literal approach is taken.

Now we can return to the `JDatabase` class, which in addition to carrying out the meta data extraction also looks after the creation of a Database RDF resource in the same fashion as `JTable`, `JCatalog`, and so on. The code appears rather involved, but we'll take each method in turn:

```
// start of JDatabase.java
package com.wrapper.dbmodel;

import java.sql.ResultSet;
import java.sql.SQLException;
import java.sql.Connection;
import java.sql.DatabaseMetaData;
import java.util.Map;
import java.util.Hashtable;
import java.util.List;
import java.util.Vector;
import java.util.Iterator;

import com.wrapper.util.TypesUtil;
```

The SQL-related imports include the `DatabaseMetaData` class, which is the crux of the whole application. The last of these imports is the utility described above:

```
public class JDatabase {

    private String name = null;
    private Connection connection = null;

    private Map attributes = null;
    private List catalogNames = null;
    private List catalogs = null;
    private List schemaNames = null;
    private List schemas = null;
    private DatabaseMetaData metadata = null;

    private static String baseUri;
```

Following the empty constructor there are three connection-related accessor methods:

```
    public void setConnection(Connection connection) {
        this.connection = connection;
    }

    public void setBaseUri(String baseUri){
        this.baseUri = baseUri;
```

```
    }

    public String getBaseUri(){
      return baseUri;
    }
```

The next setter method forwards its argument (catalogName) to the connection, which has the effect of providing a catalog name for subsequent calls to obtain meta data using the getMetaData() method below:

```
    public void setCatalog(String catalogName) {
      try {
        connection.setCatalog(catalogName);
      } catch (SQLException sqle) {
        sqle.printStackTrace();
      }
    }

    public Connection getConnection() {
      return connection;
    }
```

The next method obtains a DatabaseMetaData object through the connection:

```
    public DatabaseMetaData getMetaData() {
      try {
        if (metadata == null) {
          metadata = connection.getMetaData();
        }
      } catch (Exception e) {
        e.printStackTrace();
        return null;
      }
      return metadata;
    }
```

Obtaining the meta data uses resources, and can cause an exception to be thrown, so a familiar idiom is used so that the getMetaData() request on the connection is only sent the first time this method is called (when metadata contains its initial value of null); after then the local variable containing this value will be returned instead.

The method below gets a ResultSet containing the names of the catalogs in the database, and uses each of these to create a new Catalog object with this Database instance given as the first argument of the constructor and the name of the catalog (taken from the ResultSet) given as the second. The object created is added to a list. After all the rows in the ResultSet have been iterated through the list is returned:

```
    public List getCatalogs() {
      if (catalogs != null) {
        return catalogs;
      }
      ResultSet rsCatalogs = null;
      JCatalog catalog;
```

```
      catalogs = new Vector();
      try {
        rsCatalogs = getMetaData().getCatalogs();
        while (rsCatalogs.next()) {
          catalog = new JCatalog(this, rsCatalogs.getString(1));
          catalogs.add(catalog);
        }
      } catch (SQLException sqle) {
        catalogs = null;
        sqle.printStackTrace();
      }
      return catalogs;
    }
```

The next method looks up the named catalog from the list provided by `getCatalog()` above by simply iterating through the list, and returns the named object or `null` if no corresponding catalog is found:

```
    public JCatalog getCatalog(String named) {
      List catalogs = getCatalogs();

      if (catalogs == null) {
        return null;
      }
      JCatalog catalog;

      for (Iterator i = catalogs.iterator(); i.hasNext(); ) {
        catalog = (JCatalog) i.next();
        if (catalog.getName().equals(named)) {
          return catalog;
        }
      }
      return null;
    }
```

The `getSchemas()` method obtains a `ResultSet` from the `DatabaseMetaData` object provided by `getMetaData()` containing the names of the schemas in the database, and uses each of these to create a new `Schema` object, which is added to a list and finally the list is returned:

```
    public List getSchemas() {
      if (schemas != null) {
        return schemas;
      }
      String schemaName;
      schemas = new Vector();
      ResultSet rsSchemas = null;
      JSchema schema;
      try {
        rsSchemas = getMetaData().getSchemas();
        while (rsSchemas.next()) {
          schema = new JSchema(this, rsSchemas.getString(1));
          schemas.add(schema);
        }

      }
```

```
    } catch (SQLException sqle) {
      schemas = null;
      sqle.printStackTrace();
    }
    return schemas;
  }
```

The next part looks up the named schema from the list provided by getSchema() and returns this object:

```
public JSchema getSchema(String named) {
  List schemas = getSchemas();

  if (schemas == null) {
    return null;
  }
  String schemaName;
  JSchema schema;
  for (Iterator i = schemas.iterator(); i.hasNext(); ) {
      schema = (JSchema) i.next();
    if (schema.getName().equals(named)) {
      return schema;
    }
  }
  return null;
}
```

The following method is given a pattern for each of the first three arguments (a String, which may contain wildcards) and an array of the required table types for the fourth (we're only going to request a single type, "TABLE"). This method constructs a Table object for every table name returned, setting the object's fields as appropriate, and then adds these to a list which will be returned:

```
public List getTables(String catalog, String schemaPattern, String
                                     tablePattern, String[] types) {
  JTable table;
  List tables = new Vector();
  ResultSet rsTables;
  try {
    setCatalog(catalog);
    rsTables = getMetaData().getTables(catalog, schemaPattern,
                                        tablePattern, types);
    Object object;
    String name = "unnamed";
    String catalogName = "unnamed";
    String schemaName = "unnamed";
    String type = "unnamed";

    while (rsTables.next()) {
      object = rsTables.getObject(1);
      if(object != null) catalogName = object.toString();
      table.setCatalogName(catalogName);

      object = rsTables.getObject(2);
      if(object != null) schemaName = object.toString();
      table.setSchemaName(schemaName);
```

```
      object = rsTables.getObject(3);
      if(object != null) name = object.toString();
      table = new JTable(this, name);

      object = rsTables.getObject(4);
      if(object != null) type = object.toString();
      table.setType(type);
      tables.add(table);
    }
  } catch (SQLException sqle) {
    tables = null;
    sqle.printStackTrace();
  }
  return tables;
}
```

Note the use of getObject() rather than getString() – a test with the MySQL database driver inexplicably threw exceptions with the latter method calls, but the value obtained using object.toString() is the same.

The next method calls the method above with a wildcard in second and third arguments and null in the first and fourth (null is treated as "unspecified" – effectively another wildcard). The method will thus return all available tables as a list.

```
public List getTables() {
  return getTables(null, "%", "%", null);
}
```

We see the same basic pattern below as in getTables(,,,) above, with additional code to provide the key field value ('named', 'primary', or an identifier for the table referenced by a foreign key):

```
public List getColumns(String catalog, String schemaPattern,
                       String tablePattern, String columnPattern) {
  JColumn column;
  List columns = new Vector();
  List primaryKeys;
  Map foreignKeys;
  ResultSet rsColumns;
  try {
    setCatalog(catalog);
    rsColumns = getMetaData().getColumns(catalog, schemaPattern,
                tablePattern, columnPattern);
    primaryKeys = getPrimaryKeys(catalog, schemaPattern, tablePattern);
    foreignKeys = getForeignKeys(catalog, schemaPattern, tablePattern);
    String typeString;
    String qName;
    while (rsColumns.next()) {
      column = new JColumn(this, rsColumns.getString(4));

      typeString = TypesUtil.getTypeAsString((int) rsColumns.getShort(5));
      column.setType(typeString);
      column.setColumnSize(rsColumns.getInt(7));
```

```
            column.setTableName(rsColumns.getString(3));
            qName = column.getTableName() + "." + column.getName();
            System.out.println("foreignKeys.keySet() " + foreignKeys.keySet());
            if (primaryKeys.contains(qName)) {
              column.setKey("primary");
            } else
    //      System.out.println("qName "+qName+" get(qName)
                "+foreignKeys.get(qName)+"  foreignKeys.keySet()
                "+foreignKeys.keySet());

            if (foreignKeys.keySet().contains(qName)) {

            column.setKey(foreignKeys.get(qName).toString());
            //   System.out.println("+++qName "+qName+" get(qName)
                "+foreignKeys.get(qName)) qName;
            }
            columns.add(column);
          }
        } catch (SQLException sqle) {
          columns = null;
          sqle.printStackTrace();
        }
        return columns;
      }
```

Again we have a wildcard version of the method:

```
    public List getColumns() {
      return getColumns(null, "%", "%", "%");
    }
```

The method below returns a list of identifiers for columns that act as primary keys (as used by `getColumns()`):

```
    public List getPrimaryKeys(String catalog, String schema, String table) {

      List primaryKeys = new Vector();
      ResultSet rsKeys;
      try {
        setCatalog(catalog);
        rsKeys = getMetaData().getPrimaryKeys(catalog, schema, table);

        while (rsKeys.next()) {
          primaryKeys.add(rsKeys.getString(3) + "." + rsKeys.getString(4));
        }

      } catch (SQLException sqle) {
        primaryKeys = null;
        sqle.printStackTrace();
      }
      return primaryKeys;
    }
```

The foreign keys are returned as a hash table of [column identifier, foreign column referenced] pairs:

```java
public Map getForeignKeys(String catalog, String schema, String table) {

    Map foreignKeys = new Hashtable();
    ResultSet rsKeys;
    Object mapKey;
    Object mapValue;
    try {
      setCatalog(catalog);
      rsKeys = getMetaData().getImportedKeys(catalog, schema, table);

      while (rsKeys.next()) {
        mapValue = rsKeys.getString(3) + "." + rsKeys.getString(4);
        mapKey = rsKeys.getString(7) + "." + rsKeys.getString(8);
        System.out.println("******" + mapKey + "    " + mapValue);

        foreignKeys.put(mapKey, mapValue);
      }
    } catch (SQLException sqle) {
      foreignKeys = null;
      sqle.printStackTrace();
    }
    return foreignKeys;
}
```

The final method of this rather long class simply returns the name of the database:

```java
public String toString() {
    return name;
  }
} // end of JDatabase.java
```

Putting It All Together

The last class in the Java application provides a simple command-line way of creating the RDF meta data file. This code is provided merely as an example of how the classes above might be used. Hopefully it shows that by wrapping the external structure in an object-oriented code model, processing operations can be constructed very simply. We begin by importing everything we have seen so far:

```java
// start of ExposeDB.java

package com.wrapper.expose;

import java.util.Hashtable;
import java.util.Map;

import java.util.List;
import java.util.Vector;
import java.util.Iterator;
import java.io.FileReader;
import java.io.PrintWriter;
```

```
import java.io.FileOutputStream;
import java.sql.DriverManager;
import java.sql.Connection;
import java.sql.SQLException;

import com.wrapper.dbmodel.*;
import com.hp.hpl.mesa.rdf.jena.model.Model;
import com.hp.hpl.mesa.rdf.jena.model.Statement;

import com.hp.hpl.mesa.rdf.jena.model.StmtIterator;
import com.hp.hpl.mesa.rdf.jena.mem.ModelMem;
import com.hp.hpl.mesa.rdf.jena.model.Resource;

import com.hp.hpl.mesa.rdf.jena.vocabulary.RDF;

import com.wrapper.vocabulary.RDBE;
import com.wrapper.vocabulary.Admin;
```

The class has member variables to hold values that will be used in several methods, such as the RDF `Model` object:

```
public class ExposeDB {

   Model model = new ModelMem();
   JDatabase database = null;
   Resource dbResource = null;
   String[] tableTypes = {"TABLE"};
   String baseUri;
```

The constructor takes an array of string arguments (passed from the `main()` method below). The contents of these arguments can be seen in the `String` assignations that follow:

```
public ExposeDB(String[] args) {

   String sourceFile = args[0];
   String outputFile = args[1];
   String databaseName = args[2];
   String schemaName = args[3];
   String catalogName = args[4];
   String connectionName = args[5];
```

Next the source RDF file is read into the `Model`, a trivial task with Jena:

```
try {
  model.read(new FileReader(sourceFile), "");
```

Next the JDBC connection is obtained using parameters contained in the model, and the `baseUri` string is set up:

```
JConnection dbConnection = new JConnection();
Connection connection = dbConnection.getConnection(model,
                                            connectionName);
```

```
database = new JDatabase();
database.setConnection(connection);

baseUri = getBaseUri(databaseName);
database.setBaseUri(baseUri);
```

We can then call the database object to get pieces of the meta data, starting with the schema name. Here again a test using the MySQL JDBC driver caused a problem, as this didn't return a schema value. If such a problem occurs, a schema with a wildcard for a name is created instead:

```
JSchema schema = database.getSchema(schemaName);
if(schema == null) schema = new JSchema(database, "%");

JCatalog catalog = database.getCatalog(catalogName);
dbResource = model.getResource(databaseName);
```

We now have the higher-level (schema, catalog) characteristics of the database view, which is enough for us to obtain the details. The addToModel() method (listed below) picks up these details using JDBC and inserts them into the RDF model:

```
addToModel(schema, catalog);
model.write(new PrintWriter(System.out));

model.write(new PrintWriter(new FileOutputStream(outputFile)));

} catch (Exception e) {
e.printStackTrace();
}
}
```

The getBaseUri() method wraps up the operations needed to get this value out of the model:

```
private String getBaseUri(String databaseName){
    try{
Resource resource= model.getResource(databaseName);
baseUri = resource.getProperty(RDBE.baseUri).getString();
}
catch(Exception e){
    e.printStackTrace();
}
    return baseUri;
}
```

The addToModel() method actually calls a hierarchy of other methods to build up the corresponding model hierarchy. It first calls the addStaticMetadata() method to add the MetaVocab at the top level of the model, which is hard-coded into this class below. The contains property is used to place the schema in its rightful place in hierarchy:

```
private void addToModel(JSchema schema, JCatalog catalog) throws Exception {
    addStaticMetadata();
    dbResource.addProperty(RDBE.contains, schema.asResource(model));
    addCatalogToModel(schema, catalog);
}
```

Adding the static MetaVocab properties (defined in the `Admin` class) is another trivial operation, thanks again to Jena:

```
private void addStaticMetadata(){
    try{
    model.createResource("")
                .addProperty(Admin.errorReportsTo,
                                    "mailto:danny_ayers@yahoo.co.uk")
                .addProperty(Admin.generatorAgent, "RDBE v0.2")
                .addProperty(Admin.prefix, "rdbe");
    }
    catch(Exception e){
        e.printStackTrace();
    }
}
```

The catalog is adding to the schema resource, as another step in filling in the hierarchy:

```
private void addCatalogToModel(JSchema schema, JCatalog catalog) throws
Exception {
    schema.asResource(model).addProperty(RDBE.contains,
                                        catalog.asResource(model));
    addTablesToModel(catalog);
}
```

Getting more finely-grained, the tables are obtained and these are used in turn to insert the column details using a further `addColumns()` method:

```
private void addTablesToModel(JCatalog catalog) throws Exception {

    List tables = database.getTables(catalog.getName(), "%", "%", tableTypes);

    if (tables == null) {
        throw new Exception("No tables found.");
    }
    Vector rdfTables = new Vector();

    Resource tableResource;
    JTable table;

    for (Iterator i = tables.iterator(); i.hasNext(); ) {
        table = (JTable) i.next();
        addColumnsToModel(table);
        catalog.asResource(model).addProperty(RDBE.contains,
                                        table.asResource(model));
    }
}
```

At the most detailed level, the properties of individual columns are placed hierarchically in the model:

```
private void addColumnsToModel(JTable table) throws Exception {
    List columns = table.getColumns();
    JColumn column;
    for (Iterator i = columns.iterator(); i.hasNext(); ) {
```

```
        column = (JColumn) i.next();
        column.asResource(model).addProperty(RDBE.isKey, column.getKey());
        table.asResource(model).addProperty(RDBE.contains,
                                          column.asResource(model));
    }
}
```

Finally we have the `main()` method which acts as the entry point into the whole application:

```
    public static void main(String[] args) {
       new ExposeDB(args);
    }
}// end of ExposeDB.java
```

Running the Application

This section provides instructions on running the example application we have been discussing. The required files can all be found in the code download for this book at http://www.wrox.com.

Creating a Sample Database

First of all start up SQL Server (or your database of preference). A database called `simple` should then be created, and a user called `wrox` with the password `xorw`. This user should have database access permitted to the `simple` database. The easiest way to carry out these operations is with the SQL Server Enterprise Manager. Next we need to put something into the database. We get access to it by firing up a SQL client tool (Query Analyser) and logging in as user `wrox` (or the system administrator). Next we have to change to the `simple` database and load the file `inthewoods.sql`. This contains the following code:

```
CREATE TABLE food (id INT PRIMARY KEY, foodtype VARCHAR(10));
INSERT INTO food VALUES (1,'kapok');
INSERT INTO food VALUES (2,'honey');
INSERT INTO food VALUES (3,'campers');

CREATE TABLE bears (id INT PRIMARY KEY, name VARCHAR(10), food INT FOREIGN KEY
REFERENCES food(id));
INSERT INTO bears VALUES (1,'pooh', 2);
INSERT INTO bears VALUES (2,'teddy', 1);
INSERT INTO bears VALUES (3,'grizzly', 3);
```

Executing this should create and populate two tables. We can test this by executing the queries:

```
SELECT * FROM bears;
SELECT * FROM food;
```

which should give the results:

```
id          name       food
----------- ---------- -----------
1           pooh       2
2           teddy      1
```

```
3            grizzly     3

(3 row(s) affected)

id           foodtype
-----------  ----------
1            kapok
2            honey
3            campers

(3 row(s) affected)
```

If not, check that the correct database is selected, that the user you're logged in as has sufficient rights to the database, and that SQL Server authentication is enabled, as opposed to Windows authentication alone.

Setting up the Java Environment

In addition to the standard Java 2 class libraries (included with a default installation of the Java SDK) the code is dependent on the Jena API, which is in turn dependent on several other class libraries. The Jena package should first be downloaded and unzipped to any convenient location. The easiest way to make everything available is to copy the `.jar` files from the `jena\lib` directory into a working directory, here we use `C:\rdbexposed`, so that the directory now contains:

```
C:\rdbexposed\sax2.jar
C:\rdbexposed\rdffilter.jar
C:\rdbexposed\jena.jar
C:\rdbexposed\xerces.jar
```

A JDBC driver is needed at runtime, in the example we use the i-net SQL Server driver "Opta2000". You will need to download a fresh copy of this from http://www.inetsoftware.de as it is only available free as a 30 day evaluation. Once it is downloaded, the jar file should also be extracted to the working directory:

```
C:\rdbexposed\Opta2000.jar
```

Next, all the code has to be compiled. The source files are:

```
C:\rdbexposed\com\wrapper\dbmodel\JCatalog.java
C:\rdbexposed\com\wrapper\dbmodel\JDatabase.java
C:\rdbexposed\com\wrapper\dbmodel\JSchema.java
C:\rdbexposed\com\wrapper\dbmodel\JDataset.java
C:\rdbexposed\com\wrapper\dbmodel\JTable.java
C:\rdbexposed\com\wrapper\dbmodel\JColumn.java
C:\rdbexposed\com\wrapper\dbmodel\JConnection.java
C:\rdbexposed\com\wrapper\util\TypesUtil.java
C:\rdbexposed\com\wrapper\vocabulary\RDBE.java
C:\rdbexposed\com\wrapper\expose\ExposeDB.java
```

Here the files have been extracted into the `C:\rdbexposed` directory, which will be our working directory. The main class of the application is in `ExposeDB.java`, and entering the following at a command prompt (all on one line) will compile this and all the other files:

```
>javac -classpath .;sax2.jar;rdffilter.jar;jena.jar;xerces.jar
com\wrapper\expose\ExposeDB.java
```

(For convenience this command is supplied in the file `compile.bat`.)

Before we can run the application a suitable RDF source file needs to be available. The example in the text used the file `source.rdf`, which should also be copied into the working directory:

```
C:\rdbexposed\source.rdf
```

This file contains this data:

```
<?xml version="1.0"?>

<rdf:RDF xmlns:rdf = 'http://www.w3.org/1999/02/22-rdf-syntax-ns#'
xmlns:rdfs = 'http://www.w3.org/2000/01/rdf-schema#'
xmlns:dc= 'http://purl.org/dc/elements/1.0/'
xmlns:rdbe = 'http://www.isacat.net/ns/rdbe#'
xmlns = 'http://goldilocks/visitors/'
>

<rdbe:Database rdf:about="mydatabase" >
    <rdbe:name>Bear Diet</rdbe:name>
    <rdbe:baseUri>http://goldilocks/visitors/</rdbe:baseUri>
    <rdbe:xsdUrl>http://goldilocks/diet/diet.xsd</rdbe:xsdUrl>
    <rdbe:queryUrl>http://goldilocks/diet/query</rdbe:queryUrl>
<rdbe:description>A database of bear's preferred eating</rdbe:description>

<rdbe:hasConnection rdf:resource="#myconnection"/>
    <rdfs:seeAlso rdf:resource="http://dmoz.org/Science/Biology/Zoology/"/>
</rdbe:Database >

<rdbe:Connection rdf:about="myconnection">
    <rdbe:name>My connection</rdbe:name>
    <rdbe:driver>com.inet.tds.TdsDriver</rdbe:driver>
    <rdbe:dbcType>JDBC</rdbe:dbcType>
    <rdbe:connUrl>jdbc:inetdae:localhost:1433</rdbe:connUrl>
    <rdbe:login>wrox</rdbe:login>
    <rdbe:password>xorw</rdbe:password>
</rdbe:Connection>

</rdf:RDF>
```

Note the addition of an `rdfs:seeAlso` property, to provide a little extra information.

To run the application, a suitable command line is:

```
>java -classpath .;sax2.jar;rdffilter.jar;jena.jar;xerces.jar;Opta2000.jar
com.wrapper.expose.ExposeDB source.rdf output.rdf mydatabase wrox simple myconnection
```

(which can be found in `run.bat`).

The arguments given here are as follows:

❑ `source.rdf` – file containing meta data about the connection, etc.

❑ `output.rdf` – target filename for the program's output.

- ❑ `mydatabase` – name of the database (as specified in `source.rdf`).

- ❑ `wrox` – the database schema entity (SQL Server user).

- ❑ `simple` – the name of the catalog (database as specified in SQL Server).

- ❑ `myconnection` – the JDBC connection to use (as specified in `source.rdf`).

After a few seconds the resultant RDF text should be output to the console. It will also be saved to the file `output.rdf`.

Results

The file `output.rdf` should contain the following code, starting with all the namespaces we have added along the way:

```
<rdf:RDF
  xmlns:rdf='http://www.w3.org/1999/02/22-rdf-syntax-ns#'
  xmlns:RDFNsId1='http://webns.net/mvcb#'
  xmlns:RDFNsId2='http://www.isacat.net/ns/rdbe#'
  xmlns:RDFNsId3='http://www.w3.org/2000/01/rdf-schema#' >
```

The order of the RDF file is unimportant; it happens that the first resource happens to describe one of the tables:

```
<rdf:Description rdf:about='http://goldilocks/visitors/table.bears'>
  <rdf:type rdf:resource='http://www.isacat.net/ns/rdbe#Table'/>
  <RDFNsId2:name>bears</RDFNsId2:name>
  <RDFNsId2:tableType>TABLE</RDFNsId2:tableType>
  <RDFNsId2:contains
          rdf:resource='http://goldilocks/visitors/column.bears.id'/>
  <RDFNsId2:contains
          rdf:resource='http://goldilocks/visitors/column.bears.name'/>
  <RDFNsId2:contains
          rdf:resource='http://goldilocks/visitors/column.bears.food'/>
</rdf:Description>
```

The database resource comes next, with details specified in the source file:

```
<rdf:Description rdf:about='mydatabase'>
  <rdf:type rdf:resource='http://www.isacat.net/ns/rdbe#Database'/>
  <RDFNsId2:name>Bear Diet</RDFNsId2:name>
  <RDFNsId2:baseUri>http://goldilocks/visitors/</RDFNsId2:baseUri>
  <RDFNsId2:xsdUrl>http://goldilocks/diet/diet.xsd</RDFNsId2:xsdUrl>
  <RDFNsId2:queryUrl>http://goldilocks/diet/query</RDFNsId2:queryUrl>
  <RDFNsId2:description>A database of bear&apos;s preferred
                      eating</RDFNsId2:description>
  <RDFNsId2:hasConnection rdf:resource='#myconnection'/>
  <RDFNsId3:seeAlso
          rdf:resource='http://dmoz.org/Science/Biology/Zoology/'/>
  <RDFNsId2:contains
          rdf:resource='http://goldilocks/visitors/schema.wrox'/>
</rdf:Description>
```

Next we have one of the columns:

```
<rdf:Description
    rdf:about='http://goldilocks/visitors/column.food.foodtype'>
  <rdf:type rdf:resource='http://www.isacat.net/ns/rdbe#Column'/>
  <RDFNsId2:name>foodtype</RDFNsId2:name>
  <RDFNsId2:columnType>VARCHAR</RDFNsId2:columnType>
  <RDFNsId2:columnSize>10</RDFNsId2:columnSize>
  <RDFNsId2:isKey>none</RDFNsId2:isKey>
</rdf:Description>
<rdf:Description rdf:about='http://goldilocks/visitors/column.bears.food'>
  <rdf:type rdf:resource='http://www.isacat.net/ns/rdbe#Column'/>
  <RDFNsId2:name>food</RDFNsId2:name>
  <RDFNsId2:columnType>INTEGER</RDFNsId2:columnType>
  <RDFNsId2:columnSize>10</RDFNsId2:columnSize>
  <RDFNsId2:isKey>food.id</RDFNsId2:isKey>
</rdf:Description>
```

Jena has filled in a name where really we want to have `rdf:about=''`, referring to the current document, in use this would have to be manually edited:

```
<rdf:Description rdf:about='#RDFAnonId16'>
  <RDFNsId1:errorReportsTo>mailto:danny_ayers@yahoo.co.uk
  </RDFNsId1:errorReportsTo>
  <RDFNsId1:generatorAgent>RDBE v0.2</RDFNsId1:generatorAgent>
  <RDFNsId1:prefix>rdbe</RDFNsId1:prefix>
</rdf:Description>
```

Here we have another table:

```
<rdf:Description rdf:about='http://goldilocks/visitors/table.food'>
  <rdf:type rdf:resource='http://www.isacat.net/ns/rdbe#Table'/>
  <RDFNsId2:name>food</RDFNsId2:name>
  <RDFNsId2:tableType>TABLE</RDFNsId2:tableType>
  <RDFNsId2:contains
            rdf:resource='http://goldilocks/visitors/column.food.id'/>
  <RDFNsId2:contains
          rdf:resource='http://goldilocks/visitors/column.food.foodtype'/>
</rdf:Description>
```

Another column:

```
<rdf:Description rdf:about='http://goldilocks/visitors/column.bears.id'>
  <rdf:type rdf:resource='http://www.isacat.net/ns/rdbe#Column'/>
  <RDFNsId2:name>id</RDFNsId2:name>
  <RDFNsId2:columnType>INTEGER</RDFNsId2:columnType>
  <RDFNsId2:columnSize>10</RDFNsId2:columnSize>
  <RDFNsId2:isKey>primary</RDFNsId2:isKey>
</rdf:Description>
```

Now we have the higher-level schema resource, which contains the catalog:

```
<rdf:Description rdf:about='http://goldilocks/visitors/schema.wrox'>
  <rdf:type rdf:resource='http://www.isacat.net/ns/rdbe#Schema'/>
  <RDFNsId2:name>wrox</RDFNsId2:name>
  <RDFNsId2:contains
          rdf:resource='http://goldilocks/visitors/catalog.simple'/>
</rdf:Description>
```

Another couple of columns:

```
<rdf:Description rdf:about='http://goldilocks/visitors/column.food.id'>
  <rdf:type rdf:resource='http://www.isacat.net/ns/rdbe#Column'/>
  <RDFNsId2:name>id</RDFNsId2:name>
  <RDFNsId2:columnType>INTEGER</RDFNsId2:columnType>
  <RDFNsId2:columnSize>10</RDFNsId2:columnSize>
  <RDFNsId2:isKey>primary</RDFNsId2:isKey>
</rdf:Description>
<rdf:Description rdf:about='http://goldilocks/visitors/column.bears.name'>
  <rdf:type rdf:resource='http://www.isacat.net/ns/rdbe#Column'/>
  <RDFNsId2:name>name</RDFNsId2:name>
  <RDFNsId2:columnType>VARCHAR</RDFNsId2:columnType>
  <RDFNsId2:columnSize>10</RDFNsId2:columnSize>
  <RDFNsId2:isKey>none</RDFNsId2:isKey>
</rdf:Description>
```

Now the connection details:

```
<rdf:Description rdf:about='myconnection'>
  <rdf:type rdf:resource='http://www.isacat.net/ns/rdbe#Connection'/>
  <RDFNsId2:name>My connection</RDFNsId2:name>
  <RDFNsId2:driver>com.inet.tds.TdsDriver</RDFNsId2:driver>
  <RDFNsId2:dbcType>JDBC</RDFNsId2:dbcType>
  <RDFNsId2:connUrl>jdbc:inetdae:localhost:1433</RDFNsId2:connUrl>
  <RDFNsId2:login>wrox</RDFNsId2:login>
  <RDFNsId2:password>xorw</RDFNsId2:password>
</rdf:Description>
```

Finally the catalog resource:

```
<rdf:Description rdf:about='http://goldilocks/visitors/catalog.simple'>
  <rdf:type rdf:resource='http://www.isacat.net/ns/rdbe#Catalog'/>
  <RDFNsId2:name>simple</RDFNsId2:name>
  <RDFNsId2:contains
          rdf:resource='http://goldilocks/visitors/table.bears'/>
  <RDFNsId2:contains
          rdf:resource='http://goldilocks/visitors/table.food'/>
</rdf:Description>
</rdf:RDF>
```

After the application has run, the RDF generated has the following structure:

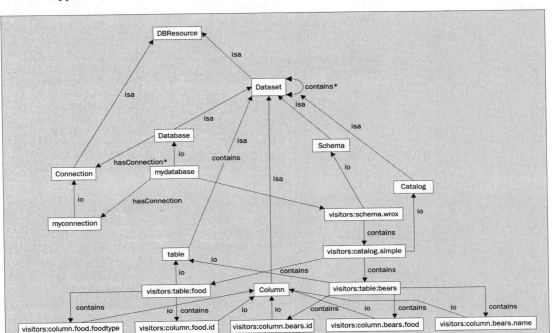

Looking at one branch of this tree in more detail, we can see some of the meta data that has been incorporated into the RDF:

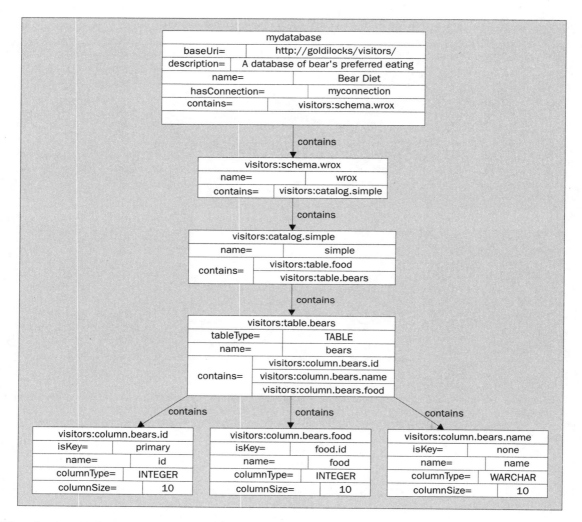

Viewing the Output with Protégé-2000

To view the RDF in graphical forms like those above, we can use Protégé-2000. First, of course, the Protégé application has to be downloaded and installed. In addition it will be necessary to install the Ontoviz tab, which depends on the Graphviz application included in the Ontoviz download. Full up-to-date instructions may be found on the Protégé site at http://smi-web.stanford.edu/projects/protege/. The readme file included in the Ontoviz download is also useful as it has step-by-step instructions.

When Protégé is run, an empty window will appear with a toolbar and menu bar. From the menus select Project... and then Import... This will bring up a box offering a choice of import formats:

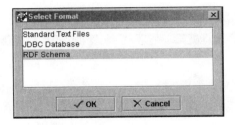

Select **RDF** and click **OK**.

Now fill in the text entry lines as follows (you can use the + button to navigate to `rdbe.rdfs` for the **Classes** file name and `output.rdf` for the **Instance** file name – they do not have to be moved into the Protégé directory):

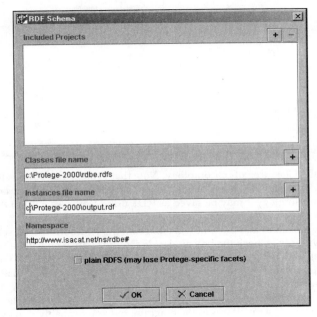

Note that the namespace is that specified in our instances file.

Clicking **OK** will bring up:

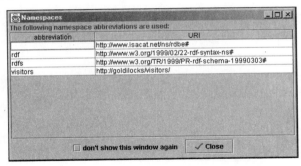

which you can then close to reveal Protégé's Classes view:

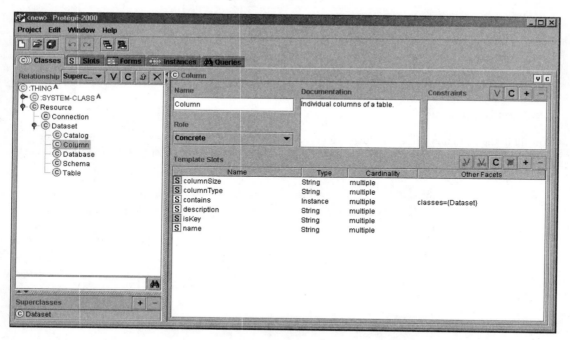

Here we may explore the Class tree of our ontology. Note that Protégé has various features that can't be directly expressed in RDF, so a little care is needed when using it to edit ontologies destined for this model. If you make changes to the ontology it may be saved as RDF using **Save As…** from the **Project** menu.

To get a graphic view we need to add the Ontoviz tab. From the **Project…** menu select **Configure…** You will see a list of 'Tab Widgets'. Check the box alongside **OntovizTab**. You will be returned to the classes view, except that now there will be an additional tab for Ontoviz. Click on this. If you now click on the **C** button just to the left of the centre divider, near the top of the window, a simple diagram will appear in the right-hand pane. On the left a row of checkboxes should also have appeared. Drag the centre divider across until they are all visible. These select which aspects of the knowledge base to display. The checkbox on the right includes all the Protégé system classes in the diagram, but you probably don't want these. If you check all the others and click the **C** button again, you should see something like this:

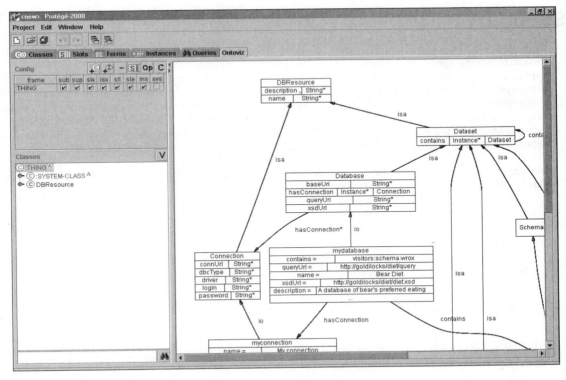

Unless you have a monitor with a resolution of at least 1600x1200 you will have to scroll to see other parts of the diagram.

Further Information

❑ Despite a profusion of book advertisements and not a little venom, the "Database Debunking" site contains good information on how today's system implementations and current practices match up to the theory of relational databases: http://www.firstsql.com/dbdebunk.

❑ Work on database meta data standards in XML has been done by the Meta Data Coalition, http://www.mdcinfo.com/, unfortunately not using RDF, though a mapping between their standards and RDF may provide a good route to future interoperability.

❑ Other RDF-related information is available in Chapters 4 and 5 of this book and from the W3C: http://www.w3.org/RDF/.

Summary

In an ideal world the communication channels between relational databases and other entities on the Web such as reasoning agents would fully maintain the semantics contained in the database. As it is, we can approach this transparency by passing through such information in RDF meta data and other XML. The prototype application described here shows one possible approach to this. The Jena API makes the construction of an RDF model very straightforward, allowing us to concentrate on the structure and content of our meta data. The flexibility of the API has allowed us to construct a single model with information from three different sources – a manually entered RDF file, some hard-coded properties and the actual database details dynamically obtained using JDBC and programmatically inserted into the RDF model.

In Chapter 13 we'll be looking, briefly, at a different use of meta data – that of using a Schematron schema to check XML data against a set of validation rules.

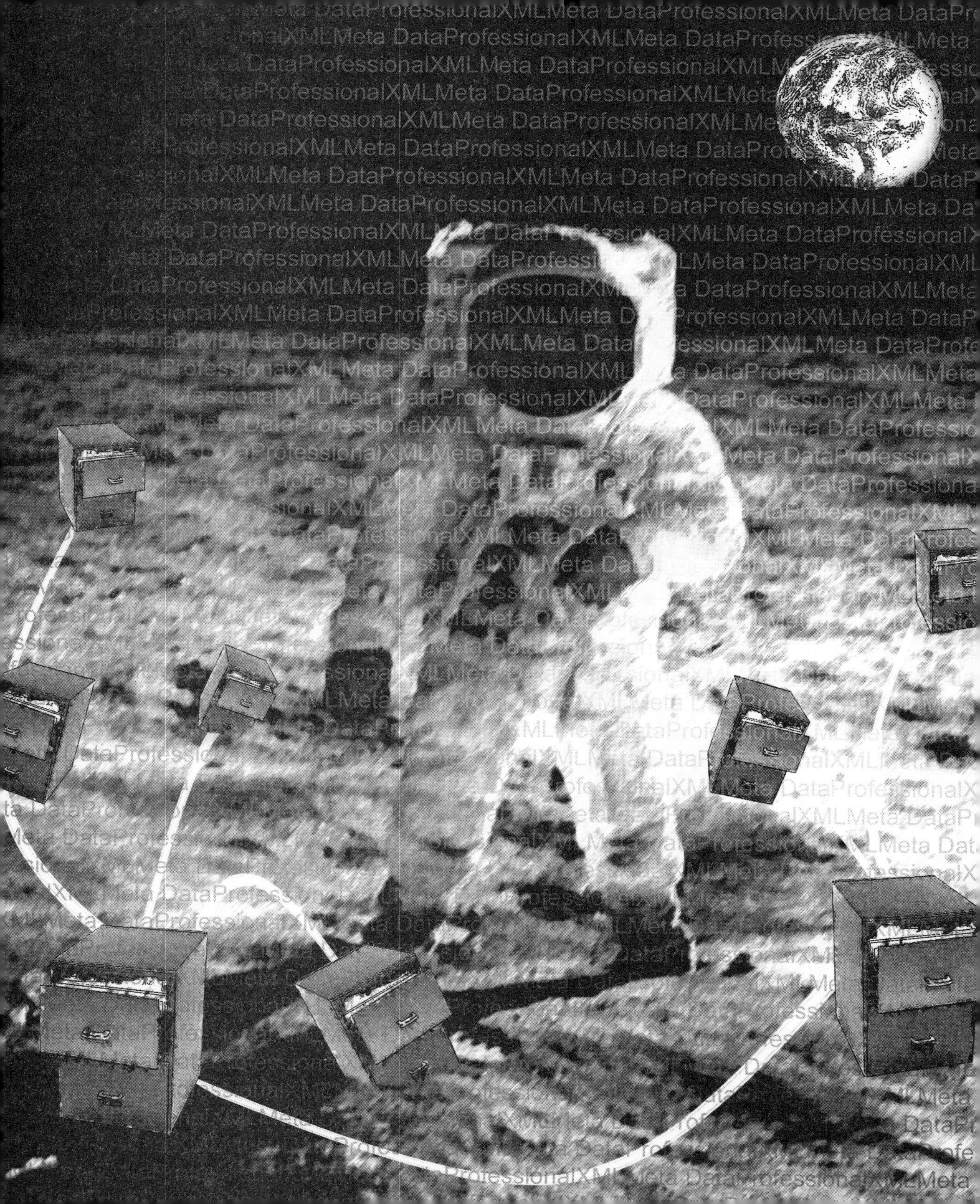

13

Data Validation and Mining with Schematron

Every developer strives for data consistency, but this can be an elusive beast. Experience tells us that the most obvious errors are the most difficult to find, and you can almost guarantee that your boss will open your project report on the one page with an idiotic mistake, despite the fact that you proof-read the thing at least ten times.

Wouldn't it be nice if we could automatically detect such errors and save ourselves the embarrassment? Although the automatic discovery of every conceivable error is somewhat out of the reach of current technology, it is still possible to detect a variety of common slip-ups. If we are aware of error-prone areas, we may be able to devise a suitable method for detecting and reporting problems likely to arise. The obvious approach would be to write a specialized program for each document, database, or program we wish to validate, but clearly this would not be a very efficient use of our time.

The provision of universal tools for data validation is one of XML's strong points. In fact, the fundamental concept of well-formedness itself can be very useful for detecting certain classes of error. An XML processor must issue a fatal error if a document is not well-formed, and so successful document parsing is an indication that particular types of inconsistencies are not present.

But obviously not every problem will be picked up at this level. In our fight for data consistency, a very useful ally can be found in validation languages. These let us specify further document constraints and so automatically detect many hidden errors. XML is employed in a huge range of different areas, so it is not a practical proposition to expect a validating language to be applicable everywhere with the same efficiency. The size of documents, the required validation speed, and the checks to be performed vary dramatically and an optimal trade-off must be sought.

Thus, there is space for several languages each offering different benefits. However, only a masochist would want to learn a completely new language for every task encountered, so it follows that there should be only a restricted, complementary set of such languages, and it would seem wise to build on the XML expertise that many of today's developers have spent so long acquiring.

In this chapter, we shall discover the basics of **Schematron**, a validating tool that can be applied to the sorts of scenario discussed above (for general Schematron information see http://www.ascc.net/xml/resource/schematron/schematron.html). I believe it has an important place in every XML expert's tool portfolio, and that moreover it is especially valuable in the XML meta data areas covered by this book. Schematron is very easy to learn; it builds on XPath (which anyone wishing to work seriously in the XML field will need to have a good understanding of) to create a very powerful validation language indeed.

Several Schematron implementations are already available, mostly built from **Extensible Stylesheet Language for Transformations (XSLT)**. XSLT processors are becoming very popular and are even being built into the next generation of Internet browsers, which will provide an enormous user-base with the software necessary for Schematron processing. In this chapter you will see that the power of XSLT processors in browsers can be harnessed in a way not possible with other validation languages.

Schematron does not impose any special requirements on the document to be validated, and can be used together with other tools as it does not introduce any unwanted side effects. Rick Jelliffe, the creator of Schematron, describes it as "a feather duster for the furthest corners of a room where the vacuum cleaner (the DTD) cannot reach" – a very fitting analogy.

A few days after Schematron was unveiled by Rick Jelliffe, the Zvon Schematron tutorial was announced to the xml-dev mailing list with this mail from the 27th October 1999:

> *"If I can speak for myself with Schematron a dream come true. This was precisely the tool I was looking for. And I actually missed it for the first time I have seen the announcement some time ago. Then, on this Friday, I have seen it mentioned in a message at comp.text.xml, peeped in and was trapped. This week I have started to play with it and I have realized that it solves many problems I had so far with XML validation. It is superbly simple, elegant, XPath based and already implemented!"*

By the end of this chapter you will have acquired the knowledge and skills to use Schematron in your everyday work. We will firstly stress some important points to be aware of when using Schematron, then we will introduce XPath basics for the benefit of uninitiated readers. Schematron will be introduced and its power will be illustrated using a short sample rendering a family tree. This book is focused on meta data processing and so, in the closing part of the chapter, we will rewrite the family tree using topic map syntax (XTM) – we can then use Schematron to check the topic map code for consistency.

DTD Drawbacks

Before we start on Schematron let's recapitulate some important points to keep in mind when working through this chapter. **Document Type Definitions (DTDs)** form part of the **Extensible Markup Language (XML) 1.0 standard** and have become the most widely used validation language. As such, they are likely to continue to be used for some time yet and a good working knowledge of DTDs is essential for anyone seriously dealing with XML. However, as we saw in Chapter 2, they have some disadvantages that make them unsuitable for certain applications.

DTDs predate the XML Namespaces specification, and are therefore not namespace aware. So if, for example, we have our own namespace and are using the namespace prefix `"family"` in some documents but only the prefix `"f"` in others, from a DTD point of view `f:mother` and `family:mother` would denote different elements. The result is that validation will fail unless the DTD is changed for every set of documents.

And this is not all: all elements and attributes used in the documents to be validated must be defined in the DTD. This is not a problem if we have a strictly defined vocabulary, but in the real world that's not always the case. We can write the DTDs and, while some elements can be defined beforehand, such as author or title, we may also define elements which are to contain formatted text of a more general kind (XHTML, WML, OurCompanyML, RandomML, and so on). If we want to validate such documents, we must provide the validating processor with the DTDs for all such inserted languages, which can lead to name clashes and a host of other problems.

Creating associations within documents is a very common task, and validating these associations is given to being performed automatically. So, for example when we are writing a project report, we need to make sure that all materials mentioned in the text are actually in the list of references, that footnote comments are all present, and that links to figures and tables really do lead to a figure or a table. The DTD specification defines an ID/IDREF mechanism for this kind of validation but it has several disadvantages. Its power is limited by not distinguishing the *context* of the identifier, making it hard to differentiate between a table and a figure. The range of possible values of these attributes is restricted also, for instance values cannot start with a number. It quite often happens that in the later stages of document writing you realize that there are associations which would be nice to validate and that you have attributes well suited for that, but they have some problems with their names/values. You cannot just change the DTD, you must change the source document if you want to use this mechanism.

XML Schema Drawbacks

We also discussed in Chapter 2 that XML Schema became a W3C Recommendation on the 2nd May 2001, bringing about many improvements over DTDs. XML Schemas (or XSD Schemas as we are referring to them in this book) are namespace aware and they are substantially more expressive than DTDs.

But this standard too has its disadvantages. While the basics of XSD Schema are reasonably simple, and selection can be used as a powerful DTD substitute, the specification as a whole offers many possibilities which are not really very easy to grasp and implement. Because of its size and complexity it can be expected that it will be some time before reliable and vigorously tested, fully compliant XSD Schema processors become available. This is a particular issue in regard to the advanced features which bring new possibilities to the XML validation armory, as these new features will take the longest for processor developers to implement, therefore delaying their use in the discovery of errors.

Personally, I think it's a little bit of a pity that the specification was not prepared in a more modular way so that individual processors could specify the subsets they are fully conformant with and indicate the areas where problems are to be expected.

Because of their importance and position in the overall W3C effort, we can be sure that XSD Schema will become commonly used and hence we will access more and more reliable processors. But even when these processors are available and knowledge of XSD Schemas is widespread, they will still not always be the right solution for every task.

Most of the validation demonstrated in the following text would not be trivial to implement in XSD Schema. I won't use the term "impossible" as there is always some bright spark who can make any tool perform unbelievable tricks, but for common usage a tool must offer a natural and simple solution. We cannot assume that everybody has a top class XSD Schema expert lying around!

So to conclude this section, XSD Schema is very important, powerful, and useful, but there remain plenty of reasons for exploring other approaches. And in fact, because Schematron is based on different premises, it is a superb *complement* to XSD Schema: not an opponent.

XSLT and Schematron

Most Schematron engines are implemented as XSLT stylesheets. The way this works is that a Schematron document is transformed with XSLT to create a general XSLT stylesheet that can then be used to validate source documents against the original Schematron document. We can use an analogy with programming languages. The first stylesheet implementing Schematron serves as a compiler, which produces the second stylesheet which can be considered as a native code for actual validation. Nowadays there are several excellent XSLT engines available which fully implement both the XSLT 1.0 and XPath 1.0 specifications. I personally prefer Saxon by Michael Kay, available from http://users.iclway.co.uk/mhkay/saxon/, because of its very good performance and exceptional standards compliance.

There are two ways in which we can perform both steps – compilation and validation – of the Schematron model.

❑   All required files can be specified from the command line and therefore neither the Schematron file nor the XML source to be validated need contain a URL for a Schematron implementation or a compiled stylesheet. The stylesheet to be used can also be specified directly in the source document using the relevant processing instruction directive. Both approaches can be combined and both steps do not have to be applied at the same time.

❑   Alternatively, we can compile a Schematron schema with a standalone processor and then make the resulting compiled stylesheet available over the web on our server. As I have already mentioned, XSLT processors are being incorporated into the latest generation of web browsers, so if you publish your commonly used stylesheets on the web, you can effectively use these built-in parsers to validate your documents from any computer connected to the Internet (or intranet).

But you must be careful with your choice of browser. The XSLT engine which shipped with Internet Explorer 5.5 does not conform to the current XSLT and XPath standards, but to a very old draft of them. Stylesheets produced by most Schematron implementations require the standards-compliant versions and so the final release of the XML tools component, MSXML 3.0, must be installed to use Internet Explorer in this way. You can easily check that you have the right version set up correctly by pointing your browser at http://www.zvon.org and choosing its View as XSLT option. The Zvon site will only be visible in this mode when used with a standards-compliant browser.

Introduction to XPath

As we saw in Chapter 3, **XPath** (http://www.w3.org/TR/xpath) is one of the basic building blocks of the XML world. It offers very powerful methods for addressing nodes in an XML "tree": something that is of paramount importance to XML processing. XPath is a base for both the XSLT and XPointer specifications, it will become part of the Document Object Model (DOM) Recommendation, and it will be very important for the XML Query Language. Schematron is another specification which draws on its enormous power.

While real mastery of XPath requires plenty of practice, the basics are really quite simple. We will demonstrate the syntax on several simple examples so that a reader who has not encountered XPath before will understand the Schematron examples. At the Zvon site previously mentioned, you will find many different examples and a handy interactive feature called XLab, which should help you master the more advanced syntax.

We'll be using the following trivial XML document to illustrate the principles of XPath:

```
<AAA>
  <BBB aaa="1" bbb="aaa"/>
  <BBB aaa="2"/>
  <BBB aaa="3"/>
  <CCC>
     <BBB/>
     <DDD/>
  </CCC>
</AAA>
```

The basic XPath syntax is similar to the means for addressing a file system, so should be familiar to most developers already. So, `"/AAA/CCC/DDD"` specifies the path to the `<DDD>` element, and `"/AAA/BBB"` gives the path to all `<BBB>` elements which are immediate children of the root element `<AAA>` but not the one given by the XPath `"/AAA/CCC/BBB"`.

It is possible to use XPath to say which one of the three `"/AAA/BBB"` elements we need to work with. Its position can be given in square brackets – the **predicate** – so for example the first and the third are specified as `"/AAA/BBB[1]"` and `"/AAA/BBB[3]"` respectively. Quite often the last of a set of elements is of interest, and there is a special function called `last()` to select this one:

```
"/AAA/BBB[last()]"
```

An XML document can contain not only elements but attributes as well. Attribute names are distinguished from element names in XPath with the "at sign" `"@"`. So the bbb attributes can be selected like this:

```
"/AAA/BBB/@bbb"
```

Quite often we are interested in elements which have something in common (for example, they are all children of the same parent) but that do not have the same name. The wildcard `"*"` character can be used in such cases. This allows us to select *all* children of the root element `<AAA>` with the following expression:

```
"/AAA/*"
```

We can even count them with the `count()` function:

```
count(/AAA/*)
```

In our case the result is 4.

The concept of axes is very important for XPath processing. We have already used two of them. The most commonly used is the `child` axis, and so is designated as the default in the XPath specification. In other words, an expression like `"/AAA/CCC/BBB"` uses only the `child` axis and, as the default, need not be explicitly specified. This notation is equivalent to the following, where the name of the axis is used:

```
"/child::AAA/child::CCC/child::BBB"
```

The `attribute` axis is also commonly used; attributes written using the shorthand `"@"` can be alternatively written like this:

```
"/AAA/BBB/attribute::bbb"
```

If we have children we obviously have parents as well. The root node `"/AAA"` can be selected with a slightly more verbose statement, involving the use of the `parent` axis:

```
"/AAA/CCC/BBB/parent::CCC/parent::AAA"
```

Other important axes include the `ancestor` and `descendant` axes. The `descendant` axis selects all elements which are descendants of the given element, that is, including all children's children and so on. So `"/AAA/descendant::*"` selects all elements from the document except for the root element `<AAA>`. Elements `"/AAA"` and `"/AAA/CCC"` can be selected using the `ancestor` axis as in the following:

```
"/AAA/CCC/DDD/ancestor::*"
```

XPath defines several other axes but this section is intended as only a brief introduction – a whole book would be required to describe all the possibilities that XPath offers.

Schematron Basics

Schematron is a very simple language that consists of a few core elements and attributes belonging to the namespace `"http://www.ascc.net/xml/schematron"`. In this chapter we will use the prefix `sch` for every element in this namespace.

The root element of a Schematron document is `<sch:schema>`. Several attributes can be specified for it but these are not required, so we can safely ignore them here.

Each Schematron schema must have at least one `<sch:pattern>` element with a required `name` attribute. These `pattern` elements mean that validation tests can be grouped into subsets, with the `name` attribute determining individual patterns.

The actual processing is specified by `<sch:rule>`, `<sch:report>`, and `<sch:assert>` elements. With `<sch:rule>` one or several nodes of an XML document are selected. These nodes then create context from which tests can be applied.

The elements `<sch:report>` and `<sch:assert>` are very similar to each other. The contents of a `<sch:report>` element will be output when the specified test succeeds, whereas the contents of a `<sch:assert>` element are output when its test fails. The examples given below will clarify these concepts.

After this short summary it is time for some examples that I hope will demonstrate that Schematron is very simple indeed in practice.

Firstly we will investigate the relationships in an XML document representing a family tree. We are always talking in XML about children, descendants, and parents so this example has been deliberately chosen to reflect this terminology. There are some differences, of course. An XML element has only one parent and we can always be sure of that parent's identity. To keep the parallel as clear as possible we will start with just women family members, introducing men later in the chapter. To keep the code to a reasonable size we will just consider a small section of a fictional family tree. Let us imagine that we are talking about ancestors from the very distant past and we are trying to distill their history from sometimes contradictory and faded fragments discovered in an old wine cellar.

According to one of our fragments, the founder of our family was Ann, and she had two daughters, Alice and Claire. These daughters are to be represented as XML elements, and daughters shall be ordered according to age. Although you'd be unlikely to use XML in this form for such a document – it would make more sense to use elements like `<family-member name="Ann" sex="female"/>` – the form used here keeps the code simple. Here is the content of `ann.xml`, which also shows details of her daughter's daughters:

```
<Ann>
  <Alice>
    <Kate/>
    <Julie/>
  </Alice>
  <Claire>
    <Maria/>
  </Claire>
</Ann>
```

The fact that Alice's daughters were called Kate and Julie was found in another document, so we want to validate this fact is consistent in our XML tree – for this we can use `daughters.xml`:

```
<sch:schema xmlns:sch="http://www.ascc.net/xml/schematron">
  <sch:pattern name = "Daughters">
    <sch:rule context="/Ann/Alice">
      <sch:report test="Kate">Kate is Alice's daughter.</sch:report>
      <sch:report test="Julie">Julie is Alice's daughter.</sch:report>
    </sch:rule>
  </sch:pattern>
</sch:schema>
```

The first `<sch:report>` element tests whether there is a path `"/Ann/Alice/Kate"` in the document, displaying its child text if there is, and the second `<sch:report>` tests for the XPath `"/Ann/Alice/Julie"`.

When running this test we would get the following output:

```
Kate is Alice's daughter.
Julie is Alice's daughter.
```

We can demonstrate this at the command prompt using the Saxon utility mentioned earlier and the latest Schematron schema, Skeleton1-5.xsl (http://www.ascc.net/xml/schematron/1.5/).

Firstly we must produce a stylesheet called daughters.xsl from daughters.xml using the following command line entry, where the attribute -o represents output:

saxon -o daughters.xsl daughters.xml skeleton1-5.xsl

Then we use Saxon again to test ann.xml against our newly produced stylesheet, daughters.xsl, to create the stated output:

saxon ann.xml daughters.xsl

This is illustrated in the following screenshot:

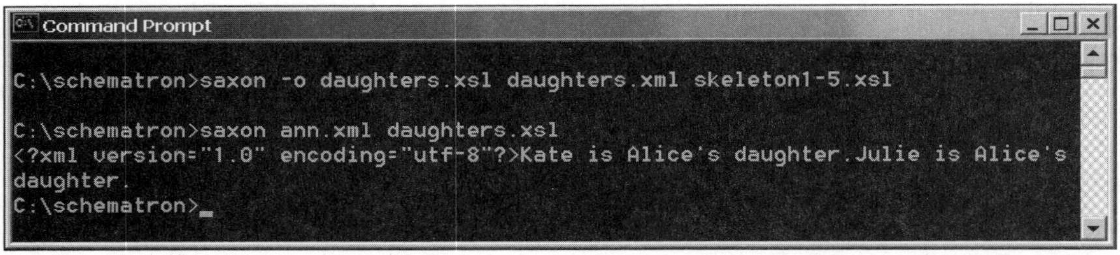

The test has evidently succeeded, so we can move on. Now let's suppose that we have found a report elsewhere suggesting that both Alice and Kate had two daughters. We can use both <sch:assert> and <sch:report> to validate this fact, illustrating the way these Schematron elements differ. This is the schema, in file grandchildren.xml:

```
<sch:schema xmlns:sch="http://www.ascc.net/xml/schematron">
  <sch:pattern name = "Ann grandchildren count">
    <sch:rule context="/Ann/*">
      <sch:report test="count(*)=2">A child with 2 daughters</sch:report>
      <sch:assert test="count(*)=2">A child with more or less than 2
                daughters</sch:assert>
    </sch:rule>
  </sch:pattern>
</sch:schema>
```

The output will confirm that there is a child who has two daughters but also that there is another one who does not. Schematron also offers the possibility to print the name of elements that satisfy a particular test condition, using the <sch:name> element, so we could know which daughter had two children and which did not. We will discuss this further later.

If you consider both these short schemas given above you can see that, while the first test could be specified equally as easily in other validation languages such as DTDs, the second would require expert knowledge of these other validation languages and could not even be specified with a DTD at all. Schematron makes this sort of validation very natural and simple.

The following sample has been chosen as it would really stretch other languages but is not much harder than the one we've already seen in Schematron. If we want to confirm that the older child, Alice, had more daughters than the younger one, Claire, we can use the following (count.xml):

```
<sch:schema xmlns:sch="http://www.ascc.net/xml/schematron">
  <sch:pattern name = "Child count comparison">
    <sch:rule context="/Ann/*[1]">
      <sch:report test="count(*) &gt; count(parent::*/*[2])">Test
                  succeeded.</sch:report>
    </sch:rule>
  </sch:pattern>
</sch:schema>
```

We will now consider another fragment of our family tree, starting with Kate, this time including the year every girl was born as attributes. The listing for kate.xml is:

```
<Kate born="1601">
  <Maria born="1623">
    <Susan born="1642"/>
  </Maria>
  <Jane born="1627"/>
  <Julie born="1627"/>
</Kate>
```

We know that a mother must always be older than her children, so we will now perform a test using agecheck.xml to make sure we have not made a typing error when creating the document:

```
<sch:schema xmlns:sch="http://www.ascc.net/xml/schematron">
  <sch:pattern name = "Age check">
    <sch:rule context="*">
      <sch:assert test="@born &gt; parent::*/@born">A daughter is older
                  than mother!!!</sch:assert>
    </sch:rule>
  </sch:pattern>
</sch:schema>
```

After running this test, Schematron will announce that there is one daughter older than her mother. But we know that isn't true, so we need to look at the source document to find out what's going on. You can see that all the ages are correct. If we encounter a problem like this it's a common mistake to think that our Schematron implementation is broken, but that is not always the case. Let's think again about how the schema works. Kate is the root element, so she has no mother in this document, and therefore there is no born attribute for elements on the parent axis and the assertion fails. But as this was the only case reported, we can be sure the rest are valid.

Schematron and Data Mining

So now we have used Schematron as a validating language we will move on to see how it can be used for data mining as well. The following schema (`several.xml`) prints out the names of all women who had several children:

```
<sch:schema xmlns:sch="http://www.ascc.net/xml/schematron">
  <sch:pattern name = "Print women with several children">
    <sch:rule context="*">
      <sch:report test="count(*)>1">
        <sch:name/>
      </sch:report>
    </sch:rule>
  </sch:pattern>
</sch:schema>
```

In this example we have used another Schematron element, `<sch:name>`, to report the name of the element satisfying the current test. Schematron correctly reports that there is only one mother with several children, Kate.

We can even use Schematron for a preliminary screening of data before time-consuming final tests are applied. Say, for example, we want to investigate if there are any twins amongst our ancestors. We know the year of birth and twins will obviously have been born in the same year. There could of course be some cases when one child is born in January and the second one in December, but these cases will be rare, and preliminary Schematron screening will highlight any likely candidates for further investigation. The listing for our schema (`twins.xml`) is:

```
<sch:schema xmlns:sch="http://www.ascc.net/xml/schematron">
  <sch:pattern name = "Twins">
    <sch:rule context="*">
      <sch:report test="@born = preceding-sibling::*/@born"><sch:name/> may
                 have had a twin</sch:report>
    </sch:rule>
  </sch:pattern>
</sch:schema>
```

Schematron reports "Julie may have had a twin" and we may now go back to the source document, find the element for Julie and the name of the possible twin (or triplet, etc.). Then we can further investigate the documents to confirm our hypothesis.

Schematron and Associations

Thanks to the use of XPath, Schematron is very strong when some form of association between elements is to be tested. We are now going to introduce men into our family and perform some typical tests. In the first case we shall have both men and women in the same document:

```
<family>
  <women>
    <Ann>
      <Alice>
```

```
          <Kate/>
          <Julie/>
        </Alice>
        <Claire>
          <Maria/>
        </Claire>
      </Ann>
    </women>
    <men>
      <Charles wife="Ann"/>
      <Tom wife="Alice"/>
      <John wife="Claire"/>
    </men>
  </family>
```

We would like to find out which women are married. The following schema prints out the names of married women. In this schema we are using slightly more advanced features of XPath and so a short explanation is needed before proceeding.

The context is selected with the expression "*[ancestor::women]". This expression uses another important feature of XPath: the possibility of testing the properties of individual nodes along the path. In this case, we want all elements with an ancestor element of <women>.

The attribute test of <sch:report> uses an important XPath function, name(), not to be confused with the Schematron <sch:name> element used previously. This function prints out the name of the element in the context in which the function is being used.

```
<sch:schema xmlns:sch="http://www.ascc.net/xml/schematron">
  <sch:pattern name = "Married women">
    <sch:rule context="*[ancestor::women]">
      <sch:report test="/family/men/*/@wife = name()"><sch:name/> is
                married.</sch:report>
    </sch:rule>
  </sch:pattern>
</sch:schema>
```

The report generated by Schematron will be:

```
Ann is married.
Alice is married.
Claire is married.
```

and so the test has been performed successfully.

Schematron even allows us to keep men and women in separate documents. We will use our first example as the source of women relatives:

```
<Ann>
  <Alice>
    <Kate/>
    <Julie/>
  </Alice>
```

```
      <Claire>
        <Maria/>
      </Claire>
    </Ann>
```

and the men will be found in a separate document, men.xml:

```
<men>
  <Charles wife="Ann"/>
  <Tom wife="Alice"/>
  <John wife="Claire"/>
</men>
```

As we have already discussed, most Schematron implementations are built on top of an XSLT engine. XSLT enhances XPath with several functions, among them the document() function. With its help a second external XML document can be used as the source to which an XPath expression is applied. We need a slight change to the previous schema to make use of this new arrangement:

```
<sch:schema xmlns:sch="http://www.ascc.net/xml/schematron">
    <sch:pattern name = "Married women">
      <sch:rule context="*">
        <sch:report test="document("men.xml")/men/*/@wife =
                    name()"><sch:name/> is married.</sch:report>
      </sch:rule>
    </sch:pattern>
</sch:schema>
```

and we will get the same output. Just a word of warning: the document() function is not part of the XPath standard so not all Schematron implementations are required to recognize it. But as it brings about many new possibilities, it is appropriate to mention it in this overview.

Schematron and Topic Maps

Because of its versatility, Schematron can be usefully applied to many different areas and topic maps are no exception. In the last example we shall demonstrate how to validate references in a short topic map document. As you saw in Chapter 7, topic map syntax is rather verbose and so we will use only a very short fragment of our family tree in topic map syntax:

```
<Alice>
  <Kate/>
  <Julie/>
</Alice>
```

This fragment can be rewritten according to XTM grammar as:

```
<topicMap xmlns:xlink="http://www.w3.org/1999/xlink">

  <topic id="alice-1">
    <baseName>
      <baseNameString>Alice</baseNameString>
```

```
      </baseName>
    </topic>

    <topic id="kate-1">
      <baseName>
        <baseNameString>Kate</baseNameString>
      </baseName>
    </topic>

    <topic id="julie-1">
      <baseName>
        <baseNameString>Julie</baseNameString>
      </baseName>
    </topic>

    <association>
      <member>
        <roleSpec><topicRef xlink:href="http://family.org/mother"/></roleSpec>
        <topicRef xlink:href="#alice-1"/>
      </member>
      <member>
        <roleSpec><topicRef
                  xlink:href="http://family.org/daughter"/></roleSpec>
        <topicRef xlink:href="#kate-1"/>
      </member>
    </association>

    <association>
      <member>
        <roleSpec><topicRef xlink:href="http://family.org/mother"/></roleSpec>
        <topicRef xlink:href="#alice-1"/>
      </member>
      <member>
        <roleSpec><topicRef
                  xlink:href="http://family.org/daughter"/></roleSpec>
        <topicRef xlink:href="#julie-1"/>
      </member>
    </association>

</topicMap>
```

The following schema will test whether there is a link to a non-existent topic inside the document. It uses some XPath string functions, as the internal links start with the fragment identifier "#" that we must filter out:

```
<sch:schema xmlns:sch="http://www.ascc.net/xml/schematron"
xmlns:xlink="http://www.w3.org/1999/xlink">
  <sch:pattern name = "Topic links">
    <sch:rule context="@xlink:href[starts-with(.,"#")]">
      <sch:assert test="/topicMap/topic/@id = substring(.,2)">Referred
                  topic does not exist.</sch:assert>
    </sch:rule>
  </sch:pattern>
</sch:schema>
```

Summary

This chapter has presented a brief overview of the sorts of features offered by Schematron. We have not discussed some of the more advanced features that further increase the power of Schematron, like the use of keys, ways of making your schemas more modular, or the use of phases, which enable us to use the same stylesheet in different phases of the work flow to validate different pieces of data.

Interested readers will find up to date information at the homepage of Schematron, at http://www.ascc.net/xml/resource/schematron/schematron.html. You will also find several related materials at the Zvon site (http://www.zvon.org) including Schematron and XPath tutorials, interactive code labs, and references.

So we have touched on a few areas where Schematron excels but I hope that you will be able to use Schematron in the course of your everyday work, as it can solve many problems not easily addressed by other approaches. Schematron can be used almost like a hammer to nail just about anything in good and hard, but a more judicious user will combine it with power of DTDs, XSD Schemas, and further languages to achieve the required results.

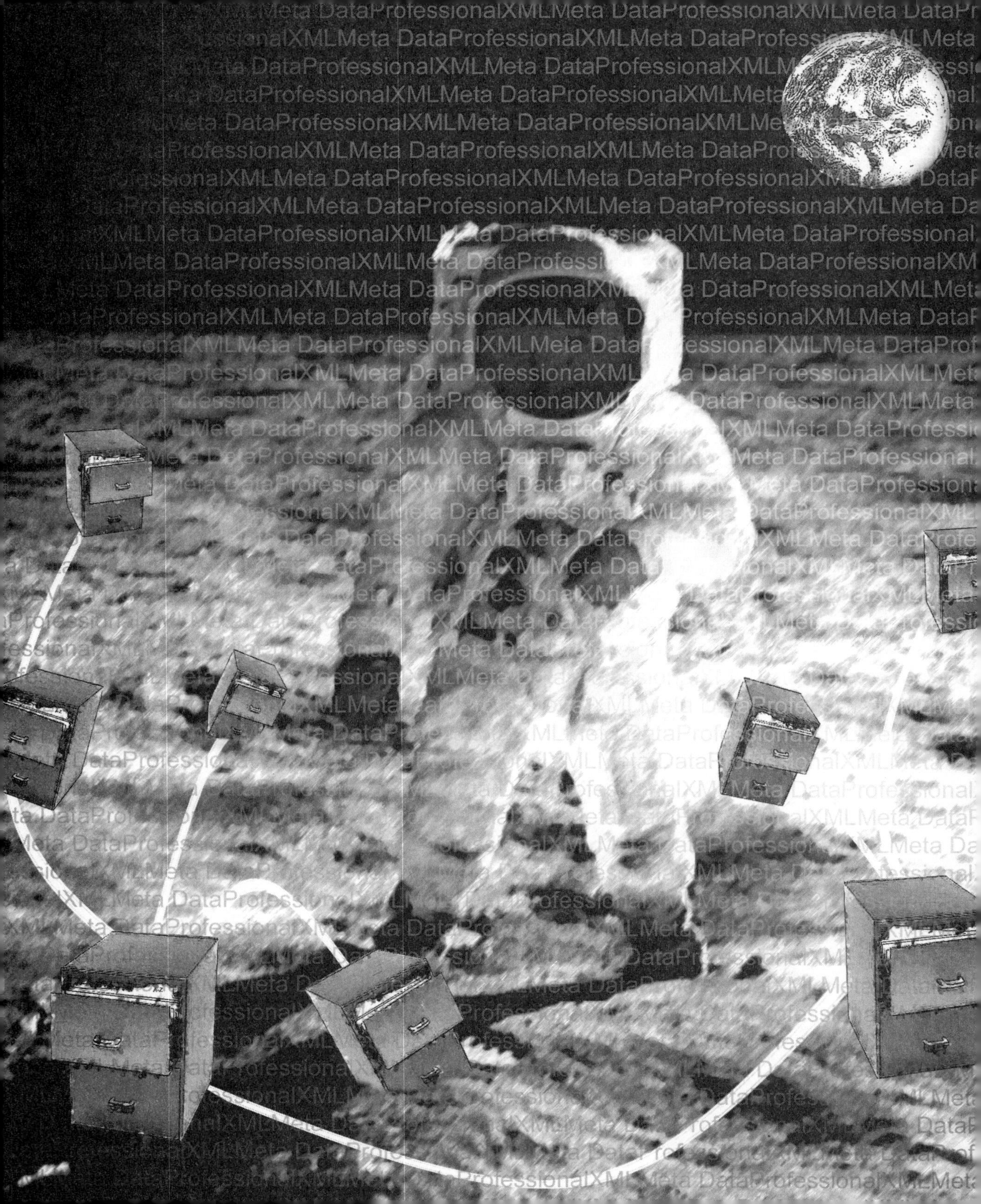
Meta DataProfessionalXML

14

Process Descriptions

So far in this book the uses of meta data we have considered have mainly been related to data or document storage/retrieval, but in the real world we also want to represent and exchange process information. In this chapter we will discuss the use of XML for applications involving **discrete processes**; that is, processes described as individually distinct sequences of events. Examples of such processes include production scheduling, process planning, workflow, business process re-engineering, simulation, process realization, process modeling, and project management.

*We do not address **process characterization**, which we define as the representation of a process independent of any specific application. For example, we are not concerned with representing a process's dynamic or kinematic properties, such as numerical models capturing limits on a process's performance. Since process characterizations employ methods (for example, differential equations) that are quite different from the techniques used to describe sequences of discrete events, a discussion on representing process characterizations in XML would require its own chapter (if not its own book).*

We'll start the chapter by considering what process meta data is and how it can be used, before looking at an example of how to design an XML vocabulary for the exchange of process meta data.

This chapter is a contribution of the National Institute of Science and Technology.

What is a Process Description?

Consider that there are two sides to a process:

- ❑ The sequence of *what* will be done.

- ❑ The description or explanation of *how* each "what" is accomplished.

Let's look at a simple example of a process description – a recipe to make chocolate fudge brownies. Recipes are process descriptions, they say what objects or material to use and what operation or activity to apply to these objects at each step, such as *add* or *mix*.

A recipe assumes that the user knows how to execute/perform/do the activity mentioned in the recipe. Such activities might be *add*, *pour in*, *stir*, *fold*, *blend*, etc. *Add*ing and *pour*ing *in* are pretty obvious, *stir*ring is common in many cultures for various kinds of processing. But what about *blend*ing? An inexperienced cook might take this to mean "take the heap of stuff you have arrived at so far in your brownie making, place it in a blender, and go!" Perhaps the term *blend* isn't quite as universally known as *stir*. And then there is *fold*! What on earth does that mean? "Folding-a-piece-of-paper" knowledge doesn't make sense in the context of mushy brownie dough.

The problem with recognizing what the activity *fold*ing means is pertinent because computer systems are as yet unable to generally and competently determine metaphorical equivalences, in processes or elsewhere. *Fold*ing would become a kind of *stir*ring were it possible for the computer (or the inexperienced cook) to be able to recognize metaphorical equivalences in processes.

Components of Process Descriptions

Process descriptions include information about some or all of the following:

- ❑ Objects and materials that are to receive processing.

- ❑ Activity or action names ("add", "pour", "stir").

- ❑ Sequence indication.

- ❑ Time indication, of the types: Start time, End time, and Duration.

- ❑ Rate ("stir quickly", "12000 bits per second", "3000 revolutions per minute").

- ❑ Conditional execution ("start p29 if p12 has completed successfully").

Although the syntax of these various representations may be different, they each specify common concepts such as the objects and materials to be used in processing, relationships between objects and activities, and the sequence or order of processing. These are indications of *who* (receives the processing), *what* (the name or nature of the processing to be done), and *when* (the duration of the processing).

What is Process Data?

Many applications use process descriptions. The problem is that these applications work with process descriptions in their own internal representations. Therefore communication between them, a growing need for industry, is nearly impossible without some kind of translator. Since an environment with n applications needing to exchange data potentially requires n* (n-1) translators, we clearly need some sort of exchange standard for process data in order to avoid having to implement a point-to-point translator for every pair of applications.

XML is a natural syntax choice for the exchange of process data; XML defines a well-tested and extensible standard syntax for representing structured data, it is text-based and non-proprietary, and processing software for XML is widely available. However, any useful XML formulation of process information should be based upon well-defined semantics. One such definition, which we will use in this chapter as a source of semantics for process representation, is the **Process Specification Language (PSL)**. When we discuss how to use XML to represent process data later on in this chapter, PSL semantics will influence our guidelines, although (to keep matters simple) we won't attempt to formally derive our XML vocabulary from PSL.

The PSL project (http://www.nist.gov/psl) began as a collaborative effort led by the **National Institute of Standards and Technology (NIST),** a US government agency working with industry to develop and apply technology, measurements, and standards. The project's goal is to create a standard language for process specification, in order to integrate multiple process-related applications throughout their life cycle. PSL has recently been proposed as an international standard (ISO 18629).

Although we choose PSL to guide our foray into the XML representation of process descriptions, PSL is not the only source of process semantics. Two other possible sources for semantics are the Unified Modeling Language (UML) and the Workflow Management Coalition's Workflow Reference Model. We briefly discuss these later in the section *"Alternative Process Representation Approaches"* near the end of this chapter.

About PSL

Most computer-interpretable languages are rigorous when it comes to specifying their syntax but fuzzy when it comes to semantics. Language specifications often describe syntax unambiguously using grammar rules, but state the meaning of the terms in the syntax using ambiguous prose. Unlike most languages, PSL has formally defined semantics. However, PSL doesn't specify a single syntax. Rather, PSL allows for the possibility of multiple syntaxes, with the choice of syntax depending on factors such as the nature of the process being described and the data source and destination.

Key to PSL is the formal definitions (the *ontology*) that underlie the language. Because of these explicit and unambiguous definitions, information exchange can be achieved without relying on hidden assumptions or subjective mappings. PSL semantics are represented using **Knowledge Interchange Format (KIF)**. Briefly stated, KIF (http://logic.stanford.edu/kif) is a formal language developed for the exchange of knowledge among disparate computer programs. KIF is a declarative language, it can express arbitrary logical assertions and rules, and it allows for the representation of knowledge about knowledge (meta knowledge). Thus KIF provides the level of rigor necessary to unambiguously define concepts, a necessary characteristic to exchange process information using the PSL ontology.

The primary components of PSL are KIF expressions constituting the PSL ontology for processes. We can include as many terms as we like in our ontology, but they can only be shared if we agree on their definitions. It is the definitions that are being shared, not simply the terms. For example, consider the KIF term (between a b c). This term tell us that one thing is "between" two other things, whatever *that* means. To make the term meaningful, we need to supplement it with definitions, such as the following:

```
(defrelation between (?p ?q ?r) :=
    (and (before ?p ?q) (before ?q ?r)))
```

This KIF definition says that if you have three things: ?p, ?q, and ?r, and that ?p is before ?q and ?q is before ?r, then ?q is between ?p and ?r. The definition adds some semantics to "between". Of course, it does not specify any semantics for "before". The meaning of "before" could be specified in other definitions, or, as is the case with PSL, "before" might be part of our **primitive lexicon**. The primitive lexicon consists of those terms for which we do not give definitions; rather, we specify **axioms** that constrain the interpretation of the terms. An example of an axiom constraining the interpretation of "before" is the statement that the "before" relation is irreflexive (in other words, nothing can be before itself). This axiom is formally specified in KIF as follows:

```
(forall (?p)
        (not (before ?p ?p)))
```

The PSL ontology (available on-line at http://www.nist.gov/psl/psl-ontology) consists of primitive terms, definitions, and axioms for the concepts of PSL. However, this is not simply an amorphous set of sentences. The figure below gives an overview of the semantic architecture of the PSL ontology. There are three major components:

- ❑ **PSL Core** – the most basic elements of the PSL ontology.
- ❑ **Core theories** – very widely applicable extensions to PSL Core.
- ❑ **Extensions** – Definitions capturing the semantics of process terminology for different applications.

The PSL ontology is organized modularly in order to facilitate the addition of new extensions as future industrial requirements for PSL emerge. PSL's modularity also makes it possible for applications to support a subset of extensions responding to a particular class of process specifications, without having to support the entire PSL ontology. The PSL semantic architecture is represented in the following diagram:

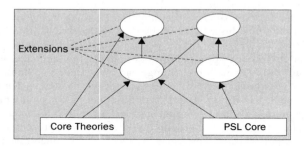

PSL Core specifies the concepts in the PSL ontology corresponding to fundamental intuitions about activities. The extensions are organized by logical dependencies – one extension depends on another if the definitions of any terms in the first extension require terms defined in the second extension. PSL Core is therefore intended as the basis for defining terms of the extensions in the PSL ontology. PSL extensions often define new terms by specifying constraints on core terms.

Supplementing PSL Core is a set of core theories (also known as the "outer core"). This special set of extensions provides building blocks common to a wide variety of applications of PSL. Some of these extensions introduce new primitive concepts, because the concepts introduced in PSL Core are not sufficient for defining the terms introduced in the extension. Therefore, new primitive concepts are introduced within the extensions to ensure that all other terms within the extension can be completely defined.

As we mentioned earlier, PSL does not mandate a single syntax for exchanging process descriptions. However, the PSL project proposes to standardize an XML framework for the exchange of process specifications. The framework has not yet been developed, but one idea suggested is to determine an appropriate XML vocabulary for an application based on meta data associated with the application describing the kinds of processes supported. The approach we take in the remaining sections of this chapter is less ambitious, but probably a good first step toward understanding how one might describe processes using XML. Rather than try to create a custom-built XML exchange syntax, we instead develop an (admittedly limited) XML vocabulary that captures some of the more fundamental concepts from the PSL ontology.

Basic Characteristics of Process Data

To guide our design of an XML vocabulary for process data, we'll begin by enumerating some key concepts defined in PSL core. These are:

- **Activity** – A class or type of action. For example, painting a house is an activity. It is the class of actions in which houses are being painted.

- **Activity occurrence** – An event or action that takes place at a specific place and time, in other words an instance or occurrence of an activity. For example, painting John's house in Baltimore, Maryland at 2 PM on May 25, 2001 is an occurrence of the "paint house" activity.

- **Time point** – An instant separating two states, for example the point at which the first coat of paint is dry but before the second coat has been started.

- **Object** – Anything that is not a time point or an activity, for example John's house.

Some other ideas, introduced in some of the more fundamental PSL extensions, are:

- **Ordering** – Activities occur in ordered sequences delimited by time points.

- **Parallelism** – Activities can occur at the same time.

- **Decomposition** – Activities can contain sub-activities. Occurrences of such activities contain sub-occurrences.

- **Objects versus resources** – A resource is an object being used by an activity. For instance, a paintbrush could be a resource of the "paint house" activity.

These are just some of the most basic PSL ontological concepts. There are many others including resource contention, states and conditions, complex ordering relationships, and many more.

An area not included in the PSL ontology, but nevertheless necessary for representing processes, is **object structure**. Since process specifications need to be able to describe an activity's resources, or at least refer to object descriptions specified elsewhere, PSL simply assumes that objects are described using methods outside of PSL's scope. In the guidelines for XML representation of processes discussed in the next section, we suggest using RDF to describe objects.

XML Representation of Process Data

Now that we have extracted some process representation concepts from the PSL ontology, the next step is to come up with a set of guidelines for describing processes in XML. The business case for doing this is compelling. Vendors of mainstream software applications such as Internet browsers, database environments, and business productivity tools are either already supporting or intend to support XML in their products. Mapping PSL instances to XML will enable process specifications to be interpreted by these generic applications, lowering the barriers to data sharing.

What XML Can and Cannot Do

An XML markup scheme for process data should take advantage of what XML does best, while minimizing the impact of where XML falls short. XML's "tag-centric" syntax makes it a natural fit for representing ordered sequences and hierarchies. Thus it is well suited for ordering time points and occurrences of activities. It is also good at representing sub-activities and sub-occurrences. Another capability of XML, useful for process representation, is XML's modularity. For example, using XML namespaces we can embed an arbitrary object description into a process specification and leave it up to a software tool, separate from the process specification interpreter, to parse the object description. We can also employ namespaces to modularize our process markup language itself (perhaps mirroring PSL's modularization).

Although XML has many advantages for representing processes, it has a major disadvantage. While XML excels as a serialization syntax for exchanging data structures between applications, XML is not very good at expressing the kinds of complex constraints needed for process descriptions. For example, it might be difficult for an XML schema for a process description language to enforce scheduling constraints involving shared resources. Such constraints could be more easily expressed in a rich language for knowledge representation such as KIF.

Because XML is deficient when it comes to representing complex constraints on populations of data elements, its process representation capabilities are limited. However, this does not mean that we cannot use XML to exchange process descriptions. Rather, it means that we probably would not want to exchange all of a process description's underlying ontology in XML, and we cannot count on an XML language to enforce all constraints on process data. It also means that XML would be a poor authoring environment for all but the most simple process descriptions.

Guidelines for Representing Process Data in XML

To maximize XML's strengths while minimizing its weaknesses, use the following guidelines for representing process descriptions in XML. These guidelines are not exhaustive or even optimal for the subset of process descriptions they cover; however, they may prove useful if you are new at developing XML process description vocabularies.

Use RDF to Represent a Process's Resources

RDF is probably the best choice for representing the objects used in a process. RDF can be embedded into process descriptions as needed, and RDF Schema is useful for specifying object structure, classes and instances, and inheritance relationships. An alternative to using RDF would be to write an XML "mini-language" to describe your objects, but it might be hard to develop a single mini-language that would satisfy all possibilities for objects in a process description.

As a matter of fact, RDF/RDF Schema could be used to represent not just the objects, but also the entire process description. However, these guidelines choose to limit the use of RDF to representing objects used in a process, mainly in order to make the XML syntax more human-readable.

Represent Time Points as Sequences of Elements

Represent time points as sequentially ordered groups of elements, with each time point element having a unique identifier. If the XML application uses a DTD or schema, the unique identifier should be represented using an ID attribute so that references to the time point can be made using IDREF, or alternatively using a URI reference. Each time point element may optionally contain character data (intended for human consumption, not machine processing) documenting the meaning of the time point.

If we were to use these sample markup declarations:

```
<!ELEMENT   timepoints    (timepoint+)                                    >
<!ELEMENT   timepoint     (#PCDATA)                                       >
<!ATTLIST   timepoint
            id            ID                                 #REQUIRED >
```

An example of time point data might be:

```
<timepoints>
    <timepoint id="t1">start</timepoint>
    <timepoint id="t2">end</timepoint>
</timepoints>
```

Incidentally, we use DTD syntax in this chapter rather than XML Schema syntax because DTD syntax is less verbose and is adequate enough for our examples. XML Schema syntax may be a better choice for real world applications. See the section *"Choosing an XML Schema Language"* for further discussion of this issue.

Create Hierarchies for Activities

For each activity, specify a unique identifier (with an ID attribute if using a DTD) and an activity name. If the activity contains sub-activities, specify these within a container element. If the activity has no sub-activities, specify the resources used with references to the appropriate class defined in the RDF Schema.

So our sample markup declarations might look like this:

```
<!ELEMENT   activity      (name, (activity+ | resource*))             >
<!ATTLIST   activity
            id            ID                                 #REQUIRED >
<!ELEMENT   name          (#PCDATA)                                    >
<!ELEMENT   resource      EMPTY                                        >
<!ATTLIST   resource
            rdf:resource
                          CDATA                              #REQUIRED >
```

Consider the activity of preparing a meal of leftovers. We represent this activity as having two sub-activities: reheating the leftover food and reading a newspaper (while waiting for the food to be ready). Let us further suppose that reheating requires two resources (an oven and a frozen meal), and that reading the newspaper requires a newspaper as a resource. Data representing this activity might appear as follows. The values of the `rdf:resource` attributes assume that `Oven`, `FrozenMeal`, and `Newspaper` are defined as classes in an RDF schema, the RDF schema and the activity data are in a file whose relative URI is `leftovers.rdf`, and that the entire process description is enclosed in a wrapper element as follows:

```
<processdesc xmlns:rdf="http://www.w3.org/1999/02/22-rdf-syntax-ns#">

   ...

</processdesc>
```

Here is XML markup for the "prepare leftovers" activity:

```
<activity id="a4">
   <name>prepare leftovers</name>
   <activity id="a5">
      <name>reheat food</name>
      <resource rdf:resource="leftovers.rdf#Oven"/>
      <resource rdf:resource="leftovers.rdf#FrozenMeal"/>
   </activity>
   <activity id="a6">
      <name>read newspaper</name>
      <resource rdf:resource="leftovers.rdf#Newspaper"/>
   </activity>
</activity>
```

Create Hierarchies for Occurrences, and Allow for Parallelism

Specify occurrences of activities in sequential order with sub-activities enclosed inside parent activities. Each activity occurrence should have a beginning and ending time point unless they can be inferred from a parent activity occurrence. If the activity occurrence cannot be decomposed into sub-activities, it should contain a list of any RDF-defined resource instances it uses. References to time points and activities should refer to their respective unique identifiers (and should be of type `IDREF` if using a DTD).

A `<fork>` element, whose content is one or more activity occurrences, can represent activities taking place in parallel that start and end at the same time.

The markup declarations for this example could be:

```
<!ELEMENT    occurrence    ((occurrence | fork)+ | resource*)        >
<!ATTLIST    occurrence
             activity       IDREF                        #REQUIRED
             begin          IDREF                        #IMPLIED
             end            IDREF                        #IMPLIED   >
<!ELEMENT    fork          (occurrence+)                             >
<!ATTLIST    fork
             begin          IDREF                        #IMPLIED
             end            IDREF                        #IMPLIED   >
```

An occurrence of the activity "prepare leftovers", with reheating and reading taking place in parallel, might appear as follows. We assume that myMicrowave is an instance of Oven, tunaCasserole is an instance of FrozenMeal, and that 2001May29WashingtonPost is an instance of Newspaper.

```
<occurrence activity="a4" begin="t1" end="t2">
   <fork>
      <occurrence activity="a5">
         <resource rdf:resource="leftovers.rdf#myMicrowave"/>
         <resource rdf:resource="leftovers.rdf#tunaCasserole"/>
      </occurrence>
      <occurrence activity="a6">
         <resource rdf:resource="leftovers.rdf#2001May29WashingtonPost"/>
      </occurrence>
   </fork>
</occurrence>
```

Omit Underlying Ontologies and Foundational Theories

As we discussed earlier in the section *"What XML Can and Cannot Do"*, XML is not designed to be a general-purpose knowledge representation language. An XML representation of a process description should not attempt to encode the entire PSL ontology. For example, the axiom that "before" is irreflexive probably does not need to be part of an XML vocabulary for processes. Such axioms and other underlying definitions and assumptions should probably be omitted from the XML representation, unless they describe "containing" or "ordering" relationships that can be easily represented by XML markup.

Extended Example: a Finishing Process

To illustrate the use of these guidelines in a single complete process description, consider a simple manufacturing scenario consisting of an activity "Finish product". "Finish product" involves a "Paint" activity, followed by "Clean brush" and "Sand" activities, followed by another "Paint" activity, and concluding with final "Clean brush" and "Sand" activities. "Paint" has two sub-activities: "Mix paint" and "Apply paint". "Clean brush" can be done while waiting for the paint to dry. The first coat of paint is a primer coat, and the second coat uses the color blue. Sanding is performed the first time using 100 grit sand paper and the second time using 200 grit sand paper. Mixing is done using a paint mixer, and cleaning the brush is done using paint thinner.

This process, when drawn as a UML activity diagram, looks something like this:

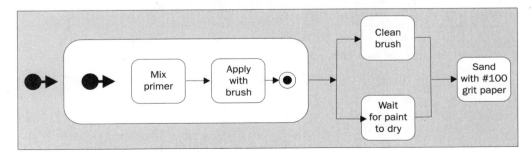

Specifying Objects in RDF

We begin by defining classes for the paint, brush, mixer, thinner, and sand paper objects. We also define classes for paint colors and sandpaper grit numbers. RDF (Resource Description Framework), discussed at length in Chapter 4, is an XML-serializable language for expressing meta data for resources on the Web. The RDF data model is essentially a labeled directed graph, and an arc or node label may either be a URI or a literal. RDF Schema, defined using RDF, is a type system for use in RDF models (see Chapter 5 for a full description). The following diagram shows the RDF graph:

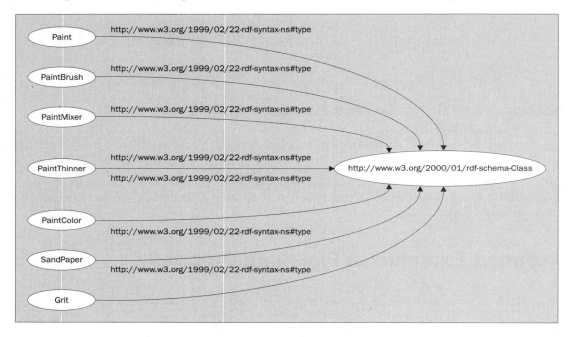

The XML serialization (using the abbreviated syntax) is as follows:

```
<rdfs:Class rdf:ID="Paint" />
<rdfs:Class rdf:ID="PaintBrush" />
<rdfs:Class rdf:ID="PaintMixer" />
<rdfs:Class rdf:ID="PaintThinner" />
<rdfs:Class rdf:ID="PaintColor" />
<rdfs:Class rdf:ID="SandPaper" />
<rdfs:Class rdf:ID="Grit" />
```

Next we specify instances of the brush, mixer, and thinner. The RDF graph appears as follows:

The XML serialization for these instances is:

```
<PaintBrush rdf:ID="brush"/>
<PaintMixer rdf:ID="mixer"/>
<PaintThinner rdf:ID="thinner"/>
```

In order to specify instances of the paint and sand paper, we need to define some properties. We define a property `paintColor` whose domain is the `Paint` class and whose range is the `PaintColor` class. We use the convention of beginning class names with an upper case letter and beginning other names with a lower case letter. The RDF graph is:

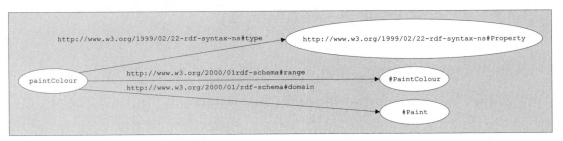

The XML serialization for this property is:

```
<rdf:Property ID="paintColor">
    <rdfs:range rdf:resource="#PaintColor"/>
    <rdfs:domain rdf:resource="#Paint"/>
</rdf:Property>
```

Similarly, we define a `grit` property with a domain of `SandPaper` and a range of `Grit`. The RDF graph is:

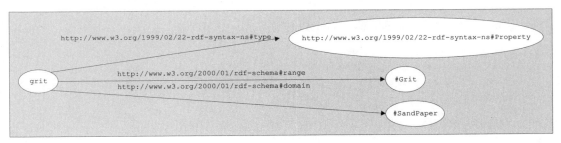

The XML serialization is:

```
<rdf:Property ID="grit">
    <rdfs:range rdf:resource="#Grit"/>
    <rdfs:domain rdf:resource="#SandPaper"/>
</rdf:Property>
```

Now let us specify an instance for the primer coat of paint using the `paintColor` property we defined. The RDF graph is as follows:

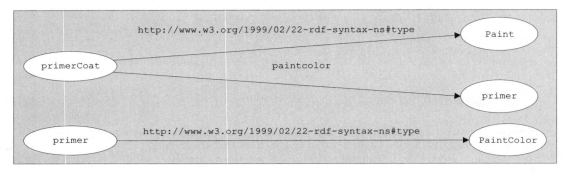

The XML serialization for the instance of the `PaintColor` property is:

```
<PaintColor rdf:ID="primer"/>
<Paint rdf:ID="primerCoat">
    <paintColor rdf:resource="#primer"/>
</Paint>
```

The RDF graph specifying the second coat of (blue) paint looks like:

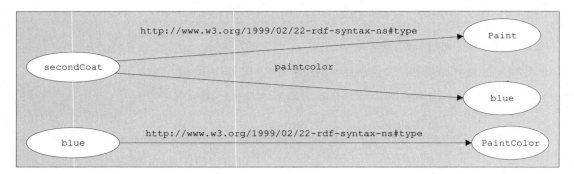

The corresponding XML serialization would be:

```
<PaintColor rdf:ID="blue"/>
<Paint rdf:ID="secondCoat">
    <paintColor rdf:resource="#blue"/>
</Paint>
```

The RDF graph for the 100 grit sandpaper instance is:

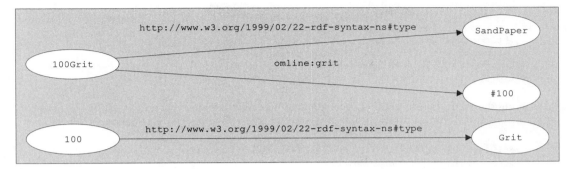

and the XML serialization would look like:

```
<Grit rdf:ID="100"/>
<SandPaper rdf:ID="100Grit">
  <grit rdf:resource="#100"/>
</SandPaper>
```

Finally, the RDF graph for the 200 grit sandpaper instance is:

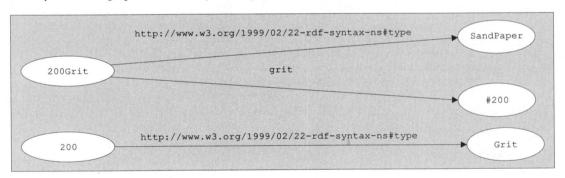

The XML serialization would be:

```
<Grit rdf:ID="200"/>
<SandPaper rdf:ID="200Grit">
   <grit rdf:resource="#200"/>
</SandPaper>
```

The Process Description

We can now specify the process's time points, activities and activity occurrences.

Here is what the time points for our scenario might look like:

```
<timepoints>
   <timepoint id="t1">start</timepoint>
   <timepoint id="t2">done mixing paint</timepoint>
```

```
    <timepoint id="t3">done applying paint</timepoint>
    <timepoint id="t4">done cleaning brush and drying</timepoint>
    <timepoint id="t5">done sanding</timepoint>
    <timepoint id="t6">done mixing paint</timepoint>
    <timepoint id="t7">done applying paint</timepoint>
    <timepoint id="t8">done cleaning brush and drying</timepoint>
    <timepoint id="t9">done sanding</timepoint>
</timepoints>
```

Assuming the RDF representation of the resource objects is contained in a file with the relative URI `finish.rdf`, the "Finish product" activity from our scenario could be represented as follows:

```
<activity id="a1">
    <name>Finish product</name>
    <activity id="a2">
        <name>Paint</name>
        <activity id="a3">
            <name>Mix paint</name>
            <resource rdf:resource="finish.rdf#Paint" />
            <resource rdf:resource="finish.rdf#PaintMixer" />
        </activity>
        <activity id="a4">
            <name>Apply paint</name>
            <resource rdf:resource="finish.rdf#Paint" />
            <resource rdf:resource="finish.rdf#PaintBrush" />
        </activity>
    </activity>
    <activity id="a5">
        <name>Clean brush</name>
        <resource rdf:resource="finish.rdf#PaintBrush" />
        <resource rdf:resource="finish.rdf#PaintThinner" />
    </activity>
    <activity id="a6">
        <name>Dry</name>
    </activity>
    <activity id="a7">
        <name>Sand</name>
        <resource rdf:resource="finish.rdf#SandPaper" />
    </activity>
</activity>
```

The XML representing the first occurrence of the "Paint" activity from our scenario might look like this:

```
<occurrence activity="a2" begin="t1" end="t3">
    <occurrence activity="a3" begin="t1" end="t2">
        <resource rdf:resource="finish.rdf#primerCoat"/>
        <resource rdf:resource="finish.rdf#mixer"/>
    </occurrence>
    <occurrence activity="a4" begin="t2" end="t3">
        <resource rdf:resource="finish.rdf#primerCoat"/>
        <resource rdf:resource="finish.rdf#brush"/>
    </occurrence>
</occurrence>
```

Next we have the first occurrences of the concurrent "Clean brush" and "Dry" activities:

```
<fork begin="t3" end="t4">
   <occurrence activity="a5">
       <resource rdf:resource="finish.rdf#brush"/>
       <resource rdf:resource="finish.rdf#thinner"/>
   </occurrence>
   <occurrence activity="a6"/>
</fork>
```

The next activity occurrence is the sanding of the primer coat with 100 grit paper. Then there are second occurrences of the "Paint", "Clean brush", "Dry", and "Sand" activities. Because the XML markup of these activity occurrences looks a lot like that of the activity occurrences already shown, we will not present it in this section. However, it is included in the code listing for this chapter (along with the full process specification DTD).

Representation Issues

In the section *"XML Representation of Process Data"*, we presented process representation guidelines that attempt to maximize XML's strengths while minimizing its weaknesses. However, XML developers should consider the following issues as well. There are no "one-size-fits-all" answers for these issues.

Late Versus Early Binding

In a late binding, the named components of the XML vocabulary do not directly correspond to specific constituents in the process. Instead, they correspond to meta-concepts such as "activity", "time point", etc. The leftovers preparation and finishing process examples from the previous sections are both specified in a late-bound manner.

In an early binding, the named components of the XML vocabulary directly correspond to specific items. For example, an early-bound representation of the leftovers preparation activity occurrence from the *"Guidelines for Representing Process Data in XML"* section might look like this:

```
<prepareLeftovers xmlns:rdf=http://www.w3.org/1999/02/22-rdf-syntax-ns#
                   concurrentSubActivities="true">
   <reheatFood>
       <oven rdf:resource="#myMicrowave"/>
       <frozenMeal rdf:resource="#tunaCasserole"/>
   </reheatFood>
   <readNewspaper>
       <newspaper rdf:resource="#2001May29WashingtonPost"/>
   </readNewspaper>
</prepareLeftovers>
```

Because reheating the food and reading the newspaper can occur in parallel, the content model for <prepareLeftovers> should specify that <reheatFood> and <readNewspaper> can occur in any order.

Early bindings tend to be more succinct and human-readable than late bindings. However, each early binding requires its own DTD or schema. A late binding, on the other hand, allows for a single vocabulary to be used for multiple process descriptions. Thus, late bindings are best suited for applications involving a class of processes while early bindings may be best for situations involving a single process.

Choosing an XML Schema Language

We used DTD syntax in our examples from the *"Guidelines for Representing Process Data in XML"* section. Alternatively, we could have used W3C XML (XSD) Schema definitions, RELAX NG patterns, or some other XML schema language (see Chapter 2 for further information). Although a DTD was adequate for specifying the vocabulary used in our examples, there are times when you need features that DTDs lack. For example, if you want to use multiple namespaces in your document (perhaps to combine your process vocabulary with another vocabulary), you will need a schema language that supports namespaces. You also might need more powerful data typing.

The ability to define context-dependent element types can also be useful. For example, consider the content model for the `<prepareLeftovers>` element in our early binding example specifying that its sub-activities can occur in any order. This could be represented using DTD syntax as:

```
<!ELEMENT prepareLeftovers
        ((reheatFood, readNewspaper) | (readNewspaper, reheatFood))>
```

Although this isn't too bad for only two sub-activities, imagine how clumsy it would be to use DTD syntax to specify that ten sub-activities can occur in any order. Clearly, W3C XML Schema (using `<all>`) or RELAX NG (using `<interleave>`) would be better suited for representing arbitrarily large collections of unordered elements.

XLink Versus ID/IDREF

In our examples, we used attributes of type ID to uniquely identify time points and activities. Activity occurrences used attributes of type IDREF to reference their beginning time point, ending time point, and associated activity. Alternatively, we could have used XLinks for cross-references. XLinks are more powerful than IDREF in that they allow references to things outside the XML document, permit us to associate semantics with links, and support aggregation of links. On the other hand, unlike ID/IDREF, XLink applications don't detect dangling cross-references.

While ID/IDREF may be best for process descriptions contained in a single document, XLink may be best for process descriptions spread across multiple documents, lightweight applications where no DTD or schema is available for the process description, or applications with sophisticated cross referencing requirements.

Hierarchical Versus Flat Descriptions

Although our XML representation guidelines suggest using hierarchies of elements to represent activities and activity occurrences, sometimes this is not practical. For example, if multiple activities share a common sub-activity, a hierarchical representation would require that the same information be repeated multiple times. Also, processes with complex timing relationships between activities (for example, activities that overlap but have different starting and/or ending times) might be difficult to represent in a hierarchical form.

An alternative to using hierarchies is to represent containment relationships using a "relationship" element whose content is one or more cross-references. For example, suppose we wanted to represent our early binding example such that the <reheatFood> and <readNewspaper> elements are not children of <prepareLeftovers>. We could do this using a <subactivities> element to specify the relationship, <reheatFood-ref> to cross-reference <reheatFood>, and <readNewspaper-ref> to cross-reference <readNewspaper>. The result would look like this:

```
<process xmlns:rdf="http://www.w3.org/1999/02/22-rdf-syntax-ns#">
    <prepareLeftovers concurrentSubActivities="true">
        <subactivities>
            <reheatFood-ref ref="rf1"/>
            <readNewspaper-ref ref="rn1"/>
        </subactivities>
    </prepareLeftovers>
    <reheatFood id="rf1">
        <oven rdf:resource="#myMicrowave"/>
        <frozenMeal rdf:resource="#tunaCasserole"/>
    </reheatFood>
    <readNewspaper id="rn1">
        <newspaper rdf:resource="#2001May29WashingtonPost"/>
    </readNewspaper>
</process>
```

Alternative Process Representation Approaches

We have used the concepts defined in PSL as the foundation for our ideas for XML representation of processes. Two other sources of process representation semantics that may be worth considering are the **Unified Modeling Language (UML)** and the **Workflow Management Coalition's (WfMC) Workflow Reference Model**.

UML

UML (http://www.omg.org/technology/uml/index.htm), an **Object Management Group (OMG)** standard, is actually a family of graphically oriented modeling languages intended to be used for software design. Just as XML has become the dominant language for serializing and transporting data, UML has become the dominant modeling language. Unfortunately for process modelers, no single type of UML diagram captures all of the information needed to describe a process. UML activity diagrams (see the figure at the beginning of the section *"Extended Example: A Finishing Proces*s" for an example) do a good job modeling complicated sequences and parallelism. However, activity diagrams are not the best choice for representing the relationships between activities and objects. UML interaction diagrams do a much better job describing how actions and objects collaborate.

The OMG's **XML Meta Data Interchange (XMI)** standard provides a way to represent UML models in XML. Thus it is possible (although probably not easy) to obtain an XML representation of a process by modeling it both as an activity diagram and as an interaction diagram, generating XMI from the two diagrams, and using XSLT to convert the exported XMI into a single XML process description.

The WfMC's Workflow Reference Model

The WfMC (http://www.wfmc.org/) is a consortium of workflow vendors, users, and researchers developing interoperability and connectivity standards for workflow products. The WfMC's Workflow Reference Model is a specification identifying the characteristics, terminology and components of workflow management systems. The Workflow Reference Model provides the context for other WfMC specifications.

One such WfMC specification is the **XML Process Definition Language (XPDL)**, a format for the exchange of workflow process definitions. The XPDL DTD defines an XML syntax for workflow-related concepts such as state transitions, activities, participants, etc. Although XPDL is (at the time of this writing) in "Draft" status, it is further along than PSL in the sense that a specific XML vocabulary has already been specified. For representing process descriptions involving workflow, XPDL may well be worth a look.

Summary

In this chapter we discussed the design of XML vocabularies for describing discrete processes. Taking PSL concepts as a starting point, we established some guidelines and demonstrated their use with examples. We then enumerated some additional design issues and additional sources of process semantics.

For PSL or any other process specification language to achieve widespread success, there needs to be some sort of "killer app". This killer app, if and when it emerges, is certain to use XML for exchanging process descriptions. The application could be a web-based process visualization tool, perhaps employing the W3C's **Scalable Vector Graphics** standard (**SVG** – see http://www.w3.org/Graphics/SVG/Overview.htm8). Or maybe it could be a framework for distributed workflow management that makes workflow tools affordable for the masses. Only time will tell.

Now we've looked at meta data applied to processes, we're going to return to look at processing that can be applied to meta data. We'll be expanding on one of the topics in Chapter 10 and looking in more detail at logical inferencing.

XMLMeta DataProfessionalXMLMeta DataProfessionalXMLMeta DataProfessionalXMLMeta

15

Inferencing Systems

This (short) chapter discusses the concept of inferencing and inferencing systems, which have been mentioned on occasion earlier in the book. Inferencing is all about drawing conclusions from the data or meta data that we do possess in order to derive data or meta data that we do not. This is in fact something that we all do every day in our normal lives. For instance, if I plan to go out I may look out of the window before doing so. If I see that it is getting cloudy I can infer that it might rain. Using this inference I can then make a choice – whether I take an umbrella with me or not. If I do and it rains then I'll be OK. If I don't and it rains then I'll get wet.

Although they are not as good at it as humans, computers programs can do this sort of thing too. This is not to suggest that computers are capable of intelligent thinking, but that they can be programmed to apply rules to facts or data to deduce new facts or data.

By the end of this chapter you will have an understanding of the concept of inferencing and inferencing systems, as well as some of their uses.

Introduction to Inferencing

Logical inferencing can be defined as a formal means or process by which propositions are examined and conclusions using them are reached. Stated another way, somewhat informally, it is a consistent process used to go from the state of knowing some facts to obtaining or deriving the additional state of knowing some follow-on facts, which fall out or are realized as a result of the process being applied.

Inferencing can be illustrated in terms of "*if I know this, this and this, what does this tell me?*" As an example let me say "*If it walks like a duck, quacks like a duck, looks like a duck, then it probably is a duck.*"

In addition to its light-hearted entertainment value, this "duck" expression from common folklore illustrates the public consciousness of the nature of inferencing itself. In the duck expression the "*this*" things that I know are:

- ❑ Walks like a duck.
- ❑ Quacks like a duck.
- ❑ Looks like a duck.

These are our givens, what logicians call the **antecedents** and what a computer program would call **inputs**.

In this duck expression it was said: "If ... it probably is a duck." The version I have heard most often includes the word *probably*, but I have heard some versions of this expression which omit the "probably". If we look at the duck expression *without* the presence of "probably" we can say that our conclusion or inference – "It is a duck" – is either true or false. This means either 100% true or 100% false. This could be expressed in pseudo-code as follows:

```
IF    objectx (walks like a duck)
AND   objectx (quacks like a duck)
AND   objectx (looks like a duck)
THEN  objectx IS ["a duck"]
```

Now if we look at our duck expression *with* the word "probably" included, we can say that the presence of the word is a signal to the inferer that the statement cannot now be 100% true. The word *probably* conveys that the likelihood or tendency for the statement to be "true" is there, and therefore the likelihood of it being "false" is less likely. This would then be expressed as:

```
IF    objectx (walks like a duck)
AND   objectx (quacks like a duck)
AND   objectx (looks like a duck)
THEN  objectx IS PROBABLY ["a duck"]
```

One of the ways we deal with assertions made about the world, like this duck expression, is to include the possibility of error or that of incompleteness, instead of pounding the table with simplistic "*all assertions made are either (100%) true or false.*" In this way we can deal with certainty and uncertainty.

In classical logic, if all of the antecedent conditions are true then we can state that the **consequent** (what we concluded) is also 100% true. This assumes both perfect knowledge and perfect logic. For simple things this can be assumed to be the case and we can construct and use logic in our daily lives that have simple true or false outcomes.

The answer to the earlier question "*What does this tell me?*" is that by knowing those three things about some object I know, or at least recognize, that the object is a duck.

So, what does any of that duck stuff have to do with meta data? Here is the connection, in the form of an XML example:

```xml
<objectx name="unknown">
  <feature appearance="duck appearance"/>
  <feature locomotion="duck walk"/>
  <feature sound="duck quack"/>
</objectx>
```

The name of `objectx` is unknown. Whoever created the data set did not specify the name of the object and put "`unknown`" instead. By using the data contained within the `<feature>` elements, we can use inference to determine that `objectx` is a duck.

If in our normal daily lives we see an object which "walks like a duck, quacks like a duck and looks like a duck", we generally do not need to be explicitly told that it is a duck by, for instance, the object wearing a sign that says "I am a duck", before we are able to recognize it as a duck.

This is in fact what the process of inferencing is all about – how to recognize ducks that aren't wearing signs which explicitly say "I am a duck".

Currently, most computerized systems require that all such "duck" data sets explicitly state somewhere in the data structure "I am a duck". This might be through a value assigned to an "id" field or XML element or attribute.

Just as it is very powerful (although taken for granted) for you to be able to recognize a duck without a sign on it, it is very powerful for a computer to be able to recognize data (or a process on data) without having to have an element in the data structure saying explicitly what it is. Inferencing allows a computer program to recognize things without needing to be told explicitly what it is that's being recognized.

What we see in inference is the ability to detect data which are implicit, by virtue of processing the data or meta data that are explicit. The computer program can then detect tacit information through the process of inferencing.

Inferencing Systems

Reasoning Systems

Early computer-based "reasoning" systems were based upon **simple algebraic condition logic** of the type:

```
If A Then B
```

This could also be described as "A implies B"; by this we mean that if A is true then B is also true. These early systems, often written in languages such as LISP and Prolog, consisted of a series of simple logic "rules" which could be applied.

With **cascaded algebraic conditional logic** the concept of "Else If" is introduced, taking the form:

```
If A Then B
Else If C Then D
Else If …
```

This form of logic can be further implemented in logic programs via a series of switch or case statements:

```
Case of A
  1: B
  2: C
  3: D
  …
```

While it is possible to take this approach in inferencing, it is really only amenable to simple problems. The approach, while compact and fast to execute, is difficult to maintain for real-world sized problems due to the complexity of the branching involved.

Expert Systems

The inferencing statements and mechanisms used by **expert systems** differ from the algebraic conditional logic used in reasoning systems. In the previous algebraic approach, each of the IF statements acted on its own, making its own contribution to the solution. In the case of expert system rules they act as a kind of collective.

Another way in which expert system rules are different from the cascaded algebraic conditionals, is that they are designed to make assertions into a special location in the memory of the expert system program. In the case of an inferencing system simulated by means of cascaded algebraic conditionals, it is the duty of the constructing agent, whether a hand-coding human, or a diagram-driven text substitution system, to be sure that any variable named in the actions of an output must also recur in the conditional A part of at least one downstream or down sequence statement. Why? If a given statement sets variable degrees to a value of 60.2 that information is lost, effectively having been forgotten, if none of the successor statements test degrees in their conditional A parts. It would be like reaching a conclusion, and then immediately forgetting it.

The rules are stored in a **knowledge base**, in a form suitable for processing by the application. The expert system "engine" is able to examine any rule. If the "If A Then..." condition (the "antecedent") is true, the rule is "fired", or activated, meaning that the rest of the rule, or "consequent", is asserted or acted upon. When the program is run, the engine iterates through all the rules.

When a rule fires, when its antecedent or conditional is true, then the rule may "make an assertion". By this it is meant that the rule causes information to be placed into the **assertion base**. The assertion space is the collective (active) memory of the knowledge base, like a big blackboard. This assertion space is visible to all the rules in the knowledge base and it is automatically examined by the search engine as it iterates round through the rules in the knowledge base, performing the inferencing steps.

Since the inference engine does the inferring using the inference rules (originally specified by the programmer) and specifically examines all the assertions in the assertion base for each rule being tested, there is no need for the programmer to necessarily name all the variables and also to check that those names are being tested by down sequence inference (conditional) statements. This alone means that many more rules and many more outputs assertions can viably be made in an expert system than can in a cascade of algebraic conditionals.

One of the results of a rule's firing could be a "**retraction**", the opposite of an assertion, of some information. This causes the removal of that information from the assertion space, and hence none of the rules in the rule base use that retracted information further.

In the cascaded algebraic conditionals based system, inferencing starts at the top of the inverted branching structure and proceeds unidirectionally through it, arriving at some end-point, which ends the inferring behavior. Whatever values have been set in all the variables visited in that cascade constitute its "response". It is important to note that in that type of system the flow of execution is always only unidirectional. This places certain restrictions on the logical processing capability of that ensemble.

In expert system things are importantly different from that. In this expert system the engine iterates over *all* of the rules on each inference cycle. It also makes the values or contents of *all* the assertions in the assertion base available to each rule as the engine iterates through all the rules. In the expert system, unlike in the cascaded algebraic conditionals, a rule is used more than once.

The way the expert system obtains its response is to continue iterating through the rules in the knowledge base until no more assertions can be made, subject to any time-out restrictions.

Fuzzy Logic

The traditional expert system does its inferencing on "crisp" values or content. The use of the term crisp here means discrete values such as the Boolean values of true or false. A system of computation called **fuzzy logic**, as developed by Dr Zadet of the University of California at Berkeley in the 1960s, can be considered a superset of conventional (Boolean) logic, having been extended to handle the concept of partial truth or partial correctness. This means that fuzzy values are not just true or false, yes or no, 0 or 1.

Uses of Inferencing

In this section we'll take a look at some areas where inferencing can be used. One major use of inference is as a mechanism of implementing learning, in which learning may be thought of as detecting, remembering (storing), and recalling (retrieving). As there is a mountain of books on this subject, I will concentrate on another important use – the development of plans.

One example of a planning program is that of the SHRDLU program by Terry Winograd (see http://hci.stanford.edu/~winograd/shrdlu/). It was written in LISP and was quite a sensation when first published in the early 1970s. It operated in a closed "Block's World" in a graphics-based system. The user of SHRDLU typed English questions and English sentence based commands, such as "Put the blue pyramid on top of the large green block". SHRDLU would examine the current world/scene, figure out which block best corresponded to "the large green block" and then located "the blue pyramid". Usually there were other blocks and pyramids in the scene, of various colors and sizes, in addition to the two in the request. Once SHRDLU had located the blue pyramid it would use its planning program to figure out how to move it from where it was to the top of the desired block. If, during figuring this out, SHRDLU detected an object already on top of the goal object (the large green block), and that object wasn't the one that was to be put there, then the planning program temporarily suspended the "move the blue pyramid" plan and started a "clear top" plan. This was used to figure out what to do about the condition that the top of the large green block wasn't clear, and hence the blue pyramid could not be put there. SHRDLU would, of its own accord, figure out that it had to move the object from the top of the large green block to some other location. Then it would resume the "move the blue pyramid".

SHRDLU had the appearance of understanding, because a surprised visiting user could type "Why did you move that object, I didn't ask you to?" SHRDLU would display back, "I moved the [whatever] because it was in the way". Eyebrows raised, the visitor was suitably impressed. (If the visitor had looked at the code, though, he would have seen that the phrase "I moved the * because it was in the way" was hard coded, so no abstract mentalization needed to be somehow magically transformed into meaningful, syntactically elegant English.)

I have mentioned SHRDLU in the planning discussion because there are occasions where present day users could well benefit from an agent assistant during their web usage and perhaps at other times too. We can see that while a successor planning system to implement today's web agent would still need to have the capability of performing planning behavior, it would not completely consist of predefined or hard coded actions, nor would the objects it dealt with likely be as simple as the blocks world. And, the web is not a closed world.

Summary

In this chapter we briefly illustrated the concept of inferencing. We looked at simple and cascaded algebraic conditional logic and how these concepts were built upon to develop expert systems. We saw how SHRDLU was an early example of a planning program.

Having now been introduced to inferencing, in the next chapter we will look at some advanced use cases for meta data.

ProfessionalXMLMeta DataProfessionalXMLMeta DataProfessionalXMLMeta D

16

Advanced Meta Data Use Cases

The increasing necessity to interchange fragments of data between applications and across the Web means a new era in program-to-program communication, and this will require the use of more advanced meta data than has been the practice so far. This chapter builds on the topics covered throughout the rest of this book and presents some futuristic use cases of applications employing meta data, in order to demonstrate how meta data might be used by applications in the future.

The use cases presented discuss the use of meta data embedded inside files themselves, but the first also describes how meta data that is kept at a URI remote to a particular XML file is used in conjunction with local information embedded in the file itself.

These use cases are:

❑ Self-describing XML files, using a **Scalable Vector Graphics (SVG)** file.

❑ Meta data for picture document security, detection of change, and recovery of original content.

The first use case discusses self-describing XML files, which may in turn be used by other programs to "understand" the contents of the file. As far as our picture file example is concerned, this means that the visual objects and sub-objects in the picture, and their co-locations, are recognized by the software, and not just by a human viewing the picture. This particular example uses a simple picture file coded using SVG. SVG is a vector graphics format for use on the Web, which is currently at Candidate Recommendation stage at the W3C; see http://www.w3.org/Graphics/SVG/. It is essentially a language for describing two-dimensional graphics in XML. SVG, rather than some other XML language, is used here to provide a clear example of why self-describing files are of interest to the programmer and user of the Web. You should understand that not all SVG files are self-describing, nor is it required that a given SVG picture file necessarily contains meta data.

In the second use case, the section on advanced meta data for document security, we will consider the issue of original content recovery. Digital signature technology is mentioned but rudimentary knowledge of it is taken for granted so it is not discussed in detail. We discuss a simple visual illustration, reasons why it might be altered, and how the approach in this chapter allows the original to be recovered.

In order to view the output from the SVG XML files used in this chapter, you'll need an SVG browser plug-in or viewer. Mozilla.org is working on including SVG support in its browser, and Microsoft may incorporate SVG functionality in a future version of Internet Explorer. In the meantime, however, there are just a few viewers available. One of the best is a plug-in that may be obtained from the Adobe web site at www.adobe.com/svg, which enables you to view SVG files in your browser. A list of other SVG viewers may be found at www.w3.org/Graphics/SVG/SVG-Implementations.

Self-Describing XML Files – An SVG Example

In this first example we will be considering how to make use of inferencing (which was discussed in the previous chapter) to allow a computer to recognize what it is that the data in an XML file represents. We will be looking at an SVG file that contains, amongst other things, code to be rendered as picture components – in this case we will be studying a very simple example, that of a bar graph. We will first consider how a human being infers information from what is visually represented, and then we'll look at how we might implement logic to do something similar on a computer.

Let's take a look at the rendered SVG before we start examining the code to produce it. The following screenshot shows an instance of a rendering of our sample SVG file, barchart.svg (which is available in the code download):

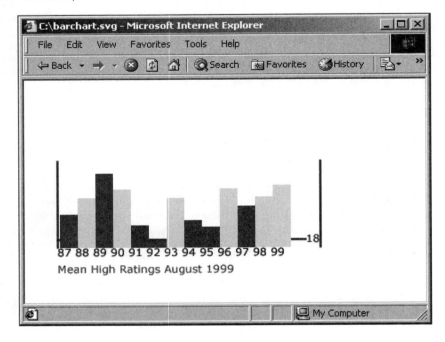

While looking at the rendered SVG, we see that it consists of a number of colored bars (or shaded bars for the screenshot in this book), all parallel with each other, numbers underneath the bars, a title, and two end lines at either end of the chart. This could be the output of a database, for instance, but in this case was actually created by hand.

We know that the picture itself just consists of a bunch of colored dots on the screen, and what we "see" is a bar graph. But while it is perfectly straightforward for our brains to make this leap from dot to chart, it isn't so straightforward for a computer, and we would need to explain to the computer how to go from the colored dots to perceiving the bar graph. This is where **self-describing XML files** can be useful. Self-describing XML files allow meta data, which carries a description of the semantics of the file, to be used by programs to do useful things – such as index picture contents according to what the picture *conveys*, rather than only by what the picture title or caption says or what the author put in a tag as a description.

There are two ways of providing the computer with a means of "understanding" the content of the picture:

❑ We can provide the computer with a means whereby the computer can examine the pixels (dots) of the actual picture itself on the screen.

❑ We can provide the computer with a means whereby the computer can examine the XML that was the source of the picture.

The word "understanding" here means that the computer can recognize the constituents of the picture and their visual relationships, and does not mean that the computer has a mental concept of the picture as a result of the processing.

"Examine the Dots" Approach

It is sometimes possible for a computer to understand a picture by logically examining the pixels (dots) that make up that picture. However, the computer requires that the logic that enables the understanding must exist prior to the time when the computer attempts to "see what is there" in the picture.

One possible approach involves simply providing a template, a data structure, which contains a description of pixels in some pattern. The template can be "laid over" the picture dots for matching. This process does work for line-drawing illustrations like business graphs, such as the example above, because these types of picture have a very stereotyped location of picture objects, unlike an image such as a photograph, which would be far too complicated to examine using an approach such as this one.

In the case of completely computer-generated pictures it is not always possible to match pictures with this "cookie-cutter" template capability because convincing computer graphics are often created by software that uses some fractal or probabilistic method. These methods rule out the possibility of using a fixed pattern template approach, because the pattern of pixels is not repeatable.

Of course, it is possible for computers to generate graphics/pictures with content that is highly repeatable, and which are thus amenable to the template approach. The bar graph picture that we're considering in our example is such a regular picture. However, the code required to examine even this simple picture and gather information from it would be complex and very inflexible, so let's consider another approach.

"Examine the XML" Approach

The "examine the dots" approach relies on pre-defined pixel placement logic code, and only really works for very simple graphics. When the objects are more complex or novel a different tactic is required. Instead of examining the picture in terms of the pixels on the screen, the computer can examine the XML source file to infer what the picture represents. We call this the "examine the XML" approach.

Picture Grammar Approach

Due to the visual regularity and relatively simple content of our bar graph picture, it seems reasonable for **picture grammars** to be used to figure out that this "collection of lines " is in fact a bar graph.

A picture grammar is a set of statements comprising a **context-free grammar** (**CFG**), which is used to "recognize" a picture object based on the syntactical description of its visual constituents. It is called context-free because each rule always holds, regardless of context. Here is a very simple example of such a grammar:

```
bargraph ::= bars + xaxisdata + title + endlines
bars ::= rectangle*
bars ::= line + line + line + line
xaxisdata ::= content*
endlines ::= line + line
title ::= content*
content ::= a:z | A:Z | 0:9
```

The above is a simplified and stylized picture grammar example; however, it should be enough to show what these grammars look like.

A picture grammar, as shown here, is a series of statements that have a term to the left of the ::= and one or more terms to the right of it. The terms on the right hand side are those that comprise the left hand term, for example, head::= eye + eye + mouth + nose. In turn, each of the terms on the right hand side is "explained" by being a term on the left hand side on another line. At some point a term on the right hand side of the ::= cannot be simplified any more. These terms are called **leaves** in the tree of the grammar. They are also called **terminals**.

Both rectangle and line are leaves in the example given above and have corresponding SVG elements. This example of CFG bar graph grammar does not explicitly deal with the **spatial co-relationships** of the objects that make up the picture. For example, it says nothing about the positioning of the bars, or the text of xaxisdata ("87 88 ..99"), or the title ("Mean High ratings August 1999"), other than say that they must be present (and that the text must only contain the characters a to z, A to Z, or the numbers 0 to 9). In this respect, our example picture grammar is probably a little deficient, because it does not say anything about the bars being next to each other, or that they should be vertical, aligned with the x-axis line, and so on. This is not good enough, because to recognize that the picture is a bar chart and not something else the various parts of the bar graph must not only be present, they must also have certain visual relationships.

It would, however, be easy enough to add spatial co-location restrictions (for example, the bars in the bar graph have to be above the x-axis line, and the x-axis line has to be above the title of the graph) to the grammar, just by putting in **DAXSVG elements** like AtRight-content instead of content. DAXSVG is an RDF Schema-based vocabulary whose terms include spatial co-location items, see Chapter 11 for more details. Thus the system that processed the picture grammar would now have leaves (like AtRight-content) to give extra positional information to the grammar.

For example, our grammar could be changed to something like:

```
bargraph  ::= xaxisdata + title + endlines
endlines  ::= line + AtRight-bars + AtRight-line
bars  ::= rectangle*
bars  ::= line  + line + line + line
xaxisdata  ::= content*
title  ::= content*
content  ::= a:z | A:Z | 0:9
```

The occurrence of the DAXSVG term `AtRight` in the SVG code, occurring in conjunction with several items, could provide tokens to match to the picture grammar. A sophisticated system would be able to examine the x-y locations of objects in the picture and determine which spatial terms in DAXSVG (`AtRight` for example), were relevant in a "linearized" description of the picture.

Using the graphical location (coordinates) of the objects we could then use logical inferencing (see the previous chapter for details of inferencing systems) to apply all of the spatial terms found in DAXSVG (such as `AtRight`, `Below`, `IsNear`, etc.) to these object locations. We would then examine this built-up description, which would now include spatial meta data, with knowledge about objects through the view of their constituents, and compare the results against our picture grammar.

This is an excerpt from the `barchart.svg` XML document, showing two SVG `<rect>` elements, called `line2` and `line3`:

```
<rect id="line2" x="60" y="140" width="20" height="60"
      style="stroke:yellow; fill:yellow; stroke-width:0" />
<rect id="line3" x="80" y="111" width="20" height="89"
      style="stroke:red; fill:red; stroke-width:0" />
```

The SVG `<rect>` element produces the rectangles that make up the bars on our chart. The `id` property defines a name for the object, which can be used to reference it. The `x` and `y` properties give the x and y coordinates of the origin of the rectangle. The `width` and `height` properties define the width and height of the rectangle. The `style` attribute can be used to determine aspects like the fill color of the object, and how thick its outline can be.

Thus the `line2` object has its origin located at position 60, 140, has a width of 20, and a height is 60. The `line3` object has its origin located at 80, 111, has a height of 89, and also has a width of 20. The reason that the y coordinates for the origin of the two bars are not the same is that the y coordinates in SVG increase the further down the screen the element is (in other words, the origin is at the top of the screen), and the height value of the rectangle can't be negative, because that would be an error according to the SVG Candidate Recommendation. If you add the y coordinate to the height of each of the bars, you come up with the same figure for both, 200, which is the y coordinate position of the x-axis line of the bar chart. Using this data, we can locate the edges of the SVG objects.

Next, let's take a look at how the logical inferencing can be done.

There are two pieces of software that are needed to play with the DAXSVG schema and the inferencing rules themselves. The first is **XSLT**, and the second is a **rule-based processing system**. This could be an expert system, which allows Java constructs interspersed with expert system-like "rules". Examples of the rules will be given below.

You would need to write some XSLT code which can input the syntax of an RDF statement like this:

```
<rdf:Description about="#text2">
    <daxsvg:below resource="#text1" />
</rdf:Description>
```

The system would then need to follow a series of steps to do the logical inferencing:

1. Examine the SVG source code (in this case `barchart.svg`) and locate the RDF statements in it, like the one shown above containing `text1` and `text2`.

2. Get the element names out of each RDF statement, in this case `text2` and `text1`.

3. Locate the SVG statement which has the `id` attribute `text2` and get the x and y coordinate values out of it, in this case 37 and 210.

4. Locate the SVG statement which has the `id` attribute `text1` and get the x and y coordinate values out of it, in this case 37 and 230.

5. Locate the URI for the function for the DAXSVG relationship term in the RDF expression, which in this case is `<daxsvg:below>` (see the RDF statement above). In the DAXSVG RDF Schema, there is an `<rdfs:comment>` in each entry. Within that comment is the URI for the calculation to determine that the statement is correct.

In the knowledge base of our inferencing system we would have a piece of knowledge that might look like this:

```
IF Object2.x > Object1.x THEN Relationship = "AtRight"
```

In these examples, x and y are variables which represent the x and y coordinate location of the graphics origin of the SVG object. All SVG objects have an origin, thus the relationships about the objects shown in the rules concern only the location of the origins of each object in the relationship. Humans take into account the size and shape of things when they think of spatial relationships, but to explain how to do that in graphics systems and then how to do the inferencing on those shapes and sizes would take pages of explanations, and would serve no better purpose than the simplification of using point origins for illustrative purposes.

Note that it would be necessary for a human to have programmed these concepts into the knowledge base.

What this piece of logic says is that when some graphical object, say `line3` from the example above, is bound to the temporary name `Object2`, and `line2` is bound to the temporary name `Object1`, if the origin x coordinate value of `line3` is greater than the origin x coordinate of `line2` then `line3` has the relationship of `AtRight` to `line2`.

For example, see the following excerpt from `barchart.svg`:

```
<rdf:Description about="#line2">
    <daxsvg:AtRight resource="#line3" />
</rdf:Description>
```

We would carry on in this manner for the rest of the components in the picture. At this point we'd have the inferred logical relationships identified, such as `line3` is to the right of `line2`. We can see that those objects constitute a logical and spatial description. If we then had, in our knowledge base, a bar graph term such as:

```
IF
(AND
(ParallelBars.count > 2
    Text  under ParallelBars     <!-- Text1 -->
    Text  under  Text             <!-- Text2 Text1 -->
    EndBarLeft and EndBarRight)
)
THEN  Object = "Bargraph"
```

we could compare our logical/spatial description to it and determine whether we're looking at a bar graph or not.

This still might not be enough to determine that what we are looking at is, in fact, a bar graph. For instance, it could be the barcode from the back of this book! We could add further rules to check that, for example, the bars were of equal thickness, and other things to refine our check.

Next, we will look at a more widely applicable approach using the application of RDF Schema meta data (and inferencing) to the self-describing of XML files.

Meta Data and Inferencing Approach

This section shows how the combination of meta data and inferencing can be applied so that a computer can recognize the data presented in a picture, in this case the bar graph created by our SVG code. The following code is again taken from the `bargraph.svg` XML file used to produce the output we saw earlier – the complete code is available in the code download.

```
<rect id="xbaseline" x="37" y="190" width="280"
      height="1" style="stroke:black; stroke-width:1" />
<text id="text3" x="317" y="194"
      style="font-family:Verdana; font-size:12.333; fill:indigo">
18
</text>
<rect id="endlineright" x="333" y="96" width="1"
      height="104" style="stroke:black; stroke-width:1" />
<rect id="endlineleft" x="37" y="96" width="1"
      height="104" style="stroke:black; stroke-width:1" />
<rect id="line1" x="40" y="160" width="20"
      height="40" style="stroke:green; fill:green; stroke-width:0" />
<rect id="line2" x="60" y="140" width="20"
      height="60" style="stroke:yellow; fill:yellow; stroke-width:0" />
<rect id="line3" x="80" y="111" width="20"
      height="89" style="stroke:red; fill:red; stroke-width:0" />
<rect id="line4" x="100" y="130" width="20"
      height="70" style="stroke:yellow; fill:yellow; stroke-width:0" />
<rect id="line5" x="120" y="173" width="20"
      height="27" style="stroke:green; fill:green; stroke-width:0" />
<rect id="line6" x="140" y="191" width="20"
      height="09" style="stroke:green; fill:green; stroke-width:0" />
<rect id="line7" x="160" y="140" width="20"
```

```
          height="60" style="stroke:yellow; fill:yellow; stroke-width:0" />
<rect id="line8" x="180" y="167" width="20"
      height="33" style="stroke:green; fill:green; stroke-width:0" />
<rect id="line9" x="200" y="175" width="20"
      height="25" style="stroke:green; fill:green; stroke-width:0" />
<rect id="line10" x="220" y="129" width="20"
      height="71" style="stroke:yellow; fill:yellow; stroke-width:0" />
<rect id="line11" x="240" y="150" width="20"
      height="50" style="stroke:green; fill:green; stroke-width:0" />
<rect id="line12" x="260" y="139" width="20"
      height="61" style="stroke:yellow; fill:yellow; stroke-width:0" />
<rect id="line13" x="280" y="125" width="20"
      height="75" style="stroke:yellow; fill:yellow; stroke-width:0" />

<text id="text1" x="37" y="210"
      style="font-family:Verdana; font-size:12.333; fill:black">
87  88  89  90  91  92  93  94  95  96  97  98  99
</text>
<text id="text2" x="37" y="230"
      style="font-family:Verdana; font-size:12.333; fill:brown">
Mean High Ratings August 1999
</text>
```

What we are looking at is the SVG code that creates a number of lines, colored rectangles and text objects. Note that the SVG code items have an id and other various properties, including x and y coordinates. When an SVG engine renders these lines of code into actual graphics on the screen, we see the bar graph object as in the previous screenshot.

Also present in the SVG file is the following RDF material. When the SVG drawing code was created, RDF code that gives spatial descriptions (in other words, RDF meta data about some aspects of the content of the picture) was also added. This could have been added by the author of the SVG by hand (as in this case), by the authoring tool, or by some external processor. Here we see RDF code that defines the semantic spatial relationship information about the text representing the title and x-axis labeling, the lines that frame the left and right sides of the bar graph, and the named lines (rectangles). It uses DAXSVG's AtRight, Below, and IsNear terms, which we met briefly earlier and will discuss in greater detail in a moment:

```
<rdf:Description about="#text1">
  <daxsvg:Below resource="#xbaseline"/>
</rdf:Description>
<rdf:Description about="#text1">
  <daxsvg:IsNear resource="#xbaseline" />
</rdf:Description>
<rdf:Description about="#text2">
  <daxsvg:Below resource="#text1"/>
</rdf:Description>
<rdf:Description about="#text2">
  <daxsvg:IsNear resource="#text1" />
</rdf:Description>
<rdf:Description about="#endlineleft">
  <daxsvg:AtRight resource="#line1"/>
</rdf:Description>
<rdf:Description about="#endlineleft">
  <daxsvg:IsNear resource="#line1" />
```

```
    </rdf:Description>
    <rdf:Description about="#endlineright">
       <daxsvg:AtLeft resource="#bar13"/>
    </rdf:Description>
    <rdf:Description about="#endlineright">
       <daxsvg:IsNear resource="#bar13" />
    </rdf:Description>
    <rdf:Description about="#line1">
       <daxsvg:AtRight resource="#line2" />
    </rdf:Description>
    <rdf:Description about="#line2">
       <daxsvg:AtRight resource="#line3" />
    </rdf:Description>
    <rdf:Description about="#line3">
       <daxsvg:AtRight resource="#line4" />
    </rdf:Description>
    <rdf:Description about="#line4">
       <daxsvg:AtRight resource="#line5" />
    </rdf:Description>
    <rdf:Description about="#line5">
       <daxsvg:AtRight resource="#line6" />
    </rdf:Description>
    <rdf:Description about="#line6">
       <daxsvg:AtRight resource="#line7" />
    </rdf:Description>
    <rdf:Description about="#line7">
       <daxsvg:AtRight resource="#line8" />
    </rdf:Description>
    <rdf:Description about="#line8">
       <daxsvg:AtRight resource="#line9" />
    </rdf:Description>
    <rdf:Description about="#line9">
       <daxsvg:AtRight resource="#line10" />
    </rdf:Description>
    <rdf:Description about="#line10">
       <daxsvg:AtRight resource="#line11" />
    </rdf:Description>
    <rdf:Description about="#line11">
       <daxsvg:AtRight resource="#line12" />
    </rdf:Description>
    <rdf:Description about="#line12">
       <daxsvg:AtRight resource="#bar13" />
    </rdf:Description>
```

DAXSVG Schema

DAXSVG's `AtRight` term is defined in the DAXSVG schema (`daxsvg-schema-rdf.xml`) as:

```
<rdf:Property ID="AtRight">
<rdfs:comment>has a degree of to the right (by value).   (uses context)
www.openmeta.org/2001/g15(x)</rdfs:comment>
<rdfs:range rdf:resource="#SvgEntity" />
<rdfs:domain rdf:resource="#SvgEntity" />
</rdf:Property>
```

It uses a function, `g15()`, which computes a scalar return value. That scalar value is used to signify the degree to which a particular relationship is `AtRight`, or how close one SVG element is to another.

The calculation is simple. For two objects, let's say `line1` and `line2` (from the SVG code), with SVG graphic x origins at 40 and 60, respectively, the calculation is: Object2.x – Object1.x = 20. The graphic distance separating the two x origins is 20. Then the value of `g15(20)` is calculated, using a specific formula. The value returned from this calculation is the degree to which `line2` is `AtRight` of `line1`, which can be a number between 0 and 1.

The value returned from the calculation `g15(x)` can then be used in a process known as **hedging**, which was developed by Professor Lotfi Zadeh, the creator of fuzzy logic. What hedging provides is a means of using a controlled English vocabulary to relate numeric values as meaningful English words.

To encode the hedging rules in XML syntax, we use **UKL**.

> *UKL is the Unified Knowledge Language, a meta-representation system that has been under development for some time. Briefly, the purpose of UKL is to provide a representation that can express information and knowledge in a vendor-neutral way. There are vendors, such as iLog and Blade, who have commercial rule-based products. UKL is a representational language where rule-type information may be expressed in UKL instead of tying one's rules to a specific syntax (and rule engine) of any commercial rule based system vendor.*

Here we see the `<setVal>` element being used to define a variable and its value, the name of the variable is `True` and its value is `1.0`. There is also a synonym defined for the name, `completelyTrue`. A datatype is included indicating that this variable is of type `real`:

```
<setVal>
    <variablename>True</variablename>
    <synonym>completelyTrue</synonym>
    <variablevalue>1.0</variablevalue>
    <variabletype>real</variabletype>
</setVal>
```

Here's another instance of the `<setVal>` element being used to define a variable and its value, the name of the variable is `sortOfTrue` and its value is `0.3`. Its datatype is also defined as `real`:

```
<setVal>
    <variablename>sortOfTrue</variablename>
    <variablevalue>0.3</variablevalue>
    <variabletype>real</variabletype>
</setVal>
```

We then go on to define further variables in the same way:

```
<setVal>
    <variablename>somewhatTrue</variablename>
    <variablevalue>0.5</variablevalue>
    <variabletype>real</variabletype>
</setVal>

<setVal>
    <variablename>nearlyTrue</variablename>
```

```
      <variablevalue>0.8</variablevalue>
      <variabletype>real</variabletype>
   </setVal>

   <setVal>
      <variablename>occasionallyTrue</variablename>
      <synonym>vaguelyTrue</synonym>
      <variablevalue>0.2</variablevalue>
      <variabletype>real</variabletype>
   </setVal>

   <setVal>
      <variablename>False</variablename>
      <synonym>completelyFalse</synonym>
      <synonym>totallyFalse</synonym>
      <variablevalue>0.0</variablevalue>
      <variabletype>real</variabletype>
   </setVal>
```

What we see above is a set of `<setVal>` elements that have defined a collection of variables, giving each a name, value, and datatype. At this point we have defined a few terms for use as hedges, such as `sortOfTrue`. Later we can use these names as levels in a thresholding or conditional statement.

If the value returned by the calculation `f(x)` was, say, 0.8, then the system would be able to compute that the relevant English term would be `nearlyTrue`, as found in the `variablename` content. That explains how the UKL processor, given the XML SVG code, and all of the stated rules, could examine the two lines `line1` and `line2` and output a meaningful statement such as "*It is nearly true that line2 is at the right of line1*".

If we look further into the DAXSVG vocabulary we can see that, using the vocabulary item `IsNear`, we could do another calculation, this time `g1(x)`, using the result obtained from `g15(x)` (the calculation from `AtRight`), and get a degree of nearness. This definition is taken from the DAXSVG schema (`daxsvg-schema-rdf.xml`):

```
   <rdf:Property rdf:ID="IsNear">
   <rdfs:comment>has a degree of nearness (by value). (uses context)
   www.openmeta.org/2001/g1(x)</rdfs:comment>
   <rdfs:range rdf:resource="#SvgEntity" />
   <rdfs:domain rdf:resource="#SvgEntity" />
   </rdf:Property>
```

Let's say that `IsNear` uses the same `f(x)` function. The resulting upshot is that the system would be aware that the two objects have the relationship "*It is nearly true that line2 is at the right of line1*", and also simultaneously has the relationship "*line1 is rather near line2*". The *rather* term comes from the calculation for `IsNear` using different values for the hedging but within the same process.

Bridging the Gap Between Human and Computer 'Vision'

If we compare our experience of the picture with the multiple lines of SVG markup, it's clear that when we receive the picture we see it as a whole entity (a picture) but in the code it exists as a series of objects which look nothing like a single, graphical or visual unit. So how can we bridge this difference, between what a human infers and what a computer might?

So far we have a collection of colored rectangles we have named "line such and such", we have an RDF-based meta data section in the same file which indicates that these "lines" are to the right of each other – it is even able to capture by how much to the right. Let's now turn our attention to how this inferred information, RDF vocabulary, and code, all come together to detect a bar graph picture.

Now, we have all the visual components of the bar graph defined in the picture and we have the RDF-based spatial relationship of all these visual components defined. All that is left to tie up the bag is the logic that detects that this information constitutes a bar graph object or picture.

Here's how that logic looks. Each of the SVG elements provides a *name*, from its id. These names also appear in the RDF statements, (RDF meta data!) which explicitly give the spatial relationship semantic information, such as "AtRight", for all of the SVG graphic objects that constitute the bar graph.

Here are some logic statements that the UKL processor will use to examine this information and provide an inference as to the implications of it expressed in UKL. These are the XML-encoded rules that provide the logic for inferencing:

```
<?xml version="1.0" standalone="no"?>
<ukl width="100%" height="100%" xmlns = 'http://www.openmeta.org/2001/UKLnom'>
<ruleset>
```

Here we are defining an object, which is used to express and test conditions in the logic of the rule set being built. The name of the object is CondObj39. There is no special significance to that particular name. It has four object model variables (Condition1, Condition2, Condition3, and Condition4) defined as being associated with this model structure. They all have the data type of real. No values are defined at this point for any of the variables.

```
<defineNOM>
<defineNOMname>CondObj39</defineNOMname>
<defineNOMvar>
    <varname>Condition1</varname>
    <vartype>real</vartype>
</defineNOMvar>
<defineNOMvar>
    <varname>Condition2</varname>
    <vartype>real</vartype>
</defineNOMvar>
<defineNOMvar>
    <varname>Condition3</varname>
    <vartype>real</vartype>
</defineNOMvar>
<defineNOMvar>
    <varname>Condition4</varname>
    <vartype>real</vartype>
</defineNOMvar>
```

Here we see a second object being defined, CondObj23:

```
<defineNOMname>CondObj23</defineNOMname>
```

This object has four variables defined as being associated with it:

```
<defineNOMvar>
```

```
        <varname>Condition10</varname>
        <vartype>real</vartype>
</defineNOMvar>
<defineNOMvar>
        <varname>Condition20</varname>
        <vartype>real</vartype>
</defineNOMvar>
<defineNOMvar>
        <varname>Condition30</varname>
        <vartype>real</vartype>
</defineNOMvar>
<defineNOMvar>
        <varname>Condition40</varname>
        <vartype>real</vartype>
</defineNOMvar>
</defineNOM>
```

Next we see a **path statement**, in the <setPath> element. The path statement is used to specify where the value of a variable can be obtained, like a URI. The detailed path name can be given an alias by using the <pathname> element.

```
<setPath>
        <pathname>Condition1</pathname>
        <pathvalue>SVG.fnsvg9.id.line1</pathvalue>
</setPath>
```

The equivalent URI for SVG.fnsvg9.id.line1 is www.openmeta.org/2001/svg9#id="line1". These paths link the named variable, such as Condition1, with an actual data item, SVG.fnsvg9.id.line1 in this case. These paths are resolved into complete URIs by the UKL processor so that the variables referenced can be used.

Further paths are defined for the other conditions:

```
<setPath>
        <pathname>Condition2</pathname>
        <pathvalue>SVG.fnsvg9.id.line2</pathvalue>
</setPath>
<setPath>
        <pathname>Condition3</pathname>
        <pathvalue>SVG.fnsvg9.id.line3</pathvalue>
</setPath>
<setPath>
        <pathname>Condition4</pathname>
        <pathvalue>SVG.fnsvg9.id.line4</pathvalue>
</setPath>
<setPath>
        <pathname>Condition10</pathname>
        <pathvalue>SVG.fnsvg9.id.text1</pathvalue>
</setPath>
<setPath>
        <pathname>Condition20</pathname>
        <pathvalue>SVG.fnsvg9.id.text2</pathvalue>
</setPath>
<setPath>
        <pathname>Condition30</pathname>
```

```
    <pathvalue>SVG.fnsvg9.id.endlineleft</pathvalue>
</setPath>
<setPath>
<pathname>Condition40</pathname>
<pathvalue>SVG.fnsvg9.id.endlineright</pathvalue>
</setPath>
```

An enumerated list with the name `truth` is defined as having the two values, `true` and `false`.

```
<defineEnumList>
    <enumlistname>truth</enumlistname>
        <enumvalue>true</enumvalue>
        <enumvalue>false</enumvalue>
</defineEnumList>
```

Next, `<setVal>` elements are defined for use in the hedging process, as described above:

```
<setVal>
    <variablename>True</variablename>
    <synonym>completelyTrue</synonym>
    <variablevalue>1.0</variablevalue>
    <variabletype>real</variabletype>
</setVal>

<setVal>
    <variablename>sortOfTrue</variablename>
    <variablevalue>0.3</variablevalue>
    <variabletype>real</variabletype>
</setVal>

<setVal>
    <variablename>somewhatTrue</variablename>
    <variablevalue>0.5</variablevalue>
    <variabletype>real</variabletype>
</setVal>

<setVal>
    <variablename>nearlyTrue</variablename>
    <variablevalue>0.8</variablevalue>
    <variabletype>real</variabletype>
</setVal>

<setVal>
    <variablename>occasionallyTrue</variablename>
    <synonym>vaguelyTrue</synonym>
    <variablevalue>0.2</variablevalue>
    <variabletype>real</variabletype>
</setVal>

<setVal>
    <variablename>False</variablename>
    <synonym>completelyFalse</synonym>
    <synonym>totallyFalse</synonym>
    <variablevalue>0.0</variablevalue>
  <variabletype>real</variabletype>
</setVal>
```

Next is a statement that is used to define a rule, which is a kind of conditional statement. The condition part of the rule has four conditions to it, connected together by an <andconnector> element. It uses the object model defined above (CondObj39), together with the four paths associated with it (Condition1 through Condition4) in tests, which look to see if the variable corresponding to the paths have values greater than somewhatTrue. Note the escaped character > used to represent the greater than (>) symbol in XML:

```
<definerule>
    <rulename>Rule55</rulename>
    <rulepriority/>
    <rulegroup/>
    <rulecondition>
        <andconnector>
            <Cond>
                Condobj39.Condition1 &gt; somewhatTrue
            </Cond>
            <Cond>
                Condobj39.Condition2 &gt; somewhatTrue
            </Cond>
            <Cond>
                Condobj39.Condition3 &gt; somewhatTrue
            </Cond>
            <Cond>
                Condobj39.Condition4 &gt; somewhatTrue
            </Cond>
        </andconnector>
    </rulecondition>
```

Next, we see the rule action part of the rule (comparable with the THEN part of a conditional IF...THEN statement in a programming language such as Java).

If the tests above are satisfied, the UKL processor can make an assertion, in this case that the bars are parallel and adjacent to each other. In this case it makes an assertion name of parallelbars and sets the topic (a topic in a topic map) to have a base string name of parallelbars, with a topic name of t_parallelbars, and a topic map association element of adjacentlines. The topic maps base is given as tm.033. See Chapter 7 for more information on topic maps and their syntax.

```
<ruleaction>
    <setvariable>
        AssertName = "parallelbars"
            <settopic>
                topicbasestring="parallelbars"
                topicname = "t_ parallelbars"
                synassoc = "adjacentlines"
                tbase = "tm.033"
            </settopic>
    </setvariable>
</ruleaction>
</definerule>
```

Here a second rule is defined, to test whether there is title text under the graph and end lines at either end of the graph:

```
<definerule>
    <rulename>Rule27</rulename>
    <rulepriority/>
    <rulegroup/>
    <rulecondition>
        <andconnector>
            <Cond>
                Condobj23.Condition1 &gt; somewhatTrue
            </Cond>
            <Cond>
                Condobj23.Condition2 &gt; somewhatTrue
            </Cond>
            <Cond>
                Condobj23.Condition3 &gt; somewhatTrue
            </Cond>
            <Cond>
                Condobj23.Condition4 &gt; somewhatTrue
            </Cond>
        </andconnector>
    </rulecondition>
    <ruleaction>
        <setvariable>
            AssertName = "textunderandendbars"
                <settopic>
                    topicbasestring="textunderandendbars"
                    topicname = "t_ textunderandendbars"
                    synassoc = ""
                    tbase = "tm.033"
                </settopic>
        </setvariable>
    </ruleaction>
</definerule>
```

The final rule that we're going to define here is that if all of the conditions defined above are true, then the system will assert that the SVG image we're studying is, in fact, a bar chart.

```
<definerule>
    <rulename>Rule3</rulename>
    <rulepriority/>
    <rulegroup/>
    <rulecondition>
        <andconnector>
            <Cond>
                Condobj39.all = True
            </Cond>
            <Cond>
                Condobj23.all = True
            </Cond>
        </andconnector>
    </rulecondition>
    <ruleaction>
        <setvariable>
            AssertName = "bargraph"
                <settopic>
                    topicbasestring="bargraph"
                    topicname = "t_ bargraph"
```

```
            synassoc = "linegraph"
            tbase = "tm.033"
         </settopic>
      </setvariable>
   </ruleaction>
</definerule>
```

Finally, we close the UKL rule set:

```
</ruleset>
```

When a UKL processor runs these rules the relative position of the objects in the bar chart are compared with the positions needed if the logic is to recognize that this collection of SVG graphic objects actually constitutes a bar chart.

What this amounts to is that if the SVG graphical objects (rectangles) are found in a series to the right of each other, with an x-axis base line having text below it, with text below that text, and the whole thing has a left vertical line and a right vertical line, then the object qualifies as a bar graph according to our rules, and the system can make an assertion that this is the case. Further information could be inferred from the graph if other rules were defined.

Summary of Self-Describing XML Files

By applying logical inferencing to the SVG code file using the spatial vocabularies in DAXSVG we can arrive at certain assertions in our inferencing system, for instance that a picture of a bar chart actually is a bar chart, and we could also use this meta data to get further machine understandable description of the picture.

It is viable to design a schema or vocabulary that expresses relationships about two objects. It's important to note that this relationship doesn't have to be a spatial relationship as we have shown here with our SVG example; it could be spatial, financial, physical, or whatever. In this way, files can be passed between applications in an intelligent manner, because the meta data present in the file can contain semantic information about the contents of the file.

Meta Data for Document Integrity and Recovery

A common way to add security to data and documents is to **encrypt** the contents. An additional way to add integrity recovery is to use meta data to contain **semantic descriptions of vital parts**. The semantic descriptions can be used to check that the document has not been tampered with in an "illegal" way. Of course, those descriptions, in turn, must be protected from loss or alteration. The easiest way to do that is to digitally sign these semantic descriptions – in that way any alteration is detectable.

In this use case we will look at the document security of an SVG-based picture. There are other means of securing text documents and general data but in this example we will just focus on one approach. What we will see in this section is that meta data can be combined with XML SVG graphics code to protect a document, in this case an XML-based picture, which can be secured against loss through deletion or alteration of the SVG code in the file.

Using Meta Data to Preserve Intention

Consider the following picture:

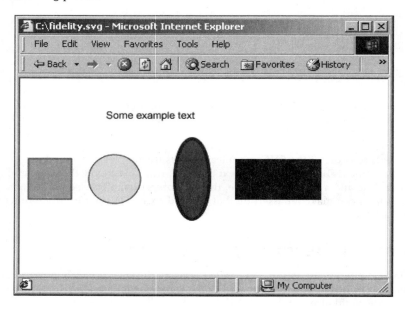

If we look at the following sample code that produced this picture, `fidelity.svg` (which is available in the code download), we see that meta data has been placed into the SVG description (<desc>) element having a group name of `object`. The three `$Fidelity` statements and the one `$Group` meta data statement perform some useful functions, which we'll discuss in a moment:

```
<?xml version="1.0" standalone="yes"?>
<svg xmlns="http://www.w3.org/2000/svg">
    <desc>
        $Fidelity{idname:Object1 fill:orange stroke:blue
            fractal:1.379152 lacunarity:0.32719}
        $Fidelity{idname:Object3 stroke:purple}
        $Fidelity{sign:93761822507052D35A}
        $Group{gname:Group1 group:Object1 Object2 Object3 Object4
            leftof:Object2 Object3}
    </desc>

    <g id="Group1">
        <text id="Object1" x="100" y="50">
            Some example text
        </text>

        <rect id="Object2" height="50" width="50" x="10" y="100"
            style="stroke:blue; fill:orange; stroke-width:1" />

        <circle id="Object3" cx="110" cy="125" r="30"
```

```
                style="fill:yellow; stroke:purple; stroke-width:1" />

      <ellipse id="Object4" cx="200" cy="125" rx="20" ry="50"
              style="fill:red; stroke:blue; stroke-width:4" />
   </g>

   <rect id="Object5" height="50" width="100" x="250" y="100" />

</svg>
```

In the SVG <desc> element we can see that there are three $Fidelity statements and one $Group statement, all within the <desc> element.

$Fidelity Statements

The $Fidelity statement is used to capture and retain particular information about an XML statement. In the case of this example the XML information that is captured is SVG code.

Consider the case of an SVG file in which the author would like to protect some elements from being modified permanently by a user, while allowing other elements to be modified. By using the $Fidelity statement as a guide, a program could automatically recover the elements in the picture if they were altered, or use the information to stop the data being changed.

The first statement:

```
$Fidelity{idname:Object1 fill:orange stroke:blue fractal:1.379152
     lacunarity:0.32719}
```

names SVG graphic object Object1 as the XML statement that it is going to secure. The SVG attributes of Object1 that are being secured are listed in the $Fidelity statement. This is the fill:orange and stroke:blue part. Neither fractal nor lacunarity are SVG attributes, they are security attributes that are inserted for the purpose of invoking numerical calculations. What these mathematically-based measures provide is a kind of "rubber template" which allows the shape of the object to vary within a certain range and still be considered the same shape. This provides permission for a certain range of object modification in terms of shape without setting off an alarm, as it were.

The fractal attribute fractal:1.379152 is used to store a calculation of the "fractal dimension" of the figure that is rendered in object1. Fractal geometry allows us to specify the shape of something mathematically, by giving its fractal dimension. Those interested in learning more about fractal geometry might wish to read material on the subject by Benoit Mandelbrot.

The lacunarity attribute lacunarity:0.32719 is used to permit a calculation of the "wiggliness" or "spacefillingness" of the figure (for more information on lacunarity, see http://www.swiss.ai.mit.edu/~rauch/lacunarity/lacunarity.html). It provides a numeric measure of the first and second order graphical "inflections" in the figure. In other words it provides a succinct mathematical description of the visual object.

Using the fractal dimension and lacunarity of a graphical object as a description permits a visual, morphological description, instead of a "cookie cutter" template, which is valid only for an exact, particular pattern of pixels. The use of the fractal geometry measures allows the figure to be altered slightly so long as the measures are maintained. This means that there are a range of changes that may be made to the figure which are considered "legal", so long as the figure resulting from the changes still has the same fractal measurements as were stated in the $Fidelity statement.

The second $Fidelity statement:

```
$Fidelity{idname:Object3 stroke:purple}
```

names SVG graphic object Object3 as the XML statement that it is going to secure. The SVG attributes of Object3 that are being secured are listed in the $Fidelity statement. This is the stroke:purple part. If the actual fill color gets changed for some reason it can be recovered. There are no fractal geometry considerations in the security aspects in this statement.

The third $Fidelity statement:

```
$Fidelity{sign:93761822507052D35A}
```

states the "value" of the digital signature which occurred when the $Fidelity and $Group statements used were digitally signed.

The single $Group statement makes an assertion that a logical group exists, called Group 1, and that it has constituents named Object1 through Object4. It further states that it is intended that Object3 should be to the left of Object 2:

```
$Group{gname:Group1 group:Object1 Object2 Object3 Object4
    leftof:Object2 Object3}
```

The picture file itself has a <g> group element, defined in SVG, but that element's placement has certain syntactical and hence functional effects on SVG files. As a result it is not always available to indicate "just so" logical groupings intended by an SVG author. The $Group meta data statement may be used to achieve this goal. An author may define named logical groupings of his SVG graphical objects. In this way we can avoid entanglements with the SVG <g> group element, where the particular use of an SVG <g> group element means to treat the SVG code statements a particular way, which is different from the conceptual grouping intended or desired by the picture author. It is also possible for the author to declare that he intends particular relationships, especially appearance and location relationships, to be logically assigned that are independent of the operation of SVG's grouping behavior.

If, for example, "Object2" gets coded in SVG into a location which is not to the right of "Object3" then, when the security/intention pass is made of the code in the SVG file, the system can display a message that the author intended such and such, but the actual SVG code in the file has something else coded.

If we take another look at the SVG markup, we can see that Object5 has no security statements made about it, and hence the user is allowed to change this element as much as they like.

Summary of Document Security

To summarize what we have learned in this use case, we saw that:

❏ It is possible to capture and retain important XML statement values, such as those of attributes in statements conveying information which the generator of the file considers important or worth recovery, or those which convey "intent", such as a blue logo color.

❑ Meta data can be used to add further security properties to those attributes, by adding attribute-value pairs to the secured XML information. (In this use case we saw the use of the fractal geometry concepts of fractal dimension and lacunarity, neither of which exist in the SVG language itself.)

❑ It is legitimate to consider some changes as "permissible" and to specify the nature of these changes.

❑ It is possible to recover or redisplay the rendered XML file so as to display the visual "intent" of the picture's author, automatically by means of meta data-based $fidelity statements.

Summary

In this chapter we've taken a look at a couple of areas where the application of meta data might enhance our future applications.

We saw how, in conjunction with logical inferencing, we can use meta data to enable computers to recognize and understand self-describing XML files, and in particular diagrams, opening up the possibility of greater use of the wealth of diagrammatic information available via the Web.

We also saw how meta data can be used to secure and preserve a web page author's intentions concerning the presentation of a document, but at the same time allowing the end user to modify the file within specified limits.

These use cases are both currently quite speculative, but hopefully they have rounded off our study of XML meta data and the possibilities it offers, both now and into the future.

Meta DataProfessionalXMLMeta DataProfessionalXMLMeta DataPro

Glossary

Acquired infoset: In XInclude, the infoset that results from an include process or series of include processes.

Activity: In PSL, a class or type of action.

Activity occurrence: In PSL, an instance or occurrence of an activity (an event or action taking place at a specific place and time).

Aggregation: The process of converting the embedded meta data within a set of resources into a meta data repository.

Annotations: Structured or unstructured data attached to specific points or sections within a document.

Anonymous resource: In RDF, a description element that exists for no other reason than to be given properties.

Application profiles: In PSL, meta data describing the kinds of processes the systems support.

Arc: In XLink, information about how to traverse a link. An arc that has a local starting resource and a remote ending resource goes outbound. An arc that has a remote starting resource and a local ending resource goes inbound. In the case that neither the starting resource nor the ending resource is a local resource, the arc is termed a third party arc.

Association: In topic maps, a defined relationship between topics, in which each topic plays a specified role.

Association nodes: In MDL, nodes that denote instances of an association between objects, in any XML representation.

Association templates: In topic maps, a specification of a set of constraints on associations of a given type.

Attribute information item: Exists for each attribute of each element in an XML document.

Axis: A direction in an XPath expression.

Bag: In RDF, the simplest type of container.

Base name: In topic maps, the first kind of characteristic that may be assigned to a topic. A base name is guaranteed to refer to only one topic.

BizTalk Mapper: Microsoft's XML-to-XML mapping tool.

Cardinality: In a DTD, defines how often an element may occur in a particular position in an XML document.

Casting: Sometimes called re-casting or transcoding, the process of generating a topic map rendition from some other representation.

Centralized meta data: Meta data that may be retrieved from a single source.

Character information item: Exists for each data character in an XML document whether literally, as a character reference, or in a CDATA section.

Choice list: In a DTD, specifies the elements which may be present, and is typically used with a cardinality operator to indicate how many times the elements in the choice list may be used.

Codasyl: A 1970s navigational model for databases.

Comment information item: Is present in the infoset for each comment appearing in the XML document, with the exception of any comments present within the DTD, which are not represented.

Complex type elements: Elements that contain other elements or that have attributes.

Composite Capabilities/Preference Profiles (CC/PP): A specification for the use of XML/RDF to describe user preferences and the capabilities of the device and software used to access the Web.

Conceptual Knowledge Markup Language (CKML): An application of XML that extends the capabilities of Ontology Markup Language (OML).

Container: In RDF, a list, or collection, of resources.

Container membership property: In RDF, a property that relates to the members of a container.

Content model: In DTDs, describes the category to which an element in an XML document belongs, which in turn defines what type of content the element is permitted to have.

Context: The information or structure that surrounds the focus of interest.

Context node: A defined starting point in an XPath expression.

Conversion: The stage of the aggregation process that attempts to turn raw meta data into quality meta data by enforcing a degree of consistency amongst possibly diverse meta data vocabularies and meta data instances.

Core theories: In PSL, the theories that provide building blocks necessary to define concepts.

DAML+OIL: Combination of OIL (Ontology Interchange Language, based on RDF and RDF Schema), and DAML (DARPA Agent Markup Language, a framework providing information to web-agents).

Data mart: A smaller, more localized version of a data warehouse.

Data warehouse: A large database designed for the fast storage, retrieval, and management of any type of data.

Decision graphs: Diagrams which show the flow or sequence of the logical conditions necessary to reach end points in a graph structure.

Decomposition: In PSL, the theory that activities can contain sub-activities, and occurrences of such activities can contain sub-occurrences.

Definitions and **relations**: The primary components of PSL expressed in KIF.

Discovery: The process by which resources containing embedded meta data are located.

Distributed meta data: Meta data that must be retrieved from a number of sources external to the processing system.

Document information item: In an XML document, corresponds to the document entity itself, plus, typically, a number of element and other information items.

Document instance: Each individual XML document belonging to a particular document type.

Document Object Model (DOM): A formal definition of what the XML syntax represents in terms of data objects that can be manipulated in memory once the XML document has been parsed.

Document type: A class of XML documents which share a common vocabulary and structure.

Document type declaration: Incorporates the DTD (Document Type Definition) directly into the document. Commonly called the DOCTYPE declaration.

Document type declaration information item: Is present in the XML infoset if the XML document has a document type declaration.

Document type definition (DTD): An XML schema that describes the content and structure of a class of XML documents, written according to the W3C's DTD specification.

Dublin Core: A standard for the content of meta data. Comprises a core set of elements that are common to most types of document.

ebXML (Electronic Business Extensible Markup Language): An initiative for developing XML specifications for global business exchanges.

Element information item: Exists for each element that appears in an XML document.

Embedded meta data: Meta data that is contained within the body of the resource that it describes, for example in <META> and <TITLE> tags in HTML.

Enterprise Application Integration (EAI): An architecture for the unrestricted sharing of data and business processes within an organization.

ECMA: European Computer Manufacturer's Association.

ECMAScript: An object-oriented programming language derived from JavaScript for computation and object manipulation within a host environment.

Extended-type links: In XLink, a link that associates any number of resources.

XHTML (Extensible Hypertext Markup Language): A reformulation of HTML 4 as an XML 1.0 application.

XSL-FO (Extensible Stylesheet Language – Formatting Objects): A language that enables the precise definition of page layout of XML documents.

XSLT (Extensible Stylesheet Language for Transformations): A language for transforming the structure of XML documents.

External meta data: Meta data that is contained in a data store that is separate from the resource that it describes. The data store for external meta data may be a database application, a flat file, or a structured file format (such as XML).

Extraction: The process of filtering out meta data from the resource content.

Fragment identifier: Identifies a piece of an XML document.

Fuzzy logic: A system of computation that uses values between 0 and 1, in other words not just the logic values 0/1, yes/no, true/false.

GML (Generalized Markup Language): The predecessor of SGML.

Global attributes: In XLink, attributes that can be attached to elements from different namespaces, and that provide all XLink functionality. There are type, locator, semantic, behavior, and traversal attributes.

Grove model: A formal model of the objects held in memory once an SGML document has been parsed. A key part of the HyTime specification.

Hedging: A technique used in inferencing, that provides a means of using a controlled English vocabulary to relate numeric values as meaningful English words.

HyTime: The application of SGML to multimedia and hyper-documents.

ID – IDREF mechanism: In a DTD, an attribute can be declared to be of type ID, so that its value is the unique identifier for that element instance. The IDREF attribute type refers to the element with an ID attribute with the same value as the IDREF.

Included items: The information items referenced by the XInclude <include> element.

Include location: An absolute IURI that specifies where the item to be included can be located.

Inclusion transformation: A specific type of XML infoset transformation, which uses XInclude to merge one or more infosets.

Inferencing engine: A program that uses inference rules to infer new facts from known facts. Commonly found as part of a Prolog interpreter, expert system, or knowledge based system.

Information item: An abstract representation of some part of a well-formed XML document. Each individual information item has a number of associated properties.

Input problem: In MDL, extracting the information from an "incoming" XML document and viewing that information directly in terms of the classes, simple properties, and associations of the semantic model.

Internationalized Uniform Resource Identifier (IURI): A URI that directly uses Unicode characters.

JDBC (Java Database Connectivity) API: Contains straightforward methods for getting meta data out of virtually any database.

KIF (Knowledge Interchange Format): KIF is a formal language developed for the exchange of knowledge among disparate computer programs, and used to represent PSL semantics.

Linearization: The logic used in the inferencing of English statements.

Link: An explicit relationship between two resources or portions of two resources.

Link database or linkbase: An XML document which contains a collection of inbound or third-party links.

Local resource: In XLink, an XML element that participates in a link by virtue of having as its parent, or being itself, a linking element.

Location paths: An important subset of XPath expressions. A location path consists of one or more location steps.

Location step: Consists of an axis, a node test, and zero or more predicates.

Logical inferencing: A formal means or process by which propositions are examined and conclusions using them are reached.

MathML (Mathematical Markup Language): A low-level specification for describing mathematics as a basis for machine-to-machine communication.

MDL (Meaning Definition Language): XML-based language for bridging the gap between XML structure and meaning.

MDF (Metadata Processing Framework): An application framework that enables the modular creation of meta data processing utilities.

Namespace information item: In an XML infoset occurs for each element information item for each namespace that is in scope for that element.

NITF (News Industry Text Format): An XML vocabulary used to transfer news articles between organizations.

Node factory: A module in the RDF API to create resources, literals, and statements with the structure that is specific for a particular application.

Nominals: In topic maps, objects in the source representation from which topic items are derived.

Non-addressable subjects: In topic maps, things that are not directly accessible to a computer system – people, places, physical objects, organizations, abstract concepts, and so on.

Notation information item: In the XML infoset, exists for each notation in the DTD.

Object: In PSL, anything that is not a time point or an activity.

OMG (Object Management Group): A consortium formed to set standards in object-oriented programming.

Occurrence: In topic maps, an information resource that is relevant to the topic subject in some way.

Occurrence type: In topic maps, indicates to the user the nature of the relevance of the resource to the topic.

XOL (Ontology Exchange Language): An XML-based language designed to provide a format for exchanging ontology definitions among a set of interested parties.

OML (Ontology Markup Language): An evolution of Simple HTML Ontology Extensions (SHOE) to Extensible Markup Language (XML).

XSU (Oracle's XML SQL Utility): Generates XML documents from SQL queries and writes data from an XML document into a database table or view.

Ordering: In PSL, the theory that activities occur in ordered sequences delimited by time points.

OASIS: The Organization for Advancement in Structured Information Standards. A useful source of XML related information.

Output problem: In MDL, 'packaging' the information in an instance of the semantic model into an 'outgoing' XML document which conveys that information.

Parallelism: In PSL, the theory that activities can occur at the same time.

PCDATA (Parsed character data): Character data left after data has been parsed and entity references have been replaced with their text.

Participation: In XLink, when a link associates two resources, the resources are said to participate in the link.

Picture grammar: A set of statements used to 'recognize' a picture object based on the syntax of its visual constituents.

P3P (Platform for Privacy Preferences): W3C specification that enables a browser to compare a web site's privacy policy (expressed in RDF) against the user's preferences and to take appropriate actions when that site is visited.

Point: In XPointer, a position in XML information. A point may be a node (although it is not identical to a node in XPath), a location within text content, even an individual character.

Predicate: Description of the final destination in an XPath expression.

Process characterization: The representation of a process, independent of any specific application.

Processing instruction information item: In the infoset, it exists for each processing instruction in the corresponding XML document.

PSL (Process Specification Language): A language for process specification, allowing integration of multiple process-related applications throughout their life cycle.

PSL Core: A module which captures the high-level, primitive concepts inherent to process specification, and the base upon which the modules of the PSL ontology are built.

Property: In RDF, a specific aspect, characteristic, attribute, or relation used to describe a resource.

Protégé 2000 expert system: An integrated knowledge-base editing environment, and an extensible architecture for the creation of customized knowledge-based tools.

Published subject indicator (PSI): In topic maps, a subject indicator that is explicitly made available at a known address so it can reliably be addressed using a stable URL or other referencing mechanism, for the purposes of being used by the authors of multiple topic maps.

QNames (Qualified Names): A primitive datatype that defines an element name using a namespace, a colon, and the local name.

Range: In XPointer, the XML structure and content between two end points.

Recognition: The process of extracting the content from an initial representation ready for casting.

RELAX (Regular Language description for XML): A proposed specification for describing XML-based languages, now replaced by RELAX NG.

RELAX NG: A schema for identifying a class of XML documents matching a pattern of content and structure. Formerly existed as two draft proposals for XML schemas, TREX and RELAX.

Reification: Creation of a model of a statement, for example in RDF or topic maps.

Remote resource: In XLink, any resource or resource portion that participates in a link by virtue of being addressed with a URI reference.

repat: A C version of the Java-based RDF filter by David Megginson, creator of SAX.

Resource: In RDF, all things being described by RDF expressions. Resources are always named by URIs plus optional anchor ids.

Resource: In XLink, any addressable unit of information or service, including files, images, or query results.

Resource: In topic maps, things that are directly accessible to a computer system.

Resource-based meta data: Data which is intended to describe the whole (or a designated part) of an information resource.

RDF (Resource Description Framework): Integration of a number of web-based meta data activities to support the exchange of knowledge on the web.

RDF API: Provides a generalized framework for parsing and accessing RDF models as sets of statements.

RIL (RDF Inference Language): A way to create and exchange inference rules using XML for RDF models.

RDF Model and Syntax (RDFMS) Specification: One of the two documents (the other being RDFS) making up the RDF specification; this breaks RDF into two parts. The first is a *model* for meta data, and the second is an XML *syntax* for expressing meta data.

RDF Schema (RDFS) Specification: One of the two documents (the other being RDFMS) making up the RDF specification, this specifies the mechanisms needed to define a vocabulary of descriptive elements; it provides a basic type system for use in RDF models.

RDDL (Resource Directory Description Language): An extension of XHTML Basic 1.0 with an added element, which serves as an XLink to the referenced resource, and that contains a human-readable description of the resource and machine-readable links which describe the purpose of the link and the nature of the resource being linked to.

Result infoset: The output from an inclusion transformation.

SVG (Scalable Vector Graphics): A language for describing two-dimensional graphics in XML.

Schema: A means of describing or constraining the structure and content of some data. That data may be in the form of structured documents or may be highly complex relational or other data.

Schema adjuncts: Provide additional meta data for schema-validated XML documents.

Schematron: XML validating tool based on patterns in the XML tree.

Scope: In topic maps, the context within which the assignment of a characteristic is valid.

Semantic Web: the idea of having data on the Web defined and linked in a way that it can be used by machines not just for display purposes, but for automation, integration and reuse of data across various applications, for finding services, drawing inferences, determining trustworthiness, etc.

Sequence: In RDF, ordered lists of resources.

Sequence list: In a DTD, ensures that child elements are in a particular order.

SHOE (Simple HTML Ontology Extensions): A small extension to HTML that allows web page authors to annotate their web documents with machine-readable knowledge.

Simple-type links: In XLink, provide the same functionality as HTML hyperlinks. They are one-way links, involving two resources: the source and the destination.

SiRPAC (Simple RDF Parser and Compiler): The most widely used RDF parser.

Source infoset: The input for an inclusion transformation.

SGML (Standard Generalized Markup Language): A generic language for writing markup languages, of which XML is a subset.

Statement: In RDF, a specific resource (the **subject**), together with a named property (the **predicate**) plus the value of that property for that resource (the **object**). The object of a statement (the property value) can be another resource or it can be a literal.

Structural mappings: Organization of meta data between two or more complex documents or data structures.

SQL (Structured Query Language): The de facto standard for working with RDBMS.

Subject-based meta data: Data organized principally by subject, which also associates these subjects with information resources.

SMIL (Synchronized Multimedia Integration Language): An XML language that enables simple authoring of interactive audio-visual presentations.

Three-node model: In MDL, each instance of an association in a document involves three nodes – the two elements representing the objects at either end of the association instance, and the association node itself. The three-node model represents all possible associations.

Time point: In PSL, a point in time (obviously!).

Topic: In topic maps, an information object representing a specific subject of interest.

Topic characteristics: In topic maps, the topic characteristics are the names, occurrences, and roles in associations. It is the topic characteristics that make the topic intelligible to the topic map system.

Topic identity: Provides the bridge between the topic map and the subjects that the topics represent. It is these that make the topics intelligible to human beings, or to computer systems beyond the topic map system itself.

TMQL (Topic Map Query Language): A proposal for a language to allow the querying of topic maps.

Topic maps: Provide a 'navigation layer' over a set of information resources. They consist of topics, associations, and occurrences.

Topic naming constraint: In topic maps, a rule which states that when two topics have the same base name in the same scope, they are to be considered identical, and are merged into one.

Traversal: In XLink, using or following a link for any purpose. Traversal takes place from the starting resource to the ending resource.

Tree diagram: Illustrates XML structure by showing the possible nesting structure of elements.

TREX (Tree Regular Expressions): A proposed language for validating XML documents, now replaced by RELAX NG.

Triples: In RDF, simple statements for expressing meta data, consisting of the name/value pair that contains the actual meta data, plus an indicator of what document this meta data is referring to.

Unconstrained scope: In topic maps, a characteristic with unconstrained scope can validly be assigned in all contexts within the topic map.

Unexpanded entity reference information item: In an XML infoset, is used as a placeholder to indicate whether or not an XML processor has expanded a referenced external parsed entity.

UML (Unified Modeling Language): A family of graphically oriented modeling languages intended to be used for software design.

URI (Uniform Resource Identifier): Uniquely identifies the resource to which a link is made.

UDDI (Universal Description, Discovery, and Integration): A specification for distributed web-based information registries of web services. UDDI is also a publicly accessible set of implementations of the specification that allow businesses to register information about the web services they offer so that other businesses can find them.

Unparsed entity information item: In an XML infoset, exists for each unparsed general entity declared in the DTD.

WAI (Web Access Initiative): W3C initiative promoting usability of the Web for people with disabilities.

WSDL (Web Services Description Language): An XML format for describing network services.

Workflow Management Coalition's (WfMC) Workflow Reference Model: A specification identifying the characteristics, terminology, and components of workflow management systems.

W3C (World Wide Web Consortium): Organization maintaining web standards.

XDR (XML-Data Reduced): A subset of ideas described in the XML-Data specification. XDR schemas form the basis for the BizTalk initiative promoted by Microsoft.

XInclude (XML Inclusions): A W3C language that enables the information sets (infosets) of two or more XML documents to be merged.

XML Infoset: W3C specification that defines the meaningful information structures that are represented by the syntactic structures of XML itself.

XLink (XML Linking Language): A W3C language that provides a syntax for defining links in XML, including links that involve multiple XML (and non-XML) resources, and multiple traversal directions between those resources. Doesn't have any elements of its own, instead it uses global attributes on other XML elements.

XMI (XML Metadata Interchange): OMG standard XML language that provides a way to save UML models in XML, designed for the interchange of meta data.

XPath (The XML Path Language): A W3C language for addressing sections of an XML document.

XPointer (The XML Pointer Language): A W3C XML-based syntax, built on XPath, that enables linking to fragments of XML documents.

XPDL (XML Process Definition Language): A format for the exchange of process definitions, specified by the WfMC.

XQuery (XML Query Language): A W3C proposed language that provides for searching and retrieving data from XML documents.

XML schema: Describes in XML syntax the ordering and inter-relationships of XML elements and attributes in the class of XML documents to which the schema applies.

XTM (**XML Topic Maps**): A DTD for creating topic maps as an XML document.

XMuLator: An XSLT translation tool.

XSD Schema: The W3C's XML Schema Recommendation – an XML language for describing the syntactic structure of one or more elements within an XML document.

X-Smiles: An open source XML browser.

XSLT Standards-conformant processors: xt, Saxon, Xalan

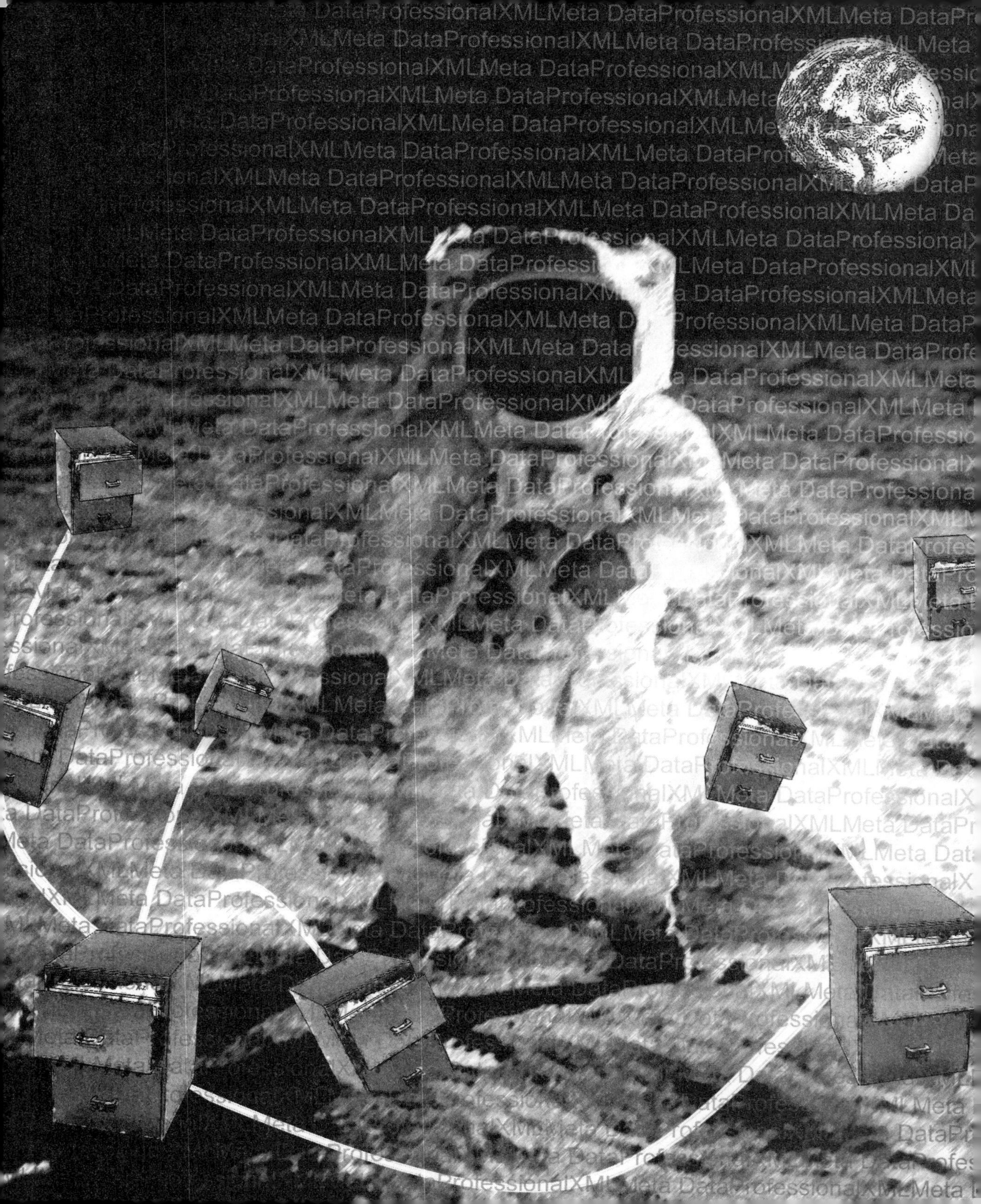
DataProfessionalXMLMeta DataProfessionalXMLMeta

B

Useful Resources

Books and Articles

Professional XML Schemas (Wrox Press, ISBN 1-861005-47-4)

Professional XSL (Wrox Press, ISBN 1-861003-57-9)

XSLT Programmer's Reference 2nd Edition (Wrox Press, ISBN1-861005-06-7)

Professional XML 2nd Edition (Wrox Press, ISBN 1-86100-5-05-9)

Professional Java XML (Wrox Press, ISBN 1-86100-401-X)

RELAX NG Tutorial:
http://www.oasis-open.org/committees/relax-ng/tutorial.html

Topic Maps: Introduction and Allegro (Dr Hans Holger Rath and Steve Pepper):
http://www.topicmaps.com/content/resources/mt99/hhr-stp.pdf

Discussion of work to define the relationship between topic maps and RDF (Graham Moore):
http://www.topicmaps.com/topicmapsrdf.pdf

Sergey Melnik's article on storing meta data in a database:
http://www-db.stanford.edu/~melnik/rdf/db.html

Specifications

XSD Schema home page:
http://www.w3.org/XML/Schema.html

XSD Schema Recommendation: Part 0: Primer:
http://www.w3.org/TR/xmlschema-0/

XSD Schema Recommendation: Part 1: Structures:
http://www.w3.org/TR/xmlschema-1/

XSD Schema Recommendation: Part 2: Datatypes:
http://www.w3.org/TR/xmlschema-2/

TREX:
http://www.thaiopensource.com/trex/

RELAX:
http://www.xml.gr.jp/relax/

RELAX NG Technical Committee at OASIS:
http://www.oasis-open.org/committees/relax-ng/

RELAX NG Technical Committee mailing list at OASIS:
http://lists.oasis-open.org/archives/relax-ng/

Uses of Schema adjuncts:
http://www.extensibility.com/resources/saf.htm

Schematron homepage:
http://www.ascc.net/xml/resource/schematron/schematron.html

MDL draft specification:
http://www.charteris.com/mdl/

XLink (XML Linking Language):
http://www.w3.org/TR/xlink/

XInclude specification Working Draft:
http://www.w3.org/TR/xinclude/

XML Query language home page:
http://www.w3.org/XML/Query

XQueryX:
http://www.w3.org/TR/xqueryx

XML Query Requirements:
http://www.w3.org/TR/xmlquery-req

XML Query Use Cases:
http://www.w3.org/TR/xmlquery-use-cases

XML Query Data Model:
http://www.w3.org/TR/query-datamodel

The XML Query Algebra:
http://www.w3.org/TR/query-algebra

XPath 2.0 requirements Working Draft:
http://www.w3.org/TR/xpath20req

XSLT 2.0 requirements Working Draft:
http://www.w3.org/TR/xslt20req

RDF Model and Syntax Recommendation:
http://www.w3.org/TR/REC-rdf-syntax

RDF Schema Recommendation:
http://www.w3.org/TR/rdf-schema/

RDF-related information available from the W3C:
http://www.w3.org/RDF/

The RDF Interest Group's page:
http://www.w3.org/RDF/Interest/

DAML+OIL:
http://www.daml.org/2001/03/daml+oil-index

General topic map information:
http://www.topicmaps.org

XML Topic Maps (XTM) 1.0 Specification:
http://www.topicmaps.org/xtm/1.0/

TMQL mailing list and archives:
http://groups.yahoo.com/group/tmql-wg

Uniform Resource Identifiers (URI) generic syntax:
http://www.ietf.org/rfc/rfc2396.txt?number=2396

Simple HTML Ontology Extensions (SHOE):
http://www.cs.umd.edu/projects/plus/SHOE/

Ontology Exchange Language (XOL):
http://www.ai.sri.com/~pkarp/xol/

Dublin Core (DC) initiative:
http://dublincore.org/documents/dces/

XML Signature:
http://www.w3.org/Signature/

Document Object Model (DOM):
http://www.w3.org/DOM/

Namespaces in XML Recommendation:
http://www.w3.org/TR/REC-xml-names

XML Base specification:
http://www.w3.org/TR/xmlbase

XML Information Set specification:
http://www.w3.org/TR/xml-infoset/

NewsML standard:
http://www.newsml.org

cXML protocol and data formats:
http://www.cxml.org/

W3C MathML Specification:
http://www.w3.org/Math/

The Composite Capabilities/Preference Profiles specification:
http://www.w3.org/Mobile/CCPP/

The Metadata Processing Framework (MDF):
http://www.techquila.com/mdf.html

Software and Tools

RELAX NG tools:
http://www.thaiopensource.com/relaxng/

Jing, a validator for RELAX NG:
http://www.thaiopensource.com/relaxng/jing.html

RDF parsers:
http://www.w3.org/RDF/

SiRPAC RDF parser:
http://www.w3.org/RDF/Implementations/SiRPAC/

Jason Diamond's XSLT stylesheet for transforming RDF into a list of triples:
http://injektilo.org/rdf/rdft.xsl

Jonathan Borden's RDF extractor:
http://www.openhealth.org/RDF/rdf_Syntax_and_Names.htm

David Megginson's repat RDF parser toolkit:
http://injektilo.org/rdf/repat.html

RDF Filter:
http://www.megginson.com/Software/

Stanford University's RDF API, maintained by Sergey Melnik:
http://www-db.stanford.edu/~melnik/rdf/api.html

The Jena API and documentation:
http://www-uk.hpl.hp.com/people/bwm/rdf/jena

Processing model for topic maps:
http://www.topicmaps.net

Michel Biezunski's XTM knowledge base:
http://ep.open.ac.uk/PubSys/resources/html/dodd0000.html

SVG viewers:
www.w3.org/Graphics/SVG/SVG-Implementations

Adobe SVG Viewer:
http://www.w3.org/Graphics/SVG/Overview.htm8

The X-Smiles processor:
http://www.xsmiles.org

Michael Kay's Saxon XSLT processor:
http://users.iclway.co.uk/mhkay/saxon/

Apache Xerces XML parser and Xalan XPath implementation:
http://xml.apache.org/

XML Spy authoring tool:
http://www.xmlspy.com

Java SDK 1.3:
http://www.java.sun.com

NetBeans Java IDE:
http://www.netbeans.org

The Java implementation of the MDF framework:
http://www.techquila.com/mdf.html

Protégé KB:
http://smi-web.stanford.edu/projects/protege/

Ontoviz tab for Protégé:
http://protege.stanford.edu/plugins/ontoviz/ontoviz.html

Graphviz (needed for Ontoviz):
http://www.research.att.com/sw/tools/graphviz

Princeton University's WordNet Project:
http://www.cogsci.princeton.edu/~wn/

Riboweb:
http://riboweb.stanford.edu/

DAXSVG RDF Schema:
http://www.openmeta.org/daxsvg-schema-rdf.html

The SHRDLU program by Terry Winograd:
http://hci.stanford.edu/~winograd/shrdlu/

CYC:
http://www.cyc.com

Stanford's Protégé 2000 expert system:
http://protege.stanford.edu/

Microsoft SQL Server:
http://www.microsoft.com

Opta2000 JDBC Driver:
http://www.inetsoftware.de

Oracle's XML SQL Utility (XSU):
http://technet.oracle.com/tech/xml/oracle_xsu/

'Database Debunking' site:
http://www.firstsql.com/dbdebunk

Organizations

W3C Semantic Web Activity:
http://www.w3.org/2001/sw/

SemanticWeb.org index page:
http://www.semanticweb.org

XML.org:
http://www.xml.org/

Zvon site (useful XML related tutorials):
http://www.zvon.org

The xml-dev mailing list:
http://lists.xml.org/archives/

International Organization for Standardization (ISO):
http://www.iso.ch/iso/en/ISOOnline.frontpage

Information on the Extreme Markup Languages conference series:
http://www.gca.org

UK GovTalk Homepage:
http://www.govtalk.gov.uk

Empolis:
http://www.empolis.co.uk/technology/tech_tmo.asp

Infoloom:
http://www.infoloom.com

Mondéca:
http://www.mondeca.com

Ontopia:
http://www.ontopia.net/topicmaps/index.html

Exel Ltd:
http://www.exel.com/

BizTalk.org:
http://www.biztalk.org/.

Business & Accounting Software Developer's association (BASDA):
http://www.basda.org/

Open Applications Group (OAG):
http://www.openapplications.org/

The Meta Data Coalition:
http://www.mdcinfo.com/

The Open Directory Project:
http://dmoz.org

Web Access Initiative (WAI):
http://www.w3.org/WAI/

Text Encoding Initiative (TEI) home page:
http://www.tei-c.org/

Object Management Group (OMG):
http://www.omg.org/

Workflow Management Coalition (WfMC):
http://www.wfmc.org/

The International Press Telecommunications Council (IPTC):
http://www.iptc.org

Association for Computing Machinery (ACM):
http://www.acm.org/

The Society of Manufacturing Engineers (SME):
http://www.sme.org/cgi-bin/getsmepage.pl?/new-sme.html&&&SME&

International Electrotechnical Commission (IEC)
http://www.iec.ch/

IEEE:
http://www.ieee.org/

Meta DataProfessionalXMLMeta DataProfessionalXMLMeta DataPr
XMLMeta DataProfessionalXMLMeta DataProfessionalXMLMeta
DataProfessionalXMLMeta DataProfessionalXML
DataProfessionalXMLMeta DataProfessionalXMLMeta
Meta DataProfessionalXMLMeta DataProfessionalXMLMe
ProfessionalXMLMeta DataProfessionalXMLMeta DataProfes
ProfessionalXMLMeta DataProfessionalXMLMeta DataProfessionalXM
ProfessionalXMLMeta DataProfessionalXMLMeta DataProfessionalXMLMeta Da

Index

p2p.wrox.com
The programmer's resource centre

A unique free service from Wrox Press
with the aim of helping programmers to help each other

Wrox Press aims to provide timely and practical information to today's programmer. P2P is a list server offering a host of targeted mailing lists where you can share knowledge with your fellow programmers and find solutions to your problems. Whatever the level of your programming knowledge, and whatever technology you use, P2P can provide you with the information you need.

ASP Support for beginners and professionals, including a resource page with hundreds of links, and a popular ASP+ mailing list.

DATABASES For database programmers, offering support on SQL Server, mySQL, and Oracle.

MOBILE Software development for the mobile market is growing rapidly. We provide lists for the several current standards, including WAP, WindowsCE, and Symbian.

JAVA A complete set of Java lists, covering beginners, professionals,and server-side programmers (including JSP, servlets and EJBs)

.NET Microsoft's new OS platform, covering topics such as ASP+, C#, and general .Net discussion.

VISUAL BASIC Covers all aspects of VB programming, from programming Office macros to creating components for the .Net platform.

WEB DESIGN As web page requirements become more complex, programmer sare taking a more important role in creating web sites. For these programmers, we offer lists covering technologies such as Flash, Coldfusion, and JavaScript.

XML Covering all aspects of XML, including XSLT and schemas.

OPEN SOURCE Many Open Source topics covered including PHP, Apache, Perl, Linux, Python and more.

FOREIGN LANGUAGE Several lists dedicated to Spanish and German speaking programmers, categories include .Net, Java, XML, PHP and XML.

How To Subscribe

Simply visit the P2P site, at **http://p2p.wrox.com/**

Select the 'FAQ' option on the side menu bar for more information about the subscription process and our service.

Programmer to Programmer™

Wrox writes books for you. Any suggestions, or ideas about how you want
information given in your ideal book will be studied by our team.
Your comments are always valued at Wrox.

Free phone in USA 800-USE-WROX
Fax (312) 893 8001

UK Tel.: (0121) 687 4100   Fax: (0121) 687 4101

Professional Meta Data – Registration Card

Name _____

Address _____

_____

_____

City _____ State/Region_____

Country _____ Postcode/Zip_____

E-Mail _____

Occupation _____

How did you hear about this book?

☐ Book review (name) _____

☐ Advertisement (name) _____

☐ Recommendation _____

☐ Catalog _____

☐ Other _____

Where did you buy this book?

☐ Bookstore (name) _____ City_____

☐ Computer store (name) _____

☐ Mail order_____

☐ Other _____

What influenced you in the purchase of this book?

☐ Cover Design ☐ Contents ☐ Other (please specify):

How did you rate the overall content of this book?

☐ Excellent ☐ Good ☐ Average ☐ Poor

What did you find most useful about this book? _____

_____

What did you find least useful about this book? _____

_____

Please add any additional comments. _____

_____

What other subjects will you buy a computer book on soon?

_____

What is the best computer book you have used this year?

_____

Note: This information will only be used to keep you updated
about new Wrox Press titles and will not be used for
any other purpose or passed to any other third party.

Check here if you DO NOT want to receive support for this book ■   4516

wrox

Programmer to Programmer™

Note: If you post the bounce back card below in the UK, please send it to:

Wrox Press Limited, Arden House, 1102 Warwick Road,
Acocks Green, Birmingham B27 6HB. UK.

Computer Book Publishers